SOMETHING ABOUT THE AUTHOR

SOMETHING ABOUT THE AUTHOR

Facts and Pictures about Authors

and Illustrators of Books for Young People

Anne Commire

VOLUME 18

GALE RESEARCH
BOOK TOWER
DETROIT, MICHIGAN
48226

Also Published by Gale

CONTEMPORARY AUTHORS

*A Bio-Bibliographical Guide to Current Writers in
Fiction, General Nonfiction, Poetry, Journalism,
Drama, Motion Pictures, Television,
and Other Fields*

(Now Covers Nearly 57,000 Authors)

Associate Editors: Agnes Garrett, Helga McCue

Assistant Editors: Kathryn T. Floch, Mary F. Glahn,
D. Jayne Higo, Linda Shedd, Susan L. Stetler

Consultant: Adele Sarkissian

Sketchwriters: Dianne H. Anderson, Rosemary DeAngelis Bridges,
Catherine Coray, Gail Schermer

Research Assistant: Kathleen Betsko

Editorial Assistants: Susan Pfanner, Elisa Ann Sawchuk

Library of Congress Catalog Card Number 72-27107

ISBN 0-8103-0099-0

Table of Contents

Introduction   vii   Illustrations Index   313

Acknowledgments   ix   Author Index   323

Nadema Agard 1

Floyd Akers
   see L. Frank Baum 7

Joseph A. Alvarez 2

Ted Anderson
   see Waldo T. Boyd 35

Madeline Angell 3

Martha Sherman Bacon 4

Laura Bancroft
   see L. Frank Baum 7

Lucy Bate 6

L. Frank Baum 7

Nina Beachcroft 31

Charles Austin Beard 32

Evelyn Bolton
   see Anne Evelyn Bunting 38

Lucia Merecka Borski 34

Waldo T. Boyd 35

H. F. Brinsmead 36

Lewis Buck 37

A. E. Bunting
   see Anne Evelyn Bunting 38

Anne Evelyn Bunting 38

Eve Bunting
   see Anne Evelyn Bunting 38

Em Burgess
   see Mary Wyche Burgess 39

Mary Wyche Burgess 39

Bonnie Carey 40

Seymour Chwast 42

Frank J. Clark 43

Columella
   see Clement Clarke Moore .. 224

Walter Crane 44

Countee Cullen 64

Morgan Dennis 68

Wesley Dennis 70

Derry Down Derry
   see Edward Lear 182

Charles Dougherty 74

Alexandre Dumas 74

Dale Fife 110

Captain Hugh Fitzgerald
   see L. Frank Baum 7

Ruth Franchere 111

Robert Edward Gard 113

Alan Garner 114

Eleanor Graham 116

John Gretzer 117

Richard Hallas
   see Eric Knight 151

Janice Holland 117

Donald Honig 119

Leonora Hornblow 120

Robert J. Houlehen 121

Geoffrey Hoyle 121

Pixie Hungerford
   see H. F. Brinsmead 36

Robert Utley Hyndman 123

Elizabeth Orton Jones 123

Robert W. Kane 131

John Kaufmann 132

Walt Kelly 135

Eric Knight 151

Beth Krush 162

Joe Krush 163

Paul Kuttner 165

Jean de la Fontaine 166

Sidney Lanier 176

Edward Lear 182

Jack London 195

John Griffith London
   see Jack London 195

Anson C. Lowitz 214

Anthony D. Marshall 215

David McCord 217

Suzanne Metcalf
   see L. Frank Baum 7

Kazue Mizumura 222

Clement Clarke Moore 224

Janet Gaylord Moore 236

Ann Nicol
   see Ann Turnbull 281

Mary Norton 236

Robert Parker
   see Waldo T. Boyd 35

Charles Payzant 239

Ann Merriman Peck 240

Richard Peck 242

Kathy Pelta 245

Illa E. Podendorf 247

Janet Quin-Harkin 247

Renée Reggiani 248

Johanna de Leeuw Reiss 250

Becky Reyher
   see Rebecca Hourwich
   Reyher 253

Rebecca Hourwich Reyher 253

Nicole Rubel 255

Johanna Sengler 255

Ernest Thompson Seton 257

Nicolas Sidjakov 272

Schuyler Staunton
   see L. Frank Baum 7

William Steig 275

David Swift
   see John Kaufmann 132

Gustaf Tenggren 277

Peter Thayer
    see Rose Wyler 303

Roy Eugene Toothaker 280

Ann Turnbull 281

Salaman Van Abbé 282

Janet Van Duyn 283

Edith Van Dyne
    see L. Frank Baum 7

Hendrik Willem Van Loon 284

John H. Vogel, Jr. 292

Audrey Walters 293

Joyce W. Warren 294

Thompson Watson
    see David McCord 217

Adelle Weiss 296

Rosemary Wells 296

Garth Williams 298

Donald Emmet Worcester 301

Rose Wyler 303

Robert Wyndham
    see Robert Utley Hyndman . 123

Gene Zion 305

Introduction

Beginning with Volume 15, the time span covered by *Something about the Author* was broadened to include major children's writers who died before 1961, which was the former cut-off point for writers covered in this series. This change will make *SATA* even more helpful to its many thousands of student and professional users.

Authors who did not come within the scope of *SATA* have formerly been included in *Yesterday's Authors of Books for Children,* of which Gale has published two volumes.

It has been pointed out by users, however, that it is inconvenient to have a body of related materials broken up by an arbitrary criterion such as the date of a person's death. Also, some libraries are not able to afford both series, and are therefore denied access to material on some of the most important writers in the juvenile field.

It has been decided, therefore, to discontinue the *YABC* series, and to include in *SATA* at least the most outstanding among the older writers who had been selected for listing in *YABC*. Volumes 1 and 2 of *YABC* will be kept in print, and the listings in those two volumes will be included in the cumulative *SATA* index.

GRATEFUL ACKNOWLEDGMENT

is made to the following publishers, authors, and artists,
for their kind permission to reproduce copyrighted material.

ADDISON-WESLEY PUBLISHING CO. Drawing by Edward Gorey from *The Dong with a Luminous Nose* by Edward Lear. Illustrations © 1969 by Edward Gorey. Reprinted by permission of Addison-Wesley Publishing Co.

AMERICAN LIBRARIES. Sidelight excerpts from an article, "In the Country of Teenage Fiction" by Richard Peck, April, 1973 in *American Libraries*. Reprinted by permission of *American Libraries*.

AMS PRESS. Sidelight excerpts from *Young la Fontaine* translated by Philip Wadsworth. Reprinted by permission of AMS Press.

ATHENEUM PUBLISHERS. Illustration by John Gretzer from *The Beggar King of China* by Dale Carlson. Copyright © 1971 by Dale Carlson. Reprinted by permission of Atheneum Publishers.

ATLANTIC MONTHLY CO. Sidelight excerpts from an article "Dotty Dimple and the Fiction Award" by Martha Bacon, March, 1963 in *Atlantic*. Reprinted by permission of the Atlantic Monthly Co.

ERNEST BENN LTD. Illustration by Arnold Bond from *Head O'Mey* by Eleanor Graham. Reprinted by permission of Ernest Benn Ltd.

BERKLEY PUBLISHING CORP. Illustration by Garth Williams from *The Rescuers* by Margery Sharp. Copyright © 1959 by Margery Sharp. Illustration © 1959 by Garth Williams. Reprinted by permission of Berkley Publishing Corp.

THE BOBBS-MERRILL CO. Illustration by Larry Veeder from *The Fantastic Variety of Marine Animals* by Madeline Angell. Copyright © 1976 by Madeline Angell. Illustrations copyright © 1976 by Larry Veeder./ Illustration by Richard Rosenblum from *A Kidnapped Santa Claus* by L. Frank Baum. Introduction copyright © 1969 by The Bobbs-Merrill Co., Inc. Illustration copyright © 1969 by Richard Rosenblum. Both reprinted by permission of The Bobbs-Merrill Co.

R. R. BOWKER CO. Sidelight excerpts from an article "Thirteen in the Children's Book Field Explore Cuba's New Publishing Industry," May 1, 1978 in *Publisher's Weekly*. Copyright © 1978 by Xerox Corp. Reprinted by permission of R. R. Bowker Co.

GEORGE BRAZILLER, INC. Sidelight excerpts from *La Fontaine and His Friends* by Agnes Mackay. Reprinted by permission of George Braziller, Inc.

CURTIS BROWN, LTD. Sidelight excerpts from the forward to *Song on Your Bugles* by Eric Knight. Reprinted by permission of Curtis Brown, Ltd.

JONATHAN CAPE, LTD. Sidelight excerpts from *The Titans* by Andre Maurois. Copyright © 1957 by Andre Maurois. Reprinted by permission of Jonathan Cape, Ltd.

THE CARDAVON PRESS, INC. Illustration by Edy Legrand from *The Three Musketeers* by Alexandre Dumas. Copyright © 1953 by the George Macy Companies, Inc./ Reprinted by permission of The Cardavon Press, Inc.

CHAPMAN & HALL. Sidelight excerpts from *Portrait of a Flying Yorkshireman: Letters from Eric Knight in the U.S. to Paul Rotha in England* edited by Paul Rotha. Reprinted by permission of Chapman & Hall.

CHILDRENS PRESS. Illustration by Darrell Wiskur from *Living Things Change* by

Illa Podendorf. Copyright © 1971 by Regensteiner Publishing Enterprises, Inc. Reprinted by permission of Childrens Press.

CITATION PRESS. Sidelight excerpts from *Books Are by People* by Lee Bennett Hopkins. Reprinted by permission of Citation Press, a division of Scholastic Press.

WILLIAM COLLINS, LTD. Sidelight excerpts from *Edward Lear: The Life of a Wanderer* by Vivien Noakes./ Illustration by Charles Keeping from *Elidor* by Alan Garner. Copyright © 1965 by William Collins, Ltd. Both reprinted by permission of William Collins, Ltd.

CONTEMPORARY BOOKS. Sidelight excerpts from *The Magic of Oz*, preface by L. Frank Baum. Copyright © 1919./ Sidelight excerpts from *Ozma of Oz*, introduction by L. Frank Baum. Copyright © 1907./ Sidelight excerpts from *To Please a Child: A Biography of L. Frank Baum, Royal Historian of Oz* by Frank Joslyn Baum and Russell P. MacFall. Copyright © 1961. All reprinted by permission of Contemporary Books.

THE COUNTRYMAN PRESS. Illustration by Janice Holland from *The Blue Cat of Castle Town* by Catherine Cate Coblentz. Copyright 1949 by Catherine Cate Coblentz. Reprinted by permission of The Countryman Press.

COWARD, McCANN AND GEOGHEGAN, INC. Illustration by Paul Galdone from *Who Goes There, Lincoln?* by Dale Fife. Copyright © 1975 by Dale Fife and Paul Galdone./ Sidelight excerpts from *Life of Sidney Lanier* by Lincoln Lorenz./ Illustration by Margot Tomes from *Five Children and a Dog* by Renée Reggiani. Copyright © 1965 by Renee Reggiani. All reprinted by permission of Coward, McCann and Geoghegan, Inc.

THOMAS Y. CROWELL, INC. Illustration by Earl Thollander from *Cesar Chavez* by Ruth Franchere. Copyright © 1970 by Ruth Franchere. Illustrations copyright © 1970 by Earl Thollander./ Illustration by John Kaufmann from *Coyote in Manhattan* by Jean Craighead George. Copyright © 1968 by Jean Craighead George./ Illustration by Kazue Mizumura from *If I Were a Mother* by Kazue Mizumura. Copyright under Berne Convention./ Sidelight excerpts from *The Journey Back* by Johanna Reiss./ Sidelight excerpts from *The Upstairs Room* by Johanna Reiss. Copyright © 1972 by Johanna Reiss. All reprinted by permission of Thomas Y. Crowell, Inc.

CROWN PUBLISHERS. Illustration by Diane de Groat from *Little Rabbit's Loose Tooth* by Lucy Bate. Text copyright © 1975 by Lucy Bate. Illustrations copyright © 1975 by Diane de Groat. Reprinted by permission of Crown Publishers.

J. M. DENT & SONS, LTD. Illustration by Charles Pickard from *White Fang* by Jack London. Illustrations copyright © 1967 by J. M. Dent & Sons, Ltd./ Illustrations by S. Van Abbé from *Tanglewood Tales* by Nathaniel Hawthorne./ All reprinted by permission of J. M. Dent & Sons, Ltd.

THE DEVIN-ADAIR CO., INC. Sidelight excerpts from *Ernest Thompson Seton's America* edited by Farida Wiley. Copyright © 1954 by Devin-Adair. Reprinted by permission of The Devin-Adair Co., Inc.

THE DIAL PRESS. Illustration by Anita Lobel from *Peter Penny's Dance* by Janet Quin-Harkin. Copyright © 1976 by Janet Quin-Harkin and Anita Lobel./ Illustration by Rosemary Wells from *Noisy Nora* by Rosemary Wells. Copyright © 1973 by Rosemary Wells. Both reprinted by permission of The Dial Press.

DODD, MEAD & CO. Illustrations by Mead Schaeffer from *The Count of Monte Cristo* by Alexandre Dumas./ Illustrations by Maurice Leloir from *The Three Musketeers* by Alexandre Dumas./ Illustrations by Edward Lear from *The Complete Nonsense Book* by Edward Lear. Copyright 1912 by Constance, Lady Strachery./ Illustration by Anne Merriman Peck from *A Vagabond's Provence* by Anne Merriman Peck. Copyright 1929 by Dodd, Mead & Co., Inc. All reprinted by permission of Dodd, Mead & Co.

DOUBLEDAY & CO. Illustration by Richard Scarry from *Best in Children's Books,* selections from *The Wonderful Wizard of Oz* by L. Frank Baum. Copyright © 1960 by Nelson Doubleday, Inc./ Sidelight excerpts and photograph from *Five Boyhoods* edited by Martin Levin. Copyright © 1962 by Martin Levin./ Sidelight excerpts and photographs from *By a Thousand Fires* by Julia M. Seton. Copyright © 1967 by Julia M. Seton. All reprinted by permission of Doubleday & Co.

E. P. DUTTON & CO., INC. Illustrations by S. Van Abbé from *Tanglewood Tales* by Nathaniel Hawthorne. Reprinted by permission of E. P. Dutton & Co., Inc.

FARRAR, STRAUS & GIROUX, INC. Photographs from *The Incredible Marquis, Alexandre Dumas* by Herbert Gorman. Copyright 1929 by Farrar, Rinehart./ Illustration by William Steig from *Dominic* by William Steig. Copyright © 1972 by William Steig./ Illustration by William Steig from *Abel's Island* by William Steig. Copyright © 1976 by William Steig. All reprinted by permission of Farrar, Straus & Giroux, Inc.

FOLCROFT LIBRARY EDITIONS. Sidelight excerpts from *La Fontaine* translated by Monica Sutherland. Reprinted by permission of Folcroft Library Editions.

GROSSET AND DUNLAP, INC. Illustration by Tomi Ungerer from Lear's *Nonsense Verse* by Edward Lear. Copyright © 1967./ Illustration by Kyuzo Tsugami from *The Call of the Wild and Other Stories* by Jack London. Copyright © 1965 by Grosset and Dunlap, Inc./ Illustration by Evelyn Copelman from *The Wizard of Oz* by L. Frank Baum. Copyright © 1956 by Grosset and Dunlap, Inc. All reprinted by permission of Grosset and Dunlap, Inc.

HARCOURT BRACE JOVANOVICH, INC. Illustration by Beth and Joe Krush from *The Borrowers* by Mary Norton. Copyright © 1952, 1953 by Mary Norton./ Illustration by Erik Blegvad from *Bedknob and Broomstick* by Mary Norton. Copyright © 1943, 1957, 1971 by Mary Norton. Both reprinted by permission of Harcourt Brace Jovanovich, Inc.

HARMONY BOOKS. Photograph by Seymour Linden from *The Call of the Wild* by Jack London. Photographs copyright © 1977 by Seymour Linden. Reprinted by permission of Harmony Books, a division of Crown Publishers.

HARPER AND ROW PUBLISHERS, INC. Sidelight excerpt from *Caroling Dusk* edited by Countee Cullen./ Illustrations by Charles Sebree from *The Lost Zoo* by Christopher Cat and Countee Cullen. Copyright 1940 by Harper & Bros./ Illustration by Robert Reid Macguire from *My Lives and How I Lost Them* by Christopher Cat in collaboration with Countee Cullen. Copyright 1942 by Harper & Brothers./ Sidelight excerpts from *The Titans* by Andre Maurois. Copyright © 1957 by Andre Maurois./ Illustration by John Kaufmann from *The Letter on the Tree* by Natalie Savage Carlson. Text copyright © 1964 by Natalie Savage Carlson. Pictures copyright © 1964 by John Kaufmann./ Illustration by Nancy Ekholm Burkert from *The Scroobious Pip* by Edward Lear. Completed by Ogden Nash. Illustration copyright © 1968 by Nancy Ekholm Burkert./ Illustration by Hilary Knight from *The Night Before Christmas* by Clement C. Moore. Pictures copyright © 1963 by Hilary Knight./ Illustration by Garth Williams from *Charlotte's Web* by E. B. White. Copyright 1952 by E. B. White./ Illustration by Garth Williams from *Little House on the Prairie* by Laura Ingalls Wilder. Text copyright 1935 by Laura Ingalls Wilder. Picture copyright 1953 by Garth Williams./ Illustration by Margaret Bloy Graham from *Harry the Dirty Dog* by Gene Zion. Text copyright © 1956 by Eugene Zion. Pictures copyright © 1956 by Margaret Bloy Graham./ Illustration by Margaret Bloy Graham from *The Plant Sitter* by Gene Zion. Text copyright © 1959 by Eugene Zion. Pictures copyright © 1959 by Margaret Bloy Graham. All reprinted by permission of Harper and Row Publishers, Inc.

HARVARD UNIVERSITY PRESS. Sidelight excerpts from *In Sight of Sever: Essays from Harvard* by David McCord. Reprinted by permission of Harvard University Press.

HARVEY HOUSE. Illustration by Audrey Walters from *Just Like You....* by Leonore Klein. Copyright © 1968 by Harvey House. Reprinted by permission of Harvey House.

HEINRICH HANAU PUBLICATIONS, LTD. Illustration by Owen Wood from *The Owl and the Pussycat* by Edward Lear. Reprinted by permission of Heinrich Hanau Publications, Ltd.

HOLIDAY HOUSE, INC. Illustration by Nadema Agard from *The Chichi Hoo Hoo Bogeyman* by Virginia Driving Hawk Sneve. Text copyright © 1975 by Virginia Driving Hawk Sneve. Illustrations copyright © 1975 by Holiday House, Inc. Reprinted by permission of Holiday House, Inc.

HOLT, RINEHART AND WINSTON. Sidelight excerpts from *The Incredible Marquis: Alexandre Dumas* by Herbert Gorman. Copyright 1929 by Farrar & Rinehart, Inc. Reprinted by permission of Holt, Rinehart and Winston.

HORN BOOK, INC. Sidelight excerpts from *Illustrators of Children's Books: 1946-1956* compiled by Bertha M. Miller and others. Copyright © 1958 by The Horn Book, Inc./ Sidelight excerpts from *Illustrators of Children's Books: 1957-1966* compiled by Lee Kingman and others. Copyright © 1968 by The Horn Book, Inc./ Sidelight excerpts from an article, "Caldecott Award Acceptance" by Nicolas Sidjakov, August, 1961, in *Horn Book*./ Sidelight excerpts from an article "Illustrating the Little House Books" in *Horn Book*. Copyright © 1953 by The Horn Book, Inc. All reprinted by permission of Horn Book, Inc.

HOUGHTON MIFFLIN CO. Illustration by Jesse Willcox Smith from *Twas the Night Before Christmas: A Visit from St. Nicholas* by Clement C. Moore. Copyright 1912 by Houghton Mifflin Company./ Illustration by Nicole Rubel from *Sleepy Ronald* by Jack Gantos. Copyright © 1976 by John B. Gantos, Jr. Copyright © 1976 by Leslie Rubel./ Illustration by Gustaf Tenggren from *A Wonder-Book and Tanglewood Tales* by Nathaniel Hawthorne. Copyright 1951 by Houghton Mifflin Co. Copyright 1923 by Houghton Mifflin Co. All reprinted by permission of Houghton Mifflin Co.

HOWELL, SOCKIN, PUBLISHERS. Illustration by Garth Williams from *I Married Them* by Janet Van Duyn. Copyright 1945 by Janet Van Duyn. Reprinted by permission of Howell, Sockin, Publishers.

INDIANA UNIVERSITY PRESS. Illustration by Guy Fleming from *Baba Yaga's Geese and Other Russian Stories* translated and adapted by Bonnie Carey. Copyright © 1973 by Indiana University Press. Reprinted by permission of Indiana University Press.

P. J. KENEDY. Sidelight excerpts from *Edward Lear: Landscape Painter and Nonsense Poet* by Angus Davidson. Reprinted by permission of P. J. Kenedy, a division of Macmillan Publishing Co.

ALFRED A. KNOPF, INC. Illustrations from *The Worlds of Ernest Thompson Seton* edited by John G. Samson. Copyright © 1976 under the International Union for the Protection of Literary and Artistic Works./ Illustration by Gustaf Tenggren from *The Ring of the Nibelung* by Gertrude Henderson. Copyright 1932 by Alfred A. Knopf, Inc./ Illustration by Nicolas Sidjakov from *A Loadstone and a Toadstone*. Copyright © 1969 by Irene Elmer. Illustrations copyright © 1969 by Nicolas Sidjakov. All reprinted by permission of Alfred A. Knopf, Inc.

LERNER PUBLICATIONS CO. Illustration by Johanna Sengler from *The Wandering Shoe* by Clemens Parma. Copyright © 1966 by Lerner Publications Co. Reprinted by permission of Lerner Publications Co.

LIBRA PUBLISHERS. Sidelight excerpts from *Roots of Negro Racial Consciousness* by Stephen Bronz. Reprinted by permission of Libra Publishers.

LIBRARRIE GALLIMARD. Sidelight excerpts from *La Fontaine Oeuvres Diverses* translated by Pierre Clarac. Copyright © 1942 by Editions Gallimard. Reprinted by permission of Librarrie Gallimard.

THE LIMITED EDITIONS CLUB. Illustration by Lynd Ward from *The Count of Monte Cristo* by Alexandre Dumas. Reprinted by permission of The Limited Editions Club.

J. B. LIPPINCOTT CO. Sidelight excerpts from *The Story of Hendrik Willem Van Loon* by Gerard Willem Van Loon. Copyright © 1972 by Gerard Willem Van Loon. Reprinted by permission of J. B. Lippincott Co.

LITTLE, BROWN AND CO. Illustration by Richard Cuffari from *In the Company of Clowns* by Martha Bacon. Copyright © 1973 by Martha Bacon Ballinger./ Illustration by Henry B. Kane from *All Day Long* by David McCord. Copyright © 1966 by David McCord./ Illustration by Leslie Morrill from *Away and Ago: Rhymes of the Never Was and Always Is* by David McCord. Copyright © 1968, 1971, 1972, 1973, 1974 by David McCord./ Illustration by Henry B. Kane from *For Me to Say* by David McCord. Copyright © 1970 by David McCord./ Illustrations by Morgan Dennis from *Portrait of Dog* by Mazo de la Roche. Copyright 1930 by Little, Brown and Co./ Illustration by Barbara Cooney from *The Owl and the Pussy-Cat* by Edward Lear. Illustration copyright © 1961 by Barbara Cooney./ Illustration by Marc Simont from *The Star in the Pail* by David McCord. Illustrations copyright © 1975 by Marc Simont./ Illustration by Gustaf Tenggren from *The Tenggren Tell-It-Again Book* with text edited and adapted by Katharine Gibson. Copyright 1942 by Artists and Writers Guild, Inc. All reprinted by permission of Little, Brown and Co.

LONGMANS, GREEN & CO. (London). Illustration by Frank Utpatel from *Wisconsin Is My Doorstep* by Robert E. Gard. Copyright 1948 by Robert E. Gard. Reprinted by permission of Longmans, Green & Co.

LOTHROP, LEE AND SHEPARD CO. Photograph by Harnischfeger from *Jobs in Manufacturing* by Robert J. Houlehen. Copyright © 1973 by Robert J. Houlehen./ Illustrations by Ruth Gannett from *My Mother Is the Most Beautiful Woman in the World* by Becky Reyher. Copyright 1945, 1973 by Becky Reyher and Ruth Gannett. Both reprinted by permission of Lothrop, Lee and Shepard Co.

MACMILLAN PUBLISHING CO. Illustration from *The History of the American People* by Charles A. Beard and William C. Bagley. Copyright 1918, 1920 by The Macmillan Co./ Illustration by James Daugherty from *The Three Musketeers* by Alexandre Dumas. Illustration by Elizabeth Orton Jones from *Big Susan* by Elizabeth Orton Jones. Copyright 1947 by the Macmillan Company./ Illustration by Elizabeth Orton Jones from *Prayer for a Child* by Rachel Field. Copyright 1941, 1944 by Macmillan Publishing Co., Inc./ Illustration by Elizabeth Orton Jones from *The Scarlet Oak* by Cornelia Meigs. Copyright 1938 by the Macmillan Co. All reprinted by permission of the Macmillan Publishing Co.

McGRAW-HILL BOOK CO. Illustration by Paul Galdone from *A Visit from St. Nicholas* by Clement C. Moore. Reprinted by permission of McGraw-Hill Book Co.

McINTOSH & OTIS, INC. Illustration by Ruth Gannett from *My Mother Is the Most*

Beautiful Woman in the World by Becky Reyher. Copyright 1945, 1973 by Becky Reyher and Ruth Gannett. Reprinted by permission of McIntosh & Otis, Inc.

DAVID McKAY, INC. Illustration by Erica Gorecka-Egan from *Good Sense and Good Fortune* compiled and translated by Lucia Merecka Borski. Copyright 1970 by Lucia Merecka Borski. Reprinted by permission of David McKay, Inc.

MICHIGAN STATE UNIVERSITY PRESS. Sidelight excerpts from *The Wizard of Oz and Who He Was* by Martin Gardner and Russel B. Nye. Copyright © 1957 by the Michigan State University Press. Reprinted by permission of Michigan State University Press.

MOREHAUS-GRAHAM CO. Sidelight excerpts from *The Poet of Christmas Eve: A Life of Clement Clarke Moore, 1779-1863* by Samuel White Patterson. Reprinted by permission of Morehaus-Graham Co.

PETER OWEN LTD. Sidelight excerpts from *My Memoirs* by Alexandre Dumas, translated by A. Craig Bell. Copyright © 1961 by Peter Owen Ltd. Reprinted by permission of Peter Owen Ltd.

OXFORD UNIVERSITY PRESS (London). Illustration by Brian Wildsmith from *The Lion and the Rat* by La Fontaine. Copyright © 1963 by Brian Wildsmith. Reprinted by permission of Oxford University Press.

PARABEL VERLAG. Illustration by Johanna Sengler from *The Wandering Shoe* by Clemens Parma. Copyright © 1966 by Lerner Publications Co. Reprinted by permission of Parabel Verlag.

PARENTS' MAGAZINE PRESS. Illustration by Grambs Miller from *Wetlands—Bogs, Marshes, and Swamps* by Lewis Buck. Illustrations copyright © 1974 by Grambs Miller./ Illustration by Imero Gobbato from *Barney the Beard* by Eve Bunting. Illustration copyright © 1975 by Imero Gobbato./ Illustration by Alasdair Anderson from *2010 Living in the Future* by Geoffrey Hoyle. Text copyright 1973 by Parents' Magazine. Illustration copyright 1972 by William Heinemann, Ltd./ Illustration by Harold Berson from *The Pelican Chorus* by Edward Lear. Copyright © 1967 by Harold Berson./ Illustration by Tàlivaldis Stubis from *Funny Magic* by Rose Wyler and Gerald Ames. Text copyright © 1972 by Rose Wyler and Gerald Ames. Illustrations copyright © 1972 by Tàlivaldis Stubis. All reprinted by permission of Parents' Magazine Press.

CLARKSON N. POTTER. Sidelight excerpts from *The Annotated Wizard of Oz*, introduction and annotation by Michael Patrick Hearn. Reprinted by permission of Clarkson N. Potter.

PRENTICE-HALL, INC. Illustration by Tom Dunnington from *A Wild Goose Chase* by Roy Toothaker. Copyright © 1975 by Roy Toothaker and Tom Dunnington. Reprinted by permission of Prentice-Hall, Inc.

G. P. PUTNAM'S SONS. Illustration by Charles Dougherty from *I Know a Policeman* by Barbara Williams. Copyright © 1966 by Barbara Williams. Reprinted by permission of G. P. Putnam's Sons.

RAND McNALLY AND CO. Illustrations by Wesley Dennis from *Album of Horses* by Marguerite Henry. Copyright 1951 by Rand McNally & Co. Copyright 1951 under International Copyright Union by Rand McNally & Co./ Illustration by Tasha Tudor from *The Night Before Christmas* by Clement Clarke Moore. Copyright © 1975 by Rand McNally & Co. All reprinted by permission of Rand McNally and Co.

RANDOM HOUSE, INC. Sidelight excerpts from *The Oz Scrapbook* by David L. Greene and Dick Martin. Illustration by Seymour Chwast from *The House That Jack Built* by Seymour Chwast./ Illustration by Michael K. Frith from *Reptiles Do the Strangest Things* by Leonora and Arthur Hornblow. Copyright © 1970 by Random House./ Illustration by Grandma Moses from *The Night Before Christmas* by Clement C. Moore. Copyright © 1948, 1960, 1961 by Grandma Moses Properties, Inc. All reprinted by permission of Random House, Inc.

HENRY REGNERY CO. Illustration by John R. Neill from *The Emerald City of Oz* by L. Frank Baum. Copyright 1910, 1927, 1938./ Illustration by John Neill from *The Lost Princess of Oz* by L. Frank Baum. Copyright 1917, 1944./ Illustration by John Neill from *The Road to Oz* by L. Frank Baum. Copyright 1909, 1927, 1937. All reprinted by permission of Henry Regnery Co., a division of Contemporary Books.

SCHOLASTIC BOOK SERVICES. Illustration by Beth and Joe Krush from *The Cat Sitter Mystery* by Carol Adorjan. Text copyright © 1973 by Carol Adorjan. Illustration copyright © 1973 by J. Philip O'Hara, Inc. Reprinted by permission of Scholastic Book Services.

CHARLES SCRIBNER'S SONS. Sidelight excerpts from *Writers and Writing* by Robert

Van Gelder. Copyright 1946 by Charles Scribner's Sons./ Illustration by N. C. Wyeth from *The Boy's King Arthur* by Sidney Lanier. Copyright 1917, 1924 by Charles Scribner's Sons; renewal copyright 1945 by N. C. Wyeth and 1952 by John Lanier, David Lanier and Sterling Lanier./ Illustration by E. B. Russell from *The Boys' Percy* edited and an introduction by Sidney Lanier. Copyright 1882 by Charles Scribner's Sons./ Illustration by Ernest Thompson Seton from *Lives of the Hunted* by Ernest Thompson Seton. Copyright 1901 by Ernest Seton-Thompson. All reprinted by permission of Charles Scribner's Sons.

SEA CLIFF PRESS LTD. Illustration by Jerry Lang from *A Mouse to Be Free* by Joyce W. Warren. Text copyright © 1973 by Joyce W. Warren. Illustrations copyright © 1973 by Jerry Lang. Reprinted by permission of Sea Cliff Press Ltd.

SIMON AND SCHUSTER, INC. Illustrations by Walt Kelly from *Pogo Revisited* by Walt Kelly. Copyright © 1957, 1959, 1960, 1961, 1962, 1966, 1974 by Walt Kelly./ Illustrations by Walt Kelly from *Walt Kelly's Pogo Revisited* by Walt Kelly. Copyright © 1957, 1959, 1961, 1962, 1966, 1974 by Walt Kelly./ Illustrations by Hendrik Van Loon from *The Last of the Troubadours* by Grace Castagnetta. Copyright 1939 by Hendrik Willem Van Loon and Grace Castagnetta. All reprinted by permission of Simon and Schuster, Inc.

STEIN AND DAY. Illustration by Anson Lowitz from *The Pilgrims' Party: A Really Truly Story* by Sadyebeth and Anson Lowitz. Copyright © 1931 by Sadyebeth and Anson Lowitz. Copyright renewed 1959 by Sadyebeth and Anson Lowitz. Reprinted by permission of Stein and Day.

STERLING PUBLISHING CO. Illustration by Charles H. Paraquin from *Eye Teasers* by Charles H. Paraquin. Copyright © 1977 by Sterling Publishing Co. Reprinted by permission of Sterling Publishing Co.

THE THIMBLE PRESS. Sidelight excerpts from an article "An Interview with Alan Garner" by Aidan Chambers, September, 1978 in *Signal*, #27. Reprinted by permission of The Thimble Press.

UNIVERSITY OF NORTH CAROLINA PRESS. Sidelight excerpts from *Sidney Lanier* by Aubrey Starke. Copyright © 1933 by the University of North Carolina Press. Reprinted by permission of University of North Carolina Press.

THE VIKING PRESS. Illustration by Elizabeth Orton Jones from *Small Rain* by Jessie Orton Jones. Copyright 1943 (renewed 1971) by Jessie Orton Jones and Elizabeth Orton Jones./ Illustration by Don Freeman from *Monster Night at Grandma's House* by Richard Peck. Copyright © 1977 by Richard Peck and Don Freeman. Both reprinted by permission of The Viking Press.

HENRY Z. WALCK. Illustration by Harper Johnson from *Lone Hunter's First Buffalo Hunt* by Donald Worcester. Copyright © 1958 by Henry Z. Walck, Inc. Reprinted by permission of Henry Z. Walck.

FRANKLIN WATTS, INC. Illustration by Sam Fink from *The Journal of One Davey Wyatt* by Donald Honig. Copyright © 1972 by Donald Honig./ Illustration by Brian Wildsmith from *The Lion and the Rat* by La Fontaine. Copyright © 1963 by Brian Wildsmith. Both reprinted by permission of Franklin Watts, Inc.

WESTERN PUBLISHING CO., INC. Sidelight excerpts from *Letters from Jack London* edited by King Hendricks and Irving Shepard. Copyright © 1965 by King Hendricks and Irving Shepard. Reprinted by permission of Western Publishing Co., Inc.

THE WESTMINSTER PRESS. Illustration by Beth and Joe Krush from *Petey* by Betty Cavanna. Copyright © 1973 by Betty Cavanna. Reprinted by permission of The Westminster Press.

THE JOHN C. WINSTON CO. Illustration by Marguerite Kirmse from *Lassie Come Home* by Eric Knight. Copyright 1940 by The John C. Winston Co./ Illustration by Everett Shinn from *The Night Before Christmas* by Clement Clarke Moore. Copyright 1942 by John C. Winston Company. Both reprinted by permission of The John C. Winston Company.

YEARLING BOOKS. Illustration by David Omar White from *Sophia Scrooby Preserved* by Martha Bacon. Copyright © 1968 by Martha Bacon Ballinger./ Illustration by Garth Williams from *The Adventures of Benjamin Pink* by Garth Williams. Copyright © 1951 by Garth Williams. Reprinted by permission of Yearling Books, a division of Dell Publishing.

Illustration by Erik Blegvad from *Bedknob and Broomstick* by Mary Norton. Copyright © 1943, 1957, 1971 by Mary Norton. Reprinted by permission of Erik Blegvad./ Sidelight excerpts from The General Manuscripts Collection, Rare Book and Manuscript Library, Columbia University. Reprinted by permission of Columbia University Library./ Illustration by Joseph Low from *The Lost Zoo* by Christopher Cat and Countee Cullen. Text copyright renewed 1968 by Ida M. Cullen. Illustration copyright © 1969 by Follett Publishing Co. Reprinted by permission of Mrs. Ida M. Cullen./ Sidelight excerpts from "The Papers of Countee Cullen, 1921-1969," The Schomberg Center for Research in Black Culture. Reprinted by permission of Amistad Research Center, Dillard University./ Illustration by Arthur Rackham from *The Night Before Christmas* by Clement C. Moore. Reprinted by the kind permission of Mrs. Barbara Edwards./ Illustration by Arnold Lobel from *The New Vestments* by Edward Lear. Illustration copyright © 1970 by Arnold Lobel. Reprinted by permission of Arnold Lobel./ Photograph by Anthony D. Marshall from *Trinidad—Tobago* by Anthony D. Marshall. Copyright © 1975 by Franklin Watts. Reprinted by permission of Hon. Anthony D. Marshall./ Illustration from *What Does a Lifeguard Do?* by Kathy Pelta. Copyright © 1977 by Kathy Pelta. Reprinted by permission of Dennis McCarbery, Los Angeles County, Department of Beaches./ Sidelight excerpts from an article "I Went to Noke and Somebody Spoke" by David McCord, October, 1974 in *Horn Book*. Reprinted by permission of David McCord./ Sidelight excerpts from an introduction to *What Cheer* by David McCord. Reprinted by permission of David McCord./ Sidelight excerpts from an article "The Magic of Mary Norton" by Jean de Temple, November, 1958 in *Ontario Library Bulletin*. Reprinted by permission of *Ontario Library Bulletin*./ Sidelight excerpts from an article "Unforgettable Walt Kelly" by Joseph P. Mastrangelo, July, 1974 in *Reader's Digest*. Reprinted by permission of *Reader's Digest*./ Sidelight excerpts from an article "Pogo Looks at the Abominable Snowman" by Walt Kelly, August 30, 1958 in *Saturday Review*. Reprinted by permission of *Saturday Review*./ Sidelight excerpts from *Trail of an Artist-Naturalist* by Ernest Thompson Seton. Reprinted by permission of Mrs. Ernest Thompson Seton./ Photograph by W. Brindle from *New at the Zoo* by Terry Shannon and Charles Payzant. Picture courtesy of the Australian News and Information Bureau. Copyright © 1972 by Terry Shannon. Reprinted by permission of Terry Shannon./ Sidelight excerpts from an article "Printer's Life Is the Life for Me!" by Elizabeth Orton Jones in *Imprint: Oregon,* Volume I. Reprinted by permission of University of Oregon Library./ Sidelight excerpts from *Report to Saint Peter* by Hendrik Van Loon. Copyright 1947 by Helen Van Loon. Reprinted by permission of the Van Loon Estate./ Sidelight excerpts from an article "How to Submit a Manuscript" by Martha Bacon, May, 1956 in *The Writer*. Reprinted by permission of *The Writer*./ Sidelight excerpts from letters and manuscripts of Clement C. Moore. Reprinted by permission of The General Theological Seminary, New York, N.Y.

Thanks also to the Performing Arts Research Center of the New York Public Library at Lincoln Center for permission to reprint the following theater stills: "Count of Monte Cristo" and "The Wizard of Oz."

PHOTOGRAPH CREDITS

Madeline Angell: Phil Revoir; Charles A. Beard: Walter Sanders, *Life Magazine;* Dale Fife: John Armstrong White; Paul Kuttner: L. Jefferson Siegel; David McCord: Thomas Garland Tinsley; Mary Norton: Fred Daniel; Richard Peck: Nancy K. Smith; Kathy Pelta: Edmond Pelta; Johanna Sengler: Foto Lockemann; William Steig: Nancy Crampton; John H. Vogel, Jr.: Judd Studio; Rosemary Wells: Richard W. Germann; Garth Williams: Berko; Gene Zion: William Grigsby.

SOMETHING ABOUT THE AUTHOR

"We didn't dare tell about the man 'cause then you'd know we'd waded across the river when you told us not to." ■ (From *The Chichi Hoo Hoo Bogeyman* by Virginia Driving Hawk Sneve. Illustrated by Nadema Agard.)

AGARD, Nadema   1948-

PERSONAL: Born September 10, 1948, in New York, N.Y.; daughter of James E. (a baker) and Frieda (Phillips; a receptionist) Agard; married Melvin Ray Tubby (a student), August 29, 1975; children: Brandon Marc. *Education:* New York University, B.S., 1970; Teachers College, New York University, M.A., 1973. *Home:* 50 Park Terrace East, New York, N.Y. 10034. *Office:* 103 West 107th Street, New York, N.Y. 10025.

CAREER: New York Public Schools, New York, N.Y., teacher, 1970-75; Red School House, Minneapolis, Minn., curriculum developer for Native American children, 1974. *Exhibitions:* Bahai Spiritual Assembly, October, 1976; Interlochen, Michigan, April, 1977; Teachers College Alumni Show, 1977. *Member:* American Indian Community House. *Awards, honors:* Proclamation from city of Albany for Representation on American Indian Day, September, 1975.

WRITINGS: (Co-advisor) *Guidelines for Fair and Accurate Representation of Women and Minorities*, Silver Burdett, 1976.

Illustrator: Virginia D. Sneve, *Chi Chi Hoo Hoo Bogey Man*, Holiday House, 1975.

SIDELIGHTS: "I illuminate the influence and beauty of the Native American Indian culture, art, philosophy and history. Motivated by the spirituality of Edward Munch, the respect for third world cultures painted by Gauguin.

"Have travelled to Europe five times and speak fluent Spanish, semi-fluent Italian."

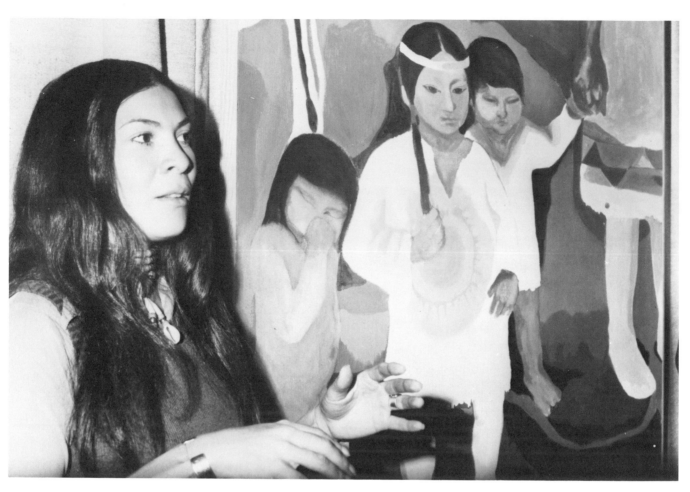

NADEMA AGARD

FOR MORE INFORMATION SEE: New York *Post,* May 14, 1975; *51 News Magazine,* September 12, 1975; *Knicker-bocker News,* Albany, N.Y., September 29, 1975; *Traverse City Record-Eagle,* Michigan, May 12, 1977.

ALVAREZ, Joseph A. 1930-

PERSONAL: Born October 2, 1930, in New York, N.Y.; son of Raul (a utility company supervisor) and Helen (Woehl) Alvarez; married Marianne Besser, December 17, 1955 (died November 14, 1971); children: Krista. *Education:* City College, New York, N.Y., B.A., 1955; Sonoma State University, Calif., M.A. (English), 1975, M.A. (psychology), 1979. *Residence:* Santa Rosa, Calif. *Agent:* Curtis Brown Ltd., 575 Madison Ave., New York, N.Y. 10022.

CAREER: Writer's Digest, Cincinnati, Ohio, circulation director, 1955-58; Book-of-the-Month Club, New York, N.Y., advertising executive, 1958-61; Santa Rosa Junior College, Santa Rosa, Calif., English instructor, 1972—; professional writer, 1961—. *Member:* Author's Guild.

WRITINGS: (With C. W. Mattison) *Man and His Resources in Today's World,* Creative Education Press, 1967; *Vice Presidents of Destiny,* Putnam, 1969; *Politics in America,* Creative Education Press, 1971; *From Reconstruction to Revolution: The Black Struggle for Equality,* Atheneum, 1971; *The Elements of Technical Writing,* Harcourt, 1980.

Educational film strips: "Streets, Prairies and Valleys: The Life of Carl Sandburg"; "The World of Mark Twain"; "The Regulatory Agencies"; "Mass Media"; "The Puritan Legacy"; "From Colony to Country: Early American Literature"; "We Are Indians: American Indian Literature"; "Do We Really Have Freedom of the Press?".

WORK IN PROGRESS: A biography of Shakespeare.

SIDELIGHTS: "When I began to write, I wanted to describe things as clearly and interestingly as possible. And I wanted the recognition that goes with being a writer. Twenty-five years later, I am less concerned with recognition. Now I write basically for myself. What I mean is that for me writing is a way of expressing myself, of learning, of sorting things out for myself. This applies whether I write a book or make an entry in my journal.

"I am a curious person: I like to explore feelings, ideas, relationships. I like to know. This is sometimes dangerous, often painful, but I do it anyway, taking my cue from poet T. S. Eliot's lines from *Little Gidding:*

'We shall not cease from exploration
And the end of all our exploring
Will be to arrive where we started
and know the place for the first time.'"

HOBBIES AND OTHER INTERESTS: Tennis, guitar, running.

All living things depend upon the natural world for their existence. ■ (From *Man and His Resources* by C.W. Mattison and Joseph Alvarez. Photo courtesy of U.S. Forest Service.)

MADELINE ANGELL

ANGELL, Madeline 1919-

PERSONAL: Born January 6, 1919, in Devils Lake, N.D.; daughter of Bernard Oscar and Evelyn (Smith) Angell; married Kenneth F. Johnson (a vice-president in men's retail clothing business), August 31, 1940; children: Mark Frederick, Randall David. *Education:* University of Minnesota, B.S. (cum laude), 1940. *Politics:* Independent. *Religion:* Lutheran. *Home and office:* R.R.4, Cardinal Dr., Red Wing, Minn. 55066.

CAREER: Sears, Roebuck & Co., Duluth, Minn., advertising manager, 1944-45; writer. Former co-chairman of local mayor's citizens committee for the state training school. *Member:* American Association of University Women (co-president, 1956-58). *Awards, honors:* Humanities award from McKnight Foundation, 1966, for unpublished novel *The October Horse.*

WRITINGS: One Hundred Twenty Questions and Answers About Birds, Bobbs-Merrill, 1973; *America's Best Loved Wild Animals,* Bobbs-Merrill, 1975; *The Fantastic Variety of Marine Animals,* Bobbs-Merrill, 1976; *Red Wing, Minnesota, Saga of a River Town,* Dillon Press, 1978; *Snakes and Frogs and Turtles and Such,* Bobbs-Merrill, 1979. Contributor to popular magazines, including *Parents' Magazine, Better Homes and Gardens,* and *Science World.*

WORK IN PROGRESS: A book on identification of wild berries for Bobbs-Merrill; a biography of J. W. Hancock,

Sea otter

How does a sea otter swim?

If it is not in a hurry, it swims on its back, propelling itself with strokes of the tail. If it is in a hurry, it turns over and uses its feet as well as its tail for swimming. ■ (From *The Fantastic Variety of Marine Animals* by Madeline Angell. Illustrated by Larry Veeder.)

Minnesota pioneer, to be written in collaboration with Mary Miller.

SIDELIGHTS: "I started writing for young people with my book on birds. I found that in spite of being a bird watcher for many years, I had many questions in my mind about birds, such as why they raise their heads to drink water, and why the black throat patch of an English sparrow shows more in late winter than it does at other times of the year.

"The children I know share with me an insatiable curiosity and a delight in learning something new. So I decided to write a book based on my questions and their answers, and aim it at young readers. One nature book led to another, and the last one published, on amphibians and reptiles, is dedicated to my two young grandsons.

"Although I consult authorities on various aspects of nature study, much of my source material comes from direct observation. My husband and I are fortunate in having friends who share our interest in roaming the woods, enjoying the sights and sounds and smells of the outdoors, and speculating on the meaning of what we observe. I also share my love of the outdoors with a group of biking friends who get together every Monday, weather permitting, and bike the back roads, stopping to admire wildflowers, autumn leaves, bird songs and the like."

HOBBIES AND OTHER INTERESTS: Nature study and natural history, biking, bridge, reading (biography, history, fiction), travel.

BACON, Martha Sherman 1917-

PERSONAL: Born in 1917, in California; daughter of Leonard Bacon (a poet); married Philip Oliver-Smith; later married Ronald Ballinger (a history professor). *Education:* Attended the American Academy of Dramatic Arts, New York City. *Residence:* Rhode Island.

CAREER: Member of the staff for the *Atlantic Monthly;* Rhode Island College, Providence, lecturer in English; novelist and poet.

WRITINGS: Lament for the Chieftains, and Other Poems, Coward, 1942; *Things Visible and Invisible* (poems), Coward, 1947; *A Star Called Wormwood,* Random House, 1948; *A Masque of Exile,* C. N. Potter, 1962; *Puritan Promenade,* Houghton, 1964; *Sophia Scrooby Preserved* (illustrated by David Omar White), Little, Brown, 1968; *The Third Road* (illustrated by Robin Jacques), Little, Brown, 1971; *In the Company of Clowns: A Commedia,* Little, Brown, 1973. *Moth Manor,* Little, Brown, 1978.

SIDELIGHTS: Born in California in 1917, Bacon attended schools in Massachusetts and in Italy. Her father was Leonard Bacon, a poet. ". . . When I was a child I preferred to think of my books as just books, not children's books. I was highly privileged in childhood, and I had every imaginable book—*Pilgrim's Progress, Peter Rabbit, Alice in Wonderland, The Wind in the Willows, Ingoldsby Legends* (nobody seems to have *The Ingoldsby Legends* anymore), and books by E. Nesbit, Dickens, Scott, and Louisa May Alcott. I disliked Miss Alcott. How can you write a book about children and then populate it with watchful loving parents like Marmee? I compared Marmee unfavorably with Henry the Eighth in *The Prince and the Pauper* and the wolves in the Jungle Books and left *Little Women* out in the rain. Besides the above-mentioned volumes I had a shelfful of historical novels, illustrated with macabre steel engravings and dealing loosely with the names and reputations of Mary Queen of Scots, Catherine the Great, Goethe, Schiller, and Sans Souci, to name only a few. They were the work of a woman named Maria Louisa Mühlbach, an expert in the field of prolonged horror. Every chapter began with a conspiracy and ended with a supernatural visitation. Purveyors of this kind of thing could learn much from Maria Louisa." [Martha Bacon, "Dotty Dimple and the Fiction Award," *Atlantic,* March, 1963.[1]]

In the grand tradition of the commedia dell' arte Ginestra led the troupe into Castellino. Her horse lifted his knees like a thoroughbred and the applause of the multitude was sweet in her ears. She had found her vocation. From that time forth she included horses in her prayers.
■ (From *In the Company of Clowns* by Martha Bacon. Illustrated by Richard Cuffari.)

The disembarkation was festive in the sunshine and Pansy and her companions found themselves the center of a most enjoyable scene. ■ (From *Sophie Scrooby Preserved* by Martha Bacon. Illustrated by David Omar White.)

Bacon's first published works were poetry books. She began writing in the early 1940's when she was in her mid-twenties. "When I first began my struggles with the literary profession, I wrote a poem and was then faced with the problem of getting it published. I hit upon a solution. I mailed it to an editor. It worked and I've been doing just that ever since. However, at the time that I met this challenge I had no thoughts of becoming an editor, and for the next decade and a half I simply went on mailing things to editors and forgetting them until they either came back or appeared in print. It was all fairly satisfactory. Then fate in the shape of more children than money closed in on me, and in an attempt to come to terms with this condition, I became an editor. It was then that I discovered how many gins, snares, pitfalls and blind alleys exist between the author's desk and the editor's." [Martha Bacon, "How to Submit a Manuscript," *The Writer*, May, 1956.[2]]

In 1948 her first novel, *A Star Called Wormwood* was published. Her first marriage was to Philip Oliver-Smith; later married Ronald Ballinger. "It occurred to me after I had children of my own that I might contribute to their pleasure and support by writing a book for children. The book I wrote

took a hero and two heroines through a zoo full of mythological animals, a haunted abbey and a circus; dealt exhaustively with dwarfs, royalty, the Spanish inquisition, merry-go-rounds, an apostate nun, thunderstorms, and cowboys. I solved the problem of the parents by sending them around the world on a second honeymoon. The children liked it, but no publisher would touch it. They said that unicorns and griffins were out of style, that children couldn't identify with royal personages, and that much of it would give their readers nightmares. As one, they advised me to cut out the apostate nun.

"But there was one publisher, more constructive than the rest, who sent along with the rejection slip a list of the standards by which a children's book should be judged.

"'If you really want to write for the juvenile trade,' his letter said in part, 'here are some of the criteria which our editors apply to manuscripts submitted to us. Emotional appeal, values for today's living, humor, stimulation for the imagination, sense of security, inspiration, significant and lasting appeal.' The publisher concluded by offering an award for a book that should contain all this and a plot and characters too.

"The letter interested me chiefly for negative reasons. I could not think of any book, classic or contemporary which could be measured successfully by these standards. At least, not any good book. *Alice in Wonderland* has significant and lasting appeal, but I defy anyone to find a sense of security in it. You may find stimulation for the imagination in *The Princess and the Goblin,* but the 'values for today's living' are as far from George MacDonald's mind as from Prince Harelip's. *The Ingoldsby Legends* has humor, but it is a gallows humor.

"I began amusing myself by reading to the children, trying to find a possible award winner among the fireside favorites, but nothing that we really enjoyed came close."[1]

"To write a great book for children—as opposed to an amusing, commendable, or useful book evidently requires a volatile mixture of contradictions in the personality and a wide measure of irresponsibility. The foregoing is not to suggest that such people are not concerned with morality. But moral earnestness is skeletal to their work. They are priests in harlequinade, moralists in motley. Almost against their wills their sermons are entertainments." [Martha Bacon, "Puppet's Progress," *Atlantic Monthly*, April, 1970.[3]]

FOR MORE INFORMATION SEE: Christian Science Monitor, April 26, 1947; *Saturday Review of Literature,* May 31, 1947; *Kirkus,* September 15, 1948; *New York Herald Tribune Weekly Book Review,* November 14, 1948; *The Writer,* May 1956; *Atlantic,* March, 1963; *Horn Book,* October, 1968, June, 1973; *New York Times Book Review,* October 20, 1968; *Atlantic Monthly,* April, 1970.

BATE, Lucy   1939-

PERSONAL: Born March 19, 1939, in Washington, D.C.; daughter of Immanuel (a musician) and Ruth (Schmerler) Neumark; married Michael Bate (a computer scientist), March 15, 1965; children: Gabrielle, Rebecca. *Education:* Brandeis University, B.A., 1960. *Politics:* Liberal. *Home:* 195 Lakeview Ave., Cambridge, Mass. 02138.

"I think she will save my tooth and give it to a baby rabbit that was just born, and that's how little baby rabbits get teeth. Do you think that, Daddy?"

"Ah—" said Father Rabbit.

"Or," said Little Rabbit, "I think she will put my tooth up in the sky because it is such a shiny tooth, and that's how stars get made. Do you think that, Daddy?"

"We-l-l," said Father Rabbit.

"Really," said Little Rabbit, "I think she says a magic spell and she turns the tooth into a penny, I mean a dime. Do you think that, Daddy?"

(From *Little Rabbit's Loose Tooth* by Lucy Bate. Pictures by Diane de Groat.)

LUCY BATE

CAREER: Crown Publishers, New York City, editorial assistant, 1961; American Book Co., New York City, assistant editor, 1962-63; Hart Publishing Co., New York City, writer, 1964-65; freelance writer, 1965—. *Member:* Overseas Press Club. *Awards, honors:* New plays award from Skidmore College, 1969, for "The Great Silkie of Sule Skerry"; Evansville, Indiana Book Award, 1978 and Young Reader's Medal, 1978, both for *Little Rabbit's Loose Tooth*.

WRITINGS: Little Rabbit's Loose Tooth (juvenile), Crown, 1975.

Plays: "The Great Silkie of Sule Skerry" (radio play), first produced by Liberi Artisti, 1973; "Little Red Riding Hood" (juvenile), first produced in Cambridge, Mass. by Tobin Players, 1974; "An Antigone Play" (one-act), first produced in Boston, Mass. by Octopus, 1974; "King David" (three-act), first produced in Boston by Jewish Repertory Theatre, 1975; "A Long Drive to Quincy" (one-act), first produced in Cambridge by Tobin Players, 1975; "Events in a Beerhall" (one-act), first produced in Cambridge by Tobin Players, 1975.

Poem: "Wwolf: The Midnight Train," broadcast in translation by Radio Belgrade, Yugoslavia, 1977.

HOBBIES AND OTHER INTERESTS: Jazz piano, anthropology.

BAUM, L(yman) Frank   1856-1919
(Floyd Akers, Laura Bancroft, Captain Hugh Fitzgerald, Suzanne Metcalf, Schuyler Staunton, Edith Van Dyne)

PERSONAL: Born May 15, 1856, in Chittenango, New York; died May 6, 1919; son of Benjamin Ward (an oil

L. FRANK BAUM

dealer) and Cynthia (Stanton) Baum; married Maude Gage, November 9, 1882; children: Frank Joslyn, Robert Stanton, Henry Neal, Kenneth Gage. *Education:* Privately tutored at home; also attended Peekskill Military Academy. *Home:* Hollywood, California.

CAREER: Playwright, novelist, journalist, author of books for children. Began as a newspaper reporter in New York City; manager of a chain of small theaters (in which he occasionally acted and had four of his own plays produced), 1880-83; worked in a family business in Syracuse, New York, 1883-88, also raising fancy poultry, writing a textbook on chickens, and collaborating in the production of a new brand of axle grease; operator of a variety store, "Baum's Bazaar," and later editor of the newspaper *Saturday Pioneer,* both in Aberdeen, South Dakota, 1888-90; held a variety of positions in Chicago, Illinois, including newspaper reporter, traveling salesman, and crockery buyer, beginning 1891; founded a national association of shop window decorators, and edited and published *The Show Window* (a trade magazine), Chicago, 1897-1902; full-time writer, 1902-19. *Awards, honors:* Lewis Carroll Shelf Award, 1968, for *The Wizard of Oz.*

WRITINGS—"Oz" series: *The Wonderful Wizard of Oz* (illustrated by William Wallace Denslow), G. M. Hill, 1900, later published as *The Wizard of Oz,* reissued, Rand McNally, 1971 [other editions include those illustrated by Leonard Weisgard, Junior Deluxe Editions, 1955; Evelyn Copelman, Grosset & Dunlap, 1956; Maraja, Grosset & Dunlap, 1958; Anna Marie Magagna, Grosset & Dunlap, 1963; Balint Biro, Dutton, 1965; Roy Krenkel, Airmont, 1965; Brigitte Bryan, Childrens Press, 1969; abridged versions include those adapted by Allen Chaffee, Random House, 1968; Jean Kellogg, Reilly & Lee, 1961; Albert G. Miller, Random House, 1968; dramatic adaptations include those written by

Elizabeth Fuller Chapman, Samuel French, 1956; Adele Thane, Children's Theatre Press, 1957; Anne Coulter Martens, Dramatic Publishing, 1963; Alfred Bradley, D. Dobson, 1971].

Other "Oz" books; all illustrated by John R. Neill: *The Marvelous Land of Oz,* Reilly & Britton, 1904, reissued, Dover, 1969, later published as *The Land of Oz: A Sequel to "The Wizard of Oz,"* reissued, Rand McNally, 1971 [abridged versions include the adaptation by Jean Kellogg, Reilly & Lee, 1961; dramatic adaptations include those written by Elizabeth Fuller Goodspeed, Samuel French, 1956; Adele Thane, Children's Theatre Press, 1963]; *Ozma of Oz,* Reilly & Britton, 1907, reissued, Rand McNally, 1971; *Dorothy and the Wizard in Oz,* Reilly & Britton, 1908, reissued, Rand McNally, 1971; *The Road to Oz,* Reilly & Britton, 1909, reissued, Rand McNally, 1971; *The Emerald City of Oz,* Reilly & Britton, 1910, reissued, Rand McNally, 1972.

The Patchwork Girl of Oz, Reilly & Britton, 1913, reissued, Rand McNally, 1972; *The Little Wizard Stories of Oz,* Reilly & Britton, 1914; *Tik-Tok of Oz,* Reilly & Britton, 1914, reissued, Rand McNally, 1973; *The Scarecrow of Oz,* Reilly & Britton, 1915, reissued, Rand McNally, 1972; *Rinkitink in Oz,* Reilly & Britton, 1916; *The Lost Princess of Oz,* Reilly & Britton, 1917; *The Tin Woodman of Oz,* Reilly & Lee, 1918, reissued, Rand McNally, 1971; *The Magic of Oz,* Reilly & Lee, 1919, reissued, Rand McNally, 1972; *Glinda of Oz,* Reilly & Lee, 1920, reissued, Rand McNally, 1973; *The Royal Book of Oz* (enlarged and edited by Ruth Plumly Thompson), Reilly & Lee, 1921.

(From *Dorothy and the Wizard in Oz* by L. Frank Baum. Illustrated by John R. Neill.)

(Fred Stone and David Montgomery, the original Scarecrow and Tin Man in the 1902 musical comedy "The Wizard of Oz.")

(An original water-color painting by John R. Neill from *The Emerald City of Oz* by L. Frank Baum.)

(Original drawing by John Neill from *The Road to Oz* by L. Frank Baum.)

Tommy Tucker

Tommy hesitated, but when he glanced at the white bread and butter his mouth watered in spite of himself. ■ (From *Mother Goose in Prose* by L. Frank Baum. Illustrated by Maxfield Parrish.)

"Oz" series continued by other authors—written by Ruth Plumly Thompson; illustrated by J. R. Neill; published by Reilly & Lee: *Kabumpo in Oz*, 1922; *The Cowardly Lion of Oz*, 1923; *Grampa in Oz*, 1924; *The Lost King of Oz*, 1925; *The Hungry Tiger of Oz*, 1926; *The Gnome King of Oz*, 1927; *The Giant Horse of Oz*, 1928; *Jack Pumpkinhead of Oz*, 1929; *The Yellow Knight of Oz*, 1930; *Pirates in Oz*, 1931; *The Purple Prince of Oz*, 1932; *Ojo in Oz*, 1933; *Speedy in Oz*, 1934; *The Wishing Horse of Oz*, 1935; *Captain Salt in Oz*, 1936; *Handy Mandy in Oz*, 1937; *The Silver Princess in Oz*, 1938; *Ozoplaning with the Wizard of Oz*, 1939.

Written and illustrated by John R. Neill; published by Reilly & Lee: *The Wonder City of Oz*, 1940; *The Scalawagons of Oz*, 1941; *Lucky Bucky in Oz*, 1942.

Written by Jack Snow; illustrated by Frank Kramer; published by Reilly & Lee: *The Magical Mimics in Oz*, 1946; *The Shaggy Man of Oz*, 1949.

Written by Rachel Cosgrove; illustrated by Dirk; published by Reilly & Lee: *The Hidden Valley of Oz*, 1951.

Other writings by Baum for children: *Mother Goose in Prose* (illustrated by Maxfield Parrish), Way & Williams, 1897; *Father Goose: His Book* (illustrated by W. W. Denslow), G. M. Hill, 1899; *The Songs of Father Goose for the Kindergarten, the Nursey, and the Home* (music by Alberta N. Hall), G. M. Hill, 1900; *A New Wonderland* (illustrated by Frank Ver Beck), R. H. Russell, 1900, later published as *The Surprising Adventures of the Magical Monarch of Mo and His People*, Bobbs-Merrill, 1903, reissued, Dover, 1968 [another

edition under the latter title illustrated by Evelyn Copelman, Bobbs-Merrill, 1947]; *The Army Alphabet* (illustrated by Harry Kennedy), G. M. Hill, 1900; *The Navy Alphabet* (illustrated by Kennedy), G. M. Hill, 1900.

American Fairy Tales (illustrated by George Kerr), G. M. Hill, 1901; *Dot and Tot of Merryland*, G. M. Hill, 1901; *The Master Key: An Electrical Fairy Tale Founded Upon the Mysteries of Electricity and the Optimism of Its Devotees* (illustrated by Fanny Y. Cory), Bowen-Merrill, 1901, reissued, Hyperion Press, 1971; *The Life and Adventures of Santa Claus* (illustrated by Mary Cowles Clark), Bowen-Merrill, 1902, reissued, Exposition Press, 1971; *The Enchanted Island of Yew* (illustrated by F. Y. Cory), Bobbs-Merrill, 1903; *The Woggle-Bug Book*, Reilly & Britton, 1905; *Queen Zixi of Ix; or, The Story of the Magic Cloak* (illustrated by Frederick Richardson), Century, 1905, reissued, Dover, 1971; *John Dough and the Cherub* (illustrated by John R. Neill), Reilly & Britton, 1906, reissued, Dover, 1974; *Father Goose's Year Book: Quaint Quacks and Feathered Shafts for Mature Children* (illustrated by Walter J. Enright), Reilly & Britton, 1907.

L. Frank Baum's Juvenile Speaker: Readings and Recitations in Prose and Verse, Humorous and Otherwise (illustrated by J. R. Neill and Maginel Wright Enright), Reilly & Britton, 1910; *The Sea Fairies* (illustrated by Neill), Reilly & Britton, 1911, reissued, Reilly & Lee, 1969; *The Daring Twins: A Story for Young Folk* (illustrated by Pauline M. Batchelder), Reilly & Britton, 1911; *Sky Island* (illustrated by J. R. Neill), Reilly & Britton, 1912, reissued, Reilly & Lee, 1970; *Jaglon and the Tiger Fairies*, Reilly & Lee, 1953; *Animal Fairy Tales* (illustrated by Dick Martin; first published in the *Delineator*, January-September, 1905), International Wizard of Oz Club, 1969; *A Kidnapped Santa Claus*, (illustrated by Richard Rosenblum; first published in the *Delineator*, December, 1904), Bobbs-Merrill, 1969.

Under pseudonym Floyd Akers; "Boy Fortune Hunters" series, published by Reilly & Britton: *Boy Fortune Hunters in Alaska*, 1908; . . . *in Egypt*, 1908; . . . *in Panama*, 1908; . . . *in China*, 1909; . . . *in Yucatan*, 1910; . . . *in the South Seas*, 1911.

Under pseudonym Laura Bancroft; all illustrated by Maginel Wright Enright; all published by Reilly & Britton: *Bandit Jim Crow*, 1906; *Mr. Woodchuck*, 1906; *Prairie-Dog Town*, 1906; *Prince Mud-Turtle*, 1906; *Sugar-Loaf Mountain*, 1906; *Twinkle's Enchantment*, 1906; *Policeman Bluejay*, 1907; *Twinkle and Chubbins: Their Astonishing Adventures in Nature-Fairyland*, 1911; *Babes in Birdland*, 1911.

Under pseudonym Captain Hugh Fitzgerald; all published by Reilly & Britton: *Sam Steele's Adventures on Land and Sea* (illustrated by Howard Heath), 1906; *Sam Steele's Adventures in Panama*, 1907.

Under pseudonym Suzanne Metcalf: *Annabel: A Novel for Young Folks*, Reilly & Britton, 1906 [a later edition illustrated by Joseph Pierre Nuyttens, 1912].

Under pseudonym Schuyler Staunton: *The Fate of a Crown*, Reilly & Britton, 1905; *Daughters of Destiny*, Reilly & Britton, 1906.

Under pseudonym Edith Van Dyne; "Aunt Jane's Nieces" series; published by Reilly & Britton: *Aunt Jane's Nieces*, 1906; . . . *Abroad*, 1907; . . . *at Millville*, 1908; . . . *at Work*,

1909; . . . *in Society*, 1910; . . . *and Uncle John*, 1911; . . . *on Vacation*, 1912; . . . *on the Ranch*, 1913; . . . *out West*, 1914; . . . *in the Red Cross*, 1915.

The Flying Girl (illustrated by J. P. Nuyttens), Reilly & Britton, 1911; *The Flying Girl and Her Chum* (illustrated by Nuyttens), Reilly & Britton, 1912; *Mary Louise*, Reilly & Britton, 1916; *Mary Louise in the Country*, Reilly & Britton, 1916; *Mary Louise Solves a Mystery*, Reilly & Britton, 1917; *Mary Louise at Dorfield*, Reilly & Lee, 1920; *Mary Louise and Josie O'Gorman*, Reilly & Lee, 1922; *Josie O'Gorman*, Reilly & Lee, 1923; *Josie O'Gorman and the Meddlesome Major*, Reilly & Lee, 1924.

Plays: "The Maid of Arran," first produced in New York City, 1881; "Matches," first produced in New York City, 1882; "Kilmorne," first produced in Syracuse, New York, 1884; "The Queen of Killarney," first produced in Rochester, New York, 1885; "The Wizard of Oz" (musical), first produced in Chicago, Illinois, 1902; "The Woggle-Bug" (musical), first produced in Chicago, 1905; "The Radio-Play," produced in Chicago and New York City, 1908-09; "The Tik-Tok Man of Oz," first produced in Los Angeles, California, 1913.

Other: *By the Candelabra's Glare* (poems), privately printed, 1898; *The Last Egyptian: A Romance of the Nile* (illustrated by Francis P. Wightman), E. Stern, 1908. Also author of *The Art of Decorating*, 1900, and illustrator of Clement Clarke Moore's *The Night before Christmas*, Reilly & Britton, 1905.

ADAPTATIONS—Movies and filmstrips: L. Frank Baum, "The Patchwork Quilt," Thomas A. Edison, Inc., 1913; "The Magic Cloak" (motion picture), Oz Film Manufacturing Co., 1914; "The Wizard of Oz," Chadwick Pictures Corp., 1925; "The Wizard of Oz" (motion picture), Loew's Inc., 1939; "Scarecrow Man" (filmstrip), Stillfilm, Inc., n.d.; "Scarecrow Man: Wizard of Oz" (filmstrip), Stillfilm, Inc., 1949; "The Wizard of Oz" (filmstrip), Teaching Resources Film, 1975.

SIDELIGHTS: **May 15, 1856.** Born the seventh child of Benjamin Ward Baum, an oil man, and Cynthia Stanton in Chittenango, New York.

1861. Family moved to residential farm property just north of Syracuse, New York known as "Rose Lawn." "The cool but sun-kissed mansion seemed delightful after the formal city house. It was built in a quaint but pretty fashion, and with many wings and gables and broad verandas on every side. Before it were acres and acres of velvety green lawns, sprinkled with shrubbery and dotted with beds of bright flowers. In every direction were winding paths covered with white gravel, which led to all parts of the grounds, looking for all the world like a map." [*The Annotated Wizard of Oz*, introduction and annotation by Michael Patrick Hearn, Clarkson N. Potter Inc., 1973.[1]]

1868-1870. Sent to Peekskill Military Academy. "I complained to my father about the brutal treatment I felt I was receiving at the school. I said the teachers were heartless, callous and continually indulging in petty nagging. I told father they were about as human as a school of fish. In those days, of course, instructors were quick to slap a boy in the face, or forcibly use a cane or ruler to punish any student who violated in the slightest way any of the strict and often unreasonable rules." [Frank Joslyn Baum and Russell P.

Little Boy Blue

For she had slipped upon the stile and fallen, and her leg was broken. ■ (From *Mother Goose in Prose* by L. Frank Baum. Illustrated by Maxfield Parrish.)

MacFall, *To Please a Child: A Biography of L. Frank Baum, Royal Historian of Oz*, Reilly & Lee, 1961.[2]]

May, 1871-1874. Began, with younger brother, Harry, to put out an amateur newspaper, *The Rose Lawn Home Journal*, using a hand press and a supply of type provided by their father. The project lasted three years. He wrote his sister, Harriet: "It was you, I remember, who first encouraged me to write. Years ago you read to father an incomplete 'novel' which I, in my youth and innocence, had scribbled, and you declared it was good."[2]

1873. Published an eleven-page pamphlet, "Baum's Complete Stamp Dealer's Directory."

1874. Published a literary monthly, *The Empire*, with a friend, Thomas G. Alfords. They described *The Empire* as "a first class amateur monthly newspaper, containing poetry, literature, postage stamp news, amateur items, etc."[1]

That same year, he broke into the theatre by joining a stock company under the name George Brooks.

1875. Bred "Hamburg chickens" at nearby Spring Farm.

1877. Secured a job with a paper, *The New Era*, in Bradford, Pennsylvania.

1878. Opted to become a professional actor by joining Albert M. Palmer's Union Square Theatre in New York.

(From the movie "The Wiz" based on the book *The Wizard of Oz,* starring Ted Ross, Michael Jackson, Diana Ross and Nipsey Russell. Copyright © 1978 by Universal City Studios, Inc.)

1880. Became manager of a chain of opera houses owned by his father in Olean and Richburg, New York and in Bradford and Gillmor, Pennsylvania. Shortly after this, his father deeded them to him. "We had a lot of trouble getting shows for the playhouses, hidden away in the oil fields, because the towns were too small to provide profitable patronage for a one-night stand. So I decided to organize my own company and produce some of Shakespeare's better known plays.

"About that time we were asked to give a special performance of *Hamlet* in the town hall of a small oil settlement. When we got there we found the hall had no stage—not even a raised platform. We asked the oil workers to arrange some saw horses at one end of the room and cover them with one by twelve inch planks that were stacked outside for use in a building under construction.

"They soon had a make-shift stage in place, but because they refused to nail the boards to the saw horses for fear of spoiling them for use in the new building, the footing was very uncertain. It was necessary to make this wobbly platform answer the purposes of a stage, but we had to be careful not to walk too heavily or jar the boards, lest they shift under our feet.

"That night everything went well until Scene Four was under way. Horatio had just said: 'Look, my lord, it comes,' and at this cue the Ghost entered and started across the loose planks. I, playing Hamlet, exclaimed: 'Angels and ministers of grace, defend us' and jumped, stumbled and displaced the ends of two of the boards.

"The Ghost was covered with a white sheet and could not see where he was walking. He veered to one side and stepped on a plank I had dislodged. It tipped and before anyone could stop him, the Ghost slipped from sight through the floor of our make-shift stage.

"None of the oil workers in the audience knew the plot of *Hamlet*. They thought the disappearance of the Ghost in this slapstick manner was part of the play and they roared with laughter. They shouted and whistled, stamped their feet and called 'More—more' until we had to repeat the scene five times before we could continue with the show.

"The old actor who played the part of the Ghost took his work very seriously, and he was still angry the following morning. He claimed his arms and legs were skinned from the rough boards because he had been required to repeat this

(From the MGM movie "The Wizard of Oz," starring Jack Haley, Ray Bolger, Frank Morgan, Judy Garland and Bert Lahr. Copyright 1939 by Loew's, Inc.)

performance of the accidental fall so many times. He quit the company in spite of the fact that we tried to make him see he should have felt highly honored. He had received more encores than all the other members of the cast together. But his spirit was bruised, like his body, and we had to get a new man for the Ghost before we could put on *Hamlet* again."[2]

1882. Wrote his first plays, including a modestly successful Irish melodrama, *The Maid of Arran,* which he produced, directed, and starred in as the romantic lead. "We opened *The Maid of Arran* in the opera house at Gillmor. It was an immediate success. This encouraged me to engage the Grand Opera House in Syracuse for two performances. The first was on May 15, 1882, my twenty-sixth birthday. A correspondent for a New York newspaper sent a favorable account of the play to his editor, and through this notice the Windsor Theater in New York booked us for the week of June 19 through 24.

"Apparently our play appealed to the big city folk as much as it had back home. We had a well filled theater all week. But I soon found that playing the principal part and managing the company, too, had become too much for me. When I asked father what to do, he assigned his brother, John Wes-ley Baum, to us as business manager for the road tour. It started in Ithaca. We played in Toronto and Rochester and several other cities in northern New York State. Then we took the train west to Columbus, Ohio, and Milwaukee, arriving in Chicago for ten performances at the Academy of Music beginning October 9. It was my first sight of Chicago, which was very busy and energetic after rebuilding from the great fire."[2]

November 9, 1882. Married Maud Gage, a daughter of Matilda Joslyn Gage, a leading suffragette. " . . . Show business doesn't leave me much time to run around with girls. You know I've never found one yet I could stay interested in."[2]

Nevertheless, "During the following summer my show had some free time between bookings. At every opportunity I returned to Syracuse, borrowed a horse and buggy from father, and drove the eight miles to Fayetteville. The Gage home there was an attractive house with colonial pillars, built in 1805, roomy and comfortably furnished. There were front and back parlors with sliding doors between. We were in the front parlor when Maud finally consented to become my wife. Then she asked me to wait there while she told her mother.

After it had boiled for a time the maple syrup became stringy, and the Prince quickly threw a string of it across the river. It hardened almost immediately, and on this simple bridge the Prince rode over the stream.
■ (From *The Magical Monarch of Mo* by L. Frank Baum. Illustrated by Frank Ver Beck.)

"Mrs. Gage was in the back parlor and, although the doors were closed, I could not avoid hearing what was said. The old lady told Maud in no uncertain terms that she objected to her marrying an actor who was on the road most of the time, jumping from town to town on one-night stands, and with an uncertain future.

"I heard Mrs. Gage say: 'I won't have my daughter be a darned fool and marry an actor.' Maud snapped back: 'All right, mother, if you feel that way about it, good bye.' 'What do you mean, good bye?' Mrs. Gage demanded. 'Well,' Maud replied, 'you just told me I would be a darned fool to marry an actor, and you wouldn't have a daughter of yours do that. I'm going to marry Frank, so, naturally you don't want a darned fool around the house.'

"Then Mrs. Gage laughed and said: 'All right, Maud. If you are in love with him and really determined to marry him, you can have your wedding right here at home.'"[2]

1884. Lost the opera house chain.

1885. Became a superintendent and salesman for Castorine, an axle oil.

1886. Published his first book, a seventy-page disquisition on chicken-raising entitled *The Book of the Hamburgs.*

1887. Father died after a decline in family fortunes.

July, 1888. Arrived in Aberdeen, the Dakota Territory, with his wife and two sons. There he opened a general store, "Baum's Bazaar" which lasted nearly two years.

January, 1890. Assumed control of a local weekly, *The Aberdeen Saturday Pioneer,* and began writing a satirical column, "Our Landlady." In the October 18, 1890 *Saturday Pioneer* he blasted the organized church: "When the priests acknowledge their fallibility; when they abolish superstition, intolerance and bigotry; when they abhor the thought of a vindictive and revengeful God; when they are able to reconcile reason and religion and fear not to let the people think for themselves, then, and then only will the Church regain its old power and be able to draw to its pulpits the whole people."[1]

His outspoken views did not win him many friends. It was about this time that Baum developed an interest in Theosophy. Baum claimed that the basic belief of Theosophy was that "God is Nature, and Nature God." As editor of the *Pioneer* (February 22, 1890) he wrote: "Of all that is inexplicable in our daily lives, we can only say that they are Nature's secrets, and a sealed book to ignorant mortals; but none the less do we marvel at their source and desire to unravel their mystery."[1]

In his article on Theosophy (January 25, 1890) Baum described his own era as an "'Age of Unfaith,' this is not atheism of the last century. It is rather an eager longing to penetrate the secrets of nature—an aspiration for knowledge we have thought is forbidden. The Theosophists are 'searchers for Truth' and 'admit the existence of God—not necessarily a personal God.'"[1]

March, 1891. Forced to give up the *Pioneer* because of financial difficulties. Baum recognized—"The sheriff wanted the paper more than I did—so I let him have it."[2]

Years later, he would be able to look back on the Dakota experience with "mingled sighs and smiles."[2]

Spring, 1891. Took a job with Chicago's *Evening Post* and searched for a home for his family. "One afternoon I was walking slowly down State Street. I stopped at the corner of Adams to look in the windows of the Fair department store and admire the skillful window decorating.

"As I looked I was half aware that a street car had passed me and stopped where the rails ended at State Street. The driver unhitched the horses, led them to the other end of the car and hitched them again for the outbound trip.

"Just as the car started, I impulsively ran into the street and jumped aboard. I had no idea where I was going as I paid my five cent fare and looked out the window. We left the business district, crossed a bridge over the river, and were soon in a residential neighborhood. Later I learned that I had taken the Harrison Street line and ridden into Chicago's great West Side.

"When we came to a section of good average American homes, about as far from the business district as I desired to live, I got off and began walking. A half hour later I discovered quite an attractive street only a block long. Down the center of a wide thoroughfare was a grassy parkway; large shade trees grew along the curbs, and the street radiated a feeling that here lived warm-hearted, contented folks. A sign post on the corner was lettered Campbell Park and halfway down the block was a cottage with a *For Rent* sign in the window.

"This was before the day of electricity in houses and very few, including this cottage, even had gas fixtures. However, in most respects it was the sort of house I wanted and felt I could afford. I hunted up the owner and signed a lease."[2]

Fall, 1891. Became a crockery buyer for Siegel, Cooper & Co., a Chicago department store. "Prices were in line with my income. Steak cost us ten cents a pound, chickens were twenty-five cents each, eggs ten cents a dozen, and butter a dime a pound. Ice cost us three cents a pound, but we did not use much of it. Food that had to be kept cool we buried in a box of clean sand from the shores of Lake Michigan. When we wanted a cold drink on a hot summer evening we would send one of the older boys down to the corner to 'rush the growler.' A quart pail of cool, foaming beer was a nickel, and it tasted mighty good as we sat on the small front porch hunting for a stray breeze.

"Clothing for myself and boys were comparatively cheap, too. Boys in those days wore what were called combination suits—knee breeches that buttoned to a shirt, with coat and cap to match. When I told one of the boys that I was buying him a combination suit he wanted to know what it was like. Jokingly I told him it was a combination of green pants, yellow coat, purple hat and blue shirt. Picturing himself parading to school in such an outfit while his classmates jeered, he began to sob. He was not much comforted until I explained what I really planned to get him and let him see it."[2]

1892-1897. Worked as a travelling salesman for Pitkin and Brooks, a china and glassware firm. "If everything is satisfactory then they will keep me the whole year. I am starting in very well and have not much fear but what I shall be able to get bread and butter anyhow, although I'm afraid we can't indulge in many luxuries."[2]

1896-1900. Developed a brief interest in politics when he supported William Jennings Bryan after hearing the "Cross of Gold" speech at the 1896 Democratic Convention. He also supported Bryan in the presidential election in 1900.

1897. Published his first children's book, *Mother Goose in Prose*, which was also the first book illustrated by Maxfield

(From *The Magical Monarch of Mo* by L. Frank Baum. Illustrated by Frank Ver Beck.)

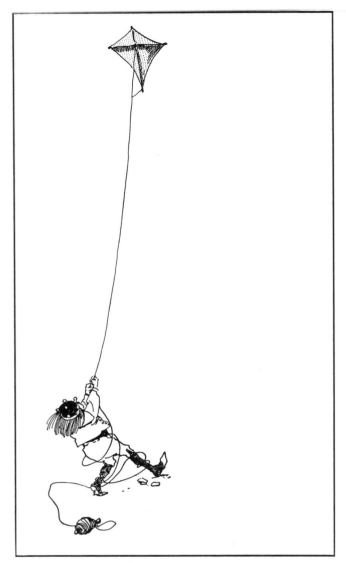

(From "The Land of the Civilized Monkeys" in *The Magical Monarch of Mo* by L. Frank Baum. Illustrated by Frank Ver Beck.)

Parrish. "When I was young I longed to write a great novel that should win me fame. Now that I am getting old my first book is written to amuse children. For, aside from my evident inability to do anything 'great,' I have learned to regard fame as a will-o'-the-wisp which, when caught, is not worth the possession; but to please a child is a sweet and lovely thing that warms one's heart and brings its own reward. I hope my book will succeed in that way—that the children will like it." [Martin Gardner and Russel B. Nye, *The Wizard of Oz and Who He Was*, Michigan State University Press, 1957.[3]]

As to his rewriting established stories Baum wrote, "I have thought the children might like the stories told at greater length, that they may dwell the longer upon their favorite heroes and heroines."[2]

"Modern education includes morality; therefore the modern child seeks only entertainment in its wonder-tales."[3] His stories would be stripped of "fearsome" morality at least, and aimed simply to "excite laughter and gladden the heart."[3]

The fellow at once busied himself untying the knots that bound Santa Claus and unlocking the chains that fastened him to the wall. Then he led the way through a long tunnel until they both emerged in the Cave of Repentance. ■ (From *A Kidnapped Santa Claus* by L. Frank Baum. Illustrated by Richard Rosenblum.)

He also vowed that his tales would "bear the stamp of our times and depict the progressive fairies of today."[3]

Later, he would recall in a letter to Frank K. Reilly of December 16, 1916, "the book was not appealing to children, although adults went wild over the beautiful drawings."[1]

Baum wrote his wife: "I know at times you get impatient with me for telling stories instead of working at other jobs when we need money so badly. But we have broken ice with *Mother Goose in Prose*. I hope to publish other books that will please the children—and make life easier for us, too. Right now I am thinking of writing a long story about Dorothy and the Scarecrow; something like the story I was telling the children tonight. Now that I have coined a good name for my magic land I am sure it will make the extra money we need."[2]

Also published his own slim volume of poetry, *By the Candelabra's Glare*. In the foreward he commented, "My best friends have never called me a poet . . . nevertheless this little book has an excuse. Unassisted I have set the type and turned the press and accomplished the binding. Such as it is, the book is 'my very own.'"[2]

November, 1897. Became the editor for his own magazine, *The Show Window*, a trade publication for window dressers. He wrote his sister, Mary Louise: "I have been more worried than usual over business matters this summer. Writing of all kinds I have been forced to neglect and the result, after all my labors, has profited me but little. I have wanted to quit traveling and find some employment that would enable me to stay at home, and I conceived the idea of a magazine devoted to window-trimming, which I know is greatly needed and would prosper if ever I could get it going.

"I wrote Mr. Neal [his brother-in-law] to loan me the money to start it, but he bluntly refused. Next I interested a Chicago man who promised to put ample means into the business and when the first number was ready to go to press he failed in business and left me just where I started. I have been nearly

a month now trying to find someone with money to pick up the enterprise and carry it through. . . ."[2]

Baum described his magazine as "a journal of practical, up-to-date window trimming."[2]

September, 1899. Published *Father Goose* with illustrations by W. W. Denslow and it became an immediate success. Of verse writing Baum noted: "Poetry doesn't pay today—especially good verse [but] doggerel will sometimes command a price, if it is witty and pointed and on humorous lines."[2]

"The financial success of my books is yet undetermined, and will only be positively settled after the coming fall season. We only had three months sale of *Father Goose,* and though it made a hit and sold plenteously we cannot tell what its future might be. . . . I have been grateful for its success. The money has been a pleasure to me and my work is sought by publishers who once scorned my contributions. Harper Bros. sent a man here last week to try to make a contract for a book next year. Scribner's writes offering a cash advance for a manuscript. Appleton's, Lothrop's and the Century have asked for a book—no matter what it is. This makes me proud, especially as my work in *Father Goose* was not good work, and I know I can do better. But I shall make no contracts with anyone till next January. If my books succeed this year I can dictate terms and choose my publishers. If they fall down I will try to discover the fault and to turn out some better work.

"A lady here, Mrs. Alberta N. Hall, has written some charming music to the *Father Goose* verses. *The Songs of Father Goose* was the result and is now in preparation, being announced for publication June 1st. *The Army Alphabet* wonderfully illustrated by Harry Kennedy, will be issued May 15. The book surely *ought* to catch on. *The Navy Alphabet,* also illustrated by Kennedy, will appear August 1st. I have received some proofs of the illustrations Frank Verbeck has made for my Phuniland book, which appears July 1st from R. H. Russell's, New York. The work is splendid. This is the man who has illustrated Kipling's new book of

And, strangest of all, these people were all made of china, even to their clothes, and were so small that the tallest of them was no higher than Dorothy's knee. ■ (From *The Wonderful Wizard of Oz* by L. Frank Baum. Illustrated by W.W. Denslow.)

Chapter VI. The Cowardly Lion.

(From *The Wonderful Wizard of Oz* by L. Frank Baum. Illustrated by W.W. Denslow.)

animal stories, having been selected over all other American artists to do that work. The title of the book will be *A New Wonderland.*"[1]

1900. Published his tales of "Phuniland" under the title, *A New Wonderland.*

Baum also published two alphabet books, *The Army Alphabet* and *The Navy Alphabet.* "Perhaps some of those big, grown-up people will poke fun at us—at you for reading these nonsense tales. . . .and at me for writing them. Never mind. Many of the big folk are still children—even as you and I. We can not measure a child by a standard of size or age. The big folk who are children will be our comrades; the others we need not consider at all, for they are self-exiled from our domain."[3]

The Wonderful Wizard of Oz, with illustrations by W. W. Denslow, published. "I was sitting . . . in the hall, telling the kids a story and suddenly this one moved right in and took possession. I shooed the children away and grabbed a piece of paper that was lying there on the rack and began to write. It really seemed to write itself. Then I couldn't find any regular paper, so I took anything at all, even a bunch of old envelopes.

"It was pure inspiration. It came to me right out of the blue. I think that sometimes the Great Author has a message to get across and He has to use the instrument at hand. I happened

to be that medium, and I believe the magic key was given me to open the doors to sympathy and understanding, joy, peace and happiness. That is why I've always felt there should never be anything except sweetness and happiness in the Oz books, never a hint of tragedy or horror. They were intended to reflect the world as it appears to the eyes and imagination of a child.

"I have a little cabinet letter file on my desk in front of me. I was thinking and wondering about a title for my story, and I had settled on 'Wizard' as part of it. My gaze was caught by the gilt letters on the three drawers of the cabinet. The first was A-G; the next drawer was labeled H-N; and on the last were the letters O-Z. And Oz it at once became.

". . . The best thing I have ever written, they tell me [is] *The Wonderful Wizard of Oz.* It is now on the press and will be ready soon after May 1st. Denslow has made profuse illustrations for it and it will glow with bright colors. Mr. Hill, the publisher, says he expects a sale of at least a quarter of a million copies on it. If he is right, that book alone solves my problem. But the queer, unreliable Public has not yet spoken. I only need one hit this year to make my position secure, and three of these books seem fitted for public approval. But there—who knows anything! I'm working at my trade, earning a salary to keep my family and holding fast to a certainty until the fiat has gone forth."[1]

In his introduction to *The Wonderful Wizard of Oz* Baum wrote: "Folk lore, legends, myths and fairy tales have followed childhood through the ages, for every healthy youngster has a wholesome and instinctive love for stories fantastic, marvelous and manifestly unreal. The winged fairies of Grimm and Andersen have brought more happiness to childish hearts than all other human creations.

Now, the Wicked Witch of the West had but one eye, but it was as powerful as a telescope. ■ (From *Best in Children's Books* selections from *The Wonderful Wizard of Oz* by L. Frank Baum. Illustrated by Richard Scarry.)

"Yet the old-time fairy tale, having served for generations, may now be classed as 'historical' in the children's library; for the time has come for a series of newer 'wonder tales' in which the stereotyped genie, dwarf and fairy are eliminated, together with all the horrible and bloodcurdling incident devised by their authors to point a fearsome moral to each tale. Modern education includes morality; therefore the modern child seeks only entertainment in its wonder-tales and gladly dispenses with all disagreeable incident.

"Having this thought in mind, the story of *The Wonderful Wizard of Oz* was written solely to pleasure children of today. It aspires to being a modernized fairy tale, in which the wonderment and joy are retained and the heart-aches and nightmares are left out."[3]

1901. Published *The Master Key: An Electrical Fairy Tale,* a science fiction novel for teenage boys.

In a prophetic mood, Baum described his book, in the preface, as "a fairy tale founded upon the wonders of electricity and written for children of this generation. Yet when my readers shall have become men and women my story may not seem to their children like a fairy tale at all."[2]

On the fly leaf of the copy of *The Master Key* that Baum presented to his second son, Robert, he wrote: "This book, dedicated to Robert, is due in its inception to his love of electrical toys. For his workshop first gave me the idea of an electrical story and *The Electrical Demon* was a natural sequence. The book has been so well received that I am sorry, now, I did not end it differently and leave an opening for a sequel."[2] Previously, in a letter to his brother, Baum had mentioned that "Rob fills the house with electrical batteries and such truck and we are prepared to hear a bell ring whenever we open a door or step on a stair."[2]

1901. The final Baum-Denslow book published. *Dot and Tot of Merryland.* He admitted in the preface of *Dot and Tot of Merryland* that, "the success achieved last year by *The Wonderful Wizard of Oz*—a book that not only ran through many large editions but brought to the author hundreds of letters from interested little folk—has induced me to follow that tale with another, herein presented."[2]

Baum and Denslow soon had a falling out over infringements on each other's copyrights. Baum admitted with some bitterness in a letter of August 10, 1915, to his publishers: "Denslow was allowed to copyright his pictures jointly with my claim to authorship, [and] having learned my lesson from my unfortunate experiences with Denslow, I will never permit another artist to have an interest in the drawings he makes of my described characters, if I ever can help it."[1]

Many years later, he was in a more tolerant mood. "Perhaps no author is satisfied with his illustrations, and I see my characters and incidents so differently from the artist that I fail to appreciate his talent. I used to receive many compliments on Denslow's pictures when he was illustrating my books, from children and others."[1]

1902. The first musical version of *The Wizard of Oz* was performed in Chicago and was a wild success. Later, it was done in New York to great acclaim and the show survived on various American stages for nine years. "But after Julian Mitchell [the show's producer] had seen the manuscript he urged my adapting it to a modern extravaganza, on account of the gorgeous scenic effects and absurd situations suggested by the story."[1]

Ugu the Shoemaker

(From *The Lost Princess of Oz* by L. Frank Baum. Illustrated by John Neill.)

Baum was quoted as saying in an interview in an unidentified newspaper. "This I accomplished after much labor, for I found it necessary to alter materially the story of the book. When I wrote the fairy tale I allowed my imagination full play, so that a great deal of the action is absolutely impossible to adapt to the limitations of the stage. So I selected the most available portions and filled the gaps by introducing several new characters and minor plots which serve to throw the story of Dorothy and her unique companions into stronger relief. The main plot of the book is retained, and its readers will have little difficulty in recognizing the well-known characters as they journey in search of the Emerald City and the wonderful Wizard. . . . I was told that what constituted fun in a book would be missed by the average audience, which is accustomed to a regular gatling-gun discharge of wit—or what stands for wit. So I secured the assistance of two experts in this line of work, selected by the advice of Manager Hamlin, and they peppered my prosy lines with a multitude of 'laughs.' "[1]

For the 1902 musical of *The Wizard of Oz* the dog Toto was replaced by a spotted calf named Imogene. "I regret that one favorite character of the children—the dog Toto—will be missing."[1]

Baum was quoted in an interview in an unidentified newspaper just prior to the opening of the production: "We found Toto an impossibility from the dramatic viewpoint, and reluctantly abandoned him. But we put the cow in his place. It may seem a long jump from a dog to a cow, but in the latter animal we have a character that really ought to amuse the youngsters exceedingly, and the eccentric creature accompanies Dorothy on her journey from Kansas just as Toto did in the book."[1]

As to the experience of an opening night: "Few people can understand the feelings of an author who for the first time sees his creations depicted by living characters upon the stage. The Scarecrow, the Tin Woodman, and the Cowardly Lion were real children of my brain, having no existence in fact or fiction until I placed them in the pages of my book. But to describe them with pen and ink is very different from seeing them actually live. When the Scarecrow came to life

on the first night of *The Wizard of Oz* I expected strange sensations of wonder and awe; the appearance of the Tin Woodman made me catch my breath spasmodically, and when the gorgeous poppy field, with its human flowers, burst on my view—more real than my fondest dreams had ever conceived—a big lump came into my throat and a wave of gratitude swept over me that I had lived to see the sight. I cannot feel ashamed at these emotions."[1]

Baum made the following curtain speech: "Kind friends, thank you for your enthusiasm. It is heart-warming. You have been generous enough to call for the author, but I do not need to remind you that he is only one of many whose efforts you are enjoying tonight. If you will pardon a homely comparison, our play is like a plum pudding, which combines the flavor of many ingredients. The author contributes only the flour—necessary, of course, but only to hold the other good things together."[2]

Baum later refuted tales of rancor between himself and the show's management. "As a matter of fact, I am in perfect harmony with both Julian Mitchell and Mr. Hamlin. . . . Few authors of successful books are ever fully satisfied with the dramatization of their work. . . . This was my own experience. I myself made *The Wizard of Oz* into an extravaganza, and it was accepted by Mr. Hamlin. . . . But when Julian

(From the stage production of "The Wiz," starring Stephanie Mills and Hinton Battle, which opened at the Majestic Theater, 1975. Photo by Martha Swope.)

(The cyclone scene from the first act of the musical "The Wizard of Oz," which opened at the Grand Opera House in Chicago, 1902.)

Mitchell came to go over the script he declared it would never do in the world for the stage.

"Through deference to the opinion of so experienced a stage director, I labored hard to remodel the play and even called in the assistance of professional dramatists. Mr. Mitchell then took a hand in the reformation itself. The original story was practically ignored, the dialogue rehashed, the situations transposed, my Nebraska Wizard made into an Irishman, and several other characters forced to conform to the requirements of the new schedule.

"A story has been circulated by the press that I was heartbroken and ashamed of my extravaganza when it was finally produced, but that is not true. I was filled with amazement, indeed, and took occasion to protest against several innovations that I did not like, but Mr. Mitchell listened to the plaudits of the big audiences and turned a deaf ear to my complaints.

"I confess, after two years of success for the extravaganza, that I now regard Mr. Mitchell's views in a different light. The people will have what pleases them and not what the author happens to favor, and I believe that one of the reasons Julian Mitchell is recognized as a great producer is that he faithfully tries to serve the great mass of play goers—and usually succeeds.

"My chief business is, of course, the writing of fairy tales, but should I ever attempt another extravaganza, or dramatize another of my books, I mean to profit by the lesson Mr.

Mitchell has taught me, and sacrifice personal preferences to the demands of those I shall expect to purchase admission tickets."[2]

1903. Purchased a cottage at Macatawa on Lake Michigan and dubbed this home, "The Sign of the Goose."

July, 1904. The second Oz book, *The Marvelous Land of Oz*, published. "After the publication of *The Wonderful Wizard of Oz* I began to receive letters from children, telling me of their pleasure in reading the story and asking me to 'write something more' about the Scarecrow and the Tin Woodman. At first I considered these little letters, frank and earnest though they were, in the light of pretty compliments; but the letters continued to come during succeeding months, and even years.

"Finally I promised one little girl, who made a long journey to see me and prefer her request—and she is a 'Dorothy,' by the way—that when a thousand little girls had written me a thousand little letters asking for another story of the Scarecrow and the Tin Woodman, I would write the book. Either little Dorothy was a fairy in disguise, and waved her magic wand, or the success of the stage production of *The Wizard of Oz* made new friends for the story. For the thousand letters reached their destination long since—and many more followed them.

"And now, although pleading guilty to a long delay, I have kept my promise in this book." [L. Frank Baum, introduction to *The Land of Oz,* Sirmont Publishing Co., n.d.[4]]

It was not as high as the first, however, and by standing upon the Lion's back they all managed to scramble to the top. ■ (From *The Wonderful Wizard of Oz* by L. Frank Baum. Illustrated by W.W. Denslow.)

"To write fairy stories for children, to amuse them, to divert restless children, sick children, to keep them out of mischief on rainy days, seems of greater importance than to write grown-up novels. Few of the popular novels last the year out, responding as they do to a certain psychological demand, characteristic of the time; whereas, a child's book is, comparatively speaking, the same always, since children are always the same kind of little folks with the same needs to satisfy."[1]

August, 1904-February, 1905. Published a weekly newspaper comic page entitled "Queer Visitors from the Marvelous Land of Oz." A contest connected with this comic—"What did the Woggle-Bug Say?"—became a national craze.

1905. *The Woggle-Bug Book* appeared and met with some success, although a stage play, *The Woggle-Bug* failed. On the very day of the play's opening, Baum had insisted that he had written an extravaganza, with "the dignity that clings ever to the real fairy tale, and which must carry with it its own quota of awe and wonderment,"[2] and not a musical comedy, which he described out of the side of his mouth as a "burlesque of grand opera, a jest.

"It isn't through opera that I hope to live, that I base any hope that I may have of seeing my name written in bronze. My important work I consider to be my fairy tales, not my plays."[2]

1905. Wrote *The Fate of a Crown,* an adult novel under the pseudonym "Schuyler Stanton." "This book I wrote under an assumed pen name because I did not think it wise to produce a novel to compete with my fairy tales, which occupy a field of their own. The name Schuyler Stanton is taken from that of my mother's brother, the modern 'Stanton' having been formerly written 'Staunton.' As Uncle Schuyler is long since dead I took the liberty of perpetuating his name in this way. As I write this the book is well received and going into a second edition."[2]

Published a tale about a magic cloak entitled *Queen Zixi of Ix* with illustrations by Frederick Richardson. "In some ways *Queen Zixi* is my best effort, and nearer to the 'old-fashioned' fairy tale than anything I have yet accomplished."[2]

Baum mentioned that the illustrator, Frederick Richardson, should "be induced to make the small pictures broadly humorous even to the verge of burlesque—it would be a good time all around. He seems to have a distinctly humorous

quality . . . but is afraid [to] 'let it out.' In other words, Mr. Richardson is so much an artist that he is fully impressed with the dignity of his calling and hesitates to lend his talents to the grotesque." [From a letter to Mr. Ellsworth, September 4, 1904, from Special Collections, Butler Library, Columbia University.[5]]

1906. Went abroad. Stops included France, Switzerland, Egypt, Greece, Italy, and North Africa.

Published *John Dough and the Cherub,* featuring John Dough, a gingerbread man, and Chick the Cherub, the world's first incubator baby. ". . . I, too, like to hear about my funny creatures. I never know what strange characters are going to pop into my head when I begin telling a story. You know, I think up things for them to do, but when I start telling the story to the children, these characters seem to develop a life of their own. They often surprise *me* by what they do—just like living people."[2]

Wrote *Policeman Bluejay,* under the pseudonym, Laura Bancroft. "If a little tenderness for the helpless animals and birds is acquired with the amusements, the value of the tales will be doubled.

"The question is often asked me whether Twinkle and Chubbins were asleep or awake when they encountered these wonderful adventures; and it grieves me to reflect that the modern child has been deprived of fairy tales to such an extent that it does not know . . . that in a fairy story it does not matter whether one is awake or not. You must accept it as you would a fragrant breeze that cools your brow, a draught of sweet water, or the delicious flavor of a strawberry, and be grateful for the pleasure it brings you, without stopping to question its source."[1]

"If you see any house, or any place where we can pass the night," she said, "you must tell me; for it is very uncomfortable walking in the dark." ■ (From *The Wizard of Oz* by L. Frank Baum. Illustrated by Evelyn Copelman.)

September, 1907. The third Oz book published, *Ozma of Oz.* "My friends the children are responsible for this new 'Oz Book,' as they were for the last one, which was called *The Land of Oz.* Their sweet little letters plead to know 'more about Dorothy'; and they ask: 'What became of the Cowardly Lion?' and 'What did Ozma do afterward?'—meaning, of course, after she became the Ruler of Oz. And some of them suggest plots to me, saying: 'Please have Dorothy go to the Land of Oz again'; or 'Why don't you make Ozma and Dorothy meet, and have a good time together?' Indeed, could I do all that my little friends ask, I would be obliged to write dozens of books to satisfy their demands. And I wish I could, for I enjoy writing these stories just as much as the children say they enjoy reading them.

"Well, here is 'more about Dorothy,' and about our old friends the Scarecrow and the Tin Woodman, and about the Cowardly Lion, and Ozma, and all the rest of them; and here, likewise, is a good deal about some new folks that are queer and unusual. One little friend, who read this story before it was printed, said to me: 'Billina is *real Ozzy,* Mr. Baum, and so are Tiktok and the Hungry Tiger.'

"If this judgment is unbiased and correct, and the little folks find this new story 'real Ozzy,' I shall be very glad indeed that I wrote it. But perhaps I shall get some more of those very welcome letters from my readers, telling me just how they like *Ozma of Oz.* I hope so, anyway." [L. Frank Baum, introduction to *Ozma of Oz,* Reilly & Britton, 1907.[6]]

1908. Bobbs-Merrill published *Baum's American Fairy Tales.* In the foreword to *Baum's American Fairy Tales* he explained his intentions in writing "modern tales about modern fairies: They are not serious in purpose, but aim to amuse and entertain, yet I trust the more thoughtful readers will find a wholesome lesson hidden beneath such extravagant notion and humorous incident.

"I once asked a little fellow, a friend of mine, to tell me what a 'fairy' is. He replied, quite promptly: 'A fairy has wings, and is much like an angel, only smaller.' Now that, I believe is the general conception of fairies; and it is a pretty conception, is it not? Yet we know the family of immortals generally termed 'fairies' has many branches and includes fays, sprites, elves, nymphs, ryls, knooks, gnomes, brownies and many other subdivisions. There is no blue book or history of the imaginative little creatures to guide us in classifying them, but they all have their uses and peculiar characteristics; as, for example, the little ryls, who carry around paintpots, with which they color, most brilliantly and artistically, the blossoms of the flowers."[1]

Of Hans Christian Andersen, Baum wrote: "The great Dane had not only a marvelous imagination but was a poet as well, and surrounded his tales with some of the most beautiful descriptive passages known to our literature. As children you skipped those passages—I can guess that, because as a child I skipped them myself."[1]

1908. Began a series of books for boys, *The Boy Fortune Hunters,* under the pseudonym, Floyd Akers. "I've got twenty-four feet, four-and-a-half inches of boys myself. Four of them, and every one over six feet."[2]

Wrote a romantic adult novel, *The Last Egyptian,* anonymously. "Based upon material I picked up in Egypt. . . . It will have to be published under a pen name . . . because I cannot interfere with my children's books by posing as a novelist. But I wanted to write this Egyptian tale."[2]

1908. Invested heavily in his "Fairylogues and Radio Plays" which were short, hand-painted films of his stories. The venture was a colossal failure. "One of the simplest of [tricks] is the introduction to my fairy story entertainment, when my little characters step from the pages of an Oz book preparatory to becoming the moving actors of my little tales. A closed book is first shown, which the fairies open. On the first page is disclosed a black and white picture of little Dorothy. . . . I beckon, and she straightway steps out of its pages, becomes imbued with the colors of life and moves about. The fairies then close the book, which opens again and again until the Tin Man, Scarecrow and all the others step out of the pages and come, colored, to life. . . .

"How is it done? Well, grooves were cut to the exact shape of each character [who stood within the book] and so was photographed in black and white. At the signal each steps forth, and the groove, being backed by white, no grotto can be seen. . . . Between each character the camera is stopped, [and] the new character is arranged in his grotto, [and] the camera starts again. [It was] necessary to color the figures . . . artificially, as we found a difficulty in changing from black and white to colors on the one film, but even this needed ingenuity. [When] figures are enlarged from three-quarters of an inch to eight feet high . . . smudges of tint would occur upon the screen. So the films had to be colored under a great magnifying glass. . . .

"There is another illusion . . . which required a good deal more ingenuity. Little Dorothy in a chicken coop is seen to be dashed about in the middle of a storm at sea—[and the] little girl was never at sea in her life. [First] I took motion pictures of a storm at sea. [Then,] in the studio, I draped with black cloth a space in which I placed Dorothy in her chicken coop. This was built upon rockers, which were fitted with a series of casters, and invisible wires were attached, all being concealed beneath the black cloth except the coop and the child. [Next] I projected upon a screen at one side the picture of the sea, and as the waves rolled in we made the chicken coop follow its curve and float across the black space, at the same time taking another motion picture of it. . . .

"When this strip was developed it showed the girl in the coop plainly, but the dead black surrounding made the film transparent. . . . We next placed the chicken coop film above the film containing the sea scene and printed them together against the strip of positive film which is now used for projection. The result is that the child appears to be floating upon the sea since the sea scene is pictured through the transparent portion of the film, while the child in her coop is shown upon the surface. To make the chicken coop follow the roll of the waves was quite difficult and seven trials were required to obtain a satisfactory result.

"In another scene some characters build a flying machine under the roof of a palace and fly away in it. They first drag in two sofas, which are placed with the seats together and bound with a clothesline. They place a stuffed . . . deer head at one end and a broom at the other to serve as a tail. Then they run off the stage and fetch some big palm leaves [for] wings. When the characters have all climbed into this queer flying machine and begin to wave the palm leaf wings, the machine rises into the air and flies away with them.

"The effect is startling—but easily explained. When the characters leave the stage, the camera is stopped and then workmen come and attach invisible wires to the sofa. These wires extend into the flies where they are joined to a runway.

F RICHARDSON

And the dog Ruffles ran through the city, crying to every Roly-Rogue he met: "Hurry and get your soup before it is gone." ■ (From *Queen Zixi of Ix or The Story of the Magic Cloak* by L. Frank Baum. Illustrated by Frederick Richardson.)

When everything is [ready] the workmen leave the stage and the camera again begins taking the succession of minute pictures, and the characters appear with their palm leaf wings and climb aboard the sofas. Next moment the invisible wires pull them into the sky and the effect is complete.

"[Another] class of illusion in fairy photography is bewitchment. Thus a boy is changed into a little girl. He melts before your eyes, [and] out of the mist appears a girl, and vague and shadowy at first, until she at length stands before you, solid

as she can be. Moving picture film is prepared for a tremendously quick exposure. Should the exposure be made longer—that is, the camera to be made to go more slowly—the film becomes overexposed and the picture becomes more shadowy. So . . . to efface the boy we gradually slow down the camera till it finally stops. Then we take the boy away and put the little girl in exactly the same place. . . . [Then] we slowly start the camera again, gradually increasing its speed [to normal, taking care, however, to make the two 'slows' overlap]. Thus the little girl will gradually strengthen on the film until . . . she appears as her little solid self. . . . A camera can be made a fine liar!''[1]

1908. The fourth Oz book, *Dorothy and the Wizard of Oz,* published. ''They (the children) have flooded me with thousands of suggestions, and I have honestly tried to adopt as many of these suggestions as could be fitted into one story. . . . The children won't let me stop telling tales of the Land of Oz. I know lots of other stories, and I hope to tell them sometime or another, but just now my loving tyrants won't let me.''[2]

Of Dorothy herself, Baum wrote: ''She had accomplished all these wonders not because she was a fairy, or had any magical powers whatsoever, but because she was a simple and sweet little girl who was honest to herself and to all whom she met. In this world in which we live, simplicity and kindliness are the only magic wands that work wonders.''[2]

1909. *The Road to Oz* published.

1910. Decided to conclude the ''Oz'' series with the publication of *The Emerald City of Oz.* ''They won't do what I want them to,''[3] Baum once said of his Oz characters. But he soon solved this writer's block: ''By letting them do what they wanted to.''[3]

Moved to Hollywood and built a large frame house there called ''Ozcot.'' ''Mrs. Baum and I go out the fifteenth of January and will stay at the Hotel del Coranado. We can't think of any place that suits us better.''[5]

There, because he suffered from a heart ailment, Baum took up golf. Of one game he quipped: ''Oh, I made it in about ninety-eight. Of course, that's for the first nine holes.''[2]

1911. The first Trot book, *The Sea Fairies,* about a little California girl and her constant companion, Cap'n Bill Weedles, appeared. ''I hope my readers who have so long followed Dorothy's adventures in the Land of Oz will be interested in Trot's equally strange adventures.''[2]

June, 1911. Declared bankruptcy. Against debts of $12,600 he listed as assets two suits of clothing, ''one in actual use and another kept in his room at 149 North Magnolia Avenue,''[2] eleven second-hand books and a five-year-old typewriter.

1912. Wrote *Sky Island,* which he considered his finest work. Baum confessed to his readers that *Sky Island* is one of his stories that ''wrote itself,'' and he mentioned in his preface that it had astonished him considerably.

''The sky country is certainly a remarkable land. After reading about it I am sure you will agree that our old Mother Earth is a good place to live on.''[2]

1913. Baum revived the Oz stories with the publication of *The Patchwork Girl of Oz.* ''A lot of thought is required on one of these fairy tales. The odd characters are a sort of inspiration, liable to strike me any time, but the plot and plan of adventures take considerable time to develop. When I get at a thing of that sort I live with it day by day, jotting down on odd slips of paper the various ideas that occur and in this way getting my material together. The new Oz book *Patchwork Girl* is in this stage. I've got it all—all the hard work has been done—and it's a dandy I think. But laws-a-massy! It's a long way from being ready for the printer yet. I must rewrite it, stringing the incidents into consecutive order, elaborating

the characters, etc. Then it's typewritten. Then it's revised, retypewritten and sent on to Reilly & Britton [Baum's publisher].'' [David L. Greene and Dick Martin, *The Oz Scrapbook,* Random House, 1977.[7]]

Baum gave a whimsical explanation for continuing with the Oz series. ''. . . After two long years of waiting, another Oz story is now presented to the children of America. This would not have been possible had not some clever man invented the 'wire-less' and an equally clever child suggested the idea of reaching the mysterious Land of Oz by its means.'' [L. Frank Baum, introduction to *The Patchwork Girl of Oz,* Reilly & Britton, 1913.[8]]

The author conceded that he would be ''The royal historian of Oz''[7] for the rest of his life.

Promising that ''as long as you care to read them I shall try to write them,''[3] he resigned himself to at least one Oz story a year.

The musical ''The Tik-Tok Man of Oz'' opened in Los Angeles then went on tour.

1914. Wrote what would be his favorite Oz book, *The Scarecrow of Oz.* ''. . . I am deeply grateful to my little readers for their continued enthusiasm over the Oz stories, as evinced in the many letters they send me, all of which are lovingly cherished. It takes more and more Oz Books every year to satisfy the demands of old and new readers, and there have been formed many 'Oz Reading Societies,' where the Oz Books owned by different members are read aloud. All this is very gratifying to me and encourages me to write more Oz stories. When the children have had enough of them, I hope they will let me know, and then I'll try to write something different.'' [L. Frank Baum, introduction to *The Scarecrow of Oz,* Reilly & Britton, 1914.[9]]

Baum was well aware that romance might have been out of place in his children's stories. ''In the *Scarecrow* I introduced a slightly novel theme, for me, in the love and tribulations of Pon the gardener's son and the Princess Gloria. It smacked a bit of the Andersen fairy tales and I watched its effect upon my readers. They accepted it gleefully, with all the rest, it being well within their comprehension.''[1]

Founded the ''Oz Film Manufacturing Company'' to make silent movies of his books. Although five films were made, the company was a failure.

1916. Wrote *Rinkitink in Oz.*

1917. Wrote *The Lost Princess in Oz.* ''. . . Imagination has brought mankind through the Dark Ages to its present state of civilization. Imagination led Columbus to discover America . . . Franklin to discover electricity. Imagination has given us the steam engine, the telephone, the talking-machine and the automobile, for these things had to be dreamed of before they became realities. So I believe that dreams—day dreams, you know, with your eyes wide open and your brain-machinery whizzing—are likely to lead to the betterment of the world. The imaginative child will become the imaginative man or woman most apt to create, to invent, and therefore to foster civilization. . . .'' [L. Frank Baum, introduction to *The Lost Princess of Oz,* Reilly & Britton, 1917.[10]]

February, 1918. Went to the hospital for a gall bladder operation. Despite his illness he continued his work. ''I want to

Ozcot, Hollywood, California, 1911.

tell you, for your complete protection, that I have finished the writing of the *second* Oz book—beyond *The Tin Woodman of Oz*—which will give you a manuscript for 1919 and 1920. Also there is material for another book, so in case anything happens to me the Baum books can be issued until and including 1921. And the two stories which I have here in the safety deposit I consider as good as anything I have ever done, with the possible exception of *Sky Island,* which will probably always be considered my best work.''[1]

1918. Published *The Tin Woodman of Oz.*

1919. Wrote *The Magic of Oz* and the last Oz book, *Glinda of Oz.* ''Curiously enough, in the events which have taken place in the last few years in our 'great outside world,' we may find incidents so marvelous and inspiring that I cannot hope to equal them with stories of The Land of Oz.

''However, *The Magic of Oz* is really more strange and unusual than anything I have read or heard about on our side of The Great Sandy Desert which shuts us off from The Land of Oz, even during the past exciting years, so I hope it will appeal to your love of novelty.

''A long and confining illness has prevented my answering all the good letters sent me—unless stamps were enclosed—but from now on I hope to be able to give prompt attention to each and every letter with which my readers favor me.'' [L. Frank Baum, introduction to *The Magic of Oz,* Reilly & Britton, 1919.[11]]

''I believe, my dears, that I am the proudest story-teller that ever lived. . . . To have pleased you, to have interested you, to have won your friendship, and perhaps your love, through my stories, is to my mind as great an achievement as to become President of the United States.''[2]

Baum wrote his son, fighting in Europe:

''My dear son:

''Your last letter from 'somewhere in France' was very welcome, for it let us know you were still in good health.

''Your descriptive account of recent army activities is fascinating and vital—and gives an extremely vivid picture of what goes on around you. In descriptive writing you do a job far superior to anything I have ever done or am capable of doing.

''We were sorry to learn of your great disappointment in certain phases of your military assignment. But do not be too down-hearted, my boy, for I have lived long enough to learn that in life nothing adverse lasts very long. And it is true that as the years pass, and we look back on something which, at that time, seemed unbelievingly discouraging and unfair, we come to realize that, after all, God was at all times on our side. The eventual outcome was, we discover, by far the best solution for us, and what then we thought should have been to our best advantage, would in reality have been quite detrimental.

Slowly the glass cylinder rose to the surface of the waves, and Jac saw just beside her the boat containing her parents. ■ (From *John Dough and the Cherub* by L. Frank Baum. Illustrated by John R. Neill.)

"I have lately been much improved in health and trust that before many weeks the doctors will allow me to leave my bed and at least move about the house.

"We all send you much love, and I continually pray for a speedy end to this terrible war and your safe return to our beloved country."[2]

May 6, 1919. Died in his Hollywood home. His last words were: "Now I can cross the Shifting Sands."—The Shifting Sands being the desert region that lies outside the Land of Oz. [*TV Guide*, March 19, 1977.[12]]

FOR MORE INFORMATION SEE: Jack Snow, *Who's Who in Oz,* Reilly & Lee, 1954; *L. Frank Baum: The Wonderful Wizard of Oz; an Exhibition of His Published Writings in Commemoration of the Centenary of His Birth, May 16, 1856,* Columbia University Libraries, 1956; Martin Gardner and Russell B. Nye, *The Wizard of Oz and Who He Was,* Michigan State University Press, 1957; Frank Joslyn Baum and Russell P. MacFall, *To Please a Child: A Biography of L. Frank Baum, Royal Historian of Oz,* Reilly & Lee, 1961; D. P. Mannix, "Father of the Wizard of Oz," *American Heritage,* December, 1964.

"I am the Princess Fluff," said Meg to the sailor; **"and your necktie is part of my magic cloak. So please give it back to me."** ■ (From *Queen Zixi of Ix or The Story of the Magic Cloak* by L. Frank Baum. Illustrated by Frederick Richardson.)

Laura Benét, *Famous Storytellers for Young People,* Dodd, 1968; Brian Doyle, editor, *Who's Who of Children's Literature,* Schocken Books, 1968; Doris de Montreville and Donna Hill, editors, *Third Book of Junior Authors,* Wilson, 1972; R. Sale, "L. Frank Baum and Oz," *Hudson Review,* Winter, 1972-73; Baum, *The Annotated Wizard of Oz* (introduction, notes, and bibliography by Michael P. Hearn), C. N. Potter, 1973; Raylyn Moore, *Wonderful Wizard, Marvelous Land* (preface by Ray Bradbury), Bowling Green University, 1974; David L. Greene and Dick Martin, *The Oz Scrapebook,* Random House, 1977; *TV Guide,* March, 1977.

BEACHCROFT, Nina 1931-

PERSONAL: Born November 10, 1931, in London, England; daughter of Thomas Owen (a writer) and Marjorie Evelyn (Taylor) Beachcroft; married Richard Gardner (a physician), August, 1954; children: Helen, Katy. *Education:* St. Hilda's College, Oxford, B.A. (honors), 1953. *Agent:* Harold Ober Associates, Inc., 40 East 49th St., New York, N.Y. 10017; and David Higham Associates Ltd., 5-8 Lower John St., London W1R 4HA, England.

CAREER: Has worked as an editorial assistant; writer.

*WRITINGS—*Juveniles: *Well Met by Witchlight,* Atheneum, 1973; *Under the Enchanter,* Atheneum, 1974; *Cold Christmas,* Atheneum, 1974; *A Spell of Sleep,* Atheneum, 1976; *A Visit to Folly Castle,* Heinemann, 1977; *A Farthing for the Fair,* Heinemann, 1978.

NINA BEACHCROFT

SIDELIGHTS: "I have always wanted to write, but apart from a few short stories I had nothing published until my oldest child was ten and I thought of turning to children's books. Now I have no plans for writing anything else!"

BEARD, Charles Austin   1874-1948

PERSONAL: Born November 27, 1874, near Knightstown, Ind.; died September 1, 1948, in New Haven, Conn.; buried in Ferncliff Cemetery, Hartsdale, New York; son of William Henry (a building contractor and banker) and Mary (Payne) Beard; married Mary Ritter (an author), March 8, 1900; children: Miriam (Mrs. Alfred Vagts; an author), William (an author). *Education:* De Pauw University, Ph.B., 1898; Columbia University, M.A., 1903, Ph.D., 1904; additional study at Oxford University, 1898-99 and Cornell University, 1899-1900. *Home:* New Milford, Connecticut.

CAREER: Author, historian, and educator. Following graduation from high school, Beard and his brother successfully ran the *Knightstown Sun* (weekly newspaper), purchased for them by their father; while at De Pauw University, he was a reporter for the *Henry County Republican;* Columbia University, New York City, adjunct professor of politics, 1907-10, associate professor, 1910-15, professor of politics, 1915-17, visiting professor of government, 1939; director of the Training School for Public Service, New York City, 1917-22; lecturer at Dartmouth College, 1922; advisor at the Institute of Municipal Research, Tokyo, Japan, 1922, and to Viscount Geto, Japanese minister of home affairs, after the earthquake in 1923; head of the New York Bureau of Municipal Research, 1923-27; adviser to the Yugoslav government in Belgrade, Yugoslavia, 1927-28; professor of American politics, Johns Hopkins University, 1940. Co-founder of Ruskin College at Oxford University and the New School for Social Research, 1918; also ran a successful dairy farm, selling

300,000 quarts of milk yearly, and helped to organize the milk producers.

MEMBER: American Historical Association (president, 1926), National Association for Adult Education (president, 1936), Phi Beta Kappa, Phi Gamma Delta. *Awards, honors:* New York City Association Award for teacher of social studies, 1940; American Academy of Arts and Letters gold medal award, 1941; LL.D., from De Pauw University, 1917, D.Litt., from Columbia University, 1944.

WRITINGS—For young people: (With William C. Bagley) *The History of the American People,* Macmillan, 1918, 2nd revised edition, 1934; (with Bagley) *A First Book in American History,* Macmillan, 1920, revised edition, 1934; (with Bagley) *Our Old World Background,* Macmillan, 1922, revised edition, 1925 [a revised and simplified edition published as *Elementary World History,* Macmillan, 1932]; *The Presidents in American History,* J. Messner, 1935, 10th revised edition, 1977.

The Industrial Revolution, S. Sonnenschein, 1901, Macmillan, 1905, reprinted, Scholarly Press, 1976; *The Office of Justice of the Peace in England, in Its Origin and Development,* Columbia University Press, 1904, reprinted, Scholarly Press, 1976; *An Introduction to the English Historians,* Macmillan, 1906, reprinted, B. Franklin, 1968; *American Government and Politics,* Macmillan, 1910, 10th edition, 1949; *American City Government: A Survey of Newer Tendencies,* Century, 1912, reprinted, Arno, 1970; *The Supreme*

CHARLES AUSTIN BEARD

The first settlers in Virginia did not bring wives with them, and it was some little time before any women appeared in the colony. ■ (From *The History of the American People* by Charles A. Beard and William C. Bagley.)

Court and the Constitution, Macmillan, 1912, reissued, Prentice-Hall, 1962; *An Economic Interpretation of the Constitution of the United States,* Macmillan, 1913, reprinted, 1968; (with wife, Mary R. Beard) *American Citizenship,* Macmillan, 1914; *Contemporary American History, 1877-1913,* Macmillan, 1914, reprinted, Kennikat, 1971; *Economic Origins of Jeffersonian Democracy,* Macmillan, 1915, reprinted, Free Press, 1965.

(With M. R. Beard) *History of the United States,* Macmillan, 1921, revised edition, 1941; *The Economic Basis of Politics,* A. Knopf, 1922, 3rd revised edition, Books for Libraries, 1972; *Cross Currents in Europe Today,* M. Jones, 1922; *The Administration and Politics of Tokyo: A Survey and Opinions,* Macmillan, 1923; (with M. R. Beard) *The Rise of American Civilization* (illustrated by Wilfred Jones), Macmillan, 1927, new enlarged and revised edition, 1956; *The American Party Battle,* Macmillan, 1928, reprinted in *The Party Battle,* Arno, 1974; (with George Radin) *The Balkan Pivot: Yugoslavia: A Study in Government and Administration,* Macmillan, 1929.

(With son, William Beard) *The American Leviathan: The Republic in the Machine Age,* Macmillan, 1930; (with George H. E. Smith) *The Future Comes: A Study of the New Deal,* Macmillan, 1933, reprinted, Greenwood Press, 1972; *The Nature of the Social Sciences in Relation to Objectives of Instruction,* Scribner, 1934, reprinted, Arno, 1974; (with G.H.E. Smith) *The Idea of National Interest: An Analytical Study in American Foreign Policy,* Macmillan, 1966; (with Smith) *The Open Door at Home: A Trial Philosophy of National Interest,* Macmillan, 1934, reprinted, Greenwood Press, 1972; *Jefferson, Corporations, and the Constitution,* National Home Library Foundation, 1936; *The Discussion of Human Affairs,* Macmillan, 1936; *The Devil Theory of War:*

An Inquiry into the Nature of History and the Possibility of Keeping Out of War, Vanguard, 1936, reprinted, Greenwood Press, 1969; (with M. R. Beard) *The Making of American Civilization* (illustrated by Stanley M. Arthurs), Macmillan, 1937; (with M. R. Beard) *America in Midpassage* (illustrated by W. Jones), Macmillan, 1939, reissued, P. Smith, 1966; *Giddy Minds and Foreign Quarrels: An Estimate of American Foreign Policy,* Macmillan, 1939.

(With James H. Robinson and Donnal V. Smith) *History of Civilization: Our Own Age,* Ginn, 1940, reissued, 1965; *A Foreign Policy for America,* A. Knopf, 1940; *Public Policy and the General Welfare,* Farrar & Rinehart, 1941; (with M. R. Beard) *The American Spirit: A Study of the Idea of Civilization in the United States,* Macmillan, 1942, reissued, Collier Books, 1962; *The Republic: Conversations of Fundamentals,* Viking, 1943, reprinted, 1968; (with M. R. Beard) *A Basic History of the United States,* Doubleday, Doran, 1944 [a new edition revised by William Beard and published as *New Basic History of the United States,* Doubleday, 1968]; *American Foreign Policy in the Making, 1932-1940: A Study in Responsibilities,* Yale University Press, 1946, reprinted, Archon Books, 1968; *President Roosevelt and the Coming of the War, 1941: A Study in Appearances and Realities,* Yale University Press, 1948, reprinted, Archon Books, 1968; *Charles A. Beard and the Social Studies: A Book of Readings* (selections; edited by Raymond A. Ducharme, Jr.), Teachers College Press, 1969.

Contributor: "Inside of Germany's War Politics," in *Essays in Intellectual History, Dedicated to James Harvey Robinson by His Former Seminar Students,* Harper, 1929; "Recent Gains in Government," in *Recent Gains in American Civilization,* edited by Kirby Page, Harcourt, Brace, 1930; (with William Beard) "Government in a Technological So-

CHARLES A. BEARD

ciety,'' in *Essays in Contemporary Civilization,* edited by Charles W. Thomas, Macmillan, 1931; ''Politics,'' in *Roads to Knowledge,* edited by William A. Neilson, Norton, 1932; ''Myth of Rugged American Individualism,'' in *Essays of Today,* edited by Raymond W. Pence, Macmillan, 1935; ''What Is This Sea Power?'' in *American Points of View, 1936,* edited by William H. Cordell and Kathryn Cordell, Doubleday, Doran, 1937; ''Historiography and the Constitution,'' in *Constitution Reconsidered,* edited by C. Read, Columbia University Press, 1938; (with Mary R. Beard) ''Guilded Age,'' in *America through the Essay,* edited by A. Theodore Johnson and Allen Tate, Oxford University Press, 1938; ''Education under the Nazis,'' in *Essays of Three Decades,* edited by Arno L. Bader and Carlton F. Wells, Harper, 1939; ''Idea of Progress,'' in *Of Time and Truth: Ideas and Values for College Students,* edited by Fred W. Lorch and others, Dryden Press, 1946; ''Whom Does Congress Represent?'' in *Running the Country: An Anthology of American Politics in Action,* edited by Asher N. Christensen and Evron M. Kirkpatrick, Holt, 1946.

Editor: *An Introduction to the English Historians,* Macmillan, 1906, reprinted, B. Franklin, 1968; (with James H. Rob-

inson) *Development of Modern Europe,* two volumes, Ginn, 1907; (with Robinson) *Readings in Modern European History,* Ginn, 1909; *Readings in American Government and Politics,* Macmillan, 1909; *Loose Leaf Digest of Short Ballot Charters: A Documentary History of the Commission Form of Municipal Government,* [New York], 1911; (with Birl E. Shultz) *Documents on the State-Wide Initiative, Referendum, and Recall,* Macmillan, 1912, reprinted, De Capo Press, 1970; *Whither Mankind: A Panorama of Modern Civilizations,* Longmans, Green, 1928, reprinted, Greenwood Press, 1973; *Toward Civilization,* Longmans, Green, 1930; *A Century of Progress,* Harper, 1932, reprinted, Books for Libraries, 1970; *America Faces the Future,* Houghton, Mifflin, 1932, reprinted, Books for Libraries, 1969; (with G.H.E. Smith) *Current Problems of Public Policy,* Macmillan, 1936; *The Enduring Federalist,* F. Ungar, 1959.

FOR MORE INFORMATION SEE: Hubert Herring, ''Charles A. Beard,'' *Harper's,* May, 1939; Stanley J. Kunitz, editor, *Twentieth Century Authors,* H. W. Wilson, 1942, 7th edition, 1973, first supplement, 1955; M. Lerner, ''Charles Beard's Stormy Voyage,'' *New Republic,* October 25, 1948; Lerner, ''Charles Beard: Civilization and the Devils,'' *New Republic,* November 1, 1948; Matthew Josephson, ''Charles A. Beard, A Memoir,'' *Virginia Quarterly Review,* Autumn, 1949; Richard E. Banta, compiler, *Indiana Authors and Their Books, 1816-1916,* Wabash College Press, 1949; B. C. Borning, ''Political Philosophy of Young Charles A. Beard,'' *American Political Science Review,* December, 1949; A. W. MacMahon, ''Charles Austin Beard as a Teacher,'' *Political Science Quarterly,* March, 1950; H. B. Phillips, ''Charles Beard, Walter Vrooman, and the Founding of Ruskin Hall,'' *South Atlantic Quarterly,* April, 1951; Howard K. Beale, editor, *Charles A. Beard: An Appraisal* by Eric F. Goldman, et. al., University of Kentucky Press, 1954, reprinted, Octagon, 1976; Mary R. Beard, *Making of Charles A. Beard: An Interpretation,* Exposition, 1955.

Bernard C. Borning, *Political and Social Thought of Charles A. Beard,* University of Washington Press, 1962; Lee Benson, *Turner and Beard: American Historical Writing Reconsidered,* Free Press, 1965; Robert E. Brown, *Charles Beard and the Constitution,* Norton, 1965; David W. Noble, *Historians against History,* University of Minnesota Press, 1965; Cushing Strout, *Pragmatic Revolt in American History: Carl Becker and Charles Beard,* Cornell University Press, 1966; Frank E. Hill, *Famous Historians,* Dodd, Mead, 1966; Richard Hofstadter, *Progressive Historians,* A. Knopf, 1968; Marcus Cunliffe and Robin W. Winks, editors, *Pastmasters,* Harper, 1969; Ronald Radosh, *Prophets on the Right,* Simon & Schuster, 1975; Thomas C. Kennedy, *Charles A. Beard and American Foreign Policy,* University Presses of Florida, 1975.

Obituaries: *New York Times,* September 2, 1948; *School and Society,* September 11, 1948; *Newsweek,* September 13, 1948; *Publishers Weekly,* September 18, 1948; *Public Management,* November, 1948; *Wilson Library Bulletin,* November, 1948; *Current Biography Yearbook, 1948; American Historical Review,* January, 1949.

BORSKI, Lucia Merecka

PERSONAL: Born in Warsaw, Poland; emigrated to the United States after World War I; married Stephen Borski Szczepanowicz. *Education:* Attended private Polish and Russian schools. New York University, B.A.; Columbia

University Library School, B.S. *Home:* Forest Hill Manor, Forest and Gibson Avenues, Pacific Grove, Calif. 93950.

CAREER: Translator of Polish folk tales. Worked for the New York Public Library, 1922-44, and for the Library of Congress, 1944-46, 1949-65.

WRITINGS: (Translator from the Polish with Kate B. Miller) *The Jolly Tailor, and Other Fairy Tales,* Longmans, Green, 1928, reissued, McKay, 1966; (translator from the Polish with K. B. Miller) Marya Gawalewicz, *The Queen of Heaven,* Dial, 1929; (translator from the Polish with K. B. Miller) *The Gypsy and the Bear, and Other Fairy Tales,* Longmans, Green, 1933; (translator from the Polish) Janina Porazinska, *In Voytus' Little House,* Roy, 1944; (translator from the Polish) Janina Porazinska, *My Village,* Roy, 1944; (translator and adaptor) *Polish Folk Tales,* Sheed & Ward, 1947; (translator and compiler) *Good Sense and Good Fortune,* McKay, 1970; (translator from the Polish) Jerzy Ficowski, *Sister of the Birds and Other Gypsy Tales,* Abingdon, 1976.

WORK IN PROGRESS: Jerzy Ficowski's volume of Gypsy tales as well as an amusing dog story by Ludwik Jerzy Kern.

The fish and mollusks came in multitudes to feed on the noodles. ■ (From *Good Sense and Good Fortune* compiled and translated by Lucia Merecka Borski. Illustrated by Erica Gorecka-Egan.)

SIDELIGHTS: "Even as a pre-school child, I read both Polish and Russian and translated to myself from Russian to Polish, so that now I do not recall which books I read in what language. As a children's librarian in the New York Public Library, I found few Polish tales available in English and began translating with the encouragement of Mary Gould Davis, who was in charge of storytelling in the New York Public Library."

Polish Folk Tales are all deeply religious. *Saturday Review* said, "In translating the old Polish legends Mrs. Borski preserves their curious simplicity and their humor. They are not told for children, but there is a great deal in them that boys and girls will enjoy.... It is a handsome book and one that forms an important record for anyone who is interested in folklore." The *New York Herald Tribune* commented, "Beautifully printed and characteristically illustrated in brilliant colors, this is one of the handsomest of the recent folklore books. It is also one of the most distinctive in spirit, for these stories are Catholic to the core.... In each there is a sense of race and religion, one coloring the other." The *New York Times* added, "Striking illustrations in three colors enhance the folk quality of the tales and supply the humor lacking in the text."

BOYD, Waldo T. 1918-
(Ted Andersen, Robert Parker)

PERSONAL: Born February 4, 1918, in Wiergor Township, Wis.; son of Walter S. (a farmer) and Mary S. (Reid) Boyd; married Anna B. Anker (an accountant and bookkeeper), July 19, 1941; children: Tahirih Ann (Mrs. Lowell Bell), Anna Ruhiyyih (Mrs. John Vasquez). *Education:* Attended high school in West Des Moines, Iowa. *Politics:* None. *Religion:* Baha'i. *Address:* P.O. Box 86, Geyserville, Calif. 95441.

CAREER: U.S. Navy, 1936-40, 1941-45, served as warrant radio electrician (radar) in South Pacific during World War II; teacher of electronics at technical high school in Des Moines, Iowa, 1945-47; Philco Corp., field electronics engineer in Germany, 1948-50; Dianetic Foundation, Wichita, Kan., director of public relations and publications, 1950-53; Aerojet-General Corp., Sacramento, Calif., manager of publications department, 1956-65; Baha'i School, Geyserville, Calif., manager, 1967-71. Holds Federal Communications Commission radiotelephone operator's license, first class, and is a licensed radio amateur, advanced class. *Member:* Authors League of America, Science Fiction Writers of America, California Writer's Club (president, 1966).

WRITINGS: Your Career in the Aerospace Industry (Junior Literary Guild selection), Messner, 1966; *Your Career in Oceanology,* Messner, 1968; *The World of Cryogenics,* Putnam, 1968; *The World of Energy Storage,* Putnam, 1977. Contributor to *Popular Electronics, Popular Science, IF Science Fiction, Scholastic Magazines,* and other publications, some articles under pseudonyms; author of a weekly syndicated science column, "Science in the Service of Man," *Feature Associates,* 1977—.

WORK IN PROGRESS: Science and Religion: The Wings of Mankind.

SIDELIGHTS: "I was the first of five children in a family with a very stern father. My first love was the Thornton W. Burgess stories, which my mother read to me from the daily paper from my earliest months, and the poems of Edgar

WALDO T. BOYD

Guest. She would point to each word as she read, by which unlikely system of pattern recognition I learned to read at an unbelievably early age. When I entered kindergarten I was already an avid reader of fairy tales, stories from the *Saturday Evening Post* (then a household weekly!) *Colliers,* and all the pulp magazines I could beg, borrow, or trade for marbles, frogs, and garter snakes. Upon entering kindergarten I was immediately 'skipped' to first grade, and from then on read my way to excellent grades in all subjects. (If I may digress briefly, my philosophy of education is this: first learn to read well, and all else will come with relative ease!)

"The country was struggling to overcome the severe economic depression of the thirties when I graduated from high school and since jobs for graduates were virtually non-existent and financial backing for college the privilege of the wealthy, I joined the Navy and saw the world. I kept a daily log of my life and times, an important step in my eventual development as a writer.

"I have always been primarily a seeker of truth, that is, I would seek to pry away the layers of illusion from things and events to get at the kernel of truth which usually lies forgotten. This undoubtedly led to my becoming a non-fiction writer, although I have had a few bits of poetry and fiction published. To this day I delight in the discovery of a new facet of truth, wherever it may lie, and in a new realization that much reality lies in the imagination, by asking 'what if? . . .' and watching in fascination as a story develops form and substance, its characters taking on a life of their own.

"My writing always stems from personal experience, although even those who know me well would hardly recognize me or themselves from the writing. Not that I try to hide them, but simply that the story characters have the kernel of

truth and reality that lies mostly hidden from the view of one's closest friends, and therefore is virtually lost to the individual himself, pending intensive reflection and introspection.

"I am a stickler for research. Even in fiction, I must have the story true to science and reason. This is not to say that the imagery cannot range to the far reaches of the universe—but it must 'ring true.'

"As I approach the age of 60, I feel that my writing career is only just now beginning to flower, built upon the hundreds of articles and stories behind me, and upon my observations of life as it is lived by self and others. As an avid science fiction fan, I feel most comfortable writing science fiction, and of course, fantasy as well. I sometimes feel that science fiction is the only good fiction left in the mass of experimental writing that passes for fiction today. A 'slice of life' is not a story. But then it will all come out in the wash, as my mother used to say."

HOBBIES AND OTHER INTERESTS: "Having long since resigned from the 'race for riches,' I consider myself truly wealthy in interests and friendships and constantly expanding horizons of understanding. I have built and driven an electric automobile, I do all sorts of work around the home and acre with my home-built electric tractor and its implements, and I am continuing my experiments with electrical effects on plant growth and into the psi-functions of human beings. I develop craft projects for youth in my workshop, and one of these days I'll catch up on my filing and routine work . . . maybe."

BRINSMEAD, H(esba) F(ay) 1922-
(Pixie Hungerford)

PERSONAL: Born March 15, 1922, in Blue Mountains, New South Wales, Australia; daughter of Edward K. G. (missionary to Indonesia and saw-mill operator) and May (Lambert) Hungerford; married Reginald Brinsmead (now owner of spray contracting company), February 11, 1943; children: Bernard Hungerford, Ken Hungerford. *Education:* Lived in isolated area as a child and received early schooling through a correspondence school; attended high school at Wahroonga, near Sydney, Australia, and then Avondale College, one year. *Politics:* Country Party ("anti-war; humanitarian"). *Religion:* Seventh-day Adventist. *Home:* 36 Menin Rd., Nunawading, Melbourne, Victoria, Australia. *Agent:* Dorothy Blewett Associates, View Hill Crescent, Melbourne, Victoria, Australia.

CAREER: Governess for two years in Tasmania, where she continued her study of speech therapy; teacher of speech therapy in western Victoria, Australia, 1945-48; later was kindergarten supervisor in Melbourne, Australia, for two years; did amateur acting with Box Hill City Drama Group, Melbourne, Australia, 1950-60; began writing after a trip to Indonesia, 1957, and has been writing more or less full time, 1960—. *Member:* International P.E.N. (committee member), Quill Club of Victoria, Victoria League. *Awards, honors:* Marg Gilmore Award for manuscript of *Pastures of the Blue Crane,* 1963, and Children's Book of the Year Award of Australian Children's Book Council for the same book, 1965.

WRITINGS: Pastures of the Blue Crane, Oxford University Press, 1964, Coward, 1966; *Season of the Briar,* Oxford University Press, 1965, Coward, 1966; *Beat of the City,* Oxford University Press, 1966, Coward, 1967; *A Sapphire for

H. F. BRINSMEAD

September, Oxford University Press, 1967; *The Wind Harp,* Macmillan, 1967; *Isle of the Sea Horse,* Oxford University Press, 1969; *Listen to the Wind,* Oxford University Press, 1970; *Who Calls from Afar?,* Oxford University Press, 1971; *Longtime Passing,* Angus & Robertson, 1971; *Echo in the Wilderness,* Oxford University Press, 1972; *Under the Silkwood,* Macmillan, 1975; *The Ballad of Benny Perhaps,* Macmillan, 1977.

Anthologies: *Beneath the Sun,* Collins, 1972; *The Cool Man,* Angus & Robertson, 1973; *A Handful of Ghosts,* Hodder & Stoughton, 1976, reissued, 1977; *A Swag of Australian,* edited by Leon Garfield, Ward Lock. Author of two children's serials, "The Honey Forest," 1960, and "The Apple Ship," 1962; has written short stories for Australian Broadcasting Commission; and articles and stories, some under name Pixie Hungerford, for *People, Country, Women's Weekly, Australian Letters,* and other periodicals.

WORK IN PROGRESS: A teen-age novel, *Isle of the Sea Horse.*

SIDELIGHTS: "[In 1971] my husband and I moved from Melbourne to our farm near Tweed Heads on the Queensland border, though it was being sold. We built a new house a few miles further into the hills, at Terranora, our present home.

"The move disrupted my writing very much and I am only just now beginning to get a proper routine. Still, we live in a beautiful place, a hilltop, overlooking the Pacific coast on one side, and behind us, the Tweed Valley, with the river winding through the fields of sugar cane, and in the distance the Numinbah Range and Mount Warning against the sky, dominating the country for many miles around. It is the old

volcanic plug of the monstrous volcano that produced this system of rugged mountains and lush river valleys. Originally it was all dense rain forest, semi-tropical. The cedar getters came from the 'red gold,' as they called the timber, and now the hills are denuded, turned into pasture country, and sown by alien laurel trees.

"On our two acres of land, my husband and I hope to reproduce a micro-rain forest. We are collecting and planting all the trees that still thrive in isolated pockets and on the slopes of Warning—teak, rose wood, white and red cedar, red barabeen, plum wood, laburnum and more than I can remember. My husband is a 'keep-fit' man, and every evening goes for a run on the long, straight white beach of Fingal, with the two dogs, Barney the Dalmation, who should live down the hill but comes every day to be taken for his run and often forgets to go home—and Fred, the old and grey-nosed Bitsa, who came to us fourteen years ago and has seen all our ups and downs.

"Our son, Ken, works in Brisbane as a psychologist and comes home at week ends. At present, our eldest son, Bernie, with his wife and four children, are in Michigan while he completes a doctorate in theology; but we hope that it will not be too long before the four children can enjoy our garden and infant forest and the long white beaches that line the coast for a hundred miles or more."

BUCK, Lewis 1925-

PERSONAL: Born February 16, 1925, in Norfolk, Va.; son of Ernest Robert (a mechanic) and Florence (Thompson)

LEWIS BUCK

Marshes have been used as dumps. They have been filled with trash, bottles, wrecked cars, and old refrigerators. ■ (From *Wetlands—Bogs, Marshes, and Swamps* by Lewis Buck. Illustrated by Grambs Miller.)

Buck; married Georgia Allen Weaver, June 26, 1953; children: Eric Banning, Peter Carson. *Education:* Duke University, A.B., 1947; College of William and Mary, M.F.A., 1952. *Home address:* 13 Pearl St., Camden, Me. 04843.

CAREER: High school teacher of English and art in Poquoson, Va., 1952-53; tour guide in Europe and North Africa, 1953-54; Barney Neighborhood House, Washington, D.C., art teacher and social worker, 1954-57; American University, Washington, D.C., draftsman and illustrator for Human Relations Area Files, 1957-59; National Rehabilitation Association, Washington, D.C., administrative assistant, 1960-67; *Journal of Rehabilitation,* Washington, D.C., editor, 1967-70; Craignair at Clark Island, Spruce Head, Maine, innkeeper and artist, 1970—. *Military service:* U.S. Naval Reserve, 1943-59. *Member:* Mid Coast Audubon Society (member of board of directors, 1976-77).

WRITINGS: Wetlands: Bogs, Marshes, and Swamps (juvenile), Parents' Magazine Press, 1974.

SIDELIGHTS: "The book, *Wetlands,* was done at the suggestion of friends, Rose Wyler and Gerald Ames, who have written many science books for children. From our many field trips together, they felt that I was qualified to write this one that they knew Parents' Magazine Press hoped to produce. To my surprise, the editor accepted my initial chapter and outline, and I wrote the book in a month.

"While our sons were small we took them often to the woods and mountains and became interested in natural history and ecology. When we moved to Maine, we continued to lead guests at our inn on natural history field trips. All of this was volunteer work. We made our living in other ways.

"Both of our sons are now away at college. With our jobs as parents over, we expect to pursue art careers fulltime. We have opened the Pearl Street Printmakers etching workshop in Camden, Maine.

BUNTING, Anne Evelyn 1928-
(Evelyn Bolton, A. E. Bunting, Eve Bunting)

PERSONAL: Born December 19, 1928, in Maghera, Ireland; daughter of Sloan Edmund (a merchant) and Mary (Canning) Bolton; married Edward Davison Bunting (a medical administrator), April 26, 1951; children: Christine, Sloan, Glenn. *Education:* Methodist College, Belfast, graduate, 1945. *Politics:* Democrat. *Religion:* Protestant. *Home:* 1512 Rose Villa St., Pasadena, Calif. 91106. *Agent:* Larry Sternig, 2407 North 44th St., Milwaukee, Wis. 53210.

CAREER: Free-lance writer, mainly for young people. *Member:* P.E.N. International, California Writer's Guild,

ANNE EVELYN BUNTING

A silver car stood by the curb, and crossing the footpath toward it was a small man in a black striped suit and a round black hat. ■ (From *Barney the Beard* by Eve Bunting. Illustrated by Imero Gobbato.)

Southern California Council on Writing for Children and Young People. *Awards, honors:* Golden Kite Award, 1976, for *One More Flight; Ghost of Summer* received an award for Best Work of Fiction, published in 1977, by Southern California Council on Literature for Children and Young People, 1978.

WRITINGS—Under name Eve Bunting, except as noted: *The Two Giants,* Ginn, 1972; *A Gift for Lonny,* Ginn, 1973; *Box, Fox, Ox and the Peacock,* Ginn, 1974; *Say It Fast,* Ginn, 1974; *The Wild One,* Scholastic Book Services, 1974; (under name A. E. Bunting) *Pitcher to Center Field,* Elk Grove, 1974; *We Need a Bigger Zoo,* Ginn, 1974; (under name A. E. Bunting) *Surfing Country,* Elk Grove, 1974; *The Once-A-Year Day,* Golden Gate, 1974; *Barney the Beard,* Parents' Magazine Press, 1975; (under name A. E. Bunting) *High Tide for Labrador,* Childrens Press, 1975; *Springboard to Summer,* Childrens Press, 1975.

The Dinosaur Machine series—all published by E.M.C., 1975: *The Day of the Dinosaurs, The Dinosaur Trap, Escape from Turannasaurus, Death of a Dinosaur.*

One More Flight, Warne, 1976; *The Skateboard Four,* Whitman, 1976; *The Creature of Cranberry Cove,* E.M.C., 1976; *The Ghost,* E.M.C., 1976; *Josefina Finds the Prince,* Garrard, 1976; *The Tongue of the Ocean,* E.M.C., 1976; *Ghost of Summer* (Junior Literary Guild selection), Warne, 1977; *The Big Cheese,* Macmillan, 1977; *Winter's Coming,* Harcourt, 1977; (with Glenn Bunting) *Skateboards: How to Make Them, How to Ride Them,* Harvey House, 1977; *Blacksmith at Blueridge,* Scholastic Book Services, 1977; *Magic and the Night Rider,* Harper, 1978; *The Haunting of Kildoran Abbey,* Warne, 1978; *The Big Red Barn,* Harcourt, 1979; *Yesterday's Island,* Warne, 1979; *The Cloverdale Switch,* Lippincott, 1979; *The Robot Birthday,* Dutton, 1979; *The Seaworld Book of Sharks,* Seaworld Press, 1979.

Under name Evelyn Bolton—all published by Creative Educational Society, 1974: *Stable of Fear, Lady's Girl, Goodbye Charlie, Ride When You're Ready, The Wild Horses, Dream Dancer.*

Author of stories for basal readers published by Heath, Lyons & Carnahan and other educational houses. Contributor to children's magazines in United States and Canada, including *Jack and Jill* and *Cricket.* Adult articles and stories have been published in United States and Australia.

WORK IN PROGRESS: The Seaworld Book of Whales.

SIDELIGHTS: "I like to write, and I particularly like to write about Ireland. As an immigrant, although I appreciate the ever-blue skies of California I sometimes long for the misty greys of Ireland. Perhaps I sublimate my homesickness and my heartsickness by writing about Northern Ireland at peace, the way I knew it as a child and growing up."

FOR MORE INFORMATION SEE: Horn Book, June, 1977.

BURGESS, Mary Wyche 1916-
(Em Burgess)

PERSONAL: Born November 6, 1916, in Greenville, S.C.; daughter of Cyril Granville (an attorney) and Mary (Wheeler) Wyche; married Alfred Franklin Burgess (an attorney), June 25, 1938; children: Mary Wyche (Mrs. Arthur Ervin Lesesne), Caroline (Mrs. Benjamin R. Ansbacher), A. Franklin, Jr., Granville Wyche, Victoria (Mrs. Anthony R. Pitman). *Education:* Randolph-Macon Woman's College, A.B., 1937; Furman University, M.A., 1970. *Politics:* Democrat. *Religion:* Episcopal. *Home:* 308 West Faris Rd., Greenville, S.C. 29605.

CAREER: Greenville Piedmont (daily newspaper), Greenville, S.C., city reporter, 1937-38; *Greenville News,* Greenville, part-time feature writer, 1941-43. *Member:* Phi Beta Kappa, Junior League (Greenville, S.C.), United Way, Girl Scouts of America, Family Service, Symphony Association, Civic Ballet.

WRITINGS: Women in Education, Dillon, 1975. Columnist for *Greer Citizen* (weekly newspaper), 1941-43. Contributor,

Jack and Jill, Sandlapper, South Carolina Historical Magazine, and religious publications.

WORK IN PROGRESS: Women in Music; Biography of Creek Indian, Alexander McGilliveay; historical articles on South Carolinians; editing letters of a confederate soldier for South Carolina historical magazine; children's stories; short stories; *Signers of U.S. Constitution;* and a novel about murder.

SIDELIGHTS: "When I was growing up in a small southern town, I had, in addition to freedom to explore woods and nearby mountains, access to the city library, a mile from home. Regularly I would choose a dozen books, the limit allowed, and walk slowly home, reading the one opened up on top of the stack. Of course, there was little traffic in those days, the Twenties, and the practise posed no hazards. Fairy tales, Sir Walter Scott's romances, Robert Louis Stevenson's stories were favorites. I must have read *Treasure Island,* a dozen times—its all-male cast appealed to my tomboy soul. And how I looked forward to the arrival of the *Youth's Companion* magazine!

"Yet, reading solely for entertainment, I did not give much thought to the structure of the stories. I gained a good vocabulary, spelling accuracy, and a facility for writing but little knowledge of the drama and action necessary in a good story. Now, forty years later, I am trying to learn. The wealth of anecdotes in any lawyer's family furnishes a mine of material, but oh! how hard it is to give them the proper structure!

"Journalistic training and a love of history have steered me toward research articles, which demand much time but little plotting. With nine grandchildren as inspiration, however, I earnestly desire to write for children. They have such marvelous imaginations and such honest responses that I am ambitious to write something they will accept. My motto is 'Better late than never!' "

HOBBIES AND OTHER INTERESTS: Music (violinist with Greenville Symphony for twenty-six years), vegetable gardening, tennis, politics, hiking.

CAREY, Bonnie 1941-

PERSONAL: Born June 9, 1941, in Concord, N.H.; daughter of Sumner E. (a florist) and Agnes (McNeill; a secretary) Marshall; married John J. Carey (a computer design engineer), August 25, 1962; children: Lorrie Jean, Peter Dean. *Education:* Boston University, B.A. (summa cum laude), 1962; Assumption College, M.A.T., 1966; attended North Carolina State University, 1969, Moscow State University, certificate, 1975; currently attending University of North Carolina. *Home and office:* 4221 Redington Drive, Raleigh, N.C. 27609. *Agent:* Am-Rus Literary Agency, 25 West 43rd St., New York, N.Y. 10036.

CAREER: Literary translator; writer; teacher; folklorist. Hale High School, Raleigh, N.C., Russian and English teacher, 1972-77; Student Theatre Guild, Raleigh, N.C., production adviser and script writer, 1973-75; free-lance literary translator from Russian and author, 1969—. Book reviewer for *World Literature Today* (Russian and Serbo-Croatian books); guest speaker on Slavic and children's literature at local schools and clubs; judge for script writing and poetry contests. *Member:* Creative Writer's Group of the Raleigh Woman's Club (chairwoman, 1972-73), Phi Beta

Kappa, Long View Writers, Boston University Women Graduates' Club, American Association of Teachers of Slavic and East European Languages (secretary-treasurer of Carolinas Chapter, 1973-74), North Carolina Writer's Conference. *Awards, honors:* Registered on list of qualified writers by North Carolina Arts Council; Chicago Book Clinic Certificate of Award for *Baba Yaga's Geese and Other Russian Stories,* 1974; *Search Behind the Lines* nominated for 1976 Mildred Batchelder Award; *Grasshopper to the Rescue,* Junior Literary Guild selection, 1979; Graduate Student-Young Faculty Exchange between the U.S.A. and the U.S.S.R., 1978-79.

WRITINGS—All translations: *Baba Yaga's Geese and Other Russian Stories,* Indiana University Press, 1973; Yevgeny Ryss, *Search Behind the Lines,* Morrow, 1974; Anatoli Aleksin, *Alik the Detective,* Morrow, 1977; *Grasshopper to the Rescue,* Morrow, 1979.

Plays: Catherine Chernyak, *Vassilissa the Beautiful,* performances: Raleigh, N.C., 1972, Durham, N.C., 1972, Chapel Hill, N.C., 1972, Boone, N.C., 1972, 1973, Danville, Va., 1974, toured by professional actors throughout the schools of N.C. as part of a cultural enrichment project, 1975; L. Brausevich and I. Karnaukhova, *The Scarlet Flower,* performances: Raleigh, N.C., 1975, Durham, N.C., 1975.

Work has appeared in *The Long View Journal, Gleanings, Jack and Jill, The Christian Science Monitor, Poetry Parade, Poet Lore, Michigan Quarterly Review, Festival Poets, Poetry Ventura, The News Observer* and others.

WORK IN PROGRESS: Animals Stories from the Soviet Union; It's Not Easy to Steal from a Gypsy and Other Yugoslav Folktales.

SIDELIGHTS: "I was raised on a New England farm on fairy tales, first as oral tradition and then as written litera-

BONNIE CAREY

(From *Baba Yaga's Geese and Other Russian Stories* translated and adapted by Bonnie Carey. Illustrated by Guy Fleming.)

ture. Books were one of the few ties a farm girl could have with civilization, and my reading passed from folk tales to mysteries to French literature and finally to Russian literature. At eleven, I made fledgling attempts at writing poetry. My educational activities and the raising of two children of my own reinforced my enthusiasm for literature.

"My activities have always been connected in some way with languages, folklore, writing, and the theater. Because I went to high school in a small New Hampshire town (Penacook) named after an extinct Indian tribe, I developed an interest in Indian lore and lived in the shadow of strong, legendary, pioneering heroines like Hannah Duston, who was reputed to have escaped from and scalped her Indian captors, whose statue still stands in our town, and about whom I've written several poems.

"After receiving a sound foundation in Russian at Boston University and Assumption College, I applied my knowledge to literary translations in hopes of exposing American youth to the folk tales and children's literature of Russia. Since it is only within recent years that alphabets have been developed for many of the Soviet ethnic groups, the recording of their folklore is in a state of evolution, and it is exciting to be involved in pioneering efforts to render new folktales into English.

"The children's theater has been an arena for my literary activities. The Student Theatre Guild, Inc., of North Carolina, for which I've written scripts and served as production adviser, has experimented with authentic Russian children's plays. One of them, *Vassilissa the Beautiful,* was endorsed and subsidized by the North Carolina State Department of Public Instruction to be shown in the schools as a cultural enrichment project.

"At the same time, I initiated the only existent Russian language program in the secondary schools of North Carolina at Hale High School in Raleigh. There I taught Russian, English, folklore, creative writing and drama.

"During the summer of 1975 I was chosen to represent our country as one of a group of thirty exchange teachers with the Soviet Union, an experience that gave me new insights into teaching Russian and increased my proficiency in Russian and knowledge of literature.

"Now I am enrolled in a Ph.D. program at the University of North Carolina, where my interests have expanded into the area of Yugoslav folklore.

"For me, life and scholarship have always been inseparable facets of the same coin. My approach to literature, too, has been a combination of the spontaneity of a creative artist and an analytical scholar. My efforts, in general, are always focused on undeveloped areas, because to work in such areas is a true adventure."

FOR MORE INFORMATION SEE: *North Carolina Leader,* February 16, 1972; *The Wake Weekly,* March 2, 1972; *Watauga Democrat,* August 9, 1973.

CHWAST, Seymour 1931-

PERSONAL: Surname rhymes with Quast; born, 1931, in N.Y.; *Education:* Cooper Union Art School, New York, N.Y. *Home:* New York, N.Y. *Office:* Push Pin Studios, 207 East 32nd St., New York, N.Y. 10016.

SEYMOUR CHWAST

CAREER: Founding partner of the Push Pin Studios; helped develop the distinctive Push Pin style. Was an originator of the *Push Pin Graphic,* a studio publication. Cooper Union Art School, New York, N.Y., visiting professor; American Institute of Graphic Arts, New York, N.Y., vice-president. *Exhibitions:* "A Century of American Illustration," Brooklyn Museum; American Institute of Graphic Arts; Art Directors Club of New York; Society of Illustrators; Type Directors Club of New York; Art Directors Club of Chicago; Lincoln Center for the Performing Arts, New York, N.Y.; California State University; Galerie Delpire, Paris, France; Louvre's Musee des Arts Decoratifs, March, 1970. *Member:* Alliance Graphique Internationale. *Awards, honors: New York Times* Choice of Best Illustrated Book of the Year, *Sara's Granny and the Groodle,* 1969; Cooper Union Citation for Excellence.

WRITINGS—Self-illustrated: (With Martin Moskof) *Still Another Alphabet Book,* McGraw, 1969 (with Martin Moskof) *Still Another Number Book,* McGraw, 1971.

Illustrator: Gill, *Sara's Granny and the Groodle,* Doubleday, 1969; Eve Merriam, *Finding a Poem,* Atheneum, 1970; Phyllis La Farge, *The Pancake King,* Delacorte, 1971; *Rimes De La Mere Oie: Mother Goose Rhymes,* Little, 1971; *The House That Jack Built,* Random House, 1973.

His illustrations, posters, typographic designs and animated commercials have been created for print and television advertising, book jackets, record albums, package designs, brochures and magazines.

FOR MORE INFORMATION SEE: *Idea,* Japan, October, 1973; *Horn Book,* October, 1973.

This is the cock that crowed in the morn,
That waked the priest all shaven and shorn,
That married the man all tattered and torn,
That kissed the maiden all forlorn,
That milked the cow with the crumpled horn,
That tossed the dog,
That worried the cat,
That killed the rat,
That ate the malt
That lay in the house that Jack built.

(From *The House that Jack Built* by Seymour Chwast. Illustrated by the author.)

FRANK J. CLARK

CLARK, Frank J(ames) 1922-

PERSONAL: Born August 4, 1922, in Brooklyn, N.Y.; son of J. Franklin and Anna (Koch) Clark; married Betty Schulte, November 8, 1946; children: John, Donald. *Education:* New York University, B.A., 1953, further study, 1966-72; Columbia University, M.A., 1961; further study, Mannes College of Music, 1961-62; Electronic Computer Programming Institute, certificate, 1965; also attended State University of New York at New Paltz, Dutchess Community College, and Genessee Community College, 1966-70. *Home:* 205 Grandview Terr., Batavia, N.Y. 14020. *Office address:* Department of Data Processing, Box 718, Genessee Community College, College Rd., Batavia, N.Y.

CAREER: Trumpeter with Boston Pops Orchestra, Boston, Mass., 1953, Band of America, New York, N.Y., 1964-65, and Gershwin Orchestra, American Album of Famous Music Orchestra, and others; music teacher in public schools, Plainview, Long Island, N.Y., 1958-64; teacher of mathematics in other schools; Dutchess Community College, Poughkeepsie, N.Y., assistant professor of data processing, 1965-68; Genessee Community College, Batavia, N.Y., director of data processing and associate professor of data processing, 1968-1978; Rochester Institute of Technology, Rochester, N.Y., associate professor of computer science; programmer, International City Manager's Association, spring, 1967; designer of several city and county data processing systems. *Military service:* U.S. Navy, 1942-45; musician on U.S.S. "Iowa"; received twelve battle stars, Presidential Unit Citation. *Member:* New York State Association of Junior Colleges, American Technical Education Association, Authors Guild, Federation of Musicians (president, local 575, Batavia, N.Y., 1976-1977).

WRITINGS: (With Melvin Berger) *Science and Music: From Tom-tom to Hi-fi,* McGraw, 1961; (with Alan Vorwald) *Computers: From Sand Table to Electronic Brain,* McGraw, 1961, 3rd edition, 1970; (with Berger) *Music in Perspective,*

S. Fox, 1962; *Contemporary Studies for the Trumpet*, Adler, 1963; *Contemporary Math*, F. Watts, 1964; *Contemporary Math for Parents*, F. Watts, 1965; *Speed Math*, F. Watts, 1966.

Information Processing, Goodyear Publishing, 1970; *Introduction to PLH Programming*, Allyn & Bacon, 1970, new edition, 1971; (with Robert L. Gray) *Accounting Programs and Business Systems: Case Studies*, Goodyear Publishing, 1971; *Business Systems and Data Processing Procedures*, Prentice-Hall, 1972; (with Joseph M. Whalen) *RPG I and RPG II Programming*, Addison-Wesley, 1974; *Mathematics for Data Processing*, Reston, 1974; *Data Recorder*, Reston, 1974. Also author of television scripts.

SIDELIGHTS: There is a collection of Clark's writings at the University of Mississippi.

CRANE, Walter   1845-1915

PERSONAL: Born August 15, 1845, in Liverpool, England; died March 15, 1915, in London, England; son of Thomas (an artist) and Marie Crane; married Mary Frances Andrews, 1871; children: two sons, one daughter. *Education:* Privately tutored; mostly self-taught. *Politics:* Socialist. *Home:* West Kensington, London, England.

CAREER: Artist, writer, and illustrator of children's books. Started sketching animals as a child, became an apprentice to wood-engraver, W. S. Linton, 1858-61; illustrated his first book at the age of seventeen; designed the covers of railway novels, 1863; began association with color engraver, Edmund Evans, 1865; director of design, Manchester School of Art, 1893-96; principal, Royal College of Art, South Kensington, 1898-99. His works have been exhibited at the Dudley Gallery, London, 1866-82, the Grosvenor Gallery, London, and in several galleries in the United States; many of his frieze and mosaic decorations can be seen in several private and public buildings in Britain; some of his tapestry designs are exhibited at the Victoria and Albert Museum in London.

MEMBER: Royal Institute of Painters in Oil and Water Colour, Royal Society of Painters in Water Colours, Art Workers' Guild (past master), Arts and Crafts Society (founder; first president, 1888), Dresden Academy of Fine Arts (honorary member), Munich Academy of Fine Arts (honorary member), Societe Nationale des Beaux Arts (Paris), Fabian Society. *Awards, honors:* Silver medal (Paris), 1889, for *The Diver;* gold medal (Munich), 1895, for *Chariot of the Hours;* honorary art director, Reading College, 1898; gold medal (Paris), 1900, for mural tile design; Commendatore of the Order of the Royal Crown of Italy, 1903; Albert Gold Medal, Society of Arts, 1904; gold medal and grand prize, Milan International Exhibition, 1906; Cavaliere, Order of S. S. Maurizio e Lazzaro (Italy), 1911.

ILLUSTRATOR—"Toy Book" series, all published by Routledge, 1867-1876, except as noted: *Absurd ABC; Alladin; Alphabet of Old Friends; Annie and Jackie in Town; Baby's Own Alphabet; Beauty and the Beast; Bluebeard; Chattering Jack; Cinderella; Cock Robin*, Warne, 1865-66; *Dame Trot and Her Comical Cat*, Warne, 1865-66; *Fairy Ship; Farmyard Alphabet*, Warne, 1865-66; *Forty Thieves; Frog Prince; Gaping Wide-Mouth Waddling Frog; Goody Two Shoes; Grammar in Rhyme; Hind in the Wood; House That Jack Built*, Warne, 1865-66; *How Jessie Was Lost; Jack and the Beanstalk; King Luckieboy's Party; Little Red Riding Hood; Mother Hubbard; Multiplication Table in Verse;*

My Mother; Noah's Ark Alphabet; Old Courtier; One, Two, Buckle My Shoe; Princess Bell Etoile; Puss-in Boots; Railroad Alphabet, Warne, 1865-66; *Sing a Song of Sixpence*, Warne, 1865-66; *Sleeping Beauty; This Little Pig; Three Bears; Valentine and Orson; Yellow Dwarf.*

"Picture Book" series, all published by John Lane, except as noted: *King Luckieboy's Picture Book*, Routledge, 1871; *The Marquis of Caraba's Picture Book*, Routledge, 1874; *Bluebeard Picture Book*, Routledge, 1875; *Aladdin's Picture Book*, Routledge, 1876; *The Three Bears' Picture Book*, Routledge, 1876; *This Little Pig Picture Book*, 1895; *Cinderella's Picture Book*, 1897; *Mother Hubbard Picture Book*, 1897; *Red Riding Hood's Picture Book*, 1898; *Beauty and the Beast Picture Book*, 1900; *Goody Two Shoes' Picture Book*, 1901; *The Buckle My Shoe Picture Book*, 1910, reissued, Watts, 1967; *The Sleeping Beauty Picture Book*, 1911.

Walter Crane's Picture Book, Routledge, 1872; (with Kate Greenaway) *The Quiver of Love: A Collection of Valentines*, Marcus Ward, 1876; (and editor with sister, Lucy Crane) *The Baby's Opera: A Book of Old Rhymes*, Routledge, 1877; (and editor with L. Crane) *The Baby's Bouquet: A Fresh Bunch of Old Rhymes and Tunes*, Routledge, 1879; *Slate and Pencil-Vania: Being the Adventures of Dick on a Desert Island*, Marcus Ward, 1885; *Pothooks and Perseverance; or, The ABC Serpent*, Marcus Ward, 1886; *A Romance of the Three Rs*, Marcus Ward, 1886 (contains *Little Queen Anne, Pothooks and Perseverance*, and *Slate and Pencil-Vania*).

Legends for Lionel, Cassell, 1887; *Flora's Feast: A Masque of Flowers*, Cassell, 1889; *Queen Summer; or, the Tourney of the Lily and the Rose*, Cassell, 1891; *Columbia's Courtship: A Picture History of the United States*, L. Prang, 1892; *Eight Illustrations to Shakespeare's "Tempest,"* Dent, 1893; *Eight Illustrations to Shakespeare's "Two Gentlemen of Verona,"* Dent, 1894; *Shakespeare's Comedy of "The Merry Wives of Windsor" Presented in Eight Pen Designs*, George Allen, 1894; *A Floral Fantasy in an Old English Garden*, Harper, 1899.

John R. de Capel Wise, *The New Forest: Its History and Its Scenery*, Southeran, 1863; Agnes DeHavilland, *Stories from Memel*, W. Hunt, 1864; Henry and Augustus Mayhew, *The Magic of Kindness*, Cassell, Petter, 1869; Henry C. Selous, *Sunny Days; or, A Month at the Great Stowe*, Griffith & Farran, 1871; Dinah Maria Mulock, *Agatha's Husband: A Novel*, Macmillan, 1875; D. M. Mulock, *The Head of the Family: A Novel*, [London], 1875; (with George Du Maurier) Jemmett Browne, *Songs of Many Seasons*, Simpkin, Marshall, 1876; Mary A. DeMorgan, *The Necklace of Princess Fiorimonde*, Macmillan, 1880, reissued, Gollancz, 1963; J. R. de Capel Wise, *The First of May: A Fairy Masque*, Southeran, 1881.

(With father, Thomas Crane) Lucy Crane, *Art and Formation of Taste: Six Lectures*, Macmillan, 1882; Theo Marzials, *Pan Pipes: A Book of Old Songs*, Routledge, 1882; Jakob Ludwig Karl and Wilhelm Karl Grimm, *Household Stories from the Collection of the Brothers Grimm*, translation by Lucy Crane, Macmillan, 1882, reissued, McGraw, 1966; John M. D. Meiklejohn, *The Golden Primer*, W. Blackwood, 1884; Constance C. Harrison, *Folk and Fairy Tales*, Ward & Downey, 1885; *The Baby's Own Aesop*, edited by L. Crane, Routledge, 1887; Homer, *Echoes of Hellas: The Tale of Troy and the Story of Orestes*, Marcus Ward, 1887.

(With G. P. Jacomb Hood) Oscar Wilde, *The Happy Prince and Other Tales*, Nutt, 1888; *The Turtle Dove's Nest and*

CRANE, 1909.

Other Nursery Rhymes, Routledge, 1890; Francois L. Schauermann, *Wood Carving in Practice and Theory*, Chapman & Hall, 1891; Nathaniel Hawthorne, *A Wonder Book for Girls and Boys*, Osgood & McIlvaine, 1892; Margaret W. Deland, *The Old Garden and Other Verses*, Osgood & McIlvaine, 1893; *History of Reynard the Fox*, translation from the Dutch by William Caxton, Nutt, 1894; Elizabeth Harrison, *The Vision of Dante: A Story for Little Children*, Chicago Kindergarten College, 1894.

Edmund Spenser, *Faerie Queene*, edited by Thomas J. Wise, George Allen, 1894; William Morris, *The Story of the Glittering Plain*, Kelmscott Press, 1894; *Book of Christmas Verse*, edited by H. C. Beeching, Methuen, 1895; Miguel de Cervantes Saavedra, *Don Quixote of the Mancha*, edited by Edward Abbott Parry, Blackie, 1900, reissued, Dodd, 1960; Charles Lamb, *A Masque of Days: From the Last Essays of Elia*, Cassell, 1901; William Shakespeare, *Flowers from Shakespeare's Garden: A Posy from the Plays*, Cassell, 1906; Beatrice Crane, *The Procession of the Months*, R. H. Bath, circa 1908; Arthur Kelly, *The Rosebud and Other Tales*, Arthur Unwin, 1909.

Alfred C. Calmour, *Rumbo Rhymes; or, The Great Combine*, Harper, 1911; Thomas Malory, *King Arthur's Knights*, edited by Henry Gilbert, Jack, 1911; Henry F. B. Gilbert, *Robin Hood and His Merry Men*, Jack, 1912; Mary MacGregor, *The Story of Greece Told to Boys and Girls*, Jack,

1913; H.F.B. Gilbert, *The Knights of the Round Table*, Jack, 1915; *Best Loved Fairy Tales of Walter Crane*, Watts, 1967.

Stories by Mary L. Molesworth, published by Macmillan, except as noted: (Under pseudonym Ennis Graham) *Carrots: Just a Little Boy*, [London], 1876; (under pseudonym Ennis Graham) *The Cuckoo Clock*, [London], 1877; *Grandmother Dear*, 1878; *The Tapestry Room*, 1879; *A Christmas Child: A Sketch of Boy Life*, 1880; *The Adventures of Herr Baby*, 1881; *Rosy*, 1882; *Christmas-Tree Land*, 1884; *Us: An Old-Fashioned Story*, 1885; *Four Winds Farm*, 1887; *Little Miss Peggy*, 1887; *A Christmas Posy*, 1888; *The Rectory Children*, 1889; *The Children of the Castle*, 1890.

Writings—Nonfiction, except as noted: *Lines and Outlines*, Marcus Ward, 1875; *The Sirens Three: A Poem* (self-illustrated), Macmillan, 1886; *The Claims of Decorative Art*, Lawrence & Bullen, 1892; *Of the Decorative Illustration of Books Old and New*, G. Bell, 1896, reprinted, Gale, 1968; *The Bases of Design*, G. Bell, 1898; *Line and Form*, G. Bell, 1900; *Moot Points: Friendly Disputes on Art and Industry*, (self-illustrated), Batsford, 1903; *Ideals in Art: Papers, Theoretical, Practical, Critical*, G. Bell, 1905.

An Artist's Reminiscences (autobiographical; self-illustrated), Macmillan, 1907, reprinted, Singing Tree Press, 1968; *India Impressions* (self-illustrated), Macmillan, 1907; *William Morris to Whistler: Papers and Addresses on Art and Craft and the Commonwealth* (self-illustrated), G. Bell, 1911, reprinted, Norwood, 1976; *Walter Crane Hazelford Sketch Book* (self-illustrated), John Barnard, 1937.

SIDELIGHTS: **August 15, 1845.** Born in Liverpool, England. His early ability and interest in art stemmed from his father, Thomas Crane, who was a well-known painter of portraits. "My father and mother went to live in Liverpool in the early 'forties,' and my father became Secretary and Treasurer of the Liverpool Academy of Art, a post which he resigned on being ordered to Torquay on account of his health, as consumption was feared.

"[My mother] had remarkable energy and sense, and devoted herself in the most self-sacrificing way to her family. Her maiden name was Kearsley. Her father was a 'maltster,' a prosperous man in a good position in Chester.

"I cannot say that I have any recollection of my birthplace—Liverpool; but this is accounted for by the fact of my transportation from thence at the early age of three months, when, in October 1845, on account of my father's state of health, the family removed to Torquay—then coming into high repute as a health resort.

"It was in Maryland Street, Liverpool, however, that I first saw the light—the same street, I believe, which claims to have been the birthplace of Mr. W. E. Gladstone.

"The 15th of August was my natal day—a day marked in the calendar as the date of the death of Napoleon the First and that of the birth of Sir Walter Scott.

"I cannot say whether the latter circumstance had any influence over the choice of my name, however.

"I can claim, without any special egoism, to have made a noise in the world at a very early period. The journey to South Devon from Liverpool in the 'forties' must have been somewhat trying. The last part of the journey, I think from Exeter, was performed by stage coach, and the legend is that

(From *Wonder Book for Girls and Boys* by Nathaniel Hawthorne. Illustrated by Walter Crane.)

it was here that the voice of my crying made the coach impossible for any inside passengers unconnected with the family, who must have been very long-suffering, and it was said only a particular aunt of the party had the power of soothing my inarticulate infantine troubles.

"My memory, fortunately perhaps a blank as to this period, cannot discover any distinct visual impressions until at least three years later. The very earliest, I think, is one of sitting in a swing suspended between two elm trees in the old garden of the first house we inhabited on settling in South Devon. This was at Tor, and known as Beanland Place. The house is vague, but the garden, where, probably, with brother and sisters, most of this time was spent, seems more distinct, and there was in one corner the woodhouse, where the garden tools were kept—a dark and shadowy temple in a world of wonder and mystery.

"I have a very early recollection—a strange one—of being seized with 'croup' and waking my parents in the middle of the night with strange squeaking sounds from my throat, and being dimly conscious of lights being struck and carried about, and the doctor being sent for.

"My next primitive memory picture is of a tall house on the side of a hill—Walden or Waldon Hill, with a long sloping walled garden, and a good many stone steps, rather perilous to us children, and I do not think residence there could have been very lengthy, and probably recollections of the place are merged in later memories of the aspects of the town and harbour, of which Waldon Hill commanded a fine view.

"The next move was inland again to the village of Upton, then quite distinct from Torquay. Here memory is much less vague and impressionistic, and, in fact, becomes almost pre-Raphaelite. I have a distinct picture of a rather pretty villa, one of a pair in early Victorian taste, with a verandah having light trellis supports, which were covered with climbing white roses in great profusion. French casement windows opened out on to this verandah from the drawing-room, which was decorated by a plaster cast of Thorvaldsen's popular circular relief 'Night' on the mantelpiece, the companion 'Day' occupying a corresponding position in the dining-room, which, according to a usual plan in those days, was divided from the drawing-room by folding doors.

"I remember that another room was converted into a studio for my father by having a skylight inserted, and recall seeing the workmen cut the hole through the plaster ceiling for the purpose.

"Upton was a pretty, old-fashioned Devonshire village of thatched cottages with whitewashed walls, nestling among tall hedgerow elms. I remember a stream flowing across the road and a foot-bridge over it, an attractive place from which to watch the fish and the ducks. Near by was a cider press—a most mysterious affair, turned by a horse in the recesses of a dark shed. It was joy to see the heaps of apples and to taste the new sweet cider. Amid such scenes and with such surroundings a very happy child-life was passed, not oppressively shadowed by much governessing or schooling.

"The years went by happily enough at Upton, at least from the irresponsible child's point of view, pleasantly varied by excursions on donkeys, combined with picnics in the pleasant and romantic places with which the neighbourhood abounded, such as Anstey's Cove and Babbicombe. These outings were an institution on birthdays, and as there was no great disparity of years in the little family of five, we could all

join in the same childish pleasures and were quite companionable. My father was very fond of walking, too, and often took us for long rambles among those pleasant Devonshire lanes and hills.

"I daresay my early efforts with the pencil may have been encouraged by some of my father's friends who visited at Laureston Villa (the name of the Upton house) about this time. I remember he and a few other artists formed an evening sketching club, meeting at each other's houses or studios and making sketches in charcoal by lamplight.

"Meanwhile I picked up in my father's studio and under his eye a variety of artistic knowledge in an unsystematic way. I was always drawing, and any reading, or looking at prints or pictures, led back to drawing again. *Nash's Mansions* was one of the books I loved to pore over. It was a folio, and rather heavy and unwieldy for a small person, but such difficulties were always solved by the use of the floor. Then there was another folio, *Liversege's Works,* a book of mezzotints of romantic and dramatically treated figure-subjects, chiefly illustrations to Walter Scott's novels, as far as I remember; also the *Art Journal* in its original form in the buff-covered parts, with a more or less classical design on the wrapper and bound in thickish volumes of plain green cloth. The designs which attracted me the most in these were not the elaborate steel engravings from modern pictures, but the woodcuts.

(From "Rapunzel" in *Household Stories* by Jacob and Wilhelm Grimm. Illustrated by Walter Crane.)

(From *Beauty and the Beast* illustrated by Walter Crane.)

CRANE, 1865.

"Impressions from such designs had no doubt an unconscious effect in forming one's future tendencies and style. For a time they became obscure and displaced by other influences." [Walter Crane, *An Artist's Reminiscences,* Singing Tree Press, 1968.[1]]

1856. Sent to a private boy's school. Crane had been privately tutored at home before this first school experience. "It was presently thought advisable to send my brother and myself to school. The principal boys' school was then under the mastership of a Mr. Page. It was commonly called 'Page's school,' and was situated upon the Teignmouth road in the upper part of Torquay, quite in the suburbs, and almost in the fields at that time. The schoolhouse was a large square block connected with the master's suburban-looking residence in a garden, facing a large bare-looking playground with what was called a Giant's Stride in one corner. . . .

"My brother Tom was about two years older than I, and had already had some school experience at another school in the town, but it was my first acquaintance with a boys' school. We were, however, only 'day-boys,' and were regarded rather as in a different class by the boarders, though duly officially named Crane Major and Crane Minor. I cannot say my recollections of school life were at all happy. The brutality of it struck me very much. A herd of boys in a gaunt bare room, the walls relieved only by one or two varnished maps; the floor bare, and rows of much-worn and well-inked wooden double-sloped desks, and forms without backs for the boys, and a master's desk or two. The constant use of the cane for quite trifling faults or mistakes was disgusting. Mr. Page was a severe man and seemed to enjoy using the cane, or at least did not seem to think his authority could be maintained without it. He was rather short but sturdily built, and he generally appeared in a black alpaca coat and a black smoking-cap with a tassel hanging on one side, and there was generally a hush at his entry into the schoolroom. There was one poor chap, a Jew and a foreigner, who was always catching it, perhaps because he did not understand so well as the others. I do not think the other masters were empowered to use the cane, however. The second master was very harsh and unsympathetic. I was hopeless in arithmetic always, and at this school on Monday mornings a class was taken by the aforesaid severe master, what was called 'mental arithmetic.' There were no slates or pencil and paper allowed, and the problems which were read out by the master had to be done in the head. After a pause each boy was asked in turn for the answer. If a boy could not answer, or made the wrong answer, it was promptly, 'Next boy!'

"I got on better with the Latin master (Mr. Stuart, a Scotchman with a characteristic accent), with writing on themes which were set by the same master, who was much more sympathetic to me than the others.

"There was a midday dinner served in a long room on the ground floor, also used as a classroom. The food was abundant, certainly, plain roast and boiled with vegetables. A standing dish was roast beef and Yorkshire pudding. The second master would carve for the boys, and each boy could indicate his choice, if he had any, vocally. This was done in a sort of chanted response to the carver's look, generally this form: 'Any way, no fat, please sir.' We day-boys, a very small group, sat at the Principal's table with his own family. He had a son of his own as one of the scholars.

"Writing from dictation, generally some well-known poem, such as, 'On Linden when the sun was low,' I liked well enough, and writing generally, but we had a lot of lessons to take home, and these grew to be such a burden on my spirit, and the anxiety to get them creditably done was such that an attack of congestion of the brain came on and stopped my school career temporarily.

"I do not remember making any very fast friendships among my schoolfellows, but this may be accounted for by the short and interrupted time one spent at the school, and also being a day-boy. The chief opportunities of becoming acquainted with one another were of course in the playground, where we played football and hockey.

"My schooldays, however, were destined to be very short. The last incident I can remember in connection with them was the distribution of some of my early drawings among my schoolfellows as mementoes on the last day of our attendance, when we bade farewell to Mr. Page and his school. Some of these were illustrations to Walter Scott's novels and ballads, chiefly combats and fights, such as that between young Morton and Balfour of Burleigh in *Old Mortality* (or Lord Cranstoun and William of Deloraine in the Ballads), which, curiously enough, I met with in the rooms of one of our old schoolfellows who had settled in London years afterwards, and who had carefully preserved this relic, which was crude enough."[1]

Spring, 1857. Moved to London with his family. ". . . A great change took place in the family. My parents decided to remove to London. I fear my father's professional prospects

Crane's studio at Beaumont Lodge, 1885.

were not improving in Torquay, where his art met with very little encouragement, and he was advised to take up his residence in London, as offering the best field for an artist. His health, which had been a difficulty from the first, had improved very much at Torquay, and no doubt his residence there had prolonged his life. It was not without risk that the new departure was resolved upon. It entailed, of course, the giving up of the house in Park Place, and also the sale of the furniture and effects, so that the break with the old days was complete, and it was like beginning life again in a new world.

"My father had taken a furnished house in what is now called Goldhawk Road—the address was No. 2 Alfred Villas, Starch Green. The house was a semi-detached one, of the early Victorian builders' quasi-Greek-fronted type in painted cement, with Mr. Ruskin's abomination—a Doric portico—and a small flight of steps to the front door, and a small forecourt or front garden, defended from the pavement by an outer wooden gate with posts and balustrade, and there was a long narrow strip of garden at the back divided from the neighbours' on each side by low brick walls, which, so to speak, kept the word of privacy to the eye but broke it to the hope.

"The outlook in front across the road was a brickfield. This at least had the charm of novelty, and I began to sketch the shed with the horse going round, the men laying the bricks of London clay in the long rows under straw to dry, and the smoking pile when they were baked, emitting that curious stuffy oven odour which used to permeate the suburbs of London.

"The education question troubled my parents a good deal, and as want of means was a difficulty, they were advised to try and obtain nominations to Christ's Hospital School for my elder brother and myself. Letters were duly written to certain influential governors or patrons . . . but they brought nothing but more or less courteous replies expressing inability to help in the matter, which was not encouraging; so the idea was given up, and we remained at home—to my great relief, privately, it must be confessed."[1]

1858. Family moved to Lambton Terrace, which was then on the outskirts of Westbournia. At thirteen Crane drew a set of colored page designs for Tennyson's *Lady of Shalott* which were shown to John Ruskin and W. J. Linton, the London

WALTER CRANE

wood-engraver. "Mr. Ruskin was fairly encouraging, and praised particularly the colour of this Lady of Shalott set.

"The same drawings were shown about the same time, however, to Mr. W. J. Linton, who was considered the head of his craft as a wood-engraver at that time, besides being a writer and a poet and an ardent champion of political freedom. . . .

"He seemed so taken with the drawings that he very generously at once offered to take me into his office without the usual premium, with the idea of my learning the craft of drawing on the wood, at that time necessary for those who sought a career in book illustrating. He evidently thought more of my possible capacity as a designer, and praised the Tennyson set for their conception and arrangement, which he said was their chief merit, not so much the colour, as Ruskin had thought."[1]

January, 1859. Apprenticed to W. J. Linton of London. "Well, as it was necessary to consider my prospects of making a living, and as I was quite willing, the offer was accepted by my father; and finally . . . an indenture of apprenticeship to W. J. Linton for a period of three years was signed and sealed, and I remember being instructed to place my thumb upon the little red seal, and say the mystic words, 'I deliver this as my act and deed.' There was no compulsion, as I was eager to begin my new career, and seemed fully aware of what it might lead to, as I carefully recorded the date in a pocket-book, and added in boyish round hand, 'One of the most important events of my life.'

"W. J. Linton was in appearance small of stature, but a very remarkable-looking man. His fair hair, rather fine and thin, fell in actual locks to his shoulders, and he wore a long flowing beard and moustache, then beginning to be tinged with grey. A keen, impulsive-looking, highly sensitive face with kindly blue eyes looked out under the unusually broad brim of a black 'wideawake.'

"He had abundance of nervous energy and moved with a quick, rapid step, coming into the office with a sort of breezy rush, bringing with him always a stimulating sense of vitality. He spoke rapidly in a light-toned voice, frequently punctuated with a curious dry, obstructed sort of laugh. Altogether a kindly, generous, impulsive, and enthusiastic nature, a true socialist at heart, with an ardent love of liberty and with much of the revolutionary feeling of '48 about him. He had a curious way of breaking off his sentences, leaving the listener to supply the last word.

"He never obtruded his opinions, however, and such maxims as he may have given me at times were quite incontrovertible: such as, 'A man cannot be a great man unless he is also a good man,' which I recall his saying once; and on hearing about some people rather under a cloud through impecuniosity, and not being able to pay their rent, he said, 'They may be very good people, and yet not able to pay their rent.' A gentle way, perhaps, of correcting bourgeois sentiment.

"My chief work at first was making little drawings, on fragments of boxwood, for the apprentices to practise upon. The outside edges of the boxwood, after the square block had been sawn out of a cross section of the tree, were used up in this way.

"Wood-engraving was, however, rapidly entering a mechanical stage, and engravers were becoming specialised for different sorts of work. There was a 'tint' man and a 'facsimile' man, for instance. Work for the weekly press necessitated speed, and the blocks used were jointed and screwed together so that they could be taken apart by the use of nuts and spanners, and put together again. By these means a block could be distributed among several different engravers, so that the work could go on simultaneously, and of course much more quickly than if the block was engraved throughout by one pair of hands. Before the block was separated the joints were cut, so that the drawing at the edges of each piece should not be lost and that the work on each should fit together properly. It was usual in a block containing figures and faces for the heads to be cut by the master hand, and what was called the less important 'facsimile' work by the apprentices. In the vignetted drawings then popular there was a good deal of more or less meaningless scribble and cross-hatching to fill up, or to balance, or to give a little relief and colour to the subject.

"Out of office hours I carried on a certain amount of practice in painting and study of various kinds, my models being chiefly members of the family.

"I used to walk every day, except Sundays, from Westbourne Park to Essex Street and back in the evening, taking my lunch with me. I had government office hours—ten to four, and a half-holiday on Saturdays."[1]

Summer, 1859. Father died. Crane was approaching his fourteenth birthday. ". . . A sad sorrow fell upon us in the death of my father. The change and the air of London, and no doubt increased anxieties, had told upon his health, and so seriously that the end came in July. It was, of course, a terrible blow. A kinder father never lived, and with his death the family lost their bread-winner. He had never been able to win a secure position by his art, though always at work; and

She went to the tailor's
    To buy him a coat,
But when she came back,
    He was riding a goat.

She went to the cobbler's
    To buy him some shoes,
But when she came back,
    He was reading the news.

(From *Old Mother Hubbard* illustrated by Walter Crane.)

(From "The Sleeping Beauty" in *Grimm's Household Stories* by Jacob and Wilhelm Grimm. Illustrated by Walter Crane.)

although he maintained his position and kept his family in comparative comfort, he was not able to leave any provision, dying as he did at the early age of fifty-one, and we were none of us of an age to be able to earn a living, but it became more necessary than ever to regard our pursuits as a means towards this end.

"We were greatly indebted to the kindness of an uncle at this sad time, my mother's brother, Mr. Edward Kearsley, then member of a firm of wholesale woollen cloth merchants in the City. Arrangements were eventually made that he should live with us, and a removal from Lambton Terrace was decided on. A house was taken in Westbourne Park Villas, one of a pair of semi-detached, with a small front garden and a large back one which extended to the embankment of the Great Western Railway. From here my uncle could get his omnibus from the 'Royal Oak' to the City in the morning easily enough—and they used to run special express ones in those days for business men. My elder brother was engaged in a lawyer's office in Gray's Inn Square, and a school was found for my younger brother close by; my elder sister found some teaching work, and my younger sister at a school near Chester; so that we were all disposed of in a way—though not provided for."[1]

January, 1862. Completed his three-year apprenticeship at the age of seventeen. "On leaving Linton I was pretty much thrown on my own resources, though I continued to do small works for the office from time to time; among other things, I remember having to put upon the wood a series of rather vague sketches of Faröe and Iceland by the author of a small book bearing that title.

"I used, in seeking for work, to call on different publishers to whom I had obtained introductions and hawk round my poor little folio of designs and proofs, and through an old clergyman friend of my mother's I did some work for one or two firms of publishers of religious tracts—miserable things and miserably paid. I was so inexperienced that on one occasion, having to sign a receipt for my little account,—which must have actually run over two pounds, for a wonder,—I so respected the design of the inland revenue stamp as to leave it untouched by my signature, on which the publisher remarked on the necessity of obliterating it to some extent, as it had been so ordered by 'the wisdom of our legislators.' Another highly evangelical publisher once exacted 5 per cent. for paying me cash. The amount was a little over a pound, I think, but he had to do the sum himself, as I was quite innocent of what 5 per cent. might be.

"I was engaged, too, by a Mr. Orr to make some drawings for an Encyclopaedia—I think Chamber's—and in order to get at the proper authorities it was necessary to obtain a ticket for the British Museum Reading Room. . . . As I was under age, an exception to the rules had to be made in my favour, and my ticket was endorsed in red ink.

"I was deeply impressed on being admitted to the great temple of authorship, reference, and research, and, duly initiated in the mysteries of the catalogue and writing on slips for works required, took my place at one of the desks for the first time. The curious hush of the place, broken only by the occasional coughing of the readers, or the soft fall of a book upon a desk, exaggerated by reverberation in the circular building, combined with savour of morocco bindings, was quite peculiar; the atmosphere perhaps a little stuffy, but otherwise undoubtedly a very comfortable place to read and work in.

WALTER CRANE

"Here I drew a variety of subjects from various authorities for the Cyclopaedia, ranging from the bust of Shakespeare to the scenery of Honolulu."[1]

1865. Associated with the color engraver, Edmund Evans. Continued his art studies in evening classes at Heatherley's. "Mr. Evans was one of the pioneers in the development of colour-printing, and not only did a quantity of ordinary trade work in this way, but also choice books. One of the 'mustard plaisters.' Designs of this kind were my principal work for Mr. Evans at first, but later . . . I began to design for him the children's picture-books published by the house of George Routledge & Sons which afterwards attained such popularity.

"In the evenings I had joined the classes at 'Heatherley's,' the well-known art school at 79 Newman Street, for the study of the life and costume model. Many well-known artists had worked here, at different times.

"There was a sketch club among the students, and we had exhibition nights, when the sketches which had been made in response to a given subject were displayed. The end of the terms, too, would be celebrated by evening entertainments, in which generally some theatricals formed the *pièce de résistance*, the parts being taken by different students, and the orchestral accompaniment generally supplied by a musical student with a guitar, who would sit on the steps in front of what formed the stage till the green baize curtain which divided the classrooms was 'rung up,' or rather pulled apart, and the performance began before a merry crowd of young men and maiden students."[1]

February, 1866. ". . . I had my first glimpse of France and Paris. My eldest brother held at that time a clerkship in the General Post Office, and he taking his holidays at that time, I joined him and two friends for the trip across the Channel.

(From *Don Quixote* retold by Stephanie Green. Illustrated by Walter Crane.)

"Paris then was under the Second Empire. The old Palace of Tuileries was intact and the Vendôme Column, and there was a general pervading air of reverence and glorification of the Napoleonic legend about the public places and monuments, and the big N surrounded with a laurel wreath was a very frequent emblem. The military were much in evidence, and there was a great display of various uniforms and of crinoline on the part of the ladies. We had a series of rapid and vivid impressions of Paris and its life as we flitted from its public monuments to theatres, Cirque Napoleon and Bal masque, with intervals of cafés and restaurants,—all singularly fresh and strange to our young and insular party. I recall, too, above all, the deep impression I had from the great masterpieces of the Louvre, and worshipped at the shrine of the Venus of Milo. These remain, but what of the Empire?"[1]

1869-1870. Continued illustrating for Edmund Evans and began illustrating children's toy books, published by Routledge. In 1870 Crane became engaged to Mary Frances Andrews. "The demand for new picture-books went on at the rate of two a year. About 1869-70 they began to show something like a distinct decorative treatment and style, as I endeavoured to adapt them more both to the conceptions of children and to the conditions of colour-printing. In this I found no little helpful and suggestive stimulus in the study of certain Japanese colour prints, which a lieutenant in the Navy I met at Rode Hall, who had recently visited Japan in his ship, presented me with. He did not seem to be aware of their artistic qualities himself, but regarded them rather as mere curiosities. Their treatment in definite black outline

and flat brilliant as well as delicate colours, vivid dramatic and decorative feeling struck me at once, and I endeavoured to apply these methods to the modern fanciful and humorous subjects of children's toy-books and to the methods of wood-engraving and machine-printing. *The Fairy Ship, This Little Pig went to Market,* designed in 1869, and *King Luckieboy's Party* (the verses and idea of which were supplied by me), in 1870 made this new departure, and led on to their successors, which shortly became numerous enough to be put in a separate category and labelled with my name by Messrs. Routledge.

"Amid all this work, with improving prospects it was natural that being 'over head and ears in love' I should be anxious to gain the consent of my . . . beloved to marriage.

"I was successful in this in the course of time. The lady with her mother and sisters were in the spring of 1870 staying at Carisbrooke, Isle of Wight, and my sister and myself were asked down to stay, and the quiet garden of a delightful old-fashioned house below the old Castle saw the consummation of my hopes, and at last I was actually—engaged!"[1]

September 6, 1871. Married Mary Frances Andrews. The couple went to Italy for a long stay and later Crane admitted that the trip had somewhat of an "Italianising" influence on his work. "There were wedding breakfasts in those days, and even speeches,—but all was over at last, and escaping from the friendly shower of shoes and rice, we were soon rumbling through darkest London in a brougham and tell-tale pair of greys to Liverpool Street Station. Somewhere in the wilds of the City one of the horses fell, and we were soon surrounded by a grinning London crowd, some members of which, however, lent willing hands to get the horse up, and this at last accomplished, presented themselves at the carriage window for tips.

"We had planned an extensive tour to Italy by way of the Rhine and the Brenner Pass, but the journey was to be taken in easy stages.

"On Thursday, October 12, we started on the last stage of our journey to Rome, on a wet morning, 'and though our way lay through a most interesting and lovely country—orchards, vineyards, and maize-covered land with mountains beyond—the view was spoiled by a mosaic of raindrops on the railway-carriage window.' Arezzo, Perugia, Assisi were passed, and the lake of Trasimeni; a mountainous part was entered soon after Foligno, and very fine landscape. Nearing Rome, we crossed the great plain of the Campagna, where we saw herds of cattle. 'All roads lead to Rome,' but we arrived in pouring rain when it was almost dark, and nothing was to be seen from beneath the hood of the carrozze which took us to our quarters in the Piazza di Spagna. Even here from our window next morning we could only see a bit of the 'Collegium Urbanum de Propaganda fide' and the top of the church of St. Andrea delle Frate.

"Arrived in Rome, the next step was to find an *appartement,* and we commenced our search the very next morning, and, by the assistance of a compatriot, found one in the Via San Nicolo Tolentino.

"I soon found myself in quite a circle of artists, chiefly English and American, who were then living in Rome. . . . A sort of sketching club was presently formed which met at different studios, each member being host in turn. A subject was given out by the host of the evening, and the members then set to work to realise it in paint, clay, charcoal, or other media. Then the sketches were shown, and the evening finished in talk and smoke.''[1]

May 18, 1872. ''We quitted Rome and travelled to Naples, intending, despite the heat, to spend our summer in Southern Italy. It certainly was the strongest sunshine we had ever experienced. I shall never forget my first sight of the bay, the blue sea sparkling with the sun's diamonds, the clear horizon, the deep blue vault rapidly melting into the dazzling light of the lower sky.''[1]

October 10, 1872. Returned to Rome. ''After much getting up and down flights of stone steps in search of apartments we found one in the Via San Giuseppe (a little street running into Capo le Case from the Babuino, opposite the church of the same name). Here we settled ourselves quite comfortably for the winter, and I was able to carry on my work in the sitting-room, the windows of which looked towards the north. Several of the early series of children's picture-books were designed here—*Mother Hubbard,* for instance, whose famous dog I took the liberty of depicting as a poodle, that type flourishing at that time in Rome. The drawings were made on card in black and white and sent to London through the post to Mr. Evans, who had them photographed on to the wood and engraved, returning me the proofs to colour. This method of working now beginning to supersede the old practice of drawing direct on the block for the engraver. It certainly had its advantages, not the least among which was that of being able to retain the original drawings.

''Drawing for publishers was varied by making water-colour studies out of doors, or finished drawings to send home to London exhibitions.

''We looked up our friends, too, and made new ones, My wife set up 'At Home' days, and we soon had quite a circle about us.''[1]

February, 1873. ''It was just past the middle of February . . . that an important event happened in our little household—the arrival of our first born.

''The event necessitated a visit to the British Legation . . . for registration purposes, as well as to the Roman authorities; 'L'Ufficiale Sanitario,' afterwards paying us a visit to verify the fact and to see that no deception had been practised upon S.P.Q.R.

''It was a somewhat anxious time, and though in the end all went well, and the kindness and solicitude of our friends was most gratifying, I do not know that I should be prepared to recommend anyone to be born in Rome!''[1]

May, 1873. Returned home to England. ''At last the day of our departure came, and, after a farewell glimpse of the Coliseum by moonlight, we said good-bye to Rome, and started on our way back to England, breaking the journey first at Florence, where one renewed one's acquaintance with some of the art treasures, also at Turin . . . at Macon, and at Paris, as with a nurse and a baby it had to be taken rather easily. However, in due time we reached Charing Cross, and were put up for the first few weeks at my mother's house at Hammersmith, until we could find a home for ourselves.

''Woodlane, Shepherd's Bush, where we had decided to make our home, at that time only had an irregular line of old-fashioned detached houses along a part of its east side. These houses mostly dated from the early years of the nineteenth century, and they all possessed gardens of various and some of considerable extent, with the further advantage of orchards and meadow-land, bounded by a fine belt of trees which effectually shut out 'the hideous town,' and made a pleasant oasis in the midst of brick fields.

The Frog seemed to relish his dinner much, but every bit that the King's daughter ate nearly choked her.... ■ (From *Best Loved Fairy Tales of Walter Crane* illustrated by Walter Crane.)

"I soon settled down to work, and commenced the processional picture commissioned by Mr. Somerset Beaumont in Rome, which I entitled 'The Advent of Spring.'

"Work for the publishers, too, was resumed, and the series of coloured picture-books for children which, in association with Mr. Edmund Evans as the engraver and printer, had been commenced in 1865 for the house of Routledge, and a new and larger series started, which included *Aladdin, The Yellow Dwarf, Beauty and the Beast, Princess Belle-etoile, Goody Two Shoes,* and *The Hind in the Wood.*

"While I was away in Italy, the publishers, who at first were by no means converted to the efforts we were making to get more artistic colour and treatment in these books, perceiving a growing demand for them, issued a set of my six-penny books bound together, and called it *Walter Crane's Picture Book,* but without my knowledge. This volume, though far from being what I should have approved in its general format, certainly served as a poster for me, and was, I believe, a commercial success, but as I had no rights in it, it was of no benefit to me in that respect.

"My drawings for these books were done for a very modest sum and sold outright to the publishers. The engraving and printing was costly, and very large editions had to be sold in order to make them pay—as many as 50,000 of a single book, I was told, being necessary. However, if they did not bring in much money, I had my fun out of them, as in designing I was in the habit of putting in all sorts of subsidiary detail that interested me, and often made them the vehicle for my ideas in furniture and decoration.

"This element, indeed, in the books soon began to be discovered by architects and others interested in or directly connected with house decoration, and this brought me some occasional commissions for actual work in that way in the form of friezes or frieze panels."[1]

Autumn, 1874. Mother died. "I experienced one of the saddest losses in life—the death of my mother. She has struggled with remarkable fortitude against ill-health and adverse circumstances for years, suffering from a distressing cough, but her energy, spirit, and self-sacrifice were wonderful. She began to fail towards the end of the summer, and after a few weeks passed away at Sussex House in September of that year, the house being afterwards given up."[1]

Winter, 1874. Began illustrating the well-known series of children's books by Mrs. Molesworth for the Macmillan Company.

1875. Apart from his successful illustration work, began designing wallpapers. Several public and private buildings in Britain contained his friezes, mosaics, panels, wallpapers and tapestry designs. "Mr. Metford Warner, of the famous firm of Jeffrey & Co. (the same who printed all William Morris's papers), called upon me and commissioned me to design a nursery wallpaper—no doubt in consequence of seeing my children's books. The design was in three columns divided by a narrow border, each column containing a group illustrative of a nursery rhyme,—Bo Peep and Boy Blue and the Queen of Hearts figured in it,—and it was for machine-printing, which necessitated the outlines of the faces being formed of brass wire (which was not particularly favourable to subtlety of expression), but one relied more upon the decorative effect of the general distribution and colour.

"It seemed to be successful, and was even imitated in its main motive in a paper brought out by a rival firm—a compliment of very doubtful advantage. With this design, however (the forerunner of many), a connection was established with the firm of Jeffrey & Co., which has continued up to ... a period of thirty years.

"I continued to paint in oil, and to offer at least one picture each year to the Royal Academy, but had met with nothing but rejection since 1872.... The Dudley Gallery, however, enabled me to show my water-colour work, and I continued to send there, eventually serving on the Committee...."[1]

May, 1876. Son, Lionel, born.

1877. *The Baby's Opera* published. Crane illustrated about forty of his elder sister's, Lucy Crane's, rhymed versions of old nursery and fairy stories. These books were best sellers in their day. "*The Baby's Opera* turned out a great success, although at first 'the Trade' shook its head, as the sight of a five-shilling book not decently bound in cloth and without any gold on it was an unheard-of thing, and weighing it in their hands and finding it wanting in mere avoirdupois weight, some said, 'This will never do!'—but it *did.* The first edition of 10,000 copies was soon exhausted, and another was called for, and another, and another. It has long passed its fortieth thousand, and, like 'Charley's Aunt,' is still running.

"No doubt the combination of favourite nursery rhymes with pictures, as well as the music of the old airs, made it attractive, and commended it to mothers as well as children.

"I was indebted to my sister for the arrangement of the tunes, which she collected with considerable care and research; but she was a pianist of much taste and skill, and possessed a considerable knowledge of music, both ancient and modern, and the task was a congenial one, I feel sure."[1]

1878. "Mr. Sidney Colvin introduced to me Mr. Robert Louis Stevenson, who was just about to publish, through Messrs. Kegan Paul & Co., his first book, and they wanted a frontispiece for it.

"The frontispiece was duly designed and engraved on wood. It shows Pan among the reeds by a riverside, with his pipes, resting after the classical river-god manner on a hydria from the mouth of which the water flows. R.L.S. and his friend are seen paddling their canoes beyond the reeds, and on the crest of a hill in the distance a ploughman appears against the rays of a setting sun.

"The subject is framed by an architectural border in which the two canoes *Arethusa* and *Cicarette* figure, and a medallion of a centaur bearing off a nymph, all of which details are allusive to passages in the book, which was very charmingly written. So that I may be said to have helped to launch Stevenson's first (canoe) book, which was to be the forerunner of such a remarkable literary career. The following year Stevenson brought out, through the same house, another book, *Travels with a Donkey in the Cevennes,* and again I was called upon to furnish a frontispiece, in which I introduced various incidents in the travels in what one reviewer described as a 'Bunyanesque' way.

"I met Stevenson once or twice about this period at the Savile Club, in its old quarters in Savile Row. He used to stand on the hearthrug in the smoking-room, the centre of an admiring circle, and discourse very much in the same style as

April Fool (as my young lord's jester) took upon himself to marshal the guests, and wild work he made with it.   It would have posed old Erra Pater to have found out any given Day in the year, to erect a scheme upon —

(From *A Masque of Days: From the Last Essays of Elia* by Charles Lamb. Illustrated by Walter Crane.)

Crane's sketch of his son, Lancelot.

that in which he wrote. It gave one the impression of artificiality rather—I mean his manner of speaking and choice of words, as if carefully selected and cultivated.

"His personal appearance was quite as unusual as his speech. A long, pale thin face and lank hair, quick and penetrating eyes, and a rather sardonic smile.

"I never saw him afterwards nor was I called upon again to illustrate anything of his."[1]

Christmas, 1878. *The Baby's Bouquet,* a companion to *The Baby's Opera,* was published. "It was a book of the same size, and my sister again selected and arranged the musical accompaniment. The rhymes and songs included one or two French and German ones. This book, like *Baby's Opera,* however, is still before the public, and though it never quite reached the same numbers as its predecessor, it was quite successful, and keeps fairly up with it in popular favour."[1]

January, 1884. Infant son died. Crane had two sons and a daughter. "Before that January was past a sad sorrow fell upon us in the death of our fourth child, a little son who had been born in the previous June. The heavy fogs which visited London at that time proved fatal in their effects, and our child, who never seemed very strong from the first, succumbed to a cold which settled on the lungs.

"This upset us so much that, after laying him to rest at Kensal Green, we determined to leave our house for some time.

"We went, in the first place, to Eastbourne with our two little boys [their daughter, Beatrice, was away at school] and a nurse, but after stopping there a while turned inland, and eventually discovered a retreat near Sevenoaks Weald. It had been an old manor-house, and retained a fine old Gothic hall with open-timbered roof. This and the house, however, had been 'restored' and added to, with the idea of making it a modern country residence, and there had been no attempt to make the modern part harmonise with the old hall. There was a farm attached of about two hundred acres in extent,

and this was managed by a steward, who with his family lived in a part of the house.

"We had abundance of room, and the old hall was a delightful place for the children to play in in bad weather. One of the rooms had a good north light, and I was able to paint and carry on my work. So we stayed on here through the spring, until the copses were blue with hyacinths and the valley filled with the song of nightingales.

"This year saw the appearance of *Grimm's Household Stories,* which my sister had translated, and for which I had furnished a large number of illustrations in the form of full pages with headings and tail-pieces to each story. These were engraved on wood by Messrs. Swain, and the book was printed by Messrs. R. & R. Clark, and no pains were spared upon it. It was called 'The Crane Edition,' and has been reprinted several times, remaining still a favourite with the public.

"Another book published this year was *Pan-pipes,* a book of old songs with the tunes. In this I had the advantage of the cooperation of Mr. Theo. Marzials, himself a most charming song composer. The book was in oblong form, so as to be convenient on a piano, and to each song there was a coloured design, taking the form of a decorative border enclosing the music. It opened with the delightful 'Tudoresque' melody, as Marzials called it, of Mr. Malcolm Lawson's setting of Marlowe's words, 'Come live with me and be my love'; but this was the only modern exception, as the rest of the airs were all arranged by Mr. Marzials from the old traditional ones. Marzials himself seemed really more like a troubadour than a modern person, and was always most delightful to meet, apart from his musical gifts.

"While at Wickhurst the sad news arrived of the sudden death of my sister [Lucy Crane]. She was at the time among her friends in the north of England, engaged in giving the series of lectures which were afterwards published by Macmillan & Co. under the title of *Lectures on Art and the Formation of Taste,* with a memorial Introduction by my brother and myself. It was in March, and my sister, never very strong, must have rather over-tasked herself, as after one of the lectures she fell suddenly ill, and died very shortly afterwards at the house of the friends she was with."[1]

1885. Joined the Fabian Society. Crane was an active Socialist. "I joined the Society, and lectured for them on several occasions—once, I remember, in Westminster Town Hall, to a large audience, when Mr. G. Bernard Shaw took the chair, and Oscar Wilde was among the speakers in the discussion which followed.

"The Fabian Society certainly has done very useful educational work by its economic lectures and tracts. The Society has addressed itself more to the middle classes, and as regards Socialism has advocated a waiting or Fabian policy, relying rather on the effects of a gradual permeation of society by new ideas than emphatic protest and revolt—the name 'Fabian' being an allusion to the Roman general who opposed Hannibal. Representatives of the other Socialist bodies, however, frequently attended their meetings and spoke—Morris himself among the number."[1]

1886. "I added another little book to the *Baby's Opera* Series. This was *Baby's own Æsop.* For the text I was indebted to my old friend and master, W. J. Linton, who sent it [to] me from America, where he had been living for many years. He had treated the Fables in verse; compressing them into very succinct lines with still shorter morals, 'for the use of railway travellers and others,' as he said.

''I was occupied a good deal in the spring and early summer . . . with the design of a series of tableaux—a scheme of Professor Warr's of King's College to illustrate the text of his translations from Homer, *The Tale of Troy* and *The Wayfaring of Ulysses,* and also some scenes from the *Agamemnon of Æschylus.*

''. . . I was considerably engaged in an agitation for a really representative National Exhibition of Art as distinct from

(From *Cock Robin* illustrated by Walter Crane.)

the Royal Academy and its methods, and on much broader and more comprehensive lines, including a better representation of architecture and sculpture, as well as decorative design and handicraft.

"There had been rather more than the usual crop of surprising rejections at the Royal Academy that year, and the group of artists who then formed the leading spirits of the New English Art Club felt that something ought to be done—if only to bring their own forms of art more prominently before the public."[1]

Spring, 1886. After much agitation, the Painter's Movement was created, but it failed to form a National Exhibition of Art. From the ashes, however, sprang the Arts and Crafts Exhibition Society, of which Crane was one of the originators. Crane resigned his membership to the Royal Institute of Painters and Water Colours and Oil.

1888. Arts and Craft Society formed. ". . . We held our first exhibition in the autumn . . . at the New Gallery. William Morris had joined us by this time, and Burne-Jones became a member not long afterwards, and their work was an important feature of our earlier exhibitions."[1]

Spring, 1888. Became a member of the Old Water Colour Society. "Being duly elected as Associate I exhibited that year 'Flora' and 'Pegasus,' both of which ultimately found homes out of this country—one in Germany, and one in Belgium."[1]

September, 1890. Made a return trip to Italy with his wife. "So about the end of September my wife and I found ourselves once more in Italy. . . . It was the beginning of November before we turned homewards, and the cold had descended. Snow had appeared on the mountains at Florence before we left, and snow now covered the Friuli mountains, and the air over the canals had a peculiar penetrating chill, which one had never experienced there before.

"We were glad to get back to our children, and had only to regret the loss of a little pet dog which had disappeared in our absence."[1]

March, 1891. Infant daughter died. "We had a sad sorrow during this year . . . in the death of our little daughter from diphtheria. . . . She was born in the summer of 1888, and had been a great joy to us. . . . This cast a shadow over our home, and we decided to leave it for a time at least. We had already been rather unsettled by the prospect of the Central London Railway scheme swallowing up our house and garden. Our thoughts turned towards America, which my wife had a great wish to see. Other things, too, tended in that direction.

"Mr. Henry Blackburn—the pioneer of illustrated exhibition catalogues and the terror of artists, from whom he demanded black-and-white sketches of their own works—at the time of my exhibition in Bond Street strongly advised me to send it to the States afterwards, assuring me that it would be welcomed at the Boston Art Museum, the Director (General Loring) of which he knew, and to whom he gave me an introduction.

"Although many works found purchasers at the Fine Art Society's, I had a considerable collection left, and I decided to take Mr. Blackburn's advice. He very kindly gave me every information in regard to Boston, having been on a lecturing tour in the States himself. I wrote to General Loring,

and received a cordial invitation in reply to send the collection. . . .

"This removed all difficulties, and so the collection on leaving Bond Street was packed and duly forwarded across the Atlantic.

"We arranged to go ourselves early in October."[1]

Autumn, 1891. "We landed at Boston on Monday the 19th October—the eleventh day from Liverpool.

"The ordeal of landing and passing the customs is a severe one for the stranger to U.S. ports. To begin with, there was a sort of religious ceremony or solemn parade of all the passengers before certain officials on board, when a kind of oath was taken that nothing excisable of any consequence was concealed in their baggage; but this did not prevent the wild scene on the custom-house wharf which followed, when the heavy baggage began slowly to slide down the planks, and the passengers gradually collected their belongings, and after a long wait, their treasured worldly goods were ruthlessly exposed to the eagle eyes of the U.S. custom-house officers. I saw a handsome new bicycle lying comfortably on the top of a clothes' trunk, and one lady was discovered to have an outfit of no less than twenty-five water-proofs, a supply which perhaps might not have been considered excessive if she had been landing in England—although, as it happened, it was a wet day in Boston.

"Kind friends assisted in our rescue from the customs wharf, and we were presently landed in the comfortable 'Brunswick,' where we made the acquaintance of the negro—the hotel being manned by black servants. The negro is of course 'free' in the States, but he seems to do all the waiting. The 'Brunswick' was at the west end of Boston, close to the Art Museum and to Richardson's famous church, and the new Library, then in [the] course of building.

"Our first impressions were a little damp and dismal, as we arrived in a heavy downpour of rain, which kept us in the hotel the rest of the day. The aspect of the streets and the character of the buildings struck one at first as very un-English. There was just a faint suggestion of Piccadilly and the Green Park (on a quiet Sunday) about Mount Vernon Street and the Common, with a touch of Bloomsbury here and there about the older houses, but it was soon lost among the electric trams—'the broomstick train' of Oliver Wendell Holmes—and the 'sky-scrapers' of the business end of the town.

"I was made free of the leading Clubs, and duly plied with 'cocktails'—which certainly deserved their name. . . . My views as a Socialist were well known, and I was earnestly invited to attend and speak at a memorial meeting on the anniversary of the death of the Chicago men, who certainly had fought hard for the cause of the workers generally, and were regarded as martyrs. The meeting took place at Paine Hall. . . . I was asked to say a few words by the chairman, and shortly explained my views to the meeting, expressly stating that I sympathised with the struggle of the workers for improved conditions at Chicago as everywhere else, but not with the use of explosives, and that, in common with English Socialists and other lovers of freedom and justice in England, I considered the men had been done to death wrongfully, and other imprisoned for their opinions, which was a sad thing to think of in 'free' America, and I concluded by reading this sonnet, which had appeared in my recently published book of verse, *Renascence:*—

"FREEDOM IN AMERICA

"Where is thy home, O Freedom? Have they set
  Thine image upon a rock to greet
  All comers, shaking from their wandering feet
The dust of old world bondage, to forget
The tyrannies of fraud and force, nor fret,
  When men are equal, slavish chain unmeet,
  Nor bitter bread of discontent to eat,
Here, where all races of the earth are met?

"America! beneath thy banded flag
  Of old it was thy boast that men were free
    To think, to speak, to meet, to come and go.
What meaneth then the gibbet and the gag,
  Held up to Labour's sons who would not see
    Fair Freedom but a mask—a hollow show?

"Since those days considerable light has been thrown upon the conditions of labour in Chicago—the terrible disclosures, for instance, made by Mr. Upton Sinclair in *The Jungle*. The revolting facts about the meat-canning business and the stock-yards, which the author has really under-stated, have, however, rather diverted public attention from the frightful conditions of labour, to draw attention to which was, however, the main purpose of the book.

"We visited Cambridge (Mass.) and Harvard College, and were duly impressed by its extensive buildings and educational arrangements, though it lacked the historic charm and green seclusion of the Cambridge on this side the water."[1]

December, 1891. Lectured on art in New York and Hartford, Conn.

December 14, 1891. Visited Chicago. "My collection followed me from Boston like my shadow, and was duly unpacked and exhibited at the Chicago Art Institute, where an art school and museum were under the same roof. Here also I was induced to give a lecture on Art, which I illustrated by charcoal sketches on paper."[1]

January, 1892. "From Chicago my collection was invited to St. Louis, and towards the middle or end of January we went on there, a journey of some three hundred miles farther south, for the most part through a flat agricultural country of maize fields, which spreads west and south of Chicago—a great grain centre. At length we reached the big rivers Mississippi and Missouri, at the junction of which is the city of St. Louis. A tremendous bridge in three tiers crosses the river, carrying the railroad, a road for ordinary traffic, and a footway. There was a sort of rivalry between St. Louis and Chicago as to which should be considered the premier town. Kansas was, I believe, also in the running at one time, but has been knocked out by the enormous commercial progress of its bigger and more advantageously situated rivals. St. Louis was in many ways more pleasantly situated than Chicago, being on a rising ground with a fine wooded country towards the west. As regards planning and architectural character and general aspects, American towns, however, suffer from a certain sameness as well as the want of historic background. Everything which is not of the moment seems to belong to yesterday, or at most to the day before."[1]

February, 1892. Visited California. "Los Angeles, where we made out first stay in South California, showed a strange mixture of elements—American, Chinese, Spanish—though the American, of course, prevailed; and the main street was of the usual type, decked with tramcars, overhead wires, and hotels.

"The Chinese quarter was quite distinct, with its native shops, vertical orange labels, lanterns, and pigtails.

"From Los Angeles we went on to Santa Barbara, which brought us close to the Pacific in a beautiful bay enclosed by rocky islands, the town trailing away from the sea in a long wide street of scattered houses and hotels.

"San Francisco was our next stop, and our farthest point westward. Again one's impressions were of a city of strangely mixed elements—a touch of New York, a dash of Liverpool, a whiff of Glasgow, a strong flavour of opium, and a Chinese quarter so complete that its influence seemed to be felt all over the American quarter, giving a quaint touch to the mansard roofs, the much whittled woodwork porches; and even the steep hills, over which the cable cars popped so suddenly, and the long flights of steps leading up to the terraced dwellings and gardens with their palm trees, in some parts, might have been worked into a sort of willow pattern."[1]

Summer, 1892. After visiting New York and completing a wall-paper design for the Chicago World Fair which was to be held the following year, Crane and his wife sailed for home.

Autumn, 1893. Accepted the post of director of design of the Manchester School of Art. "I found it a little difficult to graft the kind of study I had found practically useful in my own work as a designer on to the rather cut and dried and wooden courses prescribed by the Department, or rather, to dovetail new methods with the existing curriculum. To obtain grants or to compete for prizes in the national competition certain works had to be done in certain ways by the candidates, and the rules for the exercises necessary for winning certificates had to be strictly followed. Under these circumstances it was difficult for students working with the aim of gaining the official distinctions which were supposed to qualify them for the teaching of art, to give much time to experiments in or to master new methods."[1]

1894. Began illustrating Edmund Spenser's *Faerie Queene*. "The *Faerie Queene* had long been known to me—indeed, I might say that it had been a cherished dream of mine to illustrate it—to follow the poet through the six books, and to endeavour to embody the extraordinarily rich invention and complexity of much of his allegory, with its historic, mythical, and classical allusions, as well as to depict the incidents and characters of the story, was no light undertaking, but the task was a congenial one, and I commenced with a light heart.

"The work was to be issued in parts, and I was able to deliver my designs in instalments. These consisted of one or more full-page illustrations to each canto and headings and tailpieces besides, as well as title-pages to each book. Altogether the work extended over three years, as it was not complete until 1897."[1]

1896. "The years now seemed to be rather emphatically marked by the holidays which, what with lectures at the Manchester School and work there every month, and one's studio and deskwork at home, were welcome enough when they came, and dwelt pleasantly in the memory."[1]

1897. Resigned his post at Manchester School of Art.

1898. Served as principal of the Royal College of Art in South Kensington. "This post, just as my Manchester appointment had done, necessarily precluded my acting as examiner or assisting in the awards of medals and prizes in the National Competition of the art schools of the country, in which I had taken part for many years, and in which, on resigning my position at Manchester, I had again served.

"While on the Council I drew up a Primary Schools' Syllabus on drawing, giving a series of progressive exercises calculated to assist teachers in this now compulsory subject, and to initiate those who might not possess any previous knowledge on the subject, and this was issued, and is now in use.

"I was requested by my colleagues, and actually commissioned by the Board, to prepare a second illustrated syllabus for the evening schools, which I accordingly did, adapting the exercises to the various trades and handicrafts with a view to the cultivation of trade in design, and to assist teachers, many of which would be quite inexperienced in such subjects.

1899. Retired from his position as principal of the Royal College of Art.

1903. Made Commendatore of the Order of the Royal Crown of Italy. In January of that year Crane was also made a member of the Royal Society of Painters in Water Colours.

1904. Given the Albert Gold Medal of the Society of Arts. "[The Medal is given] . . . in recognition of the services rendered to Art and Industry by awakening popular interest in Decorative Art and Craftsmanship, and by promoting the recognition of English Art in the forms most material to the commercial prosperity of the country. This medal has usually been won by men eminent in science and mechanical invention."[1]

1906. Won the gold medal and grand prize at the Milan International Exhibition.

1911. Made Cavaliere of the Order of S. S. Maurizio e Lazzaro, an Italian honor.

March 15, 1915. Died in London, England at the age of sixty-nine. "The thought of the enormous indebtedness of the individiual, however capable, to the community at large and to the fellow-workers who have constructed the ladder by which a man rises, or the scaffolding by means of which he is able to build, should keep his estimate of his own powers modest."[1]

FOR MORE INFORMATION SEE: Walter Crane, *An Artist's Reminiscences,* Macmillan, 1907, reprinted, Singing Tree Press, 1968; Jacqueline Overton, "Illustrators of the Nineteenth Century in England," *Illustrators of Children's Books: 1744-1945,* edited by B. E. Mahony and others, Horn Book, 1947; Brian Doyle, editor, *Who's Who of Children's Literature,* Schocken Books, 1968; Rodney K. Engen, *Walter Crane as a Book Illustrator,* St. Martin, 1975; Isobel Spencer, *Walter Crane,* Macmillan, 1976.

Cullen, 1925. From the painting by Winold Reiss.

CULLEN, Countee 1903-1946

PERSONAL: Born May 30, 1903, in New York City; died January 9, 1946, in New York City; buried in Woodlawn Cemetery, New York; son of Frederick Asbury (a Methodist minister) and Carolyn Belle (Mitchell) Cullen; married Yolande Du Bois, April, 1928 (divorced, 1930); married Ida Mae Roberson, September 27, 1940. *Education:* New York University, B.A., 1925; Harvard University, M.A., 1926; studied abroad on a Guggenheim fellowship, 1928. *Home:* Tuckahoe, New York.

CAREER: Poet, teacher, and author of stories for children. Assistant editor of *Opportunity: Journal of Negro Life,* 1926-28. French teacher, Frederick Douglass Junior High School, New York City, 1934-45. *Member:* Phi Beta Kappa, Alpha Delta Phi, and the Civic Club.

WRITINGS—All poems, except as noted: *Color,* Harper, 1925, reprinted, Arno, 1969; *Copper Sun* (illustrated by Charles Cullen), Harper, 1927; *The Ballad of the Brown Girl* (illustrated by C. Cullen), Harper, 1927; (editor) *Caroling Dusk: An Anthology of Verse by Negro Poets* (illustrated by Aaron Douglas), Harper, 1927, reissued, 1974; *The Black Christ, and Other Poems* (illustrated by C. Cullen), Harper, 1929; *One Way to Heaven* (novel), Harper, 1932, reprinted, AMS Press, 1975; *The Medea and Some Poems,* Harper, 1935; (with Arna Bontemps) "St. Louis Woman" (musical comedy; based on Bontemps' novel, *God Sends Sunday),* first produced on Broadway at the Martin Beck Theatre, March 30, 1946; *On These I Stand: An Anthology of the Best Poems of Countee Cullen,* Harper, 1947, reissued, 1966.

For children: *The Lost Zoo* (ALA Notable Book; illustrated by Charles Sebree), Harper, 1940 [another edition illustrated by Joseph Low, Follett, 1969]; *My Lives and How I Lost Them* (illustrated by Robert R. MacGuire), Harper, 1942 [another edition illustrated by Rainey Bennett, Follett, 1971].

ADAPTATIONS—Recordings: "To Make a Poet Black: The Best Poems of Countee Cullen," read by Ossie Davis and Ruby Dee, Caedmon Records, 1972.

SIDELIGHTS: **May 30, 1903.** Born to Elizabeth Lucas of Louisville, Kentucky.

1912. Brought to New York City by a Mrs. Porter, who was probably his grandmother.

1917. Entered DeWitt Clinton High School. Wrote his first poem, which was published in *Modern School Magazine.*

1918. After Mrs. Porter's death he was informally adopted by the Reverend Frederick Asbury Cullen and his wife, Carolyn. "[I] was reared in the conservative atmosphere of a Methodist parsonage." [Stephen Bronz, *Roots of Negro Racial Consciousness,* Libra Publishers, 1964.[1]]

1921 Wrote and presented the speech which won him the Douglas Fairbanks Oratorical Contest.

1922. Entered New York University. His first poem published in a commercial magazine was in the *Crisis*.

1925. Received A.B. degree from New York University. First volume of poetry, *Color,* was published. ". . . Good poetry is a lofty thought beautifully expressed. . . . Poetry should not be too intellectual; it should deal more . . . with the emotions. The highest type of poem is that which warmly stirs the emotions, which awakens a responsive chord in the human heart. Poetry, like music, depends upon feeling rather than intellect, although there should, of course, be enough to satisfy the mind, too." [Margaret Perry, *A Bio-Bibliography of Countee P. Cullen,* Catholic University, 1959.[2]]

1926. Received M.A. degree from Harvard University.

1926-1938. Went abroad each summer, acting as interpreter and guide for his father.

1926-1927. Studied at the Sorbonne in Paris.

1926-1928. Appointed assistant editor for *Opportunity.* Wrote editorials and book reviews. "American life is so constituted, the wealth of power is so unequally distributed, that whether they relish the situation or not, Negroes should be concerned with making good impressions. They cannot do this by throwing wide every door of the racial entourage. . . . Let art portray things as they are, no matter what the consequences, no matter who is hurt, is a blind bit of philosophy. . . . Every phase of Negro life should not be the white man's concern."[1]

1927. Compiled *Caroling Dusk,* an anthology of verse by blacks. "I have called this collection an anthology of verse by Negro poets rather than an anthology of Negro verse, since this latter designation would be more confusing than accurate. Negro poetry, it seems to me, in the sense that we speak of Russian, French, or Chinese poetry, must emanate from some country other than this in some language other than our own. Moreover, the attempt to corral the outbursts of the ebony muse into some definite mold to which all poetry by Negroes will conform seems altogether futile and aside from the facts. This country's Negro writers may here and there turn some singular facet toward the literary sun, but in the main, since theirs is also the heritage of the English language, their work will not present any serious aberration from the poetic tendencies of their times. The conservatives, the middlers, and the arch heretics will be found among them as among the white poets; and to say that the pulse beat of their verse shows generally such a fever, or the symptoms of such an ague, will prove on closer examination merely the moment's exaggeration of a physician anxious to establish a new literary ailment. As heretical as it may sound, there is the probability that Negro poets, dependent as they are on the English language, may have more to gain from the rich background of English and American poetry than from any nebulous atavistic yearnings toward an African inheritance. . . .

"While I do not feel that the work of these writers conforms to anything that can be called the Negro school of poetry, neither do I feel that their work is varied to the point of being sensational; rather is theirs a variety within a uniformity that is trying to maintain the higher traditions of English verse. I trust the selections here presented bear out this contention.

(From *The Lost Zoo* by Christopher Cat and Countee Cullen. Illustrated by Charles Sebree.)

COUNTEE CULLEN

The poet writes out of his experience, whether it be personal or vicarious, and as these experiences differ among other poets, so do they differ among Negro poets; for the double obligation of being both Negro and American is not so unified as we are often led to believe. A survey of the work of Negro poets will show that the individual diversifying ego transcends the synthesizing hue." [Countee Cullen, editor, *Caroling Dusk*, Harper & Brothers, 1927.[3]]

1928. Awarded Guggenheim fellowship to study in Paris "to complete a group of narrative poems and a libretto for an opera."

April 10, 1928. Married Yolande DuBois, daughter of W.E.B. DuBois, black educator and sociologist.

1929. *The Black Christ and Other Poems* published while he was abroad. "Mrs. Roosevelt certainly likes *The Black Christ,* for I believe this is about the third time that I have seen where she has mentioned it." ["The Papers of Countee Cullen, 1921-1969," The Schomberg Center for Research in Black Culture.[4]]

March, 1930. Divorced in Paris.

November 16, 1930. While traveling to a lecture engagement, he was barred from eating in the restaurant at the New York Central terminal in Buffalo, New York. Cullen retaliated by quoting his poem, "Incident in Baltimore," dealing with a similar experience. "In spite of myself . . . I find that I am actuated by a strong sense of race consciousness. This grows upon me, I find, as I grow older, and although I struggle against it, it colors my writing, I fear, in spite of everything I can do. There may have been many things in my life that have hurt me, and I find that the surest relief from these hurts is in writing.

"Most things I write, I do for the sheer love of the music in them. Somehow or other, however, I find my poetry of itself treating of the Negro, of his joys and his sorrows—mostly of the latter, and of the heights and the depths of emotion which I feel as a Negro." [Houston Baker, *A Many Colored Coat of Dreams: The Poetry of Countee Cullen,* Broadside Press, 1974.[5]]

1931. Continued to write as much as possible. Began series of poetry readings and lectures.

1932. Only novel for adults, *One Way to Heaven,* was published.

September, 1932. Became teacher of English, French and creative writing at Frederick Douglass Junior High in New York City. There he fostered the literary ambitions and abilities of his pupils. "The way the Board of Education is piling up work on us teachers, I am going to need special taking care of. . . . My new class was angelic today but I am not going to allow that to fool me. They were probably just trying me out."[4]

1935. Served on the Mayor's Commission to study conditions in Harlem.

September 27, 1940. Married Ida Mae Roberson Parker. He wrote to his bride to-be: "It would be fine, as you say, to be married and established by the time my work begins, but I have grave doubts that we can do that.

"Another drawback is that I have to cash in an insurance policy before the event. I can possibly get about two thousand dollars on it, and that should enable me to clear up all my outstanding debts, marry you correctly, and still have a small nest egg for us to keep on hand for that inevitable rainy day. . . ."[4]

1940. Cullen's first children's novel, *The Lost Zoo,* was published. "Out of all the things I read yesterday, the extract from *The Lost Zoo* went over the best. Many people, at the end of the reading, asked for the name of the book—and said they were certainly going to buy it for their sons, daughters, nieces and nephews—and a few just for themselves."[4]

We were a large family, the eight of us, and a noisy one! As young as we were, each of us Kittens was already showing those cateristics which were to mark us for the rest of our lives. ■ (From *My Lives and How I Lost Them* by Christopher Cat in collaboration with Countee Cullen. Illustrated by Robert Reid Macguire.)

1941. *My Lives and How I Lost Them,* the autobiography of Christopher the Cat published. "Christopher came to Pleasantville today for the first time and hasn't quite become accustomed to this strange house as yet. . . . They say he traveled from New York all the way to the door here. To make matters worse my aunt already had another cat here (name's Minnie and Minnie is in the family way which doesn't help matters any) and Christopher and she haven't been able to decide who is boss of the ranch. I told Christopher that as a gentleman he ought to defer to the lady but he doesn't seem to think so. . . . The book is going along splendidly and I'm sure I'll have it all ready by the end of July and ready to begin the sequel. . . .

". . . While it is interesting and fanciful, the language seems to be for children older than those for whom I meant it; but it seems to me that I simply am not able to write for children in the lower reading brackets. You see what happened to *The Lost Zoo.* It got out of hand. . . . I am now well into my second chapter and going strong. Christopher is really quite a liver or quite a liar! . . . Poor little Christopher, the one here who reminded me of my Christopher, he was killed last week. The poor little fellow ran out into the road straight into the path of an automobile, and that was the end of a very lively career. . . .

"At least my book has been published and sent away. . . . I am learning a great deal from little Christopher and his little brother. I am especially anxious to have this second Christopher book finished by the end of the year and in my publisher's hands because I read in the paper yesterday where someone had written a book about a rabbit, and I don't want to be accused of copying anyone."[4]

1944. Presented poetry reading at the American Missionary Association's Race Relations Institute at Fisk University. "I gave my reading before the largest group yet assembled for this period. Everybody was gracious and complimentary. There were far more white than colored present. Many of the students from the surrounding white universities were on hand, and although I read some very bitter things, they took it very well. . . ."[4]

1944-45. Served on committee for Mass Education in Race Relations. "I have met with very few instances of discrimination during my life. I don't mean to convey the impression that I'm still not aware that I'm a Negro and being a Negro there are some things which will always be closed to me. I'm speaking now of every day experiences and how little actual difference it makes in New York if you are a Negro or white."[1]

March, 1945. "Byword for Evil," an adaptation of Euripides' *Medea* by Cullen, presented at Fisk University.

Summer, 1945. Visited Los Angeles, worked on "St. Louis Woman," musical adaptation of *God Sends Sunday.* "The work I am doing here is progressing constantly although not with the speed I had hoped it would. It is very tedious work, but if all goes well, it will in the end be well worth all the pains taken. Fortunately the people I have to work with are all fine and sympathetic, so that when I have to take time out for my headaches nothing is said about it.

"I am writing this letter on a typewriter loaned to me by Mr. Harold Arlen, a very pleasant person to know as is Mr. Lemuel Ayres. (They both call me Countee, although in spite of their invitations to do otherwise I still Mr. them. . . .) The music Arlen has done so far is very lovely and catchy and the ideas he has for songs to come are equally fine. Mr. Gross . . . insists that he was on the verge of giving up the play once or twice but held on because he wants me to make some money. He thinks I am a deserving person. I don't know whether he thinks so because we both went to DeWitt Clinton or not, but whatever the reason, hallelujah I say."[4]

January 9, 1946. Died after a three week illness, several months prior to the Broadway opening of "St. Louis Woman". "My life has been most uneventful. If anyone should gather otherwise from my poems, they must remember that we singers live largely in the realm of the imagination."[4]

FOR MORE INFORMATION SEE: Ralph W. Bullock, "Countee Cullen," in his *In Spite of Handicaps,* Association Press, 1927; Benjamin G. Brawley, "Protest and Vindica-

We're at a loss how to describe
This very quaint and curious tribe.
■ (From *The Lost Zoo* by Christopher Cat and
Countee Cullen. Illustrated by Joseph Low.)

tion,'' in his *Negro Genius,* Dodd, 1937; Jay S. Redding, ''Emergence of the New Negro,'' in his *To Make a Poet Black,* University of North Carolina Press, 1939; Horace Gregory and Marya A. Zaturenska, ''Negro Poet in America,'' in their *History of American Poetry, 1900-1940,* Harcourt, 1946; Stephen H. Bronz, *Roots of Negro Racial Consciousness,* Libra, 1964; Charlemae Rollins, *American Negro Poets,* Dodd, 1965; Blanche E. Ferguson, *Countee Cullen and the Negro Renaissance,* Dodd, 1966; Margaret Perry, *Bio-Bibliography of Countee P. Cullen, 1903-1946,* Greenwood, 1971; Darwin T. Turner, *In a Minor Chord: Three Afro-American Writers and Their Search for Identity,* Southern Illinois University Press, 1971; E. W. Collier, ''I Do Not Marvel, Countee Cullen,'' in *Modern Black Poets,* edited by Donald B. Gibson, Prentice-Hall, 1973; Houston Baker, *A Many Colored Coat: Countee Cullen,* Broadside Press, 1974; Arthur P. Davis, *From the Dark Tower,* Howard University Press, 1974.

Obituaries: *New York Times,* January 10, 1946; *Newsweek,* January 21, 1946; *Time,* January 21, 1946; *Publishers Weekly,* January 26, 1946; *Saturday Review of Literature,* February 23, 1946; *Current Biography,* March, 1946; *Wilson Library Bulletin,* March, 1946; *Poetry,* April, 1946; *Opportunity,* Spring, 1946; *Current Biography Yearbook, 1946.*

DENNIS, Morgan   1891?-1960

PERSONAL: Born February 27, (1891 or 1892, according to some sources) in Boston, Mass.; died October 22, 1960, in New York; brother of Wesley Dennis (an illustrator); *Education:* Studied at New School of Design, Boston; studied with

various artists and illustrators including W.H.W. Bicknell and Stanhope Forbes. *Home:* Key West, Florida in winter; Shoreham, Long Island in summer.

CAREER: Illustrator, author of books for children. Worked as an illustrator for various Boston newspapers including the *Globe, American, Herald,* and *Transcript,* 1915-25; published the first of a series of dog etchings which became his specialty, 1924; lectured two seasons for the W. Colston Leigh Bureau; began writing and illustrating books for children about 1940. *Military service:* U.S. Marine Corps during World War II.

WRITINGS—All for children; all self-illustrated: *The Pup Himself,* Viking, 1943; *Burlap,* Viking, 1945; *The Morgan Dennis Dog Book (with Some Special Cats),* Viking, 1946; *Skit and Skat,* Viking, 1951; *Himself and Burlap on TV,* Viking, 1954; *Pure Breds,* Winston, 1954; *The Sea Dog,* Viking, 1958; *Kitten on the Keys,* Viking, 1961.

Illustrator: Ruth Adams Knight, *Friend in the Dark,* Grosset, 1937; Thomas Pendleton Robinson, *Pete,* Viking, 1941; Edward Anthony, *Every Dog Has His Say,* Watson-Guptill, 1947; Frances Mary Frost, *Cat That Went to College,* Whittlesey House, 1951; David Malcolmson, *Yipe: The Story of a Farm Dog,* Little, 1955.

You were at the door. You were angry with us for not being there to meet you. ■ (From *Portrait of a Dog* by Mazo de la Roche. Illustrated by Morgan Dennis.)

There you stood fastened to the handle of a trunk. ■ (From *Portrait of a Dog* by Mazo de la Roche. Illustrated by Morgan Dennis.)

SIDELIGHTS: February 27, (1891 or 1892). Born in the South End of Boston, Mass. Morgan's father had come to the United States from England as a shorthand reporter and worked on the Boston *Globe* at night. Dennis' brother, Wesley, became an illustrator, specializing in books about horses.

1915-25. "I worked on Boston newspapers . . . doing general illustrating, while studying etching summers with W.H.W. Bicknell at Provincetown. I studied painting with Stanhope Forbes in England." [Bertha M. Miller and others, compilers, *Illustrators of Children's Books: 1946-1956,* Horn Book, 1958.[1]]

1924. Published a series of etchings of dogs which became his specialty. "Shortly after my return to America I made a small etching of my Airedale puppy for my Christmas card. Mr. Macbeth, of the Macbeth Galleries, suggested that I sell such etchings, and published an ad in the Fifth Avenue Shopping Section of Scribner's. That was the beginning of my going to the dogs! People, it seemed, wanted pictures of dogs, and I've been doing them ever since." [Walter Joseph Wilwerding, *Animal Drawing and Painting,* Watson-Guptill, 1946.[2]]

1937. Illustrated his first book. A few years later he wrote and illustrated his first book for children. Dennis was best known for his dog illustrations and one of his best known dog portraits was of Fala, President Roosevelt's Scotty. "Probably the best known picture of mine is that used by the Texaco Company—a pair of Scotties. I lectured two seasons for the W. Colston Leigh Bureau, using as a basis a story I did for *Cosmopolitan* called *Autobiography of a Scottie.* I have had articles and illustrations on dog subjects in *Cosmopolitan, This Week, American, Good Housekeeping,* and *Saturday Evening Post.*"[1]

October 22, 1960. Died in a New York bookshop. Morgan and his wife lived on a houseboat in Key West, Florida, during the winter and spring, and the rest of the year in Shoreham, Long Island.

FOR MORE INFORMATION SEE: Walter Joseph Wilwerding, *Animal Drawing and Painting,* Watson-Guptill, 1946; Bertha E. Mahony and others, *Illustrators of Children's Book: 1744-1945,* Horn Book, 1947; Bertha M. Miller and others, *Illustrators of Children's Books: 1946-1956,* Horn Book, 1958; Loring Holmes Dodd, *Generation of Illustrators and Etchers,* Chapman and Grimes, 1960; Muriel Fuller, editor, *More Junior Authors,* Wilson, 1963.

DENNIS, Wesley 1903-1966

PERSONAL: Born May 16, 1903, in Falmouth, Massachusetts; died September 5, 1966, in Falmouth, Massachusetts; son of John W. and Ida (Morgan) Dennis; brother of Morgan Dennis (a painter); married Dorothy Schiller Boggs; children: two sons. *Education:* Studied art at the New School of Design in Boston. *Home:* Warrenton, Virginia.

CAREER: Author and illustrator of books for children. Worked in the art departments of several Boston newspapers; also employed by department stores, doing fashions at Jordan Marsh, and Christmas cards and portraits at Filene's. *Awards, honors: King of the Wind,* written by Marguerite Henry and illustrated by Dennis, was awarded the Newbery Medal, 1949.

WESLEY DENNIS

WRITINGS—All self-illustrated: *Flip,* Viking, 1941, reissued, 1969; *Flip and the Cows,* Viking, 1942; *Holiday,* Viking, 1946; *Flip and the Morning,* Viking, 1951, reissued, 1968; *A Crow I Know,* Viking, 1957; *Tumble: The Story of a Mustang,* Hastings House, 1966.

Illustrator: Anna Sewell, *Black Beauty,* World Publishing, 1946; Theodore J. Waldeck, *Golden Stallion,* Viking, 1947; Marguerite Henry, *Benjamin West and His Cat, Grimalkin,* Bobbs-Merrill, 1947; M. Henry, *Misty of Chincoteague,* Rand McNally, 1947; M. Henry, *Always Reddy,* Whittlesey House, 1947; M. Henry, *King of the Wind,* Rand McNally, 1948; Dorothy Lyons, *Harlequin Hullabaloo,* Harcourt, 1949; M. Henry, *Little-or-Nothing from Nottingham,* Whittlesey House, 1949; M. Henry, *Born to Trot,* Rand McNally, 1950; (and editor) *Palomino and Other Horses,* World Publishing, 1950; M. Henry, *Album of Horses,* Rand McNally, 1951, reissued, 1965; Mary Martin Black, *Summerfield Farm,* Viking, 1951; Henry V. Larom, *Bronco Charlie, Rider of the Pony Express,* McGraw-Hill, 1951; Ruth Adams Knight, *Halfway to Heaven,* Whittlesey House, 1952; M. Henry, *Brighty of the Grand Canyon,* Rand McNally, 1953.

Watty Piper (pseudonym), *Animal Story Book,* Platt & Munk, 1954; M. Henry, *Justin Morgan Had a Horse,* Rand McNally, 1954; M. Henry, *Wagging Tales: An Album of Dogs,* Rand McNally, 1955; Mildred Mastin Pace, *Old Bones,* Whittlesey House, 1955; M. Henry, *Cinnabar: The One O'Clock Fox,* Rand McNally, 1956; M. Henry, *Black Gold,* Rand McNally, 1957; Doris S. Garst, *Crazy about Horses,* Hastings House, 1957; H. V. Larom, *Ride Like an Indian,* McGraw-Hill, 1958; Belle Coates, *That Colt Fireplug,* Scribner, 1958; Jocelyn Arundel, *Simba of the White Mane,* McGraw-Hill, 1958; Wilma Pitchford Hays, *Little Horse That Raced a Train,* Little, Brown, 1959; Lilian Moore, *Tony the Pony,* McGraw-Hill, 1959; J. Arundel, *Jin-*

Oystermen, clam diggers, and boat builders live on Chincoteague, but the outer island is left to the wild things, the wild ponies and the birds. ■ (From *Album of Horses* by Marguerite Henry. Illustrated by Wesley Dennis.)

(From *Album of Horses* by Marguerite Henry. Illustrated by Wesley Dennis.)

(From *Album of Horses* by Marguerite Henry. Illustrated by Wesley Dennis.)

(From *Album of Horses* by Marguerite Henry. Illustrated by Wesley Dennis.)

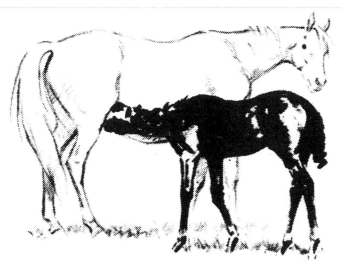

(From *Album of Horses* by Marguerite Henry. Illustrated by Wesley Dennis.)

go, *Wild Horse of Abaco*, McGraw-Hill, 1959; John Steinbeck, *The Red Pony*, Viking, 1959.

J. Arundel, *Dugan and the Hobo*, McGraw-Hill, 1960; W. P. Hays, *Little Lone Coyote*, Little, Brown, 1961; J. Arundel, *Mighty Mo: The Story of an African Lion*, McGraw-Hill, 1961; Jane S. McIlvaine, *Cammie's Choice*, Bobbs-Merrill, 1961; J. S. McIlvaine, *Cammie's Challenge*, Bobbs-Merrill, 1962; J. Arundel, *Whitecap's Song*, McGraw-Hill, 1962; M. Henry, *Five O'Clock Charlie*, Rand McNally, 1962; M. Henry, *Stormy: Misty's Foal*, Rand McNally, 1963; Maureen Daly, *The Ginger Horse*, Dodd, 1964; Marjorie Reynolds, *A Horse Called Mystery*, Harper, 1964; J. Arundel, *Shoes for Punch*, McGraw-Hill, 1964; M. Henry, *White Stallion of Lipizza*, Rand McNally, 1964; J. Arundel, *The Wildlife of Africa*, Hastings House, 1965; Pauline B. Innis, *The Ice Bird: A Christmas Legend*, R. B. Luce, 1965; Suzanne Wilding, *The Book of Ponies*, St. Martin's Press, 1965; Maureen Daly McGivern, *The Small War of Sergeant Donkey*, Dodd, 1966.

(From *Album of Horses* by Marguerite Henry. Illustrated by Wesley Dennis.)

SIDELIGHTS: Born in 1903 in Falmouth, Massachusetts, Dennis was raised in that small, Cape Cod town. His mother, Ida Morgan, encouraged her son to become a clam digger or a postmaster in Falmouth, but he had other career aspirations. A newsreel about a polo game spurred his interests in horses. Eventually, Dennis was offered the job of assistant postmaster in Falmouth but he had already determined to become an artist and to paint horses.

Dennis left Falmouth for Boston where he studied art at the New School of Design. He drew fashion sketches for Jordan Marsh, portraits at Filene's in Boston, and worked in the art departments of several Boston newspapers. He learned how to play polo and was able to study horses when he joined a National Guard cavalry unit.

In 1941 his first juvenile, *Flip* was published. He was encouraged to write and illustrate the book by a juvenile editor, May Massee, of Viking Press, whom he had met in Santa Fe while honeymooning with his bride, Dorothy Schiller Boggs.

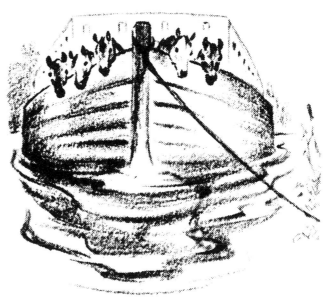

(From *Album of Horses* by Marguerite Henry. Illustrated by Wesley Dennis.)

Flip was the beginning of a series which established his reputation.

In 1947 he illustrated Marguerite Henry's *Misty of Chincoteague* and the team eventually collaborated on fifteen books, including *King of the Wind* which was awarded the Newbery Medal in 1949. Their admiration for each other's talent was mutual. He once remarked: "Marguerite's a demon for detail. When we were working on the illustrations for 'Misty,' she wanted full rigging in perfect detail on a ship drawing that would be no more than an inch high in the book. Besides that, she wanted a small boy high up on that rigging with his hand shading his eyes as he looked out over the horizon. She's a perfectionist all the way." [Alberta R. Semrad, "Marguerite Henry, Newbery Medal Winner," *Publishers Weekly,* March 26, 1949.[1]]

The Dennis family divided their time between Virginia (where he enjoyed fox hunting) and Cape Cod. He died at sixty-three, having illustrated over forty-five children's books. He is especially remembered for his illustrations of children's books about horses.

(From *Album of Horses* by Marguerite Henry. Illustrated by Wesley Dennis.)

FOR MORE INFORMATION SEE: Bertha E. Mahony and others, compilers, *Illustrators of Children's Books: 1744-1945*, Horn Book, 1947; Alberta R. Semrad, "Marguerite Henry, Newbery Medal Winner," *Publishers Weekly*, March 26, 1949; B. E. (Mahony) Miller and others, compilers, *Illustrators of Children's Books: 1946-1956*, Horn Book, 1958; Muriel Fuller, editor, *More Junior Authors*, H. W. Wilson, 1963; Lee Kingman and others, compilers, *Illustrators of Children's Books: 1957-1966*, Horn Book, 1968. Obituaries—*New York Times*, September 5, 1966; *Publishers Weekly*, October 3, 1966.

(Died September 5, 1966)

DOUGHERTY, Charles 1922-

PERSONAL: Born May 1, 1922, in Chicago, Ill.; son of James (a musician) and Inez (Lilgegren; a musician) Dougherty; married Elizabeth (Lear; a singer), June 1, 1945. *Home:* R.D. 4, Box 231, Sussex, N.J. 07461.

CAREER: Artist, 1945—.

ILLUSTRATOR: Louis Wolfe, *Let's Go to the Louisiana Purchase*, Putnam, 1963; Louis Wolfe, *Let's Go to the Klondike Gold Rush*, Putnam, 1964; Barbara Williams, *I Know a Policeman*, Putnam, 1967; Barbara Williams, *I Know a Mayor*, Putnam, 1967; Charles Mercer, *Let's Go to Europe*, Putnam, 1968; Kirk Polking, *Let's Go to an Atomic Energy*

I wave goodbye to the safety patrol boy as I hurry on my way. ■ (From *I Know a Policeman* by Barbara Williams. Illustrated by Charles Dougherty.)

Town, Putnam, 1968; Barbara Mitchell, *Let's Go to the Peace Corps*, Putnam, 1968; *Let's Go to a Hospital*, Putnam, 1968; David C. Cooke, *Let's Go to India*, Putnam, 1969; Muriel Stanek, *I Know a Dairy Man*, Putnam, 1970; Naomi Buchheimer, *I Know a Ranger*, Putnam, 1971; Andrew Bronin, *I Know a Football Player*, Putnam, 1973. Has also illustrated several text books and fishing and camping books for Time-Life, Inc.

SIDELIGHTS: "Major interest in painting watercolors and printmaking. I do as little illustration as possible. I was strongly influenced by Winslow Homer."

DUMAS, Alexandre (the elder) 1802-1870

PERSONAL: Born July 24, 1802, in Villers-Cotterets, France; died December 5, 1870, in Puys, France; buried at Villers-Cotterets; son of Thomas Alexandre (a general in Napoleon's army) and Marie Louise Elizabeth (Labouret) de la Pailleterie; married Ida Ferrier, 1840; children: Alexandre (an author and playwright), Marie Alexandrine, Henry Bauer, Micaella Cordier. *Education:* Attended school for a while, but was largely self-educated and taught by his mother and sister. *Politics:* Republican. *Home:* Chateau de Monte-Cristo, Paris, France.

CAREER: Novelist and playwright. At age 15, he was apprenticed to a local notary; in 1823 he went to Paris to work for the Duc d'Orleans, first as a copyist and later as a librarian. Dumas aided LaFayette when revolution threatened in 1830 and became a hero in his hometown, only to be exiled by the new king, Louis Philippe (the former Duc d'Orleans). Fought for Italian independence with Garibaldi, 1860, living in Naples for four years afterward. Most of Dumas' writings first appeared serially in various periodicals.

*WRITINGS—*Novels, except as noted: *La Salle d'Armes* (three stories: *Pauline, Pascal Bruno,* and *Murat*), Dumont, 1838, translations published separately as *Pauline: A Tale of Normandy*, J. Winchester, 1842, *Pascal Bruno*, Colburn, 1837, and *Murat*, Methuen, 1907; (with Adrien Dauzats) *Le Capitaine Paul* (based on James Fenimore Cooper's novel, *The Pilot*), Dumont, 1838, translation published as *Captain*

Paul the Pirate: A Tale of the Sea, G. Pierce, 1848 [another translation by Henry L. Williams published as *Paul Jones: A Nautical Romance,* F. Warne, 1889]; *La Comtesse de Salisbury,* Dumont, 1839; *Acte,* Dumont, 1839, translation by Henry W. Herbert published as *Acte of Corinth; or, The Convert of St. Paul,* E. P. Williams, 1847; *Aventures de John Davys,* Dumont, 1840; *Maitre Adam le Colabrais,* Dumont, 1840, translation by Harry A. Spurr published as *Master Adam the Calabrian,* R. F. Fenno, 1902; *Othon l'Archer,* Dumont, 1840, translation published as *Otho the Archer,* H. Lea, 1860; *Le Maitre d'Armes,* Dumont, 1840, translation by G. Griswold published as *The Fencing Master; or, Eighteen Months in St. Petersburg,* Stretton & Burnard, 1850 [other translations by the Marquis of Ormonde published as *Memoirs of a Maitre d'Armes; or, Eighteen Months in St. Petersburg,* Longmans, 1854; *The Fencing Master; or, Life in Russia,* Methuen, 1904]; *Le Capitaine Pamphile,* Dumont, 1840, translation by James Herald published as *Captain Pamphile,* J. Winchester, 1850, new edition translated by Douglas Munro published as *Captain Pamphile's Adventures* (illustrated by William Papas), Oxford University Press, 1971.

La Chasse au Chastre, [Paris], 1841, translation published as *The Bird of Fate,* Methuen, 1906; *Jehanne la Pucelle, 1429-1431,* Magen & Cormon, 1842, translation published as *Joan the Heroic Maiden,* J. S. Pratt, 1847; *Aventures de Lyderic,* Dumont, 1842, translation published as *Lyderic, Count of Flanders,* R. B. Johnson, 1903; *Albine,* C. Maquardt, 1843, reissued as *Le Chateau d'Eppstein,* de Potter, 1844, translation published as *The Spectre Mother,* Clarke, 1864 [another translation published as *The Castle of Eppstein,* Methuen, 1903]; *Georges,* Dumont, 1843, translation by G. J. Knox published as *George; or, The Planter of the Isle of France,* Simms & MacIntyre, 1846; (with Paul Meurice) *Ascanio,* Petion, 1843-44, translation published as *Ascanio,* Simms & MacIntyre, 1861; (with Auguste Maquet) *Le Chevalier d'Harmental,* Dumont, 1843, translation by H. L. Williams published as *The Orange Plume; or, The Bride of the Bastille,* E. D. Long, 1860 [another translation published as *The Conspirators; or, Chevalier d'Harmental,* G. Munro, 1878].

(With P. Meurice) *Amaury,* H. Souverain, 1844, translation published as *Amaury,* Harper, 1854 [another translation by A. Allinson published as *Amaury* (illustrated by Gordon Browne), Methuen, 1904]; *Cecile,* Dumont, 1844, translation published as *Cecile,* Methuen, 1904; *Gabriel Lambert,* H. Souverain, 1844, translation published as *Gabriel Lambert,* Methuen, 1904; (with Hippolyte Auger) *Fernande,* Dumont, 1844, translation published as *Fernande,* Methuen, 1904; *Les Freres Corses,* Cans, 1844, translation by Gerardus van Dam published as *The Corsican Brothers,* G. Munro, 1883; (with A. Maquet) *Sylvandire,* Dumont, 1844, translation by T. Williams published as *The Disputed Inheritance,* Clarke, 1847 [other translations published as *Beau Tancrede; or, The Marriage Verdict,* Clarke, 1861; *Sylvandire: A Romance of the Reign of Louis XIV,* Little, Brown, 1897].

(With Maquet) *Les Trois Mousquetaires,* Baudry, 1844, translation by William Robson published as *The Three Musketeers,* Routledge, 1853, new edition based on the translation by William Barrow, Pan Books, 1974 [other English editions illustrated by Maurice Leloir, T. Y. Crowell, 1894; Frank Adams, with an introduction by Andrew Lang, Methuen, 1903; Rowland Wheelwright, Dodd, 1920; Milo Winter, Rand, McNally, 1923; George M. Richards, Macmillan, 1925; Mead Schaeffer, Dodd, 1925; Edward R.

ALEXANDRE DUMAS, 1832.

Higgins, J. C. Winston, 1931; Pierre Falke, Limited Editions, 1932; Valenti Angelo, Three Sirens, 1935; Arthur Jameson, Whitman, 1945; Hookway Cowles, Coward-McCann, 1950; Daniel Rasmusson, Doubleday, 1952; Norman Price and E. C. Van Swearingen, Grosset & Dunlap, 1953; Hamilton Greene, Simon & Schuster, 1957; C. Walter Hodges, World Publishing, 1957; Edy Legrand, Heritage Press, 1960; James Daugherty, Macmillan, 1962].

(With Maquet) *Le Comte de Monte Cristo,* Petion, 1844-45, translation by William Thiese published in two parts as *Edmond Dantes, The Count of Monte Cristo* and *The Count of Monte Cristo; or, The Revenge of Edmond Dantes,* M. J. Ivers, 1892, new edition published as *The Count of Monte Cristo* (illustrated by Bill Sokol), Platt & Munk, 1968 [other English editions illustrated by G. Staal and J. A. Beauce, Routledge, 1888; Sybil Tawse, Black, 1920; Riou, G. W. Jacobs, 1922; M. Schaeffer, Dodd, 1928, reprinted, 1968; Lynd Ward, with an introduction by Andre Maurois, Limited Editions, 1941; Joseph Camana, Webster, 1949]; *Une Fille de Regent,* Cadot, 1845, translation by Charles H. Town published as *The Regent's Daughter,* Harper, 1845; (with A. Maquet) *La Reine Margot,* Garnier Freres, 1845, translation published as *Marguerite de Valois,* R. Griffin, 1850 [another translation published as *Queen Margot,* Routledge, 1856]; (with Maquet) *Vingt Ans Apres,* Baudry, 1845, translation by W. Barrow published as *Twenty Years After; or, The Further Feats and Fortunes of a Gascon Adventurer,* Bruce & Wyld, 1846, new edition, Collins, 1962 [other English editions illustrated by F. Adams, Methuen, 1904; R. Wheelwright, Dodd, 1923; Fred Money, M. Smith, 1928; E. Legrand, Limited Editions, 1958].

La Guerre des Femmes, de Potter, 1845-46, translation published as *Nanon,* Routledge, 1867 [another translation published as *The War of Women,* Little, Brown, 1895]; (with A. Maquet) *Le Chevalier de Maison-Rouge,* Cadot, 1846, translation published as *Marie Antoinette; or, The Chevalier of the Red House: A Tale of the French Revolution,* G.

Pierce, 1846 [another translation published as *The Chevalier de Maison Rouge*, G. Munro, 1877]; (with Maquet) *La Dame de Monsoreau*, Petion, 1846, translation published as *Chicot the Jester*, Clarke, 1857, new edition, Collins, 1956 [other translations published as *Diana of Meridor; or, The Lady of Monsoreau*, T. B. Peterson, 1860; *La Dame de Monsoreau*, Little, Brown, 1889]; (with Maquet) *Le Batard de Mauleon*, Cadot, 1846, translation published as *The Bastard of Mauleon*, Appleyard, 1848 [another translation by L. Lawford published as *The Half Brothers*, Routledge, 1858]; (with P. Meurice) *Les Deux Diane*, Cadot, 1846-47, translation published as *The Two Dianas*, Simms & MacIntyre, 1857; (with A. Maquet) *Memoires d'un Medecin: Joseph Balsamo*, Cadot, 1846-48, translation published as *Memoirs of a Physician*, Clarke, 1854.

(With Maquet) *Les Quarante-Cinq*, Cadot, 1848, translation published as *The Forty-Five Guardsmen*, Clarke, 1861 [another translation published as *The Forty-Five*, Little, Brown, 1894]; (with Maquet) *Le Vicomte de Bragelonne; ou, Dix Ans Plus Tard*, M. Levy Freres, 1848-50, translation published as *The Vicomte de Bragelonne; or, Ten Years Later*, Routledge, 1857, a later translation by H. L. Williams published under three separate titles as *The Vicomte de Bragelonne, the Son of Athos; or, Ten Years Later, Louise de La Valliere; or, The Love of Bragellone*, and *The Man in the Iron Mask*, F. M. Lupton, 1892 [*The Man in the Iron Mask* reissued separately (illustrated by E. Legrand, with an introduction by A. Maurois), Limited Editions, 1965]; (with Paul Bocage) *Les Mille et un Fantomes: Une Journee a Fonlenay-Aux-Roses* (stories about the occult), Cadot, 1849, translation published as *Tales of the Supernatural, Tales of Strange Adventure, and Tales of Terror*, Methuen, 1907-09; (with A. Maquet) *Le Collier de la Reine*, Cadot, 1849-50, translation published as *The Queen's Necklace*, Clarke, 1861, new edition under the same title (illustrated by Cyril Arnstam), Limited Editions, 1973.

(With P. Bocage) *Les Marriages du Pere Olifus*, Cadot, 1850, translation published as *The Marriages of Pere Olifus*, Methuen, 1907; (with A. Maquet and Paul Lacroix) *La Tulipe Noire*, Baudry, 1850, translation published as *Rosa; or, The Black Tulip*, Clarke, 1861, new edition published as *The Black Tulip*, Mayflower, 1970; *Le Testament de Monsieur de Chauvelin*, Cadot, 1850, translation by Mary Stuart Smith published as *Monsieur de Chauvelin's Will*, G. Munro, 1900; *Le Trou de l'Enfer*, Cadot, 1850-51, translation published as *The Mouth of Hell*, Methuen, 1906; (with P. Lacroix) *La Femme au Collier de Velours*, Cadot, 1851, translation by M. S. Smith published as *The Woman with the Velvet Collar*, G. Munro, 1900; *La Colombe*, Cadot, 1851, translation published as *The Dove*, Methuen, 1906; *Dieu Dispose*, Cadot, 1851-52, translation published as *God's Will Be Done*, Methuen, 1909 [another translation by Alexandre Dumas, the younger, published as "The Pigeon Prize," *Golden Book Magazine*, September, 1930].

(With Lacroix) *Olympe de Cleves*, Cadot, 1852, translation published as *Olympe de Cleves*, Little, Brown, 1893; *Conscience l'Innocent*, Cans, 1852, translation published as *The Conscript: A Tale of War*, T. B. Peterson, 1863; *Les Drames de la Mer* (sea stories), Cadot, 1852; *La Maison de Savoie*, C. Perrin, 1852-56; *Le Pasteur d'Ashbourne*, Cadot, 1853; *L'Horloger*, [Paris], 1853, translation published as *The Watchmaker*, Clarke, 1862; *Isaac Laquedem*, Marchant, 1853; (with A. Maquet) *Ange Pitou*, Cadot, 1853, translation published as *Six Years Later; or, Taking the Bastile*, G. Munro, 1878 [another translation published as

Ange Pitou, Little, Brown, 1890]; *La Comtesse de Charny*, Cadot, 1853-55, translation published as *The Countess de Charny*, Lea, 1860; *Catherine Blum*, Cadot, 1854, translation published as *The Foresters*, D. Appleton, 1854 [another translation published as *Catherine Blum*, G. Munro, 1878]; *Le Salteador*, Cadot, 1854, translation published as *The Brigand*, Dent, 1897; *La Princesse de Monaco*, Cadot, 1854; (with P. Lacroix) *Ingenue*, Cadot, 1854, translation by Julie de Marguerittes published as *Ingenue; or, The First Days of Blood*, Lippincott, 1855 [another translation published as *Ingenue; or, The Socialists of Paris*, G. Munro, 1878].

(With P. Bocage) *Les Mohicans de Paris* [et] *Salvator*, Cadot, 1854-59, translations published separately as *The Mohicans of Paris*, T. B. Peterson, 1859 and *Salvator*, G. Munro, 1882; *Le Page du Duc de Savoie*, Cadot, 1855, translation published as *Emmanuel Philibert; or, The European Wars of the Sixteenth Century*, D. Appleton, 1854 [another translation published as *The Page of the Duke of Savoy*, G. Munro, 1878]; *Madame du Deffand*, Cadot, 1856-57, reissued as *Memoires d'une Aveugle* [et] *Confessions de la Marquise*, M. Levy Freres, 1862; *Les Compagnons de Jehu*, Cadot, 1857, translation by Katharine Prescott Wormeley published as *The Company of Jehu*, Estes & Lauriat, 1894; *Le Meneur de Loups*, Cadot, 1857, translation by A. Allinson published as *The Wolf-Leader*, Methuen, 1904, reissued (with illustrations by Mahlon Blaine), Prime Press, 1950; *Le Capitaine Richard*, Cadot, 1858, translation by H. L. Williams published as *The Twin Lieutenants; or, The Soldier's Bride*, Peterson Brothers, 1862; *Black*, Cadot, 1858, translation published as *Black: The Story of a Dog*, Little, Brown, 1895; *L'Horoscope*, Cadot, 1858, translation published as *The Horoscope: A Romance of the Reign of Francois II*, Little, Brown, 1897; *Herminie*, Cans, 1858, reissued as *Une Aventure d'Amour*, M. Levy Freres, 1863.

Ammalat-Bey, Cadot, 1859, reissued as *Sultanetta*, M. Levy Freres, 1862, translation by A. Allinson published as *Sultanetta* (illustrated by F. Adams), Methuen, 1904; *Charles le Temperaire*, M. Levy Freres, 1859, translation published as *Charles the Bold*, Hodgson, 1860; *L'Histoire d'un Cabanon et d'un Chalet*, Meline, Cans, 1859, reissued as *Monsieur Coumbes: Roman Marseilles*, M. Levy Freres, 1860, translation published as *The Convict's Son*, Methuen, 1905; *Les Louves de Machecoul*, Cadot, 1859, translation by K. P. Wormeley published as *The Last Vendee; or, The She-Wolves of Machecoul*, Estes & Lauriat, 1894; *La Princesse Flora*, Meline, Cans, 1859; *Ainsi Soit-il!*, Meline, Cans, circa 1859, reissued as *Madame de Chamblay*, Cadot, 1862, translation published as *Madame de Chamblay*, Turner Brothers, 1869; *La Chasseur de Sauvagine*, Cadot, 1859, translation published as *The Wild Duck Shooter*, Methuen, 1906; *Marianna*, Meline, Cans, 1859, translation published as *Marianna*, Methuen, 1905; *Le Medecin de Java*, [Brussels], circa 1859, reissued as *L'Ile de Feu*, M. Levy Freres, 1870, translation published as *Doctor Basilius*, Routledge, 1860; *Jane*, Meline, Cans, 1859, translation published as *Jane*, Methuen, 1903.

La Maison de Glace, M. Levy Freres, 1860, translation published as *The Russian Gipsy; or, The Palace of Ice*, Clarke, 1861; *Le Pere la Ruine*, M. Levy Freres, 1860, translation published as *Pere la Ruine*, Methuen, 1905; *Jacquot sans Oreilles*, Meline, Cans, 1860, translation by A. Allinson published as *Crop-Eared Jacquot* (illustrated by G. Browne), Methuen, 1905; *Les Drames Galants*, M. Levy Freres, 1860; *Une Nuit a Florence sous Alexandre de Medi-*

Dumas' Milady was suggested to him by a figure in the *Memoirs of Monsieur d'Artagnan*, an English lady of rank, maid of honor to Henrietta Maria, the Queen of England (who was at that time in exile in France); d'Artagnan had an affair with her and outwitted a rival much as in *The Three Musketeers*. With this Dumas combined the historic incident, described by La Rochefoucauld, of the diamond pendants, which Lady Carlisle cut from Buckingham's clothing, to avenge herself on him and serve Cardinal Richelieu. The character and history of Milady Clarik are of course Dumas' invention. ■ (From *The Three Musketeers* by Alexandre Dumas. Illustrated by Maurice Leloir.)

(From the movie "The Count of Monte Cristo," starring Robert Donat. Copyright 1934 by Reliance Pictures, Inc.)

(From the movie "The Prince of Thieves," starring Jon Hall and Alan Mowbray. Released by Columbia Pictures, 1947.)

(From the movie "Black Magic," based on the novel *Memoirs of a Physician,* starring Orson Welles. Copyright 1949 by United Artists Corp.)

(From the movie "The Story of the Count of Monte Cristo," starring Louis Jourdan. Released by Warner Bros.-Seven Arts, 1962.)

cis, M. Levy Freres, 1861; *La Boule de Neige*, M. Levy Freres, 1862, translation by A. Allinson published as *The Snow Ball* (illustrated by F. Adams), Methuen, 1904; *La Dame de Volupte: Memoires de Mademoiselle de Luynes*, M. Levy Freres, 1863; *Les Deux Reines*, M. Levy Freres, 1864; *La Peche aux Filets*, [Paris], 1864, translation published as *Netting the Waters*, Methuen, 1904; *La San-Felice [et] Emma Lyonna*, M. Levy Freres, 1864-65, translation by H. L. Williams published as *The Lovely Lady Hamilton; or, The Beauty and the Glory*, [London], 1903 [another translation published as *The Neapolitan Lovers [and] Love and Liberty*, S. Paul, 1916-18].

(With Charles Nodier) *Les Blancs et Les Bleus*, M. Levy Freres, 1867-68, translation by K. P. Wormeley published as *The First Republic; or, The Whites and the Blues*, Estes & Lauriat, 1894; *La Terreur Prussienne*, M. Levy Freres, 1867, translation by R. S. Garnett published as *The Prussian Terror*, S. Paul, 1915; (with Gaspard de Cherville) *Parisiens et Provinciaux*, M. Levy Freres, 1868; *The Count of Moret* (translated from the French by H. L. Williams), Peterson Brothers, 1868; *Le Docteur Mysterieux*, M. Levy Freres, 1872; *La Fille du Marquis*, M. Levy Freres, 1872; *Le Prince des Voleurs*, M. Levy Freres, translation by A. Allinson published as *The Prince of Thieves* (illustrated by F. Adams), Methuen, 1904; *Robin Hood le Proscrit*, M. Levy Freres, 1873, translation by A. Allinson published as *Robin Hood, the Outlaw* (illustrated by F. Adams), Methuen, 1904, new edition translated by Lowell Blair published as *Robin Hood, Prince of Outlaws*, Dell, 1965.

Plays: (With Adolphe de Leuven and P. J. Rousseau) *La Chasse et L'Amour* ("The Chase and Love"; one-act; first produced in Paris at the Theatre de l'Ambigu-Comique, September 22, 1825), Duverois, 1825; *La Noce et L'-Enterrement* ("The Wedding and the Burial"; three-scene; first produced in Paris at the Theatre de la Porte-Saint-Martin, November 21, 1826), Bezou, 1826; *Henry III et Sa Cour* ("Henry III and His Court"; five-act; first produced in Paris at the Comedie-Francaise, February 11, 1829), Vezard, 1829; *Christine; ou, Stockholm, Fontainebleau, et Rome* ("Christine; or, Stockholm, Fontainebleau, and Rome"; five-act; first produced in Paris at the Theatre de l'Odeon, March 30, 1830), J. N. Barba, 1830; *Napoleon Bonaparte; ou, Trente Ans dans l'Histoire de France* ("Napoleon Bonaparte; or, Thirty Years in the History of France"; six-act; first produced in Paris at the Theatre de l'Odeon, January 10, 1831), Tourachon, Molin, 1831; *Antony* (five-act; first produced in Paris at the Theatre de la Porte-Saint-Martin, May 3, 1831), A. Auffray, 1831, translation by H. A. Spurr published as *Antony*, Tuten, 1904; *Charles VII chez Ses Grands Vassaux* ("Charles VII and His Chief Vassals"; five-act; first produced in Paris at the Theatre de l'Odeon, October 20, 1831), Lemesle et la Veuve Bechet, 1831.

Richard Darlington (three-act; first produced in Paris at the Theatre de la Porte-Saint-Martin, December 10, 1831), J. N. Barba, 1832; (with Auguste Anicet-Bourgeois) *Teresa* (five-act; first produced in Paris at the Theatre Royal de l'Opera-Comique, February 6, 1832), C. Lemesle, 1832; *Le Mari de la Veuve* ("The Widow's Husband"; one-act; first produced in Paris at the Comedie-Francaise, April 4, 1832), A. Auffray, 1832; (with Frederic Gaillardet) *La Tour de Nesle* (five-act; first produced in Paris at the Theatre de la Porte-Saint-Martin, May 29, 1832), J. N. Barba, 1832, translation by A. L. Gowans published as *The Tower of Nesle*, Gowans & Gray, 1906; "Le Fils de l'Emigre" ("The Son of the Emigrant"; four-act), first produced in Paris at the

And he hanged her to a tree. ■ (From *The Three Musketeers* by Alexandre Dumas. Illustrated by Maurice Leloir.)

Theatre de la Porte-Saint-Martin, August 28, 1832; *Perinet Leclerc; ou, Paris en 1418* ("Perinet Leclerc; or, Paris in 1418"; five-act; first produced in Paris at the Theatre de la Porte-Saint-Martin, September 3, 1832), J. N. Barba, 1832.

Angele (five-act; first produced in Paris at the Theatre de la Porte-Saint-Martin, December 28, 1833), Charpentier, 1834; *La Venitienne* ("The Venetian Woman"; five-act; first produced at the Theatre de la Porte-Saint-Martin, March 18, 1834), J. N. Barba, 1834; *Catherine Howard* (five-act; first produced in Paris at the Theatre de la Porte-Saint-Martin, June 2, 1834), Charpentier, 1834, translation by W. D. Suter published as *Catherine Howard*, Lacy's Plays, 1859; *La Tour de Babel* ("The Tower of Babel"; one-act; first produced in Paris at the Theatre des Varietes, June 24, 1834), Marchant, 1834; (with E.C.H. Cordellier-Delanoue) *Cromwell et Charles I* ("Cromwell and Charles I"; five-act; first produced in Paris at the Theatre de la Porte-Saint-Martin, May 21, 1835), Marchant, 1835; (with M.E.G. Theaulon de Lambert and E. Rousseau) *Le Marquis de Brunoy* ("The Marquis of Brunoy"; five-act; first produced in Paris at the Theatre des Varietes, March 14, 1836), J. N. Barba, 1836; *Don Juan de Marana; ou, La Chute d'un Ange* ("Don Juan of Marana; or, The Fall of an Angel"; five-act; first produced in Paris at the Theatre de la Porte-Saint-Martin, April 30, 1836), Marchant, 1836; (with Theaulon de Lambert) *Kean; ou, Desordre et Genie* (five-act; first produced in

Paris at the Theatre des Varietes, August 31, 1836), J. N. Barba, 1836, translation published as *Edmund Kean; or, The Genius and the Libertine*, Vickers, 1847.

(With Gerard de Nerval) *Piquillo* (three-act opera; music by Hippolyte Monpou; first produced in Paris at the Opera Comique, October 31, 1837), Marchant, 1837; *Caligula* (five-act; first produced in Paris at the Comedie-Francaise, December 26, 1837), Marchant, 1838; (with Hippolyte Romand) *Le Bourgeois de Gand; ou, Le Secretaire du Duc d'Albe* ("The Man from Ghent; or, The Duke of Alba's Secretary"; five-act; first produced in Paris at the Theatre de l,Odeon, May 21, 1838), [Paris], 1838; *Paul Jones* (five-act; first produced in Paris at the Theatre du Pantheon, October 12, 1838), Marchant, 1838; (with A. Maquet) *Bathilde* (three-act; first produced in Paris at the Theatre de la Renaissance, January 14, 1839), Marchant, 1839; *Mademoiselle de Belle Isle* ("The Lady of Belle Isle"; three-act; first produced in Paris at the Comedie-Francaise, April 2, 1839), Dumont, 1839; (with G. de Nerval) *L'Alchimiste* ("The Alchemist"; five-act; first produced in Paris at the Theatre de la Renaissance, April 10, 1839), Dumont, 1839; (with Nerval) *Leo Burckart* (five-act; first produced in Paris at the Theatre de la Porte-Saint-Martin, April 16, 1839), J. N. Barba, 1839.

(With Charles Lafont) *Jarvis l'Honnete Homme; ou, Le Marchand de Londres* ("Jarvis the Gentleman; or, The Merchant of London"; two-act; first produced in Paris at the Theatre du Gymnase-Dramatique, June 3, 1840), Henriot, 1840; *Un Mariage sous Louis XV* (five-act; first produced in Paris at the Comedie-Francaise, June 1, 1841),

Marchant, 1841, translation by S. Grundy published as *A Marriage of Convenience: Period Louis XV*, Lacy's Plays, 1899; (with Eugene Bourgeois) *Jeannil le Breton; ou, Le Gerant Responsable* ("Jeannil the Breton; or, The Responsible Manager"; five-act; first produced in Paris at the Theatre de la Porte-Saint-Martin, November 27, 1841), Beck, 1842; *Lorenzino* (five-act; first produced in Paris at the Comedie-Francaise, February 24, 1842), Marchant, 1842; (with C. Lafont) *Le Seducteur et le Mari* ("The Seducer and the Husband"; three-act; first produced in Paris at the Theatre des Delassements Comiques, November 5, 1842), Marchant, 1842; *Halifax* (three-act; first produced in Paris at the Theatre des Varietes, December 2, 1842), Marchant, 1842.

(With A. de Leuven and Leon Lherie) *Le Mariage au Tambour* ("Marriage to Drumbeats"; three-act; first produced in Paris at the Theatre des Varietes, March 9, 1843), C. Tresse, 1843; *Les Demoiselles de Saint-Cyr* (five-act; first produced in Paris at the Comedie-Francaise, July 25, 1843), Marchant, 1843, translation published as *The Ladies of Saint-Cyr*, Lacy's Plays, 1870; (with Louis Lefevre) *L'-Ecole des Princes* ("The School of Princes"; five-act; first produced in Paris at the Theatre de l'Odeon, September 29, 1843), C. Tresse, 1843; (with A. de Leuven and L. Lherie) *Louise Bernard* (five-act; first produced in Paris at the Theatre de la Porte-Saint-Martin, November 18, 1843), Marchant, 1843; (with Leuvin and Lherie) *Le Laird de Dumbicky* ("The Laird of Dumbicky"; five-act; first produced in Paris at the Theatre de l'Odeon, December 30, 1843), Marchant, 1844.

"I have always been told that a Catalan is not a man to be supplanted by a rival." ■ (From *The Count of Monte Cristo* by Alexandre Dumas. Illustrated by Mead Schaeffer.)

(With Leuven and Lherie) *Le Garde-Forestier* ("The Forester"; two-act; first produced in Paris at the Theatre des Varietes, March 15, 1845), Beck, 1845; (with Leuvin and Lherie) *Un Conte de Fees* ("A Fairy Tale"; three-act; first produced in Paris at the Theatre des Varietes, April 29, 1845), Beck, 1845; (with Leuven and Louis-Emile Vanderburch) *Sylvandire* (four-act; first produced in Paris at the Theatre du Palais-Royal, June 7, 1845), Marchant, 1845; (with A. Maquet) *Les Mousquetaires* ("The Musketeers"; five-act; first produced in Paris at the Theatre de l'Ambigu-Comique, October 27, 1845; based on Dumas' novel, *Vingt Ans Apres*), Marchant, 1845; *Une Fille du Regent* ("The Regent's Daughter"; five-act; first produced in Paris at the Theatre de l'Odeon, May 23, 1846), Marchant, 1846; (with Octave Feuillet and P. Bocage) *Echec et Mat* ("Check and Checkmate"; five-act; first produced in Paris at the Theatre de l'Odeon, May 23, 1846), Jerome, 1846.

(With A. Maquet) *La Reine Margot* ("Queen Margot"; five-act; first produced in Paris at the Theatre Historique, February 20, 1847; based on Dumas' novel of the same title), M. Levy Freres, 1847; *Intrigue et Amour* ("Love and Intrigue"; five-act; first produced in Paris at the Theatre Historique, June 11, 1847; based on Johann Schiller's play), M. Levy Freres, 1864; (with A. Maquet) *Le Chevalier de Maison-Rouge* ("The Knight of Maison-Rouge"; five-act; first produced in Paris at the Theatre Historique, August 3, 1847), M. Levy Freres, 1847; (with P. Meurice) *Hamlet, Prince de Danemark* ("Hamlet, Prince of Denmark"; five-act; first produced in Paris at the Theatre Historique, December 15, 1847; based on William Shakespeare's play), M. Levy Freres, 1848; (with A. Maquet) *Monte-Cristo, I* (five-act; first produced in Paris at the Theatre Historique, February 3, 1848), C. Tresse, 1848; (with Maquet) *Monte-Cristo, II* (five-act; first produced in Paris at the Theatre Historique, February 4, 1848), C. Tresse, 1848; (with Maquet) *Catalina* (five-act; first produced in Paris at the Theatre Historique, October 14, 1848), M. Levy Freres, 1848.

(With Maquet) *La Jeunesse des Mousquetaires* ("The Youth of the Musketeers"; five-act; first produced in Paris at the Theatre Historique, February 17, 1849), Dufoyr et Mulat, 1849; (with Maquet) *Le Chevalier d'Harmental* ("The Chevalier of Harmental"; five-act; first produced in Paris at the Theatre Historique, July 26, 1849), Cadot, 1849; (with Maquet) *La Guerre des Femmes* ("The War of Women"; five-act; first produced in Paris at the Theatre Historique, October 1, 1849), Cadot, 1849; (with Eugene Grange and Xavier de Montepin) *Le Connetable de Bourbon; ou, L'Italie au Seizieme Siecle* ("Constable Bourbon; or, Italy in the Sixteenth Century"; five-act; first produced in Paris at the Theatre de la Porte-Saint-Martin, October 20, 1849), Cadot, 1849; (with Jules Lacroix) *Le Testament de Cesar* ("The Testament of Caesar"; five-act; first produced in Paris at the Comedie-Francaise, November 10, 1849), M. Levy Freres, 1849; *Le Comte Hermann* ("Count Hermann"; five-act; first produced in Paris at the Theatre Historique, November 22, 1849), Marchant, 1849.

(With Eugene Nus) *Le Cachemire Vert* ("The Green Cashmere"; one-act; first produced in Paris at the Theatre du Gymnase, December 15, 1849), Marchant, 1850; *Trois Entr'actes pour "L'Amour Medecin"* ("Three Intermissions for 'Love, the Doctor'"; first produced in Paris at the Comedie-Francaise, January 15, 1850), [Paris], 1864; (with A. Maquet) *Urbain Grandier* (five-act; first produced in Paris at the Theatre Historique, March 30, 1850), Marchant, 1850; *Le Vingt-Quatre Fevrier; ou, L'Auberge de Schwasbach* ("The Twenty-fourth of February; or, The Tavern of

Schwasbach"; one-act; first produced in Paris at the Theatre de la Gaite, March 30, 1850; based on Zacharias Werner's play), Marchant, 1850; (with A. Maquet) *La Chasse au Chastre* (three-act; first produced in Paris at the Theatre Historique, August 3, 1850), Marchant, 1850; (with E. Grange and X. de Montepin) *Pauline* (five-act; first produced in Paris at the Theatre Historique, June 1, 1850), Dondey-Dupre, 1850; (with Grange and Montepin) *Les Chevaliers du Lansquenet* ("The Chevaliers of Lansquenet"; five-act; produced, 1850), Marchant, 1850; (with Grange and Montepin) *Les Freres Corses* ("The Corsican Brothers"; first produced in Paris at the Theatre Historique, August, 1850; based on Dumas' novel of the same title), Dondey-Dupre, 1850.

(With A. Maquet) *Le Vampire* ("The Vampire"; five-act; first produced in Paris at the Theatre de l'Ambigu-Comique, December 20 or 30, 1851), [Paris], 1865; (with Maquet) *Le Comte de Morcerf* ("The Count of Morcerf"; five-act; first produced in Paris at the Theatre de l'Ambigu-Comique, April 1, 1851), C. Tresse, 1851; (with Maquet) *Villefort* (five-act; first produced in Paris at the Theatre de l'Ambigu-Comique, May 8, 1851), C. Tresse, 1851; (with P. Meurice) *La Barriere de Clichy* ("The Clichy Gate"; five-act; first produced in Paris at the National Theatre, April 21, 1851), Marchant, 1851; (with Meurice) *Benvenuto Cellini* (five-act; first produced in Paris at the Theatre de la Porte-Saint-Martin, April 1, 1852), M. Levy Freres, 1852; *La Jeunesse de Louis XIV* ("The Youth of Louis XIV"; five-act; first produced in Brussels at the Vaudeville Theatre, January 20, 1854), Kiessling, Schnee, 1854; (with L. Lherie and P. Bocage) *Le Marbrier* ("The Marble Polisher"; three-act; first produced in Paris at the Theatre du Vaudeville, May 22, 1854), M. Levy Freres, 1854; *La Conscience* ("The Conscience"; six-act; first produced in Paris at the Theatre de l'Odeon, November 4, 1854), Taride, 1854; *Romulus* (one-act; first produced in Paris at the Comedie-Francaise, January 13, 1854), Librairie Theatrale, 1854, translation by Barnett Shaw published as *Romulus,* Samuel French, 1971.

L'Orestie ("The Oresteia"; three-act; first produced in Paris at the Theatre de la Porte-Saint-Martin, January 5, 1856), Librairie Theatrale, 1856; (with X. de Montepin) *La Tour Saint-Jacques* (five-act; first produced in Paris at the Theatre Imperial, November 15, 1856), Marchant, 1856; *Le Verrou de la Reine* ("The Queen's Bolt"; three-act; first produced in Paris at the Theatre du Gymnase-Dramatique, December 15, 1856), M. Levy-Freres, 1865; (with Charles Gabet) *Les Compagnons de Jehu* ("Jehu's Companions"; five-act; first produced in Paris at the Gaite Theatre, July 2, 1857), Beck, 1857; *L'Invitation a la Valse* ("The Invitation to the Waltz"; one-act; first produced in Paris at the Theatre du Gymnase-Dramatique, August 3, 1857), Beck, 1857, translation by C. L. Young published as *Childhood's Dreams,* Lacy's Plays, 1881; *L'Honneur est Satisfait* ("Honor is Satisfied"; one-act; first produced in Paris at the Theatre du Gymnase-Dramatique, June 19, 1858), Librairie Theatrale, 1858.

L'Envers d'une Conspiration; ou, Le Fils de Donald le Noir ("Behind a Conspiracy; or, The Son of Black Donald"; five-act; first produced in Paris at the Theatre du Vaudeville, January 4, 1860), [Paris], 1860; (with A. de Leuven) *Le Roman d'Elvire* ("The Romance of Elvire"; three-act opera; music by M. Ambroise Thomas; first produced in Paris at the Opera Comique, February 4, 1860), M. Levy Freres, 1860; *Le Gentilhomme de la Montagne* ("The Gentleman of the Mountain"; five-act; first produced in Paris at the Theatre de la Porte-Saint-Martin, June 12, 1860), M.

The Ambuscade. ■ (From *The Three Musketeers* by Alexandre Dumas. Illustrated by Maurice Leloir.)

(From the movie "Start the Revolution Without Me," a backhanded salute to the novels of Dumas, starring Donald Sutherland and Gene Wilder. Copyright © 1970 by Warner Bros., Inc.)

Levy Freres, 1860; (with A. Maquet) *La Dame de Monsoreau* ("The Lady from Monsoreau"; five-act; first produced in Paris at the Theatre de l'Ambigu-Comique, November 19, 1860), M. Levy Freres, 1860; (with Maquet) *Le Prisonnier de la Bastille: Fin des Mousquetaires* ("The Prisoner of the Bastille: End of the Musketeers"; five-act; first produced in Paris at the Theatre Imperial du Cirque, March 22, 1861), Calmann-Levy, 1861.

(With Bernard Lopez) *La Veillee Allemande* ("The German Vigil"; one-act; first produced in Paris at the Theatre Belleville, November 21, 1863), E. Dentu, 1864; (with P. Bocage) *Les Mohicans de Paris* ("The Mohicans of Paris"; five-act; first produced in Paris at the Gaite Theatre, August 20, 1864), M. Levy Freres, 1864; *Les Forestiers* ("The Foresters"; five-act; first produced in Marseilles at the Grand Theatre, March 23, 1858; based on his novel, *Catherine Blum*), M. Levy Freres, 1865; (with Amedee de Jallais) *Gabriel Lambert; ou, Gabriel le Faussaire* ("Gabriel Lambert; or, Gabriel the Forger"; five-act; first produced in Paris at the Theatre de l'Ambigu-Comique, March 16, 1866), M. Levy Freres, 1866; *Madame de Chamblay* (five-act; first produced in Paris at the Salle Ventadour, June 4, 1868), M. Levy Freres, 1869; *Les Blancs et Les Bleus* ("The Whites and the Blues"; five-act; first produced in Paris at the Theatre du Chatelet, March 10, 1869), M. Levy Freres, 1874; "Joseph Balsamo" (completed by Alexandre Dumas, the younger), first produced in Paris at the Theatre de l'Odeon, March 18, 1878.

Also author of the following plays, neither published nor produced: "Ivanhoe" (three-act); "Fiesque de Lavagna" (five-act); "L'Ecossais" (five-act); "La Jeunesse de Louis XV" (five-act); (with P. Meurice) "Romeo et Juliette" (five-act); and "La Femme sans Amour" (three-act).

Children's stories: *Histoire d'un Casse-Noisette*, J. Hetzel, 1845 (based on Ernst Hoffmann's story, *The Nutcracker and the Mouse King*), translation published as *The Story of a Nutcracker*, Chapman & Hall, 1846 [another translation published as *The Nutcracker of Nuremberg* (illustrated by Else Hasselriis), McBride, 1930]; *La Bouille de la Comtesse Berthe*, J. Hetzel, 1845, translation published as *Good Lady Bertha's Honey Broth*, Chapman & Hall, 1846; *La Jeunesse de Pierrot; ou, Le Roi de Boheme*, Coulon-Pineau, 1854, translation by H. A. Spurr published as "When Pierrot Was Young," in *Fairy Tales by Dumas* (edited by Spurr; illustrated by Harry Rountree), F. A. Stokes, 1904; *Le Lievre de mon Grand-Pere*, Cadot, 1857; *L'Homme aux Contes* (fairy tales), Meline, Cans, circa 1858; *Contes pour les Grands et les Petits Enfants*, Meline, Cans, 1859; *Le Pere Gigogne: Contes pour les Enfants* (collection of fairy tales), M. Levy Freres, 1860; *Fairy Tales by Dumas* (translated from the French and edited by H. A. Spurr; illustrated by H. Rountree), F. A. Stokes, 1904.

Historical works: *Gaule et France*, A. Auffray, 1833, translation published as *The Progress of Democracy*, J. & H. G. Langley, 1841; *La Vendee et Madam*, Guyon & Canel,

(From the movie "The Four Musketeers," based on the novel *The Three Musketeers,* starring Faye Dunaway and Michael York. Copyright © 1975 by Twentieth Century-Fox Film Corp.)

1833, translation published as *The Duchess of Berri in La Vendee,* Bull & Churton, 1833; *Isabel de Baviere,* Dumont, 1836, translation by W. Barrow published as *Isabel of Bavaria; or, The Chronicles of France for the Reign of Charles VI,* Bruce & Wyld, 1846; *Napoleon,* Delloye, 1839, translation by John B. Larner published as *Napoleon,* Putnam, 1894; *Crimes Celebres,* Querard, 1839-40, translation by I. G. Burnham published as *Celebrated Crimes* (illustrated by de Los Rios), G. Barrie, 1895; *Les Stuarts,* Dumont, 1840; *L'Armee Francaise,* [Paris], 1841-45; *Louis XIV et Son Siecle,* Dufour et Fellens, 1844-45; *Trois Maitres,* Recoules, 1844-46.

Les Medicis, Recoules, 1845; *L'Histoire des. Peintres,* Cans, 1845; *Souvenirs d'Antony,* M. Levy Freres, 1848; *Louis XV et Sa Cour,* Cadot, 1849; *Louis XVI et la Revolution; ou, Louis XVI et Marie Antoinette,* Cadot, 1850-51; *Montevideo; ou, Une Nouvelle Troie,* N. Chaux, 1850; *Le Drame de Quatre-Vingt-Treize: Scenes de la Vie Revolutionnaire,* H. Souverain, 1851-52; *Histoire de la Vie Politique et Privee de Louis-Philippe,* Dufour & Mulat, 1852; *Le Dernier Roi des Francais, 1771 a 1851,* H. Souverain, 1852, translation by R. S. Garnett published as *The Last King; or, The New France,* S. Paul, 1915; *Les Grands Hommes en Robe de Chambre: Henri IV, Louis XIII, et Richelieu,* Cadot, 1856; *Les Grands Hommes en Robe de Chambre: Cesar,* Cadot, 1857-58; *Les Garibaldiens: Revolution de Sicile et de Naples,* M. Levy Freres, 1861, translation published as *The Garibaldians in Sicily,* Routledge,

1861; *Italians et Flamands,* M. Levy Freres, 1862; *Les Souvenirs d'une Favorite,* M. Levy Freres, 1865; *Les Hommes de Fer,* M. Levy Freres, 1867.

Travel: *Impressions de Voyage: En Suisse,* [Paris], 1833-34, translation by R. W. Plummer and A. Craig Bell published as *Adventures in Switzerland,* Chilton, 1960; *Nouvelles Impressions de Voyage: Quinze Jours au Sinai,* Dumont, 1839, translation published as *Impressions of Travel in Egypt and Arabia Petraea,* J. S. Taylor, 1839, reprinted, Art Guild Reprints, 1968; *Nouvelles Impressions de Voyage: Midi de la France,* Dumont, 1841, translation published as *Pictures of Travel in the South of France,* Ingram, 1852; *Excursions sur les Bords du Rhin,* Dumont, 1841; *Une Anee a Florence,* Dumont, 1841; *Le Speronare,* Dumont, 1842, translation by K. P. Wormeley published as *The Speronara,* Dent, 1902; *Le Capitaine Arena,* Dolin, 1842; *Le Corricolo,* Dolin, 1843; *La Villa Palmieri,* Dolin, 1843; *De Paris a Cadix,* Garnier Freres, 1848, translation by Alma Elizabeth Murch published as *Adventures in Spain* (illustrated by Gustave Doré), Chilton, 1959.

Le Veloce; ou, Tanger, Alger, et Tunis, Cadot, 1848-51, translation by A. E. Murch published as *Adventures in Algeria,* Chilton, 1959; *Taiti-Marquises-Californie: Journal de Madame Giovanni,* Cadot, 1856, translation by Marguerite E. Wilbur published as *The Journal of Madame Giovanni,* Liveright Publishing, 1944; *La Caucase,* Librairie Theatrale, 1859, translation by A. E. Murch published as *Adven-*

tures in Caucasia, Chilton, 1962, reissued, Greenwood Press, 1975; _La Route de Varennes,_ M. Levy Freres, 1860, translation by A. C. Bell published as _The Flight to Varennes,_ Alston Books, 1962; _De Paris a Astrakan: Nouvelles Impressions de Voyage,_ A. Bourdillart, 1860, reissued as _Impressions de Voyage: En Russie,_ M. Levy Freres, 1865, translation by A. E. Murch published as _Adventures in Czarist Russia,_ Chilton, 1961; _Un Gil-Blas en Californie,_ M. Levy Freres, 1861, translation by M. E. Wilbur published as _A Gil Blas in California_ (illustrated by Paul Landacre), Primavera Press, 1933; _Un Pays Inconnu,_ M. Levy Freres, 1865.

Other: _Mes Memoires,_ 22 volumes, Cadot, 1852-54, translation by E. M. Waller published as _My Memoirs_ (with an introduction by A. Lang), Methuen, 1907-09, new edition translated by A. C. Bell published as _My Memoirs,_ Chilton, 1961, reissued, Greenwood Press, 1975; _Une Vie d'Artiste,_ Cadot, 1854, translation by R. S. Garnett published as _A Life's Ambition,_ S. Paul, 1924; _L'Art et les Artistes Contemporains au Salon de 1859,_ A. Bourdelliat, 1859; _Histoires de mes Betes,_ M. Levy Freres, 1868, translation by A. Allinson published as _My Pets_ (illustrated by V. Lecomte), Methuen, 1909, new edition translated by A. C. Bell published as _Adventures with My Pets,_ Chilton, 1960; _Souvenirs Dramatiques,_ M. Levy Freres, 1868; _Grand Dictionnaire de Cuisine,_ A. Lemerre, 1873, translation by Louis Colman published as _Dictionary of Cuisine_ (illustrated by John H. Jocoby), Simon & Schuster, 1958; _Propos d'Art et de Cuisine,_ M. Levy Freres, 1877; _Petit Dictionnaire de Cuisine,_ A. Lemerre, 1882.

Collections: _Theatre Complet,_ M. Levy Freres, 1863-65; _The Romances of Alexandre Dumas,_ 60 volumes, Little, Brown, 1893-97; _The Romances of Alexandre Dumas,_ 10 volumes, G. D. Sproul, 1896; _The Novels of Alexandre Dumas,_ 56 volumes (translated from the French by A. Allinson), Methuen, 1903-11; _Oeuvres Illustrees,_ 29 volumes, French & European Publications, 1922-35, reissued in 38 volumes, Editions Recontre, 1967; _Short Stories by Alexandre Dumas,_ W. J. Black, 1927, reprinted, Books for Libraries, 1972; _An Autobiography-Anthology including the Best of Dumas_ (edited by Guy Endore), Doubleday, 1962.

ADAPTATIONS—Movies and filmstrips: "The Count of Monte Cristo" (motion pictures), Famous Players Film Co., 1912, United Artists, 1934; "The Count of Monte Cristo [and] Cyrano de Bergerac" (filmstrip; animated, starring Mr. Magoo; with a teacher's guide), McGraw-Hill, 1972; "The Three Musketeers" (motion pictures), Edward Laurillard, 1913, Film Attractions Co., 1914, Douglas Fairbanks Pictures Corp., starring Douglas Fairbanks, 1921, Mascot Pictures (series of twelve), 1933, RKO Radio Pictures, 1935, Twentieth Century-Fox Film Corp., starring Don Ameche and the Ritz Brothers, 1939, Loew's, starring Gene Kelly, Van Heflin, June Allyson, Lana Turner, and Vincent Price, 1948, Sterling Educational Films, 1965; "The Three Musketeers" (filmstrips), Eye Gate House, 1946, McGraw-Hill (animated, starring Mr. Magoo; with a teacher's guide), 1972.

"Chicot the Jester" (motion picture), Societe Francaise des Films et Cinematographes Eclair, 1914; "The Corsican Brothers" (motion pictures), Universal Film, 1915, United Artists, starring Douglas Fairbanks, Jr., 1941; "Queen Margaret" (motion picture), adaptation of _Marguerite de Valois,_ Pathe Freres, 1915; "D'Artagnan" (motion picture), adaptation of _The Three Musketeers,_ Triangle Film Corp., 1916; "Where Is My Father?" (motion picture), adaptation

of _Black,_ Exclusive Features, 1916; "The Three Must-Get-Theres" (motion picture), based on _The Three Musketeers,_ Allied Producers and Distributors Corp., 1922; "Monte Cristo" (motion picture), Fox Film Corp., 1922; "A Stage Romance" (motion picture), adaptation of _Kean; ou, Desordre et Genie,_ Fox Film Corp., 1922; "Milady" (motion picture), Achievement Films, 1923; "The Iron Mask" (motion picture), based on _The Three Musketeers_ and _The Man in the Iron Mask,_ starring Douglas Fairbanks, Elton Co., 1929.

"The Man in the Iron Mask" (motion picture), starring Louis Hayward and Joan Bennett, United Artists, 1939; "Son of Monte Cristo" (motion picture), starring Louis Hayward and Joan Bennett, United Artists, 1941; "Fighting Guardsman" (motion picture), adaptation of _The Companions of Jehu,_ Columbia Pictures, 1945; "The Return of Monte Cristo" (motion picture), starring Louis Hayward and Barbara Britton, Columbia Pictures, 1946; "The Wife of Monte Cristo" (motion picture), Pathe Industries, 1946; "The Prince of Thieves" (motion picture), Columbia Pictures, 1947; "Black Magic" (motion picture), adaptation of _Memoires d'un Medecin,_ starring Orson Welles, United Artists, 1949.

"The Lady in the Iron Mask" (motion picture), adaptation of _The Three Musketeers,_ starring Louis Hayward and Patricia Medina, Twentieth Century-Fox, 1952; "Brigand" (motion picture), Columbia Pictures, 1952; "The Iron Mask" (motion picture), adaptation of _The Three Musketeers_ and _Twenty Years After,_ Odyssey Pictures, 1952; "The Bandits of Corsica" (motion picture), adaptation of _The Corsican Brothers,_ starring Raymond Burr, United Artists, 1954; "The Secret of Monte Cristo" (motion picture), starring Rory Calhoun, Metro-Goldwyn-Mayer, 1961; "Pris-

The Count of Monte Cristo

BY ALEXANDRE DUMAS

(From _The Count of Monte Cristo_ by Alexandre Dumas. Illustrated by Lynd Ward.)

oner of the Iron Mask" (motion picture), adaptation of *The Man in the Iron Mask,* Alta Vista Productions, 1962; "The Story of the Count of Monte Cristo" (motion picture), Warner Brothers, 1962; "Les Trois Mousquetaires" (filmstrip; to be used in French language instruction; with captions in French), Gessler Publishing Co., 1964.

Plays: Constance Cox, *The Count of Monte Cristo,* Fortune Press, 1950; Jean Paul Sartre, *The Devil and the Good Lord, and Two Other Plays* (includes *Kean,* based on Alexandre Dumas' play), A. A. Knopf, 1960; Raymond Mount, *The Count of Monte Cristo* (a play for early teenage boys and girls), [Bradford, Connecticut], 1966.

Television: "Solange," General Television Enterprises, 1950; "The Count of Monte Cristo" (series), Vision Productions, 1955-56; "The Count of Monte Cristo," starring Richard Chamberlain, Trevor Howard, and Tony Curtis, Bell System Family Theatre, NBC, January 10, 1975; "The Man in the Iron Mask," starring Richard Chamberlain, Patrick McGoohan, and Louis Jourdan, Bell System Family Theatre, NBC, January 17, 1977.

SIDELIGHTS: **July 24, 1802.** Born in the Rue de Lormet, Villers-Cotterets, a small town in the department of Ainse, France. The name Alexandre Dumas was entered in the official register and in 1813 corrected by the addition of the words Davy de la Pailleterie. "Most of the facts concerning

Drosselmayer and the astrologer had worked unceasingly for three days and nights to clear up this mysterious affair. ■ (From *The Nutcracker of Nuremberg* by Alexandre Dumas. Illustrated by Else Hasselriis.)

my life have been questioned, even my name—Davy de la Pailleterie—which I am not very tenacious about since I never use it except for official deeds.

"My mother—Marie-Louise-Elizabeth Labouret—was the daughter of Claude Labouret, commandant of the National Guard and proprietor of the Hotel del'Ecu. My father was the son of the Marquis Antoine-Alexandre Davy de la Pailleterie, colonel and commissary-general of artillery, who inherited the estate of La Pailleterie which had been raised to a marquisate by Louis XIV in 1707.

"I do not know what court quarrel or speculative motive prompted my grandfather, in about 1760, to leave France, sell his property and establish himself in San Domingo. There he purchased a large tract of land on the western side of the island, and here, on March 25, 1762, my father was born, the son of Louise-Cessette Dumas [a black slave woman] and the Marquis de la Pailleterie.

"But, brought up in the aristocratic circles of Versailles, my grandfather soon found colonial life distasteful, and after his wife's death in 1772 the estate, which she had managed, deteriorated. So he leased it and returned to France in 1780, when my father was eighteen years of age. Soon after this, when he was seventy-four, my grandfather married his housekeeper. The marriage caused an estrangement between father and son. The former tied up his money bags more closely than ever, and the latter soon discovered that life in Paris without money is a sorry one. One day he informed his father he had made up his mind to enlist.

"'In which regiment?' my grandfather demanded.

"'The first that will have me,' replied my father.

"'That is all very fine; but as I am the Marquis de la Pailleterie, a colonel and commissary-general of artillery, I will not permit my name to be dragged through the mire of the lowest ranks of the army.'

"'Then you object to my enlisting?'

"'No, but you must enlist under a different name.'

"'Very well. I will enlist under the name of Dumas.'

"So it was that in 1786 my father enlisted in a regiment of the Queen's Dragoons under the name of Alexandre Dumas. As for the marquis, he died a fortnight later as became a true aristocrat to whom the fall of the Bastille would have been unbearable. His death severed the last tie that bound my father to the aristocracy.

"At twenty-four, my father was as handsome a young fellow as could be found anywhere. Five feet nine inches tall, he was powerfully built, and his open-air life in the colonies had developed his strength and address to an extraordinary degree. He was a veritable gaucho; his skill with sword or pistol was incredible, and his strength became a by-word in the regiment. On several occasions he amused himself in the riding school by placing himself under a beam, grasping it with his arms and lifting his horse off the ground between his legs.

"At the time of his marriage, that is to say in November, 1792, my father was a lieutenant of Hussars. On July 30, 1793, he received his brevet as brigadier-general in the army of the North. On September 3 of the same year he was made a divisional general. Five days later he was appointed general commander-in-chief of the army of the Western Pyrenees. It had taken him only twenty months to rise from a junior officer to one of the highest positions in [Napoleon's] army." [Alexandre Dumas, *My Memoirs,* copyright of this translated edition, A. Craig Bell, 1961, Peter Owen Limited, London.[1]]

February, 1806. Father died. "The following day they broke the news to me.

"'My father is dead?' I repeated. 'What does that mean?'

"'It means, my poor child, that the good God has taken him from you, and that you will never see him again.'

"'Where does the good God live?' I demanded.

"'In heaven.'

"Child though I was, I sensed that something dreadful had befallen me. At the first opportunity I ran home. All the doors were open, there was a depressing atmosphere and one could tell that death was in the house. Unobserved, I slipped into the little room where the firearms were kept. I seized one of the single-barrelled guns my father had promised to give me when I was older and started to climb the stairs. On the way I met my mother, weeping bitterly.

"'Where are you going?' she asked, surprised to see me there.

"'I am going to heaven,' I replied.

"'To heaven! Whatever for?'

"'I am going to kill the good God for killing papa.'

"'Oh, my child!' she cried, 'do not say such dreadful things. We are unhappy enough as it is.'

"I had worshipped my father. Perhaps the love I felt for him was no more than an innocent and overpowering admiration for his herculean stature and physical prowess; perhaps it was only a childish pride in his braided coat, his tricoloured cockade and his large sword which I could scarcely lift. But whatever it was, I recall his every feature, and I love him still as though I had leaned on his strong arm throughout my childhood and early manhood."[1]

1807. "I had learnt to read at a very early age . . . thanks to Madame Darcourt's Buffon, M. Collard's Bible, and, above all, to my mother's kindly pains. During her holidays with us, my sister—who was at a boarding-school in Paris—completed my early education by teaching me to write.

"So at five or six years of age I was very well up in these two accomplishments, and extraordinarily conceited about them. I can still see myself, about the height of a jack-boot, in a little cotton jacket (for, like the Romans I did not leave off the *toga praetexta* until I was fifteen)—I can still see myself, pedantically joining in the conversation of grown-up people, contributing items of sacred or profane learning which I had derived from the Bible or mythology, theories of natural history cribbed from M. de Buffon and M. Daudin, geographical information borrowed from *Robinson Crusoe,* and social and political ideas culled from the sage Idomeneus, founder of Salentum.

"But mythology was my strong point. Not a god or goddess or demi-god, not a single faun or dryad, not a hero was there whose attributes I did not know. Hercules and his twelve labours, Jupiter and his twenty transformations, Vulcan and his thirty-six misfortunes, I had them all at my finger tips, and, what is still more extraordinary, I know them still."[1]

1812. Ran away from home to avoid the Seminary. "I ventured on my first wilful act. I bought a loaf and a sausage with my twelve sous, food to last me two or three days, in fact, and then I went to find Boudoux.

"Boudoux had a calling. He was an expert bird-snarer! When I found him, I unburdened my heart to him, and asked him to hide me for two or three days in one of his huts. Of course he granted my request. His only condition was that, as it was autumn, I ought to take a blanket with me, as the nights were not so warm as they had been.

"I returned home, slipped into my room, took a blanket off my bed, and wrote on a piece of paper:

"'Do not be anxious about me, mother dear, I have run away because I do not want to be a priest.'

"Then I rejoined Boudoux, who had collected his evening food and was waiting for me at the entrance to the park.

"I spent three days and three nights in the forest. At night, I rolled myself in my blanket, and I must own that I slept without any feeling of remorse. By day, I wandered from one pool to another, collecting the snared birds. We took an incalculable number of birds during those three days so that by the third day, the two pools were completely despoiled until the next breeding season.

"Those three days increased my antipathy toward the Seminary, but at the same time it gave me a keen taste for snaring.

"At the end of these three days I left, but I did not dare to go straight to the house. I went to find my good friend Madame Darcourt, and I begged her to announce to my mother the return of her prodigal son, and to smooth the way for my re-entry under her roof.

"Alas! the more prodigal the children, the warmer their reception. When the original prodigal son returned home to his father after three years' absence, they killed a calf; if he had not returned before an absence of six years, they would have killed an ox.

"My mother hugged me to her and called me a bad boy. She promised me that there should be no more talk between us of my going to the Seminary, delighted to think that I should not leave her. She reserved all her wrath for Boudoux, but the first time she saw him, poor as we were, she gave him five francs.

"It was arranged that I should go to the Abbé Grégoire's college in Villers-Cotterets instead of the Seminary. The Abbé Grégoire's school was styled a College, just as in England the illegitimate sons of noblemen are called 'lords.' It is a matter of courtesy."[1]

1814. ". . . My mother took me aside, and, looking at me more seriously than usual, but with as loving a face, said:

Athos took him by the arm, and led him into the garden. ■ (From *Twenty Years After* by Alexandre Dumas. Illustrated by Edy Legrand.)

(From the movie "The Brigand." Released by Columbia Pictures Corp., 1952.)

(From the movie "The Corsican Brothers," starring Douglas Fairbanks, Jr. A Universal Film, released by United Artists, 1941.)

(From the movie "Man in the Iron Mask," starring Louis Hayward. Released by United Artists, 1939.)

(From the movie "The Fighting Guardsman," based on the novel *The Companions of Jehu.* Copyright 1945 by Columbia Pictures Corp.)

"'Your grandfather, the Marquis de la Pailleterie, served under Louis XVI, but your father served under the Republic. Listen carefully now to what I say, for probably your whole future will depend on the decision we are about to take. Would you rather be called Davy de la Pailleterie, like your grandfather, for you are the grandson of the Marquis Davy de la Pailleterie, who was Groom of the Bed-chamber to the Prince of Conti, and Commissary-General of Artillery? In that case we could obtain a commission for you, or you could become one of the pages; and in either case you would have a position made for you in the new reigning family. If you bear the name of the republican, General Alexandre Dumas, no career will be open to you, for instead of serving those who now reign, as your grandfather did, your father served against them . . . M. Collard is going to Paris today. He knows the duc d'Orleans; in fact, he knows many people belonging to the new Court, and he will do his best for you according to your decision. Think carefully before you reply.'

"'Oh! I don't need to think, mother!' I cried—'I will be called Alexandre Dumas, and nothing else. I remember my father; I never knew my grandfather. What would my father think, if I should disown him in order to call myself by my grandfather's name?'

"My mother's face brightened.

"'Is that your opinion?' she said.

"'Yes. And yours too, is it not, mother?'

"'Alas! yes; but what is to become of us?'

"'Let us remember my father's motto: "Deus dedit, Deus dabit—God has given, God will give."'

"'Well then, my child, go off to bed. You aggravate me very much sometimes, but I am sure your heart is in the right place.'

"I went to bed without quite realising the importance of the decision my filial instinct had just prompted me to make, and that, as my mother had warned me, it might very probably mean the shaping of my whole future life.

"Meanwhile, with the approach of my 13th birthday, it was time to make my first Communion, a serious event in the life of a child. I remember that on the eve and day of the ceremony I was wrapped in a haze of emotion. When the Host touched my lips I was so overwhelmed that I burst into tears and fainted.

"It took me several days to recover from this emotional excitement, and when the abbé Grégoire next came to see me I flung myself, crying, into his arms.

"'My dear boy,' he said, 'I would far rather your feelings were less intense, but more lasting.'

"The abbé Grégoire was full of common-sense."[1]

Napolean defeated at Waterloo. "Napoleon's journey through our town dissipated any lingering doubt about the disaster at Waterloo. The mud-bespattered fugitives who had first announced it were but the forerunners of the rest of the army. They all passed through, a motley crowd: first those only slightly wounded or not at all, marching in disorder without drums and weapons; then the more severely wounded who were still able to walk or ride; and last those who had lost arms or legs or had serious body wounds, lying in wagons, some clumsily bandaged, others unbandaged. Every now and then one of them would lift himself up and, waving his blood-stained rags, cry, *'Vive l'-Empereur!'* For many, these were their last words.

"This dismal procession continued for two or three days. Where were all these men being taken? Why was their anguish prolonged by such an exposure to the burning sun, by the jolting of wagons, and by the absence of proper medical attention. Were there so many that all the towns between Waterloo and Villers-Cotterets were filled to overflowing?

"Oh! what a hideous, mad, stupid thing war is, seen divorced from the blaring of trumpets and rolling of drums, the smoke of cannon and the fusillade of guns.

"We could recognise among this debris the remains of those splendid regiments we had seen pass by, so proud, so determined, whose bands had borne witness to their enthusiasm as they marched by playing *'Veillons au salut de l'empire!'*

"Alas! the army was destroyed, and the Empire crushed."[1]

May, 1818. First encounter with a young woman. "Though only a fair dancer, I was first-rate at the waltz. The Spanish girl discovered this at the first round we made, and she gave herself up to it completely, feeling she was being well steered by a good partner.

"'You waltz very well,' she said.

"'You flatter me,' I said, 'up to now I have only had chairs to waltz with.'

"'Chairs?' she asked.

"'Yes, I learnt to waltz the year I took my first communion,' I said, 'and the abbé Grégoire forbade me to waltz with girls; so my dancing-master, thinking I really must hold something in my arms, gave me a chair.'

"My partner stopped short; I thought she would choke with laughter.

"'You really are the funniest boy; I like you very much,' she said, when she could regain her voice . . .

"'Let us waltz again.'

"And we plunged afresh into the whirlpool, which carried us with it.

"This, as I have said, was the first time I danced with a woman; it was the first time I breathed a woman's perfumed breath, or felt her hair touch my cheeks; the first time my eyes had been riveted on bare shoulders or my arm had clasped a round, full, supple waist. I heaved a shuddering sigh of delight.

"'What is the matter with you?' my partner asked, looking at me with her Spanish eyes, which shone even through her lace mantilla.

"I replied, while we waltzed on unceasingly: 'It is far nicer to waltz with you than with a chair.'

The Three Musketeers did not hesitate, therefore, to make a step forward.... ■ (From *The Three Musketeers* by Alexandre Dumas. Illustrated by Edy Legrand.)

Maximilian uttered a cry of joy and, springing forward, seized the beloved hand and imprinted on it a long and impassioned kiss. ■ (From *The Count of Monte Cristo* by Alexandre Dumas. Illustrated by Mead Schaeffer.)

"She escaped out of my arms this time, and went to sit near her friend.

"'Well, what is the matter?' asked Laurence.

"'Oh! my dear, he is so comic.'

"'It is strange, he did not strike me in that light.'

"'That is because you did not waltz with him,' she whispered.

"'I assure you I think him fascinating! Come on,' she continued. . . .

"I had grown much older within the last ten minutes, for it was no longer shame that I felt but sadness. I had stepped into the second circle of human life; I suffered.

"And yet, in spite of this pain, a mysterious hymn, an unknown song, rose from the depths of my soul; that hymn extolled pain, and for the first time cried out to the child, 'Courage! you are a man!'

"The only incontestable reality was that during the last quarter of an hour I had fallen in love.

"I had learnt much during these weeks by watching others, and my next love did not involve me with a sarcastic and sophisticated Parisienne, but with a young girl even shyer than myself, who believed in my assumed courage, and who, like the frog in the fable that jumped in the pond when a frightened hare passed by, was good enough to fear me

and to prove to me that it was possible to find someone more timid than myself. It can be seen how this gave me assurance. The roles were now completely reversed. This time I was the attacker and someone else was on the defensive, and I soon realised that I should perhaps only succeed in breaking down the serious resistance offered me after a long and patient wooing: the citadel was not to be stormed.

"Then began for me those first days, the recollection of which has lasted throughout the whole of my life: that delicious struggle of love, which asks unceasingly and is not discouraged by an eternity of refusal; the obtaining of favour after favour each of which, when gained, fills the soul with ecstasy. . . .'[1]

1820. An important friendship developed. "My meetings with Adolphe were a great event to me. What long walks we took together! How many times did I stop him as he casually spoke of this actor or actress and that, saying, after he had exhausted all the celebrities of the Gymnase, 'And Talma? And Mademoiselle Mars and Mademoiselle Duchesnois?' And he good-naturedly held forth upon the genius and talent and good-fellowship of those eminent artistes, playing upon the unknown notes of the keyboard of my imagination, causing ambitious and sonorous chords to vibrate within me that had hitherto lain dormant, the possession of which astonished me greatly when I began to realise their existence. Then Adolphe little by little conceived a singular idea, which was to make me share, on my own behalf, the hopes he had indulged in for himself; to rouse in me the ambition to become, if not a Scribe, an Alexandre Duval, an Ancelot, a Jouy, an Arnault or a Casimir Delavigne, at least a Fulgence, a Mazére or a Vulpain. And it must be admitted the notion was ambitious indeed; for, I repeat, I had never received any proper education, I knew nothing, and it was not until very much later, in 1833 or 1834, on the Publication of the first edition of my *Impressions de Voyage,* that people began to perceive I had genius. In 1820 I must confess I had not a shadow of it.

"Unluckily, Adolphe was not a very sure guide; he too, was groping blindly."[1]

1822. First trip to Paris. Went to Théâtre Francais and met the great actor, Talma. "The curtain fell to immense applause. I was stunned, dazzled, fascinated. Adolphe proposed we should go to Talma's dressing-room to thank him. I followed him through that inextricable labyrinth of corridors which wind about the back regions of the Théâtre-Francais, and which to-day unfortunately are no longer unknown to me. No client who ever knocked at the door of the original Sylla felt his heart beat so fast and so furiously as did mine at the door of the actor who had just portrayed him. The great actor's dressing-room lay before us: it was full of men whom I did not know, who were all famous or about to become famous, and in the centre of them all—Talma in his simple white robe, just despoiled of its purple, his head from which he had just removed the crown and his two graceful white hands with which he had just broken the Dictator's palm. I stayed at the door, blushing and very humble.

"'We have come to thank you, Talma,' said Adolphe.

"Talma looked round and saw me hovering at the door.

"'Come in,' he said.

"I took two steps towards him.

"'Well,' said he, 'were you satisfied?'

"'I am more than that, monsieur . . . I am wonder-struck.'

"'Very well, you must come and see me again. Ask for more seats.'

"'Alas! Monsieur Talma, I leave Paris to-morrow or the day after at latest.'

"'That is a pity! you might have seen me in *Regulus*. . . . You know I have put *Regulus* on the bill for the day after to-morrow, Lucien?'

"'Yes,' Arnault replied.

"'And can't you stay till the day after to-morrow?'

"'Impossible: I have to return to the provinces.'

"'What do you do in the provinces?'

"'I dare not tell you: I am a lawyer's clerk. . . .'

"And I heaved a deep sigh.

"'Bah! said Talma, 'you must not give way to despair on that account. Corneille was a clerk! Gentlemen, allow me to introduce you to a future Corneille.'

"I blushed to the eyes.

"'Lay your hand on my forehead: it will bring me good luck,' I said to Talma.

"Talma laid his hand on my head.

"'Alexandre Dumas,' he said, 'I baptize thee poet in the name of Shakespeare, Corneille and Schiller! . . . Go back to the provinces, go back to your office, and if you really have a vocation, the angel of Poetry will know how to find you.'

"I took Talma's hand and tried to kiss it.

"'Why, see!' he said, 'the lad has enthusiasm and will make something of himself.' And he shook me warmly by the hand.

"I had nothing more to wait for there. A longer stay in that dressing-room crowded with celebrities would have been both embarrassing and ridiculous. I made a sign to Adolphe, and we left. I wanted to fling my arms round Adolphe's neck in the corridor.

"'Yes, indeed,' I said to him, 'be sure I shall return to Paris. You may depend upon that!' "[1]

Moved to Paris. ". . . I hurried to my little rooms in the Place des Italiens. My waggon-load of furniture was waiting at the door. It took me only an hour to settle my household arrangements, at the end of which all was complete.

"Of a poet's usual equipment I now had an attic; of the possessions of the happy man, I now possessed a loft under the tiles. Better still, I was only twenty! I travelled from the Place des Italiens and the Rue Pigalle in no time. I was longing to tell Adolphe that I was working for the Duc d'Orléans; that I possessed a desk, paper, pens, ink,

ALEXANDRE DUMAS

sealing-wax, in the Palais-Royal; four chairs, a table, a bed and a yellow-papered room in the Place des Italiens."[1]

Conversed with a co-worker in the Duc d'Orléans office.

"'You want to become a man of letters?'

"'Oh, yes!' I exclaimed.

"'Not so loud!' he said, laughing, 'you know I told you not to talk so loudly about it—not here, at any rate. Well, when you do write, don't take the literature of the Empire as your model. That is my advice.'

"'But who shall I look to?'

"'Well, upon my word, I should be much puzzled to tell you. Our young dramatic authors, Soumet, Guiraud, Casimir Delavigne, Ancelot, are talented but carefully note what I say. They merely belong to a period of transition; they are links which connect the past to the future.'

"'And what is the future?'

"'Ah! there, my young friend, you ask me something I can't tell you. The public hasn't made up its mind. It already knows what it doesn't want, but it doesn't yet know what it does.'

"'Well, then, whom ought one to follow?'

"'In the first place, you should never imitate anybody; you should study. The man who employs a guide is obliged to walk behind him. Will you be content to do so?'

"'No.'

(From the movie "At Sword's Point," based on the novel *Twenty Years After,* starring Cornel Wilde. Copyright 1952 by RKO Radio Pictures, Inc.)

(From the movie "The Three Musketeers," starring Walter Able. Copyright 1935 by RKO Radio Pictures Corp.)

(From the movie "The Three Musketeers," starring the Ritz Brothers. Copyright 1939 by Twentieth Century-Fox Corp.)

(From the movie "The Three Musketeers," starring Gene Kelly and Lana Turner. Released by MGM, 1948.)

"'Then you must study. Do not attempt to produce either comedy, or tragedy, or drama; take passions, events, characters, smelt them in the furnace of your imagination, and raise statues of Corinthian bronze.'

"'What you say sounds very fine,' I replied. 'And because it is fine, it ought to be true.'

"'Have you read Æschylus?'

"'No.'

"'Do you know Shakespeare?'

"'No.'

"'Have you read Molière?'

"'Hardly at all.'

"'Well, read all that those three have written. When you have read them, re-read them; when you have re-read them, learn them by heart.'

"'And next?'

"'Next? Pass from them to their successors—from Æschylus to Sophocles, from Sophocles to Euripides, from Euripides to Seneca, from Seneca to Racine, from Racine to Voltaire, and from Voltaire to Chénier, in the realms of tragedy. In this way you will understand what transformed a race of eagles to a race of parroquets.'

"'And from Shakespeare to whom shall I turn?'

"'To Schiller.'

"'And from Schiller?'

"'To no one.'

"'And what about Molière?'

"'As to Molière, if you want to study something that is worth taking trouble over, you must ascend, not descend.'

"'From Molière to whom?'

"'From Molière to Terence, from Terence to Plautus, from Plautus to Aristophanes.'

"'Tell me, what needs to be done in fiction?'

"'Everything, just as in the drama.'

"'But I thought we had some good novelists.'

"'Then you have not read Goethe, or Walter Scott, or Cooper?'

"'No.'

"'Well, read them.'

"'And when I have read them, what shall I do?'

"'Make Corinthian bronze all the time, only try to add something of the ingredient they all lack.'

"'What is that?'

"'Passion. Goethe gives us poetry; Walter Scott character studies; Cooper the vista of prairies, forests and oceans. But it will be in vain that you look for passion among them.'

"'So, one could be a poet like Goethe, an observer like Walter Scott, a descriptive artist like Cooper. But with the addition of a touch of passion . . . ?'

"'Ah! such a man would be almost perfect.'

"'Which are the first three works I ought to read of these masters?'

"'Goethe's _Wilhelm Meister_, Walter Scott's _Ivanhoe_ and Cooper's _Spy_.'

"'I read _Jean Sbogar_ last night.'

"'Oh, that's another story altogether.'

"'What kind is it?'

"'It's a novel of manners. But France is not waiting for that.'

"'What is she waiting for?'

"'She is waiting for the historical novel.'

"'But the history of France is so dull!'

"'How do you know that?'

"I blushed.

"'People have told me it is.'

"'Poor boy! People have told you! Read for yourself and then you will have an opinion.'

"'What must I read?'

"'Why, there is a whole world of it: Joinville, Froissart, Monstrelet, Chatelain, Juvenal des Ursins, Montluc, Saulx-Tavannes, l'Estoile, Cardinal de Retz, Saint-Simon, Villars, Madame de la Fayette Richelieu . . . and so I could go on.'

"'How many volumes do those make?'

"'Probably between two and three hundred.'

"'And you have read them?'

"'Certainly.'

"'And I must read them?'

"'If you wish to write novels, you must not only read them, you must know them off by heart.'

"'Why, you frighten me! I should not be able to write a word for two or three years!'

"'Oh! longer than that, or you will write out of ignorance.'

"'Oh, my God! how much time I've lost!'

Dumas. Drawing by Maurice Leloir. ■ (From *The Three Musketeers* by Alexandre Dumas.)

(From *The Three Musketeers* by Alexandre Dumas. Illustrated by Valenti Angelo.)

"'You must retrieve it.'

"'Oh! I will read and study at night; I will work at the office, and we can talk from time to time. One word more. You have told me what I should study in the drama?'

"'Yes.'

"'In romance?'

"'Yes.'

"'In history?'

"'Yes.'

"'Well, in poetry, whom should I study?'

"'First, whom have you read?'

"'Voltaire, Parny, Bertin, Demoustier, Legouve, Colardeau.'

"'Good! forget the lot!'

"'Really?'

"'Read Homer as representative of antiquity; of the Latin poets, Virgil; of the Middle Ages, Dante. I'm giving you giants' marrow to feed on.'

"'And among the moderns?'

"'Ronsard, Mathurin Regnier, Milton, Goethe, Uhland, Byron, Lamartine, Victor Hugo.'

"'But how can I read foreign authors when I don't know either Greek or English or German?'

"'Good heavens! Why, that's simple enough; you must learn the languages.'"[1]

July 27, 1824. Son born out of wedlock to Dumas and seamstress, Catherine Laboy. Given the name Alexandre.

1825. "[Adolphe] De Leuven and I had valiantly continued to collaborate, but to no avail, so we decided to sacrifice our pride by asking Rousseau's assistance, to polish our works in such a way as would transform their rejection to acceptance. Rousseau was of the school of authors who never worked except to the sound of the popping of corks, without the vision of seething fumes of punch-bowls before their eyes. . . .

"We confided our treasures to him—two melodramas and three comic operas—and arranged to dine with him at Adolphe's rooms on the following Thursday. Conscious of its importance to us, Madame de Leuven herself undertook to supervise the dinner and Rousseau was sent a further, written invitation. At the foot of the letter, we wrote 'There will be two bottles of champagne' and naturally enough, Rousseau arrived.

"He liked neither the melodramas nor the vaudevilles. They were either borrowed from successful novels or built from dull ideas. We might well have been depressed by this opinion, but Adolphe had an idea which supported our courage and soothed our self-respect.

"'He has not read them,' he whispered to me.

"'Quite likely,' I replied.

"This semi-conviction somewhat restored our spirits. At dessert, I told several stories, among them a hunting tale.

"'What do you mean,' exclaimed Rousseau, 'by telling such amusing stories as that and yet stealing melodramas from Bouilly? Why, in that story you have just related, there is a comedietta complete in itself—*la Chasse et l'-Amour.*'

"'Do you think so?' we both exclaimed.

"'Of course I do!'

"'Let us write it then!' we cried in chorus.

"We rang for the servant, who removed the plates, dishes and cloth, leaving only the three glasses; then pens, ink and paper were put on the table, a pen was stuck into my hand, and a third bottle was produced. It was emptied in a quarter of an hour, and by the end of an hour the plan was drawn up. We divided the twenty-one scenes into three parts, of seven scenes each. Mine were to be the first seven, de Leuven's the middle seven, and Rousseau's the last. We arranged to meet again for dinner in a week's time to read the play, which we undertook to complete by then. This was how plays of the old school were composed. *La Chasse et l'Amour* was played on 22 September, 1825. It was an immense success."[1]

1826. "*La Noce et l'Enterrement* was played on 21 November, 1826. My mother and I saw my play from the orchestra. As my name was not mentioned, self-consciousness did not check my satisfaction at watching the performance. The play succeeded admirably. But, even as the Roman emperors, in their days of triumph, were reminded by a slave that they were mortal, so, lest my success should make me drunk, Providence placed a neighbour on my left who remarked as he rose at the fall of the curtain:

"'It isn't stuff like this that will keep the theatre going.'

(From *The Three Musketeers* by Alexandre Dumas. Illustrated by James Daughterty.)

James O'Neill, father of Eugene O'Neill, toured with the play, "The Count of Monte Cristo," for several years.

"He was right, and spoke from experience for he, too, was a dramatist."[1]

1829. "The salaries in the prince's offices generally, were so meagre they were not enough for us to live on, and each of us relied upon some other industry to ameliorate his constant state of penury. Some had married seamstresses who kept little shops; others had shares in livery stables; there were even some who ran cheap restaurants in the Latin quarter, and who substituted the ducal pens at five o'clock for a waiter's serviette. They were not reproached for such activities but rather these were looked upon as quite natural and ordinary. But I, who felt no vocation to marry a shopkeeper, who possessed no capital to invest in the cab trade, who was accustomed to put a serviette on my knees and not over my arm, was looked upon as a criminal because of my attempts to make a living by writing! My salary was stopped because I had had a play accepted by the Comedie-Francaise!

"I was at the theatre, where [*Henry III*] was to be produced the following Saturday, when one of M. Deviolaine's servants came hurrying to me, looking very frightened, to tell me that my mother was ill and unconscious. I rushed from the theatre, sending the property-lad to summon M. Florence, the theatre doctor. He was quickly at my mother's side. She was seated in a large armchair, her eyes open.

She had regained consciousness but could hardly speak. One side of her body was completely paralysed."[1]

Henry III opened. ". . . The enthusiasm was so unanimous that even the Duc d'Orléans himself stood up and called out the name of his employee. . . .

"Few men have been privileged to see such a rapid change in their fortunes as happened to me in the twenty-four hours which followed the performance of *Henri III*. One day, totally unknown, the next, I was the talk of Paris. From that night dated the hatreds of people whom I had never seen, hatreds roused by the unwelcome fame attached to my name. Multitudes of people envied me that night, having no idea that I spent it on a mattress on the floor by my mother's side. Next day, the room was filled with bouquets; I covered my mother's bed with them, and she touched them with the hand she could move, pulling them nearer to her or pushing them away, unconscious what all these flowers meant. . . ."[1]

After a controversial production of *Christine:* ". . . I gave a supper-party for any friends who cared to join me. If we were not fully triumphant at the victory, we were, at all events, excited by the fight. About twenty-five of us were at the supper—Hugo, de Vigny, Paul Lacroix, Boulanger, Achille Comte, Planche, Cordelier-Delanoue, Theodore Villenave—and I know not which others of the youthful band, so full of life and activity, who at that time formed my immediate circle of friends.

"The following incident I am to relate must be unique in the annals of literature. There were some hundred lines in my play which had to be altered, and various cuts which had to be made and dressed by skilful and sympathetic hands. These had to be made that same night, so that the alterations could be put into effect for the following evening. Now it was out of the question that I, with my guests to entertain, could make the amendments, but Hugo and de Vigny took the manuscript, shut themselves up in a small room, and, whilst the rest of us were eating, drinking and singing, they worked on it. For four consecutive hours they toiled as conscientiously as if it had been their own work. When at daybreak they emerged, we were all asleep, so they left the amended manuscript on the mantelpiece, and, without waking anyone, the two rivals went off arm in arm like brothers.

"The next morning we were roused from our lethargy by the bookseller, Barba, who came to offer me twelve thousand francs for the manuscript of *Christine*—that is to say, twice the sum for which I had sold *Henri III*. Unquestionably, the play was a success!"[1]

1830. Revolution. ". . . They were marching on the Tuileries.

"At the same moment the shouting and cries increased in intensity, and from my window I saw thousands of letters and papers fluttering into the Tuileries' garden. It was the correspondence of Napoleon, Louis XVIII and Charles X that they were scattering to the winds. The Tuileries had been taken.

"I rushed downstairs and joined the tail-end of the procession as it entered the Tuileries. On the pavilion in the centre the tricolour had replaced the white standard. The gates of the Carrousel had been forced open and people were pouring in at every door. Many of them were women. A student from the École Polytechnique was being drawn about astride a cannon. Another, with a bullet through his chest, was lying on the staircase. They took him up to the first storey and placed him on the throne.

"During the day tens of thousands of people took turns sitting there. Then they would go to the king's private study, then to his bedroom. The king's bed must have been very unusual. I never knew what went on in that room, but judging from the number of spectators around it and their shouts of laughter, something outrageous must have taken place in it. Perhaps it was a mock marriage of Democracy and Liberty. On and on went the crowd, following those who went ahead and being pushed by those who pressed behind.

"As I entered the library of the Duchesse de Berry I saw a copy of *Christine* bound in purple morocco and stamped with the duchess's arms lying on the table. I thought I had a right to appropriate it. . . ."[1]

March 5, 1831. Daughter, Marie-Alexandrine born out of wedlock to Dumas and Belle Krelsamer. Dumas acknowledge the child by legally giving her his name. At the same time, he acknowledged his son Alexandre which he had neglected to do for seven years. Custody battles ensued over son, Alexandre, involving Catherine Laboy, Belle Krelsamer and Dumas.

May, 1831. *Antony,* starring Marie Dorval, produced and proved to be Dumas' greatest and most innovative theatrical success. Before the production opened he wrote to one of his mistresses. "*Alexandre Dumas to Mèlanie Waldor:* You will find many things in *Antony* which have been taken from our life together, my angel, but they are things which only you and I know. So, what does it matter? The public will make nothing of them, though in us they will wake eternal memories. *Antony,* himself, will, I am pretty sure, be recognized, for he is a madman with a remarkable resemblance to me." [Andre Maurois, *The Titans,* translated from the French by Gerard Hopkins, Harper & Brothers, 1957.[2]]

Vacationed in Trouville. Credited by his contemporaries with discovering and making it a fashionable seaside resort. Returned to Paris. "Carnival time was approaching, and [the] suggestion that I should give a ball, spread throughout the artistic world and was flung back at me from all sides. One of the first difficulties was the smallness of my lodgings, which were too small for a party. A ball would necessitate three or four hundred invitations, and how could I have as many people in a dining-room, drawing-room, bedroom and study? Happily, there were four empty rooms on the same landing, still virgin of all decoration except for mirrors above the chimney-pieces, and blue-grey wallpaper. I asked the landlord for the use of these rooms to which he agreed. Next was the question of decorating them. This was the responsibility of my artist friends and they were quick to offer me their services. The decorators [included] Eugène Delacroix. . . .

"The ball had created a great stir. I had invited nearly all the artists in Paris and those I had forgotten wrote to remind me of their existence. At seven o'clock, Chevet arrived with a fifty-pound salmon, a gigantic pâté and a roebuck roasted whole, served on a silver dish which looked as if it had been borrowed from Gargantua's sideboard. Three hundred bottles of Bordeaux were put down to warm, three

(From *Les Trois Mousquetaires* (*The Three Musketeers*) by Alexandre Dumas. Illustrated by J.A. Beaucé.)

hundred bottles of Burgundy were cooling, five hundred bottles of champagne were on ice.

"At one point, there were seven hundred people present. We had supper at three in the morning in the two rooms of the empty flat which had been converted into a dining-room. Wonderful to relate there was enough to eat and drink for everyone! At nine o'clock in the morning, with music ringing in their heads, they began a final *galop* in the Rue des Trois-Fréres, the head of the procession reaching to the boulevard whilst the tail was still frisking in the courtyard of the square. I have since often thought of giving a second similar ball, but it has always seemed to me that it would be quite impossible.

"I carry about with me—where it comes from I have no idea—an atmosphere of life and excitement which has become proverbial. For three years I lived at Saint-Germain. The inhabitants, respectable subjects of the Sleeping Beauty, no longer recognised themselves. I communicated to the town a spirit of energy which they first took for a sort of epidemic, a contagious fever, such as is produced by the bite of the Neapolitan spider. I bought the theatre, and the best actors of Paris who came to have supper with me, sometimes played, before sitting down to eat, either *Hamlet* or *Mademoiselle de Belle-Isle,* or *Les Demoiselles de Saint Cyr,* for the benefit of the poor. Ravelet had not horses enough, Collinet had not rooms enough, and the railway once admitted to me an annual increase of takings of 20,000 francs since I lived at Saint-Germain. It is also true that, at election time, Saint-Germain considered me too immoral to have the honour of being its representative."[1]

"By **1832** I began to find the theatre absorbed me too much. I had . . . tried to write some short novels which I had had printed at my own expense, and sold at three francs a copy.

"I, who was already a creator of stage-scenes, found in [the histories] a tried and ready-made stage upon which to plan my characters, since all the events took place in the neighbourhood of Paris or in Paris itself. I began to compose my book, driving it before me as a labourer urges forward his plough, without knowing exactly what will result. The climax was *Isabel de Bavière.* As fast as I finished these stories I took them to Buloz, who printed them, and every fortnight the subscribers read them.

"From that time there appeared my two chief qualities, those which will give any value to my books and to my theatrical works in the future; dialogue, which is the backbone of drama and the gift of narrative, which is the foundation of the novel. These qualifications—you know how frankly and unguardedly I talk of myself—I have to a high degree.

"At that period, I had not yet discovered two other qualities in myself, none the less important, which are derived from one another—gaiety and a lively imagination. People are lighthearted because they are in good health, because they have a good digestion, because they have no reason for sadness. That is the reason for cheerfulness in most people. But with me gaiety of heart is persistent, not the lightheartedness which shines through grief. One has a lively imagination because one is lighthearted but this imagination often evaporates like the flame from spirits or the foam on champagne. A merry man, spirited and animated of speech, is often dull and uninspired when alone, pen in hand, in front of a blank sheet of paper. Now work, on the contrary, excites me. Directly I have a pen in my hand, reaction sets in. My most freakish fancies have often sprung out of my dullest days, like fiery lightnings out of a storm. But at this period of my youth, I did not recognise in myself either this imagination or this lightness of spirit."[1]

1832. Cures himself of cholera. "It was the Terror of 1793 on a grand scale. In 1793, the worst days counted their thirty or thirty-five victims. Now, the newspapers admitted to between seven and eight hundred deaths a day! Soon, there was a shortage of coffins. In the terrible steeplechase between death and the coffin-makers, the latter were outdistanced. They wrapped the bodies in tapestries; they rumbled along ten, fifteen, twenty, to the church at once. Many relatives followed the common carts and each knew the number of his own dead and mourned them. A collective mass was said, then they departed for the cemetery, where the bodies were tipped into a common grave and covered with a shroud of lime.

"One night when we had been laughing, talking, spouting verses, playing music, and having supper, I was about to see my friends off when I suddenly felt a slight trembling in my legs. I paid· no attention to it and leant against the banisters, as I shouted a cheerful *au revoir* to my friends. When the sound of their footsteps was lost in the square, I turned to go to my rooms.

"'Oh, monsieur!' Catherine, my maid, said to me, 'how pale you are!'

"'Nonsense, am I really, Catherine?' I said laughingly.

"'Go and look in the mirror, monsieur.'

"I took her advice and looked in the glass. I was, indeed, exceedingly pale. At the same time, I was seized by a fit of violent shivering.

"'It's odd,' I said, 'I feel very cold.'

"'Ah! monsieur,' cried Catherine, 'that's how it begins.'

"'What, Catherine?'

"'Cholera, monsieur.'

"'You think I have cholera?'

"'I'm sure of it, monsieur.'

"'Then lose no time Catherine. Get a lump of sugar, dip it in ether and fetch a doctor.'

"Catherine stumbled against the furniture as she left, and exclaimed:

"'Oh! *mon Dieu!* Master has cholera!'

"Meanwhile, as I felt my strength rapidly failing, I went to bed, I shivered more and more. Catherine returned, the poor girl was nearly out of her mind. Instead of bringing me a lump of sugar dipped in ether, she brought me a wineglassful of it. I hardly knew what I was doing and swallowed a whole ounce of ether at a gulp. I felt that I had swallowed the sword of the Avenging Angel. Chloroform never produced a quicker result. I was unconscious for two hours and when I reopened my eyes, I was in a vapour bath which, with a pipe, my doctor was administering to me beneath the bedclothes, whilst a good neighbour was rubbing me on the top of the sheets with a warming-pan full of embers. I do not know what I shall feel like in hell, but even there I shall never be nearer to roasting than I was that night. For five or six days I was unable, from sheer exhaustion, to put a foot out of my bed. . . ."[1]

October, 1834. Fought a duel with pistols. "After walking for five minutes we found a suitable opening, sheltered from the sun. There were only the final formalities to be arranged by the seconds. Meanwhile, in case anything should happen to me, I gave Bixio the letters intended for my mother. My final injunctions to him were delivered in so simple a manner and in such confident tones, that Bixio took my hand and pressed it, saying:

"'Bravo, dear fellow! I shouldn't have believed you could be so cool in the circumstances.'

"'It's in such situations that I am,' I replied. 'I slept badly the night after M. Gaillardet's provocation, but it is part of my temperament to be less moved by danger the nearer it approaches.'

"'I should very much like to feel your pulse when you are actually confronting one another.'

"'Just as you like—that can easily be done!'

"'We'll see how much faster it beats from excitement.'

"'I would also like to know, as a matter of personal interest.'

"'Do you think you'll hit him?'

"'I'm afraid not.'

"'Try, though.'

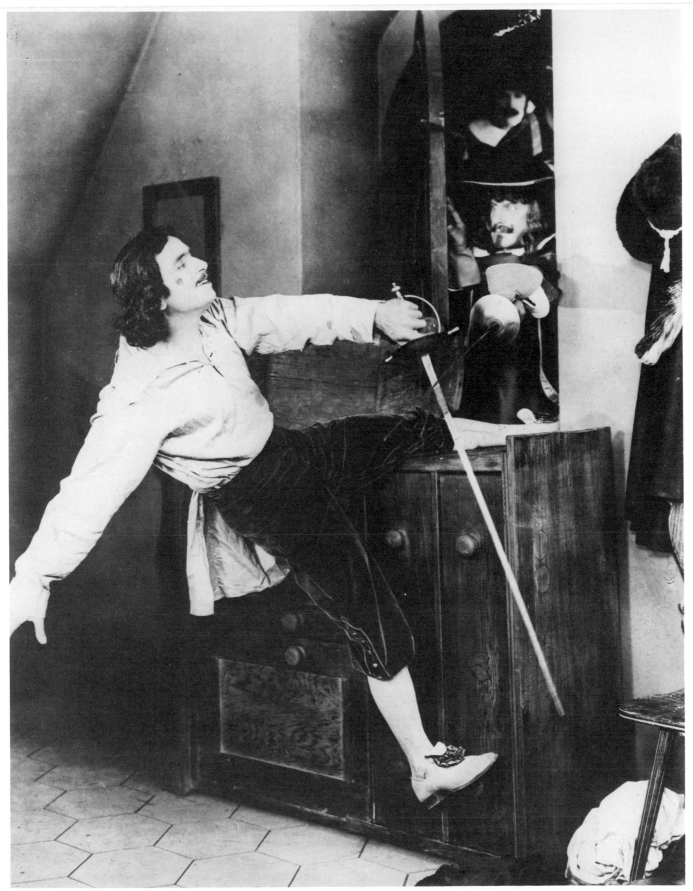

(From the movie "Man in the Iron Mask," starring Douglas Fairbanks, Sr. Released by Elton Co., 1929.)

"'I'll do my best . . . Have you a grudge against him?'

"'Not at all. I don't know him.'

"'Well, then?'

"'Have you read Mérimée's *Le Vase étrusque*?'

"'Yes.'

"'Well, he says that every man killed by a bullet turns round before he falls, and I should like to know if this is true, from the point of view of science.'

"'I shall do my best to gratify your desire.'"[1]

Shots were fired but neither man was injured. "Bixio was twice again my second; but since one of the two duels was with swords, and the other did not take place at all, he had not the chance of ascertaining whether a man wounded or killed by a bullet turns round before he falls. He had to make the experiment himself. In June, 1848, as representative of the people, Bixio was walking with his customary courage by the Panthéon barricade, a bullet, fired from the first floor of a house in the Rue Soufflet, hit him above the collar-bone, ploughed into his right lung, and after penetrating to fifteen to eighteen inches, lodged near the spine. Bixio spun round three times and fell.

"'Now I know one turns round!' he said.

"The problem was solved.

"Towards the end of September I heard of the death of Walter Scott, which made a deep impression on me. Not that I had the honour of knowing the author of *Ivanhoe* and of *Waverley,* but my discovery of that great writer, it will be remembered, much influenced my early writing. Not only had I read all the author's romances, but I had unsuccessfully tried to make two plays out of his works. Walter Scott's qualities are not dramatically suited to the stage. Admirable as a painter of manners, costumes and characters, he was quite incapable of conveying passion. With manners and characters one can concoct comedies, but passion is essential for dramas. Scott's only impassioned romance is *Kenilworth* and it is the only one which is dramatically successful. But my work on Scott had had its uses, although it had not born fruit. One only understands a man's structure by dissection; one only understands the genius of an author by analysis. A similar fidelity to manners, costumes and characters, with more lively dialogue and more natural passions, seemed to me to be what was needed. Such was my conviction, but I was yet far from feeling that I should attempt for France what Scott had achieved for Britain.'"[1]

August 1, 1836. Mother died after second stroke.

1837. Received the Cross of Chevalier, an honor which had been refused his father, General Dumas.

1839. Tried to get elected to Academy, but never succeeded. Wrote to the editor of the *Revue des Duex Mondes:* "'Do mention me in the *Review,* in connection with the Academy, and express wonder that I am not up for election, seeing that Ancelot is. . . .' **January 15th, 1841:** '. . . put a piece about me in your periodical with the Academy in view. I am not on the next list of candidates but feel pretty sure that people are surprised that I am not. . . .'"[2]

Wrote to his old friend Nodier. "Do you think I should stand a chance now? Here's Hugo in, and his friends are all, more or less, mine. . . . If you think there is anything in my suggestion, do, please, climb into the academic rostrum, and say, in my name, to your honourable fellow-members how much I should like to take my seat among them. . . . Mention your good opinion of me, if you have it, and even if you haven't. . . .'"[2]

February 1, 1840. Married Ida Ferrier. Wrote a letter in defense of his proposed marriage to his fourteen-year-old son, Alexandre.

"It is not my fault, but yours, that the relationship between us is no longer that of father and son. You came to my house, where you were well received by everyone, and then, suddenly, acting on whose advice I do not know, decided no longer to recognize the lady whom I regarded as my wife, as should have been obvious from the fact that I was living with her. From that day, since I had no intention of taking advice (even indirectly) from you, the situation of which you complain, began and has lasted, much to my sorrow, for six years.

"It can cease whenever you wish. You have only to write a letter to Madame Ida, asking her to be to you what she is to your sister: you will then be always, and eternally, welcome. The happiest thing that could happen to you is that this liaison should continue, since, having had no child for six years, I am now certain I never shall have any, so that you are now not only my eldest, but my only, son.

"I have nothing else to tell you. All that I would have you consider is this, that, should I marry any woman other than Madame Ida, I might well have three or four more children, whereas with her, I shall have none.

"I trust that in all this you will consult your heart rather than your interests, though this time—contrary to what usually happens—the two are in agreement. I embrace you with all my heart."[2]

When asked by the actor, René Luguet, why he had married Ida he replied: "My dear fellow, I did it to get rid of her."[2]

October 15, 1844. Husband and wife agreed to an amicable separation.

1845. *The Three Musketeers* serialized in the newspaper and Paris is held spellbound. "My first desire is always limitless: my first inspiration is to achieve the impossible. Only when I become infatuated, half through pride and half through love of my art, do I achieve the impossible. How? I will try to tell you, although I do not myself really understand it—by working as no one else works, cutting off all the extraneous details of life and going without sleep. Having discovered a vein of gold in the well of the beginning of the fifteenth century in which I had been digging, I never doubted, so great was my self-confidence, that at each well a century nearer our own times, I should find, if not a vein of gold, at least one of platinum or silver."[2]

Count of Monte Cristo followed. It was an even greater success. He later wrote about his desire to write novels: "I realised what could be achieved for my great and beautiful country—a picturesque and dramatic story of the past, a resurrection of great lives, a kind of last judgement of all who had worn a crown, whether of laurels, of flowers or of

(From the NBC television production of "The Man in the Iron Mask," starring Louis Jourdan and Richard Chamberlain, January, 1977.)

gold. But if I had been dazzled by this historical revelation, I was overwhelmed by the work it imposed on the historian. Yet as I worked my courage strengthened, amidst the doubt and laughter of my friends. When I met someone whom I had not seen for some time, he would say to me:

"'So it's you!'

"'Well, what's surprising in that?'

"'I thought you were dead.'

"'Why?'

"'Because you haven't been writing.'

"'Who told you that?'

"'Why, nobody is talking about you.'

"'I've written a book.'

"'Ah yes! Your *Travels in Switzerland*. I read that. It was very funny. You're a fine joker.'

"'Why?'

"'Would you have me believe you ate bear's flesh and caught trout with a bill-hook?'

"'Of course, there is absolutely nothing else in my book, I suppose. But I'm writing a history now.'

"'*You* writing a history!'

"'Why not?'

"'Stick to the theatre, my dear fellow; you know you are a dramatist to your fingertips.'

"'Does it follow that because I am essentially a dramatist I should write nothing but drama? Is nothing dramatic outside the stage, and can't one write a dramatic novel?'

"'A novel! You want to write a romance in the style of Walter Scott?'

"'Why not?'

"But then my interlocutor would shake his head.

"'Walter Scott has depicted localities, characters, manners. You must take the novel from Walter Scott's hands, as Raphael took art from Perugino's, and add the passions. But if I were you, I would stick to the theatre.'

"'Let me try, at least.'

"So my questioner would leave me with a shrug of his shoulders, as much as to say, 'There goes another lost soul!'"[1]

July 25, 1848. Built chateau called "Monte Cristo." Six-hundred guests were invited to the housewarming. Food catered by the famous restaurant, Pavillon IV.

1851. *The Lady of the Camelias* written by his son, Alexandre, about his tragic love affair with a famous courtesan, had a tremendous success. "*Dumas* père to *Dumas* fils: My

dear friend: I spent all yesterday evening with Madame Pasca, talking of you, of your success, of your laurels, of your curtain-calls, of Madame Doche's talent, of Fechter's genius. That is all splendid. Madame Pasca tells me that you have been twice to see Morny. Get him to give you the cross: once you've got it no one can take it away from you. The practical advantage I see in all this is that a certain quantity of pennies will come your way which will enable you to get washed such small quantities of dirty linen as you may have. If the amount turns out to be considerable, give the hundred francs I send you (by way of the rue d'Enghien) to the rue de Laval."[2]

January 20, 1852. Filed petition in absentia and was declared bankrupt. "*Alexandre Dumas to Auguste Maquet:* I want you to help me so far as your means will allow. In order to settle my business with Madame Dumas I have been compelled to sell the whole contents of my house, though it is my intention to buy back what I can. Can you disentangle your thousand francs from *Siècle,* and get a further thousand from your father or from Kopp; then use those two thousand to purchase certain objects which I will detail to you? Since the objects in question must be moved from the house, I want you to take them to Bougival (whence I will withdraw them). . . ."[2]

His extravagant lifestyle, generosity to friends and hangers-on caused him to spend more than the fortunes he made. One day when he finally had to leave the 'Chateau,' Dumas offered two small plums on a plate to a friend, who took one and swallowed it. "'You've just eaten a hundred thousand francs,' said Dumas.

"'A hundred thousand francs?'

"'Yes, those two small plums were all I had left of Monte Cristo. . . .'"[2]

From exile in Brussels, he wrote to the publisher, Marchant: "What would you say to an immense novel beginning with Jesus Christ and ending with the last man of creation, divided into five separate episodes: one under *Nero,* one under *Charlemagne,* one under *Charles IX,* one under *Napoleon,* and one set in the future? . . . The principal characters are to be: The Wandering Jew, Jesus Christ, Cleopatra, the Fates, Prometheus, Nero, Poppaea, Narcissus, Octavia, Charlemagne, Rolland, Vittikind, Velleda, Pope Gregory VII, King Charles IX, Catherine de Medicis, the Cardinal of Lorraine, Napoleon, Marie-Louise, Talleyrand, the Messiah, and the Angel of the Cup. I suppose this sounds mad to you, but ask Alexandre, who knows the work from end to end, what he thinks."[2]

Began to write memoirs in Brussels.

1853. Returned to Paris and started a newspaper called *The Musketeer.*

August 14, 1857. Son, Alexandre, decorated. "*Dumas* père to *Dumas* fils: My dear boy: three days ago, I received your cross, and, with it, authority to bestow on you the title of chevalier. When you get back I shall embrace you even more lovingly than usual, if that be possible, and the ceremony shall be gone through.

"I find my subjects in my dreams, my son takes his from real life. I work with my eyes shut, he with his open. I draw, he photographs. What Alexandre produces is not so much literature as music. One notices only bars, and, now and again, a few words."[2]

The Musketeer folded.

1858. Traveled through Russia. Wrote his son: ". . . I took my leave of Prince Tumaine by rubbing noses with him, which is the Kalmuck way of saying 'Yours for life.' . . .

"I had to leave the Kalmuck prince, the Kalmuck princess, the Kalmuck sister, the Kalmuck ladies-in-waiting. I tried to rub noses with the princess, but was told that that form of politeness is for use only between men. I left with a sad heart."[2]

1860. A bitter lawsuit developed between Dumas and his ex-collaborator. "*Dumas* père to *Dumas* fils, *Naples, December 29th, 1860:* Maquet is a man with whom I can have no further dealings. I trusted him, and what did he do? He got himself paid *directly*, and not through me, for one-third of *Hamlet*, on which he had done no work, and for two-thirds of *The Musketeers*, and kept every penny for himself. In my eyes he is no better than a thief.

"My works belong to me, and have cost me dear, in all conscience. They are the property of you and your sister, and, to make sure that there shall be no doubt about their ownership, *I intend to make them over to you by deed of sale* in which no money will be involved except the registration fee. But so long as I live, friend Maquet shall have no further contact with me or with my books."[2]

1864. Continued to write plays, novels, books about his travels. When the censor arrested his production of *The Mohicans of Paris,* he wrote to the Emperor: "Sire, there were in 1830, and there still are today, three men at the head of French literature. These three men are: Victor Hugo, Lamartine, and myself. Victor Hugo is exiled; Lamartine is ruined. I cannot be exiled like Hugo; nothing in my writings, in my life or in my words lends itself to proscription. But I can be ruined like Lamartine, and, in effect, I am being ruined. I do not know what malevolence animates the censor against me. I have written and published twelve hundred volumes. It is not for me to appreciate their literary value. Translated into all languages they have gone as far as steam can carry them. Though I am the least worthy of the three, these works have made me the most popular in the five parts of the world, perhaps because the first is a thinker, the second is a dreamer, while I am, myself, only a vulgarizer. Of these twelve hundred volumes there is not one that might not be safely placed in the hands of the most republican workman of the Faubourg Saint-Antoine or read by a young girl of the Faubourg Saint-Germain, the most modest of our faubourgs.

"And yet, Sire, to the eyes of the censor I am the most immoral man who ever existed. During the last twelve years the censor has successively halted:

"*Isaac Laquedem,* sold for eighty thousand francs to the *Constitutionnel.*

"*La Tour de Nesle,* after eight hundred performances (the veto has lasted seven years).

"*Angèle,* after three hundred performances (the veto has lasted six years).

ALEXANDRE DUMAS

"*Antony,* after three hundred and fifty performances (the veto has lasted six years).

"*La Jeunesse de Louis XIV,* which has been played only to foreigners and which was to be played at the Théâtre-Francais.

"*La Jeunesse de Louis XV,* received at the same theater.

"Today the censor has arrested *Les Mohicans de Paris,* which was to have been played next Saturday. He will probably halt also, under pretexts more or less specious, *Olympe de Clèves* and *Balsamo,* which I am writing at this moment. I do not complain any more for *Les Mohicans de Paris* than I do for the other dramas; only I would call Your Majesty's attention to the fact that during the six years of the reign of Charles X and during the eighteen years of the reign of Louis-Phillippe I have never had a play interdicted or suspended, and I add, always to Your Majesty alone, that it appears to me unjust to make a single dramatic author lose half a million francs while encouragement and support are extended to so many who do not merit this name.

"I appeal, then, for the first time and probably for the last, to the Prince whose hand I had the honor to shake at Arenenberg, at Ham, and at the Elysée, and who, having found me a devoted adherent on the road to exile and prison, has never found me a place-seeker on that of the Empire."

[Herbert Gorman, *The Incredible Marquis: Alexandre Dumas,* Farrar & Rinehart, 1939.[3]]

Concerned about the value of his work he started to re-read his earlier novels: "Each page reminds me of a day gone by. I am like one of those trees with bushy foliage filled with birds. They are silent at noon, but wake towards the end of the day. When evening comes they people my old age with song and the beating of wings."[2]

1869. Spent the summer at Roscoff in Brittany writing a *Dictionary of Cooking* which was published after his death.

1870. Partly paralyzed as a result of a stroke, he said to Alexandre who was taking care of him: "It has been fifty years since I came to Paris with a single louis. Why have they accused me of prodigality? I have always kept it, that louis. See, it is there."[3]

December 5, 1870. Died without suffering.

He wrote in his memoirs: "One after the other I took the works of men of genius, such as Shakespeare, Molière, Corneille, Calderon, Goethe and Schiller, laid them out as bodies on a dissecting table, and, scalpel in hand, spent whole nights in probing them to the heart, endeavouring to trace their sources of life and the secret of the circulation of their blood. Eventually, I discovered with what admirable science they galvanised nerve and muscle into life, and by what skill they modelled the differing types of flesh that were destined to cover the one unchangeable human framework of bone. For man does not invent. God has given the created world into his hands and left him to apply it to his needs. Progress simply means the daily, monthly and ever-lasting conquest of man over matter. Each individual as he appears on the scene takes possession of the knowledge of his fathers, works at it in different ways, and dies when he has added one more ray to the sum of human knowledge, one more star in the Milky Way!"[1]

FOR MORE INFORMATION SEE: Harry A. Spurr, *Life and Writings of Alexandre Dumas,* F. A. Stokes, 1902, reprinted, Haskell House, 1973; Francis Gribble, *Dumas: Father and Son,* Nash & Grayson, 1930, reprinted, R. West, 1973; F. W. Reed, *A Bibliography of Alexandre Dumas, Pere,* J. A. Neuhuys, 1933; G. R. Pearce, *Dumas Pere,* Duckworth, 1934, reprinted, R. West, 1973; Bernard Newman, *In the Trail of the Three Musketeers,* H. Jenkins, 1934, reprinted, R. West, 1973; Elizabeth Rider Montgomery, *Story behind Great Books,* McBride, 1946; Beatrice Jackson Fleming and Marion Jackson Pryde, *Distinguished Negroes Abroad,* Associated Publishers, 1946; Joel A. Rogers, *World's Great Men of Color,* The Author, 1947; A. Craig Bell, *Alexandre Dumas: A Biography and Study,* Cassell, 1950, reprinted, R. West, 1973.

Edith Saunders, *Prodigal Father: Dumas Pere et Fils and the Lady of the Camellias,* Longmans, Green, 1951; William A. DeWitt, *Illustrated Minute Biographies,* Grosset & Dunlap, 1953; Andre Maurois, *Alexandre Dumas: A Great Life in Brief* (translated from the French by Jack Palmer White), A. A. Knopf, 1955; Maurois, *Titans: A Three-Generation Biography of the Dumas'* (translated from the French by Gerard Hopkins), Harper, 1957, reissued, Greenwood Press, 1971; Alexandre Dumas, *My Memoirs,* edited and translated by A. C. Bell, P. Owen, 1961, reissued, Greenwood Press, 1975; Brian Doyle, editor, *Who's Who of Children's Literature,* Schocken Books, 1968; Richard S. Stowe, *Alexandre Dumas, Pere,* Twayne, 1976.

DALE FIFE

FIFE, Dale (Odile) 1910-

PERSONAL: Born August 24, 1910, in Toledo, Ohio; daughter of Herman and Mary (Ehret) Hollerbach; married Frank Fife, June 10, 1929 (deceased); children: Duncan. *Religion:* Catholic. *Home:* 764 Edgewood Rd., San Mateo, Calif. 94402. *Agent:* Curtis Brown, 575 Madison Ave., New York, N.Y. 10022.

CAREER: Author of children's books.

WRITINGS—All juvenile, except as noted; all published by Coward, except as noted: *Weddings in the Family* (adult fiction), Farrar, Straus, 1956; *The Unmarried Sister* (adult fiction), Farrar, Straus, 1958; *A Stork for the Belltower,* 1964; *Who's in Charge of Lincoln?,* 1965; *The Fish in the Castle,* 1965; *Cross a Narrow Bridge,* 1966; *A Dog Called Dunkel,* 1966; *The Boy Who Lived in the Railroad Depot,* 1968; *Joe and the Talking Christmas Tree,* 1968; *Bluefoot,* Lothrop, Lee & Shepard, 1967; *What's New, Lincoln?,* 1970; *Adam's ABC,* 1971; *What's the Prize, Lincoln?,* 1971; *Ride the Crooked Wind* (Junior Literary Guild selection), 1972; *Who Goes There, Lincoln?,* 1973; *The Little Park,* Whitman, 1973; *Imagine That?,* Ginn & Co., 1974; *Who'll Vote for Lincoln?,* 1976; *North of Danger,* Dutton, 1978. Contributor to periodicals.

They gathered in the darkness. Bunky had some details. Officer Roberts was calling the parents of the boys who were caught. He'd heard him say so. ■ (From *Who Goes There, Lincoln?* by Dale Fife. Illustrated by Paul Galdone.)

SIDELIGHTS: Fife commented that she always does research in the area that she's writing about. Her latest book, *North of Danger,* took her to Norway and to Spitsbergen, a group of islands north of Norway in the Artic Ocean. She has traveled extensively in Alsace, France, Germany, other areas of Europe, South America, and Mexico for research for her books.

Fife also draws upon her experiences at various Paiute reservations in Nevada. There she observed Indian students in reservation classrooms and visited the boarding school where fifty Indian tribes were represented. Her research on Indians for the book, *Ride the Crooked Wind,* was extensive and the book itself was, according to Fife, the most difficult work that she has ever written.

Fife's works are included in the Kerlan Collection at the University of Minnesota.

HOBBIES AND OTHER INTERESTS: Gardening, cooking, bridge.

FOR MORE INFORMATION SEE: Horn Book, June, 1964, December, 1965; Doris de Montreville and Elizabeth D. Crawford, editors, *Fourth Book of Junior Authors and Illustrators,* H. W. Wilson, 1978.

FRANCHERE, Ruth

PERSONAL: Born in Mason City, Iowa; daughter of H. Verne and Celta (Huffman) Myers; married Hoyt Catlin Franchere (an author), 1928; children: Julie (Mrs. E. Hugh Hinds, Jr.). *Education:* Graduated from the University of Iowa, 1930. *Home:* Lake Oswego, Oregon.

CAREER: Author of books for young people. Has taught English at the University of Oregon, University of Washington, and Portland State University. *Member:* Author's Guild, Author's League of America.

WRITINGS: Willa (illustrated by Leonard Weisgard), Crowell, 1958; *Stephen Crane: The Story of an American Writer,*

At first Cesar stayed at home with the other small children. But as soon as he was old enough he helped, too. He pulled weeds and carried water. ■ (From *Cesar Chavez* by Ruth Franchere. Illustrated by Earl Thollander.)

Crowell, 1961; *Jack London: The Pursuit of a Dream,* Crowell, 1962; *Hannah Herself,* Crowell, 1964; *The Travels of Colin O'Dae* (illustrated by Lorence Bjorklund), Crowell, 1966; *Stampede North,* Macmillan, 1969; *Tito of Yugoslavia,* Macmillan, 1970; *Cesar Chavez* (illustrated by Earl Thollander), Crowell, 1970; *Carl Sandburg: Voice of the People* (illustrated by Victor Mays), Garrard, 1970; *Westward by Canal,* Macmillan, 1972; *The Wright Brothers* (illustrated by Louis Glanzman), Crowell, 1972.

SIDELIGHTS: Franchere's first published piece of writing was *Willa,* a biography of Willa Cather. "A book with charm

RUTH FRANCHERE

for adults familiar with Miss Cather's novels, it should also interest younger readers . . . as the adventures of a lively, independent, imaginative heroine," wrote a critic for the *Chicago Sunday Tribune.* One of Franchere's later biographies, *Carl Sandburg: Voice of the People,* was reviewed by *Commonweal,* which said, "This first full biography of Carl Sandburg for young people will fill a real need . . . it is written by a gifted poetic writer . . . who understands Sandburg's unique combination of melancholy and hopefulness. . . ."

HOBBIES AND OTHER INTERESTS: Travel, swimming, and gardening.

FOR MORE INFORMATION SEE: Horn Book, 1969.

GARD, Robert Edward   1910-

PERSONAL: Born July 3, 1910, in Iola, Kan.; son of Samuel Arnold and Louisa Maria (Ireland) Gard; married Maryo Kimball, June 7, 1939; children: Maryo Gwendolyn, Eleanor Copeland. *Education:* University of Kansas, B.A., 1934; Cornell University, M.A., 1938. *Address:* 3507 Sunset Dr., Madison, Wis. 53705.

CAREER: Instructor, University of Kansas, Lawrence, Kan., 1934-37, Cornell University, Ithaca, N.Y., 1940-43; University of Wisconsin, Madison, Wis., assistant professor, 1945-48, associate professor, 1948-55, professor, 1955—; Duell, Sloan & Pearce, New York, N.Y., field director, 1958-60; writer. Director of the New York State Playwriting Project, 1938-43, and of the Alberta, Canada Folk-

lore and Local History Project, 1943-45; participant in the Survey of Cultural Arts, Great Britain, 1953; trustee of the National Theatre Conference, 1958-62, and of the Foundation of Integrated Education, 1961—; Fulbright professor, University of Helsinki, 1959-60, visiting professor, 1963; U.S. delegate to the World Theatre Congress, Vienna, Austria, 1961; president, Wisconsin House Publications, Madison, Wis., 1969; co-founder, Dale Wasserman Professional Playwright Development Laboratory, Madison, Wis., 1976.

MEMBER: National Theatre Conference, American Educational Theatre Association, American National Theatre and Academy, Wisconsin Academy of Sciences, Arts, and Letters (president, 1976-77), Wisconsin Arts Foundation and Council (president, 1957-59), Wisconsin Regional Writers Association (president, 1961-64), Pi Kappa Alpha. *Awards, honors:* Service award, Department of Speech, University of Kansas, 1958; Gold Medal of Honor from the Finnish Theatre, 1961; distinguished service award from the International Institute of Milwaukee, 1964; Governor's award for creativity, 1967; Wisconsin local history award; citation from the Wisconsin Academy of Sciences, Arts, and Letters.

WRITINGS: Raisin' th' Devil: A Comedy of Schoharie County, American Agriculturist, 1940; (editor with Alexander M. Drummond) *The Lake Guns of Seneca and Cayuga, and Eight Other Plays of Upstate New York,* Cornell University Press, 1942, reprinted, Kennikat, 1972; *Johnny Chinook: Tall Tales and True from the Canadian West* (legends), Longmans, Green, 1945, new edition, C. E. Tuttle, 1967; *Wisconsin Is My Doorstep: A Dramatist's Yarn Book of Wisconsin Lore* (legends), Longmans, Green, 1948; (with A. M. Drummond) *The Cardiff Giant,* Cornell University Press, 1949; *Midnight: Rodeo Champion* (juvenile; illus-

ROBERT EDWARD GARD

trated by C. W. Anderson), Duell, Sloan, 1951; *Grassroots Theater: A Search for Regional Arts in America*, University of Wisconsin Press, 1955; *A Horse Named Joe* (juvenile; illustrated by C. W. Anderson), Duell, Sloan, 1956; *Scotty's Mare* (juvenile; illustrated by Aaron Bohrod), Duell, Sloan, 1957; (contributor) David H. Stevens, editor, *Ten Talents in the American Theatre*, University of Oklahoma Press, 1957; *The Big One*, Duell, Sloan, 1958; *Run to Kansas* (juvenile; illustrated by Alan Moyler), Duell, Sloan, 1958; (with Gertrude S. Burley) *Community Theatre: Idea and Achievement*, Duell, Sloan, 1959, reprinted, Greenwood Press, 1975.

(With Leland G. Sorden) *Wisconsin Lore, Antics, and Anecdotes of Wisconsin People and Places*, Duell, Sloan, 1962; *Devil Red* (juvenile; illustrated by Richard W. Lewis), Duell, Sloan, 1963; *The Error of Sexton Jones*, Duell, Sloan, 1964; (with Spencer A. Gard) *The Early Background of the Gard Family in America*, [Iola, Kan.], 1965; (with David Semmes) *America's Players*, Seabury Press, 1967; (with Marston Balch and Pauline B. Temkin) *Theater in America: Appraisal and Challenge for the National Theatre Conference*, Dembar Educational Research Services, 1968; (with L. G. Sorden) *The Romance of Wisconsin Place Names*, October House, 1968; *This Is Wisconsin*, Wisconsin House, 1969; (with others) *The Arts in the Small Community: A National Plan*, [Madison, Wis.], 1969; (with Helen O'Brien) *Act Nine: Plays for Youth*, Wisconsin House, 1970; *University Madison, U.S.A.*, Wisconsin House, 1970; *Down in the Valleys: Wisconsin Back Country Lore and Humor*, Wisconsin House, 1971; *Wild Goose Marsh: Horicon Stopover*, Wisconsin House, 1972; (editor with Elaine Reetz) *The Trail of the Serpent: The Fox River Valley* (legends), Madison House, 1973; *Wisconsin Sketches* (edited by Mark E. Lefebvre), Wisconsin House, 1973; (with Allen Crafton) *A Woman of No Importance* (novel), Wisconsin House, 1974; *Wild Goose Country: Horicon Marsh to Horseshoe Island*, Wisconsin House, 1975; (editor with others) *We Were Children Then: Stories from the Yarns of Yesteryear Project*, Wisconsin House, 1976; (with Maryo Gard) *My Land, My Home, My Wisconsin*, Milwaukee Journal, 1978; *An Innocence of Prairie*, R. Bruce Allison, 1978.

SIDELIGHTS: Born in Kansas and later lived in Canada. Gard has been regional writer-in-residence at the University of Wisconsin since 1967 and director of the Wisconsin Idea Theatre, a state-wide project, at the University where he has taught since 1945. He is an all-round exponent of what he calls American "grassroots theatre. . . . The knowledge and love of place is a large part of the joy in people's lives. There

(From *Wisconsin Is My Doorstep* by Robert E. Gard. Illustrated by Frank Utpatel.)

must be plays that grow from all the countrysides of America, fabricated by the people themselves, born of their happiness and sorrow, born of toiling hands and free minds, born of music and love and reason. There must be many great voices singing out the lore and legend of America from a thousand hilltops, and there must be students to listen and to learn, and writers encouraged to use the materials." [Robert Gard, "Grassroots Theatre," *Theatre Arts*, September, 1955.[1]]

In reviewing Robert Gard's *Wisconsin Is My Doorstep: A Dramatist's Yarn Book of Wisconsin*, a *San Francisco Chronicle* critic observed: "*Wisconsin Is My Doorstep* is a collection of Wisconsin Folk Tales old and new. They are cast in a remarkably readable dramatic form that is closer to radio script than any other recognizable type of composition. In them, the author has retained the spirit and aim of folklore, which is to divert and often to amuse the audience. . . ."

Gard's contributions to children's literature includes *Midnight: Rodeo Champion*, which was reviewed by a *New York Herald Tribune Book Review* critic: "The style is crisp and authentic, the rodeo lore fascinating, the characterization excellent, and the illustrations by an expert [C. W. Anderson]."

FOR MORE INFORMATION SEE: San Francisco Chronicle, May 30, 1948; *New York Herald Tribune Book Review*, May 13, 1951; *Theatre Arts*, September, 1955, August, 1959, April, 1961.

GARNER, Alan   1934-

PERSONAL: Born in 1934, in Cheshire, England; children: five children. *Education:* Received education at local schools; attended Magdalen College, Oxford. *Home:* Blackden, Holmes Chapel, Cheshire, England.

CAREER: Author. *Military service:* Spent two years in the Royal Artillery; became a lieutenant. *Awards, honors: The Owl Service* won the Carnegie Medal in 1967, and the Guardian Award in 1978; Lewis Carroll Shelf Award, 1970, for *The Weirdstone of Brisingamen*.

WRITINGS: The Weirdstone of Brisingamen: A Tale of Alderley, Collins, 1960, published in America as *The Weirdstone: A Tale of Alderley*, F. Watts, 1961, revised edition, H. Z. Walck, 1969, Collins, 1979; *The Moon of Gomrath*, H. Z. Walck, 1963, Collins, 1979; *Elidor*, H. Z. Walck, 1965, Collins, 1979; *Holly from the Bongs*, Collins, 1966; *The Old Man of Mow* (illustrated by Roger Hill), Collins, 1967, Doubleday, 1967; *The Owl Service*, H. Z. Walck, 1967, Collins, 1979; (editor) *A Cavalcade of Goblins* (illustrated by Krystyna Turska), H. Z. Walck, 1967 (published in England as *The Hamish Hamilton Book of Goblins*, H. Hamilton, 1969); *Red Shift*, Macmillan, 1973; *The Breadhorse*, Collins, 1975; *The Guizer*, Greenwillow Books, 1976; *The Stone Book*, Collins, 1976; *Tom Fobble's Day*, Collins, 1977; *Granny Reardun*, Collins, 1977; *The Aimer Gate*, Collins, 1978; *The Golden Brothers*, Collins, 1979; *The Girl of the Golden Gate*, Collins, 1979; *The Golden Heads of the Well*, Collins, 1979; *The Princess and the Golden Mane*, Collins, 1979.

SIDELIGHTS: ". . . Everything I say *about* writing is with hindsight. At the time there are conflicting emotions—usually there is only one emotion and that is to get the thing finished. The second emotion is not to think at all but to

ALAN GARNER

modern-day settings. Garner was once quoted as saying, "The more I learn, the more convinced I am that there are no original stories: originality now means the personal colouring of existing themes."

Garner's widely acclaimed novel, *The Owl Service,* is an example that subscribes fairly well to his theory. "Mr. Garner's story is remarkable not only for its sustained and evocative atmosphere, but for its implications. It is a drama of young people confronted with the challenge of moral choice; at the same time it reveals, like diminishing reflections in a mirror, the eternal recurrence of the dilemma with each generation," wrote a reviewer for *Children's Book World.* A critic for *Christian Science Monitor* commented, "In a daring juxtaposition of legend from the *Mabinogion,* and the complex relationship of two lads and a girl, old loves and hates, are, as it were, re-enacted. Mr. Garner sets his tale in a Welsh valley and touches with pity and terror the minds of the reader who will let himself feel its atmosphere. This is not a book 'for children'; its subtle truth is for anyone who will reach for it."

HOBBIES AND OTHER INTERESTS: Archaeology and the history and folklore of Cheshire.

FOR MORE INFORMATION SEE: Brian Doyle, editor, *Who's Who of Children's Literature,* Schocken Books, 1968; *Horn Book,* October, 1968, October, 1969, February, 1970, December, 1976; John Rowe Townsend, *A Sense of Story: Essays on Contemporary Writers for Children,* Longman, 1971; Doris de Montreville and Donna Hill, editors, *Third Book of Junior Authors,* H. W. Wilson, 1972; Justin Wintle and Emma Fisher, *The Pied Pipers: Interviews with the In-*

stop everybody else making a noise so I can listen to the voices in my head. To listen to the story and watch it happening internally. That's as far as *that* goes, but after the event and probably before the event of writing, there is a very strong busker I-say-I-say-I-say feeling. I do want to stop people and grab them by the lapels.

". . . I mentioned a busker. I believe very strongly in declaring one's hand straight away . . . usually on the first page. I think if you compare all the books, you'll see they have on their first page the essence of style, plot—the indefinable quality that I know is in the book, is put on the first page. So that the reader can say 'I want to turn over' or 'I don't think it's worth going beyond the first page.'

"I think that to mess around with the question of writing for children all day would get me nowhere. There is probably a link between the twenty years—twenty-two years nearly now—that I have done nothing else but write and the first ten years of my life when I did very little but lie in bed. It is possibly a compensation for the loneliness of an only child who was paralysed. I am being very wise after the event now. But my interior world of childhood had no other criterion to measure it by, therefore I did not feel that what was happening to me was unusual. However, it was up to me to talk to myself. Now that may have resulted in my writing for children. It's the only intelligent thought I have on the subject. [Aidan Chambers, "An Interview with Alan Garner," *Signal,* The Thimble Press, #27, September, 1978.[1]]

Garner's writings have been strongly influenced by ancient legends, particularly the *Mabinogion,* a collection of old Welsh tales. The author's educational background plus his motivation to do extensive research for his books have resulted in stories that successfully weave folklore with

"I'm not the illiterate, yez'll understand. I can put a letter together with the best of them. Oh, yes. But it's a terrible night I've had. A terrible night." ■ (From *Elidor* by Alan Garner. Illustrated by Charles Keeping.)

fluential Creators of Children's Literature, Paddington Press-Two Continents Publishing, 1975; Margery Fisher, *Who's Who in Children's Books,* Holt, 1975; Aidan Chambers, "An Interview with Alan Garner," *Signal,* #27, The Thimble Press, September, 1978.

GRAHAM, Eleanor 1896-

PERSONAL: Born in 1896, in Walthamstow, London, England; daughter of P. Anderson Graham (editor of *Country Life* magazine). *Education:* Studied at North London Collegiate School for Girls.

CAREER: Author, editor, and reviewer of books for children. Early jobs included work in a London bookstore, 1927-30, where she was head of the children's department, work in a publishing house, 1930, and in a children's library. Selector and secretary of the Junior Book Club, 1934-38; editor of Penguin Books' "Puffin Story Books," 1941-62; editor of Methuen's children's books, 1943-57. Her reviews of children's books have appeared in *The Bookman, Sunday Times, Junior Bookshelf,* and *The Times Literary Supplement. Awards, honors:* Eleanor Farjeon Award, 1973.

WRITINGS: The Night Adventures of Alexis (illustrated by Winifred Langlands), Faber & Gwyer, 1925; *High Days and Holidays: Stories, Legends, and Customs of Red-Letter Days and Holidays* (illustrated by P. M. Ellingford), E. Benn, 1932, published in America as *Happy Holidays: Stories, Legends, and Customs of Red-Letter Days and Holidays,* Dutton, 1933; *Six in a Family* (illustrated by Alfred Sindall), [London], 1935; *Change for a Sixpence,* University of London Press, 1937; *When the Fun Begins,* University of London Press, 1937; *Christmas in Old England,* Silver Burdett, 1938; *The Children Who Lived in a Barn* (illustrated by J. T. Evans), Routledge, 1938, reissued, Penguin Books, 1975.

The Making of a Queen (Victoria at Kensington Palace), J. Cape, 1940; *Favorite Nursery Tales* (illustrated by Rachel Taft Dixon), Wonder Books, 1946; (adaptor) *Famous Fairy Tales: Jack and the Beanstalk, The Fisherman and His Wife, The Real Princess, and Hansel and Gretel* (illustrated by Mervin Jules), Wonder Books, 1946; (adaptor) *Bedtime Stories: Cinderella, Snow White, The Emperor's New Clothes, and Why the Sea Is Salt* (illustrated by Masha, pseudonym of Marie Stern), Wonder Books, 1946; *Head o'Mey* (illustrated by Arnold Bond), E. Benn, 1947; *The Story of Charles Dickens* (illustrated by Norman Meredith), Methuen, 1952, Abelard-Schuman, 1954; *The Story of Jesus* (illustrated by Brian Wildsmith), Hodder & Stoughton, 1960, Penguin Books, 1961, revised edition, Penguin Books, 1971; *J. M. Barrie's Peter Pan: The Story of the Play* (illustrated by Edward Ardizzone), Scribner, 1962; *Kenneth Grahame,* H. Walck, 1963.

Editor: *Welcome Christmas!* (illustrated by Priscilla M. Ellingford), E. Genn, 1931, Dutton, 1932; *A Puffin Book of Verse* (illustrated by Claudia Freeman), Penguin Books, 1953; *A Puffin Quartet of Poets: Eleanor Farjeon, James Reeves, E. V. Rieu, and Ian Serraillier* (illustrated by Diana Bloomfield), Penguin Books, 1958; *A Thread of Gold: An Anthology of Poetry* (illustrated by Margery Gill), Bodley Head, 1964, Books for Libraries, 1969; Robert Herrick, *The Music of a Feast,* Bodley Head, 1968. Also general editor, "Puffin Story Books" series, Penguin Books, 1941-62.

...The horses were loaded up and tied mane to tail so that they should not stray off the path. ■ (From *Head O'Mey* by Eleanor Graham. Illustrated by Arnold Bond.)

SIDELIGHTS: Graham came naturally into the book business. Her father, P. Anderson Graham, had been the editor of *Country Life* magazine for the first quarter of this century. When she was in her early thirties Graham joined Bumpus' famous bookshop in London as the head of the children's department. By the 1930's she had become a regular reviewer of children's books for *The Bookman* and the *Sunday Times* and had written several of her own books for children. One of her most memorable stories, *The Children Who Lived in a Barn,* was published in 1938. That same year she left her four year post as selector and secretary of the Junior Book Club.

In 1941 she became the editor of the paperback series of "Puffin Story Books" for Penguin Books, a post she held for over twenty years. In 1943 she became the editor of Methuen's children's books as well and held this position until her resignation in 1957.

After retiring from active publishing she still regularly reviews children's books for various publications and is considered a foremost authority on the subject. In 1973, at the age of 78, the author, editor, and reviewer was awarded the Eleanor Farjeon award by the Children's Book Circle (the members are children's book publishers).

The reviews of Eleanor Graham's *The Story of Charles Dickens* were very complimentary. The *Chicago Tribune* said, "It is difficult to see how anybody could produce a better life of Charles Dickens for young readers than Eleanor Graham has written. . . . Her book is saner and better balanced than many studies of Dickens intended for adult readers, and she is free of condescension toward subject and audience alike." *New Statesman & Nation* commented, "To a generation that may not know his works, this is a fascinating 'success' story. . . . Miss Graham's admirably told story is illustrated by some of the original Phiz and Cruikschank drawings." *Horn Book* added, "Covering Dickens' life from his seventh year, this straightforward biography will serve well to introduce him to young readers. . . . Its special merit is the clear revelation of specific influences of his own life on his writing. . . . Miss Graham's style is lively; her treatment of Dickens' family and friends and their effect on his career has depth." The *New York Times* said, "Miss Graham's approach is warm, sympathetic, but never sentimental—which is an achievement in itself. Her emphasis upon the social significance of Dickens' work is especially valuable."

One of Eleanor Graham's more recent books was a retelling of J. M. Barrie's play for children, *Peter Pan*, in story form. Of *Peter Pan: The Story of the Play*, a *Library Journal* critic commented, "In many ways [her] rewriting has even more immediacy for today's reader; it is less stilted and more clearly defines Peter's personality. Conversely, it lacks the economy in use of words of the original. Typical Ardizzone sketches and full-color plates maintain the British flavor."

FOR MORE INFORMATION SEE: Brian Doyle, editor, *Who's Who of Children's Literature*, Schocken Books, 1968.

GRETZER, John

EDUCATION: Attended the University of Omaha and the Kansas City Art Institute.

CAREER: Artist and illustrator of books for children. Art director for a Philadelphia publishing firm. *Military service:* U.S. Coast Guard, combat artist during World War II.

ILLUSTRATOR: G. Sentman, *Drummer of Vincennes*, Winston, 1952; Phyllis A. Whitney, *Mystery of the Black*

...Before their eyes, bearded human heads, bleeding and grimacing in the agonies of death, moved toward the stronghold. ■ (From *The Beggar King of China* by Dale Carlson. Illustrated by John Gretzer.)

Diamonds, Westminster Press, 1954; Betty Cavanna, *Touch of Magic,* Westminster Press, 1961; Molly Cove, *A Promise Is a Promise,* Houghton, 1964; S. Garst, *Hans Christian Andersen: Fairy Tale Author,* Houghton, 1965; Edna Beiler, *White Elephant for Sale,* Friendship Press, 1966; Ruth Harnden, *Summer's Turning,* Houghton, 1966; M. Cove, *The Other Side of the Fence,* Houghton, 1967; Robert Newman, *Grettir the Strong,* Crowell, 1968; Myra Scovel, *How Many Sides to a Chinese Coin?,* Friendship Press, 1969; Elizabeth G. Baker, *Stronger than Hate,* Houghton, 1969; Constance B. Hieatt, *The Knight of the Cart,* Crowell, 1969.

Bruce Mosher and Dottie Mosher, *How Do You Spell TV,* Friendship Press, 1970; Thomas Fall, pseudonym of Donald C. Snow, *Jim Thorpe,* Crowell, 1970; Bianca Bradbury, *The Loner,* Houghton, 1970; Dale B. Carlson, *Warlord of the Genji,* Atheneum, 1970; D. B. Carlson, *The Beggar King of China,* Atheneum, 1971; Ruth C. Carlson, *Sometimes It's Up,* Houghton, 1971; Evelyn S. Lampman, *Once upon the Little Big Horn,* Crowell, 1971; Teri Martini, *The Lucky Ghost Shirt,* Westminster Press, 1971; P. A. Whitney, *Mystery of the Scowling Boy,* Westminster Press, 1973; Sonia Levitin, *Roanoke,* Atheneum, 1973; R. C. Carlson, *Half-Past-Tomorrow,* Houghton, 1973; Alvin L. Ben-Moring, *Balthazar, the Black and Shining Prince,* Westminster Press, 1974; Mary Calhoun, *The Horse Comes First,* Atheneum, 1974; Mary Kay Phelan, *The Burning of Washington: August 1814,* Crowell, 1975; R. Newman, *The Shattered Stone,* Atheneum, 1975.

HOLLAND, Janice   1913-1962

PERSONAL: Born May 23, 1913, in Washington, D.C. *Education:* Studied art at Corcoran School of Art in Washington, D.C., and at Pratt Institute, School of Illustration, Brooklyn, New York. *Home:* Washington, D.C.

CAREER: Author and illustrator of books for children.

WRITINGS—All self-illustrated: *They Built a City: The Story of Washington, D.C.,* Scribner, 1953; *Pirates, Planters, and Patriots: The Story of Charleston, South Carolina,* Scribner, 1955; *Christopher Goes to the Castle,* Scribner, 1957; *The Apprentice and the Prize,* Vanguard Press, 1958; *Hello, George Washington!,* Abingdon, 1958; (adapter) *You Never Can Tell* (adapted from *The Book of Huai-nan-tzu*), Scribner, 1963.

Illustrator: Janette S. Lowrey, *Rings on Her Fingers,* Harper, 1941; Frances Cavanagh, *Our Country's Story,* Rand McNally, 1945; Mary Alice Jones, *Bible Story of the Creation,* Rand McNally, 1946; Maria C. Chambers, *Three Kings,* Oxford University Press, 1946; Andrew Lang, *Yellow Fairy Book,* Longmans, Green, 1948, reissued, McKay, 1966; Catherine C. Coblentz, *Blue Cat of Castle Town,* Longmans, Green, 1949, reissued, Countryman Press, 1974; Alberta P. Graham, *Christopher Columbus, Discoverer,* Abingdon, 1950; Siddie Joe Johnson, *Cat Hotel,* Longmans, Green, 1955; Lillian Quigley, *The Blind Men and the Elephant,* Scribner, 1959.

ADAPTATIONS—Filmstrip and record: "The Blind Men and the Elephant," a Miller-Brody Production.

SIDELIGHTS: "From the time I can remember, I aspired to be an artist—probably because my mother had such ambitions and sacrificed them for marriage. I always hoped I would illustrate children's books, but I attended a fine arts

(From *The Blue Cat of Castle Town* by Catherine Cate Coblentz. Illustrated by Janice Holland.)

school where all forms of commercial art were discouraged. For a while I accepted this view and devoted myself to water color paintings of landscapes and figures. However, the pursuit of a fine arts career ceased to attract me when I found my ideals were very different from those of the leading fashions in the fine arts. It was then I went for a few months to Pratt Institute with the idea of entering the illustration field. I had come, in the meantime, to feel that the vital arts of this period are in the commercial field. The truth is that most of the great art of the past was in its time commercial, or commissioned work, whether portrait or triptych. I saw that the limitation on the excellence of an illustration was not one imposed by the fact that it was a commissioned work, or even by the exigencies of reproduction, but the only limitation was the vision of the artist himself.

"At the time I did my first illustrations for children I knew very little about children or children's books, my background being wholly artistic. However, after many years in the field, I have learned that to work for a child audience is

the greatest of opportunities. Children are more interested and single-minded in giving themselves to what they read. I'm also convinced that children seek truth instinctively, and I'm dedicated to the old adage that 'Beauty is truth, truth, beauty.' Insofar as I am able, I try to give them these two things." [Lee Kingman and others, *Illustrators of Children's Books: 1957-1966,* Horn Book, 1968.[1]]

They Built a City: The Story of Washington was reviewed by a *Horn Book* critic who said, "The history of our nation's capital is invitingly presented for children in this informal account with a generous and colorful accompaniment of pictures. It is the story of famous landmarks and of men responsible for important developments, from Captain John Smith's visit in 1608, Washington's choice of the site, and L'Enfant's plan for the city, to notable buildings and memorials of later days." The *New York Times* added, "The colorful illustrations and maps should have brought a pleasant unity to this book, but too many pictures and sub-headings makes for typographical confusion. The result is a moderately attractive book instead of one with exceptional appeal.''

Of *Pirates, Planters and Patriots: The Story of Charleston, South Carolina, Horn Book* wrote, ''In brief text and striking pictures Miss Holland tells the story of her 'favorite city' from 1670 to the present day. She has skillfully selected episodes that are important and also of interest to children; and her illustrations are varied, as life in different parts of the city varies. They have been given beautiful color reproduction on most attractively designed pages. An introduction to Charleston that makes the reader want to know far more about the city.''

The *Chicago Tribune* described *Christopher Goes to the Moon* as, ''. . . a truly, good exciting story of a young boy learning to become a knight. It is also a book giving many facts and wonderful pictures of life as it actually was in the days of castles with moats and drawbridges, and shining knights in armor. . . .'' The *New York Times* commented, ''It's a simple, easy story, distinguished more for its information and sentiment than for its style.'' *Horn Book* added, ''. . . Ample drawings, in four colors, give clear detail, two large ones being labelled to point out parts of the castle and trappings of the Duke and his horse in full regalia.''

Kirkus called *Apprentice and the Prize* a ''sensitive, credible miracle story which grows out of historical background with charm and ease.'' The *Chicago Tribune* commented, ''Gentleness and love and the feel of Renaissance Italy are beautifully and simply expressed in story and illustrations.'' *Horn Book* added, ''The sincerity and fundamental idealism of this story make the gentle moral very natural. The backgrounds of Assisi and the country around, the festivals of Saint Francis, and the studio of the master sculptor are well integrated, and the pencil drawings emphasize the atmosphere and feeling of the story.''

Before her death, Janice Holland adapted and illustrated an old Chinese folktale translated as *You Never Can Tell*. The *New York Herald Tribune* called it, ''A philosophy of patience with a tinge of fatalism in it is embodied in the ancient Chinese tale retold here in picture-book format.'' *Horn Book*'s comments included, ''In her adaptation of this ancient Chinese legend, Janice Holland has retained its essential simplicity and philosophical wisdom. With a true storyteller's perfect economy of word and phrase, she tells a tale which gently teaches that 'sorrows sometimes bring their blessings . . .' and that 'joys many times bring their sorrows. . . . You never can tell.' The pictures in soft, mellow colors are restrained but eloquent.''

FOR MORE INFORMATION SEE: Lee Kingman and others, compilers, *Illustrators of Children's Books, 1957-1966*, Horn Book, 1968.

(Died, 1962)

HONIG, Donald   1931-

PERSONAL: Born August 17, 1931, in Maspeth, Long Island, N.Y.; son of George and Mildred (Elson) Honig; married Sandra Schindlinger (an M.B.A. candidate and marketing professional), July 11, 1965; children: Catherine Rose. *Residence:* Cromwell, Conn. *Agent:* Theron Raines, 244 Madison Ave., New York, N.Y.

CAREER: Professional writer. *Member:* Dramatists Guild, Authors League. *Awards, honors:* New York State Council of the Arts grant, 1972; Connecticut Commission on the Arts grant, 1974.

WRITINGS: Sidewalk Caesar (novel), Pyramid Books, 1958; *Walk Like A Man* (novel), Morrow, 1961; *Divide the Night* (novel), Regency Books, 1961; (editor) *Blue and Gray: Great Writings of the Civil War,* Avon, 1961; *No Song to Sing* (novel), Morrow, 1962; (editor) *Short Stories of Stephen Crane,* Avon, 1962, McGraw, 1967; *The Adventures of Jed McLane,* McGraw, 1967; *Jed McLane and Storm Cloud,*

So what he done was get behind the left-side mule and wind up with one foot and give that mule a kick square on the rump. It was such a kick like you never saw. It must've gone clear to the mule's head and lighted a memory of what it should have been doing and as if to make up for not doing it the mule and its partner suddenly lit off. ■ (From *The Journal of One Davey Wyatt* by Donald Honig. Illustrated by Sam Fink.)

McGraw, 1967; *Frontier of Fortune*, McGraw, 1967; *Jed McLane and the Stranger*, McGraw, 1968, Dell, 1976.

In the Days of the Cowboy, Random House, 1970; *Up from the Minor Leagues*, Cowles, 1970; *Dynamite*, Putnam, 1971; *Johnny Lee*, McCall Publishing, 1971; *Judgment Night*, Belmont Books, 1971; *The Journal of One Davey Wyatt*, Watts, 1972; *The Love Thief*, Belmont Books, 1972; *An End of Innocence*, Putnam, 1972; *Way to Go Teddy*, Watts, 1973; *The Severith Style*, Scribner, 1972; *Illusions*, Doubleday, 1974; *Playing for Keeps*, Watts, 1974; *Breaking In*, Watts, 1974; *The Professional*, Watts, 1974; *Coming Back*, Watts, 1974; *Fury On Skates*, Four Winds Press, 1974; *With the Consent of the Governed: Conversations with Eight U.S. Senators*, Dell, 1975; *Baseball: When the Grass Was Real*, Coward, 1975; *Baseball Between the Lines*, Coward, 1976; *Hurry Home*, Addison, 1976; *Running Harder*, Watts, 1976; *Going the Distance*, Watts, 1976; *Winter Always Comes*, Four Winds, 1977; *I Should Have Sold Petunias*, Jove Books, 1977; *The Man in the Dugout*, Follett, 1977; *The October Heroes*, Simon & Schuster, 1978.

Author with Leon Arden of play, "The Midnight Ride of Alvin Blumm," first produced in 1966. Contributor of one hundred and seventy stories and articles to various trade publications.

HORNBLOW, Leonora (Schinasi) 1920-

PERSONAL: Born in 1920, in New York City; married Arthur Hornblow (a film producer and writer); children: one son. *Home:* Los Angeles, Calif.

CAREER: Author. Has also written for magazines and newspapers. *Member:* Authors Guild.

WRITINGS: Memory and Desire, Random House, 1950; *The Love-Seekers*, Random House, 1957; *Cleopatra of Egypt* (illustrated by W. T. Mars), Random House, 1961;

LEONORA HORNBLOW

These huge reptiles live to a very old age. One is known to have lived for more than 152 years.
■ (From *Reptiles Do the Strangest Things* by Leonora and Arthur Hornblow. Illustrated by Michael K. Frith.)

(editor with Bennett Cerf) *Bennett Cerf's Take Along Treasury,* Doubleday, 1963; (with husband, Arthur Hornblow) *Birds Do the Strangest Things* (illustrated by Michael W. Frith), Random House, 1965; (with A. Hornblow) *Fish Do the Strangest Things* (illustrated by M. K. Frith), Random House, 1966; (with A. Hornblow) *Insects Do the Strangest Things* (illustrated by M. K. Frith), Random House, 1968; (with A. Hornblow) *Reptiles Do the Strangest Things* (illustrated by M. K. Frith), Random House, 1970; *Prehistoric Monsters Did the Strangest Things* (illustrated by M. K. Frith), Random House, 1974.

SIDELIGHTS: Leonora Hornblow was born in New York, a city to which she is addicted, although she lives in Los Angeles, California, with her husband, motion picture producer Arthur Hornblow, Jr., and their son Michael.

Hornblow has written since she was seven years old. Her first book, *Memory and Desire,* was published when she was thirty. In 1965 she and her husband wrote *Birds Do the Strangest Things,* which spelled the beginning for an entire series of books for children. The following year *Fish Do the Strangest Things* was published. Three other books for the popular children's series were created by the Hornblow team.

The author insists that she has no hobbies, unless reading all kinds of books, even cookbooks, can be considered a hobby. She does enjoy browsing through antique and stationery stores. In the future she hopes to write a play, live in a home on the Hudson River, and own a pet monkey.

HOULEHEN, Robert J.   1918-

PERSONAL: Born June 2, 1918, in Milwaukee, Wis.; son of John J. (a city health inspector) and Alvina E. (Bensel) Houlehen; married Marian E. McCuen (a preschool teacher), August 18, 1945; children: Patrick, Michael and Kathleen (twins), Barry. *Education:* University of Wisconsin, B.A., 1941. *Politics:* Democrat. *Religion:* Unaffiliated. *Home:* 5423 North Santa Monica, Milwaukee, Wis. 53217. *Office:* Allis-Chalmers Corp., Corporate Public Relations Dept., Box 512, Milwaukee, Wis. 53201.

CAREER: Milwaukee Journal, Milwaukee, Wis., reporter, 1945-54; Allis-Chalmers Corp., Milwaukee, Wis., general editor for corporate public relations, 1954—. Evening teacher at University of Wisconsin-Milwaukee, 1960-62, and Milwaukee Area Technical College, 1962—, University of Wisconsin-Milwaukee Extension, 1972—. *Military service:* U.S. Army Air Forces, 1941-45. *Member:* Authors Guild, Wisconsin Raconteurs, Wisconsin Council of Writers, Milwaukee Press Club, Milwaukee Council: Boy Scouts.

WRITINGS: Way to a Scout's Heart, BSA, 1965; (with Elvajean Hall) *Battle for Sales,* Lippincott, 1973; *Jobs in Manufacturing,* Lothrop, 1973; *Jobs in Agribusiness,* Lothrop, 1974. Author of hundreds of detailed technical articles and four tape series for use in schools.

WORK IN PROGRESS: Let's Get Organized, a textbook.

SIDELIGHTS: "I'm rather an unusual person to appear as a writer of young people's books, because I'm a factual writer. Yet, during seventeen years as a Scoutmaster, Cubmaster and other boy-level posts in Scouting, I also became a story teller. And even in these I drew on my extensive adventures in other parts of the world.

Like an airplane pilot, the crane operator soars up and down the production shops. ■ (From *Jobs in Manufacturing* by Robert J. Houlehen. Photo by Harnischfeger.)

"My daily work is chiefly preparation of extensive articles for the trade press of the world, all very factual, and preparation of news materials for the same. In my evening classes (three of them) I teach the skills of communication . . . real skills, not literary skills. Yet, I also coach other writers in planning and development of their own books and articles. Every year I conduct at least one private class in practical writing, ranging from reports to articles, papers and books.

"I'm not the kind of a person who invents a book, then looks for a publisher. My personal work has always been done by request; publishers who know me make suggestions. My teaching tape series arose this way and so did my career books.

"Supported by my family, I'm an inveterate camper, which is one reason I spent so much time in Scouting. Incidentally, I found that my communication skills paid off in Scouting, because I adapted or created dozens of forms, instructions, how-tos for use of my own troop and for all troops in the Milwaukee BSA Council. Many are still in use.

"Incidentally, my youngest son is definitely following in Dad's footsteps and at sixteen is a prolific, mature writer. And my oldest son, an executive chef, is planning a book on a cooking subject."

HOYLE, Geoffrey   1942-

PERSONAL: Born January 12, 1942, in Scunthorpe, Lancashire, England; son of Fred (a scientist and author) and Barbara (Clark) Hoyle; married Valerie Jane Coope (an accountant), April 21, 1971. *Education:* Attended St. John's College, Cambridge, 1961-62. *Home:* 11 Carlyle Rd., Cambridge CB4 3DN, England.

CAREER: Worked in documentary film production, 1963-67; novelist, 1967—.

WRITINGS—Novels, with father, Fred Hoyle: *Fifth Planet,* Harper, 1963; *Rockets in Ursa Major,* Harper, 1969; *Seven Steps to the Sun,* Harper, 1970; *The Molecule Men,* Harper, 1971; *Inferno,* Harper, 1973; *Into Deepest Space,* Harper, 1974.

For children: *2010: Living in the Future,* Parents' Magazine Press, 1972; *Disaster,* Heinemann, 1975.

HOBBIES AND OTHER INTERESTS: Motor racing, skiing, target-shooting.

You could spend all day watching comics, but it wouldn't be a good idea. ■ (From *2010 Living in the Future* by Geoffrey Hoyle. Illustrated by Alasdair Anderson.)

GEOFFREY HOYLE

HYNDMAN, Robert Utley 1906?-1973 (Robert Wyndham)

PERSONAL: Born about 1906; married wife, Jane Andrews Hyndman (a children's writer under pseudonym Lee Wyndham, and writing instructor), 1933 (died March 18, 1978); children: William Lee, Jane Elizabeth. *Home:* Morristown, N.J.

CAREER: Author, lecturer, editor, and critic. Has edited and rewritten more than 40 books; was also a guest lecturer at New York University.

WRITINGS—All under pseudonym Robert Wyndham: (With wife Jane Hyndman, under pseudonym Lee Wyndham) *The Little Wise Man* (illustrated by Anthony D'-Adamo), Bobbs-Merrill, 1960; (compiler with L. Wyndham) *Tales from the Arabian Nights,* Whitman, 1965; (compiler) *Chinese Mother Goose Rhymes* (ALA Notable Book; illustrated by Ed Young), World Publishing, 1968; (with Ernest Schlee Millette) *The Circus That Was: The Autobiography of a Star Performer,* Dorrance, 1971; (compiler) *Tales the People Tell in China* (illustrated by Jay Yang), Messner, 1971; *Enjoying Gems: The Lure and Lore of Jewel Stones* (illustrated by Robert Maclean), Greene, 1971.

SIDELIGHTS: Hyndman was born in the mountains of south-eastern Kentucky where his father was treasurer of a coal mine. His early years combined intensive studies at Smith Academy with instrumental and vocal training as a boy-soprano soloist in Episcopal choirs. Then, at Washington University in St. Louis, he earned his way by singing baritone roles for four seasons in light and grand opera in the famous Muny Opera Company. . . . Later, when he moved to New York, he sang professionally in various choirs to pay for further schooling.

His writing career began as an authors' representative in a New York agency located in the Flat Iron Building on lower Fifth Avenue. There he met his wife-to-be then a secretary and model. The depression era was not the best of times for agents—or writers, so he tried other fields. For a time he was chief recording engineer for the Wurlitzer Music Corporation, and then for G. Schirmer, where he supervised the master recordings for thirty-two independent record companies, and recorded many of the greats of the music and theater world, along with musicals which have become classics.

But the writing urge was always there and Hyndman had already started editing and rewriting back in his agency days. Calls for this kind of work increased through the years.

About his original creations, rewrites and editorial projects, Hyndman said, "I've done biographies, medical career books, sports stories, book condensations, historicals, novels and juveniles dealing with a wide variety of topics. Of course, I also have a whack at my wife's books, while she stands there and *screams!* and she whacks away at my writings—while I *roar.* But our marriage has survived happily the slings and arrows to which authorship is subject, and we can honestly say we're busy at the writing profession that we love."

The Hyndmans lived in a rambling white house in the hills of northern New Jersey, on a small rural road. "We try to keep 'progress' at bay, so the air is still fresh and our brook clean—most of the time. Deer wander through our orchard in the winter, pheasants feed under our bird-feeders, and we have occasional visits from 'coons, skunk, possums, squirrels, and chipmunks. Our latest and greatest thrill is hearing the exquisite singing of some new arrivals to our area—mocking birds—who serenade us at two or three o'-clock in the morning, when we take a break from our work in our separate studies."

Hyndman died at his Morristown, New Jersey home on May 24, 1973 at the age of sixty-seven. In 1973-1974, the Robert Wyndham Memorial Scholarship was transferred from the Cooper Hill (Vermont) Writers Conference to the Hofstra (New York) Writers Conference.

FOR MORE INFORMATION SEE: Horn Book, April, 1966, December, 1971. Obituaries: *Publishers Weekly,* June 11, 1973.

(Died May 24, 1973)

JONES, Elizabeth Orton 1910-

PERSONAL: Born June 25, 1910, in Highland Park, Ill.; daughter of George Roberts (a musician) and Jessie Mae (Orton) Jones. *Education:* University of Chicago, Ph.B., 1932; Ecole des Beaux Arts, Fontainebleau, France, diploma, 1932; School of the Art Institute of Chicago, student, 1932. *Residence:* Mason, N.H.

CAREER: Author, artist, and illustrator. Received commissions to do murals for the Crotched Mountain Center, Greenfield, N.H., and University of New Hampshire Library. Her works have been exhibited in numerous galleries, including O'Brien Galleries, Chicago, and the Smithsonian Institution. *Member:* New Hampshire Art Association, Cambridge (Mass.) Art Association, Delta Kappa Gamma. *Awards, honors:* Charles Muller Prize, Chicago Society of Etchers, 1939; Caldecott Medal, runner-up, 1944, for *Small*

(From *Prayer for a Child* by Rachel Field. Pictures by Elizabeth Orton Jones.)

Rain: Verses from the Bible, and winner, 1945, for *Prayer for a Child;* M.A., Wheaton College, 1955.

WRITINGS—All self-illustrated: *Ragman of Paris and His Ragamuffins,* Oxford University Press, 1937; (with Thomas Orton Jones) *Minnie the Mermaid,* Oxford University Press, 1939; *Maminka's Children,* Macmillan, 1940, reissued, 1968; *Twig,* Macmillan, 1942, reissued, 1966; *Big Susan,* Macmillan, 1947, reissued, 1967; (reteller) *Little Red Riding Hood,* Simon & Schuster, 1948; *How Far Is It to Bethlehem?,* Horn Book, 1955. Also author and editor of the *Mason Bicentennial Book, 1768-1968.*

Illustrator: Bible, *David,* Macmillan, 1937; Gladys L. Adshead, *Brownies—Hush!,* Oxford University Press, 1938, reissued, Walck, 1966; Cornelia Lynde Meigs, *Scarlet Oak,* Macmillan, 1938; Association for Childhood Education (International), *Told under the Magic Umbrella: Modern Fanciful Stories for Young Children,* Macmillan, 1939, reissued, 1967; Mabel Leigh Hunt, *Peddler's Clock,* Grosset, 1943; (her mother) Jessie Mae Jones, editor, *Small Rain: Verses from the Bible,* Viking, 1943, reissued, 1974; Rachel Field, *Prayers for a Child,* Macmillan, 1944, reissued, 1973; Eleanor Farjeon, *Prayer for Little Things,* Houghton, 1945; J. M. Jones, *Secrets,* Viking, 1945; J. M. Jones, editor, *Little Child: The Christmas Miracle Told in Bible Verses,* Viking, 1946; J. M. Jones, editor, *This Is the Way: Prayers and Precepts from World Religions,* Viking, 1951; St. Francis of Assisi, *Song of the Sun,* Macmillan, 1952; Elizabeth Bridgman, *Lullaby for Eggs,* Macmillan, 1955; Robbie Trent, *To Church We Go,* Follett, 1956.

SIDELIGHTS: **June 25, 1910.** Born in Highland Park, Illinois. Jones' father, George Roberts Jones, was a musician. As a child she grew up in an environment filled with music and literature and began to write and draw stories at an early age.

"During all the years of my childhood there were Bohemians in our home—Mamie, who cooked for us. Pantsy, our nurse, and, later Maria came from the Old Country which, by then, was part of Czechoslovakia." [From an article entitled "Printer's Life Is the Life for Me!" by Elizabeth Orton Jones, *Imprint: Oregon,* Volume I, University of Oregon Library, 1974.[1]]

1932. Received a Ph.B. from the University of Chicago. Jones studied art in France for a year where she received a diploma from the Ecole des Beaux Arts.

1937. First book, *Ragman of Paris and His Ragamuffins,* was published. The author relied heavily on her year in Paris for the material and illustrations in the book. "... *Ragman of Paris* ... grew, story and all, out of my own experience. During a time of loneliness after returning from a wonderful year in Paris, studying painting, I began writing and drawing certain things and feelings I wanted to keep. [It] wasn't a book I *decided* to do, exactly. It was a need which turned into a book."[1]

Spring, 1940. Having illustrated half a dozen books for children since *Ragman of Paris,* Jones left her home in Illinois to work on illustrations for her new book, *Maminka's Children,* which was to be published by the Macmillan Company. In New York she worked under the tutelage and inspiration of the Glasers, printers of children's books who were considered among the best in their field. "I was in New York. I had come to finish my book, *Maminka's Children,* scheduled for fall publication. I had worked on the illustrations many

weeks in my studio at home in Highland Park, Illinois, had completed the key drawings and sent them on to my editor, Doris S. Patee of the Macmillan Company. The key drawings were being photographed in the usual manner, to be reproduced in half-tone. The color would be done separately by a process which required my presence at the printers.

"The printers were Mr. and Mrs. William C. D. Glaser (Bill and Lillian). Their work, much in demand at that time, particularly for children's books, featured a special process of drawing on grained plate glass with a very hard pencil—which produced results comparable to printing from lithographic stones in the European tradition. As a matter of fact, two artists with European training and background, Willy Pogany and Miska Petersham, had aided and advised Bill Glaser in the working out of this process. Offset lithography was used rather than the traditional direct contact method of printing, making large editions possible. The drawing was done by the artist on a large rectangle of glass fitted to a specially built table. When the drawing was finished the glass was taken up and laid upon a sensitized metal plate. The drawing was transferred onto the metal plate by light passing through the transparent areas of the glass. No camera was used. The final page gave an unusual sense of directness, a 'feel' of the artist's own hand.

"The Glasers were perfectionists. Their schedule was full, their space limited. They used the facilities of the Brett Lithographic Company in Long Island City, and rented space in the Brett building. Two or three artists only could be accomodated at the glass tables at one time. It was difficult work, time-consuming and often exasperating. It required unusual patience and technical interest which every artist doesn't necessarily have. Today, of course, acetate film is available in almost any desired thickness and with many kinds of surface. It is reliable, inexpensive, and easily transportable, bringing the process, so special then, into the studio of any artist anywhere. Had this been so in 1940 I could have saved time, money, and goodness knows how many subway rides by doing my Maminka color separations at home in my own studio. I wouldn't have had to go to New York at all. But I'd have missed the whole experience of living the printer's life for a while. I might never have had a toothbrush of my own in their distinguished collection! I'd have missed all that I 'wouldn't have missed for *anything*' without even realizing what I was missing."[1]

April 13, 1940. After establishing herself in New York, the young author-illustrator wrote: "I'm having such a nice time before my job begins. I feel like a butterfly just metamorphosed from a worm. Got to N.Y. Wednesday A.M. as planned. 'The General' [Chicago train] was late, but it was a grand trip. Went to see Doris [my editor] at Macmillan's that afternoon. They're standing on their heads with enthusiasm over Maminka. Doris says I can pick any of the pictures I like and have my next Christmas card run with the book, right on the same paper. Wouldn't *that* be swell? I'm getting very excited. Then we had a beautiful dinner by the fire at Doris's house.

"Yesterday I woke up at noon! It was raining and dreary, so I had brunch and went to 'Gone With the Wind,' which I think is stupendous. Marvelous acting. But glory! what a dose! So I went to bed early."[1]

April 18, 1940. "I'm learning such a lot that I couldn't begin to tell you about, not even if I kept writing for a month, all about printing processes and the making of books. Oh, it's wonderful! I'm learning things that I've been longing to

**He did remember how he and Grandfather planned
the kite, how Grandfather had sent word to one of his
ship's captains to bring home balsa wood from South
America....** ■ (From *The Scarlet Oak* by Cornelia
Meigs. Illustrated by Elizabeth Orton Jones.)

know for *years*. I guess you can't learn these things in any
school except the school of experience! I'm *really* going to
know how to make books after this!

"Well, I go on a couple of subways & finally arrive at Long
Island City where I get off & walk across the *longest* bridge
over the Pennsylvania yards, and pretty soon there is the
Brett Lithographing Company, & on the second floor of that
is the Glasers. It's a kind of office, very nice, with big glass-
topped tables and high piles of book paper everywhere. On
the highest pile lives Brett the cat in an apartment made of
two orange crates, like a doll's house. He has 4 rooms with
little blankets in 3 of them & a catnip mouse in the other. He
rotates and takes snoozes first upstairs, then downstairs.
There's a great big front room where the Glasers work &
where the artists come to talk about their work and their
problems, which are usually the same as mine. It's fun to listen to them from where I sit in the back room at my glass table. If they're there for lunch or tea I meet them. Otherwise
not. Helene Carter [a well known author-illustrator] came in
with a book, finished. And she was raving on about how she
simply could not go through the agony of making another
unless she could get hold of herself & not be so wrapped up
in it as to be absolutely sick at her stomach all the time.
'Why must I suffer so?' says she out there. 'Why must I love
my work nearly to distraction?' And on and on, while I sat
chortling over my work, because it was me all over!

"I sit at a big glass sort of desk with a back, so that no one
can see me. There's a window beside me & a light underneath the glass. Outside the window are the Pennsy yards
and the Sunshine Biscuit Company. It's wonderful being
next door to the Sunshine Biscuit Co. The Glasers just send
a boy over, at tea time, and he comes back with a huge bag of
broken cookies, all for 10¢. At lunch time we get out the
picnic basket, set a glass table with a yellow cloth and blue
dishes, and it's a grand meal. Today: hot creamed chicken &
mushrooms, out of a thermos of course, salad, cottage
cheese, bread & butter, cake & coffee. The Glasers' maid
puts it up each morning.

"Well, they're dear. And chummy. Everybody is 'first
names.' They're Bill and Lillian & I'm Elizabeth or Liza-
betta. They aren't dirty printers at all, quite the opposite. My
goodness! Such cleanliness! A glass plate can't be left, even
for lunch, without covering it with paper and taping the paper down with Scotch tape. And at night everything, absolutely *everything* must be put *neatly* away. They're terribly
persnickety. But it's good for me. And they're quite nervous
and terribly sensitive & heart-and-soul in their work. One
has to be careful and always sweet and patient. But they
know their onions, and they *know* they know their onions!
And I know it. You'd be amazed at their huge case of books,
which they unlock for me whenever I feel like browsing.
They've done so *many* of the really beautiful books for
children published in the past five years. Things like the
d'Aulaires' *Abraham Lincoln* and *George Washington*, almost all of the Petershams' books, and Ludwig Bemelmans'
(who, by the way, Bill says, delivers drawings on any old
kind of paper, even toilet paper!), Kate Seredy's *The White
Stag*, [a 1937 Newbery Medal winner] and *Little
Ones*—remember?—with illustrations by Kurt Wiese—oh,
shelves of them! and not one is anything other than Very
High Class book making.

"Bill's taken me in hand. He says I'm a born book craftsman! Everything that goes on there he teaches me. Today,
for instance, some drawings of Marguerite Kirmse's [illus-
trator specializing in dogs] were going to be shot. They were
line drawing on Ross board. So Bill pastes them up, brings
them in, explains the photographic process of shooting for
line, shows me how the light parts of the drawings are too
light and the darks too close on the Ross board, explains why
some of the lights will probably lose in the process & some of
the darks will gain, explains what they have to do try to
avoid it, etc. Then, having saved a little corner for me, he
gives me a piece of Ross board & I make a little sketch which
is pasted up, too, to go through the process so that I can keep
it and know in the future what to avoid and what to aim for in
drawing for line reproduction. Tomorrow morning the proofs
will come down.

"Bill lets me try every process this way. He says he's even
going to let me try *stone*. And he's going to take me to the
photography department, the plate room, the press room,
etc., to teach me everything from the workman's point of
view.

"What with all this I'm really working on my job. Don't
think I'm not! The 2-color pictures are on the glass right now
. . . I draw on that frosted surface with a very hard lead-pen-
cil, 9H—that's *hard*!—but even 9H wears down so quickly
that it has to be sharpened between almost every stroke. In a
way, it's easy because the key drawings are right there & I
draw over the blue which is only a guide and doesn't show
up in the process at all. But it's *very* SLOW. There's no
hurrying at the Glasers! It takes just about a whole morning

to do one color for one picture. And when that's done, in comes Lillian with a teeny weeny magnifying glass so strong that a pencil line looks like a coal pile through it. And she goes over every square hundredth-of-an-inch & tells me where my dots are too far apart & where they're too close together. Remember once I told you how a pencil line is really a succession of dots? Well, that's what I'm working with—the dots! which are where the pencil rubs the high places or humps of the frosted glass. I have to work with a magnifier, too, but not as strong a one as Lillian's. Also, there's a little needle-kind-of-knife with which one scrapes away, carefully, the dots if there are too many or if they are too close together. Oh, it's fun! I eat it up! It's thrilling to work on that surface of glass, and Maminka and her children do look so pretty with the light underneath shining up through them.

"I don't know how long I'll be here. I don't seem to care. The longer it takes the more I'll learn. I'm delighted with the whole business.

"Yesterday Marguerite Kirmse was there all day, doing just what Doris and I did that day in Chicago at the Blackstone (cutting galleys and pasting up a dummy). Such countings of lines as I heard from the other room! Such rustlings and rattlings of paper! And Marguerite saying, 'But I *must* have a picture of the little gray rooster here! I simply must!' And Lillian saying, 'But Marguerite! You can't! It's on the wrong side of the sheet!'

"Marguerite is a peach. She's Scotch, & she plays the harp & has seven dachshunds. I told her of our passion for her dog etchings while we were in college, a great fad, really, & how I first learned to know what an etching was, from hers, & how I still have a scrapbook of her work. She was quite touched. She drove me home after work & told me about the book she made on glass last summer. 'How long did it take you to do the color?' sez I. 'Two months!' sez she.

"Oh, it's a great place. I can't possibly describe it to you. I'm sure you'd want me to be in it as long as I need to be. Bill says I must stay until everything is done, all the proving & ink-mixing etc. I'm to help mix the colors. Imagine that! So I dunno. Anyway, I feel very much at home in & part of this life.

"And then, you see, I come back here to my little room, put on my teacosy, . . . And on my window sill is a bottle of milk. And in my desk drawer are some Sunshine Biscuits. And these I drink & eat before jumping into bed.

"Poor Doris couldn't go to Rhode Island [the editor's beach house] to get rid of her bow-knot. No time. When I went there this evening, she'd been shopping all day. I think it's awful when busy people like Doris *have* to go shopping. Well, she got a sweet blue-chiffon evening gown in which to make her speech at the final dinner of the convention of all the librarians in Texas. Part of the speech is about *Maminka's Children*. At that I have to laugh—me at the Glasers' with the magnifying glass drawing it, and Doris in Texas in a blue evening gown talking about it!"[1]

April 22, 1940. Stayed at the Parkside Hotel while she wrote to her mother and father at home in Illinois: "Na! Don't worry about my living here. I don't need any clothes, I could live for months on the ones I have. I've got a box of Lux, and all I need to do is wash a pair of stockings and some pants and I'm all set to go! And I love my hotel. It is so quiet. Most people here live here, and work. Nobody goes to the theatre

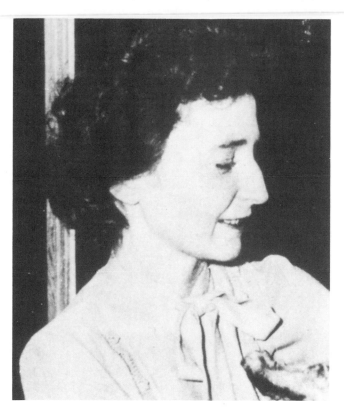

ELIZABETH ORTON JONES

much, or anything like that. Just work and go to bed early. So do I. My dear little room which I feel very much at home in is not at all hotel-y. Early American maple furniture & pewter lamps. $12.50 a week. I think I live pretty cheaply. Last week's bill was $15.95, meals & telephone included. You see, I have a few 'invited' meals. . . .

"Bill took me around for my tour of the works today, after the men had left, after four. Here they use aluminum plates instead of zinc. They look prettier than zinc because they're so shiny. For graining the plates, instead of little steel marbles, they use little balls of a very special kind of tropical wood. So smooth, *so* smooth! I wish you could see them. I wish Bill would give me one. They're installing a new press upstairs. Ach, it's big! And elegant! And complicated! I wish *Maminka's Children* could be printed on it! What fun, when the time comes, to see those huge sheets come rolling forth! We've got a swell paper, perfectly *swell*. A sort of ivory color. And tomorrow morning my first aluminum plate will be proved. I saw it up there lying in its big bath to keep nice and wet overnight.

"Why the aluminum plate? Well, it's so the printing itself can be done. Glass is unlike stone; you don't print from it. When a big glass is completely finished and inspected it's taken upstairs and laid upon a big sensitized aluminum plate and exposed like a kodak film, only without having used the camera. A lot depends on the guy who does this. If he's a guy with a hankering for getting the faintest of nuances to show he's likely to expose it too long, so the black will be too black. Or vice versa if he's the opposite kind of guy. Also a lot depends on *you*. Maybe you haven't drawn heavily enough on your light areas or delicately enough on your darks. After the exposure your drawing is on the aluminum. They give it a chemical bath and wash it with a big sponge. Then they roll it up with ink and pull a proof. And this is a

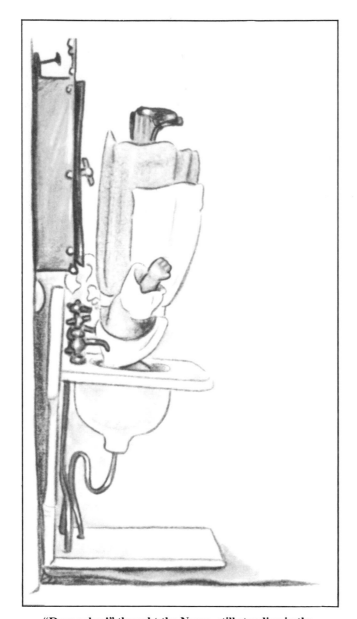

"Dear sakes!" thought the Nurse, still standing in the basin in the bathroom on her head. "Six weeks!"
■ (From *Big Susan* by Elizabeth Orton Jones. Illustrated by the author.)

very crucial moment. Sometimes they have to make another aluminum plate. Sometimes your big glass has to go downstairs and be worked on some more by you. Everybody hopes not, though. Mistakes are expensive. They're a sort of disgrace, too.

"The Glasers really love this book. Bill said today that he was going to make a Caldecott medal book of it or bust in the attempt. Doris loves it, too. She groans every time she thinks of having to go away to Texas and leave it. But then, she'll be back in a week or so! As for me, I hope it'll be beautiful. 'You big book, be beautiful!' as Nanka [Maminka's youngest child in *Maminka's Children*.] would say."[1]

April 30, 1940. She wrote her parents: "Well, we proved my tint plate, *in color*! And it's beautiful! It's the same as that pale brown watercolor background I used in the first sketches.

"You seem a bit perplexed about just what happens. So I'll tell you the story of the tint plate, as an example. So! Here's a big glass rectangle with blue-prints on it, actual size, of the key drawings of the 9 five-color pictures. O.K.? Now with a 9H pencil you draw whatever lines or areas you want to have in this tint color. You draw right on top of the blue-print. The absolutely solid places you *paint* on with thick, dirty-looking, mud-colored stuff made of graphite. The first watercolor sketches you made you use as your color guide. Wherever there is pale brown background in the sketches you duplicate it on the glass. Whatever is white you leave blank. You leave the white hen blank & the white squares in Marianka's kerchief & snowflakes & apple blossoms & candle rays & white buttons. It takes a dreadfully long time because you have to finish all the work in all the 9 pictures.

"When at last the whole glass is done you take a magnifier, a ruler, and a *terribly* sharp 9H pencil & put in the register marks which Lillian painstaking placed at the corners and edges of all the pictures before the blue-prints were made. These have to be done *precisely* and *exactly*. You have to draw your fine-pencil line along the exact center of the blue-print line. And when Lillian says center she means *center*! You *have* to get it right or you get heck. . . . At the top of each picture you have to print TOP backwards, and at the bottom of each you have to print, also backwards, the number of the page on which it will appear in the book and you had *better* get it *correct*! Then you print, *also* backwards: WILLIAM C. D. GLASER—47-07 Pierson Place, Long Island City, L.I., ORDER No. 77777 (or whatever)—*Maminka's Children*. Then you fill in one of the five empty squares on the blueprint to indicate which of the five colors this place represents. (There is a separate plate for each color, five altogether, for the 5-color pictures.)

"You go over the entire plate very thoroughly with a magnifier to make sure that no infinitesimal cinder or speck or eyelash has fallen on the surface anywhere, that no microscopic bubbles or scratches are in your solid areas, because *everything* shows! Then you say Whoopee! & call Lillian who comes to inspect it all meticulously with her tiny glass, and then, if it's O.K., she sends for Joe to come down and get it.

"Joe takes it to the 4th floor, where it is laid upon the aluminum plate and exposed. And you must now wait till day after tomorrow.

"Well! Now it *is* the day after tomorrow. When you go to work you see Joe standing by your table waiting for you with a great big smile and a great big proof of your tint plate and the aluminum plate rolled up with ink. You and Lillian now go over proof and plate with magnifiers, to see if there be any flaws. If there are, and they appear on both the aluminum plate and the proof, then you mark the aluminum plate to be corrected by the plate guy. If they are only on the proof, then you mark that for the proving guy.

"Now, say, all's O.K. It's color-mixing time! And time for proving in color. Lillian calls up Charlie the proving man, to find out if you can come up. Charlie says O.K. So up you go to the 4th floor, walk and walk until you come to a place which says GLASERS ONLY. You go in and there's Charlie with your metal plate and proof. (Joe has run up the back stairs with them!) You have your watercolor sketches in hand, to go by. The tint plate is first in order of printing. You have to plan the order of printing the colors depending on the strength and emphasis you want. We are printing: 1) Tint 2) Red 3) Brown 4) Black 5) Blue.

I am but a little child:
I know not how to go out or come in.
■ (From *Small Rain* by Jessie Orton Jones. Illustrated by Elizabeth Orton Jones.)

"Charlie has a big stone slab, many colors of ink & a big roller. You show him places in your sketches where the tint alone shows. He asks what colors the tint is made of. You say a little red, a little yellow, a smidgeon of blue and some white. Printer's ink is different from watercolor, of course. You have to interpret. Charlie mixes. Another guy wets your aluminum tint plate with a big sponge. Charlie rolls mixed ink onto the plate. Then he lays a big sheet of paper down on the bed beyond the plate. He blows on the plate and fans it. Then he says, 'Oop!' and the helper rolls a huge rubber cylinder quickly over the plate, over onto the paper and back. Everything on the aluminum plate has now been transferred to the paper, by means of the rubber cylinder. You *scrootinize*. It is too light. Do it all over again. It is too pink. Again. Too muddy. Again & again until it is just right. It's *gotta* be right. *This is it* for all time for the tint plate! You're on tenterhooks because you know that every proving session like this costs the Glasers 6 bucks. Finally—*Eureka!*—it is just right. You thank Charlie & go downstairs with your proof. You show it to Bill, then you put it in the locker marked MAMINKA'S CHILDREN, where it will wait for the moment of proving the color next in line. And so on until some fine day when all five colors shall have been mixed and proved and marked O.K. and all is ready to start printing your whole book on the big steam press.

"Clear as mud? Probably!

"Today Lillian and I got the text ready to be made into pages. For the chapter headings we picked a bold Italic Cloister face, 14 point. We went over the whole text from the master galleys and found several errors! At last away it went to be set up by the night shift. Poor guys! They're probably laboring over it this very minute!"[1]

May 3, 1940. "Maminka's page proofs are done & they look very nice. The type I mean. I'm finishing the blue plate. The red is done. In not so long now they'll all blossom forth together, the text and all the colors, and we'll have a finished book, one I do hope Bill & Lillian can be proud of."[1]

May 15, 1940. The illustrations for *Maminka's Children* were entirely executed on glass—a very difficult process. When the book was finished with text and illustrations completed, Jones enthusiastically wrote home: "*Maminka* is *Done*, and this was the day of celebration! A very hot, lovely, race-ar-oundy, sunshiny day.

"Wotta day! First I called up Wilma McFarland [editor of *Child Life,* a magazine for children published in Chicago] who is in town, to say I was sorry about the halftones. She said she was sorry, too, that they couldn't reproduce from reproductions & wasn't it too bad they couldn't have the originals! Sez I, 'You can have the whole bunch! We're not even going to use them? They're over in Doris Patee's office.' Sez she, 'Well, that changes the whole picture. Can I have those originals and a manuscript *today*?' Sure, sez I.

"Called up Doris to see if that was all right. Sure, sez she. Then I went to have my hair washed. And in the middle of that process I called up Bill. 'Come *right* over here!' sez Bill. Well, try and explain something like that to a hairdresser! But anyway, with quite damp hair I got out of there & onto the subway, over to Brett Litho. & up the stairs two-at-a-time, arriving just as Joe came triumphantly down from the proving room with the *final full-color proof!* Gosh! It was swell! Did we gloat! Everybody stopped work to gloat! We had chocolate cake and ice water, and everybody hugged everybody else & hooted I shouted & oh! those Glasers were so proud and happy!

"Then it was 'Quick! Get them to Doris!' So everybody, the Glasers, me, Lucille, Vera Neville (who is now working at my table) & Helene Carter (who happened to be there), got scissor & we all cut and pasted & in about 15 minutes *all* the pictures for *Maminka's Children* were mounted on cardboard & I was racing down the stairs & out. 'Call up when Doris sees them!' they shouted after me. 'We've got to know!'

"On and off the subway again. And over to Macmillan's. When I arrived Wilma McFarland was just leaving with the discarded originals & the manuscript. She was delighted. 'Run across the street to Longchamps as soon as you can!' she said to me at the door. 'I want you to meet somebody.' I said O.K., and away she went.

"In Doris's office I opened the package of mounted pictures. Was *she* delighted! We looked them over one by one. Then she rang for Gertrude Blumenthal, her assistant, and Miss McFee, the advertising gal. And were *they* delighted! In fact, Doris declared a holiday to celebrate *Maminka's Children.*

"At Longchamps, with Wilma McFarland, was Barbara Nolen [editor of *Story Parade,* a New York magazine for children]. Wilma took out the originals I'd given her for *Child Life* while we had tea. Right away Barbara Nolen said: 'Maminka has *got* to be in *Story Parade,* too!' Whereupon she and Wilma conferred and decided: everything that *Child Life wasn't* going to use, *Story Parade* would. So there you see! After a fine chat I flew out of Longchamps and stopped in a drug store to call up the Glasers with the good news: she *likes* them!

"On to Doris's house. In that short time she had organized a garden party! She had watered the garden & turned on the fountain & was fixing little sandwiches. In a few minutes the guests began to arrive—Macmillan people, salesmen, booksellers, Petershams. And did we celebrate! With the fountain going and the bright red tulips blooming all around, the proofs were looked at and-oh-ed and ah-ed over until there were holes in them almost. And we drank to Maminka in rum cocktails & whiskies-&-sodas and everybody was delighted.

"When they all went home Doris & I had a quiet little dinner, accompanied by smiles & the very essence of happy-ending-ness! After dinner up came Doris's very good friend Ruth Hill, [editor of *The Horn Book*] who lives in the apartment below.... She's the person who wrote that swell criticism of Maminka after reading the first version of the ms., before there were any pictures, remember? And was *she* delighted!

"So that's the end of this de-*lightful* letter, the end of printer's life for me, for the time being anyway. It's going to be awfully hard to say goodbye to those Glasers!..."[1]

1945. Although *Maminka's Children* did not receive the Caldecott Medal, the illustrator was awarded the Caldecott Medal for *Prayer for a Child,* published the previous year. In her acceptance speech the author observed, "Drawing is very like a prayer. Drawing is a reaching for something away beyond you. As you sit down to work in the morning, you feel as if you were on top of a hill. And it is as if you were seeing for the first time...."

Elizabeth Orton Jones grew up in an environment filled with music and literature. She began to write and draw stories as a child and continued to improve upon her artistic talents through college. Jones studied art in Paris, France, for a while and became so entranced with the city she later used it as the backdrop for her first book, *Ragman of Paris and His Ragamuffins.* A *New York Times* critic noted, "This little book has gayety and charm.... The delightful drawings ... have a genuine and childlike humor and together with the text present an unmistakable picture of Paris in springtime."

The author-illustrator often relied on her own childhood experiences in writing children's books. Jones' book, *Maminka's Children,* was influenced by her association with two Bohemian girls she knew as a child. "With its thoroughly childlike pictures and its descriptions of gentle homely doings, *Maminka's Children* will give pleasure to many little girls," commented a *Horn Book* reviewer.

As a young girl growing up in Illinois, the author had a vivid imagination. The author's *Twig* was about the adventures of a small girl living in a city tenement house and her encounter with an elf. "There are pictures in profusion, enchanting, funny, and full of detail," described a reviewer for *Library Journal.*

In *Big Susan* Jones told what happened when a little girl's dolls came to life. A critic for the *New Yorker* wrote "[The author] covers the fine points of doll housekeeping with a mixture of realism and imagination that little girls should enjoy."

Jones' latest book, *How Far Is It to Bethlehem?,* gave a true account of a Christmas play presented by handicapped children. A reviewer for the *New York Times* observed, "... Anyone of twelve [years] and up will find it extraordinarily moving."

FOR MORE INFORMATION SEE: Stanley J. Kunitz, editor, *Junior Book of Authors,* revised edition, H. W. Wilson, 1951; Annis Duff, "Our Miss Jones," in *Caldecott Medal Books: 1938-1957,* edited by Bertha E. (Mahony) Miller, Horn Book, 1957.

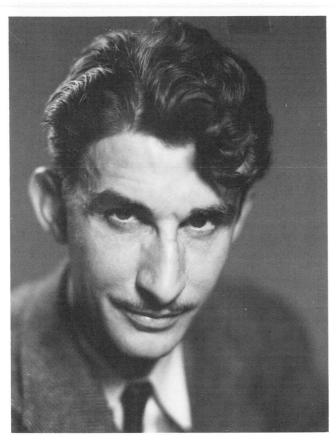

ROBERT W. KANE

KANE, Robert W. 1910-

PERSONAL: Born August 17, 1910, in New York, N.Y.; son of Matthew Joseph (a U.S. Customs official) and Selma (Koch) Kane; married Doris Hollerith (a singer; painter), February 5, 1944. *Education:* Attended Eric Pape School of Art, five years; Art Students League, three years. *Home:* 116 Pinehurst Avenue, New York, N.Y. 10033.

CAREER: Artist; illustrator. Museum of Natural History, New York, N.Y., staff artist, 1931-42, 1948-76. Project 19 East Africa, camouflage, 1942-43. *Military service:* U.S. Navy, specialist second class, 1943-45.

ILLUSTRATOR: Harold Courlander and Wolf Leslau, *Fire on the Mountain and Other Ethiopian Stories*, Holt, 1950; Harold Courlander, *Kantchil's Lime Pit and Other Stories From Indonesia,* Harcourt, 1950.

SIDELIGHTS: ''I was born in New York City where I spent my childhood and still live. I began my formal art instruction under Eric Pape and later attended the Art Students League of New York.

''I started work at the American Museum of Natural History in 1931 as assistant to William R. Leigh in Akeley African Hall. I made my first trip to Africa in 1936. Two subsequent trips covered a period of five years in the field, collecting specimens and painting studies for habitat groups. These expeditions covered all of Equitorial Africa from the east to the west coasts. On my return, I painted large backgrounds in Akeley African Hall.

(Album cover, designed by Robert Kane, for "Indonesia and Ethiopia Stories," told by Harold Courlander.)

"Contact with anthropologists at the American Museum of Natural History had stimulated a keen interest in native folk art and while in Ethiopia in 1942, I spent a great deal of time with Harold Courlander, author of *Fire on the Mountain and Other Ethiopian Folk Stories* and in the Indonesian stories of *Kantchil's Lime Pit and Other Stories From Indonesia,* also by Harold Courlander. Illustrated *Fire on the Mountain* and *Kantchil's Lime Pit* and designed album covers for Folkways records before I returned to the American Museum of Natural History in 1948 until my retirement in 1976.

"During this period at the Museum, I painted murals for the Forestry Hall, Mexican Hall, Hall of the Pacific Peoples, Children's Science Center, La Brea Tar Pits in the North American Bird Hall, dioramas and murals in the Man in Africa Hall, designed and executed a large ceramic mural in the Hall of Man and painted the black light murals in the Hayden-Planetarium. The media I use are oils, tempera, etching, black and white."

FOR MORE INFORMATION SEE: Illustrators of Children's Books, 1946-1956, Horn Book, 1958.

KAUFMANN, John   1931-
   (David Swift)

PERSONAL: Born in 1931, in New York, N.Y.; married wife, Alicia; children: two sons. *Education:* Attended the Pennsylvania Academy of Fine Arts in Philadelphia, the Art Students League in New York, and the Instituto Statale D'Arte in Florence, Italy. *Residence:* Fresh Meadows, N.Y.

JOHN KAUFMANN

CAREER: Has worked in an aircraft factory and has also done technical illustrations; author and illustrator of books for children.

WRITINGS—All for children; all self-illustrated: *Fish Hawk,* Morrow, 1967; *Wings, Sun, and Stars* (ALA Notable Book), Morrow, 1969; *Birds in Flight,* Morrow, 1970; *Robins Fly North, Robins Fly South,* Crowell, 1970; *Winds and Weather,* Morrow, 1971; *Chimney Swift,* Morrow, 1971; *Bats in the Dark,* Crowell, 1972; *Insect Travelers,* Morrow, 1972; *Flying Hand-Launched Gliders,* Morrow, 1974; *Streamlined,* Crowell, 1974; (with Heinz Meng) *Falcons Return: Restoring an Endangered Species,* Morrow, 1975; *Flying Reptiles in the Age of Dinosaurs,* Morrow, 1976; *Little Dinosaurs and Early Birds,* Crowell, 1977; (under pseudonym David Swift) *Animal Travelers,* Morrow, 1977.

Illustrator: Bernice K. Hunt, *Our Tiny Servants: Molds and Yeasts,* Prentice-Hall, 1962; Philip B. Carona, *Things That Measure,* Prentice-Hall, 1962; Eric Windle, *Sounds You Cannot Hear,* Prentice-Hall, 1963; Betty Baker, *Killer-of-Death,* Harper, 1963; Penelope Farmer, *The Magic Stone,* Harcourt, 1964; Lenore Sander, *The Curious World of Crystals,* Prentice-Hall, 1964; Raymond A. Wohlrabe, *Metals,* Lippincott, 1964; Millicent E. Selsam, *Courtship of Animals,* Morrow, 1964; Kai Soderhjelm, *Free Ticket to Adventure,* Lothrop, 1964; Natalie S. Carlson, *Letter on the Tree,* Harper, 1964; Patrick Young, *Old Abe: The Eagle Hero* (a Junior Literary Guild selection), Prentice-Hall, 1965; Lace Kendall, pseudonym of Adrian Stoutenberg, *Rain Boat,* Coward, 1965; Susan E. F. Welty, *Birds with Bracelets: The Story of Bird-Banding,* Prentice-Hall, 1965; Vincent J. Marteka, *Bionics,* Lippincott, 1965; Arthur Catherall, *Lone Seal Pup,* Dutton, 1965; N. S. Carlson, *The Empty Schoolhouse* (ALA Notable Book), Harper, 1965; M. E. Selsam, *Animals as Parents,* Morrow, 1965; Selsam, *When an Animal Grows,* Harper, 1966; Erick Berry, *The Springing of the Rice: A Story of Thailand,* Macmillan, 1966; Joseph Cottler, *Alfred Wallace: Explorer-Naturalist,* Little, Brown, 1966; Leonard S. Stevens, *The Trucks That Haul By Night,* Crowell, 1966; Robert Murphy, *Wild Geese Calling,* Dutton, 1966; Jocelyn Arundel, *Little Stripe: An African Zebra,* Hastings House, 1967; Jean C. George, *The Moon of the Salamanders,* Crowell, 1967; M. E. Selsam, *How Animals Tell Time,* Morrow, 1967; Selsam, *The Bug That Laid the Golden Eggs,* Harper, 1967; Andre Norton, pseudonym of Alice M. Norton, *Fur Magic,* World Publishing, 1968; Alonzo Gibbs, *By A Sea-Coal Fire,* Lothrop, 1968; Jean Craighead George, *Coyote In Manhattan,* Crowell, 1968; Delia Goetz, *Rivers,* Morrow, 1969; Peter Sauer, *Seasons,* Coward-McCann, 1969; Bertha S. Dodge, *Potatoes and People: The Story of a Plant,* Little, Brown, 1970; Margaret F. Bartlett, *Rock All Around,* Coward-McCann, 1970; Alfred Slote, *The Moon in Fact and Fancy,* World Publishing, 1971.

SIDELIGHTS: Born in 1931 in New York City where most of his childhood was spent. As a child his favorite subject for drawing was that of war planes. "Each was drawn in profile with its guns bristling and a fierce pilot in every cockpit." [*Illustrators of Children's Books: 1957-1966,* compiled by Lee Kingman and others, Horn Book, 1968.[1]]

Kaufmann attended the Brooklyn Technical High School where he specialized in an aeronautical course. After high school, he worked in an aircraft factory and later produced technical illustrations. He studied art at such schools as the Pennsylvania Academy of Fine Arts, the Art Students League in New York, and the Instituto Statale D'Arte in

I held my arms out and pretended that I was a bird flying over water. But most of the time I was stopping to tighten my right skate because it kept coming loose. ■ (From *The Letter on the Tree* by Natalie Savage Carlson. Illustrated by John Kaufmann.)

Tako watched it, crept out of the box, and climbed on it to get nearer to the cone. ■ (From *Coyote in Manhattan* by Jean Craighead George. Illustrated by John Kaufmann.)

Florence, Italy where he studied mural and fresco. "I crossed back into the visual arts by a strange side door. A friend, noticing my talent for painting Santa Clauses on the office doors suggested I try technical illustration. I did. After a number of years of doing isometric and perspective drawings of Cold War hardware, I got married and left for Florence with my wife Alicia."[1]

In 1962 he illustrated his first book, *Our Tiny Servants: Molds and Yeasts.* Since that time he has become an established illustrator and writer of nature books for children. His illustrations are most frequently done in black-and-white. "I use India ink for my black which allows me to work back over an area without picking up what has already been put down underneath. Often I wet my paper first and paint quickly into the moist areas before they dry."[1]

Kaufmann lives in Fresh Meadows, New York with his wife and two sons. His most recent book for children is *Animal Travelers* which was published in 1977 under his pseudonym, David Swift. He places high value on his children's books. "Because I have encountered in my technical illustrating people who have rationalized away the social consequences of their life activities, I now value my work more. To me, good books for children are diametrically opposed to the engineering of missiles and the manipulation of public opinion."[1]

The *Christian Science Monitor* called *Wings, Sun and Stars: The Story of Bird Migration,* "A technical book written simply and entertainingly. The author has drawn over 75 maps, diagrams, and sketches illustrating various experiments and theories attempting to ascertain how birds find their way across vast distances. . . ." Zena Sutherland, in *Saturday Review,* wrote the following about *Robins Fly North, Robins Fly South:* "Sharp, clear, delicate detailed pictures of robins fill these pages with movement. . . . Migration, while discussed in detail, is treated as part of the robin's life cycle and its relationship to the environment, all in the simplest of terms in straightforward style."

FOR MORE INFORMATION SEE: Lee Kingman and others, compilers, *Illustrators of Children's Books, 1957-1966,* Horn Book, 1968; *Horn Book,* October, 1969, June, 1972, October, 1975; *Christian Science Monitor,* May 1, 1969; *Saturday Review,* November 4, 1970.

KELLY, Walt(er Crawford) 1913-1973

PERSONAL: Born August 25, 1913, in Philadelphia, Pa.; son of Walter Crawford (a theatrical scene painter) and Genevieve (MacAnnulla) Kelly; children: six. *Education:* Attended public schools in Bridgeport, Conn.

CAREER: Post, Bridgeport, Conn., newspaper reporter, writer, and artist, 1928-35; Walt Disney Studios, Hollywood, Calif., animator, 1935-41; commercial artist in New York City, 1941-48; *New York Star* (newspaper), art director, political cartoonist, editorial adviser, and originator of daily comic strip, "Pogo," 1948-49; employed by Post Syndicate (later Post-Hall) to produce syndicated "Pogo" comic strip, beginning 1949. *Wartime service:* Civilian employee of the U.S. Army's foreign language unit during the Second World War. *Member:* National Cartoonist Society (president, 1954). *Awards, honors:* Reuben award ("Cartoonist of the Year"), National Cartoonists Society, 1952, invited by the Library of Congress to file a collection of original drawings of "Pogo," 1954.

Walt Kelly and Pogo.

WRITINGS—Cartoon books with captions, published by Simon & Schuster, except as noted: *Pogo,* 1951; *I Go Pogo,* 1952; *The Pogo Papers,* 1953; *Uncle Pogo So-So Stories,* 1953; *The Incompleat Pogo,* 1954; *The Pogo Stepmother Goose,* 1954; *The Pogo Peek-a-Book,* 1955; *Potluck Pogo,* 1955; *The Pogo Party,* 1956; *The Pogo Sunday Book,* 1956; *Songs of the Pogo,* 1956, reissued, 1968; *Pogo's Sunday Punch,* 1957; *Positively Pogo,* 1957; *G. O. Fizzickle Pogo,* 1958; *The Pogo Sunday Parade,* 1958; *The Pogo Sunday Brunch,* 1959; *Ten Ever-Lovin' Blue-Eyed Years with Pogo,* 1959.

Beau Pogo, 1960; *Pogo Extra,* 1960; *Gone Pogo,* 1961; *Pogo a la Sundae,* 1961; *Instant Pogo,* 1962; *The Jack Acid Society Black Book,* 1962; *Deck Us All with Boston Charlie,* 1963; *Pogo Puce Stamp Catalog,* 1963; *The Return of Pogo,* 1965; *The Pogo Poop Book,* 1966; *Prehysterical Pogo,* 1967; *Equal Time for Pogo,* 1968; *Pogo: Prisoner of Love,* 1969; *Impollutable Pogo,* 1970; *Pogo: We Have Met the Enemy and He Is Us,* 1972; (with Selby Kelly) *Pogo's Bats and the Belles Free,* 1976; (with S. Kelly) *The Pogo Candidature: A Cartoon Story for New Children,* Sheed, Andrews & McMeel, 1976.

Collections and selections; all published by Simon & Schuster: *Pogo Re-Runs: Some Reflections on Elections,* 1974; *Pogo Revisited,* 1974 (contains *Instant Pogo, The Pogo Poop Book,* and *The Jack Acid Society Black Book*); *Pogo Romances Recaptured,* 1976 (contains *Pogo: Prisoner of Love* and *The Incompleat Pogo*); *Pogo's Body Politic,* edited by S. Kelly, 1976.

THE TROUBLE WITH PEOPLE IS PEOPLE

If we could climb
    the highest steeple
And look around at
    all the people,
And shoot the ones
    not wholly good
As we, like noble
    shooters, should,
Why, then there'd be
    an only worry⋯
Who would there be left
    to bury
    us?

(From *Walt Kelly's Pogo Revisited* by Walt Kelly. Illustrated by the author.)

TERMITE OR
NOT TERMITE

To be boring within
　　And boring without
And boring again
　　And boring about
Is boring indeed
　　And boring in doubt
And the wood I would eat,
　　As I bored 'neath the bed,
Would go very neat,
　　Very straight to my head.

(From *Walt Kelly's Pogo Revisited*, written and illustrated by Walt Kelly.)

Illustrator: Inez Bertail, editor, *Complete Nursery Song Book,* Lothrop, 1947; John O'Reilly, *The Glob,* Viking, 1952; Charles Ellis and Frank Weir, *I'd Rather Be President,* Simon & Schuster, 1956.

SIDELIGHTS: **August 25, 1913.** Born in Philadelphia, Pennsylvania. "For a good part of my boyhood there occurred in the first of the dozing minutes of sleep a delicious dream or vision, in the half-wakeful glide into complete slumber, which I can only describe as a picture of a smooth ride through a gray and shadowed oval corridor. There was always a light at the end of this tunnel, a place where it seemed you should burst into daylight, and, naturally, the dream always ended about when this would have been accomplished. In the years since it happened with great frequency it has disappeared entirely, and arm-chair psychiatrists have assured me that it was a memory of birth. Whether they are right or wrong does not trouble me. I recognize in the dream a slice of symbolism, and writers are not easily discouraged from using such ready ingredients." [Martin Levin, editor, *Five Boyhoods,* Doubleday, 1962.[1]]

1916. Family moved from Philadelphia to Bridgeport, Conn., where his father was a sign painter and a factory worker. "If the trip through the tunnel started so early in dreams, it certainly continued in actuality as far as a child's mind was concerned. The trip from Philadelphia to Bridgeport was also a tunnel ride to me....

"... The part of Bridgeport that we lived in after the first year there was as new as a freshly minted dollar, but not quite so shiny. The East Bridgeport Development Company had rooted out trees and dammed up streams, drained marshes, and otherwise destroyed the quiet life of the buttercups and goldfinches in order to make a section where people like the Kellys could live. The houses were all doubles, one family living alongside another and sharing the same generous porch which ran the entire width of the building. The streets at first were bordered with plank sidewalks, and the mud in the middle was deep enough to drown a small Shetland. Surrounding us was a fairly rural and wooded piece of Connecticut filled with snakes, rabbits, frogs, rats, turtles, bugs, berries, ghosts, and legends."[1]

1918. "Shortly after Christmas one year I was informed that I was to be allowed to go to school. 'Allowed' was, to my mind, not the word they needed. I eschewed the table for once and ran away from home, into the cellar and behind the furnace. Several hours later when I'd been found and dusted off, it was made clear that nobody meant *immediately*. Next fall was to be the time. My sister had been a big success in her kindergarten and first-grade years. She had wit, grace, mature scholarly inclinations, and large brown eyes. Well, I had brown eyes.

"In the meantime the Armistice had arrived. We had two parades: one for the false Armistice and one for the McCoy. My father, cursing mildly to himself, had spent long and mysterious hours in the cellar, our common workshop. When he finally emerged, he had on poles several large signs which bore pictures of the Kaiser getting the boot, and other gentle gloatings. My memories of the parades are dim except that all of Bridgeport turned out on Main Street. One was held in the early evening and we all went down to see my father's signs go by. At about the time they were due past, some celebrant on a motorcycle ran over a neighbor's foot—and in the resulting uproar, the signs went by without a salute. Father was furious when he found that they'd gone

by unnoticed, and he never trusted the victim from that day forward. 'Damn fool anyway for standing in the gutter,' he'd mutter.

"One other memory of that war was the songs that were sung. 'Tramp, tramp, tramp, the boys are marching / Here comes the Kaiser at the door / If I had a napple core / I would knock him on the jore / And there wouldn't be no Kaiser any more.' There were others: 'Keep the Home Fires Burning,' 'Tipperary,' etc., which I liked to throw myself into. I could never understand why people laughed when I sat down after rendering a solo. (I sang 'Mama Sell from Arm and Tears' one time and didn't get any laughs from my mother. I got a spanking.)

"My interpretations at that time reflected the sort of ear I had and evidently still have. A good deal of the material in the comic strip comes from hearing incorrectly what others have said. This leads to certain incongruities useful to a cartoonist. I learned the alphabet by saying '... H I J K Elemenoe P' somewhere in the middle, and I still say it upon request. The Lord's Prayer involved 'Hallowbee Thy Name' and 'Give us to stay our daily bread' insofar as I was concerned. I wondered vaguely about 'to stay' and why the Lord should be named 'Hallowbee,' but never mentioned this to anyone for fear of being judged incapable of recognizing the obvious. Years later I was comforted when *The New Yorker* magazine reported that a child was given to saying, '... and lead us not into Penn Station, but deliver us from evil ...' It made me feel less alone."[1]

1919. Sent to Hall Grammar School in Bridgeport. "Part of that trip through the tunnel was that period during which we went to school. School was something that came in between wandering through the woods or playing frightening games beneath the porches. On rainy days we might lie around each other's houses looking at Mutt and Jeff cartoon books, all of us determining to become cartoonists and rich. Or we might read from the tattered copies of Horatio Alger and decide we'd go straight, rescue somebody beautiful with golden hair, preferably the local magnate's daughter, and become head of the firm—very wealthy, respectable, and, above all, kind to the poor. Other books were the Boy Allies series, the Battleship Boys, and, of course, the Frank and Dick Merriwell books. All of us aspired to go to Yale and become great pitchers, sing songs late at night, poke fun (kindly) at Harry Rattleton, and whip the town bully, or maybe Bruce Browning. We weren't so good with our actual, local bullies, but we were great on paper.

"The school that we went to before high school was, like the rest of the community, fairly new, having been built to accommodate the great influx of war workers' children. We were mostly factory people and our situations were all about as alike as our national origins were different. It was a bit difficult to find two families of the same nationality within a half mile. We never formed racial gangs because there was never enough of any one of us to choose up sides, so we roamed with whom we lived near. Thus we acquired a camaraderie equal to but not of the Peaceable Kingdom.

"It may be that this section of Bridgeport, or of the world, was a sort of backwater where we just never did learn the rudiments of bigotry. Our mothers, so far as I now can tell, were not inclined to look down on anyone, except, naturally, the enemy. Some of them never connected the people in our midst with the same nationalities overseas. It was evident that, once under our roof, the guest was one of us and an integral cog.

"Certainly our fathers, who worked together at boisterous and sweaty jobs, either in construction work or as factory hands—certainly they saw little difference. Racial and religious animosities, if they existed at all, broke down far below those high levels of difference and became merely personal dislike. It was not until I got into high school that I discovered that Irish Catholics are not like other people, Protestants are not like other people, the Polish are not like other people, Negroes are not like other people—Italians, Jews, the English, none of them are like other people. I finally asked my father who the hell were the other people. He said he thought they were the ones always represented by God. For a man who couldn't find his way to church, I thought it was a fairly God-loving remark.

"To keep us on our fortunate way while we were in the Hall Grammar School, there was a lady who had been a teacher for thirty years; she was the principal of the Hall School and her name was Miss Florence Blackham. She treated every one of us as if he were a newly discovered jewel. Such was the near adoration that we boys gave Miss Blackham that none of us could tell her a lie. She fixed her eyes upon you and you were done. There was a time when I had been banished to the cloakroom of Miss Lester's Room 9 for an indiscretion of some sort. The cloakroom was a separate large vestibule leading through swinging doors from the hallway into the room proper. I detected Miss Blackham's footsteps approaching and grew rigid. To have her find me there was intolerable. To hide seemed the best idea. I tried to draw myself up on a hook and make myself look like a coat, but my strength wouldn't support the effort. I dropped to the floor and decided to make a clean breast of everything. The footsteps came nearer, and as Miss Blackham opened the door, I rushed forward and cried, 'I DID IT! I DID IT!' The poor woman was flabbergasted and we finally settled what it was that I had done. But that I cannot remember now; all I know is that she was more impressed by my greeting than by my misdemeanor, whatever it had been."[1]

1923. "There is talk every once in a while that growing up is tough. If so, then perhaps I have not grown up at all. The tough part must be yet to come. That I did not know it should have been tough may have been due to a muttonheaded inability to recognize the facts. Certainly my boyhood was no Huck Finn idyl, nor is it to me now a golden dream of shores never to be seen again. My boyhood is full of pictures, not always bright with adventure, but seldom unlit.

"Possibly nobody feels that he is little when he's a boy. There is just the impression that other people are bigger. Boys my own size were curious creatures, not entirely to be trusted until centuries of adventure and misadventure had welded our hearts into one. Girls were mysteries and have remained so. One thing I was able to discover at about ten or eleven was that girls are very good to kiss. This realization came with a sense of relief. Up until that point I had despaired of their being in any way useful.

"It had to be admitted that mothers were female too, but they were ready-made adults. Once in a while one of them would let slip that she had been a girl at one time. This information was accepted with the same faith that I believed in the story of Adam and Eve. It was felt that there was something screwball about the idea, but nobody ever went so far as to voice the thought. Instead, one's mother's claim was

put in the same category with the legends of Hercules and in about the same year.

"To believe, on the other hand, that a father had been a boy in his time was comparatively a snap. Perhaps that is because most of them remain somewhat boys. . . .

"Sisters are something else. They fall between two stools, sad to say. They are neither girls, the kissing type, nor are they mothers. They are something like small mothers, but not entirely. Who belts his mother?

"Throughout the latter teens and early twenties of the century in Bridgeport, Connecticut, the state of other families in the social and economic scale was something of a puzzle, only occasionally and dimly wondered at. My own family, headed by a mother, had a kind of pride based on nothing more than the fact that we came from Philadelphia. My mother was fiercely uncertain. Nonetheless, she always felt that her family amounted to something more than any other family of equal size, weight, and age. This pride would often flush me into the open for combat with giants of my own age whose ancestry was every bit as uncertain as my own, but presumably healthier. This led to a lot of lumps, but I lost no teeth except in unequal contests with dentists, and broke nothing but the cellar door when another boy and I agreed to kill each other with coal shovels.

"It was an exercise in living in those days to aspire to owning a car that would stay in one piece and run part of the time, and to building a house on a little piece of land. The other lower middle-class hope was to send some member of the family to college. My father often said that he thought the best thing to do was to send my grandfather, because he wouldn't live for more than another two years and so it would only cost half as much. My mother said this was awful.

"With the exception of the plan for my grandfather, my parents tried to make most of these things work through those scratchy early years.

"Private enterprise roared unregulated during the twenties and among the rugged individualists of those times were entrepreneurs in knee pants who occupied themselves with painstaking projects which were either mildly successful, but operated at a loss, or failures and operated at a loss.

"Attempts in the world of commerce involved the usual paper routes, and for a time I was a sort of standout as the *Saturday Evening Post* boy with the fewest number of customers. I had seven. It should be added that none of these unfortunates ever received the *Post* until I had spent most of the day dawdling through my own copy, laughing at Florian Slappey, marveling at Norman Rockwell, and envying Charles Livingston Bull, who had the greatest name for an animal artist I have ever heard. My *Post* 'route' occupied my indifferent attention until I had saved up enough brown sales vouchers to send away for a pencil sharpener. With my pencils sharp as needles I retired to a life of drawing and writing.

"The writing led me into the theater, which was down in our cellar and as far off Broadway as you can get. D. K. Knott and Cranberry Campbell thought they were pretty fair as actors, and with me directing and writing we had an unbeatable team. We played a three-act play one Saturday afternoon to a standing-room-only audience of three-year-olds and mothers. They were standing largely because the only chairs

THE STARE WAY TO SUCCESS

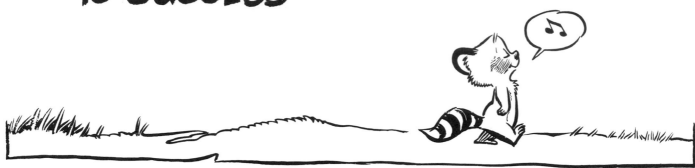

(From *Walt Kelly's Pogo Revisited*, written and illustrated by Walt Kelly.)

REQUIEM FOR AN EXAGGERATED OBITUARY

In the beginning
   Who was alone?

In any ending
   Who is unknown?

In the beginning
   There was a friend.

In the beginning
   There was the end.

(From *Walt Kelly's Pogo Revisited*, written and illustrated by Walt Kelly.)

were needed on the set. Also, our curtain had to be impounded by the company, at one point, for a costume. The three-acter would have run four acts, but the minors in the audiences were getting restless, and the mothers advised us to speed up our production, a tragedy entitled *The Frozen North*. So we quickly skipped a good deal and wound up with the finale, in which all three principals slew each other. This appealed mightily to all, and everyone left in good spirits. We made about twenty-four cents. Inasmuch as we had spent twenty-five cents on lemons and sugar for lemonade, which Campbell upset rolling off-stage in his death throes, we lost only a penny. Other shows have done worse."[1]

1927. Attended a Bridgeport high school. "My sister was an acknowledged scholar. She studied hard and her head was full of geometrical theory, more history than she needed, and grammatical rules that had never been used by man or beast. On the other hand, I was the family slob. All I did was sing and draw on paper bags. It was decided that my mother should go to work (she *had* been working, but at that lowest-paid job, that of the pre-electronics housewife) and thus we could manage to send my sister through college.

"When it came to the question of what to make of me, a puzzled look came over my father's face. 'Maybe he could learn cards,' he said to my mother, 'or to shoot dice.' My mother didn't think this was funny. I thought vaguely that I could be an artist, but experiments with my father at my elbow (he was a pretty fair painter) convinced me that the work was hard. I was asked if I liked music and, meaning no harm and trying to please, I said yes. Thereupon my mother decided that I might become another Menuhin and get to play at dances in Philadelphia. My admiration at the time for Menuhin was limited, since we had heard him only on the phonograph, whose clearest tones resembled a jungle of night noises. But knowing that Mother liked the violin, and that my father was a staunch admirer of 'Rose of Tralee' as arranged for mouth harp and fiddle, I agreed to sit through a violin concert at a friend's home one evening, as an experiment.

"For me, the most frightening thing about taking music lessons was the music itself. The English language was bad enough in print—but a sheet of music was as formidable as the Chinese Wall. Therefore, I never learned to read music well enough to play anything at sight; I would listen to the instructor a couple of times as he ran through the piece, get it down, and play it by ear.

"To convince my parents that I was practicing, I made up brand-new compositions for the fingering and bowing exercises. My friend Lux was a little against this, thought it unsporting, until he heard me try some of the actual exercises. Then he agreed that I had taken the wiser course.

"After about twenty months of this sort of hemming and hawing, an event transpired that caused me definitely to forego following in Mischa Elman's footsteps. For the first time in my checkered life I had been able to swing around and throw Rusty Coyne when he leaped on me from the rear. We were in our alley, and after rolling about in the mud a bit, we got to our feet determined to slay each other before we were called on account of darkness.

"With my back to the setting sun I had Rusty at a disadvantage and, cocking my fist, would have taken his head from his shoulders when my mother called me. 'Stop that!' she cried from the back porch. 'You'll ruin your hands for the violin.' I looked around at her and at this Rusty fetched me a

roundhouse right that destroyed my left ear for all but such noises as, in Milt Caniff's phrase, can be heard only by a tall dog. That was the end of the fight and secretly, in my heart, I knew it to be the end of my musical drift.

"In about two months I craftily contracted some still mysterious ailment which paralyzed my left side (the side you hold the violin with) and this kept me out of the music game for two years. Fortunately, it also kept me out of the alley with Rusty Coyne."[1]

1928. "In my early teens I started work as a high-school reporter for the Bridgeport *Post*. This came about because while still somewhat of a recluse, I had submitted some drawings to the Sunday *Post* for its Junior Page section. Out of this, I became the high-school reporter. When I was assigned to cover baseball games finally, it became apparent that an hereditary inability to grasp the simplest mathematical formula would never find me with the right number of men left on base."[1]

1930. ". . . After high school, there was a brief period of factory work, and then the *Post* called me back and wondered if I would lend my highly imaginative style to general assignments. By sheer drift I was next assigned to the art department—indeed, for a long spell, I was it.

"However the early thirties was a time of change. . . . When it eventually dawned on the young that the old conservatism, the old Horatio Alger formula, was not operative any longer, a good many of us became the stuff of the New Deal. But I do not think we became such because of any noble ideals; I think we were all still looking for the great American 'break.' To serve in a paternal system was still a strong motivating force in terms of service. There were few philosophers and few economists. Socialists were viewed with a bit of alarm, and Communists were thought to be madmen and dirty to boot. A changed viewpoint came later—we were still the children of our fathers.

"Maybe it was up to Dave Murphy, a friend with whom I later worked as a welfare investigator, to sum up the twenties and the start of those thirties. 'Well, I guess you can hope for one of two things in this world,' said Murphy, as he gave, with a flourish, his last dollar to a charity drive of one kind or another. 'Either you'll be poor enough to get on relief or you'll be rich enough to afford being a patsy.' "[1]

1935. Travelled to Hollywood where he gained employment as an animator with the Walt Disney Studios. For the next six years he worked and learned his cartooning art from Disney.

1941. Returned to New York to try his hand at comic books. Unhappy with the violent comic books the industry was producing, Kelly created a strip about a young boy named Bumbazine who lived in the Okefenokee Swamp of Georgia with his animal friends. Before long Bumbazine was replaced by a minor character in the strip, an opossum named Pogo because "Bumbazine, being human, was not as believable as the animals." [Joseph P. Mastrangelo, "Unforgettable Walt Kelly," *Reader's Digest,* July, 1974.[2]]

1946. When the comic book company folded Kelly worked as a commercial artist.

1948-1949. Art director, political cartoonist, editorial adviser and originator of the daily comic strip, "Pogo" for the New York *Star*. One of his fellow artists recalled those days at the

(From *Walt Kelly's Pogo Revisited,* written and illustrated by Walt Kelly.)

Star: "The *Star* was a happy paper to work on with Kelly running your shop. He wasn't a boss; he was a teacher. No idea you might have was so farfetched that he wouldn't consider it seriously.

"But the happy times didn't last. One night, Kelly came in with a long look on his face and sent us to a staff meeting in the city room. There the publisher told us we had just published the last edition. The city room ended up standing three deep at a bar. Kelly came up behind a few of his ex-staff and told the bartender to give us anything we wanted. We all switched from beer to Scotch, and it was the first dollar cigar I ever smoked."[2]

1949. After the *Star* folded Kelly devoted all his energies to "Pogo" and in four months persuaded the Post-Hall Syndicate to distribute it.

1951. With "Pogo" running in one hundred newspapers Kelly was becoming quite successful. One of his associates recalled his generosity to other less fortunate friends: "Kelly's charities were mostly of his own making. If a fellow cartoonist or writer was down and out, he might suddenly find his rent paid for the next two months—by Kelly. The morning after the papers reported a policeman shot in the line of duty, Kelly would make out a generous check for the widow. A priest running a mission on the Lower East Side in Manhattan was another beneficiary. A Jewish friend received a monthly Kelly check for a group that was hunting ex-Nazis."[2]

1952. Received the Reuben award as "Cartoonist of the Year" from the National Cartoonists Society. "Now for those who would like to crowd into a field not exactly overloaded with talent, some rules of the humor game and the possible results should be lightly pointed up. One theory about jokesmithery is that to make a joke work properly in the broad sense somebody must come out of it looking like a simpleton. This is best and most subtly handled if the teller of the tale identifies himself with the scapegoat. Then no one is hurt except the tale-teller and he is in a lather of self-employment; thus, no bones broken.

"But you are surer of success, not the best kind, but a good, heady, satisfying type of success, if you can find out what the audience is collectively against.

"For instance, if you are talking to a room full of mice, you might say, 'Why are all cats crosseyed?' This is guaranteed to convulse the group for up to three minutes. There will always be a few carping crosseyed mice in the crowd who will try to form a splinter party and claim that you are a bum. Do not listen to splinter parties. The humorist must be relentless and ruthless.

"Lay it on, because you've got them going. They are on the way. Say that not only are cats crosseyed, but they are bowlegged. Two or three bowlegged mice will leave noisily, trying to stamp out the laughter. One may even turn at the door and hurl a threat. It will not be heard above the good-humored screams. So, you will pay no attention.

"Press ahead. The crowd is in the aisles. Tell it that cats are nonentities. They are all gray in the dark. Now, you will see what happens to a humorist. You have finally told the truth, but it is a truth about mice as well as cats. You will be eaten alive. The humorist must be quick of mind, light of hand, and fleet of foot." [Walt Kelly, "Pogo Looks at the Abominable Snowman," *The Saturday Review,* August 30, 1958.[3]]

1954. Invited by the Library of Congress to file a collection of original drawings of "Pogo" there. It was the first time a comic strip artist had been invited to file material with the library. Kelly had once described Pogo as "the reasonably patient, soft-hearted, naive, friendly little person we all think we are." ["Bard of Okefenokee," *Time,* October 29, 1973.[4]]

1958. "Pogo" was syndicated in 519 newspapers and had over 44,560,000 devoted followers. A conscientious citizen, Kelly made a globe-girdling trip on behalf of Pan-American World Airways. His travels led him to believe that "those who do not believe in humans are in error. I know they exist, science to the contrary.

"In these days, when most of our heads seem rising to some sort of peak, and while summit conferences wax and wane in the manner of everybody's moon, it will be a good idea to remember the two frogs. You will recall that they lived in neighboring towns and they started out, each heading toward the other, both intent upon seeing what sort of land lay beyond the hill that separated their homelands. They met at the summit and each stood erect for a quick preview of the place he'd like to see. Naturally, with their eyes on the tops of their heads, like respectable frogs everywhere, each frog's gaze projected backward along the route that he had taken. So, with a certain amount of grumbling and complaint, they decided to return to their homes. 'For,' as one said to the other, 'everything in your country is exactly as it is in mine.'

"Of course, each had again looked at his own land, and the miracle of the story lies not in the fact that both were fooled, but that from such a vantage point neither had seen anything strange, wonderful, or new about his home country. Presumably, neither had seen his country from the top of a hill before. Both frogs, for their entire lives, had been having a frog's-eye view of their homelands, a view that leaves something to be desired by those of us who are not professional frogs.

"Perhaps the proper summit for the study of mankind and frogkind exists within every one of us. Maybe the great final joke will prove to be that in our search for the summit we never explored the crags of our individual consciences. This will be a sad development, for the view must be fine and the echoes poignant."[3]

1960. Employed six people under his direction in his studio on Madison Avenue. One of his employees recalled their New York association: "When you worked with Kelly, there was play time and deadline time. On any day of the week, he would invite the whole staff out to lunch. We would go to one of the best restaurants. He would order cocktails for everybody, thick slabs of roast beef, wine, dessert, brandy, cigars. About five o'clock a weary waiter would smile when he got a big tip. Then next day, when someone would look up from his drawing board and ask, 'Anyone for lunch?' Kelly would say, 'Those lunch hours you guys take last too long.'

"When Kelly worked, he liked to sit in a big chair, a beat-up soft hat on his head, a thick unlighted cigar in his mouth. He worked with his drawing board propped up on a big old-fashioned desk, which had letters stuffed into every pigeonhole. Pinned along the edges of his drawing board were dozens of notes."[3]

1972. The diabetic Kelly had a leg amputated. Kelly loved life, success, fame and his many friends. The cartoonist

Kelly, on a photographer's pony.

would often say hello to people by using their faces on lesser animals in his cartoon strip or by writing their names on the side of the swamp boat which Pogo and his friend sat in.

October 18, 1973. Died of complications from diabetes in Los Angeles at the age of sixty. "After a lumpy lifetime of searching for the hilarious truth in others, any rickety raconteur is delighted to find that he need not go outdoors to discover the drollness and frailty of man. In fact, the best bits of boobery can be found within oneself. If humorous writers could not find anything in ourselves to laugh at we would be in a bad way...."[3]

Pogo was twenty-four years old and appeared in over four hundred and fifty papers in the United States and Canada when his creator died. He was also known in Australia, France, New Zealand, Greece, Portugal, Italy, Lebanon, South Africa, Spain, Sweden, Thailand and South America. His books had sold close to three million copies.

The cartoonist based the storyline of his comic strips on topical subjects and even ran a "Pogo for President" campaign in both 1952 and 1956. The National Broadcasting Company took an interest in Kelly's satirical approach to social issues and hired the comic-strip artist to write some skits to brighten up the long procedures during the Democratic and Republican conventions of 1956.

By 1960, Kelly had put out *Ten Ever-Lovin' Blue-Eyed Years with Pogo,* a cartoon book commemorating the tenth anniversary of his opossum character. "As uninhibitedly inventive with language as he is gifted a draftsman, Kelly furnishes in this collection . . . the continuing story of Pogo in Pogo's world. . . . [The book] belongs on the Americana book-shelf, somewhere between Krazy Kat and Charlie Brown," noted a critic for *Commonweal.*

Metro-Goldwyn-Mayer produced "The Pogo Special Birthday Special," a thirty-minute animated television program which premiered on the National Broadcasting Network, May 18, 1969. Kelly not only wrote the story and songs for the special, but provided the voice of the character P. T. Bridgeport as well.

FOR MORE INFORMATION SEE: Current Biography Yearbook 1956; Walt Kelly, "Pogo Looks at the Abominable Snowman," *The Saturday Review,* August 30, 1958; Martin Levin, editor, *Five Boyhoods,* Doubleday, 1962; J. P. Mastrangelo, "Unforgettable Walt Kelly," *Reader's Digest,* July, 1974. *Obituaries: New York Times,* October 19, 1973; *Newsweek,* October 29, 1973; *Time,* October 29, 1973; *Current Biography Yearbook 1973.*

(Died October 18, 1973)

KNIGHT, Eric (Mowbray)   1897-1943 (Richard Hallas)

PERSONAL: Born April 10, 1897, in Menston, Yorkshire, England; emigrated to the United States in 1912; died in a plane crash during military service, January 15, 1943, in Surinam; son of Frederic Harrison (a diamond merchant) and Marion Hilda (Creasser) Knight; married Dorothy Noyes Hall, 1917; married second wife, Jere, 1932; children: (first marriage) three daughters. *Education:* Attended Boston Museum of Fine Arts School, National Academy of Design, Art Students' League, and Beaux Arts Institute. *Religion:* Quaker. *Home:* Pleasant Valley, Pennsylvania.

CAREER: Novelist, cartoonist, and author of books for children. Employed from the age of twelve, he held numerous jobs before coming to America, including work in a steel mill, cotton mill, worsted mill, sawmill, and glass-blowing factory. Worked as a copy boy for the Philadelphia *Press,* and later as a writer of feature articles for a syndicate bureau. Following World War I, he worked on several Connecticut newspapers, the *Bronx Home News,* the Philadelphia *Sun* and *Public Ledger* as a dramatic critic until 1934. Did film writing in Hollywood, 1934-36. *Military service:* Served in Princess Patricia's Canadian Light Infantry during World War I, and as a major in the Film Unit of the Special Services section of the U.S. Army during World War II. *Awards, honors:* Pacific Northwest Library Association Young Readers' Choice Award, 1943, for *Lassie Come-Home.*

WRITINGS—Fiction: Invitation to Life, Greenberg, 1934; (with others) *The Flying Yorkshireman* (novellas), edited by Whitney E. Burnett and Martha Foley, Harper, 1936; *Song on Your Bugles,* Harper, 1937; (under pseudonym Richard Hallas) *You Play the Black and the Red Comes Up,* R. M. McBride, 1938; *The Happy Land,* Harper, 1940 (published in England as *Now We Pray for Our Country,* Cassell, 1940, reissued as *This is the Land,* Morley-Baker, 1969); *This Above All,* Harper, 1941; *Sam Small Flies Again: The Amazing Adventures of the Flying Yorkshireman* (short stories;

ERIC KNIGHT

illustrated by Donald McKay), Harper, 1942, reissued as *Sam Small: The Flying Yorkshireman,* N. Spearman, 1957.

For children: *Lassie Come-Home* (illustrated by Marguerite Kirmse), J. C. Winston, 1940, reissued, Dell, 1972 [later editions include an edition abridged by Felix Sutton and illustrated by Hans H. Helweg, Grosset & Dunlap, 1957; and editions illustrated by Lilian Obligado, Junior Deluxe Editions, 1964; Cyrus L. Baldridge, Holt, 1968; Don Bolognese, Holt, 1971].

Other: *They Don't Want Swamps and Jungles* (text broadcast by the author over the Canadian Broadcasting Corporation network, March 1, 1942), Director of Public Information, Ottawa, 1942; *Portrait of a Flying Yorkshireman: Letters from Eric Knight in the United States to Paul Rotha in England,* edited by P. Rotha, Chapman & Hall, 1952.

ADAPTATIONS—Movies: "Lassie Come Home," Metro-Goldwyn-Mayer, 1943; "Son of Lassie," adaptation of *Lassie Come-Home,* Metro-Goldwyn-Mayer, 1945; "Gypsy Colt," adaptation of *Lassie Come-Home,* starring Ward Bond, Metro-Goldwyn-Mayer, 1954; "Lassie" (television series), shown on CBS, 1954-72, originally starring Tommy Rettig and Jan Clayton, and later June Lockhart and Jon Provost, among others.

Recordings: "Lassie Come-Home," read by David McCallum, Caedmon Records, 1973.

SIDELIGHTS: **April 10, 1897.** Born in Yorkshire, England of Quaker parents, the third of four boys. "I have just odd memories of places—bluebells in Yorkshire; small blue butterflies and little snail shells in Hampshire, odd bits of memories of the Isle of Man and Jersey. Obviously we were always moving up and down. Then I was away at school for several

years and didn't see my mother much. I was often going to ask her about the places we floated around in. And here I am in middle life and now no one is left to connect up the flashes of memories." [Paul Rotha, editor, *Portrait of a Flying Yorkshireman: Letters from Eric Knight in the U.S. to Paul Rotha in England,* Chapman & Hall, 1952.[1]]

1899. Knight's father, Frederic Harrison Knight, a diamond merchant, died in South Africa. Although he lived extravagantly, he passed on without leaving his family sufficient funds. "... I am a product of rich England and poor England, and was born knowing wealth, and soon dropped into slums—not an unusual story. But I know what food and diet in a slum district of a British industrial town is. I know what an orange is. I got one—once every Christmas morning."[1]

1900. His mother, Marion Hilda Creasser, went to St. Petersburg (Leningrad) as the governess to Princess Xenia's children. "My mother was a stubborn, determined and purposeful woman. As a young widow she sailed out into the world to make a living for her sons. My first remembered letters from her came from St. Petersburg, where she was governess to the children of Princess Xenia, I believe. She sent me, I remember, small blue stones picked up from some Russian seashore beach and she said they called her Gulda Feodorovna. She now had three Russian boys to take care of. A childhood grudge was that I had to remember them in my prayers, and really I was jealous of them. She had sent a picture of herself with one of them riding pick-a-back.

"I suppose we were pretty much of a nuisance to a young and pretty widow—she was only twenty-four when she went to Russia—so we all got scattered around with relatives. I suppose we were more or less an unwanted nuisance to them, too. My younger brother died—that was Noel. When I was about six I saw Fred and Ed, my older brothers, for one day as I was bundled through London on my way to still some other relative. They were almost grown men when I saw them again.

"I think my case got pretty well lost in the shuffle, and I ended up in a manufacturing town in Yorkshire with an uncle who was a carter. He was a man of sudden and furious tempers, but to me one of the kindest and most loving men who have entered my life. I was extremely happy there, went to grade school with the local lads and learned to take the upper-class drawl out of my voice and to speak good dialect. It was a very sane childhood."

1909. Began work at age twelve in a textile factory. Over the next three years, worked in a steel mill, cotton mill, worsted mill, sawmill, and a glass-blowing factory. "When I was twelve my uncle died and I passed on to still other relatives and lived at Skircoat Green in Yorkshire, which is more or less the setting of the Powkithorpe Brig in the Sam Small stories. I enjoyed life there, too, and left behind any still lingering pretensions of more polished life. I learned the change in dialect, and at twelve went half-timing in the mills as a bobbin setter, working half a day, going to school half a day. At thirteen I started work full time and became the head doffer in charge of a half-dozen other lads in their first long trousers. The days were very long, but the mill lasses sang all day, and the hours droned past.

"I got a little ambitious and was apprenticed in an engine works at Leeds. I wanted to be an artificer in the Royal Navy, but the place came out on strike a month later, and I was in my first labor struggle. I was a good striker. I never went back, but the strike dragged on and we began to get a

(From *Lassie Come Home* by Eric Knight. Illustrated by Marguerite Kirmse.)

Just a boy and his dog···

From the pages of Eric Knight's great best-seller (he wrote "This Above All" too, remember?) comes a great drama. No roar of guns, no bombs, no tanks, no planes here . . . but emotion deep, human and intense in a story you'll live and love. The kind of story real people like to pass along to their friends.

M-G-M *PRESENTS THE* TECHNICOLOR *PRODUCTION*

LASSIE
COME HOME

Screen Play by Hugo Butler
Based Upon the Novel by Eric Knight

A Metro-Goldwyn-Mayer Picture
with RODDY McDOWALL · DONALD CRISP
DAME MAY WHITTY · EDMUND GWENN
NIGEL BRUCE · ELSA LANCHESTER · LASSIE
Directed by FRED M. WILCOX · Produced by SAMUEL MARX

Magazine advertisement for "Lassie Come Home."

bit hungry. I got a job at a sawmill. Then I was taker-off at a bottle-blowing place—twelve-hour shift a night on piece work with the blowers.''

''It is curious how, after all these years, as I start to write I can find flooding back the terrible misery of the conditions in the industrial north, the children of 12 working long hours, the strikes, the hunger, the shame of poverty, of necessity paraded, the grubbing for coal during the strikes. Sights and sounds and smells of those times come stronger than those of yesterday. The speech, the actions of the people—they're all there. I enjoy writing it but don't enjoy thinking too much about it. I can't remember much of our life—beyond laburnum in spring which we don't get [in the U.S.] and the largeness of staircases; but I do remember the life of the poor people and the things they thought and talked about.''[1]

1912. Reunited with his family in the United States. ''Suddenly that most interesting part of my life came to an end, and (why I don't just know). I was headed for America. In Philadelphia, after more than a dozen years, we were all together again. We were pretty much strangers. I was homesick and we didn't get along so well. They scrubbed the dialect out of my tongue and even tried to put me back in knickerbockers. Then I was shipped off to school. Took some concentrated studying at Cambridge Latin, then at the Boston Museum of Fine Arts, and the National Academy of Design in New York.

''It was a nice period in my life, but not one-half as interesting as the looms and bobbins and forges and furnaces and rivets and kilns and power-belts of the factories. I wasted time and didn't study much. . . .''

1912-1914. Attended Cambridge Latin School and the Academy of Fine Arts in Boston.

1914. Went to Toronto at the advent of World War I and enlisted as a private in Princess Patricia's Canadian Light Infantry. ''I went out of art school to war—ran up to Canada and enlisted to get into it. Certainly I threw away all the schooling, certainly I was far too young and impressionable to have gone to war, certainly I couldn't have stayed out because I believed too fiercely in what I believed. The utter coarseness and monotony of training in the South of England, the vileness of the army system, nearly killed me outright. Today it wouldn't disturb me, but I was very young. I wasn't emotionally stable enough to get through it. I think I choked mentally. The war itself finished me up, because I wouldn't ever admit to myself that I'd let myself in for something utterly horrible and grossly wrong.

''I recall the fine, flowering flame of enthusiasm that burned in all the men I left Canada with to go overseas—an enthusiasm and high pitch of training that would have been of use. I remember our first horrible repulsion as we were lined up before British sergeants at Seaford and treated to the filthiest line of gibberish ever free men listened to.

''The stream of foul ugliness went on day after day as we were put through the same silly foolishness we had learned as recruits for a year in Canada. I think they must purposely have picked the lowest type of man in the British army to 'train' us. It was all so absolutely low and brutalized that I can remember the one man who stood out as different—a P.T. instructor. Mind you—we were all college kids or of equal ratio in my draft. I wanted to cry: 'Why? I don't mind the filthy nauseating streams of hackneyed gibberish if it had a purpose—but what is the need of it for us here? We have come because we WISH to serve. We want to serve.'

''We WANTED to get to France and serve. We found that 'being sent over' was a PUNISHMENT.

''Of course we revolted, we sank lower and lower to subterfuge equal to the training; we revolted and smashed huts, we blocked all progress, we refused to leave huts until we had more food, we evaded duties and became adept at it; we went AWOL and thought ourselves luckier to be in guardhouses when we got back than to be on dismal parade grounds.

''I think the only man we ever did anything for with one grain of goodwill was the P.T. man who took us on bayonet-fighting the first morning, lined us up around him, looked us over quietly, and said: 'I am here to teach you how to become first-class, professional murderers.'

''That man we could understand. The prospect before our own souls of killing a man had been fought out, each one of us, in private long ago—possibly before we joined up. The greater prospect of this man having to teach it was a new one, an understandable one. He was human. We understood him. We tried to learn quickly for him. But he was one man amid ugliness, pettiness, drunkenness, lead-swinging, old-soldierism, and degradation. After a few months of England, we were reduced to dumb insolence, spiritual revolt, mental uncleanliness. We went to France with relief, promptly rioted and fought with all British soldiers we could find, lynched two British M.P.'s at Boulogne, and never got into the war with that valuable fresh impact of intense enthusiasm and patriotism (call it what you will) that we had had when we landed in Britain.''[1]

1917. Married Dorothy Noyes Hall. Had three daughters by this marriage.

June, 1918. Both his brothers killed the same day in France while serving in the American Army. ''. . . After the War there was no more family. Fred and Ed were killed together in June 1918 in the 110th Pennsylvania Infantry. We never did really get that Family together and mother's masterfulness and determination seemed to leave her suddenly. I became to her always a reminder of the other two who didn't come back, I suppose. It would have been the same no matter which one of us came home. She died not long after.''[2]

''But what I wanted to admit was that after the war, I found a mental change. For ten years I sat here and never read, never heard any music. I drifted into the American army and became a good artillery expert, taught artillery, went through the courses at Sill School of Fire, Oklahoma. Suddenly at 28, it seemed as if I picked up where I had left off at 18. But I find to my sorrow that something has happened to my memory. I can't remember people's names although I remember faces. I can't remember what I write and what I read. Curious, I can reel off for you anything that happened before the war—all the names of every last boy in any class at school, any book I had read: I can quote you pages of Latin or English poetry that I read in school; I remember line after line of the Wordsworth and Longfellow I had stuffed into me at the age of 8 and 10. Yet I can't remember a thing that I read after the war. I read it—it disappears immediately. I find myself reading books I have read before and only half-suspecting it when I am nearly through.

''It's a hell of a short life though . . . and possibly a damn good one. When I got out of the last war after three years I decided that all the rest of my life was velvet to which I had no legal or moral right. We've had the supreme pleasure of finding out that most of the world is a silly fake, that the solons are cardboard and the great men really stuffed pomposities of laughable dullness. We've sworn a good swear at them once in a while. It's good to laugh at the silly prospect they present, once in a while, too.''[1]

1919-1932. Tried painting, but discovered himself to be, as he put it, ''rather color blind.'' Worked as a cartoonist but soon began newspaper writing. Held jobs with the Darien *Review*, Norwalk *Sentinel*, and Bronx *Home News*.

1932. Married his second wife, Jere Knight, also a writer. ''A woman just wrote me that I had degraded womanhood. Not me. I love womanhood. American womanhood, British womanhood, all womanhood. Womanhood keeps on being wonderful and fascinating and I can't change it one way or another. I can just be interested. I am married. I am perfectly happy with my wife in all ways.'' [Robert Van Gelder, *Writers and Writing,* Scribner, 1946.[2]]

1932-1934. Worked as a film critic for the *Philadelphia Ledger.* ''The first story sold? Oh I'd once written six columns—stories going behind small news items. A Polish woman gets thirty days for knifing her husband. What made her knife him? I tried to sell the idea of these columns as a feature to a newspaper editor. He read the samples—couldn't use 'em. I sent one called 'The Two-fifty Hat'

(From the movie "Gypsy Colt" based on the novel *Lassie Come Home.* Copyright 1954 by Loew's, Inc.)

to *Liberty* and sold it. Then one day a writer in California showed us his patio—palm trees, goldfish in a pool, all that. A perambulating typewriter table. I began fooling on his typewriter and wrote one called 'Meet Me in the Shadows.' This made an O. Henry Memorial volume—but let it alone. Please. To hell with starving-young-author-makes-his-way-in-life.''[2]

1934. Saw his first novel, *Invitation to Life,* published. ''I have word that my novel is 'being duly considered and well reported on' by publishers. They must be crazy. They want me to do the first four chapters of a cinema book with an outline which they will consider. But I can't do it. Newspaper work makes me write such a lot daily that I have to rack my brains terribly each day to keep truth and vitality and reason in my column. I find I have just completed my 3000th article on matters cinemawise in the last five years. I groan.

''This month we move out to the country—to Valley Forge where Washington wintered. God knows, I would give my left hand to get away from newspaper work with its daily quota necessities and the gabbling before clubwomen. You spend an hour outlining the structure of cinema and always some poor sweet thing ends by asking: 'What do you think of John Barrymore?' ''[1]

1934-1935. Went to Hollywood to work as a film writer. ''If I told you about this place you wouldn't believe me. If I chronicled the amazing concatenation of idiocies and irritants, you'd merely say I'd been watching one of the stage satires on Hollywood.

''It is just like the stories. I sit here in a beautiful office—my office. Having refused a secretary to do God knows what, I sit alone and contemplate my beautiful office, the marvellous carpet, the dinky lamps, the desk with doodahs on it, the comfortable chairs. Outside in this indescribable California weather strange black birds with yellow-button eyes scream on sunstriped lawns. Tropical foliage, marvellous trees, brilliant unnamable flowers stand in miraculous park-like order.

"I sit here. I have nothing to do. I have had nothing to do for days. I have had nothing to do since I came here. No one opens my office door. No one hints what might be expected of me to earn my handsome salary. No one knows I'm here, or gives a good Goddamn.

"The monotony of the sunshine gets equalled by the monotony of kindness. If only a good city-editorial voice would call me a son-of-a-bitch in lovely harsh tones, and tell me for the love of so-and-so to get something written and write it in twenty-minutes—must!

"But no! Take your time, they say. You'll be homesick at first and so we don't expect you to do anything for quite a while. Just be happy and walk around and get used to the climate. If you need anything, just ask us. And be happy!

"How can I be happy after the strange, hard, fine vigorous rush of the East? *Dolce far niente* isn't a motto—it's a curse. How I miss the cold mornings at Valley Forge when the mists lay in the valleys and the steam rose from the horses.

"But I will be hard. I won't go soft. That's why they get us fellows out here. They come out. They still have the Eastern vigor. They produce. They soften under the warm climate and the easy living. Then they're fired—through—used up.

"Nothing shall use me up. I shall give nothing away. I shall offer no ideas. I shall produce nothing from my brain. I shall give nothing of myself to this industry except competent workmanship. I shall not smash my head and spill my ideas and beliefs against the stone wall of their soft stodginess. I shall work, observe, watch—and only if I ever get a picture of my own shall I bring out any of my ideas. They don't want movies. They don't want my ideas. They want dialogue and stars. I'll write them dialogue. I'll take their money; I'll save most of the salary. I'll produce a picture of my own before I'm through."[1]

1936. Moved to an alfalfa farm in Zelzah, California to devote all his time to his own writing. "So I finally offered my resignation. In typical Hollywood fashion it was rejected. I was fired two days later.

"The curious thing is that I am now happy. I am becoming Me again. I am beginning to feel honest and can turn to a typewriter once more without apologizing to it. So starts a new chapter in life; and I get nearer to the inevitable grave.

"Now I sit in a shack, eight feet by eight, in the middle of an alfalfa field, and am completely happy and never think of

(From the movie "Son of Lassie," based on the novel *Lassie Come Home,* starring Peter Lawford. Copyright 1945 by Loew's, Inc.)

films all day long. In our wide valley the mountains reach up, always changing in the light, on three sides. I cut hay and build a house. I irrigate land and make a living alone.

"Let me tell you about my place. At night the oil lamp burns and the great pullman trains go swinging past with people sitting in them looking out. I always used to sit in trains and see a light in a shack and wonder who the person was. And now I know. He was a Me, and he didn't envy my superior luxury.

"It is the land of blue jeans."[1]

"Whit Burnett, E. E. Cummings, Ernest Hemingway, a lot of people helped me. Hemingway solved a routine-of-work problem, that of getting started each day.

"I write nine to one each morning—if I miss I don't feel good. The typewriter is modern, puts down in four hours about all you can generate in a day. I used to get stuck, each morning—have to sit down and write 'quick brown fox' or any junk for half an hour trying to get going and then throw the first five pages away. If you write or talk long enough, you'll always say something that's fairly sensible—in talking you're stuck with it all, but in writing you just throw away the bad parts.

"Hemingway said: 'I always stop when I'm going good. Right in the middle of a speech, maybe when I know what she's going to say and what he's going to answer.'

"That's a good way. Anyway, it works for me. You pick up each morning and finish those easy lines—then you're going. You don't have time to start wondering about rent or the uselessness of writing in the face of infinity or whether you really have cancer of the throat or is it smoking too much. You're right in it, and when somebody says, 'Lunch!' you say, 'By gum, where do the hours go to?'

"Then the rest of the day you get out and become a human being with other human beings to stop people from becoming something that exists only on paper. You've got to become part of other people or else you'll never know what they're laughing at and belly-aching about and thinking and feeling. You can't think humanity out in a study. If you do, you'll understand people only as they ought to exist—but not as they do exist."[3]

1936. Wrote his second novel, *Song On Your Bugles*—a story about an English mill worker who becomes an artist. "... This novel ... attempts to give you the color and feeling of a very fine spoken language. ...

"Do not be disturbed if one moment a character talks dialect and in the next uses precise English. It is natural and usual, and makes of the language a double-edged weapon.

"Yorkshire dialect itself is a mixture of corrupted English plus the remnants of a language which existed long before the tongue of the middle counties began to grow into the

(From the movie "This Above All," starring Tyrone Power and Joan Fontaine. Copyright 1942 by Twentieth Century-Fox Film Corp.)

(From the television production of "Lassie." The original cast, starring Jan Clayton and Tommy Rettig.)

English we have today. The sad thing is that the so-called education of the day frowns on Yorkshire speech as 'low-class' or 'ignorant' or 'uncouth' or many other things. So what with mass education, class-conscious and snobbish parents, sound motion pictures and radio, what is a fine and honest and most mouth-filling and expressive spoken tongue is dying out in the larger towns. Yet it is strong enough not to die quickly. Old People cannot rid themselves of it, children become bilingual and use one English for teachers and parents and another when beyond their control. Yet the rougher tongue is the stronger of the two. Often, as a child, I was punished because I used a dialectical word and couldn't remember the English word for the same thing." [Eric Knight, from the foreword to *Song On Your Bugles*, Harper and Bros., 1937.[3]]

"You can only write about what you've felt and known and thus all writing is autobiographical. How the hell can you write about hunger or violence or death when you've not seen or known any of the three. You can fake, that's all. But if you had to make the reader who never knew hunger feel a pain in his guts and a deadness of the body that is hunger, you couldn't. But why kick on that? That's swell. We write about what we know and phooey on the birds who think it all up from the eyebrows and above. You write from down in your belly, not in your head alone."[1]

1937. Returned East, to Croton-on-Hudson, New York. "Here is a Cottage. It is beside the great stone walls of a barn whose roof tumbled in years ago. Now all, even the space within the barn, is green lawn. The ruined walls are creeper-colored. Only here, of all places, can one find that feeling of quiet age that is so common in England.

"[Our collie, named Toots] with us once again, lives in a riotous new world. Gophers, jacks, she knows. But not these strange animals: cottontails who sit in the quiet of the evening on the cloistered lawn; pheasants and quail that rush up from the fields around; even a deer with great white rump and tail that went springing on india-rubber stiff legs across a swamp. Flowers I do not know, smells I had almost forgotten in the dryness of California and the dust of New York—they are too much at present. Soon I shall become used to them, and then ignore them and work better."[1]

July, 1937. Knight's popular tale, "The Flying Yorkshireman," first appeared in *Story* Magazine. "... Once I had admitted in the first line ... that Sam Small believed he could fly if he had faith, it was almost out of my hands." [*Wilson Library Bulletin*, March, 1941.[4]]

"You wonder how a man can write of England and Yorkshire when he is so removed by contrast? Good god, man, it is just the contrast that allows us to see, isn't it—or don't you get that? I only know how lush and green England is when I am in the aridness of New Mexico—or how English towns always smell of coal-smoke until I am in a Mexican village where it always smells otherwise—of *piñon* wood-smoke. I can only see how bad is the poverty of a Yorkshire town when I am in the far-more-blessed poverty of the New Mexican land. In a town, rags and dirt are an offense to man's dignity. Out on the land where earth is scratched for a living, rags and dirt ARE dignity. In a town unwashedness is a disgust—in the hot, waterless lands unwashedness is normal. (It is only in cities that men smell, and in damp climates. In the thirsty lands with dehydrated air there is little smell except of firesmoke, except after a rain. Then it soon goes.)

"No man knows England, longs for England, knows how great her clouds, blue the bluebells, sweet the lark, warm the homes, solid and pretty damned good the citizenry, law-abiding its people, offensive its smug middle-class, beautiful and neat her farmlands, prim her hedges, bad her housing, rotten her dentistry, awful her food, excellent her whisky and beer and pork pies, soft her rainsoaked air, amazing her gardens, generally polite her people, expensive her tobacco, good her tea—until he has lived in a place where all these things are not, and so longs and tastes and sees more than clearly these virtues and vices that are his own. How the hell can you know a hawthorn in blossom till you've seen the barren idiocy of palm trees in a row?"[1]

1938. Revisited Yorkshire and viewed its impoverished areas. The social inequities he saw inspired his novel with the ironic title, *The Happy Land*. "It is not as good as I wish—had I wished less it would have succeeded more. What burns in us, unworthy worms, that we wish to create something permanent, a mark our lives leave? I did want to leave some 'literature' and maybe all I shall ever do is fiction. But we try."[1]

1940. *Lassie, Come-Home*, was published. "My juvenile book is finished and a neat job of bread-and-butter workmanship is done.

"I ... now am doing the illustrations busily for it—22 pen and ink sketches of dogs. I always wanted to illustrate a book of my own.

"It was written about Toots, after a lonesome walk back of the hills you know so well as Croton."[1]

1941. Wrote *This Above All,* a realistic novel about a self-educated Englishman of lowly origin caught up in World War II. Considered by some critics to be the first great novel written about the war. "*This Above All* goes increasingly well here. Sales are biggest this week since publication, and it shows no signs of coming off the top of the best-seller list. All publishers said that Americans needed escape books and that no book dealing with war would sell. And for weeks the four top best-sellers in fiction and non-fiction have been Churchill's book, a book on Churchill, Hilton, *Random Harvest* and mine.

"I hope *This Above All* is understood in England. I am British by birth and habit, but American by training in writing. It is a curious mixture. Some people home may object to the book. But I think it succeeded for me—the writing of it. For I tried to raise all the problems concerning war that face the young man of today, brought up on 'no-more-war' and pre-Munich *laissez-faire.* And if I didn't answer all the questions—for not being God I couldn't answer some—at least I didn't ignore them.

"The White House has asked me to call at Hyde Park, and you can be sure that this is exactly the sort of matter that will meet with approving ears with Mrs. Roosevelt. I have had encouraging words from her by mail—I was honored and surprised at her request that we call.

"Over here I've been accused of anti-Semitism, anti-laborism, anti-Briticism, and anti-decency. The truth is, of course, that I am no great intellect—just an ignorant half-taught man, moved only by what I've seen in my life, by the information and misinformation I've read, colored by my prides and prejudices and experiences. I am not so anti-anything as I'm pro-humanity. The poor, bleeding, bloody, misguided, human being. Happy so infrequently! Noble so seldom! But so goddamned courageous—coming back for more all the time, always bucking fate year after year."[1]

"It doesn't matter if the writer is a ham. All that matters is that his characters shouldn't be—that he respect their integrity.

"How do I mean that? Well, you have a scene—you can see everybody there. Clive, your male character, says this. All right, it's the girl's turn. Prue's tired. She hasn't had breakfast. She says this back. Monty puts in his line—it's got to be right. Monty is alive—a real lad.

"You get up and walk around, saying it all out loud. It's no good. Clive's first line wasn't his. It was yours—something you wanted to say yourself. He couldn't say it. Throw it out and start all over—keep on saying it until it's right in origin and thought and phrase and sound. So you're walking around in a fog talking to yourself like a ham actor—but you can't let your characters ham. You can't kick them around. You've got to respect them and their limitations. Maybe that isn't the right way to write. It's the only way I know—playing it by ear.

"I don't know anything about playing by note from the classic form. I'm sorry. It's not a pose—sometimes I feel I must be missing a lot in life. I don't understand it—the good writing. I don't understand culture, maybe because I haven't got it. Listen, all those good British authors, I pick them up and it's beautiful writing, it's magnificent. And I don't know what the hell it's all about. I'm not knocking Britain. We have swell writers in Yorkshire and in Wales, too, and other

(From the television production of "Lassie," starring Jon Provost and Cloris Leachman, 1957.)

sections; but they're not the ones accepted here as British writers. It makes me wonder.

"I've been compared to D. H. Lawrence, Hemingway, everybody but Shakespeare. I'd be very happy and proud if some one would compare me to Shakespeare. Look, old man, if you could see your way clear—But have another drink. Shakespeare! There you have everything. I know what Kipling means when he's writing. I know what Dickens is writing and talking about and feeling. Shakespeare—every word and every line . . . there's nothing beyond it left to say. And he didn't have culture. By gum, no. He played by ear. He had to. There was no style. He had to make it up as he went along. He never worried about it. He was and is style. There was less barricade between him and his paper than any man who ever wrote."[2]

April, 1942. Commissioned as a major in the film unit of the Special Services section during World War II. "Frank Capra wired me to go to Washington and said: 'We need you, we need your capabilities. You can write like stinko, and you've been in on the British film end. I want you to do something for me.' I was never so gratified, because you know how I feel about Capra, as counter to about 50,000 other Hollywood bastards. He quit Hollywood, and is a major in the Films Division now, and bright and sharp as you want. So I do a script for him about Britain—what the people are like, the land, the habits—take 'em apart. It's for Army use, and they have a grand, sane plan for documentary use in Army movies. You should do the same thing there. Cultural, but outspoken everyday films made for the soldiers—what the war's about, what our enemies are like, what our allies are like. It's as sensible a procedure as I've heard of.

"Well, that makes me happy to be doing something. I was discontented just pounding on my own hook, and I like Capra and think I can work with him. That is, I know. I hope he can work with me.

"Washington is crowded so they sent me home to work here, which pleases me, as I now get up at dawn and work four hours, and then I work four hours again late in the evening. Cockeyed, but as long as the stuff flows out, I never question it.

"I know you'll get a good laugh out of me becoming a filmster after all these years of thumbing my nose at Hollywood.

"If I'm a propagandist—all right, I am—I'm tired of seeing German propaganda directed, channelized, regulated. It's time we got busy as if this were not a game but a life and death struggle.

"For we need this—propaganda in the best sense. Propaganda is best when its message is swallowed in admiration of the method—your words—in other words, a subconscious digestion. If, to show how British documentarians work and excel, I can show a film which also explains Britain's great work in this war, then I succeed. As it is, I have to use a film showing how British mail clerks worked pre-war. What a pity!

"We do need propaganda here. It is always my fate to be in centers of isolationist or Pro-German spirit—at home, and now out here. The Middle-West IS isolationist. The country at large is not. Here, at movie shows, I burn with anger and indignation as Roosevelt is laughed at on the screen, and Lindberg is applauded to the limit. Poor, weak, unseeing people to fail to see that this war, and other wars, must always go on. To stop fighting for human dignity is to surrender it—now as at Valley Forge in 1776, and as it will be in 1976, I have no doubt.

"Man has no right to victory, nor to final solutions. But he has the right to fight eternally for them.

"Let me tell you of this country as it is now. We are asking questions. We want a vision. We haven't got it.

"All men love to be heroes. We want to be great. The only way the weak willies can feel great is to take up a lost cause and get themselves oppressed for it. Me, I like the old army motto better: 'Never talk bigger than your weight.'

"I don't know much about life . . . but I know I feel healthier when I'm among men who can keep their mouths shut when they're hurt. Effeminate, weak, crying mankind—and I would swap the whole pack of intellectuals for a half-dozen puzzled young kids who didn't say a word as they walked into machine-guns and died in my outfit in France.

"There is only one approach to life, and you'll find it out for yourself. To cry: 'Where is the world going; how can we save it?' is useless.

"The answer to it all is that there is no answer to it all. We want the ideal world with every man fed and every woman content, where there is no hunger and no crime and no oppression. We can't have it. It exists only in our desire.

ERIC KNIGHT

(From the movie "Lassie Come Home," starring Elizabeth Taylor and Nigel Bruce. Copyright 1943 by Loew's, Inc.)

"The way to light is to turn inward. To say: "I, myself, shall be clean. In a world of injustice I shall be just; in a time of chaos I shall be within myself all that is order; in a time of panic I shall be alone but brave.' "[1]

1942-1943. *Lassie, Come-Home* was made into a highly successful motion picture starring Roddy McDowell and Elizabeth Taylor. "*Lassie* is becoming a super-duper-dooper at MGM, with the shooting dragging on and on, and the budget going up and up—so what was a nice little dog story maybe will be summat, lad. I can't tell. I saw the exteriors done in Technicolor—the rushes—and they begged me to say that the shores of the State of Washington looked like Scotland. I say they were exactly the same—all excepting the points where there were pelicans on the rocks in the background. They assured me they'd cut out the pelicans.

"MGM asked about cast, and to my surprise took my suggestions lightly given—I said—because you always have to base it on something they know—'Make it like *How Green Was My Valley.*' That gave them the idea. Roddy McDowall, Donald Crisp, et al, are now in the cast in leading roles. I am suggesting calling it 'How Technicolor Was My Lassie Come to My Valley Home.' "[1]

"The dog is the most magnificent collie I've ever seen—in conformation, color and brilliant sense. Oh, gladly do I call him a movie star. I coveted him more than I ever did la Fontaine, la Lamour and all the other pretty stars. (They couldn't get a bitch for the part that looked right, so he's a female impersonator—and thank God he's got a long coat that covers his manhood.) Anyhow, I've been promised a son of his for the farm." [*TV Guide,* June 10, 1972.[7]]

"My old lady Toots is getting a bit grey, more feeble. I sorrow about her, and she sorrows for us away in the war. She's a big chunk of my life and history, with all the thousands of miles she's travelled with us, and she can't understand these war-time absences.

"I am more in the Army now. I no longer have any desire to get out of uniform when I go home and put on civilian clothes to rest. That's the test—like dreaming in a foreign language shows you're living and thinking in it. Anyway, I won't see home for a long time."[1]

January 15, 1943. Died when a U.S. military transport plane en route for Cairo, Africa crashed in the Surinam jungle.

ERIC KNIGHT, 1937.

FOR MORE INFORMATION SEE: Robert Van Gelder, *Writers and Writing,* Scribner, 1946; Elizabeth Rider Montgomery, *Story behind Modern Books,* Dodd, 1949; Paul Rotha, editor, *Portrait of a Flying Yorkshireman: Letters from Eric Knight in the U.S. to Paul Rotha in England,* Chapman & Hall, 1952; Stanley J. Kunitz, *Twentieth Century Authors,* first supplement, H. W. Wilson, 1955; Frank N. Magill, editor, *Cyclopedia of World Authors,* Harper, 1958; Brian Doyle, editor, *Who's Who of Children's Literature,* Schocken Books, 1968.

KRUSH, Beth   1918-

PERSONAL: Born March 31, 1918, in Washington, D.C.; married Joe Krush (an illustrator); children: one son. *Education:* Attended the Philadelphia Museum School of Art. *Home:* Wayne, Penn.

CAREER: Illustrator of books for young people. Has taught at the Moore College of Art. *Member:* Society of Illustrators.

ILLUSTRATOR: Anne Emery, *Senior Year,* Westminster, 1949; Sally Scott, *Rip and Royal,* Harcourt, 1950; Scott, *Tippy,* Harcourt, 1950; Scott, *Little Wiener,* Harcourt, 1951; Scott, *Benjie and His Family,* Harcourt, 1952; Scott, *Binky's Fire,* Harcourt, 1952; Scott, *Jonathan,* Harcourt, 1953; Scott, *Bobby and His Band,* Harcourt, 1954; James S. Tippett, *Search for Sammie,* Abingdon, 1954; S. Scott, *Jason and Timmy,* Harcourt, 1955; Scott, *What Sally Wanted,* Harcourt, 1956; Scott, *Bitsy,* Harcourt, 1957; Scott, *Judy's Surprising Day,* Harcourt, 1957; Edna S. Weiss, *Truly Elizabeth,* Houghton, 1957; S. Scott, *Tinker Takes a Walk,* Har-

court, 1958; Scott, *There Was Timmy,* Harcourt, 1959; Scott, *Judy's Summer Adventure,* Harcourt, 1966; Rebecca Caudill, *Higgins and the Great Big Scare,* Holt, 1960; Elizabeth G. Baker, *Tammy Climbs Pyramid Mountain,* Houghton, 1962; S. Scott, *Sunny Jim: The Uppity Kitten,* Harcourt, 1962; Eudora Welty, *The Shoe Bird,* Harcourt, 1964; E. G. Baker, *Tammy Goes Canoeing,* Houghton, 1966; Baker, *Tammy Camps in the Rocky Mountains,* Houghton, 1970.

With husband, Joe Krush: Betty Cavanna, *Spring Comes Riding,* Westminster, 1950; Stuart B. Courtis and Garnette Watters, *Illustrated Dictionary for Young Readers,* Simon & Schuster, 1951, revised edition published as *Illustrated Golden Dictionary for Young Readers,* Western, 1965; Louis Untermeyer, *Magic Circle,* Harcourt, 1952; Mary Norton, *The Borrowers,* Harcourt, 1953, reissued, 1965; Lilian Moore, *Golden Picture Dictionary,* Simon & Schuster, 1954; M. Norton, *The Borrowers Afield,* Harcourt, 1955, reissued, 1970; Nora Kramer, editor, *Storybook,* Gilbert Press, 1955; Kramer, editor, *Second Storybook,* Gilbert Press, 1955; Marion Garthwaite, *Coarse Gold Gulch,* Doubleday, 1956; Florence Hightower, *Mrs. Wappinger's Secret,* Houghton, 1956; B. Cleary, *Fifteen,* Morrow, 1956; Virginia Sorensen, *Miracles on Maple Hill,* Harcourt, 1956, reissued, 1972; Elizabeth Enright, *Gone Away Lake,* Harcourt, 1957, reissued, 1966; Charlton Ogburn, Jr., *Big Caesar,* Houghton, 1958; Eleanor Cameron, *The Terrible Churnadyne,* Little, Brown, 1959; B. Cleary, *Jean and Johnny,* Morrow, 1959.

John Langstaff, *The Swapping Boy,* Harcourt, 1960; B. Cleary, *Emily's Runaway Imagination,* Morrow, 1961; M. Norton, *The Borrowers Afloat,* Harcourt, 1961, reissued, 1973; Norton, *The Borrowers Aloft,* Harcourt, 1961, reissued, 1974; E. Enright, *Return to Gone Away,* Harcourt, 1961, reissued, 1973; Irving A. Leitner, *Lady Pole and Mr. Potts,* Harcourt, 1962; B. Cleary, *Sister of the Bride,* Morrow, 1963; Harold Courlander, *The Piece of Fire,* Harcourt, 1964; E. Cameron, *A Spell Is Cast,* Little, Brown, 1964; Alberta W. Constant, *Those Miller Girls!,* Crowell, 1965; M. Norton, *Poor Stainless: A New Story about the Borrowers,* Harcourt, 1966, reissued, 1971; Norton, *Complete Adventures of the Borrowers,* Harcourt, 1967; Mary P. Warren, *A Snake Named Sam,* Westminster, 1969; A. W. Constant, *The Motoring Millers,* Crowell, 1969.

Elizabeth K. Cooper, *The Fish from Japan,* Harcourt, 1969; Ruth C. Carlsen, *Ride a Wild Horse,* Houghton, 1970; Elizabeth Hall, *Stand Up, Lucy,* Houghton, 1971; E. G. Baker, *This Stranger, My Son,* Houghton, 1971; F. Hightower, *The Secret of the Crazy Quilt,* Houghton, 1972; Sydney Taylor, *All-of-a-Kind Family Downtown,* Follett, 1972; M. P. Warren, *Ghost Town for Sale,* Westminster, 1973; Carol M. Adorjan, *The Cat Sitter Mystery,* J. P. O'Hara, 1973; B. Cavanna, *Petey,* Westminster, 1973; Helen Chetin, *Perihan's Promise, Turkish Relatives, and the Dirty Old Imam,* Houghton, 1973; Genevieve S. Gray, *Sore Loser,* Houghton, 1974; M. P. Warren, *River School Detectives,* Westminster, 1974; Jean H. Berg, *The Story of Jesus,* Christian Science Publishing, 1977; Florence and Roxanne Heide, *Brillstone Break-In,* Whitman, 1977.

SIDELIGHTS: Born March 31, 1918 in Washington, D.C. where her childhood was spent. "Washington, D.C. where I lived was a wonderful place for a child—parades, band concerts, a fine zoo, national shrines to see again and again with every visiting relative, and my favorite, the Smithsonian, where my grandmother would place herself on a bench facing a mammoth painting of the Grand Canyon and let me roam for hours among the dinosaur bones and wax Indians. I

BETH KRUSH

always loved to draw, my parents kept me supplied with paper and pencils and my 'home town' supplied me with subject material.'' [Lee Kingman and others, compilers, *Illustrators of Children's Books: 1957-1966*, Horn Book, 1968.[1]]

Krush attended the Philadelphia Museum School of Art where she met a fellow classmate and artist who became her husband and co-worker. ''Joe and I met at the Philadelphia Museum School of Art. Art school was a joy after years of being sent to the office for drawing in study hall. I won the illustration prize for the girls and Joe won the illustration prize for the boys. We also won an assortment of other prizes for water color, graphics, and drawing. We were married during World War II, and since the War we have worked at the business of making pictures together and separately. When we work together we usually pick the incidents and talk over the staging together, then Joe does the first composition and perspective sketch. Then I rework that, adding my ideas and looking up costumes, interiors, plants, animals and people. Most often Joe does the final rendering in his own decorative line. But we have our individual pride and each likes to do work that is all his or hers.''[1]

''For fifteen years I have taught Illustration and Drawing at Moore College of Art—the only woman's art college in the world to have been established before the civil war and endowed in the 1890's by the man whose name the school now carries for 'the education of young ladies in the arts.' At this time it is still a very relevant and excellent school. At present I am chairman of the Illustration Department. This takes a lot of time and I enjoy it. I also teach a course in 'Illustrating for Children' through the winter.

''Most of my art work lately has been with my husband who is a busy free-lancer doing a wide variety of art work besides children's books.

''This spring we were invited by the Smithsonian to give a slide talk on our work at the Hirshorn Museum in Washington, D. C.''

FOR MORE INFORMATION SEE: Henry C. Pitz, ''Joseph and Beth Krush: A Working Illustrative Team,'' *American Artist,* March, 1952; Bertha E. Miller and others, compilers, *Illustrators of Children's Books, 1946-1956,* Horn Book, 1958; Muriel Fuller, editor, *More Junior Authors,* H. W. Wilson, 1963; Lee Kingman and others, compilers, *Illustrators of Children's Books, 1957-1966,* Horn Book, 1968.

KRUSH, Joe   1918-

PERSONAL: Born May 18, 1918, in Camden, N.J.; married wife, Beth (an illustrator); children: one son. *Education:* Attended the Philadelphia Museum School of Art. *Home:* Wayne, Penn.

CAREER: Illustrator of books for young people. Teacher of illustration at the Philadelphia Museum School of Art. Freelancer of general illustrations to *Reader's Digest* and *Saturday Evening Post,* 1979. *Military service:* Served in the Office of Strategic Services during World War II. *Member:* Society of Illustrators.

ILLUSTRATOR: Geoffrey Trease, *Trumpets in the West,* Harcourt, 1947; G. Trease, *Secret Fiord,* Harcourt, 1950; Mary Norton, *Huon of the Horn,* Harcourt, 1951; Sally Scott, *Chica,* Harcourt, 1954; Jessamyn West, *Cress Delahanty,* Harcourt, 1954; Carl Sandburg, *Prairie Town Boy,* Harcourt, 1955; Philip Rush, *Minstrel Knight,* Bobbs-Merrill, 1956; John Langstaff, *Ol' Dan Tucker,* Harcourt, 1963.

With wife, Beth Krush: Betty Cavanna, *Spring Comes Riding,* Westminster, 1950; Stuart B. Courtis and Garnette Wat-

JOE KRUSH

He knelt down then, but Homily did not flinch as the great face came slowly closer. She saw his under lip, pink and full—like an enormous exaggeration of Arrietty's—and she saw it wobble slightly. ■ (From *The Borrowers* by Mary Norton. Illustrated by Beth and Joe Krush.)

ters, *Illustrated Dictionary for Young Readers*, Simon & Schuster, 1951, revised edition published as *Illustrated Golden Dictionary for Young Readers*, Western, 1965; Louis Untermeyer, *Magic Circle*, Harcourt, 1952; M. Norton, *The Borrowers*, Harcourt, 1953, reissued, 1965; Lilian Moore, *Golden Picture Dictionary*, Simon & Schuster, 1954; Norton, *The Borrowers Afield*, Harcourt, 1955, reissued, 1970; Nora Kramer, editor, *Storybook*, Gilbert Press, 1955; Kramer, editor, *Second Storybook*, Gilbert Press, 1955; Marion Garthwaite, *Coarse Gold Gulch*, Doubleday, 1956; Florence Hightower, *Mrs. Wappinger's Secret*, Houghton, 1956; B. Cleary, *Fifteen*, Morrow, 1956; Virginia Sorensen, *Miracles on Maple Hill*, Harcourt, 1956, reissued, 1972; Elizabeth Enright, *Gone Away Lake*, Harcourt, 1957, reissued, 1966; Charlton Ogburn, Jr., *Big Caesar*, Houghton, 1958; Eleanor Cameron, *The Terrible Churnadyne*, Little, Brown, 1959; B. Cleary, *Jean and Johnny*, Morrow, 1959.

John Langstaff, *The Swapping Boy*, Harcourt, 1960; B. Cleary, *Emily's Runaway Imagination*, Morrow, 1961; M. Norton, *The Borrowers Afloat*, Harcourt, 1961, reissued, 1973; Norton, *The Borrowers Aloft*, Harcourt, 1961, reissued, 1974; E. Enright, *Return to Gone Away*, Harcourt,

1961, reissued, 1973; Irving A. Leitner, *Lady Pole and Mr. Potts*, Harcourt, 1962; B. Cleary, *Sister of the Bride*, Morrow, 1963; Harold Courlander, *The Piece of Fire*, Harcourt, 1964; E. Cameron, *A Spell Is Cast*, Little, Brown, 1964; Alberta W. Constant, *Those Miller Girls!*, Crowell, 1965; M. Norton, *Poor Stainless: A New Story about the Borrowers*, Harcourt, 1966, reissued, 1971; Norton, *Complete Adventures of the Borrowers*, Harcourt, 1967; Mary P. Warren, *A Snake Named Sam*, Westminster, 1969; A. W. Constant, *The Motoring Millers*, Crowell, 1969; Elizabeth K. Cooper, *The Fish from Japan*, Harcourt, 1969.

Ruth C. Carlsen, *Ride a Wild Horse*, Houghton, 1970; Elizabeth Hall, *Stand Up, Lucy*, Houghton, 1971; E. G. Baker, *This Stranger, My Son*, Houghton, 1971; F. Hightower, *The Secret of the Crazy Quilt*, Houghton, 1972; Sydney Taylor, *All-of-a-Kind Family Downtown*, Follett, 1972; M. P. Warren, *Ghost Town for Sale*, Westminster, 1973; Carol M. Adorjan, *The Cat Sitter Mystery*, J. P. O'Hara, 1973; B. Cavanna, *Petey*, Westminster, 1973; Helen Chetin, *Perihan's Promise, Turkish Relatives, and the Dirty Old Imam*, Houghton, 1973; Genevieve S. Gray, *Sore Loser*, Houghton, 1974; M. P. Warren, *River School Detectives*, Westminster,

Mr. Goodall swept into the room and mounted the platform. "'All the world's a stage' after all 'and all the men and women merely players.'" ■ (From *The Cat Sitter Mystery* by Carol Adorjan. Illustrated by Beth and Joe Krush.)

Finally everything was arranged. Petey had the straw hat tied under his chin and tilted over his right eye. Totsy was bouncing in the cart, all set to go. ■ (From *Petey* by Betty Cavanna. Illustrated by Beth and Joe Krush.)

1974; Jean H. Berg, *The Story of Jesus,* Christian Science Publishing, 1977; Florence and Roxanne Heide, *Brillstone Break-In,* Whitman, 1977.

SIDELIGHTS: Born May 18, 1918, in Camden, N.J. and reared there. Krush attended the Philadelphia Museum School of Art where he met his wife.

Krush and his wife, Beth, had just begun their professional careers in illustration when he entered the army during World War II. He served in the O.S.S. where he had opportunities to design posters, graphs, displays and printed manuals and found himself present at two epoch making events—the signing of the United Nations Charter in San Francisco and the war trials in Nuremberg. Beth Krush recalled her husband's early life: "Joe and I grew up in typical row house neighborhoods of the twenties. Joe in Camden, New Jersey, where the busy Delaware River and the local airport (which had a real Ford Tri-Motor!) were major attractions. Though Joe denies any childhood ambition to be an artist, he filled notebooks with drawings of boats and won prizes for his model planes and boats. During the War Joe was with the Office of Strategic Services and attended the original meeting of the United Nations as a graphic designer, and the war guilt trials in Nuremberg, Germany." [Lee Kingman and others, compilers, *Illustrators of Children's Books: 1957-1966,* Horn Book, 1968.[2]]

Since then the Krushes have been involved in illustration as a team and separately. Beth Krush spoke of her husband's drawings which show a masculine love for gadgets and machinery: "He likes to tackle anything in the art line and has done a great variety of work in many media—posters, album covers, advertising and magazine illustrations, story books and text books."[1]

The Krushes' home is a restored Victorian summer house in Wayne, Pennsylvania, where he spends his time free-lancing, building model boats and radio-controlled planes, sailing and flying.

Krush's works are included in the Free Library of Philadelphia and in the Kerlan Collection at the University of Minnesota.

FOR MORE INFORMATION SEE: Henry C. Pitz, "Joseph and Beth Krush: A Working Illustrative Team," *American Artist,* March, 1952; Bertha E. Miller and others, compilers, *Illustrators of Children's Books, 1946-1956,* Horn Book, 1958; Muriel Fuller, editor, *More Junior Authors,* H. W. Wilson, 1963; Lee Kingman and others, compilers, *Illustrators of Children's Books, 1957-1966,* Horn Book, 1968.

KUTTNER, Paul 1931-

PERSONAL: Born September 20, 1931, in Berlin, Germany; son of Paul (a physician) and Margarete (a piano teacher; maiden name, Fraenkel) Kuttner; married Myrtil Romegialli, September, 1956 (divorced, 1960); married Ursula Timmermann, 1963 (divorced, 1970). *Education:* Educated in Berlin, Germany and Dorset, England. *Religion:* "Firm believer in the Universal Creator, but not in organized religion." *Home:* 37-26 87th St., Jackson Heights, N.Y. 11372. *Office:* Guinness *Book of World Records,* 26th floor, Two Park Ave., New York, N.Y. 10016.

CAREER: Der Weg (weekly newspaper), Bern, Switzerland, political, economic and cultural reporter, and correspondent in London, England, 1946-47; London News Chronicle, London, England, U.S. correspondent, 1948; *What's On in London—The London Week,* London, England, columnist in Hollywood, Calif. and New York City, 1948-56; affiliated as salesman with Watson-Guptill Publications, Inc., New York City, 1954-62; *Guinness Book of World Records,* New York City, publicity director, 1966-78. Social worker with Bureau of Displaced Persons (Church World Service), 1948-53.

WRITINGS—Novels; published by Sterling: *The Man Who Lost Everything,* 1977.

Juvenile; translator from the German; all published by Sterling: Katharina Zechlin, *Creative Enamelling and Jewelry*

Making, 1965; T. M. Schegger, *Make Your Own Mobiles,* 1965; A. Pfluger, *Karate: Basic Principles,* 1967; Susanne Strose, *Coloring Papers,* 1968; Susanne Strose, *Potato Printing,* 1968; Susanne Strose, *Candle Making,* 1968; Elmar Gruber, *Nail Sculpture,* 1968; Peter and Susanne Bauzen, *Flower Pressing,* 1972; Charles H. Paraquin, *Eye-Teasers: Optical Illusions and Puzzles,* 1976.

WORK IN PROGRESS: A play, "Odyssey Without End."

SIDELIGHTS: "Having been raised on the Spahn Ranch of *Mittel Europa* (Nazi Germany) in the 1930's, the melodrama and the tragedy of that era have left an indelible stamp on my mind, my writing, and the skepticism of my lifestyle. Melodrama: visiting my father at Berlin's Universum Film Aktiengesellschaft (UFA) movie studio where he was doctor-in-residence, watching Emil Jannings perform before the cameras, and my filmed conversation with Hitler, observing the political, racial, and cultural madness of the Nazi era in Berlin until 1939. Then the Tragedy: my parents murdered in a concentration camp, my sister, Annemarie, forced to live underground, and later dying of cancer, and I on my own at the age of eight, in England, where I spent my summer vacations with the Chairman of Lloyd's of London and was wounded by a V-1 Flying Bomb. These early events influenced my life more than any single work or writer.

"In the end, it was literature—Shakespeare, Tolstoy, Shaw, Forester, Greene, Salinger, Hemingway, Wolfe, Goethe—which generously and mercifully opened my eyes to look at the world with a clearer vision. Literature let me see life from a less hunted and more tranquil, contemplative perspective. It, more than any person, became my balm—the motivating factor that finally triggered my determination to settle down after a restless life and two marriages and write, write, write."

HOBBIES AND OTHER INTERESTS: Photography, amateur film-directing, oil painting.

PAUL KUTTNER

They are all the same height. The man at the right looks tallest. We expect things to look smaller when they are farther away. The man at the right is farthest away and we would expect him to look the smallest. Since he doesn't, we assume he's really larger than the others. ■ (From *Eye Teasers* written and illustrated by Charles H. Paraquin. Translated by Paul Kuttner.)

LA FONTAINE, Jean de   1621-1695

PERSONAL: Born July 8, 1621, in Château Thierry, France; died April 13, 1695, in Paris, France; buried in the Cemetery of the Holy Innocents; son of a provincial official; married Marie Héricart, 1647 (separated, 1659); children: one son. *Education:* Studied at various places, including Rheims, the seminary of St. Magloire, and l'Oratoire in Paris.

CAREER: Poet and author of fables. La Fontaine inherited his father's position with the French Civil Service as Master of Waters and Forests. Went to Paris, 1659, where he began his literary career, obtaining numerous patrons through the years. *Awards, honors:* Elected to the French Academy, 1683.

WRITINGS—Fables: *Fables* (illustrated by F. Chauveau), D. Thierry, Books I-VI, 1668, Books VII-XI, 1673-79, Book

XII, 1694, numerous English translations include *La Fontaine's Fables* (translated by Robert Thomson), [Paris], 1806; *Fables of La Fontaine* (translated by Elizur Wright, Jr.; illustrated by J. J. Grandville, pseudonym of Jean-Ignace Isidore Gerard), W. A. Coleman, 1841; *The Fables of La Fontaine* (translated by Walter Thornbury; illustrated by Gustave Doré), Cassell, 1873; *The Original Fables of La Fontaine* (translated and illustrated by Frederick Colin Tilney), Dutton, 1913; *Forty-Two Fables of La Fontaine* (translated by Edward Marsh), Heinemann, 1924, Harper, 1925, reissued as *Fables*, Dutton, 1966; *Fifty Fables from La Fontaine* (translated by Radcliffe Carter), Oxford University Press, 1928; *The Fables of Jean de la Fontaine* (translated by Joseph Auslander and Jacques LeClercq), Limited Editions, 1930; *The Fables of Jean de La Fontaine* (translated by E. Marsh; illustrated by Stephen Gooden), Heinemann, 1933; *The Fables of La Fontaine* (translated by Margaret Wise Brown; illustrated by Andre Helle), Harper, 1940; *Ten Fables* (translated by Jean Marie Sibley; illustrated by Dorothy Dey), Dorrance, 1947; *Selected Fables* (translated by Eunice Clark; illustrated by Alexander Calder), Quadrangle Press, 1948, reprinted, Dover, 1968; *The Fables of La Fontaine* (translated by Marianne Moore), Viking Press, 1954, new edition, 1965; *Fables* (translated by Marie Ponsot; illustrated by Simonne Baudoin), Grosset & Dunlap, 1957, reissued as *Selected Fables and Tales*, New American Library, 1966; *A Hundred Fables from La Fontaine* (translated by Philip Wayne), Anchor Books, 1961; *Fables from La Fontaine* (translated by Kitty Muggeridge; illustrated by J. B. Oudry), Collins, 1973.

Individual fables include *The Lion and the Rat*, 1963, *The North Wind and the Sun* (ALA Notable Book), 1964, *The

(From *Fables of La Fontaine* by Jean de La Fontaine. Illustrated by J.B. Oudry.)

JEAN DE LA FONTAINE

Rich Man and the Shoe-Maker, 1965, *The Hare and the Tortoise*, 1966, *The Miller, the Boy, and the Donkey*, 1969, all illustrated by Brian Wildsmith and published by F. Watts; other individual fable titles include *The Grasshopper and the Ant*, *The Two Pigeons*, *The Town Mouse and the Country Mouse*, *The Fox and the Stork*, *Cat into Lady*, *The Wolves and the Sheep*, *Perrette and the Jug of Milk*, *The Frogs Who Wanted to be King*, *The Crow and the Fox*, *The Two Hunters and the Bear*, *The Rabbit and the Frogs*, and *The Cockerel, the Cat, and the Young Mouse*.

Other writings: *Contes et Nouvelles en Vers* (stories; based on stories by Boccacio, Ariosto, and Rabelais), [Paris], Part I, 1664, Part II, 1668, Part III, 1671, Part IV, 1674, English translations include *Tales and Novels in Verse*, S. Humphreys, 1762; *Tales and Novels*, [New York], 1929; *Les Amours de Psyche et de Cupidon* (novel), D. Thierry, 1669, translation by John Lockman published as *The Loves of Cupid and Psyche*, H. Chapelle, 1744; *Adonis* (poem), [Paris], 1669, translation by David M. Glixon published as *Adonis* (illustrated by Ru Van Rossem), Rodale Press, 1957; (editor) *Recueil de Poesies Chrestiennes et Diverses*, [Paris], 1671-74; *Poeme de la Captivite de Saint Malo*, [Paris], 1673; *Discours a Madame de La Sabiere* (sur l' Ame des Animaux) *(poem)*, [Paris], 1679; *Poeme du Quinquina, et Autres Ouvrages en Vers*, D. Thierry et C. Barbin, 1682; *Ragotin* (play), [Paris], 1684; *Le Florentin* (one-act play; first produced July 23, 1685), [Paris], 1818; *Epitre a Huet* (poem), [Paris], 1687; *La Coupe Enchantee* (one-act play; first produced July 16, 1688), [Paris], 1803-04; *Astree* (three-act play), [Paris], 1691; *Lettres de La Fontaine a sa Femme sur un Voyage de Paris en Limousin*, Plon, 1944; *La Fontaine par Lui-Meme* (edited by Pierre Clarac), Editions du Seuil, 1961. Also author of *Elegie aux Nymphes de Vaux*.

THE SNAKE
AND THE FILE

They tell the story that a certain snake,
Living close by a man who used to make
Watches and clocks, ('twould seem a neighborhood
That for horologers was none too good)
One day in search of food entered the shop;
And finding nothing there by way of soup
Except an iron file, began to chew.
The file said kindly: "What do you mean to do,
Young ignoramus? You are tackling stuff
Harder than you. Your teeth will all break off
Before you get the fraction of a grain
From me, poor balmy serpent brain!
Only the fangs of time can eat a file."
This tale is meant for you, all spirits vile
Who, lacking talent, search without respite
For any object they can gnaw or bite.
Your industry is futile. Do you think
That on great masterpieces you can sink
Your blasphemous mark? No, they will be like bronze
Under your teeth, or steel or diamonds.

(From *Selected Fables* by Jean de La Fontaine. Illustrated by Alexander Calder.)

Collections: *Oeuvres Complettes,* six volumes (edited by J. J. Lefevre; illustrated by J. M. Moreau), Lefevre, 1814, new edition, Editions du Seuil, 1965.

ADAPTATIONS—Filmstrips: "Fables de La Fontaine" (three filmstrips, each containing several fables; with French captions), Gessler Publishing, 1958; "Fables de La Fontaine" (five filmstrips, each containing several fables; with captions), Gessler Publishing, 1959; "The Lion and the Rat [and] The Hare and the Tortoise" (color; with a text booklet), Weston Woods Studios, 1969; "The North Wind and the Sun" (color; with a script), Weston Woods Studios, 1970; "The Rich Man and the Shoe-Maker," produced by Weston Woods Studios.

SIDELIGHTS: **July 8, 1621.** Born in the French town of Château-Thierry, the son of a prosperous civil servant, La Fontaine enjoyed a relatively carefree, rustic childhood.

1641-1642. Entered the Oratory in the Rue Saint-Honoré to study for the priesthood, but was asked to leave when he was discovered writing verses about the way prayer was conducted. He returned to Château-Thierry. "[Father] Desmares wished to teach me theology, they thought he was not capable of doing so, nor that I was capable of learning it." [Agnes Mackay, *La Fontaine and His Friends: A Biography,* Braziller, 1973.[1]]

1645-1647. Studied in Paris, joined a group of literary acquaintances nicknamed 'the round table.'

1647. Married Marie Héricart, a union arranged by his father. La Fontaine was a romantic who took love more seriously than marriage. "As soon as I feel a grain of love, I don't hesitate to add to it all the explosives in my arsenal; that creates the best effect in the world; I say foolish things in verse and in prose and would be vexed if I said anything that wasn't solemnly meant; in short, I praise with all my energy.... What happens is that fickleness puts everything

back into place." [Translation of *La Fontaine: The Man and His Work,* by Monica Sutherland, Folcroft, 1974.[2]]

August, 1653. A nature lover, he became master of waterways and forest, a post inherited from his father.

> "To wander in a garden, to stray in a wood,
> To lie down among the flowers, breathe their perfume,
> To hear, while dreaming, the sound of a fountain,
> Or that of a brook rolling over pebbles,
> All this, I confess, has charms most sweet...."

[Translation of *Young La Fontaine,* by Philip Wadsworth, AMS Press, 1970.[3]]

October, 1653. La Fontaine's son, Charles, was born. He paid little attention to Charles and some years later, passed him without recognizing his own son saying, "I think I have seen that young man before."[1]

1659. He and his wife separated. "If they quarrel, if they separate, if they insist that they hate each other, there nonetheless remains a germ of love between two people who were so closely united."[2]

Enjoyed the life of French high society in the company of his patron, Nicolas Fouquet, the wealthy and powerful minister of finance. La Fontaine was dazzled by the beauty of Fouquet's Court at Vaux. "It was also this magnificent house, with its accessories and gardens, which Silvestre showed me, that my memory conserved with great care as being the most precious parts of his treasure. It was on this foundation that Dream erected its frail edifice, and tried to make me see things in their greatest perfection. [Dream] chose for this everything that was most beautiful in its stores; and, in order that my pleasure last longer, it wanted this apparition to be mixed with very remarkable adventures. I saw plants, I saw marbles, I saw liquid crystals, I saw animals and men. At the beginning of my dream, something happened which had

(From "The Town Rat and the Country Rat" in *The Fables of La Fontaine* by Jean de La Fontaine. Illustrated by Gustave Doré.)

One day, a rat walked, by accident, between a lion's paws. ■ (From *The Lion and the Rat* by Jean de La Fontaine. Illustrated by Brian Wildsmith.)

(From "The Hen with the Golden Eggs" in *La Fontaine's Fables* by Jean de La Fontaine.
Illustrated by Gustave Doré.)

happened several other times, and that often happens to everyone; that is that some of the thoughts on my mind when I had just fallen asleep, passed again through my mind first. I fancied that I had gone to look for Sleep, to ask [him] to show me Vaux, about which people had told me incredible things. The god's (i.e. Sleep's) dwelling is deep in the woods, where silence and solitude stay: it's a cave that Nature fashioned with her own hands, and whose avenues she fortified against light and sound." [Translation from *La Fontaine Oeuvres Dwerses,* by Pierre Clarac, Librairie Gallimard, 1948.[4]]

1660. Read and admired a newly issued translation of Acsop's fables. "As for Aesop, it seems to me one must number him among the great sages of whom the Greeks boasted, he who taught true wisdom, and who taught it with much more art than those who give definitions of it, and rules of it."[3]

August 17, 1661. Attended a sumptuous celebration given in honor of the King of France at Vaux. ". . . I will therefore tell you only what happened at Vaux the 17th of this month: the king, the queen mother, Monsieur, Madame, a great number of princes and lords were there: there was a magnificent supper, an excellent play, a very entertaining ballet and fireworks. . . .

> "All the senses were enchanted,
> And the feast had beauties
> Worthy of the place, worthy of the master,
> And worthy of their Highnesses,
> If anything could be. . . .

"After the noise of the fireworks came the sound of drums: because, the king wanting to return to Fontainebleau that same night, the musketeers had been ordered to be there. We then returned to the chateau, where the refreshments were prepared. While we were on our way, talking about these things, and not expecting anything more, we saw, in one moment, the sky completely hidden by a terrifying cloud of rockets and fireworks. Should I say completely hidden or lit up? It started from the light of the dome: it was at that spot that the cloud caved in first. We thought all the stars, large and small, had fallen to the earth, in order to pay hommage to Madame; but, the storm having stopped, we saw them all in their place. The catastrophe of this fracas was the loss of two horses.

> "These horses, which once pulled a carriage,
> And now pull Charon's boat,
> Fell into the trenches of Vaux
> And from there into the Acheron

"They were hitched to one of the Queen's carriages; and having reared because of the fireworks and the noise, it was impossible to restrain them. I didn't think that this account should have had such a tragic and pitiful end. Adieu. Fill your memory with all the beautiful things you will see at the place where you are. . . ."[4]

September, 1661. Fouquet was arrested. La Fontaine later pleaded unsuccessfully for his release. "I always believed that you [Monsieur Fouquet] would know how to conserve your freedom of mind even in prison, and I need for proof only your defense; there is nothing more convincing or better written than that . . . someone who looks at life with such indifference does not deserve at all to die; but perhaps you have not considered the fact that it is I who am speaking, I

LA FONTAINE

who ask a pardon that is dearer to us than to you. There are no expressions too humble, too pathetic, and too urgent, that I must not use them in this encounter. When I introduce you into the scene, I will lend you words appropriate to the greatness of your soul. In the meantime, permit me to tell you that you do not have enough passion (feeling) for a life such as yours. . . ."[4]

1663. Accompanied Monsieur Jannart, a relative of his wife's, on a trip from Paris to Limoges. He wrote to his wife: "You have never wished to read any other voyages than those of the knights of the Round Table; but our journey well deserves that you should read my account of it. However there may be things which do not suit your taste, so it is up to me to flavour them, if I can, in such a way that they will please you, and you should praise my intentions in this even when I am not successful. It may even happen that if you like this account you will afterwards enjoy more serious things. You neither play, nor work, nor do you take any care in housekeeping; and beyond the time that your good friends devote to you through charity, nothing amuses you but novels, of which the supply is soon exhausted. You have read the old ones so many times that you know them by heart; and there are very few new ones, and among the few not all are good, so you are often left high and dry with nothing to read.

"I beg you to consider, how useful it would be to you, if in amusing you I had given you the habit of reading the history of people and places; you would then have the means of diverting yourself for the whole of your life; provided that you had no intention of remembering and still less of quoting anything. It is not a good quality in a woman to be learned, and to affect to appear so is a very bad one."[1]

JEAN DE LA FONTAINE

"The fantasy of travelling had entered my mind some time before, as though I had a presentiment about the King's order. There were more than two weeks when I spoke of nothing but going to Saint-Cloud, or Charonne, and I was ashamed to have lived so long without having seen anything. This will no longer be reproached me, thank God. They told us, among other marvels, that many Limousin women of the good bourgeoisie, wear hoods made of material the color of dry roses on blocks of black velvet. If I find one of these hoods covering a pretty head, I can enjoy myself in passing, and only out of curiosity.

"Whatever the case, I have a good opinion of our trip: we have already gone three leagues without a bad accident, apart from the fact that M. Jannart's sword broke; but, since we are people who benefit from our misfortunes, we thought that it was too long anyway, and encumbered him. Soon we will be at Clamart, on top of that famous mountain where Meudon is situated; there we must refresh ourselves two or three days. In truth, it's a pleasure to travel; one always encounters some remarkable thing. You cannot believe how good the butter we eat is; I have wished for myself, twenty times, cows like these, grazing land like this, water like this, and all that follows. . . ."[4]

1664. First book published. Public controversy arose over the explicit nature of some of La Fontaine's stories.

1664-1672. Became gentleman-servant to the Duchesse of Orléans, an occupation which provided him with more free time to write.

1668. Six books of La Fontaine's fables were issued. Unlike Aesop's fables, they were written in verse.

"Since strength is a point on which I do not pride myself,
I try to turn vice into ridicule,
Being unable to attack it with the arms of Hercules.
Therein lies my talent. I don't know if it's sufficient.
Sometimes I paint, in a story,
Foolish vanity, combined with envy,
Two pivots on which turns our life today . . .
I oppose, sometimes, with a double image,
Vice and virtue, Stupidity and common sense,
Sheep and ravaging wolves. . . ."[3]

1673. La Fontaine's new patroness, Mme. de la Sablière claimed that she kept only three animals with her: her dog, her cat, and her La Fontaine.

La Fontaine was devoted to Mme. de la Sablière, his "Iris": "I kept a temple for you in my verse / That would have ended with the Universe / . . . In the inner shrine would be her lovely image: / Her features, and her smile gracious and gay / Her art of pleasing all unconsciously / Her charms to which everyone pays homage / . . . I would have made, although imperfectly, / The treasures of her soul shine in her eyes; / For this kind heart infinitely tender / For her friends only, and not otherwise, / Because this mind that's born of Heaven, / With manly beauty, womanly grace, / Cannot be fully described as I would like, / O you, Iris, who know how to charm all, / And know supremely how to please, / You whom one cherishes as oneself / Let this be said without suspicion of love / (a work that is banished from your court: / Let it alone then), grant my Muse your leave / Some day this confused project to achieve."[1]

1676. La Fontaine sold the house in which he was born, in order to pay off mounting debts.

1684. Elected to the prestigious French Academy, an honor which prompted him to take life more seriously. "What use to me are those verses composed with such care? / Did I aim at aught else but to hear them praise? / Their advice is worth little, if I do not take it, / If at least towards my end I don't begin to live; / For I have not lived; I have served two tyrants: / Vain pastimes and love have divided my years. . . . It is time to enjoy real blessings in tranquillity / To make good use of one's time and employ one's leisure; / To observe the honours due to the supreme Being: / To renounce light verse in favour of oneself, / To banish foolish love and futile vows, / Like Hydras constantly reborn in our hearts."[1]

1692. La Fontaine decided to make a full confession. "Thou mightest easily destroy me and avenge thyself / Don't do so, Lord, rather come to lighten / The burden under which I feel my soul succumb."[1]

1693. Last collection of fables, dedicated to the eight year old grandson of Louis XIV, published. "These are not unimportant subjects; animals are man's teachers in my work."[2]

Spring, 1693. Mme. de la Sablière died. La Fontaine took up residence at the home of his good friend, Monsieur de Hervart.

February, 1695. La Fontaine, in ill health, sensed his life drawing to a close. "You are mistaken, my dear friend, if . . . you think I am more ill in mind than in body. He told me that to inspire me with courage, but it is not courage that I lack. I assure you that the best of your friends (myself) cannot

(From "The Grasshopper and The Ant" in *The Fables of La Fontaine* by Jean de La Fontaine.
Illustrated by Gustave Doré.)

count on more than fifteen days of life. It is two months since I went out, except to go a little to the Academy to amuse myself. Yesterday on coming back from there, I was taken in the middle of the rue du Chantre by such an overwhelming weakness that I thought I was really dying. O my friend, to die is nothing; but do you realise that I am going to appear before God? You know how I have lived. Before you receive this note, the gates of Eternity will perhaps be opened for me."[1]

April 13, 1695. Died at the age of seventy-three. "... I would like it if, at this age, one left life the way one leaves a banquet, thanking one's host."[2]

FOR MORE INFORMATION SEE: Frank Hamel, *Jean de La Fontaine,* Brentano's, 1912, reprinted, Kennikat, 1970; Hallie Erminie Rives and G. E. Forbush, *John Book,* Beechhurst Press, 1947; Philip Adrian Wadsworth, *Young La Fontaine: A Study of His Artistic Growth in His Early Poetry and First Fables,* Northwestern University Press, 1952, reprinted, AMS Press, 1970; Monica Sutherland, *La Fontaine: The Man and His Work,* J. Cape, 1953, reprinted, Folcroft, 1974; Odette De Mourguis, *La Fontaine: Fables: Critical Analysis,* edited by W. G. Moore, Barron, 1960; Margaret Otis Guiton, *La Fontaine: Poet and Counterpoet,* Rutgers University Press, 1961; Brian Doyle, *Who's Who of Children's Literature,* Schocken Books, 1968; Ethel M. King, *Jean de La Fontaine,* Gaus, 1970; John C. Lapp, *Esthetics of Negligence: La Fontaine's Contes,* Cambridge University Press, 1971; Agnes E. Mackay, *La Fontaine and His Friends: A Biography,* Garnstone Press, 1972, reprinted, Braziller, 1973; J. Allen Tyler and Stephen M. Parrish, editors, *A Concordance to the Fables and Tales of Jean de La Fontaine,* Cornell University Press, 1974.

LANIER, Sidney   1842-1881

PERSONAL: Born February 3, 1842, in Macon, Georgia; died September 7, 1881, in Lynn, North Carolina; buried in Greenmount Cemetery in Baltimore, Maryland; son of Robert Sampson (a lawyer) and Mary Jane (Anderson) Lanier; married Mary Day, December 21, 1867; children: four sons, including Henry Wysham and Charles Day. *Education:* Graduated from Oglethorpe University, 1860. *Home:* Baltimore, Maryland.

CAREER: Poet, novelist, critic, and musician. Tutor in English at Oglethorpe University, 1860-61; after the Civil War, held various jobs, including hotel clerk, teacher, and assistant in his father's law office, 1865-73; first flutist with the Peabody Symphony Orchestra, Baltimore, Maryland, 1873; commissioned to write a cantata for the Centennial Exposition at Philadelphia, Pennsylvania, 1876; lecturer in English at Johns Hopkins University, 1879-81. *Military service:* Confederate Army, Macon Volunteers, 1861-65; was taken prisoner and spent four months in Point Lookout Prison in Maryland, 1864-65.

WRITINGS—Poetry: *Poems,* Lippincott, 1877; *Poems of Sidney Lanier,* edited by wife, Mary Day Lanier, with a memorial by William Hayes Ward, Scribner, 1884, new editions, 1891, 1916, 1920, reprinted, University of Georgia Press, 1944; *Hymns of the Marshes* (illustrated by Henry Troth), Scribner, 1907 (contains *Sunrise, Individuality, Marsh Song, At Sunset,* and *The Marshes of Glynn*); *Poem Outlines,* Scribner, 1908; *The Marshes of Glynn: A Photographic Interpretation by Mose Daniels,* Duell, Sloan, 1949, reprinted, Hannau Robinson, 1969.

SIDNEY LANIER

Prose: *Tiger-Lilies* (novel), Hurd & Houghton, 1867, reprinted, University of North Carolina Press, 1969; *Bob: The Story of Our Mocking Bird* (preface by son, Charles Day Lanier; illustrated by Arthur R. Dugmore), Scribner, 1899.

Nonfiction—Literary criticism: *The Science of English Verse,* Scribner, 1880, reprinted, Folcroft, 1973; *The English Novel and the Principle of Its Development,* Scribner, 1883, revised edition published as *The English Novel: A Study in the Development of Personality,* 1897; *Music and Poetry: Essays upon Some Aspects and Inter-Relations of the Two Arts,* Scribner, 1898, reprinted, Gordon Press, 1972; *Retrospects and Prospects: Descriptive and Historical Essays,* Scribner, 1899; *Shakespeare and His Forerunners: Studies in Elizabethan Poetry and Its Development from Early English* (based upon his lectures at Johns Hopkins University), Doubleday, Page, 1902, reprinted, AMS Press, 1966.

Travel Books: *Florida: Its Scenery, Climate, and History,* Lippincott, 1875, reprinted, University of Florida Press, 1973. Also author of *Some Highways and Byways of American Travel,* 1878.

Collections: *Select Poems of Sidney Lanier,* edited by Morgan Callaway, Jr., Scribner, 1895; *Letters of Sidney Lanier: Selections from His Correspondence, 1866-1881,* edited by son, Henry Wysham Lanier, Scribner, 1899, reprinted, Books for Libraries, 1972; *The Lanier Book: Selections in Prose and Verse from the Writings of Sidney Lanier,* edited by Mary E. Burt, Scribner, 1904; *Selections from Sidney Lanier: Prose and Verse,* edited by H. W. Lanier, Scribner, 1916; *The Centennial Edition of the Works of Sidney Lanier,* ten volumes, edited by Charles R. Anderson, Johns Hopkins Press, 1945, reprinted, 1963; *Sidney Lanier: Poems and Letters,* edited by C. R. Anderson, Johns Hopkins Press, 1970.

Editor: *The Boys' Froissart,* Scribner, 1879; *The Boys' King Arthur,* Scribner, 1880, a later edition illustrated by N. C. Wyeth, 1917, and by Florian, Grosset & Dunlap, 1950; *The Boys' Mabinogion,* Scribner, 1881; *The Boys' Percy,* Scribner, 1882; *The Boys' Library of Legend and Chivalry,* four volumes, Scribner, 1884 (contains *The Boys' Froissart, The*

Boys' King Arthur, The Boys' Percy, and *Knightly Legends of Wales*).

SIDELIGHTS: **February 3, 1842.** Born in Macon, Georgia. His father was a struggling lawyer; his mother, a thrifty and pious woman was musically gifted. Lanier delighted in researching his family tree. "If a man made himself an expert in any particular branch of human activity there would result the strong tendency that a peculiar aptitude towards the same branch would be found among some of his descendants." [Edward Mims, *Sidney Lanier,* Kennikat, 1905.[1]]

Although he was curious about Lanier ancestors in England and France, he considered Macon the perfect place for his family to have settled. "Surely, along that ample stretch of generous soil, where the Appalachian ruggednesses calm themselves into pleasant hills before dying quite away in the seaboard levels, a man can find such temperances of heaven and earth—enough of struggle with nature to draw out manhood, with enough of bounty to sanction the struggle—that a more exquisite co-adaptation of all blessed circumstances for man's life need not be sought."[1]

January 6, 1857. Entered Oglethorpe University, Midway, Georgia. Joined a literary society and delighted other students with his flute playing.

July, 1860. Graduated from college and spent summer vacation with his grandfather in Tennessee. Awed by the scenery, his interest in music also increased. "Last night we gave a magnificent concert. The house was crowded.... The orchestra was inspired, the 'Symphonie Fantastique,' as difficult and trying a piece of orchestration as was ever written, was played to a marvel...." [Aubrey Starke, *Sidney Lanier,* University of North Carolina Press, 1933.[2]]

Fall, 1860. Returned to Oglethorpe as tutor, a task he dreaded as he contemplated a future occupation. "I tremble when I think of tutorship (by the way, my rightful title of tutor here has owing to my exhibition of talents as a flutist, been corrupted into 'tooter,' it being considered that the last mentioned word euphoniously expresses whatever distinctive cognomen I ought to possess in the exercise of my two professions)."[2]

"The point which I wish to settle is merely by what method shall I ascertain what I am fit for as preliminary to ascertaining God's will with reference to me; or what my inclinations are, as preliminary to ascertaining what my capacities are—that is, what I am fit for. I am more than all perplexed by this fact: that the prime inclination—that is, natural bent (which I have checked, though) of my nature is to music, and for that I have the greatest talent; indeed, not boasting, for God gave it me, I have an extraordinary musical talent, and feel it within me plainly that I could rise as high as any composer. But I cannot bring myself to believe that I was intended for a musician, because it seems so small a business in comparison with other things which, it seems to me, I might do. Question here: 'What is the province of music in the economy of the world?' "[1]

June, 1861. After the outbreak of the Civil War, Lanier joined the Macon Volunteers in Virginia.

1863-1864. Lanier and his brother, Clifford, served as scouts in Milligan's Corps along the James River. "Our life was as full of romance as heart could desire. We had a flute and a guitar, good horses, a beautiful country, splendid residences inhabited by friends who loved us, and plenty of hairbreadth

"Now, by my faye," said jolly Robin,
  "A sweven[1] I had this night :
I dreamt me of two wighty[2] yeomen,
  That fast with me can fight.

Methought they did me beat and bind,
  And took my bow me fro';
If I be Robin alive in this land,
  I'll be wroken on them two."

   [1][*Dream.*]   [2][*Lusty.*]

(From *The Boys' Percy* by Sidney Lanier. Illustrated by E.B. Russell.)

'scapes from the roving bands of Federals who were continually visiting that Debatable Land.... Cliff and I never cease to talk of the beautiful women, the serenades, the moonlight dashes on the beach of fair Burwell's Bay...."[1]

January, 1864. When his camp was captured, Lanier lost some volumes of poetry which he counted among his choicest treasures. He contemplated his poetic inclinations. "To me, who am growing daily more in the habit of looking and hearing with the Senses of the Spirit, there is here anything *but* silence and solitude. Troops of spirits, multitudes of strange and airy shapes, wheel and hover about my hill, like sea-gulls about some lone crag in the ocean; and these, by long acquaintance, are become familiar spirits, so that I sit in the midst of them like Prospero, and am not afraid." [Lincoln Lorenz, *Life of Sidney Lanier,* Coward, 1935.[3]]

"Gradually I find that my whole soul is merging itself into this business of writing, and especially of writing poetry. I am going to try it; and am going to test, in the most rigid way I know, the awful question whether it is my vocation.

"I have frequently noticed in myself a tendency to a diffuse style; a disposition to push my metaphors too far, employing a multitude of words to heighten the patness of the image, and so making of it a *conceit* rather than a metaphor."[1]

November 2, 1864. Captured and sent to Point Lookout prison, where he was beset by the lung trouble and ill health which was to plague him for the rest of his life.

March 15, 1865. Returned to Macon. Shortly thereafter, his mother died of consumption.

January, 1866. Went to Montgomery, Alabama to take a job as a clerk in his grandfather's hotel. ''They show no life, save late in the afternoon, when the girls come out, one by one, and shine and move, just as the stars do an hour later. I don't think there's a man in town who could be induced to go into his neighbor's store and ask him how's trade; for he would have to atone for such an insult with his life. Everything is dreamy, and drowsy, and drone-y.... There's not enough attrition of mind on mind here, to bring out any sparks from a man.''[1]

Spring, 1867. Left Montgomery. Went to New York with manuscript of his novel, *Tiger Lillies*. ''The grand array of houses and ships and rivers and distant hills did not arrest my soul as did the long line of men and women, which at that height seemed to writhe and contort itself in its narrow bed of Broadway as in a premature grave.... I have not seen here a single eye that knew itself to be in front of a heart—but one, and that was a blue one, and a child owned it. 'Twas the very double of Sissa's [the name for his sister] eye, so I had no sooner seen it than I made love to it, with what success you will hear. On Saturday I dined with J. F. D. Lanier. We had only a family party.... Last and best little Kate Lanier, eight years old, pearly cheeked, blue eyed, broad of forehead, cherried i' the lip. About the time that the champagne came on I happened to mention that I had been in prison during the war.

'''Poor fellow!' says little Katie, 'and how did the rebels treat you?'

'''Rebels,' said I, 'I am a rebel myself, Kate!'

'''What!' she exclaimed, and lifted up her little lilies (when I say lilies I mean hands), and peered at me curiously with all her blue eyes astare. 'A live Reb!'

''This phrase in Katie's nursery had taken the time-honored place of bugaboos, and hobgoblins, and men under the bed. She could not realize that I, a smooth-faced, slender, ordinary mortal, in all respects like a common man, should be a live reb. She was inclined to hate me, as in duty bound.

''I will not describe the manner of the siege I laid to her: suffice it that when I rose to take leave, Katie stood up before [me], and half blushed, and paused a minute.

''With a coquetry I never saw executed more prettily, 'I know,' said she, 'that you are dying for a kiss, and you're ashamed to ask for it. You may take one.' ... And so in triumph, and singing poems to all blue eyes, I said good night.''[1]

December 21, 1867. Married Mary Day. ''Not even the wide-mouthed, villainous-nosed, tallow-faced drudgeries of my eighty-fold life can squeeze the sentiment out of me.''[1]

September, 1868. First son, Charles, born.

1869-1873. Practiced law, a career which he felt severely hampered his writing efforts. ''I have not put pen to paper in a literary way in a long time. How I thirst to do so,—how I long to sing a thousand various songs that oppress me, un-

The Lanier home on High Street.

sung,—is inexpressible. Yet the mere work that brings me bread gives me no time. I know not, after all, if this is a sorrowful thing. Nobody likes my poems except two or three friends,—who are themselves poets, and can supply themselves!''[1]

1871. Trip to New York for business and medical reasons. Lanier was captivated by the beautiful music he was treated to in the city. ''And to-night I come out of what might have been heaven. . . .

'' 'Twas opening night of Theodore Thomas's orchestra, at Central Park Garden, and I could not resist the temptation to go and bathe in the sweet amber seas of the music of this fine orchestra, and so I went, and tugged me through a vast crowd, and, after standing some while, found a seat, and the *bâton* tapped and waved, and I plunged into the sea, and lay and floated. Ah! the dear flutes and oboes and horns drifted me hither and thither, and the great violins and small violins swayed me upon waves, and overflowed me with strong lavations, and sprinkled glistening foam in my face, and in among the clarinetti, as among waving water-lilies with flexile stems, I pushed my easy way, and so, even lying in the music-waters, I floated and flowed, my soul utterly bent and prostrate.''[1]

November, 1872. In San Antonio, where he went to seek a more healthful climate, Lanier made a decision to devote his life to artistic endeavors. He wrote to his father to inform him of his decision: ''I have given your last letter the fullest and most careful consideration. After doing so I feel sure that Macon is not the place for me. If you could taste the delicious crystalline air, and the champagne breeze that I've just been rushing about in, I am equally sure that in point of climate you would agree with me that my chance for life is ten times as great here as in Macon. Then, as to business, why should I, nay, how *can* I, settle myself down to be a third-rate struggling lawyer for the balance of my little life, as long as there is a certainty almost absolute that I can do some other thing so much better? Several persons, from whose judgment in such matters there can be no appeal, have told me, for instance, that I am the greatest flute-player in the world; and several others, of equally authoritative judgment, have given me an almost equal encouragement to work with my pen. (Of course I protest against the necessity which makes me write such things about myself. I only do so because I so appreciate the love and tenderness which prompt you to desire me with you that I will make the fullest explanation possible of my course, out of reciprocal honor and respect for the motives which lead you to think differently from me.) My dear father, think how, for twenty years, through poverty, through pain, through weariness, through sickness, through the uncongenial atmosphere of a farcical college and of a bare army and then of an exacting business life, through all the discouragement of being wholly unacquainted with literary people and literary ways,—I say, think how, in spite of all these depressing circumstances, and of a thousand more which I could enumerate, these two figures of music and of poetry have steadily kept in my heart so that I could not banish them. Does it not seem to you as to me, that I begin to have the right to enroll myself among the devotees of these two sublime arts, after having followed them so long and so humbly, and through so much bitterness?''[1]

1873. Decided to give up his law career permanently and took position with the Peabody Orchestra in Baltimore. ''To write for any length of time beyond a few minutes results in very distressing consequences to me; and this effectually debars me from office practice. To speak long or often would

Lanier, in profile.

be equally injurious to me. What sort of a lawyer, then, can one be, who can neither write a bill of equity, nor make a jury speech—without a hemorrhage?''[3]

''It is therefore a *possibility* . . . that I may be first flute in the Peabody Orchestra, on a salary of $120 a month, which, with five flute scholars, would grow to $200 a month, and so . . . we might dwell in the beautiful city, among the great libraries, and midst of the music, the religion, and the art that we love—and I could write my books and be the man I wish to be.

''I am beginning in the midst of the stormy glories of the orchestra, to feel my heart sure, and my soul discriminating. Not less do I thrill to ride upon the great surges; but I am growing calm enough to see the star that should light the musician, and presently my hand will be firm enough to hold the helm and guide the ship that way. *Now* I am very quiet; I am waiting.''[1]

1874. Started to write poetry again, although physical problems made the act of writing itself a chore. Lanier experienced frustration as he attempted to sell poetry in New York. ''To carry about such a load of unwritten music and unsung songs as are in my heart, and to be only able to scratch one down occasionally—is almost intolerable.''[3]

He dealt with a rejection letter. ''I took the letter to my room—it was a high room in Brooklyn, N.Y. from whose windows I could see many things, and there, during a day whose intensity was of that sort that one only attempts to communicate to one's God, I led myself to an infinite height above myself, and meditated: and when evening came I found myself full of the ineffable content of certainty and of perfect knowledge and of decision.

''I had become aware:—not by reasoning, I could only reason about it afterwards; I know not what the process was—that my business in life was to make poems.''[3]

1875. Received a commission to write a guide book for Florida tourists. While he welcomed the money, it interfered with his poetry. ''Now, I don't work for bread; in truth, I suppose that any man who, after many days and nights of tribulation and bloody sweat, has finally emerged from all doubt into the quiet and yet joyful activity of one who *knows* exactly what his Great Passion is and what his God desires him to do, will straightway lose all anxiety as to what he is working *for,* in the simple glory of doing that which lies immediately before him. As for me, life has resolved simply into a time during which I must get upon paper as many as possible of the poems with which my heart is stuffed like a schoolboy's pocket.''[1]

''I'm sure I can't give you the least idea of the desperate run I've been making for the last two months in the attempt to get my Florida book finished in the time set me. Finally, about three weeks ago, my plans collapsed: I had a half dozen exhausting hemorrhages in succession in the course of a week, which brought me down to a point where I could only lie on a bed and look up, without being allowed the privilege of even speaking. I worried through, however, and for a week past have been again going, night and day, with the interminable pen. I never dreamed the book was going to ramify into such unearthly directions . . . for a week hence I do not expect to do aught but what I have done the week past, to wit, write at my best speed all the time betwixt waking and sleeping that isn't wasted in eating.''[3]

January, 1876. Commissioned to write cantata for the Centennial Commission. His *Centennial Meditation of Columbia* received a hostile critical reaction at first, but was eventually applauded.

August, 1876. Agreement made to publish a book of Lanier poems. It was the only volume of his poetry published before his death.

December, 1876. In declining health, Lanier was told he must go to Florida in order to save his life.

''I have at command a springy mare, with ankles like a Spanish girl, upon whose back I go darting through the green overgrown woodpaths, like a thrasher about his thicket. The whole air feels full of fecundity: as I ride I am like one of those insects that are fertilized on the wing,—every leaf that I brush against breeds a poem. God help the world when this now-hatching brood of my Ephemerae shall take flight and darken the air.

''I long to be steadily writing again. I am taken with a poem pretty nearly every day, and have to content myself with making a note of its train of thought on the back of whatever letter is in my coat-pocket. I don't write it out, because I find my poetry now unsatisfactory in consequence of a certain haunting impatience which has its root in the straining uncertainty of my daily affairs; and I am trying with all my might to put off composition of all sorts until some approach to the uncertainty of next week's dinner shall remove this remnant of haste, and leave me that repose which ought to fill the artist's firmament while he is creating.''[1]

December, 1877. Returned to Baltimore and bought a house there. ''How I wish that the whole world had a Home! I find the wish growing stronger that each poor soul in Baltimore,

whether saint or sinner, would come and dine with me. How I would carve out the merry thoughts for the old hags! How I would stuff the wall-eyed rascals till their rags ripped again!''[3]

''When I am on the street, there is a certain burgherlike heaviness in my tread; why should I skip along like a bladdery Bohemian? I am a man of substance; I am liable, like you, for water rates, gas bills, and other important disbursements incident to the possession of two gowns and everything handsome about me. . . . Our new address here is—and God grant long may be, for we are *so* tired of moving!—33 Denmead St.''[2]

February 3, 1879. Appointed lecturer in English literature at Johns Hopkins University.

November, 1879. Began writing series of books to be entitled ''The Boy's Library of Legend and Chivalry.''

November, 1880. Ill with consumption. ''For six months past a ghastly fever has been taking possession of me each day at about twelve M., and holding my head under the surface of indescribable distress for the next twenty hours, subsiding only enough each morning to let me get on my working-harness, but never intermitting. A number of tests show it not to be the 'hectic' so well known in consumption; and to this day it has baffled all the skill I could find in New York, in Philadelphia, and here. I have myself been disposed to think it arose purely from the bitterness of having to spend my time in making academic lectures and boy's books—pot-boilers all—when a thousand songs are singing in my heart that will certainly kill me if I do not utter them soon. But I don't think this diagnosis has found favor with any practical physician; and meantime I work day after day in such suffering as is piteous to see.''[1]

''Seriously, I've been ill enough; and your imagination is all I can rely on—for words are here simply exasperating—when I tell you that about three weeks ago, thinking a change might help me, I managed to crawl down to Charles Street Station and *went* to New York,—and took to bed as soon as I reached the hotel, there,—and tossed thereon for four days with a fairly flaming fever,—and finally had to crawl back to Baltimore, without having accomplished a single stroke of business, without having seen a single picture or friend, without having heard a single crash of the horns and violins,—for which I longed unspeakably.''[2]

1881. Lanier and family headed South again, planning to spend the summer near Asheville, N.C. in a last attempt to save his life.

September 7, 1881. Died. His last words were ''I can't.''

> ''Death lieth still in the way of life
> Like as a stone in the way of a brook;
> I will sing against thee, Death, as the brook does,
> I will make thee into music which does not die.''[2]

FOR MORE INFORMATION SEE: W. H. Ward, ''Memoir,'' in *Poems of Sidney Lanier,* Scribner, 1884; *Letters of Sidney Lanier,* Scribner, 1899, reprinted, Books for Libraries, 1972; Edwin Mims, *Sidney Lanier,* Houghton, 1905, reprinted, Kennikat, 1968; John W. Wayland, *Sidney Lanier at Rockingham Springs: Where and How ''The Science of English Verse'' Was Written: A New Chapter in American Let-*

And within an hour and less, he boar him four days' journey thence, till he came to a rough water the which roared, [sic] and his horse would have borne him into it. ■ (From *The Boys' King Arthur* by Sidney Lanier. Illustrated by N.C. Wyeth.)

"The King called his best archers." ■ (From *The Boys' Percy,* edited and an introduction by Sidney Lanier. Illustrated by E.B. Russell.)

ters, 1912, reprinted, Books for Libraries, 1971; Aubrey H. Starke, *Sidney Lanier: A Biographical and Critical Study,* University of North Carolina Press, 1933, reprinted, Russell & Russell, 1964; Robert Penn Warren, "The Blind Poet: Sidney Lanier," and John Crowe Ransom, "Hearts and Heads," both in *American Review,* Volume 2, 1933-34; Lincoln Lorenz, *The Life of Sidney Lanier,* Coward-McCann, 1935.

Edwin R. Coulson, *Sidney Lanier, Poet and Prosodist,* University of Georgia, 1941; Van Wyck Brooks, "The South: Lanier and Joel Chandler Harris," in his *Times of Melville and Whitman,* Dutton, 1947; Frederick Houk Law, *Great Americans,* Globe Books, 1953; Henry N. Snyder, *Sidney Lanier,* Parthenon Press, 1954; Charmenz S. Lenhart, *Musical Influence on American Poetry,* University of Georgia Press, 1956; Edmund Wilson, "The Myth of the Old South: Sidney Lanier," "The Poetry of the Civil War," and "Sut Lovingood," all in his *Patriotic Gore: Studies in the Literature of the American Civil War,* Oxford University Press, 1962.

E. W. Parks, "Lanier as Poet," *Essays on American Literature,* edited by Clarence Gohdes, Duke University Press, 1967; Parks, *Sidney Lanier: The Man, the Poet, the Critic,* University of Georgia Press, 1968; Robert E. Spiller, *Oblique Light,* Macmillan, 1968; Jack De Bellis, *Sidney Lanier,* Twayne, 1972; A. P. Antippas and C. Flake, "Sidney Lanier's Letters to Clare deGraffenried," *American Literature,* May, 1973.

LEAR, Edward   1812-1888
(Derry Down Derry)

PERSONAL: Born May 12, 1812, in Holloway, England; died January 29, 1888, in San Remo, Italy; son of Jeremiah (a stockbroker) and Ann Lear. *Education:* Tutored at home by his sister Anne; briefly attended the Royal Academy Schools, about 1850.

CAREER: Artist and author. Earned his living as an artist from the age of fifteen with zoological illustrations, landscapes, and travel books; took pupils from the age of eighteen, including Queen Victoria, to whom he gave a series of twelve lessons in 1846; best remembered for his "Nonsense Books" and for popularizing the limerick form.

WRITINGS—Books for children; all self illustrated: (Under pseudonym Derry Down Derry) *A Book of Nonsense,* McLean, 1846, revised and enlarged edition (published under his real name), Routledge, 1861, reprinted, Looking-Glass Library, 1959; *Nonsense Songs, Stories, Botany, and Alphabets,* Osgood, 1871; *More Nonsense Pictures, Rhymes, and Botany,* Aylesbury, 1872; *Laughable Lyrics: A Fourth Book of Nonsense Poems, Songs, Botany, and Music,* [London], 1877; *A Book of Limericks,* Little, Brown, 1888, a later edition published as *Limericks by Lear* (illustrated by Lois J. Ehlert), World Publishing, 1965; *Teapots and Quails, and Other New Nonsense* (edited, and with an introduction, by Angus Davidson and Philip Hofer), Harvard University

Press, 1953; *ABC: Penned and Illustrated by Edward Lear, Himself* (newly-found manuscript), McGraw, 1965.

Selections from the "Nonsense Books" published separately: *Nonsense Songs* (illustrated by L. Leslie Brooke), Warne, 1900, reprinted, 1969, another edition published as *Edward Lear's Nonsense Songs* (with illustrations by the author), Chatto & Windus, 1938, reprinted, 1953; *The Jumblies, and Other Nonsense Verses* (illustrated by L. L. Brooke), Warne, 1900, reprinted, 1954, another edition illustrated by Edward Gorey, Young Scott Books, 1968; *The Pelican Chorus, and Other Nonsense Verses* (illustrated by L. L. Brooke), Warne, 1900, reprinted, 1954, another edition illustrated by Harold Berson, Parents' Magazine Press, 1967; *Queery Leary Nonsense* (edited by Constance Lady Strachey; introduction by the Earl of Cromer), Mills & Boon, 1911; *The Owl and the Pussycat,* Warne, 1924, reprinted (illustrated by Harold King), 1975 [other editions illustrated by Margaret Jervis, Avon, 1953; William Pène Du Bois, Doubleday, 1962; Masha, Golden Press, 1964; Barbara Cooney, Little, Brown, 1969; Dale Maxey, Follett, 1970]; *The Nonsense ABC* (the original verses and pictures, with a new alphabet by Arthur L. Moore), Macmillan, 1928, [other editions published as *The Nonsense ABC's: Verses* (illustrated by Helen Endres and Robert Bonfils), Rand McNally, 1956; *A Nonsense Alphabet* (illustrated by Richard Scarry), Doubleday, 1962; *Nonsense Alphabets,* Watts, 1975].

The Duck and the Kangaroo, and Other Nonsense Rhymes (illustrated by Keith Ward), Western Printing, 1932; *Nonsense Book* (edited and illustrated by Tony Palazzo), Garden City Books, 1956; *The Two Old Bachelors* (illustrated by Paul Galdone), McGraw, 1962; *Two Laughable Lyrics: The Pobble Who Has No Toes [and] The Quangle Wangle's Hat* (illustrated by Galdone), Putnam, 1966, [other editions published as *The Pobble Who Has No Toes, and Other Nonsense* (illustrated by Dale Maxey), Collins, 1968, Follett, 1969; *The Quangle Wangle's Hat* (illustrated by Helen Oxenbury), Heinemann, 1969, Watts, 1970]; *Lear's Nonsense Verses* (illustrated by Tomi Ungerer), Grosset & Dunlap, 1967; *Scroobius Pip* (an excerpt from *Teapots and Quails;* completed by Ogden Nash; illustrated by Nancy Ekholm Burkert), Harper, 1968; *The Story of the Four Little Children Who Went Round the World* (illustrated by Arnold Lobel), Macmillan, 1968, also published in another edition with *The*

**The Scroobious Snake,
who always wore a Hat on his Head, for
fear he should bite anybody.**

■ (From *The Complete Nonsense Book* by Edward Lear. Illustrated by the author.)

EDWARD LEAR

History of the Seven Families of the Lake Pipple-Popple, Walker, 1968; *The Dong with a Luminous Nose* (illustrated by Gerald Rose), Young Scott Books, 1969, another edition illustrated by E. Gorey, Chatto & Windus, 1969; *Calico Pie, and Other Nonsense* (illustrated by D. Maxey), Collins, 1968, Follett, 1969; *Incidents in the Life of My Uncle Arly* (illustrated by D. Maxey), Collins, 1969, Follett, 1970; *The New Vestments* (illustrated by Arnold Lobel), Bradbury Press, 1970; *Edward Lear's Nonsense Coloring Book,* Dover, 1971; *Whizz: Six Limericks* (illustarted by Janina Domanska), Hamish Hamilton, 1974; *A Book of Bosh: Lyrics and Prose* (edited by Brian Alderson), Penguin, 1976.

"Nonsense" collections: *Nonsense Books,* Little, Brown, 1888, Volume I: *A Book of Nonsense,* Volume II: *Nonsense Songs, Stories, Botany, and Alphabets,* Volume III: *More Nonsense Pictures, Rhymes, and Botany,* Volume IV: *Laughable Lyrics,* reprinted, Grosset & Dunlap, 1967; *The Complete Nonsense Book* (edited by Constance Lady Strachey; introduction by the Earl of Cromer), Duffield, 1912, reprinted, Dodd, 1958; *Lear Omnibus* (edited by Rodolphe L. Megroz), Nelson, 1938; *The Complete Nonsense of Edward Lear* (edited by Holbrook Jackson), Faber, 1947, reprinted, 1961.

Letters, journals, and travel books: *Views in Rome and Its Environs,* McLean, 1841; *Illustrated Excursions in Italy,* McLean, 1846; *Journals of a Landscape Painter in Albania, etc.,* Bentley, 1851, also published as *Edward Lear in*

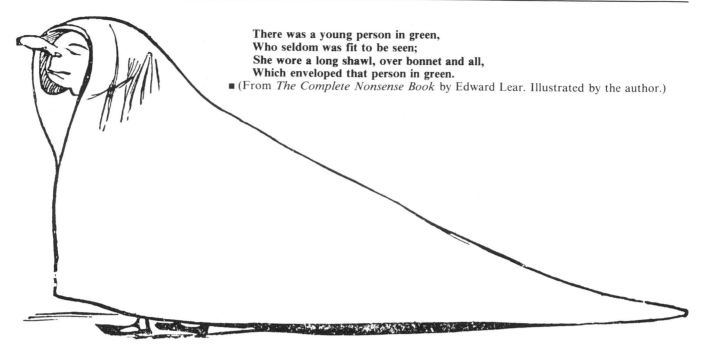

There was a young person in green,
Who seldom was fit to be seen;
She wore a long shawl, over bonnet and all,
Which enveloped that person in green.

■ (From *The Complete Nonsense Book* by Edward Lear. Illustrated by the author.)

Greece: Journals of a Landscape Painter in Greece and Albania, Kimber, 1965; *Journals of a Landscape Painter in Southern Calabria,* Bentley, 1852, also published as *Edward Lear in Southern Italy: Journals of a Landscape Painter in Southern Calabria and the Kingdom of Naples* (introduction by Peter Quennell), Kimber, 1964; *Views in Seven Ionian Islands,* [London], 1863; *Journal of a Landscape Painter in Corsica,* Bush, 1870, also published as *Edward Lear in Corsica: The Journal of a Landscape Painter,* Kimber, 1966; *Letters of Edward Lear* (edited by Constance Lady Strachey), Fisher Unwin, 1907, reprinted, Books for Libraries, 1970; *Later Letters of Edward Lear* (edited by Lady Strachey), Duffield, 1911, reprinted, Books for Libraries, 1971; *Journals: A Selection* (edited by Herbert Van Thal), Coward-McCann, 1952; *Edward Lear's Indian Journal* (extracts from the diary, 1873-75; edited by Ray Murphy), Jarrolds, 1953; *Lear's Corfu: An Anthology Drawn from the Painter's Letters* (introduced by Lawrence Durrell), Corfu Travel, 1965.

Illustrator: Lear, *Illustrations for the Family of the Psittacidae, or Parrots,* privately printed, 1832; John Edward Gray, *Gleanings from the Menagerie at Knowsley Hall,* privately printed, 1846; Gray, *Tortoises, Terrapins, and Turtles,* Sotheran, 1872; *The Lear Coloured Bird Book for Children* (facsimile reproduction of the original done for the Earl of Cromer), Mills & Boon, 1912. Also illustrator of *Indian Pheasants* and *Birds of Europe and Toucans* by John Gould, and of several volumes in the *Naturalist's Library,* edited by Sir William Jardine, published by Scribner, 1833-43.

ADAPTATIONS—Movies and filmstrips: "The Owl and the Pussycat" (motion pictures), Sterling Educational Films, 1956, Contemporary Films, 1962, Weston Woods Studios, 1971; "The Owl and the Pussycat, and Wynken, Blynken, and Nod" (filmstrip), Weston Woods Studios, 1967; "The Owl and the Pussycat, and My Shadow" (filmstrip), Cooper Films and Records, 1969; "The Pelican Chorus" (filmstrip), Reading Motivation Filmstrips, 1967; "The Table and the Chair" (filmstrip), Cooper Films and Records, 1969.

Recordings: "Anthology of Poetry for Children," read by Cecil Bellamy, Harvey Hall, Joan Hart, David King, Penel-

ope Lee, Ann Morrish and Peter Orr (cassette only), Spoken Arts; "Edward Lear's Nonsense Stories and Poems," read by Claire Bloom (six cassettes, teacher's guide; or individual records and cassettes), Caedmon; "Nonsense Verse," read by Beatrice Lillie, Cyril Ritchard and Stanley Holloway (six cassettes, teacher's guide; or individual records and cassettes), Caedmon.

SIDELIGHTS: **May 12, 1812.** Born in Holloway, England. Twentieth child of twenty-one children.

1816. Father became bankrupt. Edward given to sister Anne, twenty-one years his senior, to be looked after. "She brought me up from the leastest childhood and when she goes, my whole life will change utterly. . . . She has always been as near to Heaven as it is possible to be." [Angus Davidson, *Edward Lear: Landscape Painter and Nonsense Poet,* John Murray, 1938.[1]]

1819. Epileptic, suffered changes of mood and bouts of acute depression. "The earliest of all the morbidnesses I can recollect . . . was a rural performance of gymnastic clowns, etc. and a band. The music was good—at least it attracted me: and the sunset and twilight I remember as yesterday. And I can recollect crying half the night after all the small gaiety broke up and also suffering for days at the memory of the past scene." [Vivien Noakes, *Edward Lear: The Life of a Wanderer,* Collins, 1968.[2]]

"I suppose the everpresence of the Demon, since I was seven years old, would have prevented happiness under any sort of circumstances. It is a most merciful blessing that I have kept up as I have, and have not gone utterly to the bad mad sad."[1]

1823. At age eleven went to school. "I am almost thanking God that I was never educated, for it seems to me that 999 of those who are so, expensively and laboriously, have lost all before they arrive at my age, and remain like Swift's Stulbruggs—cut and dry for life—making no use of their earlier gained treasures: whereas, I seem to be on the threshold of knowledge. . . ."[2]

During same period he found he could make people happy with laughter. ''3 part crazy—& wholly affectionate. My Sussex friends always say that I can do nothing like other people.''[2]

1827. ''I began drawing, for bread and cheese, . . . but only did uncommon queer shop—sketches—selling them for prices varying from ninepence to four shillings: colouring prints, morbid disease drawings, for hospitals and certain doctors of physic.''[1]

1830. Took pupils in London. Engaged by Zoological Society to make drawings of parrots, called *Illustrations of the Family of Psittacidae or Parrots.* ''Should you come to town I am sorry that I cannot offer you a home pro tempore. Pro trumpery indeed it would be, if I did make any such offer—for unless you occupied the grate as a seat—I see no probability of your finding any rest consonant with the safety of my Parrots—seeing, that of the six chairs I possess 5 are

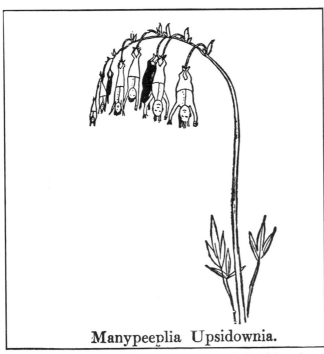

Manypeeplia Upsidownia.

(From *The Complete Nonsense Book* by Edward Lear. Illustrated by the author.)

at present occupied with lithographic prints—the whole of my exalted and delightful tenement in fact overflows with them, & for the last 12 months I have so moved—thought—looked at,—& existed among parrots—that should any transmigration take place at my decease I am sure my soul would be uncomfortable in anything but one of the Psittacidae. . . . I have just nine and twenty times resolved to give up parrots & all—& should certainly have done so had not my good genius with vast reluctance just nine and twenty times set me a going again.''[2]

1832. Asked by Lord Stanley, heir to Earl of Derby, to come and draw for him at Knowsley, England. ''The uniform apathetic tone assumed by lofty society irks me *dreadfully.* Nothing I long for half so much as to giggle heartily and to hop on one leg down the great gallery—but I dare not. The Earl of W[ilton] has been here for some days. . . . He is a very bad man, tho he looks so nicely. But what I like about him, is that he always asks me to drink a glass of champagne

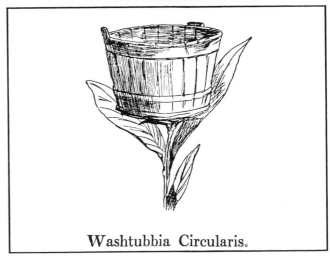

Washtubbia Circularis.

(From *The Complete Nonsense Book* by Edward Lear. Illustrated by the author.)

with him at dinner. I wonder why he does. But I don't much care as I like the champagne. . . .''[2]

Lear amused the children in the Earl's nursery by writings which were the beginnings of *The Book of Nonsense.* ''Long years ago, in days when much of my time was passed in a country house where children and mirth abounded, the lines beginning 'There was an Old Man of Tobago' were suggested to me by a valued friend as a form of verse lending itself to limitless variety for rhymes and pictures; and thenceforth the greater part of the original drawings and verses for the first *Book of Nonsense* were struck off with a pen, no assistance ever having been given me in any way but that of uproarious delight and welcome at the appearance of every new absurdity.''[1]

Lear celebrated twentieth birthday and described himself: ''Add only—that both my knees are fractured from being run over which has made them peculiarly crooked—that my neck is singularly long—a most elephantine nose—& a disposition to tumble here & there—owing to being half blind and you may very well imagine my tout ensemble.''[2]

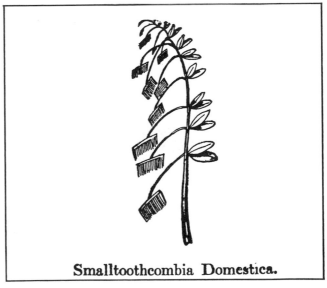

Smalltoothcombia Domestica.

(From *The Complete Nonsense Book* by Edward Lear. Illustrated by the author.)

The Scroobious Pip went out one day
When the grass was green and the sky was gray.
■ (From *The Scroobious Pip* by Edward Lear. Completed by Ogden Nash. Illustrated by Nancy Ekholm Burkert.)

(From *The Owl and the Pussycat* by Edward Lear. Illustrated by Owen Wood.)

1836. "... It is impossible to tell you *how, & how enormously* I have enjoyed the whole Autumn. The counties of Cumberland and Westmorland are superb indeed, & tho the weather has been miserable, yet I have contrived to walk pretty well over the whole ground, & to sketch a good deal besides.... My eyes are so sadly worse, that no bird under an ostrich shall I soon be able to do.

"It takes a long while to make a painter even with a good artist's education—but without one—it tries the patience of Job:—it is a great thing if one does not go backward. Meanwhile I am extremely happy as the hedgehog said when he rolled himself through a thistlebush."[2]

"I wish to goodness I could get a wife! You have no idea how sick I am of living alone!!—Please make a memorandum of any lady under 28 who has a little money—can live in Rome & knows how to cut pencils and make puddings."[2]

His views on marriage changed as they would again in later years. "I don't mean to marry—never.... I should paint less and less well; and the thought of annual infants would drive me wild. If I attain to 65, and have an 'establishment' with lots of spoons &c. to offer—I **may** chain myself:—but surely not before. And alas! and seriously—when I look around my acquaintance—and few men have more, or know more intimately, do I see a majority of happy pairs? No, I don't. Single—I may have few pleasures—but married—many risks and miseries are semi-certainly in wait-

ing—nor till the plot is played out can it be said that evils are not at hand...."[2]

1837. Left sister for Rome, Italy. "I wish we could have lived together—but it would not have done for either of us, I believe, for we are both nervous and fidgety ... and one of us—I shall not say which—has not the best temper in the world!!"[1]

1841. Returned to England for the year when *Views in Rome and Its Environs* published. "... I am very glad I took to Landscape—it suits my taste so exactly—& though I am but a mere beginner as yet—still I do hope by study and staying here to make a decent picture before I die. No early education in art—late attention & bad eyes—are all against me—but renewed health & the assistance of more kind friends than any mortal ever had: I hope will prove the heaviest side of the balance."[2]

1844. Mother died at Dover.

1845. Met one of the most intimate and beloved friends of his life, Chichester Fortescue. *Book of Nonsense* published. "I'm sure we shall be allowed to laugh in Heaven!"[2]

After publication, rumor spread that Lord Derby had written *Book of Nonsense*. Witnessing a discussion between a man and a woman concerning this, Lear responded: "Hitherto I had kept silence, but as my hat was, as well as my handkerchief and stick, largely marked inside with my name, and as I happened to have in my pocket several letters addressed to me, the temptation was too great to resist, so, flashing all these articles at once on my would-be extinguisher's attention, I speedily reduced him to silence."[1]

1846. *Illustrated Excursions in Italy* published. Resulted in a summons by the Queen to give her drawing lessons. "One of

**They took some honey, and plenty of money
Wrapped up in a five pound note.**
■ (From *Lear's Nonsense Verse* by Edward Lear. Illustrated by Tomi Ungerer.)

the Queen's Ladies-in-Waiting, who is here, has delivered to me a little print engraved from one of my drawings—of Osborne House—at Her Majesty's desire. This is one trait of many that have come under my notice that Queen Victoria has a good memory for any little condescension and kindness. I am really quite pleased with my little engraving, and shall have it placed in a good frame as soon as I can get one made...."[1]

After the Queen's lessons, Lear returned to Rome. Gave away a large part of what money he made. "I am not so rich as in other years; in fact, I have just enough to go on with—but I don't see what one wants more; and the more one gives away the better . . . I am thankful to feel that every succeeding year has fresh and fresh claims on one's mere humanity, and I trust I may never feel so less. . . . It is perfectly astonishing what comfort one may give if one only moves and does not sit torpid. But the more one does as to giving away, the more one is ashamed at not giving away *more*. I am sure I hope I shall do so more and more."[1]

1848. Travelled around the Mediterranean. ". . . We start at sunrise after a good breakfast of coffee & eggs—& we travel till 10. Then we halt at some village, or near a fountain, & a tent is pitched, & in about two hours a most capital dinner—soup & three courses—is set forth!!—so you see there is not much hardship. Then we go on till at dusk we reach some village when any house does for our night's dwell-

ing—for little iron bedsteads with mattresses are put up directly. & on these a large muslin bag tied to the ceiling, into which I creep by a hole which is tied up directly I am in it, so that no creature gets in & one sleeps soundly in a room full of vermin. I thought I should have laughed all night long the first time I crept into this strange bag, but soon grew used to it. In the morning—all is packed up & off we go again."[2]

1849. Travelled with Franklin Lushington, who became his closest friend. "I do not know when I have enjoyed so much. My fellow-traveller draws as much as I do, and we only complain that the days are too short. . . . Mr. Lushington has been so constantly the most merry and kind travelling companion. . . ."[1]

1850. Accepted at Royal Academy. ". . . He got into the Academy—he did!—Yes—so he did. . . .

"The R. Academy have sate on my drawing from the antique, and . . . I am a 'probationer'—& on my trial till April when the three drawings I have to make will be again sate on—and I shall be admitted for ten years as a student—or—rejected. *Vedermo quale sarò.*

"I tried with 51 little boys—and 19 of us were admitted. I go with a large book and a piece of chalk to school every day like a good little boy."[2]

1851. Published *Journals of a Landscape Painter in Greece and Albania*—a result of his Mediterranean journey. "I should think that little book has had as much good said of it as any ever have."[1]

1853. Sailed for Alexandria. "Of this I am sure, that had I persisted in remaining in England, my lungs would not have recovered again. So you see I am *taking it easy,* & regarding my *exile,* as a medicinal & necessary remedy."[2]

1856. Met Helena Cortazzi at Corfu. "Do you know I am half in love? . . . I begin to feel I must either run for it, or rush into extremes—and as neither they nor I have money, am not I a fool for thinking about it? Yet sometimes at 43 I cannot help believing that half and half life will get too wearisome to bear ere long. The older is my alarm,—but the younger is the prettier—o Papa! What a blasted old ass your son is. If one could only unmarry again if it didn't suit!—only one couldn't."[2]

1858. His life was a series of journeys, but he always returned to England. "You have no idea, my dear boy, what a grief this going to and fro is. I had rather, methinks, come and [settle] and die straight away, only the half life half death of physical hell and worrying is a trial one flees from as yet."[2]

1864. Visited Richard Bethel, Lord Chancellor who had a twenty-four year old daughter, Augusta. ". . . dear little Gussie, who is absolutely good & sweet & delightful. 'BOTHER.'

"Poor Gussie!—but how to decide? if her life is sad,—united to mine would it be less so? or rather—would it not be more so? . . . The risk of marriage—the marriage itself so gt. a risk of making two people more unhappy than before?"[2]

1867. Gussie declined. "I have come to the conclusion that nobody ought to marry at all, & that no more people ought ever to be born, & so we should be gradually extinguished, & the world be left to triumphant chimpanzees, gorillas, cockroaches & crocodiles. . . . I *won't* like anyone else, if I can help it, I mean, a new person, or scenes, or place, all the rest of my short foolish life."[2]

1869. In Cannes. "I can't decide 'in my mind'—if it be wiser to await death in one spot, making that spot as pleasant as may be, & varying its monotony by such pleasant gleams of older life as can be obtained—or—to hurry on through constantly new & burningly bright scenes, & then dying al'improviso as may happen."[2]

1870. "What do you think as I have been & gone & done? I grow so tired of noisy lodgings, & yet am more & more unable to think of ever wintering in England—& so unable to bear the expense of two houses & two journeys annually that I have bought a bit of ground at San Remo & am actually building a house there. . . . I shall endeavour to live upon little figs in summertime & on worms in the winter. I shall have 28 olive trees & a small bed of onions: & a stone terrace, with a gray Parrot & 2 hedgehogs to walk up & down on it by day & by night . . ."[2]

"Oh! let us be married; too long we have tarried:
But what shall we do for a ring?"

■ (From *The Owl and the Pussycat* by Edward Lear. Pictures by Barbara Cooney.)

He had walked a short way, when he heard a great noise,
Of all sorts of Beasticles, Birdlings, and Boys;

(From *The New Vestments* by Edward Lear. Illustrated by Arnold Lobel.)

Till the morning came of that hateful day
When the Jumblies sailed in their sieve away,
And the Dong was left on the cruel shore
Gazing—gazing for evermore,—

■ (From *The Dong with a Luminous Nose* by Edward Lear. Drawings by Edward Gorey.)

(From the filmstrip "Wynken, Blynken and Nod," produced by Weston Woods.)

With lovely leathery throats and chins!
Ploffskin, Pluffskin, Pelican jee!
We think no birds so happy as we!
Plumpskin, Ploshkin, Pelican jill!
We think so then, and we thought so still!

■ (From *The Pelican Chorus* by Edward Lear. Illustrated by Harold Berson.)

**"What a lovely walk we've taken
Let us dine on Beans and Bacon."**
■ (From *Nonsense Songs* by Edward Lear. Illustrated by L. Leslie Brooke.)

1873. Travelled to India. His sister, Sarah died. "We live and live and live on and perhaps so living from day to day through long years, feel these losses less."[2]

1877. Returned to England for summer, depressed and lonely. "Tears, idle tears—always in vain I resolve & re-resolve:—gloom contracts & convulses me. But I am gradually getting to see that the past must be past, & buried:—yet I can by no means think of anything to put forward as the future. Meanwhile the present is a fearful blank—cutting of heart strings the only serious order of the day.... In vain I work for an hour—tears blind me. In vain I play on the Pianno,—I get convulsed: in vain I pace the large room—or try to sleep. True, all these symptoms happened also in 1855—but then there was not the finality there is now:—then—there were unreal glimpses of light:: now—back returns the dark, 'with *no more* hope of light.' God help me. I was never nearer to utter & total madness than now. Yet, I don't mean to give way. I shall stave off worse things, if I can."[2]

1880. Had new house built in San Remo, the Villa Tennyson. His constant companions were his cat Fuss (who lived to be seventeen) and his servant. "My new land has only the road and the Railway between it & the sea, so unless the Fishes begin to build, or Noah's Ark comes to an Anchor below the site, the new Villa Eduardo cannot be spoiled. I was glad to get home again & to have the fun of gardening once more, which is really the only unchangeable pleasure now left in life.

'And this is certain, if so be
You could just now my garden see,
The aspic of my flowers so bright
Would make you shudder with delight.

And if you voz to see my roziz
As is a boon to all men's noziz,—
You'd fall upon your back and scream—
'O Lawk! O criky! it's a dream!' "[2]

1883. Servant and friend Giorgio died. "The longer I live the more I think I perceive the spaces of this life to be inexpressibly trivial and small, and that, if there be a life beyond this, our present existence is merely a trifle in comparison with what may be beyond. And that there *is* a life beyond this it seems to me the greatest of absurdities to deny, or even to doubt of."[2]

1887. Old, crippled with rheumatism, lost sight in right eye.

"He only said, 'I'm very weary,
The rheumatiz he said,
He said, it's awful dull & dreary,
I think I'll go to bed.' "[2]

Asked Gussie to come to San Remo. "More or less perplexed as to if I shall or shall not ask Gussie to marry me. Once or twice the crisis nearly came off, yet she went at five & nothing occurred beyond her very decidedly showing me how much she cared for me. . . . This I think was the day of the death of all hope."[2]

January 29, 1888. Died peacefully at San Remo. "You will render me a sacred service in telling my friends and relations that my last thought was for them, especially the Judge and Lord Northbrook and Lord Carlingford. I cannot find words sufficient to thank my good friends for the good they have always done me. I did not answer their letters because I could not write, as no sooner did I take a pen in my hand than I felt as if I were dying."[2]

FOR MORE INFORMATION SEE: Angus Davidson, *Edward Lear: Landscape Painter and Nonsense Poet, 1812-1888,* John Murray, 1938, reprinted, Kennikat Press, 1968; R. B. Heilman, "Lear World," *English Institute Essays,* Columbia University Press, 1948; Eric Partridge, "Nonsense Words of Edward Lear and Lewis Carroll," *Here, There, and Everywhere: Essays upon Language,* Macmillan, 1950; Elizabeth Sewell, *The Field of Nonsense: A Study of the Works of Edward Lear and Lewis Carroll,* Chatto & Windus, 1952; W. J. Smith, "So They Smashed That Old Man . . . ," *Horn Book,* August, 1959; Joanna Richardson, *Edward Lear,* Longmans, Green, 1965; Brian Doyle, editor, *The Who's Who of Children's Literature,* Schocken Books, 1968; Philip Hofer, *Edward Lear as a Landscape Draughtsman,* Belknap Press of Harvard University Press, 1968; Vivien Noakes, *Edward Lear: The Life of a Wanderer,* Collins, 1968; Donald Barthelme, "The Death of Edward Lear," *New Yorker,* January 2, 1971.

For children: Margaret J. Miller, *Seven Men of Wit,* Hutchinson, 1960; Laura Benét, *Famous Poets for Young People,* Dodd, 1964; Norah Smaridge, *Famous Author-Illustrators for Young People,* Dodd, 1973; Emery Kelen, *Mr. Nonsense: A Life of Edward Lear,* Nelson, 1973.

Lear, 1857. Drawing by William Holman Hunt.

LONDON, Jack   1876-1916
(John Griffith London)

PERSONAL: Born January 12, 1876, in San Francisco, California; died November 22, 1916, in Santa Rosa, California; son of W. H. Chaney (a roving astrologer) and Flora Wellman; took name of his stepfather, John London; married Bessie Maddern, April 7, 1900; married second wife, Charmian Kittredge, November 19, 1905. *Education:* London was largely self-educated, but attended public school until age 14; he returned to high school at age 19, and after a year, passed the entrance examinations to the University of California, which he attended for one semester. *Politics:* Socialist. *Home:* Glen Ellen, California.

CAREER: Novelist, short story writer, and political essayist. From the age of 14, worked on an ice wagon, in a bowling alley, as an oyster pirate, state fish patrolman, jutemill worker, coal shoveler, and on the sealing vessel, "Sophie Sutherland," traveling to the coasts of Japan and Siberia. At age 18, London joined Coxey's Army, tramping through the U.S. and Canada as a hobo, and was jailed for vagrancy in Niagara Falls. He joined the gold rush to the Klondike, 1897; traveled to London, 1902, where he made a close study of slum conditions; was a journalist and reported the Russo-Japanese War for the Hearst newspapers, 1904; ran for mayor of Oakland, California, 1905, on the Socialist ticket. London went on many sailing voyages to the Caribbean and South Seas, and in 1907-10, set off in his yacht, "Snark" with his wife on a world cruise, which was abandoned when they reached Australia.

WRITINGS—Novels: A Daughter of the Snows (illustrated by Frederick C. Yohn), Lippincott, 1902, reissued, Archer House, 1963; *The Cruise of the Dazzler,* Century, 1902, reissued, Archer House, 1963; *Call of the Wild* (illustrated by Philip R. Goodwin and Charles L. Bull), Macmillan, 1903, reissued, Washington Square Press, 1974 [other editions illustrated by Paul Bransom, Macmillan, 1912; Robert Todd, Macmillan, 1956; Leon Bishop, Scott, Foresman, 1959; Henry Varnum Poor, Heritage Press, 1960; Lee Gregori, Grosset & Dunlap, 1963; Hamilton Greene, Hart Publishing, 1963; Maurice Wilson, Longmans, Green, 1965; Ron King, Classic Press, 1968; adaptations for children include an edition adapted and abridged by Olive Price and illustrated by Douglas Allen, Grosset & Dunlap, 1961; an edition illustrated by Karel Kezer, Macmillan, 1963; an edition illustrated by Charles Pickard, Dutton, 1968; an edition adapted by Warren Halliburton and illustrated by Don Gaines, McGraw-Hill, 1968; an edition edited by Anthony L. Ariciola, with a teacher's guide, Pendulum Press, 1969; an edition edited by Virginia F. Allen, Noble, 1970; and an edition edited by Kin Platt and illustrated by Goodwin and Bull, Pendulum Press, 1973].

The Sea-Wolf (illustrated by W. J. Aylward), Macmillan, 1904, reissued, Horizon Press, 1969 [another edition illustrated by Fletcher Martin, Limited Editions, 1961]; *White Fang,* Macmillan, 1905, reissued, Scholastic Book Services, 1972 [other editions illustrated by Charles L. Bull, Grosset & Dunlap, 1914; Charles Pickard, Dutton, 1967; Dick Cole, Childrens Press, 1969; Lydia Dabcovich, Limited Editions, 1973]; *The Game* (illustrated by Henry Hutt and T. C. Lawrence), Macmillan, 1905, reissued, Literature House, 1969; *Before Adam,* Macmillan, 1906 [another edition illustrated by Leonard E. Fisher, Macmillan, 1962]; *The Iron Heel,* Macmillan, 1907, reissued, Hill & Wang, 1966; *Martin Eden* (semi-autobiographical), Macmillan,

1909, reissued, with a reader's guide, AMSCO School Publications, 1971; *Burning Daylight*, Macmillan, 1910, reissued, Manor Books, 1973; *Adventure*, Macmillan, 1911; *Smoke Bellew* (illustrated by P. J. Monahan), Century, 1912; *John Barleycorn* (semi-autobiographical; illustrated by H. T. Dunn), Century, 1913, reprinted, Greenwood Press, 1969; *The Abysmal Brute*, Century, 1913; *The Valley of the Moon*, Macmillan, 1913, reprinted, P. Smith, 1975.

The Mutiny of the Elsinore, Macmillan, 1914, reissued, Arco, 1968; *The Star Rover*, Macmillan, 1915, reissued as *The Jacket*, Horizon Press, 1969 [another edition illustrated by L. E. Fisher, Macmillan, 1963]; *The Scarlet Plague* (illustrated by Gordon Grant), Macmillan, 1915, reissued, Arno, 1975; *The Little Lady of the Big House*, Macmillan, 1916; *Jerry of the Islands*, Macmillan, 1917; *Michael, Brother of Jerry*, Macmillan, 1917; *Hearts of Three*, Macmillan, 1920; *The Assassination Bureau, Ltd.* (unfinished novel; completed by Robert L. Fish from notes by the author), McGraw-Hill, 1963.

Short stories: *The Son of the Wolf: Tales of the Far North*, Houghton, 1900, reprinted, Mss Information, 1972; *The God of His Fathers, and Other Stories*, McClure, Phillips, 1901, reprinted, Books for Libraries, 1969; *Children of the Frost* (illustrated by Raphael M. Reay), Macmillan, 1902, reissued, Arco, 1963; *The Faith of Men, and Other Stories*, Macmillan, 1904, reprinted, Books for Libraries, 1970; *Tales of the Fish Patrol* (illustrated by George Varian), Macmillan, 1905, reprinted, Books for Libraries, 1972; *Moon-Face, and Other Stories*, Macmillan, 1906, reprinted, Books for Libraries, 1970; *Love of Life, and Other Stories*, Macmillan, 1906, reissued, Chatto & Windus, 1968 [another edition with an introduction by George Orwell, P. Elek, 1946]; *The Road*, Macmillan, 1907, reprinted, Peregrine, 1970.

Lost Face, Macmillan, 1910 (includes *To Build a Fire*); *When God Laughs, and Other Stories*, Macmillan, 1911; *South Sea Tales*, Macmillan, 1911, reissued, 1961; *The House of Pride, and Other Tales of Hawaii*, Macmillan, 1912; *The Night-Born*, Macmillan, 1913; *The Turtles of Tasman*, Macmillan, 1916; *The Human Drift*, Macmillan, 1917; *The Red One*, Grosset & Dunlap, 1918; *On the Makaloa Mat*, Macmillan, 1919; *Dutch Courage, and Other Stories*, 1922.

Plays: *Scorn of Women* (three-act), Macmillan, 1906; *Theft* (four-act), Macmillan, 1910; *The Acorn-Planter: A California Forest Play*, Macmillan, 1916; *Daughters of the Rich*, Holmes Book Co., 1971.

Social commentary: *War of the Classes*, Macmillan, 1905, reprinted, Literature House, 1970; *The Apostate: A Parable of Child Labor*, The Appeal to Reason, (Girard, Kansas), 1906; *Revolution, and Other Essays*, Macmillan, 1910 (includes *Goliah: A Utopian Essay*, reprinted separately, Thorp Springs Press, 1973); *The Strength of the Strong* (illustrated by Don Sayre Groesbeck), C. H. Kerr, 1911; *London's Essays of Revolt* (edited by Leonard D. Abbott), Vanguard, 1926; *Jack London, American Rebel: A Collection of His Social Writings* (edited by Philip S. Forner), Citadel, 1947, reprinted, 1964.

Other: *The People of the Abyss*, Macmillan, 1903, reprinted, Mss Information, 1972; (with Anna Strusky) *The Kempton-Wace Letters*, Macmillan, 1903, reprinted, Haskell House, 1969; *The Cruise of the Snark*, Macmillan, 1911, reissued, Seafarer Books, 1971; *Letters from Jack*

London (edited by King Hendricks and Irving Shepard), Odyssey Press, 1965; *The Economics of the Klondike* (originally appeared in *American Monthly Review of Reviews*, January, 1900), Shorey Book Store, 1968; *The Gold-Hunters of the North* (originally appeared in *Atlantic Monthly*, July, 1903), Facsimile Reproduction, 1968; *Jack London Reports: War Correspondence, Sports Articles, and Miscellaneous Writings* (edited by K. Hendricks and I. Shepard), Doubleday, 1970; *Jack London's Articles in The Oakland High School Aegis* (illustrated by Holly Janes), [Cedar Springs, Michigan], 1971.

Selections: *Brown Wolf, and Other Jack London Stories* (edited by Franklin K. Mathiews), Macmillan, 1920, reprinted, 1967; *Selected Stories by Jack London*, World Syndicate Publishing, 1930; *Best Short Stories of Jack London*, Sun Dial Press, 1945; *The Sun-Dog Trail, and Other Stories*, World Publishing, 1951; *Tales of Adventure* (edited by I. Shepard), Hanover House, 1956; *The Call of the Wild, The Cruise of the Dazzler, and Other Stories of Adventure*, Platt & Munk, 1960; *Short Stories* (edited by Maxwell Geismar), Hill & Wang, 1960; *The Best Short Stories of Jack London*, Fawcett, 1962; *Jack London's Stories for Boys* (illustrated by C. Richard Schaare), Cupples & Leon, 1963; *The Bodley Head Jack London* (edited by Arthur Calder-Marshall), Bodley Head, 1963; *White Fang, and Other Stories*, Dodd, 1963; *The Sea-Wolf, and Selected Stories*, New American Library, 1964; *The Selected Works*, Parents Magazine's Cultural Institute, 1964.

Stories of Hawaii (edited by A. Grove Day), Appleton-Century, 1965; *Great Short Works of Jack London* (edited by Earle Labor), Harper, 1965; *The Great Adventure Stories of Jack London* (edited by Abraham Rothberg), Bantam Books, 1967; *The Game* [and] *The Abysmal Brute* (edited by I. O. Evans), Arco, 1967, Horizon Press, 1969; *The Call of the Wild* [and] *White Fang*, Cambridge Book Co., 1968; *Short Stories*, Funk & Wagnalls, 1968; *The Scarlet Plague* [and] *Before Adam* (edited by I. O. Evans), Arco, 1968; *The Call of Wild, and Other Stories* (illustrated by Robert Bates), Heron Books, 1969; *Twelve Short Stories* (edited by Jeffrey Tillett; illustrated by David Barlow), E. Arnold, 1969; *Selected Short Stories*, Airmont, 1969.

Contributor to periodicals, including *Overland Monthly*, *Atlantic Monthly*, and *Black Cat*.

ADAPTATIONS—Movies and filmstrips: "The Sea Wolf" (motion pictures), Bosworth, 1913, Famous Players-Lasky Corp., 1920, Ralph W. Ince, 1926, Fox Film Corp., 1930, Warner Brothers, starring Edward G. Robinson and Ida Lupino, 1941; "The Sea Wolf" (filmstrip; with captions), Educational Record Sales, 1969; "The Valley of the Moon" (motion picture), Bosworth, 1914; "Burning Daylight" (motion pictures), Bosworth, 1914, Metro Pictures, 1920, First National Pictures, 1928; "John Barleycorn" (motion picture), Bosworth, 1914; "An Odyssey of the North" (motion picture), Bosworth, 1914; "Martin Eden" (motion picture), Bosworth, 1914; "The Mutiny" (motion picture), adaptation of *The Mutiny of the Elsinore*, Metro Pictures, 1920; "The Star Rover" (motion picture), Metro Pictures, 1920; "The Little Fool" (motion picture), adaptation of *The Little Lady of the Big House*, Metro Pictures, 1921; "The Mohican's Daughter" (motion picture), adaptation of *The Story of Jess Uck*, P. T. B., Inc., 1922; "Jack London's Tales of the Fish Patrol" (series of eight motion pictures), Universal Films, 1922-23; "The Abysmal Brute" (motion picture), Universal Pictures, 1923; "The Call of the Wild" (motion

JACK LONDON

pictures), Pathe Exchange, 1923, Twentieth Century, starring Clark Gable and Loretta Young, 1935; "The Call of the Wild" (filmstrips), Eye Gate House, with a teacher's guide, 1958, Brunswick Productions, 1967, Universal Education and Visual Arts, 1971.

"White Fang" (motion pictures), R-C Pictures, 1925, Twentieth Century-Fox, 1936; "Adventure" (motion picture), Famous Players-Lasky, 1925; "Morganson's Finish" (motion picture), Tiffany Productions, 1926; "The Haunted Ship" (motion picture), adaptation of *White and Yellow,* Tiffany Productions, 1927; "The Devil's Skipper" (motion picture), adaptation of *Demetrious Contos,* Tiffany Productions, 1928; "Tropical Nights" (motion picture), adaptation of *A Raid on the Oyster Pirates,* Tiffany-Stahl Productions, 1928; "Stormy Waters" (motion picture), adaptation of *The Yellow Handkerchief,* Tiffany-Stahl Productions, 1928; "Prowlers of the Sea" (motion picture), adaptation of *The Lancashire Queen,* Tiffany-Stahl Productions, 1928; "Conflict" (motion picture), adaptation of *The Abysmal Brute,* starring John Wayne, Universal Productions, 1936; "Wolf Call" (motion picture), Monogram Pictures, 1939; "Torture Ship" (motion picture), adaptation of *A Thousand Dollars,* starring Lyle Talbot, Producers Releasing Corp., 1939; "Romance of the Redwoods" (motion picture), adaptation of *The White Silence,* Columbia Pictures, 1939.

"Queen of the Yukon" (motion picture), Monogram Pictures, 1940; "Sign of the Wolf" (motion picture), adapta-

tion of *That Spot,* Monogram Pictures, 1941; "North to the Klondike" (motion picture), adaptation of *Gold Hunter of the North,* starring Broderick Crawford, Universal Pictures, 1941; "The Adventures of Martin Eden" (motion picture), adaptation of *Martin Eden,* starring Glenn Ford and Claire Trevor, Columbia Pictures, 1942; "Alaska" (motion picture), adaptation of *Flush of Gold,* starring Dean Jagger and John Carradine, Monogram Pictures, 1944; "The Fighter" (motion picture), G-H Productions, 1952; "Wolf Larsen" (motion picture), adaptation of *The Sea Wolf,* starring Peter Graves and Barry Sullivan, Allied Artists Pictures, 1958; "To Build a Fire" (motion picture), Montana State College, 1963; "To Build a Fire" (filmstrip), Educational Record Sales, 1972; "The Assassination Bureau Limited" (motion picture), Paramount Pictures, 1969; "Brown Wolf" (motion picture; 26 minutes, sound, color, with a teacher's guide), Learning Corp., of America, 1972; "All Gold Canyon" (motion picture; 21 minutes, sound, color, for elementary grades), Weston Woods Studios, 1973; Piero Pieroni produced a TV series on London and the life of London's characters in the Arctic, 1976.

Recordings: "To Build a Fire," read by Robert Donley, Miller-Brody; Jack London Cassette Library (6 cassettes include "The Call of the Wild," "Martin Eden," "The Sea Wolf") read by Jack Dahlby, Listening Library, 1976; "The Call of the Wild" (2 records) read by Arnold Moss, Miller-Brody.

SIDELIGHTS: **January 12, 1876.** "My father was Pennsylvania-born, a soldier, scout, backwoodsman, trapper, and wanderer. My mother was born in Ohio. Both came west independently, meeting and marrying in San Francisco, where I was born. What little city life I then passed was in my babyhood. My life, from my fourth to my ninth years, was spent upon Californian ranches. I learned to read and write about my fifth year, though I do not remember anything about it. I always could read and write, and have no recollection antedating such a condition. Folks say I simply insisted upon being taught.

"Was an omnivorous reader, principally because reading matter was scarce and I had to be grateful for whatever fell into my hands. Remember reading some of Trowbridge's works for boys at six years of age. At seven I was reading Paul du Chaillu's *Travels,* Captain Cook's *Voyages,* and *Life of Garfield.* And all through this period I devoured what Seaside Library novels I could borrow from the womenfolk and dime novels from the farm hands. At eight I was deep in Ouida and Washington Irving. Also during this period read a great deal of American History. Also, life on a Californian ranch is not very nourishing to the imagination.

"When I was seven years old, at the country school of San Pedro, this happened. Meat, I was that hungry for it I once opened a girl's basket and stole a piece of meat—a little piece the size of my two fingers. I ate it but I never repeated it. In those days, like Essau, I would have literally sold my birthright for a mess of pottage, a piece of meat. Great God! when those youngsters threw chunks of meat on the ground because of surfeit, I could have dragged it from the dirt and eaten it; but I did not. Just imagine the development of my mind, my soul, under such material conditions.

"This meat incident is an epitome of my whole life. I was eight years old when I put on my first undershirt made at or bought at a store. Duty—at ten years I was on the streets selling newspapers. Every cent was turned over to my people, and I went to school in constant shame of the hats, shoes, clothes I wore. Duty—from then on, I had no childhood. Up at three o'clock in the morning to carry papers.

When that was finished I did not go home but continued on to school. School out, my evening papers. Saturday I worked on an ice wagon. Sunday I went to a bowling alley and set up pins for drunken Dutchmen. Duty—I turned over every cent and went dressed like a scarecrow.

"Was there any duty owing to me?

"I worked in [a] cannery, not for a vacation but for a year. For months at a time, during that year, I was up and at work at six in the morning. I took half an hour for dinner. I took half an hour for supper. I worked every night till ten, eleven and twelve o'clock. My wages were small, but I worked such long hours that I sometimes made as high as fifty dollars a month. Duty—I turned every cent over. Duty—I have worked in that hell hole for thirty-six straight hours, at a machine, and I was only a child. I remember how I was trying to save the money to buy a skiff—eight dollars. All that summer I saved and scraped. In the fall I had five dollars as a result of absolutely doing without all pleasure. My mother came to the machine where I worked and asked for it. I could have killed myself that night. After a year of hell to have that pitiful—to be robbed of that petty joy.

"My body and soul were starved when I was a child, cannot they do without a few little luxuries for me at this stage of the game?

"However, from my ninth year, with the exception of the hours spent at school (and I earned them by hard labor), my life has been one of toil. It is worthless to give the long sordid list of occupations, none of them trades, all heavy manual labor. Of course I continued to read. Was never without a book. My education was popular, graduating from the grammar school at about fourteen. Took a taste for the water. At fifteen left home and went upon a Bay life. San Francisco Bay is no mill pond by the way. I was a salmon fisher, an oyster pirate, a schooner sailor, a fish patrolman, a longshoreman, and a general sort of bay-faring adventurer—a boy in years and a man amongst men. Always a book, and always reading when the rest were asleep; when they were awake I was one with them, for I

Buck had been purposely placed between Dave and Solleks so that he might receive instruction. Apt scholar that he was, they were equally apt teachers, never allowing him to linger long in error, and enforcing their teaching with their sharp teeth. Dave was fair and very wise, and he never failed to nip him when he stood in need of it. ■ (From *The Call of the Wild and Other Stories* by Jack London. Illustrated by Kyuzo Tsugami.)

Buck threw himself forward, tightening the traces with a jarring lunge. His whole body was gathered compactly together in the tremendous effort, the muscles writhing and knotting like live things under the silky fur. His great chest was low to the ground, his head forward and down, while his feet were flying like mad, the claws scarring the hard-packed snow in parallel grooves. ■ (From *The Call of the Wild* by Jack London. Photographs by Seymour Linden.)

"Do you know what I suffered during that High School and University period? The imps of hell would have wept had they been with me. Does anyone know? Can anyone know? O the hours I have eaten out my heart in bitterness! Duty—I fought it off for two long years without cessation, and I am glad.''[1]

1898. Returned from Yukon. Began serious writing. "My father died while I was in the Klondike, and I returned home to take up the reins.

"As to literary work: My first magazine article (I had done no newspaper work), was published in January, 1899; it is now the fifth story in the 'Son of the Wolf.' Since then I have done work for The Overland Monthly, The Atlantic, The Wave, The Arena, The Youth's Companion, The Review of Reviews, etc., etc., besides a host of lesser publications, and to say nothing of newspaper and syndicate work. Hackwork all, or nearly so, from a comic joke or triolet to pseudoscientific disquisitions upon things about which I knew nothing. Hackwork for dollars, that's all, setting aside practically all ambitious efforts to some future period of less financial stringence. . . .

"Naturally, my reading early bred in me a desire to write, but my manner of life prevented me attempting it. I have no literary help or advice of any kind—just been sort of hammering around in the dark till I knocked holes through here and there and caught glimpses of daylight. Common knowledge of magazine methods, etc., came to me as revelation. Not a soul to say here you are and there you mistake.

"Of course, during my revolutionary period I perpetrated my opinions upon the public through the medium of the local papers, gratis. But that was years ago when I went to high school and was more notorious than esteemed. Once, by the way, returned from my sealing voyage, I won a prize essay of twenty-five dollars from a San Francisco paper over the heads of Stanford and California Universities, both of which were represented by second and third place through their undergraduates. This gave me hope for achieving something ultimately.''[1]

December 25, 1898. "The typewriter goes back on the thirty-first of December. Till then I expect to be busy cleaning up my desk, writing business letters of various nature, and finishing the articles I am at present on. Then the New Year, and an entire change of front.

"I have profited greatly, have learned much during the last three months. How much I cannot even approximate—I feel its worth and greatness, but it is too impalpable to put down in black and white. I have studied, read, and thought a great deal, and believe I am at last beginning to grasp the situation—the general situation, my situation, and the correlative situation between the two. But I am modest, as I say, I am only beginning to grasp—I realize, that with all I have learned, I know less about it than I thought I did a couple of years ago.

"Are you aware of the paradox entailed by progress? It makes me both jubilant and sad. You cannot help feeling sad when looking over back work and realizing its weak places, its errors, its inanities; and again, you cannot but rejoice at having so improved that you are aware of it, and feel capable of better things. I have learned more in the past three months than in all my High School and College; yet, of course, they were necessary from a preparatory standpoint.

"And to-day is Christmas—it is at such periods that the vagabondage of my nature succumbs to a latent taste for domesticity. Away with the many corners of this round world! I am deaf to the call of the East and West, the North and South—a picture such as [a friend] used to draw is before me. A comfortable little cottage, a couple of servants, a select coterie of friends, and above all, a neat little wife and a couple of diminutive models of us twain—a hanging of stockings last evening, a merry surprise this morning, the genial interchange of Christmas greeting; a cosy grate fire, the sleepy children cuddling on the floor ready for bed, a sort of dreamy communion between the fire, my wife, and myself; an assured, though quiet and monotonous, future in prospect; a satisfied knowledge of the many little amenities of civilized life which are mine and shall be mine; a genial, optimistical contemplation—''[1]

April 7, 1900. Married Bessie Maddern. "So! I am married, and I cannot start to Paris in July, dough or no dough—That's why I got married.''[1]

1901. Birth of daughter, Joan. "Well, there's no accounting for things. I did so ardently long to be a father, that it seemed impossible that such a happiness should be mine. But it is. And a damn fine, healthy youngster. Weighed nine and a half pounds at birth, which they say is good for a girl. Up to date has shown a good stomach and lack of ailments, for it does nothing but eat and sleep, or lie awake for a straight hour without a whimper. Intend to call her 'Joan.' ''[1]

1903. Separation from Bessie. Effort of Anna Strunsky and London to write a book. Bessie felt they were having an affair. "Concerning my separation from Mrs. London, I have really nothing to say except the Kempton-Wace Letters have nothing whatever to do with it. That the causes of the separation have been operative long previous to the writing of the book. As the reporters could not ascertain the real reason, they dug one out of the book, that is all. So far as the public is concerned I have no statement to make except that the Kempton-Wace Letters play no part whatever in the separation.''[1]

His wife was very jealous. London became interested in Charmian Kittredge, who was to become his second wife. "During the time I lived in the Bungalow, Charmian was often at the house. There was not the least iota even of flirtation between us. During that time I was tangled up with Anna Strunsky—in fact, during that time (and Bessie kept me informed of it), Charmian was very solicitous on Bessie's behalf. I never gave Charmian the first thought, much less a second thought. During all the time that I was away in England, Charmian was a great deal with Bessie, cheering her up and bolstering her up, and telling her that everything would come out all right regarding the Strunsky affair.

"Now, I come to the year 1903, the year of my separation. Somewhere in the latter part of June, 1903, Bessie and the children came up to Glen Ellen, camping. I was shortly to follow them. Up to this time there had never been a word exchanged between Charmian and me, nor a look. Just a short time previous to this, several weeks at the outside, one Sunday . . . in the midst of the Crowd, I felt my first impulsion toward Charmian. (This, of course I have since told her about.) But this she knew nothing about at the time. I gave no sign of it, and as I say, it was my first impulsion toward her. My first feeling about her in a sexual way. I, myself, gave no immediate further thought to it.

"As I was sayin', Henry, we've got six dogs. I took six fish out of the bag. I gave one fish to each dog, an', Henry, I was one fish short." ■ (From *White Fang* by Jack London. Illustrated by Charles Pickard.)

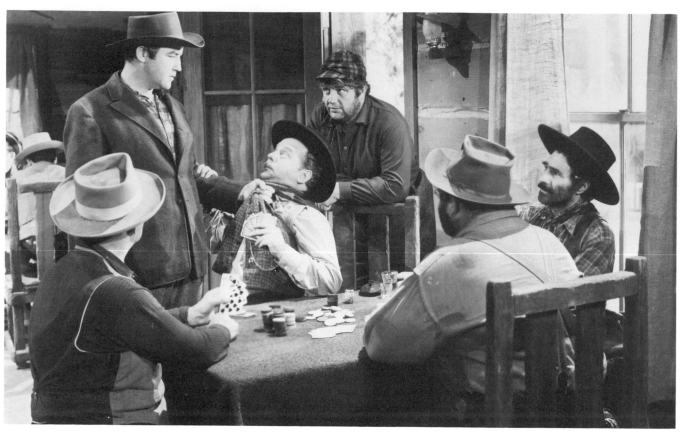

(From the movie "North to the Klondike," based on the short story "Gold Hunter of the North," starring Broderick Crawford and Andy Devine. Copyright 1941 by Universal Pictures Co., Inc.)

(From the movie "Conflict" based on the novel *The Abysmal Brute*, starring John Wayne. Copyright 1936 by Universal Productions, Inc.)

(From the movie "White Fang," starring Michael Whelan and Charles Winninger. Copyright 1936 by Twentieth Century-Fox Film Corp.)

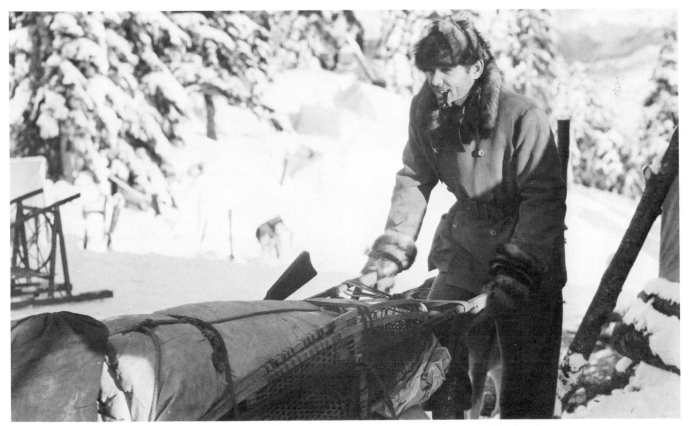

(From the movie "Call of the Wild," starring Clark Gable. Copyright 1935 by Twentieth Century Pictures, Inc.)

In a flash Buck knew it. The time had come. It was to the death. ■ (From *The Call of the Wild* by Jack London. Illustrated by Philip R. Goodwin.)

"Bessie came up, as I have said, camping at Glen Ellen the latter part of June, to be followed by me later on. In the meantime, I was going to take the *Spray* out on a cruise. Up to the time of Bessie's departure from the Bungalow on this camping-trip, I repeat, nothing had passed between Charmian and me—not a word nor a look.

"About this time I was not in a very happy state. . . . the black moods that used to come upon me at that time, and the black philosophy that I worked out at that time and afterwards put into Wolf Larsen's mouth. My marriage was eminently unsatisfactory. I was preparing to go to pieces. Said going to pieces to culminate in my separation from Bessie. While she had started on her camping-trip up here, I was going out on the *Spray* to have a hell of a time with any woman I could get hold of. I had my eyes on a dozen women—not alone in connection with the *Spray* cruise, but in any way that I could get hold of these women. It was then that my thoughts turned to Charmian amongst the rest. I was not in love with her, had never flirted with her, but I decided that she was a warm enough proposition to suit me in an illicit way. (By 'warm proposition' I don't mean to say the easy proposition that a women of loose career would mean, but by warm proposition I mean just a good warm human woman. . . .) As I say, my thoughts turned to Charmian as one of the dozen likelihoods. On the other hand, she was not a likelihood sufficiently impelling for me to go out after her then.

"Now, here's the situation: Bessie is camping at Glen Ellen, and I go out to [a] camp in the hills from Saturday night to Monday morning. I have not seen Charmian nor had a word with her nor a look with her. On Monday morning I get into the rig and drive into town with the rest of the Crowd coming in. My plan is to set about at once with the outfitting of the *Spray,* and to sail in a couple of days. No woman picked out yet. That was part of the outfitting! Coming in, in the rig on Monday morning, the fifth-wheel carried away, I lost a few inches of skin, had seven different bandages upon my carcass, and a stiff knee. I had had stiff knees before, and I knew that the last place in the world for a stiff knee was on a rolling and plunging boat. So I decided to go up to Glen Ellen until I could get myself in shape for the cruise.

"This was on Monday morning. That evening Charmian telephoned to find out if I was coming up to Glen Ellen, because Bessie had commissioned her to get some things for her to send up by me whenever I went up. These things Charmian said she had all ready for me to take. I told her I was packing that night and would start early next morning. She said she would come out right away with them. My knee was stiff, I was sick and miserable. All the places where the skin was off had stiffened up so that it was a grievous pain for me to move my arms or legs. I was looking on, directing, and [Frank] Atherton was packing my trunks for me, when Charmian arrived. She lent him a hand, packing in the things also that she had brought.

"Here was my chance,—one of the likelihoods happened opportunely to hand. But I was too darned sick and miserable to go after it very hard. I wanted to get to bed,—alone. For possibly twenty minutes or half an hour, on the porch as Charmian was leaving, we talked. We talked philosophically, and at the same time personally. I believe I was busy telling Charmian some of the things in her that I didn't like. That was all. At the end of the talk, which was unsatisfactory as I had not succeeded in explaining to her what the things were that I didn't like, as Charmian was going, I took hold of her and kissed her; and that was all, absolutely all. The conversation had no connection whatever with the kiss. It was the conversation that relieved my own miserable feelings caused by the accidents of that day. The kiss was my sole effort to go after this one likelihood in a dozen.

"I went up to Glen Ellen. I dropped a line to Charmian, rather a letter, apropos of the conversation we had had.

"Now, don't forget the basis of my life at that time. I had made up my mind to go to pieces,—to deliberately and intentionally go to pieces. Before my first trip down to town from Glen Ellen, I wrote a letter to Charmian asking to see her when I came down. Incidentally I came down. I saw her. I began to grow pretty desirous for her. At the same time that I was down, I met a girl, another man's wife, whom I had not seen for some years. I made a date with her. She was to start in a few days for Stockton and Sacramento, for a week or ten days' vacation, ostensibly to visit friends. We made it up to go together,—to go up [on] one of the river steamboats. Charmian and I came out to [a] camp on a Saturday afternoon. We returned on a Sunday afternoon. . . . We were just beginning to come together good and hard. On Sunday afternoon when we went in, I did my best to get Charmian to go out to Hayward with me that night. She said if I wanted to see her, I had to come to her house. And out to her house I came that evening in Berkeley. It was during this period, Saturday night and Sunday, that I was proceeding to fall in love with her, only I did not yet know it. I simply thought that I was growing more desirous for her to be my mistress.

"I went back to Glen Ellen. Bessie was jealous and suspicious at that time. She feared every woman. She was jealous of the nurse-girl, a scabby-faced maid. Jealous of everybody. Going through my wastepaper basket constantly, and piecing torn shreds of letters together, etc., etc. And I not caring a whoop to hell about anything she did in that way. For instance, the girl I was going up to Stockton and Sacramento with, wrote me several times (incidentally, I wasn't bothering about this girl, because I was falling in love with Charmian and didn't know it; and that took up all my interest). I did not reply to this girl's letter. Finally, came a telegram,—my last chance before she started, to let her know that I would accompany her on the trip. I received the telegram while I was eating supper. Bessie came around and wanted to see the telegram. I told her that it was for me and that I didn't think it would be good for her to see it. I had not yet read the telegram, but was tearing open the envelope. Bessie said she thought it was from her folks. I told her I thought it wasn't, and that if it was, I'd let her know. She insisted on looking at it as I opened it. I turned sideways so as to prevent her reading it. She moved around behind me so that she still could read it. And then I quit,—and let her read it. The girl's name was not signed, but the whole trip was given away. . . .

"I went down to Oakland on a second trip. I called Charmian up at Berkeley, I being at the bungalow. Incidentally, Charmian told me that Bessie had gone through my waste-basket and pieced together several shreds of the letter she (Charmian) had written me in reply to my request to see her (Charmian) and in which Charmian had told me to come to see her at Berkeley. As it was typewritten, Bessie did not know who the woman was, and had no suspicions of Charmian. All this information had come to Charmian through her aunt, as so much gossip, for to her aunt promptly had Bessie gone to relate the discovery she had made in my wastepaper basket. (It was always Bessie's way to shout all things from the housetop.)

"In this talk over the phone with Charmian, in which I made mention of the fact of trouble arising if Bessie discovered the identity of the person who had written the letter, Charmian said she would be 'game' for her share of the trouble. And in that moment, it came to me, without warning, for the first time, that I loved Charmian. And in that moment, on the very instant, spontaneously, without even thinking, I answered, 'Then you'll be game for *all* of it!' The thought I had in mind was, that I would marry Charmian.

"Now, don't forget my basis. All during this period, from before the beginning of the camping in Glen Ellen, I had made up my mind to go to pieces and get a separation. This without being in love with anybody, but from sheer disgust in life, such as I was living it.

"I came back to Glen Ellen. There was hell to pay. Bessie was suspicious of everybody. She broached the letter to me that she had got from my wastepaper basket. She didn't know but what it was from the girl from whom I had received the telegram. I was careful to steer her clear of Charmian. I had intended to bring about the separation after the camping trip was over, and when Bessie had returned to the Bungalow. But this letter which she had discovered in the wastepaper basket, plus the telegram, and her discussing the matter with me, precipitated the separa-

Three hundred weight more than half a ton he weighed; he had lived a long, strong life, full of fight and struggle, and at the end he faced death at the teeth of a creature whose head did not reach beyond his great knuckled knees. ■ (From *The Call of the Wild* by Jack London. Illustrated by Charles Livingston Bull.)

tion. She asked me if I loved somebody else. I told her that I did, though, I refused to tell that person's name. And I told her frankly that it was because of the trouble she would make for that person, if she learned that person's identity. So the separation was thus precipitated. The story is all told.

"Now, the source of this story that Charmian broke up the London household, is due directly to Bessie. It is the gossip of Oakland at the present moment."[1]

November 19, 1905. Married Charmian.

1906. Built a ship called the *Snark*. ". . .The boat is 45 feet on the water-line, 57 feet over all, and 15 feet beam. Draws 7 feet of water. It is the strongest boat ever built in San Francisco. We could go through a typhoon that would wreck a 15,000-ton steamer. Primarily it is a sailing-vessel; but it has a 70-horse-power gasoline engine. This is to be used in going up the great rivers in the different countries

(From the movie "The Sea Wolf," starring John Garfield, Edward G. Robinson and Gene Lockhart. Copyright 1941 by Warner Bros. Pictures.)

(From the movie "Adventures of Martin Eden," based on the novel *Martin Eden,* starring Glenn Ford. Copyright 1942 by Columbia Pictures Corp.)

(From the movie "Wolf Larsen," based on the novel *The Sea Wolf,* starring Peter Graves and Barry Sullivan. Copyright © 1958 by Allied Artists Pictures Corp.)

(From the movie "Jack London," starring Michael O'Shea. Released by United Artists Corp., 1943.)

we come to, in making harbors, and in getting out of ticklish positions. Otherwise we shall do nothing but sail. Practically, for every week that we are on the ocean, we will be a month in port. For instance, we expect that it will take us three weeks to sail from here to Hawaii, where we expect to remain three months—of course, in various portions of the Islands.

"Now to the crew: All of us will be the crew. There is my wife, and myself. We will stand our watches and do our trick at the wheel. Incidentally, a large portion of our time will be used in working in order to pay the expenses of the trip. My wife's uncle, Mr. Eames, will act as co-navigator with me, and devote himself mainly to the engine, and the deck,—the sailorizing, in short. The fourth member is. . .an all-round athlete from Stanford University. He is shipped, in reality, as an after-thought, and largely to do that portion of the sailorizing that would otherwise fall to me. You see, I could not do my full share of the sailorizing and at the same time do the writing and keep the pot boiling. The fifth member of the crew is the cabin-boy, a Japanese boy . . . who has been with us all summer. He is as brave as a lion, and as gentle as a lamb—in fact, he is the soul of gentleness. He is to serve as cabin-boy, serve the meals from the galley, set the table, keep things clean down below, and pay attention to the personal needs of myself and Mrs. London.

"When it comes to doing the trick at the wheel, I want to explain that this will not be arduous as it may appear at first. It is our intention, by sail-trimming, to make the boat largely sail herself, without steering. Next, in bad weather, there will be no steering for then we will be hove-to. But watches, or rather lookouts, must be kept at night, when we are sailing. Suppose we divide day and night into twelve hours each. There are six of us all-told on the boat. Each will take a two-hour turn on deck.

"Of course, when it comes to moments of danger, or to doing something ticklish, or to making port, etc., the whole six of us will then become the crew. I will not be a writer, but a sailor. The same with my wife. The cabin-boy will be a sailor, and so also the cook. In fact, when it's case for all hands, all hands it will be.

"It must be thoroughly understood that when we are on duty, the relations existing will be that of Captain and crew. Off duty, is another matter. We can then be friends, or enemies, or not speak when we pass by! But the point is, on duty is on duty."[1]

1908. Trouble on voyage. ". . . I have just returned . . . from a voyage on the *Snark* up to Lord Howe and Tasman Islands. We were gone over two months on the trip, during which the *Snark* was a hospital ship. There was never a time when some of us were not sick, and most of the time most of us were sick. Fever was the principal affliction, from which none of us escaped. One of my native sailors, a Tahitian, nearly died of it, and incidentally was crazy for a while. The cook, a Japanese, from sheer funk over the general sickness and over the fear of being eaten by the natives, went crazy and left us at Meringe Lagoon, on Ysabel Island, where he remained over two months before he could get away. I don't know whether I told you or not of the book I had been thinking of writing, sometime ago, namely, *Around the World with Two Gasoline Engines and a Wife.* I am now contemplating another book: *Around the World in the Hospital Ship Snark.* I am the navigator these days, and the doctor, and a whole lot of other things as well. Mrs. London ably performs her part as chief nurse

and A.B. She has been standing not only her own watches but some of the watches of the sick men. And all the time I think I've been the sickest of anybody on board, at least, I have accumulated several new and alarming diseases, two of which have been utterly unheard-of by any white man I have met in the Solomons."[1]

1908. Trouble with ex-wife. He wrote to her: "In all your dealings with me, it has been nothing but letter, letter, letter. I, on the other hand, have always exceeded the letter. I have always done better by you than I agreed to do. I have always given you more than was laid down in the letter of the contract. You yourself know thoroughly the spirit of my intention as regards you and the children, whether it was in agreements we made and conversations we held, or wills that I made. You know that you, Bessie London, were not to be considered at all, according to said wills, agreements, and conversations, from the moment that you contracted a second marriage. You know that in this you were placed in the same category with my second wife and with my mother. You know, absolutely, according to my will, that the moment my second wife or my mother married again, that they ceased, flatly, from participation in one cent of my money. You know that according to my will, as fast as any one of the three of you should marry, that the money that had been their share was to go to the children. And now, in the face of all this, you come back on me and try to spring a technicality about the insurance—in fact, in virtuous and magnanimous free-heartedness, point out that by all the gods you are going to have that insurance. Well, we shall see what we shall see.

"Let me point out another thing to you. As regards the children, whether I live or die, they are amply provided for. This insurance, this endowment insurance, rather, and the increased value on the house, represents sums of money which you are trying to drag out of me, not for the children, but for you and your second husband to spend or invest. Surely, your second husband will be able to take care of you without any such assistance from me.

"Then comes the funniest thing of all in your letter. You threaten, that if I do not accede to the dragging out of me of aforementioned sums of money for the benefit of you and your second husband, that you will be danged if you will get married. Why, my dear child, I don't care a whoop in high water whether you get married a second time or not. I should like to see you happily married for your own sake, but I regret that I cannot genially contribute money to finance that second marriage. I can't possibly imagine what was working in your brain that impelled you to make such a threat to me."[1]

Because of illness cancelled trip. "My sickness is of so serious a nature that I am compelled to abandon the voyage of the *Snark* and to return to my own climate of California. The doctors in Australia can do nothing for me, because they do not know what is the matter with me. My trouble is nervous in origin; and all I can prescribe for myself is to return to an environment where I maintained a stable nervous equilibrium, in the hope of regaining that equilibrium."[1]

1910. Began serious development of the Beauty Ranch. "Now, here is the way I am situated. I have got a ranch of 1000 acres here, but I have not yet built my house on it. As a result, I am renting a small house outside of the ranch for my own use. This house is too small and crowded, and this year I am starting to build. . . . but on the ranch I have a

(From the movie "Sign of the Wolf," based on the story "That Spot." Copyright 1941 by Monogram Pictures Corp.)

small comfortable cabin in a beautiful spot. This was last occupied up to several months ago by a friend of mine, a scientist and a philosopher, who wrote several books there. This is within a quarter of a mile of the farmhouse on the ranch, where my ranch foreman lives with his family."[1]

1912. Began construction of a fantastic castle, Wolf House. Costs forced him to write incessantly to pay his bills.

1913. Burning of the Wolf House.

1913. Letter to daughter, Joan.

> "Glen Ellen, Calif.
> Aug. 24, 1913

"Dear Joan:—

"I feel too miserable to write this at my desk. I am sitting up in bed to write it.

"First, please remember that I am your father. I have fed you, clothed you, and housed you, and *loved* you since the moment you first drew breath. I have all of a father's heart of love for you.

"And now we come to brass tacks. What have you done for me in all the days of your life? What do you *feel* for me? Am I merely your meal-ticket? Do you look upon me as

merely a creature with a *whim,* or *fancy,* or *fantasy,* that compels him to care for you and to take care of you?—because he is a fool who gives much and receives. . .well, receives nothing?

"Please answer the foregoing questions. I want to know how I stand with you.

"You have your dreams of education. I try to give you the best of my wisdom. You write me about the demands of the [University of California] in relation to selection of high school courses, I reply by (1) telegram, (2) by letter. And I receive no word from you. Am I dirt under your feet? Am I beneath your contempt in every way save as a meal-ticket? Do you love me at all? What do I *mean* to you?

"Answer above queries of mine.

"My home, as yet unoccupied, burns down—and I receive no word from you. When you were sick I came to see you. I gave you flowers and canary birds.

"Now I am sick—and you are silent. My home—one of my dreams—is destroyed. You have no word to say.

"Your education is mixed up by conflict between high school and university. You write me. I reply by telegram and letter. I spring to help you with my wisdom in your trouble, in the realization of your dream.

"I say, very sadly, that when my dream is ruined, I do not notice that you spring to me.

"Joan, my daughter, please know that the world belongs to the honest ones, to the true ones, to the right ones, to the ones who talk right out; and that the world does not belong to the ones who remain silent, who, by their very silence lie and cheat and make a mock of love and a meal-ticket of their father.

"Don't you think it is about time I heard from you? Or do you want me to cease forever from caring to hear from you?

"Daddy"[1]

More bitterness toward Joan. "Let me tell you a little something about myself: All my life has been marked by what, in lack of any other term, I must call 'disgust.' When I grow tired or disinterested in anything, I experience a disgust which settles for me the thing forever. I turn the page down there and then. When a colt on the ranch, early in its training, shows that it is a kicker or a bucker or a bolter or a balker, I try patiently and for a long time to remove, by my training, such deleterious traits; and then at the end of a long time if I find that these vicious traits continue, suddenly there comes to me a disgust, and I say Let the colt go. Kill it, sell it, give it away. So far as I am concerned I am finished with the colt. So it has been with all things in my whole life from the very first time that I can remember anything of myself. I have been infatuated with many things, I have worked through many things, have become disgusted with those many things, and have turned down the pages forever and irrevocably on those many things. Please believe me—I am not stating to you my strength, but my weakness. These colossal disgusts that compel me to turn down pages are weaknesses of mine, and I know them; but they are there. They are part of me. I am so made.

"Years ago I warned your mother that if I were denied the opportunity of forming you, sooner or later I would grow disinterested in you, I would develop a disgust, and that I would turn down the page. Of course, your mother, who is deaf to all things spiritual and appreciative, and understanding, smiled to herself and discounted what I told her. Your mother today understands me no more than has she ever understood me—which is no understanding at all.

"Now, do not make the mistake of thinking that I am now running away from all filial duties and responsibilities. I am not. I shall take care of you; I shall take care of Baby B., I shall take care of your mother. I shall take care of the three of you. You shall have food and shelter always. But, unfortunately, I have turned the page down, and I shall be no longer interested in the three of you.

"I do not imagine that I shall ever care to send you to the University of California, unless you should develop some tremendous desire to do specific things in the world that only a course in the University of California will fit for you. I certainly shall never send you to the University of California merely in recognition of the bourgeois valuation put upon the University pigskin.

"I should like to see you marry for love when you grow up. That way lies the best and sweetest of human happiness. On the other hand, if you want a career instead, I'll help you to pursue whatever career you elect. When you were small, I fought for years the idea of your going on the stage. I now withdraw my opposition. If you desire the stage with its consequent (from my point of view) falseness, artificiality, sterility and unhappiness, why go ahead, and I will do what I can to help you to it.

"But please, please remember that in whatever you do from now on, I am uninterested. I desire to know neither your failures nor your successes; wherefore please no more tell me of your markings in High School, and no longer send me your compositions.

"When you want money, within reason, I shall send it to you if I have it. Under any and all circumstances, so long as I live, you shall receive from me food in your stomach, a roof that does not leak, warm blankets, and clothing to cover you.

"A year from now I expect to have a little money. At the present moment, If I died, I should die one hundred thousand dollars in debt. Therefore, a year from now I may be more easy with you in money matters than I am capable of being now.

"I should like to say a few words further about the pages I turn down because of the disgusts that come upon me. I was ever a lover of fatherhood. I loved fatherhood over love of woman. I have been jealous of my seed, and I have never wantonly scattered my seed. I have (we'll say my share at least) a good body and a good brain. I had a father's fondest love and hope for you. But you know, in bringing up colts, colts may be brought up good and bad, all according to the horseman who brings up the colts. You were a colt. Time and fate and mischance, and a stupid mother, prevented me from having a guiding hand in your upbringing. I waited until you, who can dramatize 'Sohrab and Rustum,' could say for yourself what you wanted. Alas, as the colt, you were already ruined by your trainer. You were lied to, you were cheated. I am sorry; it was not your fault. But when the time came for you to decide (not absolutely between your mother and me)—to decide whether or not I might have a little hand in showing and training you to your paces in the big world, you were already so ruined by your trainer, that you declined. It is not your fault. You were so trained. It is not your mother's fault—she was born stupid, stupid she will live, and stupid she will die.

"Unless I should accidentally meet you on the street, I doubt if I shall ever see you again. If you should be dying, and should ask for me at your bedside, I should surely come; on the other hand, if I were dying I should not care to have you at my bedside. A ruined colt is a ruined colt, and I do not like ruined colts."[1]

1914. Views on writing. "In my opinion, three positive things are necessary for success as a writer. First, a study and knowledge of literature as it is commercially produced today.

"Second, a knowledge of life, and

"Third, a working philosophy of life.

"Negatively, I would suggest that the best preparation for authorship is a stern refusal to accept blindly the canons of literary art as laid down by, teachers of high school English and teachers of university English and composition.

The vessels came together before I could follow his advice. We must have been struck squarely amidships, for I saw nothing, the strange steamboat having passed beyond my line of vision. The *Martinez* heeled over, sharply, and there was a crashing and rending of timber. ■ (From *The Sea Wolf* by Jack London. Illustrated by Fletcher Martin.)

"The average author is lucky, I mean the average successful author is lucky, if he makes twelve hundred to two thousand dollars a year. Many successful authors earn in various ways from their writings as high as twenty thousand dollars a year and there are some authors, rare ones, who make from fifty to seventy-five thousand dollars a year from their writings; and some of the most successful authors in some of their most successful years have made as high as a hundred thousand dollars or two hundred thousand dollars.

"Personally, it strikes me that the one great special advantage of authorship as a means of livelihood is that it gives one more freedom than is given any person in business or in the various other professions. The author's office and business is under his hat and he can go anywhere and write anywhere as the spirit moves him."[1]

November, 1916.

"Glen Ellen, Calif.
Nov. 21, 1916

"Dear Joan:—

"Next Sunday, will you and Bess have lunch with me at Saddle Rock, and, if weather is good, go for a sail with me on Lake Merrit.

"If weather is not good, we can go to a matinee of some sort.

"Let me know at once.

"I leave Ranch next Friday.

"I leave Calif. Wednesday following.

"Daddy."[1]

November 22, 1916. Died in Santa Rosa, Calif.

FOR MORE INFORMATION SEE: Leon Ray Livingston, *From Coast to Coast with Jack London,* A-No. 1 Publishing, 1917, reprinted, Black Letter Press, 1969; Georgia Bamford, *Mystery of Jack London,* [Oakland, California], 1931, reprinted, Porter, Bern, 1975; Joan London, *Jack London and His Times: An Unconventional Biography,* Doubleday, Doran, 1939, reprinted, University of Washington Press, 1968; Shannon Garst, *Jack London: Magnet for Adventure,* Messner, 1944; William McDevitt, *Jack London's First,* Recorder-Sunset Press, 1946, reprinted, Wolf House Books, 1972; Philip S. Foner, editor, *Jack London, American Rebel: A Collection of His Social Writings, together with an Extensive Study of the Man and His Times,* Citadel, 1947, reprinted, 1964; Irving Stone, *Jack London: Sailor on Horseback,* Doubleday, 1947, reissued, New American Library, 1969.

S. S. Baskett, "Jack London on the Oakland Waterfront," *American Literature,* November, 1955; Samuel Dickson, *Streets of San Francisco,* Stanford University Press, 1955; Kenneth S. Lynn, *Dream of Success,* Little, Brown, 1955; D. E. Wheeler, "As I Remember Them," *American Mercury,* August, 1957; Saul Kussiel Padover, editor, *Confessions and Self-Portraits,* Day, 1957; S. S. Baskett, "'Jack London's Heart of Darkness," *American Quarterly,* Spring, 1958; J. Haydock, "Jack London: A Bibliography of Criticism," *Bulletin of Bibliography,* May, 1960; King Hendricks, editor, *Creator and Critic: A Controversy between*

Jack London and Philo M. Buck, Jr., Utah State University Press, 1961; Ruth Franchere, *Jack London: The Pursuit of a Dream,* Crowell, 1962; Frederick Feied, *No Pie in the Sky: The Hobo as American Cultural Hero in the Works of Jack London, John Dos Passos, and Jack Kerouac,* Citadel, 1964; Richard O'Connor, *Jack London: A Biography,* Little, Brown, 1964.

K. Hendricks and I. Shepard, editors, *Letters from Jack London: Containing Unpublished Correspondence between London and Sinclair Lewis,* Odyssey Press, 1965; Franklin D. Walker, *Jack London and the Klondike: The Genesis of an American Writer,* Huntington Library, 1966; Charles C. Walcutt, *Jack London,* University of Minnesota Press, 1966; Hensley C. Woodbridge and others, compilers, *Jack London: A Bibliography,* Talisman Press, 1966, revised and enlarged, Kraus Reprint, 1973; K. Hendricks, *Jack London: Master Craftsman of the Short Story,* Utah State University Press, 1966; Arthur Barrett, editor, *Jack London and Walt Whitman,* Odyssey Press, 1969; Joseph Gaer, *Jack London: Bibliography and Biographical Data,* reprinted from the 1934 manuscript, B. Franklin, 1971; Arthur Grove Day, *Jack London in the South Seas,* Four Winds Press, 1971; Donald Glancy, *Jack London and Norton's Nectar,* Wolf House Books, 1972; Charles V. Mosby, *Little Journey to the Home of Jack London,* reprinted from the 1917 manuscript, Wolf House Books, 1972; Dale L. Walker, editor, *The Fiction of Jack London: A Chronological Bibliography,* Texas Western Press, 1972; Walker, *The Alien Worlds of Jack London,* Wolf House Books, 1973; Walker, *Jack London, Sherlock Holmes, and Sir Arthur Conan Doyle,* A. S. Fick, 1974; Earle Labor, *Jack London,* Twayne, 1974; D. L. Walker, editor, *Curious Fragments: Jack London's Tales of Fantasy Fiction,* Kennikat, 1975; James I. McClintock, *White Logic: Jack London's Short Stories,* Wolf House Books, 1975; Andrew Sinclair, *Jack: A Biography of Jack London,* Harper, 1977; Robert Barltrop, *Jack London: The Man, the Writer, the Rebel,* Urizen Books, 1977; *Irving Stone's Jack London: Sailor on Horseback and 28 Selected Jack London Stories,* Doubleday, 1977.

For children: Elizabeth Rider Montgomery, *Story behind Great Books,* McBride, 1946; Hallie E. Rives and G. E. Forbush, *John Book,* Beechhurst Press, 1947; Frederick A. Lane, *Greatest Adventure: A Story of Jack London,* Aladdin, 1954; Robert Cantwell, *Famous American Men of Letters,* Dodd, 1956; David E. Scherman and Rosemarie Redlich, *America: The Land and Its Writers,* Dodd, 1956; Arthur Calder-Marshall, *Lone Wolf: The Story of Jack London,* Methuen, 1961, Duell, 1962; John Jakes, *Great War Correspondents,* Putnam, 1967; L. Edmond Leipold, *Famous American Fiction Writers,* Denison, 1972.

Movies: "Jack London," United Artists, 1943.

LOWITZ, Anson C. 1901(?)-1978

PERSONAL: Married Sadyebeth Heath (died, 1969); married Marion Leland; children: (first marriage) Mrs. John Ross Hamilton. *Education:* Graduated from Wesleyan University. *Residence:* Pebble Beach, Calif.; and Greenwich, Conn.

CAREER: J. Walter Thompson Co. (advertising agency), New York City, vice-president, 1937-51; Foote, Cone & Belding (advertising agency), Chicago, Ill., vice-president, 1951-53; Ted Bates & Co. (advertising agency), New York

Pilgrim Mothers loaded the life-boat with tubs full of soiled clothing. There was no laundry on the Mayflower. That whole day was spent washing clothes by the side of the sea. ■ (From *The Pilgrims' Party: A Really Truly Story* by Sadyebeth and Anson Lowitz. Illustrated by Anson Lowitz.)

City, vice-president, 1953-59. *Wartime service:* During World War II helped develop the Cadet Nursing Corps.

WRITINGS—All with wife, Sadyebeth Lowitz; all "Really Truly Story" juvenile series; all originally published by Stein & Day: (Self-illustrated) *The Pilgrims' Party,* 1931, revised edition, Lerner, 1967; *General George the Great,* 1932, revised edition, Lerner, 1967; (self-illustrated) *The Cruise of Mr. Christopher Columbus,* 1932, revised edition, Lerner, 1967; *The Magic Fountain,* 1936, revised edition, Lerner, 1967; *Mr. Key's Song,* 1937, revised edition, Lerner, 1967; (self-illustrated) *Barefoot Abe,* 1938, revised edition, Lerner, 1967; (self-illustrated) *Tom Edison Finds Out,* 1940, revised edition, Lerner, 1967.

FOR MORE INFORMATION SEE—Obituaries: *New York Times,* January 25, 1978.

(Died January 22, 1978, in Pebble Beach, Calif.)

MARSHALL, Anthony D(ryden)   1924-

PERSONAL: Born May 30, 1924; son of John Dryden (an insurance broker) and Brooke (Russell) Kuser; married Elizabeth Cryan, June, 1947; married second wife, Thelma Hoegnell, December, 1962; children: (first marriage) Alexan-der Russell and Philip Cryan (twins). *Education:* Brown University, B.A., 1950. *Politics:* Republican. *Religion:* Episcopalian. *Home and office address:* American Embassy, P.O. Box 30137, Nairobi, Kenya.

CAREER: U.S. Government, Washington, D.C., employed in various assignments, 1950-59; president, African Research & Development Co., Inc., 1959-69; NIDOCO Ltd., Lagos, Nigeria, chairman of board, 1961-69; Tucker, Anthony, & R. L. Day (stockbrokers), New York, N.Y., limited partner, 1961—; U.S. Ambassador to Malagasy Republic, 1969-71, Trinidad and Tobago, 1972-74, and Kenya, 1974—, nonresident ambassador to Seychelles, 1976—. Trustee of New York Zoological Society, Vincent Astor Foundation, Seaman's Church Institute, Astor Home for Children, and International Medical and Research Foundation. *Military service:* U.S. Marine Corps Reserve, 1942-56; active service, 1942-44; became captain; received Purple Heart.

WRITINGS: Africa's Living Arts (juvenile), F. Watts, 1969; *The Malagasy Republic: Madagascar,* F. Watts, 1972; *Trinidad and Tobago,* F. Watts, 1974. Contributor to *Explorers Club Journal, Focus* (journal of American Geographical Society), and *Animal Kingdom* (New York Zoological Society).

The Buffalypso, a crossbreed buffalo for beef is ideally suited to the Finidadian climate.
■ (From *Trinidad—Tobago* by Anthony D. Marshall. Photographs by the author.)

SIDELIGHTS: "Although I have always liked to write, and in addition to the above mentioned, have also contributed to *Africa 1960* (London), *Business International* (New York)—on Nigeria; Crowell *Colliers* (New York)—on Ethiopia, and a number of other publications, plus photographic contributions to Franklin Watts books on Africa, and even a Columbia Records album cover—the three books I have written were done for special reasons. The book on African art, for instance, was a result of my ten year business association with Nigeria. I started a business there in 1959—a food processing business: snack foods, using locally available materials. The company was a great success. It grew to 250 on the payroll and 300 on a commission basis, and I sold the company to a Nigerian who first started to work for me as an assistant to the manager. He is now Chairman of the Board. But while in Nigeria I became fascinated with the art of West Africa. I took pictures, started to think of a book, and finally produced one. I concentrated on West Africa, though including East Africa, which I had first visited in 1954—Kenya, Tanganyika, Somalia and Uganda. The theme of the book is that art in Africa all at once had a functional purpose; much still does. Having delved into the book world, Franklin Watts asked me to do a book on Madagascar. There is not much in English on Madagascar; most literature is in French. There is no over-all introductory-type of book. I felt one was needed, hence, my book; then Trinidad and Tobago. While there *is* an abundance in print on Trinidad and Tobago, I could find no simple little book which would give you the flavor of the country. I have no plans for any book on Kenya, as there is already a great deal available. My interest in photography had a great deal to do with my books. Not only were all the photographs mine, but I have thousands of photographs of Africa as well as other parts of the world.

"As the biographic sketch indicates I was in Madagascar and Trinidad and Tobago as American Ambassador; and am now in Kenya. The Seychelles would make a good book, but my visits there are short, and I have no time for concentrated research and photography. Someday—?

"Although not intending to write a book on Kenya, I have given a considerable number of speeches while here these past three years on the number of diverse subjects. I always write my own speeches. I enjoy it."

HOBBIES AND OTHER INTERESTS: Photography.

ANTHONY D. MARSHALL

McCORD, David (Thompson Watson) 1897-

PERSONAL: Born November 15, 1897, in New York City; raised in Oregon; son of Joseph Alexander and Eleanore Baynton (Reed) McCord. *Education:* Harvard University, B.A., 1921, M.A., 1922. *Politics:* Republican. *Religion:* Episcopalian. *Address:* 310 Commonwealth Ave., Boston, Mass. 02115.

CAREER: Harvard Alumni Bulletin, Cambridge, Mass., associate editor, 1923-25, editor, 1940-46; *Boston Evening Transcript,* Boston, Mass., member of the drama staff, 1923-28; Harvard Fund Council, executive director, 1925-63; poet, editor, and humorist. Phi Beta Kappa poet at Harvard University, 1938, Tufts College, 1938, College of William and Mary, 1950, and Massachusetts Institute of Technology, 1973; lecturer, Lowell Institute, 1950; staff member of the Bread Loaf Writers Conference, 1958, 1960, 1962, 1964; instructor of advanced writing courses at Harvard University during the summers of 1963, 1965, 1966; visiting professor at Framington State College, 1974; honorary curator of the Poetry and Farnsworth Rooms of the Harvard College Library; honorary associate of Dudley House, Harvard University; honorary trustee for the Boston Center for Adult Education; trustee of Historic Boston, Inc., Peter Bent Brigham Hospital, Boston, Mass., Charity of Edward Hopkins, New England College, and Boston Athenaeum; overseer, Old Sturbridge Village, Mass., and Perkins Institute for the Blind; member of the board of directors of the Association of Harvard Alumni, 1965-68; member of the usage panel of the *American Heritage Dictionary;* councilor to the Harvard Society of Advanced Study and Research, 1967-72.

MILITARY SERVICE: U.S. Army, 1918, served as second lieutenant. *Member:* International P.E.N., American Alumni Council, American Council of Learned Societies, American Academy of Arts and Sciences (fellow), Phi Beta Kappa, Colonial Society of Massachusetts, Massachusetts Historical Society, Harvard Club, St. Botolph Club, Tavern Club, Club of Odd Volumes (Boston), Faculty Club, Signet Club (Cambridge, Mass.), Century Club (New York City). *Awards, honors:* Golden Rose, New England Poetry Club, 1941; William Rose Benét award, 1952; Guggenheim fellow, 1954; Litt.D., Northwestern University, 1954, University of New Brunswick, 1963, Williams College, 1971; LL.D., Washington and Jefferson College, 1955; L.H.D., Harvard University, 1956, Colby College, 1968, Framingham State College, 1975; Art.D., New England College, 1956; National Institute of Arts and Letters grant, 1961; Sarah Josepha Hale medal, 1962; first recipient of the National Council of Teachers of English Award for Excellence in Poetry for Children, 1977.

WRITINGS: Oddly Enough, Washburn & Thomas, 1926; *Floodgate* (poems), Washburn & Thomas, 1927; *Stirabout* (essays), Washburn & Thomas, 1928; *The Crows* (poems), Scribner, 1934; *Bay Window Ballads* (illustrated by John Lavalle), Scribner, 1935; *Notes on the Harvard Tercentenary,* Harvard University Press, 1936; *And What's More* (poems), Coward-McCann, 1941; *On Occasion* (poems), Harvard University Press, 1943; *About Boston: Sight, Sound, Flavor, and Inflection* (illustrated by the author), Doubleday, 1948, reissued, Little, Brown, 1973; *A Star by Day* (poems), Doubleday, 1950; *The Camp at Lockjaw* (illustrated by Gluyas Williams), Doubleday, 1952; *The Old Bateau, and Other Poems,* Little, Brown, 1953; *Odds without Ends* (poems), Little, Brown, 1954; *Sonnets to Baedeker* (illustrated by John Lavalle), Scribner, 1963; *In Sight of Sever: Essays from Harvard,* Harvard University Press, 1963; *Notes from Four Cities, 1927-1953,* A. J. St. Onge, 1969.

DAVID McCORD

Juvenile: *Far and Few: Rhymes of the Never Was and Always Is* (illustrated by Henry B. Kane), Little, Brown, 1952, reissued, Dell, 1971; *Take Sky: More Rhymes of the Never Was and Always Is* (illustrated by H. B. Kane), Little, Brown, 1962, reissued, Dell, 1971; *All Day Long: Fifty Rhymes of the Never Was and Always Is* (illustrated by H. B. Kane), Little, Brown, 1966; *Every Time I Climb a Tree* (illustrated by Marc Simont), Little, Brown, 1967; *For Me to Say: Rhymes of the Never Was and Always Is* (illustrated by H. B. Kane), Little, Brown, 1970; *Mr. Bidery's Spidery Garden* (illustrated by H. B. Kane), Harrap, 1972; *Away and Ago: Rhymes of the Never Was and Always Is* (illustrated by Leslie Morrill), Little, Brown, 1975; *The Star in the Pail* (illustrated by M. Simont), Little, Brown, 1975.

Editor: *Once and For All* (essays), Coward-McCann, 1929; *What Cheer: An Anthology of American and British Humorous and Witty Verse*, Coward-McCann, 1945, a later edition published as *The Modern Treasury of Humorous Verse*, Garden City Books, 1951; Arthur Griffin, *New England Revisited*, Houghton, 1966; *Bibliotheca Medica: Physician for Tomorrow*, Harvard Medical School, 1966; Stow Wengenroth, *Stow Wengenroth's New England*, Barre Publishers, 1969.

Contributor to *Atlantic Monthly, Harper's, Ladies' Home Journal, New Yorker, Saturday Evening Post, Saturday Review of Literature, Theatre Arts Monthly, Virginia Quarterly*, and *Yale Review*.

SIDELIGHTS: **November 15, 1897.** Born near New York's Greenwich Village, the only child of Joseph Alexander and Eleanore Baynton (Reed) McCord, the author spent his early years on Long Island, in New Jersey and in Oregon. "Long Island was all fields and woods when I was a boy. We lived next door to a poultry farm and not far from the ocean. My love of nature began there. When I was twelve I went with my father and mother to live on a ranch in the south of Oregon on the wild Rogue River. This was frontier country then: no electric lights, oil, or coal heat. We pumped all our water out of a deep well and pumped it by hand. I didn't go to school for three years, but I learned the life of the wilderness, something about birds, animals, and wild flowers, trees and geology, and self-reliance. I learned to weather seasons of drought and weeks of steady rain. I sometimes panned gold for pocket money—a very pleasing and exciting art once you can control it! I learned to recognize a few of the constellations and to reverence the night sky—Orion is still my favorite skymark! I saw and experienced the terror of a forest fire. I can honestly say that I was a pretty good shot with a rifle, but I have never aimed at a living thing since I was fifteen. My love of all life is far too deep for that." [Lee Bennett Hopkins, *Books Are By People*, Citation Press, 1969.[1]]

Alert live reindeer galloping on air,
Those unsupported runners, and a fair-
Sized load inside old Santa's sleigh to boot:
Some shake their heads, and some don't give a
    hoot.

■ (From *Away and Ago: Rhymes of the Never Was and Always Is* by David McCord. Illustrated by Leslie Morrill.)

1915. An avid amateur wireless operator, received his operator's license. McCord once heard on a radio set he had made, "one of the original experiments in what we call radio broadcasting—a man playing the banjo!"[1]

1917. Graduated with high honors from Lincoln High School in Portland, Oregon. While a student there, McCord wrote for the school paper. As a young child he had contacted malaria and the disease caused recurrent bouts with fever which kept the honor student out of school a great deal. "One of my best high school teachers once told us, 'Never let a day go by without looking on three beautiful things.' I have tried to live up to that and have found it isn't difficult. The sky in all weather is, for me, the first of these three things."[1]

1918. McCord served in the U.S. Army as a second lieutenant.

1921. Received a B.A. in physics from Harvard University. While an undergraduate student there he was elected president of the *Lampoon*. "To be a student of Harvard requires almost an abnegation of the temporal, a long walk late at night with accredited ghosts of the place, the stab of loneliness right through a multitude of doors. Even so, the revelation may not come; there is just that whisk of the occult about it.

    'My new-cut ashlar takes the light
    Where crimson-blank the windows flare.'

Ptarmigan

O Ptarmigan, O ptarmigan,
O ptarmigan: pt
is such a funny way to start

a name. Don't you agree?
You've never had pneumonia,
though you live among the Lapps
and Eskimos inhabiting
those ice-cold ptops of maps.
There's no one here to ptell me
how you ptolerate that name!
It saddens me to think that
someone like me was to blame.
Some ancient Gael? It wasn't. No,
his word was *tārmachan*.
The Greek for feather? *pteron;* but
did Greeks know how you fan
your feathered feet to walk on snow?
You wouldn't walk on ptar;
and, anyway, the Greeks live south
and never got that far.
Some day, I guess, I'll travel north
and ask a caribou
or reindeer: How's your pterritory?
Got a Pt-V ptoo?

(From *All Day Long* by David McCord. Drawings by Henry B. Kane.)

"I wait for the flash. I watch for intimate signs of that older wilderness now vanished, as the quote from Kipling may suggest. 'It is not down in any map, true places never are,' said Melville. Yet once in a while it is. I think I became a life-long student of Harvard that bright morning in my junior year when I stepped out of Jefferson and a class in advanced physics, looked up into the cloudless blue, and saw—as not many have the luck to look and see by day—the sudden sulfurous flame out of a meteor,

"a star that spoke
In simple terms of fire and smoke,
But soundless with the stale report
Of ancient wars and dragon snort.

"Not all the visiting professors in the world could relate my clearing in the wilderness to the clearing in my mind as did that moment, awesome and unexpected." [David McCord, *In Sight of Sever: Essays from Harvard,* Harvard University Press, 1963.[2]]

1922. Completed his master's degree in Romance Languages at Harvard. For the next five years McCord was a member of the drama staff for the Boston *Evening Transcript.* He also served as associate editor for the Harvard *Alumni Bulletin* from 1923-25.

1924. The author came early into the field of children's poetry. "Two years after I finished my master's degree in English at Harvard—I had previously studied to become a physicist—I wrote a number of poems for children. One was published in the then *Saturday Review of Literature* and got into some anthologies."[1]

1925. Returned to Harvard and devoted the next thirty-seven years to serving there in various capacities but primarily as executive director of the Harvard Fund Council. During his career as a professional fund raiser, McCord raised $15,-319,872.26. He preferred to think of himself as a soft-seller. "[My technique] . . . does not stem from any personal bias, but simply out of my unshakable belief in the philosophy of using civilized language for a civil purpose." ["The Barbless Hook," *Time,* June 29, 1962.[3]]

1927. First book of serious poems, *Floodgate,* published. "Poetry is so many things besides the shiver down the spine. It is a new day lying on an unknown doorstep. It is *Peer Gynt* and *Moby Dick* in a single line. It is the best translation of words that do not exist. It is hot coffee dripping from an icicle. It is the accident involving sudden life. It is the calculus of the imagination. It is the finishing touch to what one could not finish. It is a hundred things as unexplainable as all our foolish explanations."[1]

McCord approaches his craft seriously, although he considers the numerous books he has either written or edited for children and adults a hobby rather than a vocation.

1945. When his book, *What Cheer,* a collection of witty verse was produced, McCord spoke of his regard for humor. "Much might be said in behalf of laughter, yet I shall say little. In a world late at war, none but an idiot is likely to argue the worth of a top-drawer laugh, or even one of junior grade. Possess it while you can.

"Abiding faith in laughter was the incentive for the making of this book. Fresh, saline, and cleansing as the sea, laughter is a basic commodity, an old affair in the world, an abstrac-

Me being I and what I am:
no bit of toast upon the jam,
no chance at creaming of the wheat,
or oating of the meal, to eat.

I meant to say that I'm in bed
and have the bug, the doctor said.
■ (From *For Me To Say* by David McCord. Illustrated by Henry B. Kane.)

tion and reaction about which few will quarrel. So this book is based on nothing less—on the laughter of humor, something audible and contagious; on the laughter of wit, something swift and sudden in the queer little reflex tightening about the eyes. A large but simple collection, it includes, simply enough, what to me is the happiest of available wit and humor in American and British verse from any sensible date you want to name up to the vivid present. Territorially, it covers the United States and Great Britain—touching Scotland, Ireland, Canada, Australia, and South Africa. A lot of ground, a lot of laughter; a lot of authors, a lot of anonymity; a lot of divergence, a lot of correlation.

"A book, unlike a ship, is never launched into a fully predictable medium. The ship slides down the ways, with the blessing of champagne and band music, into a sea of water. A book emerges, to the tiny dry piping of its publisher, into a world of conflicting taste and opinion. It is cheering to reflect, therefore, that at this strange immediate moment rhyme is more on the tongues of men and women than one would think. The armed services, the headline writer; the soundtrack on sports, travel features, and such in the movies; some of the national advertisers, and certain radio pro-

grams are fooling with funny and not-so-funny verses daily." [David McCord, introduction to *What Cheer*, Coward, 1945.[4]]

1952. First book for children, *Far and Few*, published. McCord was early influenced by Edward Lear and Robert Louis Stevenson. "I have a weakness for *Far and Few*. It is dedicated to my twice-pioneering mother, a lady of great imagination and courage, who died in 1956 at the age of 93.

"I seemed to know instinctively that to write for the young I had to write for myself. I write out of myself, about things I did as a boy, about things that are fairly timeless as subjects. I do not believe that one can teach the art of writing. You are born with the urge for it or you are not. Only the hardest self-discipline and considerable mastery of self-criticism will get you anywhere.

"Children still love words, rhythm, rhyme, music, games. They climb trees, skate, swim, swing, fish, explore, act, ride, run, and love snow and getting wet all over; they make things and are curious about science. They love humor and nonsense and imaginary conversation with imaginary things. I pray that I never am guilty of talking down to boys and girls. I try to remember that they are closer to the sixth sense than we who are older."[1]

1956. Received the first L.H.D. ever awarded by Harvard. McCord holds several honorary degrees and numerous awards.

1962. Retired from his post as executive director of the Harvard Fund Council. He remarked that in retirement, "Chinese, Greek, Debussy, tobacco, trout are the things I want to investigate—in that order."[3]

His wide range of hobbies and interests include, water-color painting, the theater, travel, fishing, collecting owls, wood engravings, paints and, of course, books. "I have been a fly fisherman since I was 13—trout, first; salmon, second. I am fond of professional baseball; I'm a Red Sox fan!"[1]

1977. First recipient of the National Council of Teachers of English Award for Excellence in Poetry for Children. "Today, when the lower grades in public and private schools are alive to and alive with poetry, there is no responding Blake, Lear, or Carroll to stand above the crowd and dominate the world of professional poetry for children in the way that Yeats, Pound, Eliot, Frost, and Auden have collectively dominated the adult poetry of England and America in our century. Indeed, only a handful of poets here and overseas appear to be writing largely or solely for children. Among the best of these are Eve Merriam, Marchette Chute, Rose Fyleman, Kaye Starbird, Mary O'Neill, and (perhaps most productive) Myra Cohn Livingston. The horns of elfland may blow faintly, but year by year they manage to acquire a new section of summoning brass, as they did with Housman, Belloc, Cummings, Roethke, Ogden Nash, if you but listen: Louis Untermeyer (a pioneer), John Ciardi (ahead of all), William Jay Smith (second), Phyllis McGinley (who should write more for children), Lois Lenski (for the *very* young), Maxine Kumin, Richard Wilbur (for his recent analeptic *Opposites* [Harcourt]), John Updike, Lee Bennett Hopkins, May Swenson, James Reeves, E. V. Rieu, and Ian Serraillier." [David McCord, "I Went to Noke and Somebody Spoke," *Horn Book,* October, 1974.[3]]

"Poetry for children is simpler than poetry for adults. The overtones are fewer, but it should have overtones. Basically,

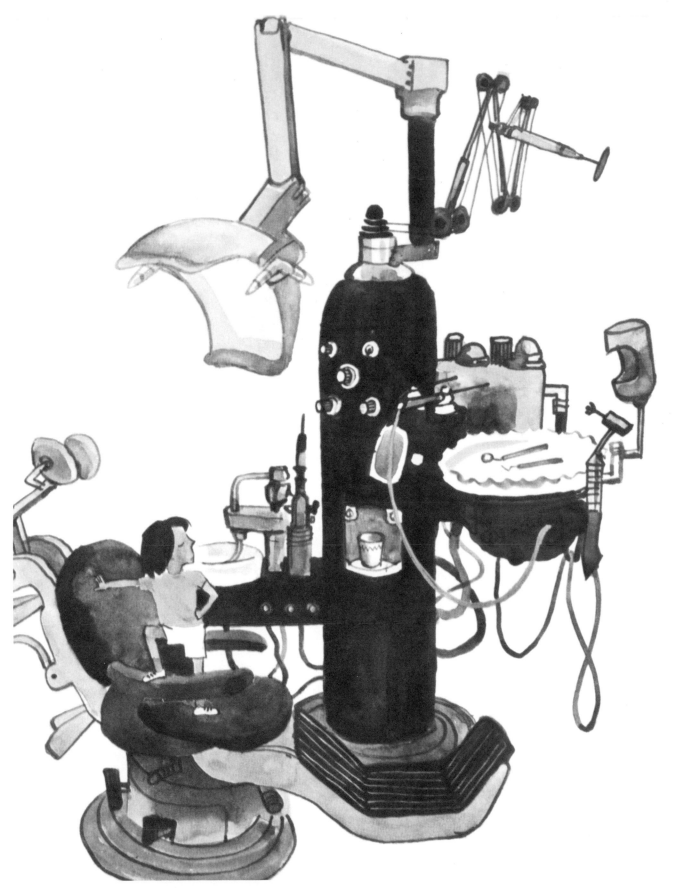

**When I see the dentist
I take him all my teeth.**

■ (From *The Star in the Pail* by David McCord. Illustrated by Marc Simont.)

of course, it isn't different. Children's verse sometimes turns out, or is turned out, to be not much more than doggerel: lame lines, limp rhymes, and poor ideas. By and large, verse written for children is rhymed; it is nearly always brief, though an occasional poem in the hands of a skilled performer like Ogden Nash may tell a story. But poetry, like rain, should fall with elemental music, and poetry for children should catch the eye as well as the ear and the mind. It should delight; it really has to delight. Furthermore, poetry for children should keep reminding them, without any feeling on their part that they are being reminded, that the English language is a most marvelous and availing instrument.

"Sometimes poems come to me full-blown—nonsense verse in particular. More often I work at them, rewriting for choice of words and for sound and smoothness. I never use an unusual word unless I can place it as a key word so that it will make the reader look it up. Poems should open new horizons. They are vistas—familiar as well as strange."[1]

FOR MORE INFORMATION SEE: Atlantic, October, 1948; *New York Herald Tribune Weekly Book Review,* October 24, 1948; *Saturday Review of Literature,* October 30, 1948, November 18, 1950; *New York Herald Tribune Book Review,* August 27, 1950, September 7, 1952; *Horn Book,* October, 1952, February, 1963, August, 1970, February, 1971, June, 1975, April, 1976; "Barbless Hook," *Time,* June 29, 1962; Lee Bennett Hopkins, *Books Are by People,* Citation Press, 1969; Doris de Montreville and Donna Hill, editors, *Third Book of Junior Authors,* H. W. Wilson, 1972; *Bulletin of the Center for Children's Books,* June, 1975.

MIZUMURA, Kazue

PERSONAL: Born in Kamakura, Japan; came to the United States in 1955; married Claus Stamm (a writer; deceased); children: one daughter (died at the age of three). *Education:* Attended Women's Art Institute, Tokyo, Japan and Pratt Institute, Brooklyn, N.Y. *Home:* Stamford, Conn.

CAREER: Began working in Japan as a commercial artist and instructor of Japanese sumi-e painting shortly after the Second World War; employed in the United States as a textile designer for four years; illustrator, beginning 1959; author of children's books, beginning 1966. *Awards, honors: The New York Times* named *If I Were a Mother* one of the outstanding picture books of 1968; Boston Globe-Horn Book Award for Illustration, 1971, for *If I Built a Village.*

*WRITINGS—*All self-illustrated; all published by Crowell: *I See the Winds,* 1966; *If I Were a Mother* (ALA Notable Book), 1968; *The Emperor Penguins,* 1969; *The Way of an Ant,* 1970; *The Blue Whale,* 1971; *If I Built a Village,* 1971; *If I Were a Cricket,* 1973; *Opossum,* 1974; *Flower Moon Snow: A Book of Haiku,* 1977.

Illustrator: Elizabeth Vining Gray, *The Cheerful Heart,* Viking, 1959; Patricia Miles Martin, *Suzu and the Bride Doll,* Rand McNally, 1960; Masako Matsuno, *A Pair of Red Clogs,* World Publishing, 1960; Claus Stamm, *The Very Special Badgers,* Viking, 1960; Janet Lewis, *Keiko's Bubble,* Doubleday, 1961; Rachel E. Carr, *The Picture Story of Japan,* McKay, 1962, reissued, 1970; M. Matsuno, *Taro and the Tofu,* World Publishing, 1962; C. Stamm, *Three Strong Women,* Viking, 1962, Penguin, 1974; Yoshiko Uchida, *Rokubei and the Thousand Rice Bowls,* Scribner, 1962; Valdine Plasmati, *Algernon and the Pigeons,* Viking, 1963; Judy Hawes, *Fireflies in the Night,* Crowell, 1963; Y. Uchida, *The*

KAZUE MIZUMURA

Forever Christmas Tree, Scribner, 1963; Roma Gans, *It's Nesting Time,* Crowell, 1964, reissued, 1972; P. M. Martin, *The Greedy One,* Rand McNally, 1964; C. Stamm, *The Dumplings and the Demons,* Viking, 1964; Y. Uchida, *Sumi's Prize,* Scribner, 1964.

M. Matsuno, *Chie and the Sports Day,* World Publishing, 1965; Frank Bonham, *Mystery in Little Tokyo,* Dutton, 1966; Nancy Serage, *The Prince Who Gave Up a Throne,* Crowell, 1966; Y. Uchida, *Sumi's Special Happening,* Scribner, 1966; Aileen Lucia Fisher, *My Mother and I,* Crowell, 1967; Jean Craighead George, *The Moon of the Winter Bird,* Crowell, 1969; Y. Uchida, *Sumi and the Goat and the Tokyo Express,* Scribner, 1969; Berniece Freschet, *Jumping Mouse,* Crowell, 1971; John Frederick Waters, *Neighborhood Puddle,* Warne, 1971; Joanna Cole, *Plants in Winter,* Crowell, 1973; B. Freschet, *Skunk Baby,* Crowell, 1973; Sigmund Kalina, *Air, the Invisible Ocean,* Lothrop, 1973; Laurence P. Pringle, *Water Plants,* Crowell, 1975; Eleanor R. Coerr, *Biography of a Giant Panda,* Putnam, 1975; May Sarton, *A Walk Through the Woods,* Harper, 1976; Lorie K. Harris, *Biography of a Whooping Crane,* Putnam, 1977; David A. Adler, *Redwoods Are the Tallest Trees in the World,* Crowell, 1978; Charlotte Zolotow, *River Winding,* Crowell, 1978.

SIDELIGHTS: Although Mizumura's interest in art began when she was a child, she never thought of pursuing it as a career. For the young Japanese girl, it was enough of a dream to lead the life of a happy wife and mother. "I always liked to draw and that was the only thing I could do really well among all the things I had to learn during my school years. Thus it was natural for me to enter the Art Institute, though I did not particularly want to be an artist. I guess I always wanted to be just an ordinary happy wife. So, for a short time, until World War II ended my dreams, I was a

Yet, like Mother Skunk,
I would dare to fight for
my children
Against all harm.
■ (From *If I Were a Mother* by Kazue Mizumura. Illustrated by the author.)

wife and mother." [*Illustrators of Children's Books: 1957-1966*, compiled by Lee Kingman and others, Horn Book, 1968.[1]]

Her ideal life came to a tragic end however, when the Second World War took the lives of her husband and infant daughter. Forced to earn her own living, Mizumura relied on her artistic talents to provide her with a source of income. "After I lost my husband and daughter, I taught traditional Japanese sumi-e painting and worked in the field of commercial art in postwar Japan. I came to the United States in 1955 on a scholarship to Pratt Institute. After Pratt, I worked as a textile designer for four years."[1]

Mizumura illustrated her first book in the late 1950's, and up until the mid 1960's was limited to illustration assignments with Japanese themes. "In 1959, I was asked to illustrate *The Cheerful Heart* and since then I have gradually established myself as an illustrator. For the first few years I was commissioned for strictly Japanese themes. In doing the illustrations for Japanese stories, there was little I could do beyond the authentic representational illustrations that were expected. Luckily, Elizabeth Riley of Crowell understood my problem and encouraged me to write my own text. The result was *I See the Wind* [1966]"[1]

Besides writing and illustrating, Mizumura has done advertising layout and Japanese brush drawing. Her workshop is in her Stamford, Connecticut home which overlooks Long Island Sound.

The author-illustrator's award-winning book, *If I Built a Village,* told the simple story of a young boy and the kind of town he would like to build. "[Mizumura's] bright, energetic designs of leaping rabbits and trout . . . are pictured in alternating black and white and sunny full-color wash-spreads. The theme is effectively expressed without becoming burdensome for the small child," noted a critic for *Horn Book.* A reviewer for *Publishers Weekly* observed, "The perfect village that a child could dream up is presented in perfect words and pictures by a distinguished artist who not only remembers how a child dreams, but has the skill to reflect the dream in beauty."

FOR MORE INFORMATION SEE: Lee Kingman and others, editors, *Illustrators of Children's Books, 1957-1966,* Horn Book, 1968; *Horn Book,* June, 1966, August, 1970, December, 1971; *Publishers Weekly,* August 9, 1971; Doris de Montreville and Donna Hill, editors, *Third Book of Junior Authors,* H. W. Wilson, 1972.

MOORE, Clement Clarke   1779-1863 (Columella)

PERSONAL: Born July 15, 1779, in New York City; died July 10, 1863, in Newport, Rhode Island; buried in Trinity Cemetery, New York City; son of Benjamin Moore (a minister; rector of Trinity Church, Bishop of New York, and President of Columbia College; participant in the Presidential inauguration of George Washington) and Charity (Clarke) Moore; married Catharine Elizabeth Taylor, November 20, 1813 (died, 1830); children: nine. *Education:* Received early schooling from father; Columbia College, B.A., 1798, M.A., 1801, LL.D., 1829. *Home:* Newport, Rhode Island.

CAREER: Poet, scholar, and educator. Diocesan Seminary, New York City, professor of Biblical Learning and the Interpretation of Scripture, beginning 1821; General Theological

CLEMENT CLARKE MOORE

Seminary, New York City, professor of Oriental and Greek literature, 1823-50, professor emeritus, beginning 1850. Member of the board of trustees of Columbia College, 1813-57, clerk of the board, 1815-50. *Member:* New York Historical Society (elected, 1813). Moore was also a member of the Knickerbocker School, made up of writers such as Washington Irving, James Fenimore Cooper, and William Cullen Bryant, living and working in the New York City area in the first half of the nineteenth century. These writers did not possess a common doctrine or practice, but all helped to make New York an important literary center.

WRITINGS: Observations upon Certain Passages in Mr. Jefferson's Notes on Virginia, [New York], 1804; *A New Translation [with notes of] The Third Satire of Juvenal* (original edition published anonymously), [New York], 1806; (under pseudonym Columella) *An Inquiry into the Effects of Our Foreign Carrying Trade upon the Agriculture, Population, and Morals of the Country,* D. & G. Bruce, 1806; *A Compendious Lexicon of the Hebrew Language,* Collins & Perkins, 1809; *A Sketch of Our Political Condition,* privately printed, 1813; *A Plain Statement,* J. Eastburn, 1818; (editor) Benjamin Moore, *Sermons by Benjamin Moore,* [New York], 1824; *A Lecture Introductory to the Course of Hebrew Instruction,* [New York], 1825; *Address Delivered before the Alumni of Columbia College,* E. Bliss & E. White, 1825; *Poems,* Bartlett & Welford, 1844; *George Castroit, Surnamed Scanderbeg, King of Albania,* D. Appleton, 1850.

For children: *A Visit from St. Nicholas* (illustrated by T. C. Boyd), H. M. Onderdonk, 1848, reprinted, Simon & Schuster, 1971 (originally appeared anonymously in the *Troy Sen-*

Clement Clarke Moore built this little brick stable in 1848 on his Chelsea farm. Photo by Lynn Karlin.

tinel on December 23, 1823; published in *The New York Book of Poetry,* 1837, and in Moore's collected *Poems,* 1844) [other editions illustrated by F.O.C. Darley, J. G. Gregory, 1862; Constance Whittemore, Macmillan, 1925; Berta and Elmer Hader, Macmillan, 1937; Valenti Angelo, Hawthorn House, 1937; Aldren Watson, Peter Pauper Press, 1945; Paul Galdone, McGraw-Hill, 1968], original edition also published as *The Night Before Christmas,* facsimile of the 1848 edition reprinted, Dover, 1971 [other editions under that title illustrated by W. W. Denslow, G. W. Dillingham, 1902; Jessie Willcox Smith, Houghton, 1912; Elizabeth MacKinstry, Dutton, 1928; Arthur Rackham, Harrap, 1931, reissued, Lippincott, 1954; Reginald Birch, Harcourt, 1937; Ilse Bischoff, Holiday House, 1937; Everett Shinn, J. C. Winston, 1942; Leonard Weisgard, Grosset, 1949; Corinne Malvern, Simon & Schuster, 1949, reissued, Golden Press, 1966; Elizabeth Webbe, Rand McNally, 1950; Gustaf Tenggren, Simon & Schuster, 1951; Roger Duvoisin, Garden City Books, 1954; Eloise Wilkin, Simon & Schuster, 1955; Catherine Barnes, Whitman, 1960; Gyo Fujikawa, Grosset, 1961; Ruth Ives, Maxton, 1961; Grandma Moses, Random House, 1961; Tasha Tudor, A. J. St. Onge, 1962, new edition, Rand McNally, 1975; Hilary Knight, Harper, 1963; Susan Perl, Dell, 1964; Ralph R. Miller, Sr., (sign language edition), Gallaudet College Press, 1973; Douglas Gorsline, Random House, 1975; Elisa Trimby, Doubleday, 1977; another edition with an introduction by L. Frank Baum, Reilly & Britton, 1905].

ADAPTATIONS—Movies and filmstrips: "A Visit from St. Nicholas" (motion picture), Coronet Instructional Films, 1949; "The Night Before Christmas" (motion pictures), Encyclopaedia Britannica Films, 1955, Amy V. Shugard, 1967, Productions Unlimited, 1972; "The Night Before Christmas" (filmstrips), Stillfilm, 1948, Filmfax, 1950, Encyclopaedia Britannica Films, 1955, Teaching Aids Service, 1956, Society for Visual Education, 1961; "'Twas the Night Before Christmas" (motion picture), Norm Drew Productions, 1975, "'Twas the Night Before Christmas" (filmstrip), Coronet Instructional Films, 1967.

Music: "'Twas the Night Before Christmas," music by Ken Darby, arranged by Harry Simeone, Words and Music Publishers, 1942.

SIDELIGHTS: **July 15, 1779.** Born in the Chelsea area of Manhattan, New York; the only child of Bishop Benjamin Moore of the Episcopalian church and Charity Clarke Moore, daughter of Major Thomas Clarke, a wealthy, retired officer of the British Army.

Moore's early days were comfortably spent with all the advantages that the position and wealth of his parents could afford. He was privately tutored by his father who later became president of Columbia University and was made an assistant at the inauguration of George Washington. These instructions took place within the family's ancestoral mansion, Chelsea House. ". . . I know nothing about my fathers ancestry, except that they were plain, honest, hard-working farmers in New-town on Long-Island; that they were of English extraction, and belonged to the Church of England; and that the graves of Moore family are now distinguishable in the burying ground of New-town, some of which are marked by tombstones so rough and shapeless as to show that under them 'The *rude* fore-fathers of the hamlet sleep. . . .' [Taken from The General Manuscript Collection, Rare Book and Manuscript Library, Columbia University.[1]]

1795. Accepted at Columbia University at the age of sixteen.

May, 1796. During an excursion to Philadelphia, in the midst of his college education, he wrote the following to his mother: "I take my pen in hand to prepare you for being very angry with me, but, before I introduce the subject, shall endeavour to expiate, in a small degree, my fault, by giving you, according to your request, a very circumstantial account of my conduct since my last letter, which, I think, was dated on Saturday evening. The next morning I went to Christ Church. . . . In the afternoon I heard Mr. Bissert preach in the African Church, and in the evening I enjoyed the happiness of hearing Mr. Pilmore's soft and melodious voice swelled to the highest pitch of harmony. . . .

"And now, with a trembling hand, I shall enter upon the subject which I dreaded so much in the beginning of my letter. This morning I went to a store of mathematical instruments. I am sure you can guess it now, and the man showed me a handsome surveying instrument upon a new construction, price 40 dollars. I had but 30 of my own, and did not know what to do, for I knew that I should not meet with such an opportunity in N. York, and it was small and neatly put up so that I could conveniently pack it in my trunk.

"Now Mama I am sure if you had been in Philadel: with me, you would not have hesitated a minute to supply the deficiency, but I am fearful that you will not be pleased with me for borrowing the money without first asking your consent; but you must consider that I had not time, if I had written, to receive an answer, and that I could not have bought one of any kind in N York. If, when I return home now, I meet your face half diffused with a smile and half contracted with a frown, I shall not only wish myself in Philadelphia, where I meet with nothing but smiles, but I shall never forgive myself, or dare to look at you with confidence again. But, if I perceive your countenance oerspread with joy at receiving me, I shall be oerjoyed once more to see you, and fly with redoubled transports to your arms. Give my love to Papa, Grandma, Mary, and Tom. And now I am sure I have trespassed long enough on the limits of decency, in regard to the length of my letter; and shall conclude with declaring myself

Your ever affectionate Son
C C Moore

"P.S. Excuse bad spelling &c, for the Post goes tomorrow morning and I have not time to be correct as it is very late." [Samuel White Patterson, *The Poet of Christmas Eve: A Life of Clement Clarke Moore, 1779-1863,* More-haus-Graham Co., 1956.[2]]

1798. Graduated from Columbia University at the head of his class as a master of Oriental and Classical literature. At nineteen, he was fluent in the French, Hebrew, Italian, Greek and Latin languages, was skilled as a violinist and organist, was a published poet, and had displayed considerable architectural talent.

1801. Received masters degree.

1804. Published an anonymous tract entitled: *Observations Upon Certain Passages in Mr. Jefferson's Notes on Virginia, Which Appear to Have a Tendency to Subvert Religion and Establish a False Philosophy.* This pamphlet was a stinging attack by Moore of Jefferson's free-thinking ideas.

Jefferson, along with the modern French philosophers of the time—Buffon, Rousseau, Voltaire—questioned the accepted ideas of "The Creation" and the sequence of events surrounding the birth of the planet. Such blatant disregard for

When what to my wondering
eyes should appear,
But a miniature sleigh
and eight tiny reindeer,

(From *The Night Before Christmas* by Clement Clarke Moore. Illustrated by Tasha Tudor.)

The children were nestled
all snug in their beds,
While visions of sugar-plums
danced in their heads;

(From *The Night Before Christmas* by Clement C. Moore. Illustrated by Grandma Moses.)

biblical accounts was unthinkable to Moore. "In Mr. Jefferson's description of the junction of the Potowmac and Shenandoah, this sentence occurs: 'The first glance of this scene hurries our senses into the opinion, that this earth has been created in time, that the mountains were formed first, that the rivers began to flow afterwards.'" [Clement C. Moore, *Observations Upon Certain Passages in Mr. Jefferson's Notes on Virginia, Which Appear to Have a Tendency to Subvert Religion, and Establish a False Philosophy,* [New York], 1804.[3]]

Outraged by any notion that the mountains were formed before the rivers, Moore quoted the scriptures to disprove Jefferson's heretical claims: "... This, however, [is] what is said in Genesis; 'And God said, Let the waters under the heaven be gathered together unto one place, and let the dry land appear: and it was so.' ..."[3]

1806. Collaborated with his friend, John Duer, on a volume of verse entitled: *A New Translation with Notes of the Third Satire of Juvenal, to Which are Added Miscellaneous Poems, Original and Translated.* Moore wrote the long introductory letter expounding his criticisms of the new poets who had dared to stray from the traditional rules of poetry writing. Moore contemptuously describes them as: "... Minds faintly glowing with the fire of genius, and unprovided with large stores of wisdom. . . .

". . . The final degradation of poetry is due to those who neglected every consideration but the sound of their produc-

tions; or who heightened by the charms of language those ideas which are dangerous to innocense. The whole race of poets have not escaped the reproaches which this last order [for I rank the nonsensical and the immodest together] have brought upon themselves. . . .

"'I hate *bainting* and *boetry* too! neither the one nor the other ever did any good,' said George the second. . . . Thus a poet is now considered as one of the useless ornaments of society . . . whose proper and original employment was to render mankind more happy. . . .

"Every admirer of genuine poetry should be anxious to see preserved all remains of her ancient dignity. No production which assumes the guise of poetry, ought to be tolerated, if it possess no other recommendation than the glow of it's expressions and tinkling of its syllables. . . . It should be scrupulously required, that whenever words are put together, they be assembled for some rational purpose. . . ." [Clement C. Moore and John Duer, *A New Translation with Notes of the Third Satire of Juvenal, to Which are Added Miscellaneous Poems, Original and Translated,* E. Sargeant, 1806.[4]]

Several of these poems and translations were credited to Moore. One of the poems entitled "Lines Addressed to the Young Ladies Who Attended Mr. Chilton's Lectures in Natural Philosophy," was intended to encourage women in scholarly pursuits.

"The beasts, that roam o'er Lybia's desert plain,
Have gentler hearts than men who dare maintain
That woman, lovely woman, hath no soul,
They too seem drench'd in Circe's pois'nous bowl,
Who grant the fair may have a soul to save,
But deem each female born an abject slave.
Give me the maiden of unfettered mind,
By thought and knowledge strengthen'd and refin'd, . . .
Ye maids, whose vows to science are addressed,
If thus your minds be fashioned, thus impressed,
With joy your course pursue, nor heed the while,
Envy's malignant grin, not folly's smile;
Trace nature's laws, explore the starry maze;
Learn why lightenings flash, or meteors blaze . . .
Then may true wisdom grace a fluttering belle."[4]

1806. Published an anonymous work entitled *An Inquiry Into the Effects of Our Foreign Carrying Trade Upon the Agriculture, Population and Morals of the Country*. This long treatise was an ardent protest against President Jefferson's embargo on foreign trade with Britain. Moore felt that battles between nations, as with individuals, were rarely worth the resulting damage and were caused by ". . . one or more of the following mental infirmities; *misapprehension, passion,* or a *false sense of honour.* . . ." [under the pseudonym Columella, *An Inquiry Into the Effects of Our Foreign Carrying Trade Upon the Agriculture, Population and Morals of the Country*, E. Sargeant, 1806.[5]]

Though he devoted over sixty pages of this pamphlet to the condemnation of the evils of money, trade and power, as well as of the evils of merchants and politicians who controlled them, he did not want the average citizen to believe that he had lost faith in America or it's people. ". . . But let it not be imagined that, while censuring the immorality of a *part* of the community, the writer of these reflections supposes this laxity of principle and practice to spring from a proneness to evil peculiarly powerful in Americans. Far be such a thought from his mind! on the contrary, he believes the great mass of his countrymen to be more virtuous than any other nation; notwithstanding the representations of travellers, who give the picture of a whole nation . . . of tavernkeepers, stage-drivers, boatmen, borderers upon the roads through which they pass, and 'from rabble senators and merchant kings.' Besides the less conspicuous virtues, they possess qualities of the brightest lustre, they are intrep-

id, enterprising beyond any other people, more jealous of freedom than of life, and roused to patriotism by every spring of principle and interest. . . ."[5]

His love of country and hope for the future were expressed as: "Never was a fairer and more extensive field opened to the domestic enterprise of any one nation than our country affords. The vast extent of our empire; the inexhaustible fertility of our immense western wilds, and the delightful climates with which they are blessed; the majestic rivers which flow through the country in every direction; the great inland seas which wash our northern boundaries; the grandeur of every natural object which strikes the eye; all conspire to fill the mind with noble thoughts, and to warm every truly patriotic heart with exultation at the prospect of our future greatness. Even the illiterate adventurers who emigrate to our western woods seem to acquire from the view of these objects an expansion of mind which the refined inhabitants of cities seldom feel. The author of this inquiry has seen in the wilderness near lake Erie a rough farmer standing bareheaded near the door of his log-house, amidst stumps and ashes, and the smoke of newly-felled trees which were burning around him, with his arm stretched out, pointing towards the vestiges of ancient lakes and rivers, and conjecturing the changes which, from natural causes, the country had probably undergone during the course of former ages. . . .

"Within [America's] borders the weary have found rest; and from her native and inexhaustible stores the needy who would exert themselves have acquired competence if not wealth. And, while peace and plenty render all smiling and happy within her dwelling, the distant sounds of war and devastation render this internal tranquillity still more desirable and delightful.

The children were nestled all snug in their beds,... ■ (From *The Night Before Christmas* by Clement Clarke Moore. Illustrated by Everett Shinn.)

"Were war to break out, what state of things would succeed to this happy condition! Our foreign commerce of every kind would be annihilated; our sea-ports blockaded and perhaps bombarded; nearly the whole present revenue of our government destroyed; half our merchants ruined, and the other half at a loss how to employ themselves; the farmers burdened with new and heavy taxes, and their produce without any market; in a word, the whole system of public and private economy throughout the country would be deranged. And all this distress and confusion would be endured by our industrious yeomen for the sake of a trade which in its very nature is detrimental to their interests; and which, by the unwarrantable practices to which it has tempted too many merchants, has excited contempt and distrust among foreigners for the American name. . . ."[5]

Moore chose to become a teacher rather than a minister like his father, but the influence of his Christian training was clear in this summation: "The writer of these reflections is well aware that when passion on one hand calls to a multitude, the mild voice of reason, on the other, has little hope of gaining immediate attention. They who work with the fire of passion, operate on materials in fusion and easily moulded; they who employ no other instruments than truth and reason, must overcome by patient labour and repeated efforts the cold resistance of the substances which they strive to fashion. But he is encouraged by the belief . . . that truth dispassionately urged will eventually prevail . . . a good man is not to adopt the opinion of too many among us, that means not perfectly pure ought sometimes to be employed for the attainment of a good end. The laws of our actions are plainly set before our eyes; the consequences are in the hand of that over-ruling Providence . . . whose mysterious counsels baffle the designs of the most sagacious; and whose operations elude the vigilance of the most clear-sighted. And may he continue to bless our country; may he give her rulers wisdom, and render her children 'kind and natural'; while other nations are harassed by war and desolation may they still cast their eyes towards her and exclaim:

"'Thy walls, remote from hostile fear,
Nor the loud voice of tumult hear,
    Nor wars wild wastes deplore;
There smiling plenty takes her stand,
And in thy courts, with lavish hand,
    Has pour'd forth all her store.'"[5]

**When what to my wondering eyes did appear,
But a miniature sleigh and eight tiny reindeer.**
■ (From *A Visit From St. Nicholas* by Clement C. Moore. Illustrated by Paul Galdone.)

When, what to my wondering eyes should appear,
But a miniature sleigh, and eight tiny reindeer.
■ (From *Twas the Night Before Christmas: A Visit From St. Nicholas* by Clement C. Moore.
Pictures by Jesse Willcox Smith.)

1809. Published a massive, two-volume work, on which he had labored for several years, containing a vocabulary of Hebraic terms with translations, entitled *A Compendius Lexicon of the Hebrew Language.* Although among the first of its kind to be published in America, it was otherwise undistinguished and was considered a text-book for beginners. The work was dedicated to the Rt. Rev. Benjamin Moore, D.D., "by his affectionate son."

1811. Moore's father suffered a paralytic stroke.

1813. Appointed a trustee of Columbia University. In response to the War of 1812, published another impassioned but anonymous political pamphlet. In "A Sketch of our Political Condition . . ." he declared: "Let us then have peace upon any terms short of dishonour. . . . This war, though not the only ill we suffer; is the great crying enormity which ought at once to be arrested."[2] To support his argument he quoted from the Old Testament: "And he shall judge among the nations, and shall rebuke many people: and they shall beat their swords into plowshares, and their spears into pruninghooks: nation shall not lift up sword against nation, neither shall they learn war any more."[2]

November 20, 1813. Married Catharine Elizabeth Taylor.

1814-1822. Six of his nine children born—Margaret, Charity, Benjamin, Mary, Clement, and Emily.

1815. Appointed clerk of the board of trustees of Columbia University.

1816. His father, Bishop Benjamin Moore died and Moore became master of the "Chelsea" estate.

> ". . . When cruel Palsy's withering blow
> Had left my father weak, forlorn,
> He yet could weep for joy, to know,
> I had a wished-for infant born.
>
> "And as he lay in death's embrace,
> You saw when last on earth he smiled;
> You saw the ray that lit his face
> When he beheld our darling child. . . ."

[Clement C. Moore, *Poems*, William Van Norden, 1944.[6]]

1819. Contributed sixty lots of ground within the city of New York to the Episcopalian Church. It was his desire that ". . . the buildings of the theological school should be erected there on." [Dumas Malone, editor, *Dictionary of American Biography,* Charles Scribner Sons, 1934.[7]]

1821. Became professor of Biblical Learning and Interpretation of Scripture in the Diocesan Seminary in New York.

Christmas Eve, 1822. As a yuletide present, he wrote "'Twas the Night Before Christmas . . .'" for his six children. Moore modelled his famous version of the myth of Saint Nicholas after a local workman. ". . . A portly, robicund Dutchman, living in the neighborhood of . . . Chelsea."[2] The poem was read aloud for the first time by Moore at the fireside of the family mansion to an audience of his children, relatives, servants and slaves.

1823. A young relative of Moore's sent the untitled poem anonymously to the *Sentinel,* a Troy, N.Y. newspaper. The editor published the verses for the first time under the heading: "An Account of a Visit from St. Nicholas." It appeared on December 23, 1823, accompanied by an editorial: "We know not to whom we are indebted for the following description of that unwearied patron of children—that *homely* and delightful personage of parental kindness—Santa Claus, —his costume and his equipage as he goes about visiting the firesides of this happy land, laden with Christmas bounties;

but from whomsoever it may have come, we give thanks for it. There is, to our apprehension, a spirit of cordial goodness in it, a playfulness of fancy, and a benevolent alacrity to enter into the feelings and promote the simple pleasures of children, which are altogether charming. We hope our little patrons, both lads and lassies, will accept it as a proof of our unfeigned good-will towards them—as a token of our warmest wish that they may have many a merry Christmas; that they may long retain their beautiful relics for those home-bred joys, which derive their flavor from filial piety and fraternal love...." [Arthur N. Hosking, *The Night Before Christmas* (facsimile of the original 1848 edition) Dover, 1971.[8]]

When the Diocesan Seminary merged with the new General Theological Seminary, Moore was appointed professor of Oriental and Greek literature.

His granddaughter, Mary Moore Sherman wrote in 1906: "The rendering of a Hebrew passage by one of his pupils in the seminary was a 'bon mot' once in student circles: 'I love justice but clemency more' and shows in what affectionate regard they held him." [Mary Moore Sherman, *Recollections of Clement C. Moore, Author of "A Visit from St. Nicholas,"* The Knickerbocker Press, 1906.[9]]

May 4, 1825. Delivered an address before the alumni of Columbia College: "... In bodies corporate and politic, as well as in individuals, early impressions are very apt to last. Let us look ahead, and see what it is best for us to be about. Let the channels of future knowledge be dug before the streams begin to flow. Let the mould be prepared before the mass is molten.

"... How many a youth may be rescued from destruction by an early taste for useful knowledge! and how many a superior genius called forth, by giving to knowledge and learning their due reward!...

"... And happy would it be for the interests of literature and of society, if the young could be made sensible of the folly of those excuses for the neglect of study which are so often heard from them. The *cui bono* recurs perpetually. 'I am destined for such a particular pursuit in life; why should I spend my time in this or that study which may never be of any use to me in my profession?' Reasoning like this is too often heard; yet no one will deny that, whatever may be his *future* destination in life, no *present* employment can be more worthy of a thinking being than to store his mind with good ideas, and to exercise and invigorate his intellectual powers by the investigation of truth. But, after all, it is to be feared that few things are more difficult than to convince and stimulate those who feel no desire for mental improvement. It has been said of old that 'the sluggard is wiser in his own conceit than seven men that can render a reason.'

"... A boy who is destined to receive a liberal education, is placed, as soon as he can read English, at a grammar school, where he is obliged, by dint of downright force and violence, to pass a number of years in the uninterrupted study of Latin and Greek, while mathematics are attended to, if at all, as matters of secondary consideration.... He is then sent to college with words and with rules for putting those words together, and possessing little more than his own native elements of mathematical science; and if he find it difficult to divert his thoughts from the studies to which they have, during a great part of his life, been accustomed, and to turn them upon subjects of a nature totally different from those studies,

he persuades himself that nature never intended him for mathematics....

"I allude to the idea entertained by many persons of the nature and relative importance of mathematics. Nothing is more common than the opinion that a peculiar turn of mind is requisite for that branch of science. While all are supposed capable of acquiring Greek and Latin, but few are considered as formed by nature to be mathematicians. Among students in college, the want of a propensity to that study is often made an excuse for neglecting it....

"The superficial man of the world may jeer at the spiderweb diagrams and mystic characters of the mathematician; but he, in his turn, may well smile; for while he acknowledges that these are but the props and steps to aid his feeble powers, he yet is conscious that his mind dwells in a world of pure intellect, and that he is engaged in the noblest of all pursuits, the pursuit of truth, and of truth changeless and eternal....

"... Whatever tends to draw men together in the bonds of harmony and friendship, is most desirable in this world of jealousy, suspicion, resentment, pride, and coldness. The asperities which may have existed among some of our number during our collegiate course, are now obliterated, or felt only as the reminiscences of boyhood; and by these our periodical reunions may be converted into friendships. The friendships too, which existed among fellow-students, and which have since decayed, may here be revived. Men, while at a distance from one another, are too apt to feel somewhat approaching to mutual dislike and suspicion, and to give way to the love of ridicule or detraction. But bring them often together by any motive which excites no jealous nor interested emotions, and they insensibly become friendly and united. Like the similar poles of different magnets, they seem embued with a power of mutual repulsion, until brought nearly into contact, when they attract and adhere to another. [Clement C. Moore, A.M., *Address Delivered Before the Alumni of Columbia College, on the 4th of May, 1825, in the Chapel of the College,* E. Bliss & E. White, 1825.[10]]

1828. Six-year-old daughter, Emily, died.

1829. Received doctoral degree.

1830. Wife, Eliza, died. She had given birth to three more children since 1822—William, Catherine and Maria Theresa (Terry)—a total of nine children in all. She died at age thirty-six of a "disordered frame." Several months later, daughter, Charity, died.

Expressed his despair over these deaths in a poem called:

"TO SOUTHEY

"... 'Tis when you sing of dear ones gone to rest,
I feel each fibre vibrate in my breast.
Alas! too well, bereavement's pangs I know;
Too well, a parent's and a husband's woe.

"To crown the num'rous blessings of my life,
I had sweet children and a lovely wife.
All seem'd so firm, so ordered to endure,
That, fool! I fancied all around secure.
Heav'n seem'd to smile; Hope wisper'd to my heart,

(From *The Night Before Christmas* by Clement C. Moore. Illustrated by Arthur Rackham.)

These love-wrought ties shall never rudely part;
But Time, with slow advance and gentle hand,
Shall loosen, one by one, each sacred band.
The old shall first drop peaceful in the tomb,
And leave the young to fill their vacant room. . . .

''But sad reality has prov'd how vain
This faithless prospect of a dreaming brain.
Death's icy hand, within three fleeting years,
Has chang'd this scene of bliss to sighs and tears.
One lovely innocent was snatch'd away—
A rose-bud, not half-open'd to the day—
I saw my wife, then, to the grave descend,
Beloved of my heart, my bosom friend.

''So interwoven were our joys, our pains,
That, as I weeping follow'd her remains,
I thought to tell her of the mournful scene—
I could not realize the gulph between.
This was not all; there was another blow
Reserv'd to put the finish to my woe.
A sweet endearing creature perish'd last,
In youth's first spring, all childhood's dangers past—
Oh! awful trial of religion's power,
To see a suffering innocent's last hour!

''But mark me well—I would not change one jot
Of Heaven's decrees, to meliorate my lot:
Farewell to earthly bliss, to all that's bright!

No thought rebels; I know, I feel 'tis right.
Nor should I mourn as though of all bereft:
Some transient pleasures, here and there, are left;
Some short-liv'd flowers that in the forest bloom,
And scatter fragrance in the settled gloom.

"I look not round, and peevishly repine,
As though no other sorrow equall'd mine.
I boast no proud preeminence of pain—
But oh! these spectres that infest my brain!
My death-struck child, with nostrils breathing wide,
Turning in vain, for ease, from side to side;
The fitful flush that lit her half-closed eye,
And burned her sunken cheek, her plaintive cry;
Her dying gasp; and, as she sank to rest,
Her wither'd hands cross'd gently o'er her breast.
My dying wife's emaciated form,
So late, with youthful spirit fresh and warm.
The deep, but noiseless anguish of her mind
At leaving all she lov'd on earth behind.

"The silent tear that down her cheek would stray,
And wet the pillow where resign'd she lay.
Her stiffen'd limbs, all powerless and weak;
Her clay-cold parting kiss; her pale damp cheek;
Her awful prayer for mercy, at the last,
Fainter and fainter, till her spirit pass'd—
The image of the next lov'd sufferer too
Is ever, ever present to my view.
Her ceaseless cough—her quick and panting breath,
With all the dreadful harbingers of death.
No anxious mother watching at her side,
To whisper consolation as she died.

"Oh! do not ask me why I thus complain
To you a stranger, far across the main—
Bear with a bleeding heart that loves to tell
Its sorrows, and on all its pangs to dwell.
A strange relief the mourner's bosom knows
In clinging close and closer to its woes.
In unheard plaints it consolation finds,
And weeps and murmurs to the heedless winds."[6]

Moore found it difficult to concentrate on every-day matters with tragedies coming one after another in his family.

His granddaughter wrote in a published recollection of Moore: "Mr. Moore never married again but lived with his widowed mother and large family in Chelsea.

"The city, however, gradually encroached on the quiet country place, and the house was finally pulled down to give way to the demands of the times. Mr. Moore then built for himself a house at the Southwest corner of 23rd St. and Ninth Avenue and one for my mother adjoining it. His summers were passed in Newport. . . ."[9]

1836. His daughter, Margaret, married John Doughty Ogden.

"For you, my Margaret dear. . . .

"I am not like the parent bird that tries
To lure its young-one from the fostering home;
That gladley sees its new-fledged offspring rise
On outspread wing, in distant shades to roam;

"Yet I were formed in Nature's sternest mood,
Did not my inmost soul with you rejoice,

To see your lot amid the wise and good,
The gentlest friends, the husband of your choice.[6]

Moore donated seven lots of ground for the erection of St. Peter's Church between 8th and 9th Avenues on 20th Street in Manhattan.

1838. The church was publicly consecrated. Moore became the first organist. His mother, Charity Clarke Moore, a deeply loved member of his household, died.

1844. A volume of his verses, *Poems,* was published. It included "A Visit from St. Nicholas." Shortly thereafter a review appeared in *Churchman.* "Everyone, nowadays, that can count his 10 digits, or can cause a few syllables to gingle (sic) together agreeably, deems himself . . . impregnated with the 'gift divine'. . . . It is really refreshing, therefore, to chance, in our barren pilgrimage, upon some beautiful exotics . . . the poems . . . exhibiting vivid powers of description, and much fertility of imagination, tempered with good taste and judgement; It is written in a happy humour, and evinces a shrewd insight of human nature. . . ." [*Churchman,* August 31, 1844.[11]]

April 18, 1845. Daughter, Margaret, died.

1848. Moore's fifth child and namesake, Clement, appeared to have suffered some mental disorders, causing his father considerable anxiety. "My son Clement is in so nervous and excitable a state of mind and body that it is impossible for him to continue the attempt to practise law. . . ."[1]

January 26, 1848. ". . . His irritability of fibre is such that any mental exertion throws him entirely off balance. When so excited, he can neither sleep nor read nor keep his attention directed to any one subject. He is now pretty well and appears to be easy and contented. But, were I to say anything to him about his office, he would, in all probability, be thrown again into a state of utter perplexity and confusion. He has agreed to remain quiet in his father's house, and endeavour to improve his mind as much as he can without over-straining it. What he may do when I am gone, God only knows; but, as long as I live, I shall feel it my duty to watch over him with parental care."[1]

1850. Resigned from his professorship at the General Theological Seminary.

Published his last major written work, a historical biography, entitled: *George Castroit, Surnamed Scanderbeg, King of Albania* a revision of an original work by Jacques Lavardin, a French historian of medieval time.

November 20, 1856. Moore began a diary. Some of its excerpts suggested his generosity.

"*Dec. 4, 1856*

. . . After tea Mr. Ball, a blind man, came to me and I gave him 20 dollars.

"*Dec. 9, 1856*

. . . Gave $5 for a Presbyterian Ch. to a chattering man.

"*Dec. 10, 1856*

. . . Sent to Mrs. Ray $5 for her ragged school.

"Jan. 15, 1857

. . . Had a visit in the evening from a long forward man with a little book. I gave him $3 for I do not exactly know what.

"Jan. 26

. . . I gave Mr. Oakley a dollar for a poor man; 3 dollars for a sabbath school to I know not who; and $5 to a young woman who brought a letter from her husband pleading sickness and want.

"March 17

. . . Gave a Jewish-looking fellow $10. Think I did wrong.

"March 30

. . . Received a letter from Mrs. Jane C. Adams of Claverack, begging for her lunatic sister. Sent her 10 dollars as a *donation* not as a *subscription.*

"Dec. 19

. . . Gave Mauri a dollar to get rid of him.

"Jan. 4, 1858

. . . A little book-man got $10 out of me. I begin to be suspicious of those men with little books.

"Jan. 6

. . . I gave $10 to a Hungarian . . . whose name I do not remember."

[Taken from the diary of Clement C. Moore.[12]]

Moore had acquired a great deal of real estate during his lifetime, both in and outside of Manhattan. Some of this property was used by his children. His son, Benjamin, and daughter-in-law Mary Elizabeth lived on the Moore estate in Sing Sing, N.Y. His house in Newport, R.I., was first a home to daughter Margaret during her marriage to John Ogden up to the time of her death and then passed to daughter Mary who married her sister, Margaret's widower in 1848.

During his retirement years, Moore travelled frequently to visit his relatives and grandchildren. His diary travelled with him.

"Nov. 19

. . . This morning we had a note from Eliza's [granddaughter's] father saying she died last night about midnight. She died very peacefully. God be praised.

"Nov. 21

. . . Eliza was buried this day next to her mother [Margaret] in my vault in St. Luke's churchyard.

"Oct. 1, 1862

I reived (sic) a letter from Ben this morning of which this is the beginning 'Sing Sing, Sept. 29th, 1862 2. O'clock P.M. My Dear Father, Elizabeth has just given us a fine bouncing girl.' "[12]

**His eyes how they twinkled!
His dimples how merry!**
■ (From *The Night Before Christmas* by Clement C. Moore. Illustrated by Hilary Knight.)

Moore's usually neat, copperplate handwriting became more untidy in the last pages of the diary: the ends of his lines began to tip, words and letters were left out and inserted later. There was no mention at all of feeling unwell. The last uneven entry occurred two days before his death, on a final visit to his daughter Mary in Newport:

"July 8, 1863

Foggy in the morning, clears off warm."[12]

July 10, 1863. Clement C. Moore died. He was buried alongside his wife and children in St. Luke's churchyard on Hudson St. However, in 1889, the entire family's resting place was moved to Trinity Church Cemetery on Upper Broadway, Manhattan. Children from the neighborhood have made annual pilgrimages on Christmas Eve to leave presents for the underprivileged at Clement C. Moore's grave and listen to the minister read out loud the famous poem, "A Visit from St. Nicholas."

Over forty editions of "The Night Before Christmas" are on record in the Library of Congress, many of them decorated by the world's finest illustrators.

FOR MORE INFORMATION SEE: R.W.G. Vail, "When Clement Clarke Moore was Young," *New York Historical Society Quarterly,* October, 1955; Vail, "Clement C. Moore's Courtship of His Laughter Loving Belle," *New York Historical Society Quarterly,* October, 1956; D. H. Hamilton, "Visit from St. Nicholas," *Hobbies,* December, 1956; Samuel W. Patterson, *Poet of Christmas Eve: A Life of Clement Clarke Moore, 1779-1863,* Morehouse, 1956; W. C. Skeath, "Night Before Christmas," *American Mercury,* December, 1957; Richard M. Ketchum, *Faces from the Past,* American Heritage Press, 1970; Clement Clarke Moore, *The Night Before Christmas* (facsimile of the original 1848 edition, with a biography of Moore by Arthur N. Hosking), Dover, 1971.

For children: Laura Benét, *Famous American Poets,* Dodd, 1950; M. Harmer, "Mr. Moore Writes a Poem," *American Childhood,* December, 1952; L. Benét, *Famous Poets for Young People,* Dodd, 1964.

MOORE, Janet Gaylord   1905-

PERSONAL: Born June 2, 1905, in Hanover, N.H.; daughter of Frank Gardner (a professor) and Anna B. (a children's librarian; maiden name, White) Moore. *Education:* Vassar College, B.A., 1927; also studied at Art Students League, New York, N.Y. *Politics:* Democrat. *Religion:* Protestant. *Home address:* Sand Beach Rd., Stonington, Maine 04681.

CAREER: Miss Hewitt's Elementary School, New York, N.Y., art teacher, 1939-43; Chance Vought Aircraft, Stratford, Conn., production illustration, 1943-45; Laurel School,

JANET GAYLORD MOORE

Shaker Heights, Ohio, head of art department, 1947-60; Cleveland Museum of Art, Cleveland, Ohio, supervisor for clubs and adult groups in the education department, 1961-72; The Cleveland Museum of Art, Department of Art History and Education, associate curator, 1967-72, curator, 1972; Case Western Reserve University, Cleveland, Ohio, adjunct assistant professor, 1967-72; writer and artist, 1973—. *Exhibitions:* May Show, The Cleveland Museum of Art and many group shows. *Awards, honors:* Newbery Honor Award for *The Many Ways of Seeing,* 1970.

WRITINGS: The Many Ways of Seeing: An Introduction to the Pleasures of Art, World Publishing, 1969; *The Eastern Gate: An Invitation to the Arts of China and Japan* (for high school students and young adults), Collins World, 1978.

SIDELIGHTS: Janet Moore has lived in Paris, Rome, and Peking. "*The Many Ways of Seeing* came out of my experience in secondary school. *The Eastern Gate* comes out of my experience with young people and adult groups in the oriental galleries at the Cleveland Museum of Art, and out of travel in China, Japan, and Taiwan. Both books owe something to my own experience as a painter."

HOBBIES AND OTHER INTERESTS: Drawing, painting, photography, European painting, Far Eastern art.

NORTON, Mary   1903-

PERSONAL: Born December 10, 1903, in London, Eng.; daughter of Reginald Spenser Pearson (a physician) and Mary Savile (Hughes) Pearson; married Robert Charles Norton (a shipping magnate) in 1927; children: Ann Mary, Robert George, Guy, Caroline. *Education:* Attended convent schools for eight years beginning at the age of eight. *Politics:* Liberal. *Religion:* Church of England. *Home:* Essex, Eng.

CAREER: Actress, author, playwright. Began acting career during the 1920's as a member of the "Old Vic" Shakespeare Company under Lillian Baylis; began writing articles, short stories, and children's books in the early 1940's; resumed acting career part-time, 1943, in London. *Wartime service:* Served two years with the British War Office, and two years with the British Purchasing Commission in New York, during World War II. *Member:* P.E.N. *Awards, honors:* Carnegie Medal, 1952, and Lewis Carroll Shelf Award, 1960, both for *The Borrowers;* American Library Association cited *The Borrowers* as one of the most distinguished books of the year, 1953.

WRITINGS: The Magic Bed-knob; or, How to Become a Witch in Ten Easy Lessons (illustrated by Waldo Peirce), Putnam, 1943; *Bonfires and Broomsticks* (illustrated by Mary Adshead), Dent, 1947; *The Borrowers* (ALA Notable Book; illustrated by Diana Stanley), Dent, 1952 [American edition illustrated by Beth and Joe Krush, Harcourt, 1953]; *The Borrowers Afield* (ALA Notable Book; illustrated by B. and J. Krush), Harcourt, 1955, reissued, 1970; *Bed-knob and Broomstick* (a combined edition of *The Magic Bed-knob* and *Bonfires and Broomsticks;* illustrated by Erik Blegvad), Harcourt, 1957, reissued, 1975; *The Borrowers Afloat* (illustrated by B. and J. Krush), Harcourt, 1959, reissued, 1973; *The Borrowers Aloft* (illustrated by B. and J. Krush) Harcourt, 1961, reissued 1974; *The Borrowers Omnibus* (illustrated by Diana Stanley), Dent, 1966, published in America as *The Complete Adventures of the Borrowers* (illustrated by B. and J. Krush), Harcourt, 1967; *Poor Stainless: A New Story about the Borrowers* (illustrated by B. and J. Krush),

The square was empty now, save for the soldiers and the huddled group of children beside the cattle pen. The ground was scattered with litter. Benches, chairs, and stools—things that people had brought to stand on—lay overturned and broken. ■ (From *Bedknobs and Broomsticks* by Mary Norton. Illustrated by Erik Blegvad.)

Harcourt, 1971; *Are All the Giants Dead?* (illustrated by Brian Froud), Harcourt, 1975; *Adventures of the Borrowers*, 4 volumes, Harcourt, 1975.

ADAPTATIONS: "Bed-knobs and Broomsticks" (motion picture starring Angela Lansbury, Roddy McDowall, and David Tomlinson), Walt Disney Productions, 1971; "The Borrowers," television special starring Eddie Albert, Tammy Grimes, and Judith Anderson, first shown December 14, 1973 on NBC; "The Borrowers" (sound recording read by Claire Bloom), Caedmon, 1974. BBC radio has also produced adaptations of *The Magic Bed-knob* and *Bonfires and Broomsticks*.

SIDELIGHTS: **December 10, 1903.** Mary Norton was born in London, England. Her father, a surgeon, could trace his ancestry back to the sixteenth century poet, Edmund Spenser.

1905. Family moved to the country. Norton's childhood was spent in a house much like the Firbank Hall described in her book, *The Borrowers*—"sunlit and creeper-hung, with lawns that sloped in terraces down to the river. There was a greenhouse which was almost a winter-garden, in which we kept (or rather, lost among the plants and flowering shrubs) a chameleon; and beyond the cedar trees there was a 'temple' with Doric pillars which later became a billiard room. We would have midnight feasts in here behind the piano which stood on a dais, making a nest of this secret corner with cushions robbed from the sofas. The great thrill was tiptoeing back across a moonlit lawn to the sleeping house—the sense of living warmth in the house and of human breath, compared with the bright, cool wilderness outside." [Roger Lancelyn Green, *Tellers of Tales*, Franklin Watts, 1965.[1]]

1911. Sent to a convent school. As the only girl among four brothers, Norton was naturally something of a tomboy. "When others saw the far hills, the distant woods, the soaring pheasant, I, as a child, would turn sideways to the close bank, the tree roots and the tangled grasses. Moss, fern-stalks, sorrel stems, created the mise en scène for a jungle drama, lacking in those days its dramatis personae. But one invented the characters—small, fearful people picking their way through miniature undergrowth; one saw smooth places where they might sit and rest: branched stems which might invite them to climb; sandy holes into which they might creep for shelter.

"All childhood has its lonely periods—the brisk 'run out and play' of harassed grown-ups: the 'stay-there-till-we-come-for-you' of elder brothers: and it was later I invented, for the sake of companionship, a way to people this tiny Eden. In those days before the First World War, one would buy small, china dolls with movable arms and flaxen hair, naked except for shoes and socks which were painted on. They stood about three or four inches high and were on sale among the lollipops in every village shop. It took no time at all to dress and disguise these and to assign to each its role. Water-colour, silver paint, odd pieces of coloured silk, tufts of black

(From the movie "Bedknobs and Broomsticks," starring Angela Lansbury and David Tomlinson. Copyright 1970 © by Walt Disney Productions.)

fur from a hearth rug—and here were one's puppets made. Infinitely docile, they played out great dramas for a child's entertainment, on smooth stages of sun-dried rock or among the green-lit shadows of the bracken—knights, ladies, fairies, witches. Joan of Arc was burned once, I remember, tied to her stake amid faggots of pine-needles. What a fire was there—with tears from me—while the bishops stood around.

"On the days when one was confined to the house, imagined excursions took place among the chair-legs and across the deep pile of the carpets. Here, the hazards were even greater: hearth and fire-irons for these tiny people took on almost nightmare properties. The sideboard, too, with its gleaming slippery silver, was rather frightening. No wonder they took to mouse-holes and the wainscot, creating their own small safety." [Jean de Temple, "The Magic of Mary Norton," *Ontario Library Bulletin,* November, 1958.[2]]

Norton later attended a more orthodox convent school for seven years. A sojourn in France followed and then she returned home to London. She recalled that "drawing turned out to be my forte, then acting and lastly, writing."

Early 1920's. Began a brief stage career. A family friend obtained an audition for Norton with the Old Vic Shakespeare Theatre. "Arthur Rose, a successful playwright and a beloved friend of the family, came to luncheon. I found, at last, the courage to say I wanted to act. 'Why not?' he said quick-

ly, before my parents could protest. If I would learn, say, two well-known speeches from Shakespeare, and recite them to him, he could gauge my chances in a flash."

1927. Stage career ended when she married Robert Charles Norton. For several years the Nortons and their four children lived in Portugal, where her husband's family of shipowners lived and traded. "We were very cut off as the roads were so bad (no government staying in power long enough to repair them) that it was a little world—with its home farm, smithy, stone mason, etc., and miles of pinewoods and cork trees. There was a man, I remember, whose only job was to paint shutters and when he reached the point at which he had started, it was time to go around again. . . . We lived an isolated life, but it was a paradise for children. We had four, Ann, Robert, Guy and Caroline."

1929. The Great Depression, which followed the American stockmarket crash, reached Europe. Norton's family suffered financial loss. "Things went very wrong with the trade and shipping and we became gradually poorer. Very gradually; it was like walking into a cold sea inch by inch, staving off with tenuous hopes the still avoidable shock. When it came at last, it was almost a relief. Everything went—houses, land, cargo, ships, tugs, lighters, copper mines. . . ."

Early 1940's. Family left Portugal when World War II erupted. Norton returned to England where she worked in

MARY NORTON

the War Office for two years until transferred to New York with her children. "We managed at last to rent a little house in Connecticut and schools were found. But none of this would have been possible without the unforgettable and amazing kindness of American friends. My job did not bring in quite enough to support a house and children, so it was here I began to write in grim earnest—at night, after the children were in bed—short stories, articles, translations from the Portuguese. Later I thought of writing down some of the stories I told my children. We stayed two years instead of one, and in 1943, London again, in the street where we still live. I wrote during the flying bomb period the book now called *Bed-knob and Broomstick*." [Edna Johnson, *Anthology of Children's Literature*, 4th edition, Houghton Mifflin, 1970.³]

1945. During the final days of World War II, Norton's eyes were injured by an explosion of a V-2 Bomb, but her sight was restored with an operation. "The operation was successful and I remember driving home through sunlit streets, looking at the world through pin-point holes in blacked-out spectacles—and an exquisite world it was."

1952. Won the Carnegie Medal for her book, *The Borrowers*. "I did not quite look upon it as a children's book: it has something of the whole human dilemma—a microcosm of our world and the powers which rule us. In each generation, only youth is restless and brave enough to try to get out from 'under the floorboards.'"

Norton lives in a cottage in Essex, England. She is a member of the P.E.N. club and reports that her list of favorite authors is endless.

HOBBIES AND OTHER INTERESTS: Swimming, riding, and unnecessary travel.

FOR MORE INFORMATION SEE: J. de Temple, "Magic of Mary Norton," *Ontario Library Review*, November, 1958; Roger Lancelyn Green, *Teller of Tales*, Franklin Watts, 1965; Brian Doyle, editor, *Who's Who of Children's Literature*, Schocken, 1968; Norah Smaridge, *Famous Modern Storytellers for Young People*, Dodd, 1969; Edna Johnson, *Anthology of Children's Literature*, 4th edition, Houghton Mifflin, 1970; Doris de Montreville and Donna Hill, editors, *Third Book of Junior Authors*, Wilson, 1972.

PAYZANT, Charles

WRITINGS: Moko, the Circus Monkey (illustrated by Ted Parmelee), Avon, 1952.

All written with Terry Shannon, pseudonym of Jessie Mercer: *Today Is Story Day: A Tale for Every Day in the Week*, Aladdin, 1954; *Project Sealab: The Story of the U. S. Navy's Man-in-the-Sea Program*, Golden Gate, 1966; *The Sea Searchers: Men and Machines at the Bottom of the Sea*, Golden Gate, 1968; *Smokejumpers and Fire Divers: Firefighters of Forests and Harbors*, Golden Gate, 1969; *Ride the Ice Down! U. S. and Canadian Icebreakers in Arctic Seas*, Golden Gate, 1970; *Zoo Safari: The New Look in Zoos*, Golden Gate, 1971; *New at the Zoo: Animal Offspring from Aardvark to Zebra*, Golden Gate, 1972; *Windows in the Sea: New Vehicles That Span the Ocean Depths*, Childrens Press, 1973; *Antarctic Challenge: Probing the Mysteries of the White Continent*, Chidrens Press, 1973.

(From *New at the Zoo* by Terry Shannon and Charles Payzant. Photograph by W. Brindle, courtesy of the Australian News and Information Bureau.)

Charles Payzant, with his wife, Terry Shannon.

Illustrator; all written by Terry Shannon, pseudonym of Jessie Mercer: *Jumper, Santa's Little Reindeer,* Jolly Books, 1952; *Wheels Across America,* Aladdin, 1954; *Little Wolf the Rain Dancer,* Whitman, 1954; *Tyee's Totem Pole,* Whitman, 1955; *At Water's Edge,* Sterling, 1955; *Among the Rocks,* Sterling, 1956; *Come Summer, Come Winter: The Picture Story of Nature's Yearly Cycle,* Whitman, 1956; *Running Fox, the Eagle Hunter* (Junior Literary Guild selection), Whitman, 1957; *Desert Dwellers,* Whitman, 1958; *Where Animals Live,* Whitman, 1958; *Kidlik's Kayak* (Junior Literary Guild selection), Whitman, 1959; *A Trip to Paris,* Whitman, 1959.

Wonderland of Plants, Whitman, 1960; *About Caves,* Melmont, 1960; *About Food and Where It Comes From,* Melmont, 1961; *A Trip to Mexico,* Childrens Press, 1961; *About Ready-to-Wear Clothes,* Melmont, 1961; *And Juan,* Whitman, 1961; *A Dog Team for Ongluk,* Melmont, 1962; *Stones, Bones, and Arrowheads,* Whitman, 1962; *Trail of the Wheel,* Golden Gate, 1962; *About the Land, the Rain, and Us,* Melmont, 1963; *A Playmate for Puna,* Melmont, 1963; *Red Is for Luck,* Golden Gate, 1963; *A Trip to Quebec,* Childrens Press, 1963; *Wakapoo and the Flying Arrows,* Whitman, 1963; *Around the World with Gogo,* Golden Gate, 1964; *Saucer in the Sea: The Story of the Cousteau Diving Saucer in Pacific Coast Waters,* Golden Gate, 1965; *Sentinels of Our Shores: The Story of Lighthouses, Lightships, and Buoys,* Golden Gate, 1969; *Children of Hong Kong,* Childrens Press, 1975.

PECK, Anne Merriman 1884-

PERSONAL: Born July 21, 1884, in Piermont-on-Hudson, N.Y.; daughter of a clergyman; children: one son. *Education:* Attended Hartford Art School and the New York School of Fine and Applied Art. *Residence:* Tucson, Ariz.

CAREER: Author and illustrator of books for children, and painter. Has taught courses in writing and illustrating for children through the University of Arizona Extension Division.

WRITINGS—All for children: *A Vagabond's Provence* (illustrated by the author), Dodd, Mead, 1929; *Storybook Europe* (illustrated by the author), Harper, 1929; *Young Germany,* R. McBride, 1931; *Roundabout Europe* (illustrated by the author), Harper, 1931; (with Enid Johnson) *Wings Over Holland* (illustrated by the author), Macmillan, 1932; (with E. Johnson) *Roundabout America* (illustrated by the author), Harper, 1933; *Young Mexico* (illustrated by the author), R. McBride, 1934, enlarged edition, 1948; (with E. Johnson) *Young Americans from Many Lands* (illustrated by the author), Whitman, 1935; (with Edmond A. Meras) *France: Crossroads of Europe,* Harper, 1936; (with E. A. Meras) *Spain in Europe and America,* Harper, 1937; *Rene and Paton* (illustrated by the author), Whitman, 1938; (with E. Johnson) *Ho for Californy!* (illustrated by the author), Harper, 1939; *Belgium* (illustrated by Alexandre Serebriakoff), Harper, 1940; *Roundabout South America* (illustrated by the author), Harper, 1940; *The Pageant of South American History*, Longmans, Green, 1941, 3rd edition, D. McKay, 1962; *Manoel and the Morning Star* (illustrated by the author), Harper, 1943; *Young Canada* (illustrated by the author), R. McBride, 1943; *The Pageant of Canadian History*, Longmans, Green, 1943, 2nd edition, D. McKay, 1963; *The Pageant of Middle American History* (illustrated by the author), Longmans, Green, 1947, reissued, D. McKay, 1963; (with E. Johnson) *Big, Bright Land*, Grosset, 1947, reissued, 1961; *Southwest Roundup* (illustrated by the author), Dodd, Mead, 1950; *Jo Ann of the Border Country*, Dodd, Mead, 1952; *The March of Arizona History* (illustrated by the author), Arizona Silhouettes, 1962; (with Dorothy and Frank Getlein) *Wings of an Eagle: The Story of Michelangelo* (illustrated by Lili Rethi), Hawthorn Books, 1963.

Illustrator: Charlotte M. Yonge, *Little Lucy's Wonderful Globe*, Harper, 1927; Alice Dussauze, *Little Jack Rabbit*, Macmillan, 1927; Rene Bazin, *Juniper Farm*, Macmillan, 1928; Enid Johnson, *Runaway Balboa*, Harper, 1938; Hope H. Newell, *Steppin and Family*, Oxford University Press, 1942; H. H. Newell, *Cinder Ike*, Nelson, 1942; Newell, *Little Old Woman Carries On*, Nelson, 1947; Newell, *Story of Christina*, Harper, 1947; Christine N. Govan, *Mr. Hermit Miser and the Neighborly Pumpkin*, Aladdin, 1949; Gertrude Crampton, *Pottlebys*, Aladdin, 1949; G. Crampton, *More Pottleby Adventures*, Aladdin, 1950; Catherine Blanton,

The street leading out to the hills. ■ (From *A Vagabond's Provence* by Anne Merriman Peck. Illustrated by the author.)

ANNE MERRIMAN PECK

Trouble on Old Smoky, Whittlesey House, 1951; G. Crampton, *Further Pottleby Adventures*, Aladdin, 1951; (with Margaret Ruse) H. H. Newell, *The Little Old Woman Who Used Her Head, and Other Stories*, Nelson, 1973

SIDELIGHTS: **July 21, 1884.** Born in Piermont, New York. Childhood was spent on Long Island and in Connecticut. "Drawing and painting were my chief interest from childhood, so that when it was a question of choosing between college and art school, I chose the latter. After studying painting and design came a period of painting portraits of children and illustrating fairy tales. Then my interest in people and my urge to see the world led to vagabond painting and study trips to Europe." [Bertha M. Miller, and others, compilers, *Illustrators of Children's Books, 1946-1956*, Horn Book, 1958.[1]]

1929. Began a life-long career in writing and illustrating books for young people. At an early age Peck developed a fondness for travel, and through her books, shared that enthusiasm with children. "Out of these trips came commissions to write travel books for young people, illustrated with my drawings. Illustrative work turned my attention to graphic arts, particularly woodcuts and lithographs. Travel in Latin America resulted in more books, among them *Round-About South America*, 1940, with art work in this period mostly confined to illustrations for my own books and those of writer friends. The artist's record of people, customs and beautiful landscapes adds to the writer's record of ways of life and history."[1]

Peck has lived in Arizona where she taught courses in illustrating and writing children's books at the University. "I have now become a permanent resident of Arizona; my home is in Tucson. The beautiful Arizona desert country is my inspiration for painting in times of leisure, and regional material of the vivid, interesting Southwest captures my mind for writing. Painting, particularly children's portraits, occupies much of my time, with some illustration added. I am active in the art organizations of Tucson, and I teach two classes in the Extension Division of the University of Arizona: Writing for Children and Young People, and Children's Book Illustration, utilizing my experiences from a good many years in the children's book field.''[1]

Among Peck's early books was *Storybook Europe*, reviewed in the *New York Times:* ''The author has managed to be replete without being verbose, and of quietly inculcating enthusiasm rather than striving for it by staccato enthusiasms of her own.'' The *New York Times* also reviewed *Vagabond's Provence:* ''Her book will be wholly delightful to people who enjoy this kind of informal traveling. . . . There is much history in the book, but all historical references are narrated in a style so fresh and lively that the whole work, whether engaged with the immediate surroundings or the ancient past, is keyed upon a human note that makes its narrative as entertaining as it is informing about a little-known place and people.''

FOR MORE INFORMATION SEE: New York Times, July 28, 1929, October 13, 1929, July 9, 1950; Stanley J. Kunitz and Howard Haycraft, editors, *Junior Book of Authors,* H. W. Wilson, 1934, 2nd edition, revised, 1951; Bertha E. Mahony and others, compilers, *Illustrators of Children's Books, 1744-1945,* Horn Book, 1947; *New York Herald Tribune Book Review,* June 4, 1950; Bertha M. Miller, and others, compilers, *Illustrators of Children's Books, 1946-1956,* Horn Book, 1958.

PECK, Richard   1934-

PERSONAL: Born April 5, 1934, in Decatur Ill.; son of Wayne M. (a merchant) and Virginia (Gray) Peck. *Education:* Attended University of Exeter, 1954-55; DePauw University, B.A., 1956; Southern Illinois University, M.A., 1959; further graduate study at Washington University, 1960-61. *Home:* 10 Mitchell Pl. #4A, New York, N.Y. 10017. *Agent:* Sheldon Fogelman, 10 East 40th St., New York, N.Y. 10016.

CAREER: Southern Illinois University, Carbondale, instructor in English, 1958-60; Glenbrook High School, Northbrook, Ill., teacher of English, 1961-63; Scott, Foresman Co., Chicago, Ill., textbook editor, 1963-65; Hunter College and Hunter College High School, New York, N.Y., instructor in English and education, 1965-71; writer, 1971—. Assistant director of Council for Basic Education, Washington, D.C., 1969-70. *Military service:* U.S. Army, 1956-58; served in Stuttgart, Germany. *Member:* Author's Guild. *Awards, honors:* National Council for the Advancement of Education Writing award, 1971; Friends of American Writers award, 1976, for *The Ghost Belonged to Me;* Edgar Allan Poe Award from Mystery Writers of America, 1976, for *Are You in the House Alone?;* named Illinois Writer of the Year, 1977, by Illinois Association of Teachers of English.

WRITINGS: (With Norman Strasma) *Old Town, A Complete Guide: Strolling, Shopping, Supping, Sipping,* 2nd edition, [Chicago], 1965; (editor with Ned E. Hoopes) *Edge of Awareness: 25 Contemporary Essays,* Dell, 1966; (editor with Ned E. Hoopes) *Sounds and Silences: Poetry for Now,* Delacorte, 1970; (editor) *Mindscapes: Poems for the Real World,* Delacorte, 1971; (editor) *Leap Into Reality,* Dell, 1972; *Don't Look and It Won't Hurt* (young adult), Holt, 1972; (with Stephen N. Judy) *The Creative Word,* Volume II (Peck was not associated with other volumes), Random

House/Singer School Division, 1973; *Dreamland Lake* (young adult), Holt, 1973; *Through A Brief Darkness* (young adult), Viking, 1973; (compiler) *Transitions: A Literary Paper Casebook,* Random House, 1974; *Representing Super Doll* (young adult), Viking, 1974; *The Ghost Belonged to Me* (young adult), Viking, 1975; *Are You in the House Alone?* (young adult), Viking, 1976; (editor) *Pictures That Storm Inside My Head,* Avon, 1976; *Monster Night at Grandma's House* (juvenile), Viking, 1977; *Ghosts I have Been,* Viking, 1977; *Father Figure* (young adult), Viking, 1978; *Secrets of the Shopping Mall* (young adult), Delacorte, 1979; *AMANDA/MIRANDA,* Viking, 1980.

Author of column on the architecture of historic neighborhoods for New York *Times.* Contributor of poetry to several anthologies *Saturday Review* and Chicago *Tribune* Magazine. Contributor of articles to periodicals including *American Libraries, PTA* Magazine and *Parent's Magazine.*

SIDELIGHTS: **April 5, 1934.** Born in Decatur, Illinois. ''I suspect that anybody who's embarked on the choppy seas of writing for a living has a different tale to tell about how he got started—and how he keeps going. I stumbled into this bewildering field by accident.

''I never was one of those young people who fell from the cradle and landed on the typewriter. I didn't write a six-hundred-page autobiographical novel in the bowels of Greenwich Village at age twenty. If I had, I'd be in another line of work today. And fortunately I never had one of those English teachers who say, 'Write what you know!' 'Write from your heart!' My teachers stressed vocabulary, the card catalogue, and the declarative sentence.

''But I was heading for a writer's career long before I went to school, when my mother read to me. This was shortly after books had been invented and well before *Sesame Street.* Without a TV to hypnotize me, I had to settle for a mother who was willing to curl up with me and a book. A satisfactory substitute for this technique has yet to be devised.''

1954-1955. Attended Exeter University in England.

1956. Received his B.A. degree from DePauw University.

1956-1958. Served in the U.S. Army. ''The Scene shifts now from my mother's knee in Decatur, Illinois, to an army field post outside Ansbach, Germany. It was in this unlikely, muddy locale, that I found out the advantage of writing. I learned that if you can type, punctuate, spell, and improvise in mid-sentence, you can work in a clean dry office near a warm stove. Otherwise, you're at the mercy of the elements and the sergeants. I became an army clerk, and then I invented a whole new career for myself. I became a ghost-writer of sermons for chaplains (all denominations). That way, I passed a pious, pleasant, and perfectly dry army hitch and sensed the power of the written word.

''The army is a more instructive experience than college, but I wouldn't sell my university days short. They were divided between a private college in Indiana—DePauw; a college in England—Exeter; and a mammoth school for graduate study—Southern Illinois University.''

1959. Received his M.A. degree from Southern Illinois University. ''I spent the waning days of my growing-up roaming among foreign cultures. And I was learning to be alone, which is of course the only way a writer can work, whenever he begins to do it in earnest.''

So, just as he did every August night, Toby climbed the tall stairs, counting the steps. ■ (From *Monster Night at Grandma's House* by Richard Peck. Illustrated by Don Freeman.)

From 1958 to 1960 Peck was an English instructor at Southern Illinois University.

1961-1963. Worked as an English teacher at Glenbrook High School in Northbrook, Illinois. ''In our country an extraordinary number of fiction writers come from three fields: journalism, advertising, and teaching. What these three fields as seedbeds seem to offer the prospective writer are evocative language, communication with strangers, and deadlines.

''I chose teaching. In the classroom I identified my potential readers: they were the students who could be won to reading. I learned that the best, most independent, most promising students are the thoughtful, quiet ones—often in the back row—who'll reach for a book in search of themselves, the ones who often get overlooked in our crisis-oriented schools.''

1963-1965. Worked as a textbook editor for Scott, Foresman Company in Chicago, Ill.

1965-1971. Instructor in English and education at Hunter College and Hunter College High School in New York City.

1969-1970. Assistant director of the Council for Basic Education in Washington, D.C. ''Many young people today are just like young people have always been—anxious to be as adult as possible. But many are not. Many are patients in the remedial reading clinic. Some of them appear to be terminal cases. The permissive home and the watered-down school curriculum have betrayed them. The basic skills were not imposed, and attention spans were not stretched. There are college freshmen abroad in the land who aren't ready for a

RICHARD PECK

seventh-grade textbook." [Richard Peck, "In the Country of Teenage Fiction," *American Libraries,* April, 1973.[1]]

1971. Resigned from teaching to pursue a writing career. "One day . . . I gave up teaching. I didn't want to, but teaching had begun to turn into something weirdly like psychiatric social work—a field in which I was not trained. I turned in my pension and hospitalization plan and my attendance book—which was, come to think of it, the first work of fiction I ever wrote. I moved my typewriter out into a sweltering, silent garden, and I began writing a novel to some of the young people I'd left behind in the schoolroom."

1972. First young adult novel, *Don't Look and It Won't Hurt,* was published. Prior to his fictional writing, Peck had edited contemporary poetry and non-fiction anthologies for young adults. "Writing for today's young has very little to do with remembering your own growing up. The underlying themes are the same, but the externals are different. Still, books are bridges—between people and between generations. When I walk into a school today and inhale that nostalgic scent of bubble gum, chalk dust, and anxiety, I slip down through a time warp. I'm suddenly back in the eighth grade again, circa 1948, hoping daily to be kidnapped by desperadoes before Miss Letty Jones's fourth-period math class. And wishing some kindly fate would hurry up and make me older. That wish came true."

1976. *Are You in the House Alone?* and *Pictures that Storm Inside My Head* were published. Received the Friends of American Writers Award and the Edgar Allan Poe Award from Mystery Writers of America for that year. "It seems to

me that trying to write a valid novel for a young reader—let's say a thirteen-year-old who is at a sensitive and troubled point in life—is at least as important and far more challenging than writing a 'real, adult novel.'

"It's a harder job because of the pitfalls. No one who has passed through adolescence can re-enter it with vision unblurred by personal nostalgia and the kind of publicity the current youth scene receives. It's a great temptation to preach, to patronize, to pander, to placate, and especially to propagandize. And, of course, most writers of juvenile fiction will never see . . . let us say, twenty-five again."[1]

1977. Named Illinois Writer of the Year by the Illinois Association of Teachers of English. Two more Peck novels, *Monster Night at Grandma's House* (juvenile) and *Ghosts I Have Been* were published. "The best juvenile novels, like all novels, are the rarities. The renegades that allow a little liberating laughter. The ones that raise human questions without providing pat solutions and stock scapegoats. Those that recognize and salute youth as a part of the continuum of life.

"In another place and age, Beatrix Potter, the creator of Peter Rabbit, wrote, 'My books were made small to fit children's hands, not to impress grown-ups.' Striking the right chord in that tentative time between childhood and adulthood is another matter. One which most authors haven't mastered."[1]

1978. *Father Figure* was published by Viking. ". . . When I was the teacher, I learned a lot about my students from what they wrote in their compositions. Today, I learn about my readers from the letters they send me. But I never can really know all I want to about those readers. Writing remains the act of reaching out in the dark, hoping for a hand to grasp. And that's where my story ends. For from that time on, my books have to speak for me—or remain silent."

In addition, "most youngsters, particularly the readers among them, are seeking shelter, or at least a place to catch their breath. In an age of sagging adult authority, they increasingly seek shelter from the tyranny of their peers. Too few books are reflecting their need to grow independently, without marching behind other people's causes and without looking back at their parents in anger. Too few books are fulfilling their need for solace and even friendship. There is sex-violence-social problems on the one hand, Tolkien fantasy on the other. And not enough middle ground."

In an *English Journal* interview Peck outlined some important elements in young adult fiction. First of all, the "signal factor" of the genre is "unreality masked as realism. One way or another, the protagonist has to do something that the reader cannot do." Whether "deadly serious" or "melodramatically absurd," the protagonist should "act on behalf of the reader in a particularly direct way." For this reason, travel is an important event for Peck's characters. "We have to remember that our readers are institutionalized twice—in homes and in schools. They set great store in mobility." Finally, Peck claimed comedy is "a major lack in young adult fiction today. We have a great deal of diversity in subject matter and approach and style, but we don't have enough humor. We need more because the young don't generate it themselves."

FOR MORE INFORMATION SEE: American Libraries, April, 1973; *Psychology Today,* September, 1975; *Horn Book,* October, 1975, February, 1977; *English Journal,* February, 1976; *Times Literary Supplement,* March 25, 1977.

KATHY PELTA

PELTA, Kathy 1928-

PERSONAL: Born October 18, 1928, in Madrid, Iowa; daughter of Edwin H. (an engineer) and Kathryn (Zenor) Birdsall; married Edmond Pelta (an engineer), February 22, 1957; children: Brian, Meg. *Education:* San Diego State College (now University), A.B., 1949; graduate study at University of California, Berkeley, 1949-51.

CAREER: U.S. Foreign Service, Bonn, Germany, 1951-54; Voice of America, Washington, D.C., secretary, 1954-55; Rand Corp., Santa Monica, Calif., technical writer, 1956-57; System Development Corp., Santa Monica, Calif., technical writer, 1957-60; free-lance writer, 1960—.

WRITINGS—For children: *What Does a Lifeguard Do?*, Dodd, 1977; *What Does a Paramedic Do?*, Dodd, 1978.

WORK IN PROGRESS: Additional juvenile books for the career series for Dodd.

SIDELIGHTS: "Writing is my first love, art my second. I enjoy working in silkscreen, woodblock, and pen and ink."

Dory races are a traditional event at lifeguard games, and a good way for lifeguards to stay in condition. ■ (From *What Does a Lifeguard Do?* by Kathy Pelta.)

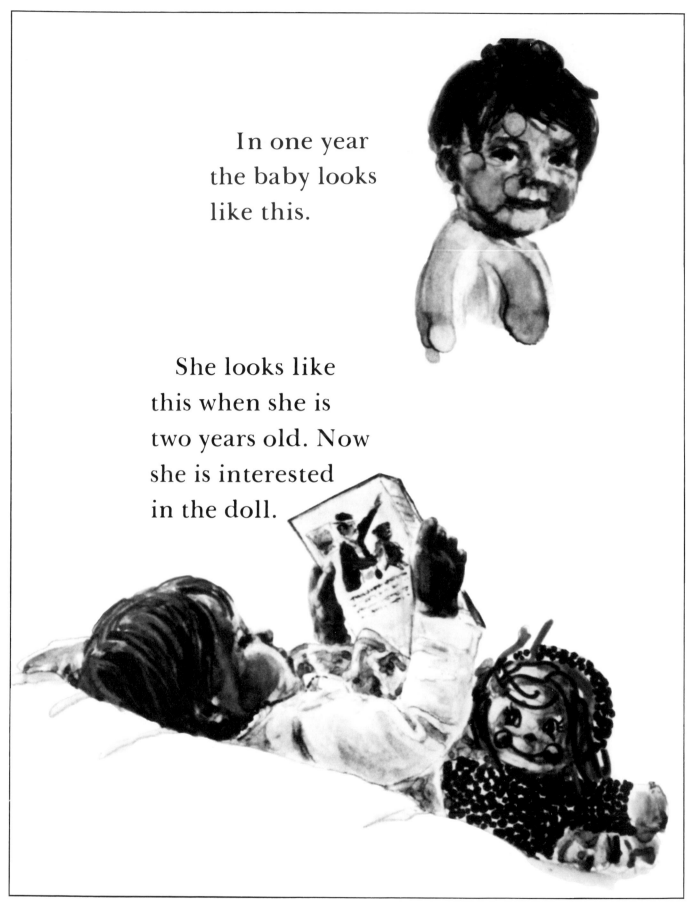

In one year
the baby looks
like this.

She looks like
this when she is
two years old. Now
she is interested
in the doll.

(From *Living Things Change* by Illa Podendorf. Illustrated by Darrell Wiskur.)

PODENDORF, Illa E.

EDUCATION: Drake University, B.S., 1934, University of Iowa, M.S., 1942. *Residence:* Chicago, Ill.

CAREER: University of Chicago Laboratory School, Chicago, Ill., chairman of science department, beginning 1954; author of non-fiction science books for children. Has lectured extensively on teaching science. *Member:* American Association for the Advancement of Science, National Science Teachers Association, Central Association of Science and Math Teachers, Council of Elementary Science Instructors.

WRITINGS—''True Book'' series, published by Childrens Press, except as indicated: *The True Book of Science Experiments* (illustrated by Mary Salem), 1954; . . . *Pebbles and Shells* (illustrated by Mary Gehr), 1954, reissued as *My Easy-to-Read True Book of Pebbles and Shells,* Grosset, 1960; . . . *Insects* (illustrated by Chauncey Maltman), 1954; . . . *Trees* (illustrated by Richard Gates), 1954, reissued as *My Easy-to-Read True Book of Trees,* Grosset, 1960; . . . *Pets* (illustrated by Bill Armstrong), 1954, reissued as *My Easy-to-Read True Book of Pets,* Grosset, 1960; . . . *Animal Babies* (illustrated by Pauline Adams), 1955; . . . *Seasons* (illustrated by M. Gehr), 1955; . . . *Sounds We Hear* (illustrated by C. Maltman), 1955; . . . *Weeds and Wild Flowers* (illustrated by M. Gehr), 1955; . . . *Animals of the Sea and Shore* (illustrated by C. Maltman), 1956, revised edition published as *The True Book of Animals of the Sea and Shore,* 1970; . . . *More Science Experiments* (illustrated by Maltman), 1956; . . . *Rocks and Minerals* (illustrated by George Rhoads), 1958, reissued as *My Easy-to-Read True Book of Rocks and Minerals,* Grosset, 1959; . . . *Space* (illustrated by Robert Borja), 1959, reissued as *My Easy-to-Read Book of Space,* Grosset, 1960; . . . *Jungles* (illustrated by Katherine Grace), 1959; . . . *Plant Experiments* (illustrated by B. Armstrong), 1960; . . . *Animal Homes* (illustrated by John Hawkinson), 1960; . . . *Weather Experiments* (illustrated by Felix Palm), 1961; . . . *Magnets and Electricity* (illustrated by R. Borja), 1961; . . . *Spiders* (illustrated by Betsy Warren), 1962; . . . *Energy* (illustrated by George Wilde), 1963, revised edition, 1971.

Other writings; all published by Childrens Press, except as noted: (Editor) Margaret R. Friskey, *Johnny and the Monarch,* 1946; (with Bertha M. Parker) *Animal World* (illustrated by Gregory Orloff), Row, Peterson, 1949; (with B. M. Parker) *The Plant World* (illustrated by Louise Fulton), Row, Peterson, 1949; (with Parker) *Domesticated Plants* (illustrated by Arnold W. Ryan), Row, Peterson, 1959; *101 Science Experiments* (illustrated by R. Borja), 1960, reprinted, Grosset & Dunlap, 1974; *Discovering Science on Your Own* (illustrated by Borja), 1962; *Animals and More Animals* (illustrated by Elizabeth Rice), 1970; *Toby on the Move* (illustrated by Roger Herrington), 1970; *Food Is for Eating* (illustrated by Margrit Fiddle), 1970; *Many Is How Many?* (illustrated by Jack Haesly), 1970; *Things Are Made to Move* (illustrated by Jane Ike), 1970; *Things Are Alike and Different* (illustrated by J. Hawkinson), 1970; *Sound All About* (illustrated by Darrell Wiskur), 1970; *Shapes: Sides, Curves, and Corners* (illustrated by Frank Rakoncay), 1970.

Predicting with Plants (illustrated by Tom Dunnington), 1971; *Shadows and More Shadows* (illustrated by D. Wiskur), 1971; *Magnets* (illustrated by Jim Temple), 1971; *Living Things Change* (illustrated by D. Wiskur), 1971; *How Big Is a Stick?* (illustrated by Richard Mlodock), 1971; *Every*

Day Is Earth Day (illustrated by J. Hawkinson), 1971; *Color* (illustrated by Wayne Stuart), 1971; *Who, What, and When* (illustrated by Sharon Elzaurdia), 1971; *Change and Time* (illustrated by Frances Eckart), 1971; *Tools for Observing* (illustrated by Donald Charles), 1971; *Touching for Telling* (illustrated by Florence Frederick), 1971; *Things to Do with Water* (illustrated by Larry Winborg), 1971; *Plant and Animal Ways,* Standard Educational Corp., 1974.

QUIN-HARKIN, Janet   1941-

PERSONAL: Born September 24, 1941, in Bath, England; came to the United States in 1966; daughter of Frank Newcombe (an engineer) and Margery (a teacher; maiden name, Rees) Lee; married John Quin-Harkin (an airline sales manager), November 26, 1966; children: Clare, Anne, Jane, Dominic. *Education:* University of London, B.A. (honors), 1963; graduate study at University of Kiel and University of Freiburg. *Religion:* Roman Catholic. *Home:* 74 Brandon Rd., Conroe, Tex. 77301.

CAREER: British Broadcasting Corp., London, England, studio manager in drama department, 1963-66; teacher of dance and drama, 1971—. Founder and director of San Rafael Children's Little Theater. *Member:* Associated Authors of Children's Literature. *Awards, honors:* Peter Penny's Dance was named outstanding book by *New York Times* and best book of the year by *School Library Journal* and Children's Book Showcase, all in 1976.

WRITINGS: (Contributor) Lawrence Carillo and Dorothy McKinley, editors, *Chandler Reading Program,* five volumes, Noble & Noble, 1967-72; *Peter Penny's Dance* (juvenile), Dial, 1976; *Benjamin's Balloon* (juvenile), Parents' Magazine Press, 1979; *Septimus Bean and His Amazing Machine* (juvenile), Parents' Magazine Press, 1979. Author of radio plays and scripts, including ''Dandelion Hours,'' for

JANET QUIN-HARKIN

Long ago on a ship of the King's Navy there lived a sailor named Peter Penny, who could dance the sailor's hornpipe better than any other man. ■ (From *Peter Penny's Dance* by Janet Quin-Harkin. Illustrated by Anita Lobel.)

British Broadcasting Corp., 1966. Contributor to education journals, *Scholastic,* and *Mother's Manual.*

WORK IN PROGRESS: Two juvenile novels, one on the past, the other on refugees in World War II.

SIDELIGHTS: "I enjoy writing for children because it is a very positive medium. You can be optimistic, indulge in fantasy and have a happy ending. What's more, you don't have to introduce sex and violence to make it sell. Also, in common with many writers for children, I don't think I ever grew up. When I write a book with an eleven year old heroine, that child is ME. I still get a very child-like delight from new experiences, from beautiful scenery, from being in the midst of nature. Children are such fine, uncomplicated beings. They accept that the world is full of magic and wonder, not try to find the scientific proof behind it. Think of the opening of Stuart Little. No child questions why Mrs. Little's second son should happen to have been born a mouse. This is what I enjoy about writing fantasy. As long as the fantasy world is true to itself, once established, it can behave in any way under the sun.

"I am particularly interested in travel. Since the first time I crossed Europe alone at the age of thirteen, I feel restless if I don't wander every few months. I have visited most parts of the globe, including a three-month stay in Greece and a year in Australia. I have made four trips to India, which I find fascinating. My love of travel is reflected in everything I write. My characters can never stay in one place."

Quin-Harkin has also written four full-length radio plays and over twelve documentary features.

REGGIANI, Renée

PERSONAL: Born in Milan, Italy; married Luciantonio Ruggieri (a playwright). *Education:* National Academy of Theatre, Rome, Italy, received diploma, 1951; University of Aix-en-Provence, degree, 1948. *Home:* Corzo Vittorio Emanuele 24, Rome, Italy. *Agent:* Nina Froud, 14 Beaumont Mews, Marylebone High St., London W1N 4HE, England. *Office:* Televisione Italiana, Viale Mazzini 14, Rome, Italy.

CAREER: Writer; creator and producer of television programs. Televisione Italiana, Rome, writer, 1955—. *Awards, honors:* Premio Ente Nazionale Biblioteche Popolari e Scolastiche, 1956, Hans Christian Andersen Award, 1962, both for *Le avventure di cinque ragazzi e un cane;* Premio Laura Orvieto, 1964, for *Domani dopodomani;* Europa-Dralon

Award, 1965, for *Il treno del sole;* Premio Villa Taranto, 1966, for *Lo Spaventapasseri;* Premio Internazionale Europeo Citta di Caorle, 1968, for *Carla degli Scavi.*

WRITINGS—In English: *Le avventure di cinque ragazzi e un cane,* L. Cappelli, 1960, translation by Mary Lambert and Anne Chisholm published as *Five Children and a Dog,* Coward, 1965, new Italian edition published as *Quando i sogni non hanno soldi* (title means "When Dreams Have No Money"), F. lli Fabbri, 1971; *Il treno del sole,* Garzanti, 1961, translation by Patrick Creagh published as *The Sun Train,* Coward, 1966; *Domani dopodomani,* Vallecchi, translation by Chisholm published as *Tomorrow and the Next Day,* Coward, 1967.

In Italian: *Strane avventure di una meravigliosa estate* (juvenile; title means "Strange Adventures of a Wonderful Summer"), Cappelli, 1963; *Lo spaventapasseri* (juvenile; title means "The Scarecrow"), L'Ariete, 1966; *Carla degli scavi* (novel; title means "Carla of the Archeological Excavations"), Garzanti, 1968; *Hanno rapito il papa* (adult novel; title means "The Pope Has Been Kidnapped"), Garzanti, 1976; (with husband, Luciantonio Ruggieri) *Processo alla guerra: Il teatro contro* (essay; title means "Trial Against the War: The Theatre in Opposition "), Bulzoni, 1976; (with Ruggieri) *La Resistenza e la Guerriglia* (essay; title means "Resistance and Guerrilla"), Venezia, 1977; *Mostri Quotidiani,* (adult novel; title means "Daily Monsters"), in press.

WORK IN PROGRESS: An adult novel; an essay on the most remarkable characters from detective stories for television.

SIDELIGHTS: "I was performing at the Greek Theater in Siracusa, a wonderful theater in the open, in the play 'Le Troiane' of Euripides. My role was that of Athena, the goddess of wisdom and arts and the favorite daughter of Jupiter. I was wearing a helmet which weighed at least thirteen or fifteen pounds and I was holding a sparkling lance. Before the play, as we walked along the waterfront on the way back to the hotel, the native children would follow us, the actors, calling us with the names of our characters: Cassandra, Menelaus, Andromache, Athena.

"These ragged, barefooted and dirty children would follow us to the restaurant and stare at us through the windows with starving eyes.

"I invited a child to come in and sit at my table, I don't remember his name, but he was the smallest, most ragged of them all. His arms and neck were full of bruises.

"I tried to question him, until finally he decided to eat, but I could hardly understand him. We were both Italians, but he was Sicilian and I was Milanese—we were speaking two different languages. I succeeded in understanding that he begged and that he had to bring home the money. His family was living on what he and his brothers could scrape together by begging the tourists, the actors of the theater, and the foreigners. He had a meal when there was a chance and was always beaten by his parents, his brothers and the bigger neighborhood boys. At the moment he was laughing; laughing and eating the big dish of spaghetti and happy as probably he had never been before.

"A dish of spaghetti. To what could that help? Solve the hunger of a day. and then? I was almost ashamed to have invited him to my table to eat with me. It was again to give 'alms,' while he had the 'right' to much more. What could I

RENÉE REGGIANI

have 'really' done to help him, the little one, and the others—his brothers and his mates in misery and hunger? Say a word? To whom?

"We should all know that there are starving, barefooted, and frightened children who beg in the streets instead of going to school. It is not their or their parents' fault, for they are all equally miserable and hungry. It is the fault of a society that allows these things. I thought that all children, those a little more fortunate and the most fortunate of children who have everything, had to know this. They should become aware that the world in which they will be grown men, shall not be like this anymore. They should know that they can and must do something to fight ignorance and injustice—the first sources of all these miseries.

"During the fascist period we went to Africa to build roads and we had the 'Africa' to colonize right here at home—our depressed areas of the South. Many things have been accomplished in Italy by democracy, but many, many more things are still to be achieved.

"We must start with children—take care of them, watch them, send them to school, teach them, and make them conscious of their dignity as future men.

"I have tried to do what I was able to do—I have started writing books."

Reggiani is a woman of a wide and varied cultural background. She graduated with a degree in French from the University of Aix-en-Provence (France) and from the National Academy of Dramatic Arts, "Silvio D'Amico" (Rome). Reggiani has travelled abroad and lived for long periods of time in different parts of Italy, especially in southern Italy.

Tufty crept away to a secret hiding place and cried and cried over the new guitar—being very careful not to wet the strings—and then began to stroke it again, and, after a while, he managed a smile! ■ (From *Five Children and a Dog* by Renée Reggiani. Illustrated by Margot Tomes.)

Theatrical performances have brought her into southern Italy and into Sicily. From this experience she personally realized the poverty and the life conditions of the people in these places. Since then the problems of the South [Italy] have become her problems. She began writing for young people, addressing herself to the younger generation.

Born in Milan where she attended a classical school, Reggiani presently resides in Rome. She is married and has for many years worked with theatrical plays and with productions (scenarios) for television.

As a journalist and writer for radio and television programs, she translates from French, German, and English. "I have therefore chosen an appropriate profession for my educational studies, my elective interests, and acquired the necessary stimulation for my writing profession. Relying on the strength of dialogue and of image, my writing involves me in a world in which human life represents itself in particularly dramatic and significant phases.

"These experiences train a novelist to an awareness of the discerning cuts of scenes, to an always concise rhythm of events, to a clear arrangement of characters, to the liveliness of dialogue and to the total production.

Reggiani has published a "black humor" novel, *Mostri Quotidiani* ("Daily Monsters"), a fantapolitical novel, *Hanno rapito il papa* ("Somebody Kidnapped the Pope") and two theatrical essays, *Processo alla guerra–Il teatro contro* ("Trial Against the War—The Theater in Opposition") and *La Resistenza e la Guerriglia* ("Resistance and the Guerrilla War").

"My last two essay books have a precise objective; besides speaking about the theater, they have a well defined theme—'against war' (keep in mind that the resistance and the guerrilla wars are one of the few possible ways of 'war against war,' war i.e. end war). These are therefore deeply pacifist books, where the study of the theater places itself in the center of the society from which it springs and that it is conditioning in its turn, and where, in a new and modern way as critics define, the figurative arts, the music and the cinema are always called 'to testify' against war. These two essays are the first of a series devoted to the same subject.

"Besides the books written for young people which are (so) rightly realistic, almost documentary books, my novels for adults, *Hanno rapito il papa* ("Somebody Kidnapped the Pope") and *Mostri Quotidiani* ("Daily Monsters"), could be defined as a "challenge" of the imagination. The critics called them an explosion of irony, a diffuse sensation of cheerfulness, a 'hilarious anger,' a 'mocking' conclusion, 'funabulatory rhythm,' a 'cheerfully disrespectful mirror,' and 'cheerful dynamite.'

Renée Reggiani was first among the living Italian and foreign authors in the classification of the Montessori's Association for the reading books in the secondary schools.

Many theses have been written about Reggiani's works at the University of Padova, Parma, etc. and a graduation thesis was written in pedagogy at the University of Bari.

REISS, Johanna de Leeuw   1932-

PERSONAL: Born in 1932; children: Julie, Kathy. *Religion:* Jewish.

CAREER: Author of books for young people. *Awards, honors: The Upstairs Room* received the Jewish Book Council's Charles and Bertie G. Schwartz Juvenile Award in 1972, was named a Newbery Medal Honor Book in 1973, and was awarded the Buxtehuder Bulle in 1976 for an outstanding children's book promoting peace.

WRITINGS: The Upstairs Room (ALA Notable Book), Crowell, 1972, G. K. Hall, 1973; *The Journey Back,* Crowell, 1976.

SIDELIGHTS: **1932.** Born in Winterswijk, Holland, the youngest of three sisters. "Winterswijk was near the German border . . . less than twenty minutes away. That's how close it was. Some farmers lived so close to the border that their cows grazed in Germany, only across the road from their houses. I knew because Father was a cattle dealer, and he often took me with him when he went to buy cows." [Johanna Reiss, *The Upstairs Room,* Crowell, 1972.[1]]

"I liked many things. Being home with my two sisters, Sini and Rachel, if they were nice to me. They were much older—adults almost. With Mother—only she was always sick. With Marie, our maid, who let me sit on her back as she cleaned the floors on all fours. And I liked being with other children, friends, with whom I climbed trees, ran, and laughed. Life went on for us, too, in Winterswijk, in the big house in which we lived." [Johanna Reiss, *The Journey Back,* Crowell, 1976.²]

1938. "I was not very old in 1938, just six, and a little thing. Little enough to fit between the wall and Father's chair, which in those days was always pulled up in front of the radio. He sat with his face close to the radio, bent forward, with his legs spread apart, his arms resting on his knees. And he listened.

"Hitler. All the man on the radio ever talked about was Hitler. He must be an important man in Germany. Why didn't he like German Jews? Because he didn't. Why else would he be bothering them. The radio said he did."¹

1939. "By the fall of 1939, Rachel had graduated from teachers' college. She found a job at one of the nursery schools in Winterswijk. Sini started to work on a farm."¹

"Then the Second World War broke out in Europe. Adolf Hitler, chancellor of Germany, wanted his country to be big and powerful and glorious again, as it had been many times in history. Many Germans agreed, and joined his Nazi party. . . .

"In less than ten months they had occupied Denmark, Norway, Belgium, Luxembourg, France, and Holland.

"Our lives did not change much—not right away. Father still went out in his car; Mother was still sick; Rachel and Sini continued to work. I was in school now, in the second grade."²

1940-1942. Conditions deteriorated for Reiss and her family as well as for all the Jews in German occupied Holland. "We couldn't rent rooms anymore in hotels. With Mother sick almost all the time now, we wouldn't have done that anyway. But why did the next poster say that Jews could no longer go to beaches and parks? That wasn't fair. Beaches and parks belonged to everybody!

"When school started again, I was in the fourth grade, but only for a few weeks: Jewish children were no longer allowed to attend school."¹

Spring, 1942. As the Jewish community became more and more persecuted by the Germans who occupied Winterswijk, Mr. de Leeuw made serious plans to place himself and his three daughters in the homes of sympathetic Dutch Christians. "There were many rumors that spring. . . . The war would be over soon, some people said. Germany should never have invaded Russia. That country was just too cold for them and too big. German soldiers were also fighting in North Africa. 'Sure, Italian soldiers are helping them there, but they don't amount to much.'

"There were other rumors, not such nice ones. Soon women could go to the labor camps too. . . ."¹

October, 1942. ". . . Father received a letter in the mail. By next week, the letter said, your family must go to a Dutch work camp. Report at the station. But they might not take us to a work camp. That letter could be lying. Father said so. Lots of times the train rode right on to Germany, or Austria or Poland, to those concentration camps."¹

November, 1942. The family scattered into Gentile homes that surrounded Winterswijk. Reiss' mother's health had

JOHANNA DE LEEUW REISS

deteriorated rapidly. She was placed in a hospital. "'We must hide,' Father said, 'if I can find Gentile people who'll take us in.' After a while he did find places for us. Secretly we left town, Father for a city near Rotterdam. 'It will not be for long,' he said. Half the world seemed to be fighting against Hitler now, and against Germany's partners, Italy and Japan. England was, France, Canada, Russia, the United States, other Allied countries. How long could the war last?

"My sister Sini and I? We went to Usselo, to live with a family named Hannink. A few weeks later, Mother died and was hurriedly buried. Only then did Rachel leave, for a small village hours from Winterswijk. She was the last Jew from our town to do so.

"It is not easy to find Usselo. On many maps of Holland you cannot find it at all, only on those that list every village, no matter how tiny. Not many people, however, care to know where Usselo is. Why, there is hardly anything there—fields, a café, a bakery, a school, a church and parsonage, a kind of dry-goods store in a house, and farmhouses, but only a handful of those. There's no more than that in Usselo. Such a quiet little village, where life was orderly and pleasant for years and years and years."²

1943. When the Hannink family were suspected of harboring Jews, Reiss and her sister, were placed in another farmhouse in Usselo. "After a few months we could no longer stay with the Hanninks. It was too dangerous, Mr. Hannink said. The Germans were suspicious of him; they thought he might be hiding Jews. 'If they find you here, we'll be murdered, too—my wife, my daughter, and myself. You must leave.'

"Late one evening, when it was dark out and no one could see us, Sini and I arrived at the Oostervelds' door. The Oostervelds lived in Usselo, and had for over fifty years. Their farm was small.

"There they were, the three of them. Frightened, I looked at the man, Johan. He was big. His face was red, and he had brown hair that grew straight up. His cheeks were thin, hollow almost, as if for years the wind and rain had beaten on them and left dents.

"'Hiya.' He smiled around a cigarette butt that hung from the corners of his mouth. 'Two Jewish girls. I'll be damned. Who would've thought it, Ma. Of all the farmers to choose from in Usselo, Mr. Hannink picked me. Ja, ja, girls, he's an important man. I bet he thought I was brave enough to take this big risk. Because that's what it is, a big risk. They could kill us all.' He shifted the cigarette butt to the other side of his mouth.

"'Let's see,' he went on, 'that little one, Annie, must be about ten or eleven. The sister's a lot older, I'd say. Sure, Ma, look for yourself. About twenty, I'd guess.' He walked over to his mother and took her by the shoulders. 'Ma, after all these years you're really an Opoe [grandmother]. Eh? You like that?'

"She did. She laughed up at him with her whole face, all her wrinkles, her toothless mouth. 'Two girls at once, Johan. Nice ones, too.'

"Now I could laugh. It was all right. They liked us.

"'*Ssht,*' Dientje [his wife] warned, 'not so loud for God's sake.' She looked scared. She reminded everybody of what Mr. Hannink had said. A few weeks, that was all. Then he'd take us back.

"But Mr. Hannink never did. No one even mentioned it. Already we had been with the Oostervelds for months. Father had been wrong. Still the war. . . .

"Sure, the Oostervelds were nice, very nice. But the days were long. So many hours in one day, so many days. On some, the sun was out; on others, not. Or it rained or not. We had to keep away from the window, so that no one could catch a glimpse of us and mention that the Oostervelds had strangers living upstairs. 'I could swear to it. I looked up and there they were—two girls. Who can they be, I wonder? Eh?'"[2]

1943-45. For two years and several months Reiss and her sister were hidden in a tiny upstairs room in the Oosterveld farmhouse living in constant fear of detection by the Germans or neighbors in sympathy with the Germans. They were unable to exercise, to go outside or to see anyone except the family they lived with. Contact with their own family was impossible. Nevertheless, the two sisters shared many happy hours with their loving "adopted" family—Johan, his wife, Dientje, and his toothless mother, whom the girls called "Opoe." "Time went on and on. Not fast, not at all. It was 1943 now, or perhaps even later. So many hours and minutes and seconds in each day. Rain or not. . . .

"The German army continued to lose, and little by little the Allied soldiers pushed them out of the countries they had occupied in the first few years of the war. The more they had to give up, the angrier Hitler became. 'Take what you can from the countries you're in,' he ordered his soldiers. 'Cloth-

ing, machines, trains, food. Send home what you can't carry.'

"Many people were wandering through the countryside, begging farmers for a turnip, an egg, a cup of milk, anything. 'Thank you, thank you,' they'd say, and shuffle on . . . the way time did.

"At night it wasn't dark. The minute the Oostervelds were finished with their work, they'd rush upstairs, ·pull the shades down, and turn on the light.

"'That's better, girls, right? Ja, ja, Dientje knows.' With a sigh she'd sit down, her hands folded on her stomach. Once in a while she'd bend forward and carefully touch my face. 'I'm so glad you're here, my little Annie,' she'd say, and nod.

"'I sure wish the other farmers could see me now,' Johan said, 'sitting here with my family.'

"I nestled deeper in his lap.'"[2]

Spring, 1945. "The war in Europe was over. It had taken the lives of twenty-five million people, from many countries, in many different ways, by bombs, on battlefields, in concentration camps.

"'. . . It was all right to make noise again, to shout, jump, run, dance. Slowly I walked to the window. My legs hurt. I had been sitting down for so long, two years and seven months. But no more, no more. It was over.

"All over Holland there was music and dancing. On country roads rusty accordions were p-u—lled and p-u—shed into waltzes and polkas. In Amsterdam a barrel organ that had been hidden from the enemy was wheeled into the streets again, pouring ting-tingly music across the canals as the man turned the wheel. Faster, louder, while skinny bodies moved to and fro, not feeling hunger, not now.

"On the other side of Holland, in Usselo, I walked outside for the first time, tightly holding on to Johan's hand. Look how well I was doing already—halfway across the road now. For a second I took my eyes off my feet and looked up. Beautiful out, especially the sky. It went on forever. . . .'"[2]

Summer, 1945. Reiss and her sister reluctantly left their "adopted" family in Usselo to return to their father and sister, Rachel, who had survived their own exiles. "For the last time we walked around the [Oosterveld] house. In the good room, on the big chest along the wall, were the family portraits. One of Opoe in her Sunday apron—the black one with the dark gray flowers. Johan's and Dientje's wedding picture—Johan grinning, in striped pants and a special jacket; Dientje holding a tiny bouquet of lilies of the valley. And now that people knew we had been hidden there, a photograph of Sini and me.

"'Our children,' Johan said proudly. 'Don't we look good there? The five of us?'

"Sini and I nodded. Yes. We hugged again and again. Until the young man who was going to give us a ride became impatient: 'Let's go.'

"Down the road we went. It was daylight now, not nighttime as it had been when we came, almost three years earlier. A tiny village, Usselo, just as Johan had said. Even tinier now.

The bakery and parsonage had been destroyed by bombs, just before the end. We went past the school Johan had gone to. It was filled with Canadian soldiers, as many schools in Holland were. The store; the café; the fields, where an occasional plow was already waiting. That was all. I turned around to catch a last glimpse of everything before we rattled across a hole and went around the bend.

"Was that Winterswijk in the distance? Already? Nervously I licked my lips. It was such a big town, hundreds of times bigger than Usselo—at least. And it had so many people, thousands and thousands, and so many children, girls my own age—just thirteen. Stealthily I pulled my skirt down as far over my legs as I could. I moved a little closer to Sini until I was sitting right next to her. She put her arm around my shoulders. What would it be like?

"We were not the only Winterswijk Jews who had come out of hiding. A few others had, too. Every day they met in the middle of the marketplace. By the tree, the same tree the enemy had marched up to during the war, carrying hammers and sharp nails, to put up notices that said Jews could no longer shop, go to restaurants, movies, parks . . . or do much of anything except get on those trains—the ones that left on Tuesdays.

"Again the tree spoke, only in hushed tones now, when a man from Town Hall put up a list of names of all the Dutch Jews who had survived the Nazi concentration camps. Trembling, the people at the marketplace searched for names that were familiar: 'Jakob Vos . . . don't see . . .' 'Please, Emma Cohen . . . no.' 'Mozes Spier. . . . His name isn't here.'

"After they had looked at the list again and again, they slowly started to leave, comforting each other, saying that maybe the next time those names would appear."[2]

The scars of war healed slowly and Reiss, her sisters, and father resumed their normal lives. Reiss was educated in Holland and after college taught school for several years before she came to the United States. "After a while both Rachel and Sini left. So did I eventually, to come to America. In my trunk was the lace cap Opoe had given me when I had gone to say goodbye."[2]

Late, 1960's. Returned for a visit to Holland. Reiss was married and had two daughters, Kathy and Julie. "I took my two children to Usselo. 'You Holland talk?' Johan asked them.

"They shook their heads. No.

"The two of them sat on Dientje's lap, staring at Opoe.

"'You really should've gotten false teeth, Opoe,' I said. 'All these years you've been miserable because you didn't.'

"'Nonsense,' she said, 'I got used to it. And now it doesn't make any sense. Soon.'

"She was ninety-two then.

"I took my girls upstairs to the front room. Johan had left the hiding place intact.

"'That's the place Mommy used to crawl into,' I said.

"'See whether you can do it now,' they asked me.

"Obediently I went over to the closet and got on the floor.

"'That's as far as I go.

"'Look, she's crying.' my girls said."[1]

1972. First book for children, *The Upstairs Room,* was published. The book was an account of her childhood ordeal in occupied Holland and was especially written for her two daughters. "I didn't think it would take me more than a week! Not until I started to write did I find out how much I remembered, things I had never talked about with anyone because they were too painful.

"I have not tried to write a historical book, although it may have some historical value. What I *did* try to write was a simple, human book, in which my sister and I suffered and complained, and sometimes found fault with the Gentile family that took us in for a few years, in which the members of that family were not heroes but people, with strengths and weaknesses."[1]

1976. *The Journey Back,* her second book for young people, was published. It is another personal account about her readjustment after World War II. "There was still something I wanted to say, something that was as meaningful to me as the story I had told in the first book, the story of a war. 'The fighting has stopped'; 'Peace treaty signed,' newspapers announce at the conclusion of every war. From a political point of view, the war is over, but in another sense it has not really ended. People are fragile. They are strong, too, but wars leave emotional scars that take a long time to heal, generations perhaps. I know this to be true of myself, and of others. And out of those feelings came *The Journey Back,* a story of the aftermath of the Second World War."[2]

1978. Lives in New York City with her two daughters. Frequently returns to Holland to visit her two sisters and the Oosterveld family.

FOR MORE INFORMATION SEE: New York Times Book Review, November 5, 1972; *Top of the News,* April, 1973; "Memories of Childhood," *Saturday Review,* June 12, 1976; *Horn Book,* October, 1976.

REYHER, Rebecca Hourwich 1897-
(Becky Reyher)

PERSONAL: Born in 1897, in New York, N.Y.; daughter of Isaac A. and Lisa (Joffe) Hourwich; married Ferdinand Reyher, July 13, 1917 (divorced, 1934); children: Faith (Mrs. Melvin Jackson). *Education:* New York School of Social Work, B.A.; also attended Columbia University and University of Chicago. *Address:* 14 Washington Place East, New York, N.Y. 10003 and Robinhood, Me. 04670.

CAREER: Suffrage worker, Women's Political Union and National Woman's Party in New York, Boston, Chicago, and 30 states, 1915-23; *Hearst's International Magazine,* feature writer in Africa, 1923-24; J. Walter Thompson Co., advertising writer and editor, 1927-29; Joseph McKee, public relations assistant, 1930-31; consultant, Sears, Roebuck and Co., 1931-33, International Institute of Women's Studies, Washington, D.C., 1971—; Federal Works Progress Administration, New York, regional director of arts projects, 1935-37, director of motion pictures information service, 1937-39; Dominican Republic Settlement Association, Inc., executive secretary and member of the board of direc-

After a while, instead of long rows of wheat, there were long rows of sheaves, standing stiffly. ■ (From *My Mother is the Most Beautiful Woman in the World* by Becky Reyher. Pictures by Ruth Gannett.)

tors, 1939-43; weekly radio show, WNYC, New York, "City Fun with Children," 1945-49 and "Behind the Scenes with the United Nations," 1946; New School of Social Research, New York, N.Y., teacher, 1963-70; writer and lecturer.

WRITINGS: (Editor) *The Stork Run: A Collection of Baby Cartoons,* Hastings House, 1944; *Babies and Puppies Are Fun!* (illustrated by Henry Stahlhut), M. Barrows, 1944; (under name Becky Reyher; reteller) *My Mother Is the Most Beautiful Woman in the World* (ALA Notable Book; illustrated by Ruth Gannett), Howell, Soskin, 1945, reissued, Lothrop, 1962; (editor) *Babies Keep Coming: An Anthology,* Whittlesey House, 1947; *Zulu Woman: The Autobiography of Christina Sibiya,* Columbia University Press, 1948, reprinted, New American Library, 1970; *The Fon and His Hundred Wives,* Doubleday, 1952.

ADAPTATIONS—Filmstrip: "My Mother Is the Most Beautiful Woman in the World," distributed by BFA Educational Media.

SIDELIGHTS: Born in 1897 in New York City, Reyher was educated at the New York School of Social Work where she received her B.A. She also attended Columbia University and the University of Chicago. When she was twenty years old she married Ferdinand Reyher. The couple have one daughter, Faith.

Reyher was very active in women's rights. As early as 1915 she worked for the Woman's Political Union and National Woman's Party, has contributed to an oral history project on the lives of the women involved in the suffrage movement and has worked for the Equal Rights Amendment to the U.S. Constitution from its inception.

From 1923 to 1924 she was a feature writer in Africa for *Hearst's International* Magazine. It was during her second visit to Zululand that she met Christina Sibiya, the subject of Reyher's book, *Zulu Woman: The Autobiography of Christina Sibiya,* which was published in 1948. Reyher went to Zululand to learn "what Zulu women felt, and did, and talked about." [Rebecca Reyher, "Christina and the King of the Zulus," *Life,* October 25, 1948.[1]]

Reyher has been actively involved in social services and taught at the New School of Social Research in New York from 1963 to 1970. Besides writing books for children she has written numerous articles for periodicals, has lectured throughout the country, and has written books on popular anthropology. She has visited Africa, Europe, Russia, Egypt, Greece, Turkey, the Near East, Pakistan, India, and Ceylon.

The Fon and His Hundred Wives (1952), a report of the polygamy of one African tribesman, was described by the *San Francisco Chronicle* as ". . . a highly readable blend of popular anthropology and straight reporting. She does not offer specific recommendations; her business is simply to report, and this she does with complete success."

Rebecca Reyher's works are included in the Kerlan Collection at the University of Minnesota.

FOR MORE INFORMATION SEE: Life, October 25, 1948; *San Francisco Chronicle,* December 30, 1952.

NICOLE RUBEL

Not even his favorite breakfast of carrot crunchies could keep him awake. ■ (From *Sleepy Ronald* by Jack Gantos. Illustrated by Nicole Rubel.)

RUBEL, Nicole 1953-

PERSONAL: Born April 29, 1953, in Miami, Fla.; daughter of Theodore (an importer) and Janice (Berman; an importer) Rubel. *Education:* Joint degree from Museum School of Fine Arts, and Tufts University B.F.A., 1975. *Home and office:* 416 Marlborough St., Boston, Mass. 02116.

CAREER: Illustrator. *Exhibitions:* "Marigold Gardens," Boston Public Library, Boston, Mass., 1977; Viewpoint Gallery, Newport, R.I., 1977. *Awards, honors:* Children Book Showcase for *Rotten Ralph,* 1977.

ILLUSTRATOR—All written by Jack Gantos; all published by Houghton: *Rotten Ralph,* 1976; *Sleepy Ronald,* 1976;

Fairweather Friends, 1977; *Aunt Bernice,* 1978; *Worse Than Rotten Ralph,* 1978.

SIDELIGHTS: "I work in watercolor. Matisse has always been a strong influence and Louis Comfort Tiffany as well, especially his lamps.

"I collect old hats from 1900 to now. I also collect, from the 1920's and 1930's, various perfume bottles, jewelry, and lamps. I also enjoy baking elaborate chocolate layer cakes with cherry, blueberry, mocha, etc. fillings all together."

SENGLER, Johanna 1924—

PERSONAL: Born September 22, 1924, in Nuremberg, Germany; daughter of Hans and Johanna (Schmitt) Sengler;

"He snatched up his bundle and took to his heels so fast that he completely forgot to put the right shoe back on again." ■ (From *The Wandering Shoe* by Clemens Parma. Pictures by Johanna Sengler.)

married Roderich Menzel, December 12, 1952; children: Roderich-Peter. *Education:* Abitür, 1943; Hochschule für Bildende Künste (an academy for artists), 1948-52. *Home:* Hubert-Reissnerstr. 5a, D-8032, Gräfelfing b., Munich, Germany.

CAREER: Illustrator. *Exhibitions:* Premio CIT, Agrigento, 1952; Palermo, 1952; Palazzo Corvaia, Taormina, 1959; Forio, Ischia, 1959; Konzerthaus, Vienna, 1962; Galleria A-A-A, Ascona, 1967, 1970, 1971, 1976, 1977, 1978; Stadttheater, Konstanz, 1968; Galerie Antoinette, Paris, 1969, 1971; Galerie Brebaum, Düsseldorf, 1969; Firma Siemens AG, Munich, 1969; Sammlung Holzinger, Munich, 1970, 1972, 1974; Städtische Galerie, Würzburg, 1970; Galerie Edelmann, Nuremberg, 1971; Galerie Centre de l'art, Den Haag, 1972; Hotel Bayrischer Hof, Munich, 1972; Kunsthaus Schaller, Stuttgart, 1972; Galerie i. d. Froschaugasse, Zürich, 1972; Galerie l'angle aigu, Brussels, 1973; Rathaus, Schweinfurt, 1973; Bijenkorf, Den Haag, 1973; Galerie Runhof, Cologne, 1974; Kunsthaus Conzen, Düsseldorf, 1975; Kunsthandel Elbers, Kleve, 1976; Munich, 1976, 1977; Städtisches Museum, Minden, 1977; Heilbadzentrum, St. Moritz, 1978; Galerie Sonnegg, Liechtenstein, 1978; Schloss Elmau, Munich, 1978; Marny's Galerie, Munich, 1978; Womanart Gallery, New York City, 1979. *Member:* Associazione-Artisti-Ascona, Verwertungsgesellschaft-Kunst (association of artists).

WRITINGS: (Self-illustrated) *Auto-Auto,* Parabel Verlag, 1971.

Illustrator: Roderich Menzel, reteller, *Der Rattenfänger von Hameln* (title means "The Pied-Piper of Hamlen"), Peter Verlag, 1961; Roderich Menzel, reteller, *Till Eulenspiegel* (title means "The Tales of Owlglass"), Peter Verlag, 1962; Roderich Menzel, *Der wandernde Schuh,* Parabel Verlag, 1963, published in the United States under the title *Wandering Shoe,* Lerner; Roderich Menzel, *Pitt und das verzauberte Fahrrad* (title means "Pitt and the Magic Bicycle"), Obpacher Verlag, 1963; Roderich Menzel, reteller, *Schneewittchen* (title means "Snow White"), Honnef, 1964; Roderich Menzel, *Neue Rubezahl-Geschichten* (title means "New Tales of Rubezahl, a Mountainspirit"), Aufstieg Verlag, 1965; Roderich Menzel, *Juri das Zauberpony* (title means "Juri the Magic Pony"), Sellier Verlag, 1966; Roderich Menzel, *Zottie der Bär* (tittle means "Shaggy the Bear"), Sellier Verlag, 1966; Roderich Menzel, *Peter und die Turmuhr,* (title means "Peter and the Towerclock"), Parabel Verlag, 1966; *Morgen Früh um 6* (title means "At 6 O'clock in the Morning"), Parabel Verlag, 1967; Roderich Menzel, *Mario und Gissi,* Sellier Verlag, 1967; Roderich Menzel, *Märchenreise ins Südetenland* (title means "Fairytale Trip into Bohemia"), Aufstieg Verlag, 1967; *Spannenlanger Hansel, nudeldicke Dirn* (title means "Skinny Johnny and the Little Fat Girl"), Parabel Verlag, 1969; Trina Korschunow, *Bubulla und der kleine Mann* (title means "Bubulla and the Little Man"), Schwaben Verlag, 1969; Trina Korschunow, *Peter geht auf Reisen* (title means "Peter Goes on Trips"), Parabel Verlag, 1970; Roderich Menzel, *Der Vogelkönig* (title means "The Bird-King"), Schneider Verlag, 1970; Günther Spang, *Ein Auto Fährt nicht von allein,* (title means "A Car Does not Drive by Itself"), Parabel Verlag, 1973. Has also illustrated Roderich Menzel, *Das Wunderauto* (Title means "The Wonder Car"), Schreiber Verlag; Maria Schmit, *Joni sucht das Paradies* (title means "Joni Searches for Paradise"), Pustet Verlag; Roderich Menzel, *Der Fliegende Teppich* (title means "The Flying Carpet"), Pustet Verlag.

JOHANNA SENGLER

ADAPTATIONS—Plays for television: "Vom Jungen, der die Zeit verstellte," (title means "About the Boy who Changes the Time"), Frankfurt, 1961; "Das Wunderauto," Stuttgard, 1963; "Bubulla und der kleine Mann," Munich, 1971.

SIDELIGHTS: Johanna Sengler began drawing at age four. In grade school she would draw over her assignments so heavily that the teachers were unable to recognize her homework.

She studied graphics, "free" drawing, and wall drawing at the academy for artists in Munich (Akademie für Bildende Künste) in 1948-1952. During this time she developed a love for the circus and captured colorful circus-life in dozens of pictures. Another of Sengler's interests was the ballet. For years she would sketch at the ballet in Munich and publish these works in newspapers and magazines.

Johanna Sengler has almost thirty books with her illustrations to her credit. Many of her picture books were made for her son, Peter—her sharpest critic.

"Before Christmas of last year (1978), I exhibited a huge collection of my works at Marny's Galerie in Munich. A few days before Christmas the gallery burnt to the ground and with it, my collection of thirty-one pieces which represent many years of work. The gallery carried no insurance."

Sengler has traveled to Italy, France, Tunisia, Yugoslavia, Holland and Switzerland. The artist lives in Munich where she has opened an art school for children.

SETON, Ernest Thompson   1860-1946

PERSONAL: Name was originally Ernest Evan Seton Thompson; born August 14, 1860, in South Shields, Durham, England; emigrated to Canada at age six; died October 23, 1946, in Santa Fe, New Mexico; buried in "Seton Village," Santa Fe, New Mexico; son of Joseph Logan (a shipping businessman) and Alice (Snowden) Thompson; married Grace Gallatin, June 1, 1896 (divorced); married Julia M. (Moss) Buttree, January 22, 1935; children: (first marriage) Anya, (second marriage) Beulah. *Education:* Attended Toronto Collegiate Institute; studied art at the Royal Academy in London, the Ontario College of Art, and at the Julian Academy in Paris, 1890-96. *Home:* "Seton Village," Santa Fe, New Mexico.

CAREER: Naturalist, author, and artist. Appointed naturalist for the Manitoba Government, November, 1892. In the United States, after 1896, he founded the Woodcraft League, 1902, and the Boy Scouts of America, 1910, serving as its Chief Scout, 1910-16. Most of his early writings were originally published under the name Ernest Seton Thompson. *Member:* National Institute of Arts and Letters, Seton Institute (past president). *Awards, honors:* Camp Fire Gold Medal, for *Life-Histories of Northern Animals;* John Burroughs Medal, 1926, and Daniel Girard Elliot Gold Medal, 1928, for *Game Animals and the Lives They Live.*

WRITINGS: The Wild Animal Play for Children, Doubleday, Page, 1900; *The Birch-Bark Roll of the Woodcraft Indians,* Doubleday, Page, 1906; *The Natural History of the Ten Commandments,* Scribner, 1907; *Boy Scouts of America: A Handbook of Woodcraft, Scouting, and Life-Craft,* Doubleday, Page, 1910; *The Arctic Prairies: A Canoe Journey of 2,000 Miles in Search of the Caribou,* Scribner, 1911; *The Forester's Manual; or, The Forest Trees of Eastern North America,* Doubleday, Page, 1912; *Manual of the Woodcraft Indians,* Doubleday, Page, 1915; *The Woodcraft Manual for Girls,* Doubleday, Page, 1916; *The Preacher of Cedar Mountain: A Tale of the Open Country,* Doubleday, Page, 1917; *The Woodcraft Manual for Boys,* Doubleday, Page, 1917; *Cute Coyote, and Other Animal Stories,* Hodder, Stoughton, 1930; *Billy the Dog,* Hodder, Stoughton, 1930; (editor) *Famous Animal Stories,* Coward-McCann, 1932; (editor) *The Gospel of the Red Man: An Indian Bible,* Doubleday, Doran, 1936, reissued, Psychic Press, 1970; *Great Historic Animals: Mainly about Wolves,* Scribner, 1937; *Biography of an Arctic Fox,* Appleton-Century, 1937; *The Buffalo Wind,* Seton Village Press, 1938; *Animal Tracks and Hunter Signs,* Doubleday, 1958.

Self-illustrated books: *Studies in the Art Anatomy of Animals,* Macmillan, 1896; *Wild Animals I Have Known,* Scribner, 1898, reissued, Grosset & Dunlap, 1966; *Lobo, Rag, and Vixon,* Scribner, 1899; *The Trail of the Sandhill Stag, and other Lives of the Hunted,* Scribner, 1899, reissued, Dutton, 1966; *The Biography of a Grizzly,* Century, 1900, reissued as *King of the Grizzlies,* Scholastic Book Service, 1973 [another edition illustrated by Clark Bronson, Rand McNally, 1969]; *Lives of the Hunted,* Scribner, 1901, reissued, New American Library, 1973; *Two Little Savages, being the Adventures of Two Boys Who Lived as Indians and What They Learned,* Doubleday, Page, 1903, reissued, Childrens Press, 1970; *Monarch, the Big Bear,* Scribner, 1904; *Animal Heroes,* Scribner, 1905, reissued, Grosset & Dunlap, 1966; *Woodmyth and Fables,* Century, 1905; *Life-Histories of Northern Animals: An Account of the Mammals of Manitoba,* Scribner, 1909; *The Biography of a Silver-Fox,* Century, 1909; *Rolf in the Woods: The Adventure of a Boy Scout with Indian Quonab and Little Dog Skookum,* Doubleday, Page, 1911; *The Book of Woodcraft and Indian Lore,* Doubleday, Page, 1912; *Wild Animals at Home,* Grosset & Dunlap, 1913; *Wild Animal Ways,* Doubleday, Page, 1916; *Sign Talk,* Doubleday, Page, 1918; *Woodland Tales,* Doubleday, Page, 1921; *Bannertail: The Story of a Gray Squirrel,* Scribner, 1922; *Lives of Game Animals,* Doubleday, Page, 1925-28; *Trail of an Artist-Naturalist: The Autobiography of Ernest Thompson Seton,* Scribner, 1940; *Santana, the Hero Dog of France,* Phoenix Press, 1945.

Selections: *Animals Worth Knowing,* Doubleday, Doran, 1934; *Johnny Bear, Lobo, and Other Stories,* Scribner, 1935; *Ernest Thompson Seton's Trail and Camp-Fire Stories,* edited by Julia M. Seton, Appleton-Century, 1940, reissued, Seton Village Press, 1965; *The Best of Ernest Thompson Seton,* edited by W. Kay Robinson, Hodder & Stoughton, 1949; *Ernest Thompson Seton's America: Selections from the Writings of the Artist-Naturalist,* edited by Farida A. Wiley, Devin-Adair, 1954; *King of the Grizzlies: Two Stories by Ernest Thompson Seton* (illustrated by Mirko Hanak), Dutton, 1972; *The Worlds of Ernest Thompson Seton,* edited by John G. Samson, Knopf, 1976.

ADAPTATIONS—Movies and filmstrips: "The Legend of Lobo" (motion picture), Walt Disney Productions, 1962; "The Legend of Lobo" (filmstrip; adapted from the Walt Disney motion picture), Encyclopaedia Britannica Films, 1964; "Lobo Takes Command" (filmstrip; adapted from the Walt Disney motion picture), Encyclopaedia Britannica Films, 1962; "Lobo, the Wolf Pup" (filmstrip; adapted from the Walt Disney motion picture), Encyclopaedia Britannica Films, 1962; "Lobo's Long Journey" (filmstrip; adapted from the Walt Disney motion picture), Encyclopaedia Britannica Films, 1962.

SIDELIGHTS: **August 14, 1860.** Born in South Shields, Durham, England; his mother nearly drowned shortly before his birth. Seton attributed his fear of water to this fact.

". . . My father built his own plain solid three-story house of brick, No. 6 Wellington Terrace, and in this his numerous progeny were born—fourteen of us in all.

"We were taught to treat [father] like the Pope, or a Roman emperor—to stand aside and at attention whenever he approached or passed. If he entered the room where we were sitting, we were trained all to rise and stand meekly behind our chairs with downcast eyes until he was seated.

"Times without number he beat me black and blue with the hard leather and sharp-cornered ironbound heel of his slipper for some trivial transgression often beyond my understanding, which was construed into disrespect, or disobedience, or loss of temper. It was generally the last, for he had commanded me to keep my temper, and therefore anger was disobedience. Yet when he flogged me, he himself was always in a rage.

"Yet it is to my father that I owe my interest in art and science; it is to him that I am indebted for a certain dogged persistence that enables me to say that I never took anything in hand without completing it. It might be well done; it might be ill done; but it was done, was the best I could do, and was always carried on to a definite prearranged finish.

"In moments of depression which, from time to time, descended on the whole family, it was always Mother who reacted first and most completely. She always led us back to happier thoughts by her smile and her ready jest. Father might see only the cloud; Mother could always see the silver lining.

"Never very strong, she spared herself not at all; broken down by overwork and over-childbearing, she continued to the last the true and loving mother—a martyr, but a joyful one, to her calling.

"Her gentle, unselfish conscientious care of us was unremitting, as it was lifelong. I do not believe there was ever a night

SETON, 1906.

when she did not creep about after hours to see that each of the younger ones was well covered in bed and sleeping the sweet sleep of healthy youth.'' [Julia Seton, *By a Thousand Fires,* Doubleday, 1967.[1]]

''I was only a child when first I heard it. My brother had made an Aeolian harp and set it in the window under the raised sash. It was silent for a time, and then began a soft low strain. This rose and fell with the wind, chimed in weird harmonies. But the wind arose, and it sang, and shrieked; then dropped to a moaning song that wrung my young soul, brought tears to my eyes. I know not why, for music was not in my gift. It gripped me with a sweet agony; it reached my inmost being. I had no words but 'I want to go! I want to go!''' [Farida Wiley, editor, *Ernest Thompson Seton's America,* Devin-Adair, 1954.[2]]

1866. Emigrated to Canada, where his father purchased one hundred acres of land in the backwoods of Ontario. ''I was not quite six when we left England. I can clearly see yet the bustle of preparation in that summer . . . Father, Mother, ten sons (for two came after I did), and my cousin Polly Burfield, then eighteen years old, adopted as a sister; I see yet the piles and piles of boxes all lashed with strong, tarry rope that told of the ship tradition. I can still smell the cats in that cheap lodging in Glasgow where we spent a day and a night before going aboard the *St. Patrick,* a steamer bound for Quebec.

''The strongest impression of this three-weeks' voyage is of rats.

''Quebec lives in my memory as a big rock that blocked the back window of the hotel, where we had sour bread to eat. There was talk of a wonderful pet bear kept by the blacksmith, but I did not see it—which left a tinge of regret.

''Of the long, five-hundred-mile journey through interminable swamps of spruce and tamarack to Lindsay, Ontario, I remember only one night. As we were preparing to sleep in the train, Father told us to look out, and we saw an amazing sight—the woods full of shooting stars. They were everywhere, some close to the train, blazing, twinkling, sailing about. When the wonder had sunk in, Father told us they were not shooting stars, but little insects called 'fire-flies,' each of which carried a lantern. It was one of those delicious rare moments when your dream fairy comes to you, and you know it is really true.''[2]

''The log schoolhouse was a mile away; but I was six years old and, with my eight-year-old brother, was sent every morning to nine o'clock school, to sit for six hours at the feet of a tremendous person. So she seemed to me, for she was grown up; she knew everything; she was the schoolmistress. I learned Agnes O'Leary better some years later. She had been only a bright young girl of sixteen then; oftentimes in winter, she had scholars much older than herself.

''An incident that profoundly impressed me was a reading from Franklin's *Polar Sea.* A white bear with two cubs had ventured near the ship. One cub was shot, the mother wounded. She led the other little one off, but she came back moaning to caress the dead one. Finding it could not follow,

A Prairie-dog cannot see well unless he is sitting up on his hind legs; his eyes are of little use when he is nosing in the grass.... ■ (From *Lives of the Hunted* by Ernest Thompson Seton. Illustrated by the author.)

The Prairie Hare, as sketched by Ernest Thompson Seton. ■ (From *The Worlds of Ernest Thompson Seton* edited by John G. Samson.)

she set out to carry it away. Meantime, the other kept calling. So she left the dead one, and ran to help the living. It came back also, and was shot. The mother fondled and licked the two little bodies. She kept looking up at the ship and moaning, as if pleading for mercy. Refusing to flee, she was herself shot dead beside them.

"The big boys reading the story were wholly engrossed with the words: P-o-l, pole, a-r, ar, Polar; w-o-u-n-d-e-d, wounded; and so on. But at the desk behind the standing line of readers was I—the only one of the crowd who seemed to feel it—with tears in my eyes and with a choking sorrow in my throat over the fate of the noble old mother bear.

"This daily two miles, to school and back, was not a serious matter in fine weather. But winter was coming, there was ice on the ditches, and soon the snow came down. At first it was fun to trudge through it; but the weather got colder, and in late November I was so benumbed coming home one dark evening that I gave up and lay down in the snow. I don't remember it very clearly. I had been terribly cold and now felt irresistibly sleepy. My older brother Arthur, with me, seemed to sense the danger; and used every means, including threats of violence, to get me home. This experience ended my winter schooling for that season." [Ernest Thompson Seton, *Trail of an Artist-Naturalist*, Scribner, 1940.[3]]

1870. Family moved to Toronto. "For four years I had seen only the big woods all about me. To the eastward, the forest was solid and unbroken. It was inconceivable that there should be anything beyond that. My childish fancy made that the end—the rim of things. I knew there was nothing that way, no clearing, nothing but woods and woods and woods.

"Mother told me we were going to Toronto to live. At my side of the schoolhouse wall hung the map of Europe, and on the lower part I made out 'Otranto.' This I proudly pointed out as the new home we were headed for. Father, now nearly fifty years of age, was quite unfitted for farm life, but he was an expert accountant of modern training, and expected to get a position as such in our new home city."[3]

April 12, 1870. "... We said good-by to the woods. The rough little cordwood railway train left Lindsay for Port Hope, forty long miles away; and with incredible speed, in half a day landed us there at noon. We stopped at a small hotel on the hill for midday meal. I stepped out on the back porch and got a marvellous thrill, for there was a great, wonderful mountain—not high, but enormously long and gloriously blue.

"As I wondered about its name, and fitted it into the fairy tales of my woods life, I noticed beautiful white gulls flying about, and then a sailboat crossing it; and slowly it dawned on me that this was no mountain—it was Lake Ontario. I was seeing it from a high hill, which, to my untrained eye, made *it* seem high. It was wonderful, beautiful, but puzzling. This was one of those moments of supreme joy, fraught with the happy sense that fairies are real after all."[3]

Of his new schoolmates, he wrote: "The attitude of this wild mob toward strangers was fundamentally hostile. They bullied and pelted us poor newcomers with brutal delight—at least for a time, until we were initiated. Those early days in that school were a nightmare of horror and misery.

"When I had been a little boy in England, four years of age, I was riding 'horsey' on the high arm of a sofa. It was covered with slippery black horsehair cloth; and I fell, landing on my

A cottontail rabbit done by Seton for a children's book. ■ (From *The Worlds of Ernest Thompson Seton* edited by John G. Samson.)

head. Of course I howled. Mother soothed me as best she could, rubbing my head as I lay on the sofa. Suddenly I exclaimed: 'Oh, I see two mammas, and two clocks, and two of everything.' Sure enough, my eyes previously all right, were now badly crossed, and continued so for years. The doctor said it had come through the accident and would slowly correct itself.

''This proved to be the case. Each year, the squint grew less, but at once returned when any one called attention to it. In this wild school the boys soon discovered my weakness, and with characteristic schoolboy delicacy and tact, found a fiendish delight in calling out: 'Now, Squinty, cross your eyes.' I could not help it—back would come the squint, and my misery was complete.

''I was not a strong boy, but the galling insult of it all used to rouse my fighting blood, the berserker streak of my wild

ancestor, Fighting Geordie. More than anything else was this the cause of my many boyish battles.

''But at the time I had no books, and I had no idea that any such existed. All that were mentioned or seemed available were books about British birds. And I groped in my darkness.

''In my father's library were two large volumes called *Knight's Pictorial Museum of Animated Nature*. These were a collection of old cuts—two pages of pictures, then two of text—one of those drawing-room table books that used to be popular.

''To me it was a riotous feast; I read every word of it that related to animals or birds, but always I wound up with a sense of loss or failure. This or that wonderful creature was invariably a foreigner. I wanted our own things, the birds and beast and flowers of our meadows; but not a book was there to meet the need.''[3]

1873. ''In the summer . . . there appeared an announcement that 'Doctor A. M. Ross's *Birds of Canada* is now published, a great work, absolutely the first and last word on the subject, now on sale at Piddington's Book Store.'

''Jingling my silver coins, I marched boldly into Piddington's store. I had a brave look, but my heart was going pit-a-pat as I walked up to the salesman and said: 'Please, sir, give me a copy of Ross's *Birds of Canada*.' He turned coldly away; I expected him to say, 'Too late, all are gone.' Or, 'The price has gone up to one hundred dollars.' But he merely said, in cold, lifeless, business tones: 'Green or brown cover?'

''I gasped, 'Green!' He took one from the shelf, looked inside the cover, and said in his melancholy way: 'One dollar, ten off for cash, ninety cents, please.'

''I laid down the ninety cents in a daze; in spite of my Scottish instincts I almost forgot to keep the dime. I seized my treasure before he could wrap it up; I hurried away, fearing he might call me back.

''Oh, how little I knew of cash discounts. Here I had suffered two months' hunger; I had delayed my entry into paradise; at last I had shocked my conscience, to raise that last, that wholly unnecessary dime.''[2]

1874. Built a log cabin in the woods—his own private getaway—which he went back to visit years later. ''There it was, the cedar logs yet good, but the roof destroyed, the timbers scattered. There it was still, the graveyard of a hope—my own dear cabin.''[1]

1875. ''The autumn . . . was a long dark valley for me. My cabin was gone, and I was absolutely alone in the world. For

Lobo, the giant cattle-killing timber wolf painted by Seton in 1894. ■ (From *The Worlds of Ernest Thompson Seton* edited by John G. Samson.)

A yellow cur would have seen the rabbit sitting there, but the hound did not, and the scent seemed stale.
■ (From *Wild Animals I Have Known* by Ernest Thompson Seton. Illustrated by the author.)

faults that may have been wholly my own, I was out of all favor at home. I was convinced now that I was not the real son of my parents, but a foundling picked up somewhere; and I felt that they were tired of me, that the end was in sight.''[3]

1876. ''In the fall . . . I, now sixteen years of age, nearly six feet high, thin as a rail, definitely faced my serious work in life, and set energetically about finding an opening as an embryo artist.

''In the streets I made sketches of business houses, and sold one or two to be used in advertising. I colored photographs, and took them to firms that dealt in such things—without much success. I made sketches of animals and birds, interesting without being remarkable.

''The intense love I had for bird life and wild life in general had been developing in childhood days when in the woods. Now, in Toronto, it ceased not to grow in spite of meager opportunities and growing opposition.

''Many times I have heard and read of boys who aspired to be artists, and had to fight their people, especially their fathers, for permission to follow such a career. Only once have I ever heard of a boy who did not wish to be an artist, and yet was compelled by his father to adopt the profession. That exception was myself.

''From my earliest years I longed to be a naturalist. I thought I had a mission—to be the prophet of outdoor life. My father said: 'No, there is no opening, no future, for such a calling. You have artistic gifts, and an artist you are going to be.' ''[3]

1879. Won gold medal at Ontario School of Art. Decided to leave Canada to study art in England. ''. . . I, a long-legged, lanky boy, stood on the deck of the *Algerian* in Toronto Harbor, bound for Montreal and England. My mother, my father and my brothers were there to see me off. A choking sensation gripped my throat, and my eyes filled with tears, as the boat swung away; I waved them good-by and watched till my mother's white hanky was lost in the crowd. I had told them, and I told myself, it was only for one year; but something deeper told me it was a final good-by. I was not yet nineteen, but I was leaving home for good.

''Thus ended the flat, stale and much overrated period called childhood. As I look over it now, it was a time of little miseries and little joys, instincts suppressed and original efforts thwarted, misunderstanding on the part of the grown-up—none of the big glorious sorrows and happinesses of the real life. I bade it farewell, not without a sigh, yet with a vast sense of ever-growing relief and escape.''[3]

1880. Received scholarship to Royal Academy School of Painting and Sculpture in London. ''My days were wholly given to my drawing at the Museum; my evenings were spent in my room, making sketches of various objects in view, or sometimes a portrait of myself in the mirror.

''Then a wonderful event took place. All my life I had been starving for books on natural history. I hardly knew that any existed; but my hunger was persistent. Through a friend, I learned that the greatest collection of natural history books in the world—two million of them—was under the very roof where I was daily at work—nothing less than the great library of the British Museum. Every book of value under the sun was housed or represented there, and access to all offered free.

''Taking advantage of an opportunity, I followed a tourist group that was being given a glimpse of this world glory. I was ablaze. All the suppressed love and hopes of my boyhood seemed renewed, reanimated with the very accumulated force of repression.''[3]

1881. Returned home to Canada. ''Home, Home! So good it sounds and so many times better it felt. Coming home, broken in body and without fame or fortune, I felt like a defeated failure slinking back, till I met my mother. With love and joy, with a welcome and words of judicious praise and thankfulness, she made me feel, in a little while, like a hero coming back in triumph.

''London had been a land of shivering cold, gloom, and starvation; all the things that I most loved, except books, were absent. Now I was in a land of sunshine, I had three good meals a day and no worry about rent. The house was warm, and something like the joy of youth was mine; and ever the inspiring thought that now I should learn the birds, now my craving for life with the Wild Things was surely to be gratified.

''I set about my natural history investigations of the region around Toronto. I was out every day with a gun—and a pair of legs that grew daily stronger. All wild life was interesting; but birds were my first love, and I followed and studied them with absolute concentration.''[3]

1882. His father presented him with bill for $537.50, itemized expenditures from Seton's birth to age of twenty-one. Shocked and saddened, Seton left home and began exploration of Manitoba. ''I was utterly staggered. I sat petrified.

Most men consider that they owe their sons a start in life. My father thought that his father owed that to him; but his case, he felt, was different.

"Oh, the blackness of that moment! Twenty-one years of age, nothing achieved, no progress in life, not a cent of money, no prospect of any—nothing but a millstone of debt bearing heavy interest; broken in health, ordered to leave and swim for myself."

"I was twenty-one, but I was like most boys of seventeen. I took a long striding walk of many miles. At the end the awful depression had passed away. I soon saw that it was all right. Of course, I must pay it off. I must strike out for myself."[3]

"I was very young then. Twenty-one snows I had seen in the woods, but my heart was sixteen."

"Oh, Father Time, steamroller, huge impulverizer, what would I not suffer to see it all again as I saw then! The eager heart, the tireless limb, the unclouded eye, the unburdenedness of a manhood late arriving."

"Now I see it all in a distant purple mist that hides the stinging vermin, singing or crawling; lights up the trees."[1]

He recalled the Manitoba experience happily, nostalgically, and rejoiced in his studies of the newly opened prairie: "The long flat grey-gold stretch in spring, the blistering wind, not wholly gone, the snowbanks in the hollows, the prairie chickens marching insouciantly on the whiteness of the hillocks, draping them over with accurately constructed toe marks, all spaced and measured, somewhat overdone around that stiff rough prairie rose that swung its last red drupes aloft—food, food, held for the hardy ones that had braved it and bested the winter. Good kind old snow that hid these rubies showing now at sun-call."[1]

May 28, 1883. "Never shall I forget . . . I had been tramping through the eastern hills and fairy groves of spruce with unusual joy, running for spells in the very exuberance of being alive, expending energy for the sheer joy of spending when energy is there in a very plethora. I was, above all, rejoicing to realize that a thousand bird voices which, three years ago, were merely tantalizing mysteries, were now the happy understandable expressions of friends whose names and lives I knew as no one else could know them.

"The very skies were brighter now, and more meaningful. A glorious, blazing prairie sunset was aglow as I crossed the familiar old slough by a log-way I myself had made, when a burst of song from a minstrel of the royalest line was heard. It was an old friend singer, and a loved old song that he sang. But now he sang as never before, and I was all a-tune. It was my old song friend, the thrasher; but this was surely the noblest singer of his race. His glorious chant from the low dead limb gripped me as never before.

"Spiritually, I knelt before him; and, when at last he climaxed, bowed, and dived into the greenery, I stood as rapt. He had me full possessed; and on my two-mile homeward sprint, my very soul seemed but the organ on which the singer king had played."[3]

October 11, 1883. ". . . We camped in a beautiful valley three miles south of Little Boggy Creek. The soil was rich, mostly open prairie, but enough timber at hand for immediate use, and plenty in sight on the mountain five miles away. So I de-

"Gazing spellbound in that window." ■ (From *Two Little Savages* by Ernest Thompson Seton. Illustrated by the author.)

cided on Section 36, Township 28, Range 31 west of the principal meridian—half for my homestead and pre-emption, and half to be entered for my brother.

"It was a beautiful region and location. There was a small lake on my half, and a running brook across both portions. It was wholly delightful; so, saying, 'I'll take this,' I drove my stake into it, with a sense of finality.

"It was now late in the day, turning very cold, and threatening rain. So we set up our tent and made supper. Then the other two boys smoked their evening pipe and turned in, leaving me alone by the fire.

"As I sat the sky cleared, and there rose above the valley a glorious full moon. A horned owl hailed it with a loud 'hoo hoohoo'; and a coyote joined in with his long-drawn acclaim. It was a scene of magic and memory; for, exactly two years before, I had stood by the River Thames in London, and seen just such a moon rise to the clang of bells and the wailing of whistles.

"It conjured up in me a mood of retrospect without regret.

The Blackbear shivered and whimpered with terror as the scraping of those awful claws ran up the trunk and up his spine in a way that was horribly suggestive. ■ (From *The Biography of a Grizzly* by Ernest Thompson Seton. Illustrated by the author.)

"My companions were sound asleep, and the pensive witchery begripped me in dreams without a jarring note to break the memory spell.

"Only two years before! And yet it seemed like ten.

"In memory, I compared my present self with the stripling of the London life. I was two years older in time, but ten years older in living. I was now in robust health. I had a little money. I had broken with the gloomy Calvinism that had darkened my boyhood. I was healed of the thorns in my flesh. I had found myself.

"But I also knew that I had bade good-by to London and its world of art."[3]

1884. After a brief trip to New York, returned for an extensive study of wildlife in Manitoba. "Eighteen eighty-four must ever stand out in memory as the climax of my Golden Age, blessed now as I was with exuberant health, strength, and spirits.

"Most athletes reach the climax of their vigor at twenty-five, and this was fully emphasized in my case, for I was admittedly the best foot-traveller in my region.

"I had my books, my birds, my dreams; and above all, my future was guaranteed safe by my recent journey to New York. There I had proved that I could face the world on my own and make a comfortable living; that I had, indeed, some gift and some product for which the hard cruel world of commerce was willing to pay cold cash.

"It was chiefly during this summer that, besides trapping and skinning many of the smaller species, I made drawings of all the wild animals found in Manitoba. . . .

"There were three periods of different and significant experience in 1884—the springtime wonderland among the birds; the building of my shanty on the Upper Assiniboine in June; and the hunting of my moose in the early winter."[3]

1885-1886. Contributed animal illustrations to *The Century Dictionary*. "During the years that I was busied illustrating *The Century Dictionary* . . . I was continually faced with the problems of animal and bird anatomy; and found that there were no books treating of the same from the artist's point of view. There were plenty of works on animal dissection and dead animals, but these had little bearing on my needs and the needs of all artists who depict animals.

"I therefore planned my *Art Anatomy;* that is to say, a careful analysis of the *visible forms* and proportions of the *living* animal, which includes the feather shapes and overlaps in the birds and the fur of animals. Color does not enter in, but measurements do.

"Having a clear field, I began with enthusiasm, measuring live dogs, cats, cows, horses and birds, cutting up dead ones."[2]

November 23, 1889. ". . . I had an adventure that marked the end of my youth—a sad, sad day for me.

"I had gone alone into the hills quite early, trotting through deep snow, with the thermometer below zero. As usual, I halted for the nooning in a sheltered hollow, lighted my fire, made some tea, and fried some bacon. I was hot when I stopped, and the wind was fierce even in that hollow. Suddenly a sharp pain struck through my right knee; and when, a little later, I packed up and tried to move on, I found the knee useless—I could not bend it. At each attempt, the pain was excruciating.

"There was no chance of any one coming for me. I had to make my way home alone and on foot, or die there. So I set out hobbling on a leg and a limp. Though barely five miles from home, it took me three hours to get there, and that with torture at every step.

"I sent for the local doctor. He said it was simply muscular, and gave prescribed treatment, with some but not conclusive results. It was some years later before a real expert told me that it was acute arthritis.

"That put an end to my far tramping afoot. I never again was the running athlete of my world. After twenty years, the pain and weakness died out with treatment, but thenceforth my travel was by horse or canoe."[3]

The musk ox, sketched by Seton on a seven-month canoe trip into the Northwest Territories of Canada in 1907. ■ (From *The Worlds of Ernest Thompson Seton* edited by John G. Samson.)

The stranger stopped atone of Rag's rubbin-trees— that is, a tree against which he used to stand on his heels and rub his chin as far up as he could reach....It lets the next one know by the scent if the last caller was an acquaintance, and the height from the ground of the rubbing-places shows how tall the rabbit is. ■ (From *Wild Animals I Have Known* by Ernest Thompson Seton. Illustrated by the author.)

"Three years I roamed and lived, and truly lived—alone, nearly always, alone but rejoicing—until I heard another, the summons back to everything I hated. The glory of the August sun was on the gold and bloom-lit plains when it came in a letter. I went across the level green—it marked the brook line. It was alive with loved and lovable things; it had held my happy thoughts for three years. And the Wind came whistling across, bending the early goldenrods, and carried a burst of song that meant but little till it struck the mosquito screen, and whistled, screamed, then dropped to a low moaning sound. And through my brain and soul it went: 'The Buffalo Wind! The Buffalo Wind is blowing!' "[3]

In this drawing of a cougar, Seton displays the single-minded concentration of the great cat.
■ (From *The Worlds of Ernest Thompson Seton* edited by John G. Samson.)

1890. Studied art at Julian Academy in Paris. "I have spent all the afternoon at the Louvre, and as I went from one great master to another, and saw all kinds of peculiarities and extremes, yet all resulting in great pictures, this is the lesson that impressed me more and more: that man who does immortal work develops *himself*. Here have I, living in Norway, been trying to grow a palm tree, because I saw that African palms were good. And each fresh frost cut down my poor, puny sprout. My wretched seedling had to contend with a great strong, frost-defying pine that kept springing up. It has only recently dawned on me that I must grow my pine. That is my timber. What a tree I might have had now had I realized this ten years ago!

"This, then, is my theory: I have something which no one else in the world has. It may be a little thing, but it is *me*. It is my pine tree, and I shall grow it, though it never exceed a foot in height. It will always be at least a living thing."[1]

1892. Appointed official naturalist to government of Manitoba. "The million little lakes, from Winnipeg to the Rockies, had so dwindled, so dried up, that the ducks had nearly disappeared—gone, we hope, to the far Northwest. But they were no more to be seen on the lovely prairie lands of the Assiniboine.

"Yes, all the sweet and wilding things were gone—the swallows from the barns to be replaced by English sparrows.

"And yet, at every step, I found new subjects for my pen and pencil, for every day in that summer I made a careful drawing; I collected a worth-while specimen; and I made a photograph that was a precious record. Also I made twelve new large paintings of animals for the Biological Survey at Washington, and found in this an ample fund for summer-long support.

"But, alas, my wings of speed no longer served me. I must hobble over the hills or hire a horse. My eyes were blurred with over use, and never ceased to give me pain. I felt the joy of youth was gone.

"Yes, the prairie and the wild things all about had changed. But the greatest change of all was in myself. Now I knew why valiant men and dreamers in the past thought this of all things precious, most worth while—youth, youth unending—and the fountain of eternal youth the noblest quest for which a man can give his life."[3]

1893. "My wolf hunt in New Mexico began October 22, 1893, and ended February 5, 1894. The country abounded in wild life. There were small herds of antelope every eight or ten miles; there were a few deer in the brakes; there were badgers, coons, jack rabbits, cottontails, and prairie dogs. A few bears frequented the wooded hills, and bird life abounded.

"But I was there for wolves, and killed over a hundred coyotes, partly by poison, partly in traps. However, I got only five of the great gray wolves—the lobos, or 'loafers' of the cattleman; and all of these I got with steel traps—not one by poison.

"I made the minutest study of trappers' ways and tricks, of the animals' reactions to each and every smell and hint of human presence; and I discovered finally a combination of devices by which I can, if I wish, catch coyotes with something like certainty. Once I discovered it, I got one or two coyotes every night.

"But I do not propose to let anyone in on the secret. I have changed from a coyote killer to a coyote protector; and the devilish secret of destruction shall perish with me."[1]

1896. Married Grace Gallatin. The union lasted as long as their interests proved to be mutually compatible. "As long as we were in New York, hobnobbing with artists and writers, among receptions and pink teas, my wife was in her element. She made a good chairman of a meeting, and quickly rose to be president of more than one club. She was a good art and literary critic, and, as said, had some literary gift, though none whatever in the pictorial line.

"As a camper she was a great success, never grumbled at hardship, or scolded any one. She was a dead shot with the rifle, often far ahead of the guides, and met all kinds of danger with unflinching nerve; was always calm and clear-headed, no matter what the stance.

"During the Great War she rendered paramount service. She raised the money to buy, equip, and operate six Ford trucks for camp and transport service between Paris and the front. For this she was decorated and highly honored by the French Government.

"I had little part in the Great War, although I offered my services at Washington, Ottawa, and London; but my age (fifty-four) ruled me out.

"After the War we saw little of each other. Our child Ann was indeed a binding link; but each winter I was compelled to take a long, hard lecture trip, during which my wife remained in New York or Greenwich, or travelled to gather book material.

"The Sleeping Wolf," perhaps the greatest single animal oil painting done by Seton in Paris, **1874.** ■ (From *The Worlds of Ernest Thompson Seton* edited by John G. Samson.)

Seton at his easel, age 14.

"These long sojourns took her to many countries and resulted in several creditable books, but they set us ever farther apart. Our home life was intermittent. Divergent interests separated us."[3] They eventually divorced.

1898. Collected his stories of animal life in *Wild Animals I Have Known*. "In the story one has greater leeway than in the scientific treatise. The following I consider to be three allowable liberties in a popular story of an animal:

"First, one may select an unusual individual.

"Second, one may ascribe to him the adventures and attributes of several of his race.

"Third, one may make him do things which his species never was known to do, because never observed under these conditions, provided that the presented case is completely hedged about by probabilities. That is, one may assume the probable as proven.

"Some will say, however, that even granting the truth of all details, I have added an atmosphere, a feeling of human sensibility, that conveys a wrong notion of the animal's way of life. To this I reply: 'The subject of my first book, and indeed of all my books, was the *personality* of the individual animal. No man can write of another personality without adding a suggestion of his own. The personal touch may be the poison of science, but may also be the making of literature, and is *absolutely inevitable.*'

"Which then is better? That which would reduce not only all animal traits but all human kindness also to a mere mathematical problem of reflex quantities and oscillating energies, or one which by the warming touch of sympathy brings the animal nearer to us, makes clear our kinship, and commends the study to the hearts of all mankind?

"Finally I maintain that my stories do convey a true notion of the ways of the animals, their troubles, their trials, their matings, their friendships, and their foes; the lives they live and the deaths they die."[1]

1900. ". . . I found myself in a position to realize the dream of my life—a dream that is common to nine men out of ten. I was blessed with means and opportunity to buy a few small abandoned farms not far from New York City. I was now absolute owner of a tract of tangled wildwood, with hills, rocks and trees in abundance, a few little meadows, and a beautiful brook that spread into an alder swamp. The swamp was easily turned into a lake, and furnished the central beauty spot to a little paradise of birds and wild life.

"I built an inexpensive cabin, and around the place put an impassable mesh wire fence ten feet high, and finished at the top with barbwire entanglements.

"Here I proposed to live most of the time. Here I meant to try out many experiments at conservation and restocking. Every native kind of wild life was to be encouraged. I rejoiced in my dream come true. I gloried in my wildwood."[3]

May, 1902. Founded the Woodcraft Indian League, dedicated to leading young people to the spiritual side of nature through recreational outdoor life. "Now we set out on what

ERNEST THOMPSON SETON

Sketches of squirrels and martens for *Lives of Game Animals* written and illustrated by Ernest Thompson Seton. ■ (From *The Worlds of Ernest Thompson Seton* edited by John G. Samson.)

was destined to be an epoch-making outing for the village boys, for myself, and for thousands of boys elsewhere.

"Our motto was 'The best things of the best Indians.' Whatever is picturesque, good, and safe in Indian life, that we used.

"The boys wanted to wear feathers. I said: 'Certainly, but remember, after the manner of the Indians. The good old Indian did not wear just any feather he could steal and stick in his hair. Each feather was conferred by the Council as the decoration for an exploit. I will give you a hundred exploits, each of which will entitle the doer to a feather.'

"It was essential that my standards should be national and *absolute,* not competitive. So, taking the interscholastic athletic rules for my standard, I allowed a feather for all who were obviously in the highest class, thus: all who could walk four miles in a hour, or run 100 yards in eleven seconds. The only cheap one was for swimming. All who could swim one hundred yards, no matter how slowly, got the swimming feather.

"In a second department, called Campercraft, I allowed honors to all who could light a campfire with rubbing sticks, could measure the width of a river without crossing it, etc.

"The third department was nature study, and honors were allowed to all who could name correctly twenty-five trees, fifty flowers, fifty birds, etc.

"I had already invented a game called Deerhunting, in which a dummy deer was pursued by its tracks of paper or corn (later with a steel tracking iron on the foot) and shot with arrows; a Hostile Spy Hunt, a Bear Hunt, a Rabbit Hunt, a Man Hunt, Spearing the Big Sturgeon, Trials of Quick Sight

Seton and his wife, Julia.

and Far Sight. The games were all prepared, and lying in wait with their insidious appeal to the primitive nature of these very primitive young persons.

"There was sanity in every part of the scheme, because it had *picturesqueness;* it made the boys *govern themselves,* and it gave them definite *things to do;* but, above all, it never failed to play on the master power of the savage, the love of glory; that was always kept in mind. It was used as the lure, the lash, and the motive power to get these boys into different ways of life and thought.

"Its success far exceeded my highest expectations. Rough and wild boys may defy the teacher, and scoff at the opinions of their elders; but they cannot scoff at the public opinion of their playmates, nor defy the companions who are able and ready to inflict condign corporal punishment."[3]

1910-1915. Served as Chief Scout of the Boy Scouts, an organization which he helped found.

1919-1927. Rewrote the mammoth four volume *Life Histories of Northern Animals.*

1930. Bought 25,000 acres of land in Sante Fe, developed as Seton Institute, and dedicated to the preservation of pristine Indian lore.

November 6, 1931. Became an American citizen.

1935. Married Julia Buttree, writer and authority on Indian life. The couple wrote and lectured together.

October 23, 1946. Died in Santa Fe, New Mexico.

FOR MORE INFORMATION SEE: Henry C. Tracy, "Ernest Thompson Seton," in his *American Naturalists,* Dutton, 1930; *Trail of an Artist-Naturalist: The Autobiography of Ernest Thompson Seton,* Scribner, 1940; R. Wallace, "Wild Animals He Has Known," *Readers Digest,* September, 1946; Bertha E. Mahony and others, compilers, *Illustrators of Children's Books, 1744-1945,* Horn Book, 1947; W. G. Vinal, "Science Janus," *School Science and Mathematics,* June, 1953; Farida A. Wiley, editor, *Ernest Thompson Seton's America,* Devin-Adair, 1954; Doris (Shannon) Garst and Warren E. Garst, *Ernest Thompson Seton, Naturalist,* Messner, 1959; *Horn Book,* June, 1966; Julia Seton, *By a Thousand Fires,* Doubleday, 1967; Brian Doyle, editor, *Who's Who of Children's Literature,* Schocken Books, 1968; Obituaries—*New York Times,* October 24, 1946; *Newsweek,* November 4, 1946; *Current Biography,* December, 1946; *Recreation,* December, 1946; *Wilson Library Bulletin,* December, 1946; *Auk,* April, 1947; *Current Biography Yearbook, 1947.*

SIDJAKOV, Nicolas 1924-

PERSONAL: Surname is pronounced *Sidge* uh koff; born December 16, 1924, in Riga, Latvia; came to the United States in 1954; son of Nicolas and Lydie (Somac) Sidjakov; married Jean McFarland, 1954; married second wife, Diane M. Sullivan, October 3, 1975; children: (first marriage) Nicolas, Gregory. *Education:* Studied at the Ecole des Beaux Arts, Paris, France. *Home:* 114 San Carlos Ave., Sausalito, Calif. 94965. *Office:* The Embarcadero, Pier 3, San Francisco, Calif. 94111.

CAREER: Freelance designer for the French movie industry, 1950-55; freelance designer in the advertising field, San Francisco, Calif., 1956—; illustrator for children's books. *Member:* San Francisco Society of Communicating Arts. *Awards, honors: Friendly Beasts* by Laura N. Baker was selected by the *New York Times* as one of the ten best illustrated children's books of 1957 and received an American Institute Graphic Arts award for one of 50 best children's books; *Baboushka and the Three Kings* by Ruth Robbins was chosen by the *New York Times* as one of the best illustrated children's books of 1960 and was also awarded the Caldecott Medal in 1961; the *New York Times* selected *The Emperor and the Drummer Boy* by R. Robbins as one of the best illustrated children's books of 1962. Recipient of awards and certificates of merit in the New York, Los Angeles, Chicago, Detroit, and San Francisco Art Directors' shows.

ILLUSTRATOR: Laura N. Baker, *The Friendly Beasts,* Parnassus, 1957; Ruth Robbins, *Baboushka and the Three Kings,* Parnassus, 1960; R. Robbins, *The Emperor and the Drummer Boy,* Parnassus, 1962; R. Robbins, *Harlequin and Mother Goose,* Parnassus, 1965; Irene Elmer, *A Lodestone and a Toadstone,* Knopf, 1969; Ross Patrick Shideler, translator, *Staffan: An Old Christmas Folk Song,* Parnassus, 1970.

SIDELIGHTS: **1924.** Born in Riga, Latvia of parents who had fled Russia during the Russian Revolution. He was still quite young when the family escaped from Latvia before the country was annexed by Russia.

1945. Studied painting at the Ecole des Beaux-Arts and then began free-lancing as an illustrator and designer.

1954. After marrying an American, Jean McFarland, Sidjakov moved to the United States. They settled in the San

Francisco area where he set up his studio. The couple have two sons, Nicolas and Gregory.

1957. First children's book illustrations appeared in *The Friendly Beasts*. The book was honored by the *New York Times* as one of the ten best illustrated children's books of the year and was included in the American Institute of Graphic Arts Children's Book Show (1955-1957). "An artist has to protect himself against routine, monotony, and the resulting sterility. Only by keeping flexible, away from the beaten paths and clichés, can he expect to maintain originality and freshness of approach. Otherwise, he gets to be strictly a technician, or a bore, or both. The dreadful prospect accounts for the enthusiasm I felt when the opportunity presented itself to work on my first children's book. A refreshing new medium to work with seemed like a welcome shot-in-the-arm. It turned out to be more like a revolution, resulting in more pioneering than I had ever expected. Accustomed as I was to working with a single piece of art, a new dimension, the thickness of a book—in other words continuity—was a new experience for me. The cover, end paper, title page, typography—all these many ingredients had to form an aesthetic unit. One wrong factor could ruin the whole project.

"*The Friendly Beasts,* my first book, surprisingly enough with-stood these laboratory-stage manipulations of mine reasonably well. To a great extent this is due to an almost boundless patience on the part of Ruth Robbins [art director of Parnassus Press and illustrator of several children's books] who led me along, pointing out all the numerous pitfalls I was so eager to tumble into." [Nicolas Sidjakov, "Caldecott Award Acceptance," *Horn Book,* August, 1961.[1]]

1960. Illustrated *Baboushka and the Three Kings.* "After a suitable recovery time, not discouraged a bit, Ruth [Robbins] came up with *Baboushka and the Three Kings.* This time I felt more at ease with the medium and its problems. I even had some energy left to give a thought or two to child psychology, as my four-year-old son was ever present when I worked on the illustrations. This contact with him on a literary and artistic plane proved to be extremely fruitful. We approached each other with a reticent caution, not being sure that we spoke the same language. I soon found out, indeed, that we did not, and had to realize with apprehension how adult I was. It is difficult to remember how wide open everything is for children of that age. They start out from scratch, feeling their way along, relying on bits of information they are being fed or that they pick up. By putting these pieces of a puzzle together, they arrive at their own conclusions with a marvelous logic that is inaccessible to adults.

"One day, perhaps being tired of hearing, 'When you grow up you can do this. . . .' and 'When you grow up you can do that. . . .' my son replied, 'When I grow up and you will be a little boy. . . .' It took me a while to realize that it seemed quite probable to him that as some people are growing taller, others must be getting shorter—to keep things balanced, I suppose. Now this type of reasoning would seem very valid to us, *if* we could forget everything we know or have experienced. It occurred to me that our adult reasoning and taste are based on an almost axiomatic acceptance of certain rules. It is impossible for an adult to break down this barrier. All this is to say that I realized how vain an attempt to foresee a child's reactions would be. Any condescending effort to conform to a child's tastes or beliefs would seem doomed to failure. So I did the only thing left do . . . I forgot all about children while trying to do the best I could and something I would be satisfied with, and then, hoping for the best, sub-

NICOLAS SIDJAKOV

mitted the final drawings to my son and his friends for approval. This method proved to be satisfactory to all parties, and when, after having manifested a quite pleased reaction to my efforts, but not wanting me to get away with it too easily, Nicolas asked me why Baboushka *always* wears tennis shoes, I merely explained patiently that this is the kind of shoe that all Russian peasants used to wear. A fact he readily accepted.

"This is one little detail that happens to be true. I did, however, take some liberties with authenticity concerning Baboushka's surroundings and her clothes, despite the extensive documentation that Ruth had gathered for me. A stricter application of reality, I felt, would make it more difficult for me to get the mood I sought. Loose interpretation is quite a dangerous thing, considering the love for accuracy and detail most children seem to have. Fortunately, the story is too far removed in time and space for them to check up on me. I will add, though, that my conscience is quite clear, since I believe that a Russian feeling has been given the book through color and style. Being Russian by birth I should know something about it. Even though I have never lived in Russia, my family was as Russian as can be—pre-Revolution, of course. Since this 'Baboushka' seems to have all the pre-Revolutionary characteristics, I can claim my experience as valid."[1]

1961. Awarded the Caldecott Medal for *Baboushka and the Three Kings.* ". . . I was, naturally, quite pleased, but, frankly, I did not even come close to realizing what it was all about. It is embarrassing to admit that I was pretty vague about the Caldecott or, for that matter, if Mr. O'Dell will forgive me, the Newbery Award. . . .

"That state did not last long. From that day on things began to happen, and they kept happening, and they are still happening. I have met many wonderful people—librarians, re-

(From *A Loadstone and a Toadstone* by Irene Elmer. Illustrated by Nicolas Sidjakov.)

viewers, and others—and have discovered that enthusiastic dedication to high standards in this field is not the prerogative of Mr. and Mrs. Parnassus Press exclusively. Ruth and Herman Schein deserve a big slice of this medal. Two people doing what they are doing the way they are doing it in this time of big organizations is a refreshing exception. The hardships of being a small publisher are largely compensated. I believe, by the finished product that has a feeling of direct concern and taste; every one of their books is a personal involvement, exhausting, but rewarding. May Parnassus Press stay small forever.

"I would like to add that it is the most gratifying experience to see the hard effort, the long, painful, and exciting work put into our book, not only did not go by unnoticed, but has been acknowledged with the greatest honor there is."[1]

Sidjakov has illustrated several other children's books since receiving the Caldecott Medal. He has established himself as a leading designer of advertising art and his work has been exhibited in leading American cities. He speaks five languages and has traveled and worked in France, Germany, Italy and Switzerland as well as in the United States.

FOR MORE INFORMATION SEE: Ruth Robbins, "Nicolas Sidjakov," *Horn Book,* August, 1961; Muriel Fuller, editor, *More Junior Authors,* H. W. Wilson, 1963; Lee Kingman, editor, *Illustrators of Children's Books, 1957-1966,* Horn Book, 1968.

WILLIAM STEIG

He was marooned on an island, nowhere near civilization, as far as he could tell; and if he was going to get off, it must be by his own devices. ■ (From *Abel's Island* by William Steig. Illustrated by the author.)

STEIG, William 1907-

PERSONAL: Born November 14, 1907, in New York, N.Y. *Education:* Attended City College, New York, N.Y. and the National Academy of Design.

CAREER: Cartoonist, illustrator; author. *Awards, honors: Sylvester and the Magic Pebble* was on the *Horn Book* honor list, nominated Children's Book of the Year, 1969, received the Caldecott Medal, 1970, and nominated for the National Book Award in the children's category; *Amos and Boris* was nominated for National Book Award in children's category, *New York Times* choice of Best Illustrated Children's Book of the Year, Children's Book Showcase Title; *Dominic* was on the *Horn Book* honor list, nominated for the National Book Award in the children's category, winner of the William White Children's Book Award, 1975; *The Real Thief* was on the *New York Times Book Review* Outstanding Book of the Year list; *Farmer Palmer's Wagon Ride* was nominated Children's Book of the Year, 1974; *Abel's Island* received the Newbery Award, 1977, was on the *Horn Book* honor list, 1977, Children's Book Showcase Title, 1977; *The Amazing Bone* received the Caldecott Medal, 1977, was on

Dominic dreamed on. Now they were flagrantly close, the would-be killers. A few had raised their deadly knives and clubs. But suddenly they stood like bewildered statues, listening. From all around them, from the whole woods, they heard voices—calling, echoing, re-echoing, repeating Dominic's name. "Dominic! Dominic! DOMINIC! Dominic! Wake up. Wake up, Dominic!" ■ (From *Dominic* by William Steig. Illustrated by the author.)

the *Horn Book* honor list, 1977, Children's Book Showcase Title, 1977.

WRITINGS—All self-illustrated: *C D B!*, Simon & Schuster, 1968; *Roland the Minstrel Pig,* Harper, 1968; *Sylvester and the Magic Pebble* (ALA Notable Book), Simon & Schuster, 1969; *The Bad Island,* Simon & Schuster, 1969; *Bad Speller,* Simon & Schuster, 1970; *Eye for Elephants,* Simon & Schuster, 1970; *Lovely Ones,* Simon & Schuster, 1970; *Male/Female,* Farrar, Straus, 1971; *Amos and Boris* (ALA Notable Book), Farrar, Straus, 1971; *Dominic* (ALA Notable Book), Farrar, Straus, 1972; *The Real Thief* (ALA Notable Book), Farrar, Straus, 1973; *Farmer Palmer's Wagon Ride* (ALA Notable Book), Farrar, Straus, 1974; *Abel's Island* (ALA Notable Book), Farrar, Straus, 1976; *The Amazing Bone* (ALA Notable Book), Farrar, Straus, 1977; *Caleb & Kate,* Farrar, Straus, 1977. Work has appeared in *The New Yorker* and other magazines.

SIDELIGHTS: "I was born in New York City in 1907. In a family where every member was engaged in some area of the arts, it was not surprising that I became an artist. After public school I went to City College and attended the National Academy of Design.

"In 1930 my work began appearing in *The New Yorker*. I published my first children's book in 1968, embarking on a new and very different career.

"I came into this second profession in the seventh decade of my life, not knowing what to expect. Cartooning, my other profession, is extremely peaceful. One submits his drawings to magazines and gets back either a check or the drawings. There are no meetings, no celebrations of anything, no medals, and almost no mail. One hardly knows for whom he is working. About three admirers write each year, and occasionally one meets one in person and is praised for something he didn't do. One has lots of time to meditate and wait for Enlightenment.

"When I create a cartoon the idea and the drawing are one. You draw whatever wants to come out. But when you illustrate, you have, for instance, to draw someone who has on a

polka-dot dress. It has to be the same dress as in the previous picture, you have to remember the facts of the story.

"You probably write for yourself as a child. As a boy I read and loved *Robin Hood, Robinson Crusoe, Pinocchio,* and the King Arthur series. I remember going to the park with friends and acting out the Arthurian tales, beating each other with cudgels and yelling, not in ancient accents, 'I'll smite thee, thou churlish knave!'

"To start a book I decide first that it's time to write a new story, and then I am most often propelled by a visual image or an idea. With *Roland the Minstrel Pig,* I had the image of a pig hanging on a string and thought, 'That's a nice picture.' The same thing happened with *Amos and Boris,* but it was one of the book's last illustrations (the picture of two elephants pushing a whale into the sea) that provided the seed from which the story grew. In the case of *Sylvester and the Magic Pebble,* I thought of doing a book with magic in it because children like magic and I do too. *Dominic* began when I decided to do a picture book about a dog who leaves home and has to choose among three roads. I thought there would be three different stories and the roads would all end up in the same place. But by the time I got around to actually writing it, the book became my first long work for children, and the story changed a lot. *The Real Thief* started with the idea of a child suffering from an injustice. That's the only time I really gave myself a theme. Otherwise, I just ramble around and discover for myself what will happen next. It's only when you're consciously aware of what you're doing in a book that you're in trouble.''

In accepting the William Allen White Children's Book Award, Steig acknowledged: "Writing for children is a different kettle of fish. Not only does one write and illustrate, but one is asked to go places and authenticate what he has written by autographing it, one is invited to attend seminars and discuss how to do what you do, one gets lots of mail (in responding to which he is saved from idleness), and so forth. Not all of it is as much fun as the writing and the drawing. But winning is definitely fun. I never understood what was missing from my life until this began to happen. It feels darn good, like being dubbed into knighthood. I've even taken to buying medals in the antique shops in my territory to have the feeling repeated.''

Steig's works are included in the Kerlan Collection at the University of Minnesota.

FOR MORE INFORMATION SEE: Selma G. Lanes, *Down the Rabbit Hole*, Atheneum, 1971; *Christian Science Monitor*, November 11, 1971; *Life*, December 17, 1971; *Time*, December 27, 1971; *Third Book of Junior Authors*, edited by Doris de Montreville and Donna Hill, H. W. Wilson, 1972; *Saturday Review/World*, December 4, 1973; *Newbery and Caldecott Medal Books: 1966-1975*, edited by Lee Kingman, Horn Book, 1975; *Horn Book*, August and October, 1975, August and December, 1976, April and June, 1977.

TENGGREN, Gustaf　1896-

PERSONAL: Born November 3, 1896, in Magra, Sweden; son of an artist. *Education:* Attended the Sloejdfoereningens School and Valand School of Fine Arts in Gothenburg, Sweden.

CAREER: Illustrator of children's books, beginning 1917; lived in Copenhagen, Denmark, 1918-19; came to the United States in 1920; held various jobs in Cleveland, Ohio, including work for an art studio, newspaper illustration, fashion drawing for a department store, and poster painting for a theater, 1920-22; designer with the Disney Studios, 1936-39; travelled and painted in Europe, Mexico, Canada, and throughout the United States. His works have been exhibited in Gothenburg and Stockholm, Sweden, and Copenhagen, Denmark. *Awards, honors: Lively Little Rabbit* by Georges Duplaix and *Tenggren's Story Book* were chosen by the American Institute of Graphic Arts for its ''Fifty Books'' Exhibit in 1943 and 1944, respectively; *New York Herald*

Gustaf Tenggren, self portrait.

(From *A Wonder-Book and Tanglewood Tales* by Nathaniel Hawthorne. Illustrated by Gustaf Tenggren.)

Tribune Spring Book Award, 1945, for *Farm Stories* by Kathryn and Byron Jackson.

ILLUSTRATOR: Bland Totmar o' Troll (fairy tale), [Stockholm], 1917; Cyrus Graner (editor), *Bland Totmar och Troll*, No. 5, Ahlen & Akerlunds [Stockholm], 1922; Nathaniel Hawthorne, *Wonder Book [and] Tanglewood Tales*, Houghton, 1923; Johanna Spyri, *Heidi*, Houghton, 1923; *Good Dog Book*, Houghton, 1924; Andrew Lang, editor, *Red Fairy Book*, McKay, 1924; Louise De La Ramee, *Dog of Flanders*, Macmillan, 1925; Frances Courtenay Baylor, *Juan and Juanita*, Houghton, 1926; Cyrus Graner (editor), *Bland Totmar och Troll*, No. 9, Ahlen & Akerlund, 1926; Ruth Campbell, *Small Fry and the Winged Horse*, Volland, 1927; Emma Miller Bolenius and M. G. Kellogg, *Mother Goose Book*, Houghton, 1929; Richard Wagner, *Ring of the Nibelung*, Knopf, 1932; Joseph Schrank, *Seldom and the Golden Cheese*, Dodd, 1933; Hans Christian Andersen, *Fairy Tales*, Appleton-Century, 1935.

Mother Goose, Little, Brown, 1940; Inez Bertail, *New Illustrated Book of Favorite Hymns*, Garden City, 1941; *Bedtime Stories*, Simon & Schuster, 1942; Katharine Gibson, editor, *The Tenggren Tell-It-Again Book*, Little, Brown, 1942, reissued, 1960; Janette Lowrey, *Poky Little Puppy*, Simon & Schuster, 1942; Ariane (pseudonym of Georges Duplaix), *Lively Little Rabbit*, Simon & Schuster, 1943; Barbara Brown and Helen Arbuthnot, *Story of England*, Random House, 1943; Helen Dike, *Stories from the Great Metropoli-*

But Tom Thumb began to run and was halfway around the world and back before the Ogre had walked a mile. ■ (From *The Tenggren Tell-It-Again Book*. Text edited and adapted by Katharine Gibson. Illustrated by Gustaf Tenggren.)

(From *The Ring of the Nibelung* by Gertrude Henderson. Illustrated by Gustaf Tenggren.)

tan Operas, Random House, 1943; Opal Wheeler, *Sing for Christmas,* Dutton, 1943; (and editor) *Tenggren's Story Book,* Simon & Schuster, 1944; H. C. Andersen, *Little Match Girl,* Grosset, 1944; Opal Wheeler, *Sing for America,* Dutton, 1944; Kathryn and Byron Jackson, *Farm Stories,* Simon & Schuster, 1946; Cathleen Schurr, *The Shy Little Kitten,* Simon & Schuster, 1946, reissued, Golden Press, circa 1960; Georges Duplaix, *The Big Brown Bear,* Simon & Schuster, 1947; Helen Bannerman, *Little Black Sambo,* Simon & Schuster, 1948; K. and B. Jackson, *Tenggren's Cowboys and Indians,* Simon & Schuster, 1948, reissued, Golden Press, 1968.

K. and B. Jackson, *Pirates, Ships and Sailors,* Simon & Schuster, 1950, reissued, Golden Press, 1971; K. Jackson, *The Little Trapper,* Simon & Schuster, 1950; Clement Clarke Moore, *The Night before Christmas,* Simon & Schuster, 1951; K. Jackson, *The Saggy Baggy Elephant,* Golden Press, 1952; *Tenggren's Jack and the Beanstalk,* Simon & Schuster, 1953; Jakob Ludwig Karl Grimm, *Tenggren's The Giant with Three Golden Hairs,* Simon & Schuster, 1955; *Tales from the Arabian Nights,* Golden Press, 1957; *Contes de Fees: Petit Poussin,* Simon & Schuster, 1958; Jane Werner, *Lion's Paw: A Tale of African Animals,* Golden Press, 1960; Geoffrey Chaucer, *The Canterbury Tales of Geoffrey Chaucer* (edited by A. Kent and Constance Hieatt), Golden Press, 1961; Thomas Malory, *King Arthur and the Knights of the Round Table* (retold by Emma Gelders Sterne and Barbara Lindsay), Golden Press, 1962; K. Jackson, *More Farmyard Tales,* Hamlyn, 1970; K. Jackson, *Tawny Scrawny Lion,* Golden Press, 1974.

SIDELIGHTS: Gustaf Tenggren was born in Magra, Sweden in 1898. He studied art in Gothenburg and began his career with exhibitions in Gothenburg, Stockholm, and Copenhagen while still a student. Beginning in 1917, he illustrated a number of children's books for Scandinavian publishers, including the annual fairy tale, "Bland Totmar o' Troll."

In 1920 Tenggren emigrated to the United States and held various jobs until he became a designer for the Walt Disney studio in 1936. There he created scenes and characters for "Snow White," "Fantasia," and "Bambi."

In 1943 *The Lively Little Rabbit,* one of the many Golden Book series that he illustrated, was chosen by the American Institute of Graphic Arts among the "Fifty Books of the Year." The following year *Tenggren's Story Book* received the same distinction.

Gustaf Tenggren lives with his wife in Dogfish Head, Maine and enjoys fishing, boating, and chess. He has travelled through Europe, Mexico, Yucatan, and Nova Scotia.

FOR MORE INFORMATION SEE: Muriel Fuller, editor, *More Junior Authors,* H. W. Wilson, 1963.

TOOTHAKER, Roy Eugene   1928-

PERSONAL: Born July 30, 1928, in Van Buren, Ark.; son of Vern Edward (a caller for a railroad company) and Birdie (Humphrey-Alcorn) Toothaker; married Norma Elnora Johnson, December 27, 1954 (divorced December 20, 1956). *Education:* Coffeyville Community Junior College, A.A., 1948; Pittsburgh State College, B.S.Ed., 1952; Wichita State University, M.Ed., 1957; further graduate study at University of Kansas, University of California, Los Angeles, University of Missouri at Kansas City, University of Wisconsin—Platteville and Madison; University of Arkansas,

ROY EUGENE TOOTHAKER

Ed.D., 1970. *Politics:* Democrat. *Religion:* Protestant. *Home:* 864 North 11th St., DeKalb, Ill. 60115. *Office:* Department of Elementary Education, Northern Illinois University, DeKalb, Ill. 60115.

CAREER: Elementary school teacher in Kansas, 1945-46, 1948-52; Beech Aircraft Corp., Wichita, Kan., accounting clerk, 1952-57; elementary school teacher in California, 1957, and Kansas, 1958-65; University of Nebraska, Omaha, instructor in English and director of Reading Improvement Laboratory, 1965-67; elementary school teacher and high school teacher of English in Cherryvale, Kan., 1968-69; Coffeyville Community Junior College, Coffeyville, Kan., instructor in English, 1969-70; University of Wisconsin—Platteville, associate professor of education, 1970-72; University of Arkansas, Fayetteville, visiting associate professor of education, 1972-73; University of Miami, Coral Gables, Fla., visiting assistant professor of education, 1973-74; supervisor and staff development person for public schools of Marianna, Ark., 1974-75; Northern Illinois University, DeKalb, assistant professor of education, 1975—.

MEMBER: Association for Childhood Education International, International Reading Association (president of local chapters, 1963-64, 1965-66, 1971-72), National Council of Teachers of English, American Library Association, Society of Children's Book Writers, Children's Reading Round Table of Chicago, Phi Delta Kappa.

WRITINGS: A Wild Goose Chase (juvenile), Prentice-Hall, 1975. Author of Spanish version of Barbara and Ed Emberley's, "Drummer Hoff" (juvenile sound filmstrip), Weston Woods Studio, 1976. Contributor of articles and reviews to literature and education journals. Editor of *Newsletter* of Kansas Council of International Reading Association, 1964-

(From *A Wild Goose Chase* by Roy Toothaker. Illustrated by Tom Dunnington.)

65; associate co-editor of *Journal for the Study of Perception*, 1967—.

WORK IN PROGRESS: The Animal's Secret (tentative title), a juvenile book, for Prentice-Hall; a historical novel for elementary school children; puzzles and quizzes for children; bibliographies of children's books; biographical essays of children's authors.

SIDELIGHTS: "Teaching and working with boys and girls brings me the greatest delight of all. I like teaching and writing about books and about authors and what they have to offer children. I like teaching others to write and have taught all grades, from first grade through graduate students. I am glad to have the opportunity to expose others to the beauty and versatility of the English language (and also Spanish and French).

"James Sterling Ayars, author of several books for children, paid me a great compliment recently when he autographed a copy of one of his books for me: 'And for Roy Toothaker, my friend and friend of *all* good authors. And I received a note from children's author Nancy Roberts; she wrote: 'Your article in *Childhood Education* embodies so many good points about children and their various kinds of curiosities that some of your observations will undoubtedly find their way into my talks. My compliments and appreciation for such an excellent and comprehensive article.'

"I did Spanish and French versions of Barbara and Ed Emberley's *Drummer Hoff*, because I wanted young Spanish and French readers to have an opportunity to enjoy that excellent but brief cumulative rhyme (and Caldecott Award winner). I wrote *A Wild Goose Chase* to help fill the need for more brief but good reading material for the very young reader, for more story-time material to read or tell to the very young child, and for more material which fulfills the young child's need to achieve and for play. (I have translated *A Wild Goose Chase* into both French and Spanish, which I hope will be published and distributed soon.)"

TURNBULL, Ann (Christine) 1943- (Ann Nicol)

PERSONAL: Born August 22, 1943, in Hertford, England; daughter of Harold Drysdale (a legal executive) and Muriel Violet (East) Turnbull; married Simon Thorne, August 6, 1966 (divorced, 1973); married Timothy Nicol (a landscape architect), August 3, 1973; children: (2nd marriage) David Ralf. *Education:* Attended Bexley Technical School, 1956-60, and Balls Park College of Education, 1971-74. *Religion:* None. *Home:* 6 Danesford, Hollinswood, Telford, Shropshire, England.

CAREER: Secretary in London and Reading, England, 1960-71, and Stevenage, England, 1974; writer.

WRITINGS: The Frightened Forest (juvenile), Kestrel, 1974, Seabury, 1975; *The Wolf King* (juvenile), Kestrel, 1975, Seabury, 1976.

WORK IN PROGRESS: Another book for juveniles.

ANN TURNBULL

HOBBIES AND OTHER INTERESTS: Folk-lore, folk-singing, archaeology, ancient history.

SIDELIGHTS: "I've been writing since I was about six years old, and started writing historical novels intended for adults when I was sixteen and sending them to publishers. It was thirteen years before I got anything accepted, and that was after being introduced to modern children's novels at college and realizing that this was where my own interest realy lay."

VAN ABBÉ, Salaman   1883-1955

PERSONAL: Born July 31, 1883, in Holland; died in 1955, in London, England. *Education:* Educated in Amsterdam, London, and Paris. *Home:* Putney, London, England.

CAREER: Painter, etcher, and illustrator. *Member:* Associate of the Royal Society of Painter-Etchers, member of the Royal Society of British Artists, Savage Club, London Sketch Club, Art Workers' Guild (president, 1941). *Awards, honors:* Paris Salon, honorable mention, 1930, Bronze Medal, 1939.

'I am your enemy,' answered the valiant Pygmy, in his mightiest squeak. **'You have slain the enormous Antaeus, our brother by the mother's side, and for ages the faithful ally of our illustrious nation. We are determined to put you to death.** ■ (From *Tanglewood Tales* by Nathaniel Hawthorne. Illustrated by S. Van Abbé.)

'Then follow me,' said Ariadne, 'and tread softly.'
■ (From *Tanglewood Tales* by Nathaniel Hawthorne. Illustrated by S. Van Abbé.)

ILLUSTRATOR: John Galsworthy, *Loyalties,* Duckworth, 1930; William R. G. Kent, *My Lord Mayor,* H. Jenkins, 1947; Louisa May Alcott, *Little Women,* Dent, 1948, Dutton, 1951, reprinted, 1961; Carola Omen, *Robin Hood,* Dent, 1949, Dutton, 1951; Nathaniel Hawthorne, *Wonder Book,* Dent, 1949, Dutton, 1951; Thomas Hughes, *Tom Brown's School Days,* Dent, 1949, Dutton, 1951; Joyce Reason, *Secret Fortress,* Dent, 1950; Hawthorne, *Tanglewood Tales,* Dutton, 1952; Alcott, *Good Wives,* Dutton, 1953; Reason, *Mad Miller of Wareham,* Dent, 1954.

SIDELIGHTS: Van Abbé's first interest was portrait painting, but the necessity of earning a living made him seek a more lucrative occupation. He devoted most of his time to illustrating books and magazines and designing book jackets. Both brought him recognition quickly. Among the famous authors for whom he designed book jackets were John Galsworthy, H. G. Wells, Edgar Wallace, and Agatha Christie.

Although generally thought of as an etcher and engraver, Van Abbé also excelled with brush, pen and pencil. He travelled extensively and studied art in Holland, Paris and England, He was particularly well known for his illustrations of such classics as *Robin Hood, Tom Sawyer,* and *Little Women.*

FOR MORE INFORMATION SEE: C. Wade, "Artists of Note," *Artist,* July, 1949; Bertha E. Miller and others, compilers, *Illustrators of Children's Books, 1946-1956,* Horn Book, 1958; (obituary) *New York Times,* March 1, 1955.

VAN DUYN, Janet 1910-

PERSONAL: Born September 23, 1910, in Auburn, N.Y.; daughter of David Montgomery and Ruth (Bartlett) Dunning; married John Van Duyn (a surgeon), December, 1935 (divorced, 1949); children: Ruth Minnich, Barbara (Mrs. Richard H. Bickerstaff, Jr.). *Education:* Vassar College, A.B., 1932. *Politics:* "Registered independent." *Religion:* "Also independent." *Home:* 135 Lyons Plain Rd. Weston, Conn. 06883.

CAREER: Writer, 1968—. Teacher of college preparatory English at Low Heywood School in Stamford, Conn.; librarian at CBS Labs in Stamford, Conn.; storyteller in the children's department of the New York Public Library in New York City.

WRITINGS: I Married Them (humorous novel), Howell, Soskin, 1945; *The Egyptians* (juvenile; early culture series), McGraw, 1970; *The Greeks* (juvenile; early culture series), McGraw, 1972; *Builders on the Desert: Stone Craftsmen of Ancient Egypt* (children's history), Messner, 1974. Editor-in-chief and chief writer of Bicentennial issue of *Fairfield County* magazine (Westport, Conn.), 1975. Contributor of articles to periodicals.

WORK IN PROGRESS: A book on the first great woman in history, Queen Hatshepsut of Egypt (c. 1500 B.C.); *The Condemned Tower,* pure fiction, "I do not know where it will go at the moment. It keeps after me".

SIDELIGHTS: "I never became a 'full time' writer. It was either a forty-eight hour day, or a two hour day, which I've shrunk to now. It began in 1968, when I was working for an

"Acting!" Doctor Mac seemed about to froth at the mouth. He stabbed a finger at her dramatically. "You're a mature woman and I insist that you behave like one." ■ (From *I Married Them* by Janet Van Duyn. Illustrated by Garth Williams.)

outfit which professed to teach people how to write. An editor asked me if I knew enough about ancient Egypt to do a book in a series. Thinking back to a tenth grade course in ancient history, I said 'Yes.' That was a marvelous course, but I know now that I'll never know enough about Egypt. I wrote the book Saturdays, Sundays, and nights, while working at my job. Now that I have all the time I need, I find that I am just as spasmodic, lazy and distraught as the rankest of amateurs.

"Research. It's homework pure and simple. It's private; the more help you get the more discouraged you become. It's lonely, but after you get into it, your world is suddenly full of people. I cannot use other people's outlines, nor indeed follow one of my own, until I have flopped about in a congenial chaos of unrelated facts. When these cut-and-dried editors ask for outlines I try to give them what they want, but I never follow them.

"For Egypt I began with simple books, worked my way up through the archaeologists like William Mathew Flinders Petrie to the scholars who wrote the *Cambridge Ancient History,* and that's pretty heady stuff. I didn't despise fiction, Lawrence Durrell, Mika Waltari. I persuaded the curator of Egyptian Art in the Metropolitan Museum of Art to check my first draft. He was great, not at all shy about writing 'utter nonsense!' in the margins. In this kind of writing one's value judgments are at stake.

"Travel, of course. Go where you can, but not for fun. I never got to Egypt until after my two books were published. But I did go to Greece and I'm glad I waited until the book

JANET VAN DUYN

was 3/4 done. Travel too soon can affect you in an exact opposite manner from a rigid outline. It overstimulates, then confuses with its wealth of material. So the point is, don't fool around; write that book!"

HOBBIES AND OTHER INTERESTS: Travel, organ music, cathedrals, medieval legends, languages, including ancient Greek, and reading hieroglyphics.

VAN LOON, Hendrik Willem   1882-1944

PERSONAL: Surname is pronounced van *lone;* born January 14, 1882, in Rotterdam, Holland; came to the United States in 1903; died March 11, 1944, in Old Greenwich, Connecticut; son of Hendrik Willem and Elisabeth Johanna (Hanken) Van Loon; married Eliza Bowditch, June, 1906; married second wife, Helen Criswell, August, 1920 (divorced, 1927); married Frances Goodrich (an actress), 1927 (divorced, 1927); remarried Helen Criswell; children—first marriage: Henry, Gerard. *Education:* Harvard University, student, 1903-04; Cornell University, A.B., 1905; University of Munich, Ph.D., 1911. *Home:* Old Greenwich, Connecticut.

CAREER: Historian, journalist, and illustrator. Associated Press, correspondent in Washington D.C., later in Poland and Russia, 1906, also in countries throughout Europe, 1914-18; lecturer on history at various American universities, 1911-16, including Cornell University, Ithaca, New York, 1915-16; Antioch College, Yellow Springs, Ohio, professor of history, 1922-23; Baltimore *Sun* (newspaper), Baltimore, Maryland, associate editor, 1923-24; lectured in New Zealand, Australia, South Africa, and South America, 1934; established a short-wave radio station from Boston to the Netherlands; radio commentator. *Member:* National Institute of Arts and Letters, Cosmos Club (Washington, D.C.), Harvard Club, Players Club (New York City). *Awards, honors:* First recipient of the Newbery Medal, 1922, for *The Story of Mankind;* Officer of the Order of Orange Nassau, 1937; Order of the Lion of Netherlands, 1942.

*WRITINGS—*Nonfiction: *The Fall of the Dutch Republic,* Houghton, 1913; *The Rise of the Dutch Kingdom, 1795-1813,* Doubleday, Page, 1915; *The Golden Book of the Dutch Navigators* (self-illustrated), Century, 1916, revised edition, Appleton-Century, 1938; *Tolerance,* Boni & Liveright, 1925, reissued, 1940 (published in England as *The Liberation of Mankind: The Story of Man's Struggle for the Right to Think,* Harrap, 1926); *To Have or to Be—Take Your Choice* (essays), John Day, 1932; *An Indiscreet Itinerary; or, How the Unconventional Traveler Should See Holland,* Harcourt, Brace, 1933; *Air-Storming: A Collection of 40 Radio Talks,* Harcourt, Brace, 1935 (published in England as *Van Loon on the Air,* Harrap, 1936); *Ships and How They Sailed the Seven Seas,* Simon & Schuster, 1935; *A World Divided Is a World Lost* (essays), Pamphlet House, 1935.

The Arts (self-illustrated), Simon & Schuster, 1937, new edition, Liveright, 1974 (published in England as *The Arts of Mankind,* Harrap, 1938); *Observations on the Mystery of Print and the Work of Johann Gutenberg,* Book Manufacturers' Institute, 1937; *How to Look at Pictures: A Short History of Painting,* Modern Age Books, 1938; *Our Battle: Being One Man's Answer to My Battle, by Adolf Hitler,* Simon & Schuster, 1938; *The Story of the Pacific,* Harcourt, Brace, 1940.

The King Is Dead—The Friend Is Gone. ■ (From *The Last of the Troubadours* by Grace Castagnetta. Illustrated by Hendrik Willem Van Loon.)

(From the movie "The Story of Mankind," starring Groucho Marx. Copyright © 1957 by Warner Brother Pictures, Inc.)

Biography: *Life and Times of Pieter Stuyvesant*, H. Holt, 1928; *Life and Times of Rembrandt*, Garden City Publishing, 1930, abridged edition, Bantam, 1957 (published in England as *R. v. R.: Being an Account of the Last Years and the Death of One Rembrandt Harmenszoon van Rijn*, Liveright, 1930); (with Grace Castagnetta) *The Last of the Troubadours: Carl Michael Bellman, 1740-1795*, Simon & Schuster, 1939; *The Life and Times of Johann Sebastian Bach*, Simon & Schuster, 1940; *Van Loon's Lives*, Simon & Schuster, 1942; *Thomas Jefferson: The Serene Citizen from Monticello* (self-illustrated), Dodd, 1943; *The Life and Times of Simon Bolivar* (self-illustrated), Dodd, 1943; the latter two books were published together as *Fighters for Freedom: Jefferson and Bolivar*, Dodd, 1962 (published in England as *Jefferson and Bolivar: New World Fighters for Freedom*, Harrap, 1966); *Adventures and Escapes of Gustavus Vasa* (self-illustrated), Dodd, 1945; *Report to Saint Peter, upon the Kind of World in Which Hendrik Willem Van Loon Spent the First Years of His Life* (autobiography; self-illustrated), Simon & Schuster, 1947.

For children: *History with a Match: Being an Account of the Earliest Navigators* (self-illustrated), McKay, 1917 [a later edition published as *The Romance of Discovery*, Carlton House, 1937]; *Ancient Man: The Beginning of Civilizations* (self-illustrated), Boni & Liveright, 1920, reissued, Modern Library, circa, 1950; *The Story of Mankind* (self-illustrated), Boni & Liveright, 1921, revised edition, Washington Square Press, 1973; *The Story of the Bible* (self-illustrated), Boni & Liveright, 1923, reissued, Grosset, 1966; *The Story of Wilbur the Hat* (self-illustrated), Boni & Liveright, 1925; *America*, Boni & Liveright, 1927 [a later edition published as *The Story of America*, Garden City Publishing, 1934, reissued, Fawcett, 1959]; *Man, the Miracle Maker*, Liveright, 1928 [a later edition published as *The Story of Inventions: Man, the Miracle Maker*, Garden City Publishing, circa, 1934; published in England as *Multiplex Man; or, The Story of Survival Through Invention*, J. Cape, 1928]; *Van Loon's Geography: The Story of the World We Live In* (self-illustrated), Simon & Schuster, 1932 (published in England as *The Home of Mankind: The Story of the*

World We Live In, Harrap, 1936); *Re: An Elephant Up a Tree* (self-illustrated), Simon & Schuster, 1933; *Around the World with the Alphabet* (self-illustrated), Simon & Schuster, 1935.

Other: *Invasion: Being the Personal Recollections of What Happened to Our Own Family and to Some of Our Friends,* Harcourt, Brace, 1940; (editor) *The Songs We Sing,* Simon & Schuster, 1936; (with G. Castagnetta) *Christmas Carols* (self-illustrated), Simon & Schuster, 1937; (editor and illustrator) *The Songs America Sings,* Simon & Schuster, 1939; (with G. Castagnetta) *Good Tidings,* American Artists Group, 1941; (editor with G. Castagnetta) *Christmas Songs,* American Artists Group, 1942; *The Message of the Bells; or, What Happened to Us on Christmas Eve* (self-illustrated), Garden City Publishing, 1942, reissued, 1962.

Illustrator: Samuel S. Fels, *This Changing World as I See Its Trend and Purpose,* Houghton, 1933; Lucy Mitchell, *Here and Now Story Book,* Dutton, 1936, revised edition, 1948; Henry C. Adams, *Wonder Book of Traveller's Tales,* Liveright, 1936; Desiderius Erasmus, *The Praise of Folly,* W. J. Black, 1942.

ADAPTATIONS—Movies: "Fight for Peace" (motion picture), Warwich War Film, 1938; "The Story of Mankind" (motion picture), starring Ronald Colman, Hedy Lamarr, and the three Marx Brothers, Warner Brothers, 1957.

SIDELIGHTS: **January 14, 1882.** "I was born on the fourteenth of January of the year 1882. I do not know whether or not Venus was in the ascendant on that fateful night, nor have I the vaguest notion in what part of the heavens Capricorn and Ursa Major were disporting themselves with Ishtar. I realize the great role astrology has played in history from the days of the original cave man to those of his descendant, Adolf Hitler. I have carefully studied and tried to make sense of the horoscopes which Johannes Kepler drew up for the Duke of Wallenstein and for the Emperor Matthias. But I feel about astrology the way I do about palmistry, numerology, bibliomancy, sciomancy, haruspicy, myomancy, orniscopy, geomancy, gastromancy, stichomancy, dactyliomancy, capnomancy, and progressive education.

"I don't want to say that there is nothing to them. A great many people brighter than I have found solace and comfort in studying the flights of birds, the lines in their hands, the behavior of mice, the way the smoke would rise from the chimney, or the way a cock would pick up grains. But I have listened to their learned arguments in the same spirit of doubt as descends upon me like a fog the moment some ardent disciple of Nostradamus tries to convince me that this French physician was something more than a clever charlatan and that his prophecies about the Emperor Napoleon and the disastrous tidal wave of Lisbon were something more than the usual abracadabra of the necromancer's trade of the early half of the sixteenth century. . . .

"[But] one of the sisters of the great Brotherhood of Star-Gazers prevailed upon me to find out something definite about the exact hour at which I had made my appearance on this planet.

"I duly wrote to one of my aunts who had been present at this occasion, and she informed me that it was shortly after three o'clock of the night of January 14, in the year of grace 1882, and that the doctor, after a long struggle with this most obstinate newcomer, said, 'Well, he seems all safe

HENDRICK WILLEM VAN LOON

and sound, but God save me from another night like this, for the brat must weigh at least nine pounds.'

"That happened, of course, in the old days when respectable housewives still bore their children in the seclusion of their own homes, and, as no hospital scales were ready at hand, my weight was merely guessed at by the midwife (for midwives still assisted physicians and often knew much more than the regular leech). But the subsequent development of this sprawling infant into a creature well over six feet two and weighing (in spite of all sorts of dietetic experiments) approximately 285 pounds makes me shiver whenever I think of what my poor mother must have suffered before at last, after hours of suffering, she was told that it was a boy and that he looked like his father.

"This has always struck me as a most unfair arrangement. For I loved my mother but never had any sincere affection for my father. . . . For, from a very early age, I tried to separate myself completely from my paternal parent, but, try as I might, I could never get rid of the imprint he had left upon my eyes and nose and the shape of my mouth. This, incidentally, will explain why I have but small love for mirrors and photographs. Both tell me something of which I want to be reminded as little as possible. And this aversion has gone so far that when occasionally a sincere lover of one of my books asks me for a photograph, I will send him a picture, not of my face, but of my hands, for those hands are the hands of my mother." [Hendrik Willem van Loon, *Report to Saint Peter,* Simon & Schuster, 1947.[1]]

Reflecting upon his parents' unhappy marriage, he placed blame upon his father who ". . . belonged to a respectable family . . . he would be able to provide for her and in those days, in our class of society, that was about all that mattered. His mania for fault-finding and his almost incredible capacity for making himself obnoxious had not yet assumed those outrageous proportions that were to make him a marked man in later life.

"[He was] quite a good-looking man, having inherited my grandfather's physical strength and a great deal of personal charm from my grandmother [but] these two personalities clashed and were at war with each other right there within his soul. . . . He came to hate the world because he so thoroughly hated himself.

"[He was also] the walking incarnation of the spiritual spoilsport. . . . If, as a child, we made ourselves a little boat out of a piece of cork and an old rag, he would wait until we had finished our craft and then he would smash it underneath the heel of his boot." [Gerard Willem Van Loon, *The Story of Hendrik Willem Van Loon,* Lippincott, 1972.²]

"In Dutch, the predicate *van* does not have the same meaning as the *von* in German. It is no indication of any kind of noble antecedent. My own name merely indicates that a certain Hendrik Willem (we are hereditarily punished with that name as other families are punished with squints or a tendency towards baldness) at some vague date moved from the county of Loon in northern Belgium to the more profitable fleshpots of Rotterdam and there settled down to make a living as a goldsmith.

"The neighborhood in which I was born still retained the aspects of what it had been in the beginning—a cloister surrounded by all kinds of buildings devoted to charitable purposes and not constructed according to a preconceived plan."

The same held true of Van Loon's home. "No two rooms were on the same floor. Short and long staircases ran every which way. My own little room (as soon as I was allowed to enjoy such a luxury) seemed to hang suspended in mid-air, since the space below it belonged to another house. The kitchen was two staircases below the living-room which also (as was customary in those days) was used as a dining-room. The back windows of that dining-room looked out upon a courtyard which was not our own but which must have been part of the old cloister garden."²

Since van Loon drew a great deal as a very young child, he was taken to the Rotterdam Art Museum. "Unfortunately, after two hundred years of neglect, peat fires and candlelight, the masterpieces of the seventeenth century all looked as if they had been painted in chocolate."²

More to his juvenile taste was the Museum of the Knowledge of This Earth and Its People, Combined with Maritime Affairs. Here he came upon a skull "of a prehistoric man who might have lived as long as thirty thousand years ago. . . . What if this had been the head of one of my ancestors? It made life so much more interesting to imagine your ancestors fighting mastodons and tigers instead of going to dull offices as everyone I knew did every day of the year.

"From my tenth year . . . I wanted more than anything to be a very famous historian. . . ."²

1897. Entered Noorthey, "a school for little snobs. I realize that everybody who writes about his youth is at this moment supposed to tell how deeply he was impressed by his Bible and William Shakespeare. The immortal William was nothing but a name to me, and a very vague name, too. He existed in an excellent Dutch translation—the labor of love of a professional botanist who had devoted all his spare time to this Herculean task. He had done a most excellent job, and we had the whole collection in our small library, for it was supposed to add considerable luster to a respectable Dutch household to have the combined efforts of William Shakespeare and L.A.J. Burgersdijk on their shelves. I did not know who Master Shakespeare had been, but when I picked up one of the volumes (bearing the intriguing name of *Hamlet*), I noticed that it had something to do with history and therefore must be something up my own little alley. But the story was beyond me, and I could make nothing of the melancholy Dane. He seemed rather silly. Very full of words and terribly sorry for himself, but without any desire to do anything about his uncomfortable position.

"I may not have thought it out that way when I was quite so young and this may be a judgment of my later days, for such things are very apt to get themselves rather badly mixed up. I remember, however, for a certainty that my first encounter with the great bard was not a success. And, if I am to be entirely honest with myself, I never got over a certain feeling of boredom when exposed to the good William of the second-best bed, either in the printed form of the endless editions which since then have been bestowed upon me or as presented on the stage in beautiful costumes that go from Brooks (the theatrical outfitters, not the haberdashers on Madison Avenue) to the theatrical storehouse of the Messrs. Eaves.

"If I had never read *Hamlet,* I should not know to this day whether Hamlet married his girl or not. For by the end of the twenty-seventh scene, I usually get so fidgety and my legs begin to shake so violently that the neighbors who are involuntarily being kicked in the posterior parts (you know how narrow our theater seats are) begin to object, and Jimmie [his second wife] takes me out to prevent a public scandal.

"The other day I decided to try again, and, since I thought that my son and Gracie [Castagnetta, a collaborator] (both of whom are still very young) needed a little Shakespeare for their education, I took them along, though I had to bribe them by the promise of a luncheon at the St. Regis, which raised the ante to quite a considerable sum. It was a fine performance by a most dignified group of mummers. But after an hour or so I got a vicious kick on the shins, and Gracie hissed at me that my snoring interfered considerably with the pleasure of the other spectators who had also paid $2.75 for the privilege of hearing the Danish prince recite his little piece about to be or not to be, and that unless I could keep awake she and Willem had better take me out and walk me around the block until I regained consciousness.

"Outside in the lobby I asked them, 'Well, do you like it?' They said no. It had bored them to extinction, and they never would have come if I had not insisted on it. Whereupon we went to the Algonquin and had tea and talked to Frank Case, who told us that since all the Hamlets of the last half century had been his patrons, he had felt duty-bound to go and see their performances. 'But did you like them?' we inquired.

"Send us a dozen prime Florentines and a half a dozen medium-priced Venetians." ■ (From *The Arts* written and illustrated by Hendrik Willem Van Loon.)

"'Oh, well,' said tactful Frank, 'it is hardly up to me to say anything against a fellow author.' And there the matter was dropped.

May 4, 1900. Mother died.

1901. To remove him from his father's influence, his uncle pressured to have him sent to a boarding school.

July 24, 1902. Sailed for America on the steamer, *Potsdam*.

Entered Cornell University where he met George Lincoln Burr, a professor who became his guide and confidante. He was admitted to the law school. "The law-studying is only a means of getting a broader view. As for the profession of a lawyer I never would be it. And the journalism for which I feel myself able is the great journalism of the world. . . . I feel myself at home in the world of great events."[2]

A female classmate recalled: "To the eye of a romantic coed, van Loon was all wrong. His hat, a soft velour, was two sizes too small. His overcoat was green. It hung perfectly straight and buttoned right up to the chin. It had horizontal braids across the front and fastened through loops into pieces of stick. He carried an encased fiddle in one hand. In the other he gripped a small bouquet, an offering to his hostess at some party to which we were both going. The boy was six feet tall or more and weighed, I should say, at least one hundred and eighty-five pounds. He was not fat but evenly larded all over, like a sleek, active seal. As a matter of fact, at this party he was pretty impressive for the first hour. Glib, though his English sounded like Dutch, perfectly at ease in meeting new people, bowing from the waist, he was never at a loss for a word or a topic. But after more people arrived and things got more general, van Loon ceased to be the center of attention and was sort of shunted off to his own devices. At that point he got out his fiddle, sat off in a corner with his back to the crowd, and softly played chords and snatches of tunes to himself. He did that often at parties."[2]

1904. Met Eliza Bowditch, a Boston Society heiress.

June, 1905. Graduated Cornell.

July 1, 1905. Met Bowditch family. "Saturday night I went to Boston, and at three went up to Jamaica Plain. . . . The mother caught me on the stoop and I was at once dragged before Loyola and the Inquisition did its work. It was not a very pleasant interview. Well, Mr. B. is an old gentleman who seems to be a little over-worked and tired and, as I am so much younger, I might as well forget some things he said and asked. For example he inquired whether, after all I had said and done, I intended to marry his daughter as soon as I had some kind of position. . . . If, after all there has been between us, I could say that it was merely a joke, I deserve to be [hung] on the highest tree . . . and to me it seemed a very strange question.

"He talked quite a good deal about position and cash-books and it would have been very pleasant to me if he had been more curious about character. . . . He wanted me not to ask any promise of his daughter and this I have not done. . . ."[2]

Accepted a position at the cable desk of the Associated Press in Washington D.C.

In December he wrote to Burr: "Of my colleagues there are not five I could introduce to Lily. I have been in this work

quite a time now. It is pleasant enough . . . but there is hardly anybody with a decent education who stays in it for any length of time. Please do not think that I am according to my nature kicking but . . . I see that this work leads to a young old-age with mighty little to live on and . . . my love for history pulls me ahead all the time."[2]

June 18, 1906. Married Eliza Bowditch. Sent as a journalist by Associated Press to St. Petersburg, Russia.

June 22, 1907. Son born, Henry Bowditch Van Loon, called Hansje. Went to Munich to work on a Ph.D.

January 16, 1911. Second son, Gerard, born.

July 19, 1911. Received his Doctorate "magna cum laude."

August 18, 1911. Returned to United States.

1913. First book published, *The Fall of the Dutch Republic*.

1914. Applied to the Netherlands Consul in New York for volunteer service in his native land. Taught history at Cornell University.

1917. Marriage unsettled. Asked to leave Cornell University.

August 3, 1920. Married Helen Criswell—called "Jimmie." "I never quite got over the feeling that all women lived on some sort of pedestal . . . and longed to be the heroines of one of these romantic episodes. It was only a great many years later and at the cost of terrific wear and tear upon my emotions and my bank account, I learned that the troubadour business had indeed gone out with Guirant Riquier (who died in the year 1294)."[2]

Taught at Antioch College. A student recalled the school and the man at that time for one of van Loon's sons: "The campus, more dangerous to cross than a minefield, was criss-crossed with great trenches, ready for the laying of pipes, and this work, I recall, was being done by the students.

"Across this very primitive stage strode the sophisticated figure of your papa. And quite a sight he was. . . . I can still see this huge Dutchman standing in front of his class, wearing a smock (the first ever seen in Ohio), a monocle (most certainly the first ever seen), white cotton gardener's gloves, a box of crayons in his left hand while, with his right, he illustrated on an enormous pad the subject of his lecture. And this was not wisdom tossed on the empty air. No student ever cut one of his classes voluntarily.

"He and Jimmie had a small cottage just off the campus and Hendrik Willem's chief joy was striding up and down the little living room, playing his fiddle as accompaniment to any Paul Whiteman record that happened to be on the record-player. (He owned them all.)"[2]

1921. *The Story of Mankind* published. "I humbly wonder that I ever wrote it for it was a fiendish job, and now that people are saying things about it, I wonder whether it can all be true? I am not telling you this because I want to impress you with my deep wisdom or [from] an asinine tendency to take these things too seriously. But I get letters these days from people who are totally unknown to me like Stuart Walker and Wyeth, the illustrator, and Donald Ogden Stuart . . . and two letters from Mencken using large words like 'stupendous' and the first edition was half sold out the first week and I really wonder is the thing going to succeed at last? For the little bit of glory that is coming in so unexpectedly has not given me the assurance that it will MEAN anything. People have said nice things about my books before. I never had quite the avalanche of approval but to what will it lead?"[2]

June, 1922. Won the first John Newbery Medal ever presented for the most distinguished contribution to American literature for children.

1925. Suffering from melancholia, as he had on and off most of his life, Van Loon engaged the services of a psychoanalyst. "The psychoanalyst fellows come to my house, look at my beautiful wife, drink my whisky and waste my evenings trying to explain something that makes no sense. They juggle with complexes and repressed desires until I am ready to fall off my chair from sheer exhaustion, and in the end they leave me as wise as I was before."[2]

Less than two years later: "It is still too soon to sum up in a single sentence what he [Freud] actually accomplished by his psychological discoveries and besides I am too hopelessly ignorant on the subject to tell you anything of the slightest value. But I think that someday the name Sigmund Freud will be placed in mankind's Hall of Fame, together with those of Copernicus, Galileo and Darwin."[2]

In a letter to a friend he wrote: "Frances, cure me of this work disease. It is a pest, a plague, it ruins everything. Booze, dope, lotus seeds would be better than this addiction to insane work. . . . I have all the money I need . . . and I don't know why I work except perhaps that it has been my refuge for so long that it was a sort of jail . . . and I did not dare look outside for fear I might be lost."[2]

October 12, 1927. Married Frances Goodrich Ames, an actress.

Began work on a long projected book, *Rembrandt van Rijn*. "The fool brain is working overtime with more pleasure than at any moment during these ghastly years and I have decided that the best way of purging myself of the whole damn mess is to write a book about it. . . . It may be something novel in the line of biography. I happen to know that seventeenth century in Holland by heart. Of course I shall take endless liberties by bringing people together who, quite reasonably, may have never met each other. Often there is no documentary evidence and the good professional historians will say, how do you know that they knew each other? To which I answer, a hundred years from now no one will be able to prove that I knew Heywood Broun. I never wrote him a single letter or postal card but what of it? Outside of that one consideration, the rest is historically correct. And anyway, I am going to write the damn thing whether there is money in it or not because I have got to. The book can be made very real by using the illustrations bestowed upon us by the late Rembrandt van Rijn. I could illustrate it myself but, on the whole, I think he is a little better than I and he won't send us a bill."[2]

November 14, 1929. Suffered a vascular spasm. The cure: rest and reduce. He now weighed over 270 lbs. "I could live by drugging myself with twelve hours' work a day. Now the drug has been removed and all the ghastly mess and the life I have got to live and hate and detest and loathe stands before me twenty-four hours a day."[2]

1930. *R.v.R.: The Life and Times of Rembrandt van Rijn* published. "It has so far had the sort of reviews that make me very happy. I want to be known for *that* book and not for any others. I don't mind being poor if I have a hell of a reputation."[2]

Time magazine saw fit to tack onto an otherwise laudatory review the following: "Hendrik Willem Van Loon . . . is fat and forty-eight. One-time newspaperman, one-time professor of history, he married his third wife after she had divorced her first husband, then left her for his second wife."[2] This rocked van Loon. "What sort of ass am I? Twenty good, terribly good reviews and one lousy, personal attack in *Time*, a scurrilous little sheet, and I am in every sort of despondency and spiritual misery."[2]

1930. During an ocean voyage he wrote his son: "This is a nice ship, 27000 crew and thirty-six passengers. Einstein is on board. I shall try and catch him in the can some day and say, Now, lieber Meister, I know that you are in a hurry but how about those parallel lines. . . . Do they really meet?"[2]

Bellman Goes Home Through The Old City. ■ (From *The Last of the Troubadours* by Grace Castagnetta. Illustrated by Hendrik Willem Van Loon.)

Hendrik Willem and Albert Einstein liked each other immediately. Both had brought along violins. They entertained themselves and the little clutch of out-of-season travelers with evening concerts.

September 8, 1932. *Van Loon's Geography* published. Hailed as a bestseller, it remained so, well into the following year.

June, 1935. Began a bi-weekly series of fifteen minute radio broadcasts for N.B.C. dispensing pieces of his mind. Subsequently published under the title *Air Storming*.

Often teamed with Fiorello La Guardia at Town Hall or Madison Square Garden, to speak or serve on committees. It was often said La Guardia had outlawed burlesque shows, but that he and Van Loon had brought back vaudeville.

Purchased a house in South Norwalk, Connecticut, he dubbed it De Onrust—the turbulence. He wrote to Eleanor Roosevelt. "This part of Connecticut is inhabited by people who, next to their dividends, cherish the Constitution and the conviction that, for some reason, they and their friends were called upon to enjoy the bountiful riches of our land and to convert them into pleasant homes, beautiful gardens and to have children who can go correctly to the correct preparatory schools to be correctly prepared for the continuation of this charming arrangement, world without end and trust-funds without limit. Amen. To confess openly to certain admiration for the achievements and intentions of your husband is almost like singing the old Russian national anthem in Moscow!"[2]

September 30, 1937. *The Arts* published. He stated the book's credo: "The man who would never approach within a thousand miles of the arts, he is the fellow I am after. I have sacrificed much which I hated to sacrifice to get this strange creature won for the arts. I did so deliberately."[2]

1941. Suffered a major heart attack.

January 14, 1942. Received the highest honor he could have hoped for from his native land—the *Order of the Netherlands Lion* conferred by Queen Wilhelmina.

1943. Joined the Unitarian Church. "I like the Unitarian Church, because the only time the name Jesus Christ is uttered is when the janitor falls downstairs."[2]

He once wrote: "God does exist in my consciousness in a late medieval form—a kind and very wise old gentleman, a sort of beneficent grandfather with whom I occasionally hold conversation and discuss my own little problems."[2]

March 11, 1944. Died of heart failure. Buried in Old Greenwich, Connecticut.

FOR MORE INFORMATION SEE: Hendrik Willem Van Loon, *Report to Saint Peter, Upon the Kind of World in Which Hendrik Willem Van Loon Spent the First Years of His Life* (autobiography), Simon & Schuster, 1947; L. Edmond Leipold, *Citizens Born Abroad,* Denison, 1967; Gerard Willem Van Loon, *Story of Hendrik Willem Van Loon,* Lippincott, 1972; A. Whitman, "Story of Hendrik Willem Van Loon," *Saturday Review,* May 20, 1972; L. E. Leipold, *Americans Born Abroad,* Denison, 1973.

JOHN H. VOGEL, JR.

VOGEL, John H(ollister), Jr. 1950-

PERSONAL: Born April 16, 1950, in New York, N.Y.; son of John H. (a banker) and Helen (a teacher; maiden name, Wolff) Vogel; married Judith Barnes (a librarian), September 28, 1974. *Education:* Attended University of Lancaster, 1970-71; Carleton College, B.A. (magna cum laude), 1972; University of Virginia, M.A., 1974; Harvard Business School, 1978. *Address:* 10 Myrtle St., Jamaica Plain, Ma. 02130. *Agent:* Curtis Brown Ltd., 60 East 56th St., New York, N.Y. 10022.

CAREER: High school English teacher in Winchester, Va., 1974-76; WICO Construction, New York, N.Y., construction superintendent, 1976-77; Ward & Ward, Cary, N.Y., construction superintendent, 1977-78. *Member:* Phi Beta Kappa.

WRITINGS: (With Martha Munzer) *New Towns: Building Cities from Scratch* (juvenile), Knopf, 1974.

WORK IN PROGRESS: With Judith Barnes, *The Wise one of Omo.*

Sunnyside—an experiment in housing. ■ (From *New Towns* by Martha E. Munzer and John Vogel, Jr.)

WALTERS, Audrey 1929-

PERSONAL: Born July 10, 1929, in Philadelphia, Pa.; daughter of George H. (a salesman) and Mary Jane (Lee) Dracup; married Henry Walters (an art director), February 24, 1953. *Education:* Attended Philadelphia Museum School of Art (now called Philadelphia College of Art), Philadelphia, Pa., four years. *Politics:* Non-Partisan. *Religion:* Episcopalian.

CAREER: Container Corporation of America, Manyunk, Pa., art director, 1952-53; *Ladies' Home Journal,* New York, N.Y., 1953-54; free-lance illustrator, 1954—. Philadelphia College of Art, Alumni Association, board of directors, 1960's; Center City Residents Association, board of directors, 1978; Cushman Club, board of directors, 1978. *Exhibitions:* Woodmere Art Gallery, Philadelphia Museum of Art,

Philadelphia Art Alliance. *Member:* Pennsylvania University Museum, Art Alliance of Philadelphia, Historic Preservation Society of America.

ILLUSTRATOR: Kate Loree, *Pails & Snails,* Harvey House, 1967; Leonore Klein, *Just Like You,* Harvey House, 1968; Lee Ryland, *Gordon and the Glockenspiel,* A. Whitman, 1966; *The Birthday Book,* Macmillan, 1969. Work has appeared in *Good Housekeeping* and *Jack & Jill.*

SIDELIGHTS: "In recent years I have become most interested in preserving and restoring old houses. Buying them and selling them along the way. Lately I have also been designing children's costumes. My art work is mostly done in acrylics or showcard colors (waterbased paints) or pen and ink. I have been influenced by Doris Lee, Lorraine Fox and painter Henri Rousseau."

(From *Just Like You....* by Leonore Klein. Pictures by Audrey Walters.)

When Johnny goes fishing,

he catches a catfish.

Danny keeps goldfish

and Sally has

guppies.

Audrey Walters, with husband.

WARREN, Joyce W(illiams) 1935-

PERSONAL: Born June 16, 1935, in Springfield, Mass.; daughter of Robert F. (a fireman) and Violet (a teacher; maiden name, Hill) Williams; married Frank A. Warren III (a professor), January 29, 1955; children: Victoria, Catherine, Charlotte. *Education:* Brown University, A.B., 1957, M.A., 1960; doctoral study at Columbia University, 1972—. *Home:* 141 Elm St., Roslyn Heights, N.Y. 11577. *Agent:* Dorothy Markinko, McIntosh & Otis, Inc., 475 Fifth Ave., New York, N.Y. 10017.

CAREER: Brown University, Providence, R.I., librarian, 1957-59; Hobart College (now Hobart & William Smith College), Geneva, N.Y., librarian, 1960-61; Queens College of the City University of New York, Flushing, N.Y., lecturer in English, 1963-71; *Roslyn News,* Roslyn, N.Y., author of environmental column, "Helpful Hints," 1971-76; free-lance writer, 1976—. Member of board of trustees of Bryant Library (Roslyn), 1971-76. *Member:* Roslyn Environmental Association (vice-president, 1970-76), Roslyn Heights Civic Association (chairman, 1969-76), Phi Beta Kappa.

WRITINGS: A Mouse to Be Free (juvenile; Child Study Association book list), Sea Cliff Press, 1973. Contributor to literary journals.

"I am warm, I am fed,
With a house just for me.
But a mouse, to be happy,
Has got to be free."
■ (From *A Mouse to Be Free* by Joyce W. Warren. Illustrated by Jerry Lang.)

WORK IN PROGRESS: Three children's books, a sequel to *A Mouse to Be Free, Dogs Don't Make You Cry,* and *The Old Man and the Toad;* research on the "American Narcissus."

SIDELIGHTS: "I grew up in Springfield, Mass., with an older brother and a little black dog. My father was from Yorkshire, England, and my mother from Nova Scotia, Canada, and they both loved to tell stories about their childhoods. My father also told me many tales of fantasy, and when I was very little, my older brother used to tell me adventure stories at night from his bedroom across the hall.

"I also did a lot of reading, and I remember weekly walks to the library. My mother did not drive, and although the walk was a long one, we both looked forward to it.

"Today I live with my husband and three daughters and a little black dog in an old house on Long Island. My principal interests are still reading and writing. Last year our family spent the year in Cambridge, England, which was a marvelous experience."

HOBBIES AND OTHER INTERESTS: Playing the guitar, songwriting, reading, writing.

JOYCE W. WARREN

WEISS, Adelle 1920-

PERSONAL: Born July 30, 1920, in New York, N.Y.; daughter of Clifford (an insurance agent) and Helen (Grossman) Nack; married Morris Weiss (an electronics engineer), October 23, 1943; children: Howard, Peter. *Education:* Cooper Union School of Art, A.A., 1943; State University of New York Empire State College, B.S., 1977. *Home and office:* 214 Carol Ave., Pelham, N.Y. 10803.

CAREER: Clothes buyer for various buying offices, 1937-39; Irving C. Krewson, New York, N.Y., fashion artist and reporter, 1939; Jack Braunstein, resident buying office, New York, N.Y., fashion artist and reporter, 1941; Brooklyn Navy Yard, New York, N.Y., draftsman, 1942; Cox & Stevens, New York, N.Y., draftsman, 1943; Webb City Foundry, Webb City, Mo., draftsman, 1944; Office of the Post Engineers, Camp Shelby, Miss., draftsman, 1945; Mrs. C. Faraday, rug designer, New York, N.Y., colorist, 1945; owner of fabric designing business, New York, N.Y., 1946-47; Palos-Orland YMCA, Palos Park, Ill., group leader and art teacher, 1958; Stamford Jewish Center, Stamford, Conn., in charge of after school art program, 1963; General Instrument Corp., draftsman, 1968; Greenwich Public Schools, Greenwich, Conn., substitute art teacher, 1968; University of Connecticut, Stamford branch, Stamford, Conn., art teacher, 1970; Pelham Public Schools, Pelham, New York, art teacher, 1974-79. *Member:* League of Women Voters, Long Island Guild of Contemporary Artists.

WRITINGS: (With Claire V. Roth) *Art Careers,* Walck, 1963; (with Vivienne Eisner) *The Newspaper Everything Book* (self-illustrated), Dutton, 1975; (with Eisner) *A Boat, a Bat, and a Beanie: Things to Make from Newspaper* (self-illustrated), Lothrop, 1977.

WORK IN PROGRESS: A book on a new kind of needlework that Weiss created.

SIDELIGHTS: "I like to bring young people and adults to an individualized view of the arts as participants and as observers. One of my chief interests is the use of materials in new ways for the sake of beauty and innovation."

WELLS, Rosemary

EDUCATION: Studied at the Museum School in Boston, Mass.

CAREER: Author, illustrator, and designer. *Awards, honors:* The American Institute of Graphic Arts selected *Impossible Possum* by Ellen Conford for their 1971-72 Children's Book Show, and *Two Sisters and Some Hornets* by Beryl Epstein and Dorrit Davis and *Noisy Nora* for their 1973-74 Children's Book Show. *Noisy Nora* was also selected for the Children's Book Showcase in 1974; Brooklyn Art Books for Children Citation, 1975 and 1977, for *Benjamin and Tulip;* Irma Simonton Black Award, 1976, for *Morris's Disappearing Bag.*

WRITINGS: John and the Rarey (self-illustrated), Funk, 1969; *Michael and the Mitten Test* (self-illustrated), Bradbury, 1969; *The First Child* (self-illustrated), Hawthorn, 1970; *Martha's Birthday* (self-illustrated), Bradbury, 1970; *Miranda's Pilgrims* (self-illustrated), Bradbury, 1970; *The Fog Comes on Little Pig Feet,* Dial, 1972, G.K. Hall, 1973; *Un-*

ROSEMARY WELLS

Jack needed drying off, so Nora had to wait. ■ (From *Noisy Nora* by Rosemary Wells. Illustrated by the author.)

fortunately Harriet, Dial, 1972; *Benjamin and Tulip* (ALA Notable Book; self-illustrated), Dial, 1973, renewed, 1977; *Noisy Nora* (ALA Notable Book; self-illustrated), Dial, 1973; *None of the Above,* Dial, 1974; *Abdul* (self-illustrated), Dial, 1975; *Morris's Disappearing Bag: A Christmas Story* (self-illustrated), Dial, 1975; *Don't Spill It Again, James,* Dial, 1977; *Leave Well Enough Alone,* Dial, 1977; *Stanley and Rhoda,* Dial, 1978.

Illustrator: William Schwenck Gilbert and Arthur Sullivan, *A Song to Sing* (from the *Yeomen of the Guard),* Macmillan, 1968; W. S. Gilbert and A. Sullivan, *W. S. Gilbert's the Duke of Plaza Toro* (from *The Gondoliers*), Macmillan, 1969; Paula Fox, *Hungry Fred,* Bradbury, 1969; Charlotte Pomerantz, *Why You Look Like You Whereas I Tend to Look Like Me,* Young Scott Books, 1969; Robert William Service, *The Shooting of Dan McGrew and The Cremation of Sam McGee,* Young Scott Books, 1969; Rudyard Kipling, *The Cat That Walked by Himself,* Hawthorn, 1970; Winifred Rosen, *Marvin's Manhole,* Dial, 1970; Ellen Conford, *Impossible Possum,* Little, Brown, 1971; Marjorie Weinman Sharmat, *A Hot Thirsty Day,* Macmillan, 1971; Beryl Williams and Dorrit Davis, *Two Sisters and Some Hornets,* Holiday House, 1972; Virginia A. Tashjian, editor, *With a Deep Sea Smile,* Little, Brown, 1974.

SIDELIGHTS: Rosemary Wells was born in New York City and raised in New Jersey. "When I was a little girl, I was most impressed one Sunday afternoon, while watching my grandmother's small, round television, with a Jean Cocteau movie about a man who walked through walls. Having wished mightily and in vain to become invisible, I thought this ability would be a delightful way to thwart teachers and North Koreans (this was in 1952). The gentleman in the movie, after using his talent in no end of lovely ways, fell in love, *of course,* and that minute lost all of his magic, *of course.* I

vowed I would never be so foolish as to fall in love as long as I lived."

Her childish vow was forgotten when she grew up, however. She married architect Thomas Wells and lived in New York City with their young daughter, Victoria.

Wells received her art training at the Boston Museum School and has worked as an art director for several publishing companies. She began illustrating books for children in 1968 and has also written and self-illustrated many other books. In 1969 Wells began working on one of these children's books, *Abdul,* while she was a book designer on the staff of a New York publishing company, but it wasn't until six years later, in 1975, that the book was published. "I think I must have tried it with two dozen different endings. It always had an intriguing beginning—an Arab finding a little white horse underneath an old mother camel, but I couldn't decide what to do with that little white horse once Feisal pulled him out. I guess it would be fair to say the book took shape because of one gesture of Feisal's, which showed expectation of finding a new baby camel and his utter despair at finding a horse instead.

"Once I had an ugly duckling plot, however, I couldn't find the trick of making Abdul a swan. I tried rescuing princesses, winning horse races across the sand, nothing worked. So I put it away for six years, looking at the drawings in the dummy wistfully every now and then. I think I was a better writer when I came back to it. I can't say I knew anything more about the Middle East, but I did take the whole tribe across the desert, had them desert Abdul, and brought in another tribe, equally fierce at the end. My editor, Phyllis Fogelman, then suggested that if the first tribe had never seen a horse, perhaps the second tribe would never have seen a camel and would think a camel hilarious. That was just what the book needed!"

Later that year another book, *Morris's Disappearing Bag,* was published. This book had been written several years before and had been rejected by two publishers. "As the book stands today, all that remains of the original *Morris* is the title. It was a nice one, and sometimes titles suggest stories.

"One day while walking my West Highland terrier and trying to think up a story and *not* think about Christmas shopping—I was reminded of the old 'Disappearing Bag,' being highly desirous of one at the very thought of going to Bloomingdale's. I remember asking myself out loud, 'Let's start with the title, at least that's good. Now why does Morris want to disappear? Because he's miserable. Why again?' I thought of my own daughter and how frustrated she'd felt in the company of two perfectly nice older children the weekend before. She'd tried so hard to keep up with them and draw their attention, but they wouldn't have any of it, and didn't want her to play with their complicated and breakable toys. 'Just a baby' is a dreadful epithet! I gave Morris a loving family with three older siblings and once I had that the story took its own course. I can't explain why they are rabbits instead of humans. It just seemed right."

Wells has received numerous awards and distinctions for her books; among them the 1976 Irma Simonton Black Award for *Morris's Disappearing Bag.*

FOR MORE INFORMATION SEE: Horn Book, August, 1969, June, 1975; *Bulletin of the Center for Children's Books,* June, 1975.

WILLIAMS, Garth (Montgomery) 1912-

PERSONAL: Born April 16, 1912 in New York, N.Y., of English parents; childhood spent in New Jersey, with visits to France, England, and Canada; son of artists; children: six.

GARTH WILLIAMS

(From *Charlotte's Web* by E.B. White. Illustrated by Garth Williams.)

Education: Attended the City of London School, Westminster Art School, 1929, and the Royal College of Art, 1931-34, all in London; studied art at the British School in Rome as a post graduate scholar; has also studied in museums of many European countries, including France, Germany, Greece, Holland, to name a few. *Address:* Apartado Postal 123, Guanajuato, Guanajuato, Mexico.

CAREER: Luton Art School, 1935-36, organizer; pursued an art career in varying capacities, making portrait busts, and art editor of a proposed woman's magazine, 1938-39; *New Yorker* magazine, 1943, artist; author and illustrator of children's books beginning 1944. *Wartime service:* Served in the British Red Cross Civilian Defense, 1939-41, until invalided out; volunteered American Services, pre-Pearl Harbor. *Awards, honors:* British Prix de Rome for sculpture, 1936.

WRITINGS—All self-illustrated: *The Chicken Book,* Howell, Soskin, 1946, reissued, Delacorte, 1970; *The Adventures of Benjamin Pink,* Harper, 1951; *Baby Animals,* Simon & Schuster, 1952; *Baby Farm Animals,* Simon & Schuster, 1953; *The Golden Animal ABC,* Simon & Schuster, 1954, new edition published as *The Big Golden Animal ABC,* 1957; *Baby's First Book,* Simon & Schuster, 1955; *The Rabbit's Wedding,* Harper, 1958.

Illustrator: E. B. White, *Stuart Little,* Harper, 1945; Ernest Poole, *Great White Hills of New Hampshire,* Doubleday, 1946; Damon Runyon, *In Our Town,* McClelland, 1946; Margaret W. Brown, *Little Fur Family,* Harper, 1946, reissued, 1970; Evelyn S. Eaton, *Every Month Was May,* Harper, 1947; M. W. Brown, *Wait Till the Moon is Full,* Harper, 1948; Brown, *The Golden Sleepy Book,* Simon & Schuster, 1948, reissued, Golden Press, 1971; Henry Gilbert, *Robin*

"Dear me!" said Miss Bianca again. "I thought you considered yourself quite a gourmet! My Persian friend, whom I may have mentioned to you, always told me mice shouldn't be hung even an *hour*! But I suppose you're forced to live coarsely." ■ (From "The Rescuers" by Margery Sharp. Illustrated by Garth Williams.)

Hood, Lippincott, 1948; Eva LeGallienne, *Flossie and Bossie,* Harper, 1949; Jane W. Watson, compiler, *The Tall Book of Make-Believe,* Harper, 1950; E. B. White, *Charlotte's Web,* (ALA Notable Book) Harper, 1952; J. Watson, *Animal Friends,* Western, 1953; *My Bedtime Book,* Golden Press, 1953; Laura Ingalls Wilder, *Little House in the Big Woods* (ALA Notable Book), Harper, 1953; Wilder, *Little House on the Prairie,* Harper, 1953; Wilder, *Farmer Boy,* Harper, 1953; Wilder, *The Long Winter,* Harper, 1953; Wilder, *By the Shores of Silver Lake,* Harper, 1953; Wilder, *Little Town on the Prairie,* Harper, 1953; Wilder, *On the Banks of Plum Creek,* Harper, 1953; Wilder, *These Happy Golden Years,* Harper, 1953; Jennie D. Lindquist, *The Golden Name Day* (ALA Notable Book), Harper, 1955, reissued, 1966.

M. W. Brown, *Three Little Animals,* Harper, 1956; Lilian Moore, *My First Counting Book,* Simon & Schuster, 1956; Charlotte Zolotow, *Over and Over,* Harper, 1957; Natalie S. Carlson, *The Happy Orpheline,* Harper, 1957; Carlson, *The Family under the Bridge,* Harper, 1958, reissued, Scholastic Book Service, 1972; *Three Bedtime Stories,* Simon & Schuster, 1958; C. Zolotow, *Do You Know What I'll Do?,* Harper, 1958; N. Carlson, *A Brother for the Orphelines* (ALA Notable Book), Harper, 1959; Margery Sharp, *The Rescuers* (ALA Notable Book), Little, Brown, 1959; J. D. Lindquist, *The Little Silver House,* Harper, 1959; Mary S. Stolz, *Emmett's Pig,* Harper, 1959; George S. Thompson, *A Cricket in Times Square,* Farrar, 1960; Russell Hoban, *Bedtime for Frances,* Harper, 1960, reissued, 1976; M. Sharp, *Miss Bianca,* Little, Brown, 1962; C. Zolotow, *The Sky Was Blue,* Harper, 1963; M. Sharp, *The Turret,* Little, Brown, 1963; Byrd, B. Schweitzer, *Amigo,* Macmillan, 1963, reissued, 1973; Else H. Minarik, *The Little Giant Girl and the Elf Boy,* Harper, 1963; Anne Colver, *Bread-and-Butter Indian,* Holt, 1964; Mirian Norton, *The Kitten Who Thought He Was a Mouse,* Golden Press, 1965; M. W. Brown, *The Sailor Dog, and Other Stories,* Golden Press, 1965.

M. Sharp, *Miss Bianca in the Salt Mines,* Little, Brown, 1966; Eugenia Garson and Herbert Haufrecht, editors, *Laura Ingalls Wilder Songbook,* Harper, 1968; Jan Wahl, *Push Kitty,* Harper, 1968; G. S. Thompson, *Tucker's Countryside,* Farrar, 1969; A. Colver, *Bread-and-Butter Journey,* Holt, 1970; L. I. Wilder, *The First Four Years,* Harper, 1971; Randall Jarrell, *The Gingerbread Rabbit,* Macmillan, 1972; G. S. Thompson, *Harry Cat's Pet Puppy,* Farrar, 1974; M. W. Brown, *The Friendly Book,* Golden Press, 1974; Brown, *Home for a Bunny,* Western, 1975; Dorothy Kunhardt, *Lucky Mrs. Ticklefeather, and Other Funny Stories,* Western, 1975; M. W. Brown, *Fox Eyes,* Pantheon, 1977.

SIDELIGHTS: Born in New York City on April 16, 1912 of parents who were artists. His father drew for *Punch* and New York publications. Until he was ten-years-old, Williams lived in New Jersey.

Williams was educated in England as a young boy and in 1929 enrolled in the Westminster Art School. After two years there, he won a scholarship for oil painting to the Royal College of Art. From 1931 to 1934 he studied mural technique and painting at the College. After graduation from the Royal College in 1934 he won a post-graduate scholarship. Beginning in 1934 he studied sculpture in the evenings at the Westminster Art School.

Upon completion of his studies, he organized Luton Art School and painted murals until 1936 when he won the British Prix de Rome for sculpture. He studied art in several European cities before returning to England from Rome in 1938.

He began to feel very unhappy. ■ (From *The Adventures of Benjamin Pink* written and illustrated by Garth Williams.)

A LONG time ago, when all the grandfathers and grandmothers of today were little boys and girls or very small babies, or perhaps not even born, Pa and Ma and Mary and Laura and Baby Carrie left their little house in the Big Woods of Wisconsin. They drove away and left it lonely and empty in the clearing among the big trees, and they never saw that little house again. ■ (From *Little House on the Prairie* by Laura Ingalls Wilder. Illustrated by Garth Williams.)

From 1938 to 1939 Williams did portraits and was an art editor for a proposed woman's magazine. When World War II erupted he joined the British Red Cross Civilian Defense, but resigned after he suffered a back injury during the London blitz. In November, 1941 he returned to the United States where he waited for his commission.

Williams began working as an artist for the *New Yorker* magazine in 1943, but by 1944 he was devoting almost all his time to book illustration. He was asked to illustrate E. B. White's *Stuart Little* in 1944. Since then he has illustrated numerous children's books, including an edition of Laura Ingalls Wilder's eight "Little House" books, for which he is probably best known. Illustrating the Wilder books took several years—exploring every possible source for background material. "When Ursula Nordstrom asked me to illustrate the new edition of the Laura Ingalls Wilder books I wanted very much to do so. I loved and admired the books myself and they had meant a great deal to my small daughters when we read them aloud together. But my knowledge of the West at that time was almost zero and I could not see myself undertaking the work happily until I had seen the country that formed the background of the stories.

"And so I decided to visit Mr. and Mrs. Wilder in Mansfield, Missouri, where they still live; and then follow the route which the Ingalls family took in their covered wagon.

"Yet even with all the data I collected it must not be assumed that every character is a portrait or that every detail is accurate. With the limited space for illustrations I could only dip into the large amount of information available and use what seemed most important.

"Illustrating books is not just making pictures of the houses, the people and the articles mentioned by the author; the artist has to see everything with the same eyes. For example, an architect would have described the sod house on the bank of Plum Creek as extremely primitive, unhealthy and unde-

sirable—nothing to seal the walls from dampness, no ventilation, no light. But to Laura's fresh young eyes it was a pleasant house, surrounded by flowers and with the music of a running stream and rustling leaves.

"She understood the meaning of hardship and struggle, of joy and work, of shyness and bravery. She was never overcome by drabness or squalor. She never glamorized anything; yet she saw the loveliness in everything. This was the way the illustrator had to follow—no glamorizing for him either; no giving everyone a permanent wave.

"It is now ten years since I began to try to recreate in pictures the lives of Laura and Mary. It has been for me a most exciting adventure." [Garth Williams, "Illustrating the Little House Books," *Horn Book*, December, 1953.[1]]

In 1950 Williams also illustrated Dorothy Kunhardt's *Tiny Library*. "Mrs. Kunhardt begged Simon & Schuster to get me to illustrate her books; twelve tiny books in a small box."

In Williams' spare time, when he is not traveling, he continues to sculpt. He has written and illustrated his own children's books as well as books by other authors.

FOR MORE INFORMATION SEE: Bertha E. Mahony and others, compilers, *Illustrators of Children's Books, 1744-1945*, Horn Book, 1947; Garth Williams, "Illustrating the Little House Books," *Horn Book*, December, 1953; B. E. Miller and others, compilers, *Illustrators of Children's Books, 1946-1956*, Horn Book, 1958; Muriel Fuller, editor, *More Junior Authors*, H. W. Wilson, 1963; Lee Kingman and others, compilers, *Illustrators of Children's Books, 1957-1966*, Horn Book, 1968; *Graphis 155*, Volume 27, the Graphis Press, 1971-72; *Contemporary American Illustrators of Children's Books*, Rutgers University Art Gallery, 1974.

WORCESTER, Donald Emmet   1915-

PERSONAL: Born April 29, 1915, in Tempe, Ariz.; son of Thomas Emmet Makemson and Maud (Lavon) Worcester; married Barbara Livingston Peck, 1941; children: Barbara Livingston and Elizabeth Stuart (twins), Harris Eugene.

Spotted Antelope's Children were hungry, and there was no food in his lodge. ■ (From *Lone Hunter's First Buffalo Hunt* by Donald Worcester. Illustrated by Harper Johnson.)

Education: University of Arizona, student, 1935-36; Bard College, A.B., 1939; University of California, M.A., 1940, Ph.D., 1947. *Religion:* Society of Friends. *Home:* 5800 Wedgworth Rd., Fort Worth, Tex. *Agent:* Paul Reynolds, 599 Fifth Ave., New York, N.Y. *Office:* Chairman, History Department, Texas Christian University, Fort Worth, Tex.

CAREER: College of Agriculture, Davis, Calif., lecturer, fall, 1946; University of California, Berkeley, lecturer, spring, 1947; University of Florida, Gainesville, assistant professor, 1947-51, associate professor, 1951-55, professor, 1955-63, history department chairman, 1955-59; Texas Christian University, Fort Worth, chairman of history department, 1963—. Visiting associate professor at University of Michigan, 1952, University of California, Berkeley, summer, 1951; visiting professor at University of Madrid in Spain, 1956-57. Board chairman, University of Florida Press. *Military service:* U.S. Naval Reserve, World War II, now commander. *Member:* American Historical Association, New Mexico Historical Society, Southern Historical Association, Florida Historical Society, Phi Alpha Theta (national president, 1960-62), Instituto Paraguayo de Investigaciones Historicos, Gainesville Parent-Teachers Association (president, 1962-63), Western Writers of America (president, 1973-74), Western History Association, (president, 1974-75), Westerners International (president, 1978—).

WRITINGS: Instructions for Governing the Interior Provinces of New Spain, 1786, Quivira Society, 1951; (co-author)

The Growth and Culture of Latin America, Oxford University Press, 1956; *Sea Power and Chilean Independence*, University of Florida monograph series, 1962; *The Three Worlds of Latin America*, Dutton, 1963; (editor) John Young Nelson, *Fifty Years on the Trail*, University of Oklahoma Press, 1963; (co-author) *American Civilization*, Allyn & Bacon, 1964; (co-author) *Man and Civilization*, Lyons & Carnahan, 1965; *Makers of Latin America*, Dutton, 1966; (co-editor) *Contemporary America: Issues and Problems*, Allyn & Bacon, 1968; *Brazil: From Colony to World Power*, Scribner, 1973; *Bolívar*, Little, 1977; also (editor and contributor) *Forked Tongues and Broken Treaties*, The Caxton Printers.

Children's books—All published by Walck, except where indicated: *Lone Hunter's Gray Pony*, 1956; *Lone Hunter and the Cheyennes*, 1957; *Lone Hunter's First Buffalo Hunt*, 1958; *Lone Hunter and the Wild Horses*, 1959; *Kit Carson: Mountain Scout*, Houghton, 1959; *John Paul Jones: Soldier of the Sea*, Houghton, 1961; *War Pony*, 1961. Contributor of articles on horses, Apache Indians, Latin American topics, to *American Thoroughbred Record*, historical and anthropological journals. Managing editor, *Hispanic American Historical Review*, 1960-65.

WORK IN PROGRESS: A book of readings on Latin American history; history of western civilization; *Chisholm Trail*.

SIDELIGHTS: "I was born in Tempe, Arizona, but grew up on my Grandfather's homestead on the edge of the Mojave

DONALD EMMET WORCESTER

Desert of southern California. About the time we moved there a drought began and soon all of the small ranchers gave up, sold their cattle, and left. They let their horses run loose on the range, and in a few years they and their descendants were as wild as deer. My brother, who was two years younger, and I learned about horses by trapping some of the wild ones in abandoned corrals, and somehow getting ropes on them. We had no saddles, so we tied a rope around them and hung on it like a surcingle. We took turns getting thrown until they were tired of bucking, then opened the gate and headed down the road. It was surprising how quickly those horses became gentle. A crippled old-time cowboy taught us a lot of tricks—one was when riding half-broken horses. I tied a rope around the horse's neck and stuck the coiled rope under my belt. If the horse spooked and threw me I grabbed the coiled rope and kept him from leaving the county. That trick saved me some twenty-mile walks.

"On a near-by ranch there was a horse from Inyo County, about one hundred miles north across the desert. It had real homing instincts; any time it got loose it headed for the range where it was born. Many years later I remembered this horse, after I had read in Lewis and Clark's accounts that they saw horses in the Oregon country with Spanish brands (from New Mexico). I put the two ideas together and wrote *War Pony*.

"Before going on to college I worked on ranches in Arizona, breaking horses and occasionally riding bulls in Indian rodeos.

"Right now we have 145 acres and fourteen or fifteen Arabian horses—two new ones arrived in the past month, and more are or should be on the way."

WYLER, Rose 1909-
(Peter Thayer)

PERSONAL: Born October 29, 1909, in New York, N.Y.; daughter of Otto Samuel and Kati (Bach) Wyler; married second husband, Gerald Ames (a writer), September 8, 1948; children: (first marriage) Joseph, Karl, (stepchildren) Eva-Lee Baird. *Education:* Barnard College, B.A., 1929, Teachers College, Columbia University, M.A., 1931. *Residence:* New York, N.Y.

CAREER: Glen Falls, N.Y. public schools, supervisor of elementary science programs, 1931-34; Teachers College, Columbia University, instructor in science education, 1934-41; has also been an elementary science consultant for Basic Books, a science script writer and adviser for Encyclopaedia Britannica Films for CBS, and science editor for Scholastic Publications; free lance writer, 1948—. *Member:* Author's Guild.

WRITINGS: Tuffy, the Truck (illustrated by Basil Davidovich), Avon Publishing, 1952; *Planet Earth* (illustrated by John Sand), Schuman, 1952; *The First Book of Science Experiments* (illustrated by Ida Scheib), Watts, 1952, revised edition, 1971; (under pseudonym Peter Thayer) *The Hungriest Robin* (illustrated by Kathleen Elgin), Messner, 1953, a new edition published as *The Flyingest Robin*, Melmont, 1965; *My Little Golden Book about the Sky* (illustrated by Tibor Gergely), Simon & Schuster, 1956; *The First Book of Weather* (illustrated by Bernice Myers), Watts, 1956, revised edition, 1966; *The Golden Picture Book of Science* (illustrated by Marjorie Hartwell and Valerie Swenson) Simon & Schuster, 1957, a later edition published as *Science: Ani-*

ROSE WYLER

mals, Plants, Rocks, Gravity, Day and Night, Rain and Snow, the Sky and the Ocean, with 45 Experiments and Activities, Golden Press, 1965; *Exploring Space: A True Story about the Rockets of Today and a Glimpse of the Rockets That are to Come* (illustrated by T. Gergely), Simon & Schuster, 1958; *Arrow Book of Science Riddles,* Scholastic, 1964 (with stepdaughter, Eva-Lee Baird) *Science Teasers* (illustrated by Jerry Robinson), Harper, 1966; *Real Science Riddles* (illustrated by Talivaldis Stubis), Hastings House, 1972; *Professor Egghead's Best Riddles* (illustrated by J. Robinson), Simon & Schuster, 1973; *What Happens If . . . ?* (illustrated by Daniel Nevins), Walker, 1974; (with E. L. Baird) *Nutty Number Riddles* (illustrated by Whitney Darrow, Jr.), Doubleday, 1977; (with Mary Elting) *The New Answer Book,* Grosset, 1977; (with Eva-Lee Baird) *Nutty Number Riddles,* Doubleday, 1977; (with Mary Elting) *The Head to Toe Answer Book,* Grosset, 1979; (with Eva-Lee Baird) *Going Metric–The Fun Way,* Doubleday, 1980.

With husband, Gerald Ames: *Life on the Earth* (illustrated by G. Ames), Schuman, 1953; *Restless Earth,* Abelard-Schuman, 1954; *The Golden Book of Astronomy* (illustrated by John Polgreen), Simon & Schuster, 1955, revised edition published as *The New Golden Book of Astronomy: An Introduction to the Wonders of Space,* Golden Press, 1965; *The Story of the Ice Age* (illustrated by Thomas W. Voter), Harper, 1956; *The Earth's Story,* Creative Educational Society, 1957, reissued, 1967; *The First People in the World* (illustrated by Leonard Weisgard), Harper, 1958; *First Days of the World* (illustrated by L. Weisgard), Harper, 1958; *What Makes It Go?* (illustrated by Bernice Myers), Whittlesy House, 1958; *The Giant Golden Book of Biology* (illustrated by Charles Harper) Golden Press, 1961, revised edition published as *The Golden Book of Biology: An Introduction to the Wonders of Life,* 1967; *Planet Earth* (illustrated by Cornelius De Witt), Golden Press, 1963; *Prove It!* (illustrated by T.

**Flip off the handkerchief,
turn the cup over in your
right hand and—there is
Little Egg!**
■ (From *Funny Magic* by Rose Wyler and Gerald Ames. Illustrated by Talivaldis Stubis.)

Stubis), Harper, 1963; *Food and Life,* Creative Educational Society, 1966; *Magic Secrets* (illustrated by T. Stubis), Harper, 1967; *Spooky Tricks* (illustrated by T. Stubis), Harper, 1968; *Exploring Other Worlds,* Golden Press, 1968; *Secrets in Stones* (photographs by G. Ames), Four Winds Press, 1970; *Funny Magic: Easy Tricks for Young Magicians* (illustrated by T. Stubis), Parents' Magazine Press, 1972; *Funny Number Tricks: Easy Magic with Arithmetic* (illustrated by T. Stubis), Parents' Magazine Press, 1976; *It's all Done with Numbers: Confounding and Astounding Feats of Mathematical Magic,* Doubleday, 1979.

WORK IN PROGRESS: With husband, Gerald Ames, three more riddle books: *Screwy Science Riddles, Haywire History Riddles, Giggly Geography Riddles*—all for Doubleday.

SIDELIGHTS: Rose Wyler was born in the Bronx, New York, and grew up in Weehawken, New Jersey. As a child, Wyler was curious about nature, but when she couldn't find adequate books on the subject, she decided, at age eleven, to write some of her own. "I always had a collection of stones, bugs, or leaves and always wanted to know more about nature. I could never find books on nature as a child, so, at 11, I decided I was going to write them." [Lee Bennett Hopkins, *Books are by People,* Citation Press, 1969.[1]]

Her school life was devoted to the study of nature. After receiving a B.A. degree from Barnard College she continued her studies at Teacher's College, Columbia University, where, in 1931, she graduated with the distinction of being the first person ever to receive a master's degree in elementary science. Before her marriage to Gerald Ames in 1948, she held a variety of jobs including writing for radio, television, educational films, and encyclopedias and actively worked in the field of science education from pre-kindergarten to college level.

Besides being the author of many non-fiction children's books, Wyler joined her husband and co-authored several scientific books. The husband-wife team have had a great deal of fun and adventure while working on their various science books for children. "In our book *The First Person in the World* [Harper, 1958], the opening words are 'Shake hands with a chimpanzee. . . .' Upon publication, the editor thought that a picture of the two of us posing with a chimpanzee would be good publicity. Well, we visited a circus out on

Long Island, and it was there that we met Chris, a three-year-old Chimp. We had arranged to borrow him for the day to take the publicity photos. The first bit of fun we had with him was en route to New York City. We let him pay a bridge toll. You can imagine the look on the collector's face!

"Even greater complications developed later when we were leaving our apartment building. We boarded the elevator and went down several flights, when all of a sudden it stopped. The superintendent's wife entered the car with her two small children. Both were drinking milk from a bottle. Chris, being a bottle-baby himself, reached for the bottle. At this, the woman began to shout and scream, 'Police! Police! Help! A gorilla, a gorilla!' The end result of this incident was much confusion—and a dispossess notice from the landlord!"[1]

To research their books, they often relied on children from their cooperative apartment in New York City, after their own three children were grown up. "Our laboratory is our living room. Children of all ages come in to watch me perform magic tricks; after I do them, I explain the 'secrets' to see if they can handle them. If they can, they go into our books; if not, we don't use them. The children actually collaborate with us. For *Magic Secrets* [1967] we ransacked the literature on magic to find material children could perform easily. *Spooky Tricks* [1968] came about because one youngster wanted some to perform on Halloween; a little girl asked, 'Show us some spooky tricks!' And that is how the volume came to be, including the title!"[1]

Funny Number Tricks: Easy Magic with Arithmetic [1976] was tried out on their grandchildren before it was published. "The arithmetic interested them to a degree, but what appealed mainly, as we had expected, was performing the magic. Our hope is that all users of the book will learn some math while enjoying the magic.

"Some children, as we gather from their letters, are content just to read our books and learn how magic is done; others eagerly perform the tricks. We think the latter surely must be stimulated by the quite theatrical illustrations of our friend and colleague, Talivaldis Stubis, who also plans advertising art for plays and films. 'After all,' Tal says, 'these books of ours are really show business for children.'"

"In recent years (the last fifteen) my interests have been in producing exciting puzzle and activity material that is easy to read in both *math* and *science*. This has led to my use of the true riddle in several books. The question provides the book and the answer [provides] information that sticks.

"In addition to a busy writing schedule, I am interested in visiting countries undergoing rapid change and studying the use of children's science and math books in such situations. This has resulted in two recent trips to Cuba."

In April, 1978 Wyler and her husband toured Cuba with other (twenty-five in all) authors of children's books. The group had interviews with librarians and publishing people. Wyler served as leader of the American group. "Since it was a group it had to have a leader, but since nobody needed any leading I could practice one-down-manship." ["Thirteen in the Children's Book Field Explore Cuba's New Publishing Industry," *Publishers Weekly*, May 1, 1978.[1]]

Wyler noted that until recently there had not been any Cuban children's book writers but that efforts were now being made to encourage the development of authors for children's books.

"Soon (May, 1979) I will be in Soviet Asia visiting schools, libraries and meeting fellow children's book writers."

Rose Wyler and her husband enjoy the outdoors and divide their year between New York City, the Maine coast and Latin America, where they usually travel in the winter. They enjoy winter snorkeling in Latin America and visiting the ancient "lost cities" there.

In collaboration with her husband, Gerald Ames, Rose Wyler has produced many scientific books for the young. A *Chicago Sunday Tribune* critic, writing about *The Golden Book of Astronomy*, noted, "Despite the complexity of the subject matter, the text is simplified to the level of understanding of young children. There are more than 200 excellent illustrations." The *New York Herald Tribune Book Review* described *The Story of the Ice Age* as, "One of the most precise and scholarly as well as one of the simplest and most effective informational books for young people this year [1956]. . . ."

In reviewing *The First Days of the World*, a *Christian Science Monitor* critic observed: "Generously illustrated by Leonard Weisgard, this book is especially aimed at youngsters under ten. It presents a scientifically complex subject in terms of its central and easily understood concepts, dropping complicated explanations in favor of clarity." Added *Kirkus*: "Though the text is generally clear and concise, there are sections . . . which might be puzzling to a young reader. On the whole, however, this natural history with its vividly colored full page illustrations . . . provides a valuable introduction to the young reader. . . ."

Writing in *Horn Book* about *The Giant Golden Book of Biology*, Isaac Asimov commented, "The illustrations are colorful and a delight to the eye . . . , but they surround the text rather than drown it. There is no need to stress the fact that a text composed by Ames and Wyler is both accurate and clear. The subject is extremely broad, and complex matters must be dealt with in a few hundred words; but the authors at least get the reader started, which is the intention."

FOR MORE INFORMATION SEE: Chicago Sunday Tribune, November 13, 1955; *New York Herald Tribune Book Review*, August 12, 1956; *Kirkus*, April 15, 1958; *Christian Science Monitor*, May 8, 1958; *Horn Book*, April, 1962, August, 1967; *Natural History*, November, 1964; Jean Poindexter Colby, *Writing, Illustrating and Editing Children's Books*, Hastings House, 1967; Lee Bennett Hopkins, *Books Are by People*, Citation Press, 1969; Doris de Montreville and Donna Hill, editors, *Third Book of Junior Authors*, H. W. Wilson, 1972.

ZION, (Eu)Gene   1913-1975

PERSONAL: Born in 1913, in New York, N.Y., died, December 5, 1975; married Margaret Bloy Graham (an artist). *Education:* Attended the New School for Social Research; graduated from Pratt Institute. *Residence:* New York, N.Y.

CAREER: Member of the staff of Esquire Publications, 1940-42; art designer, Columbia Broadcasting System, 1944-46, Condé Nast Publications, 1946-49; free-lance writer and designer, 1949-75. *Military service:* Served in the Army during World War II in the Anti-aircraft Artillery Visual Training Aids Section, designing training manuals and filmstrips. *Member:* Author's Guild. *Awards, honors:* Runner-up for the Caldecott Medal, 1952, for *All Falling Down; Really Spring* was listed among the *New York Times* Choice of Best Illustrated Children's Books of the Year, 1956.

WRITINGS—All written under name Gene Zion and all illustrated by wife, Margaret Bloy Graham: *All Falling Down*, Harper, 1951; *Hide and Seek Day*, Harper, 1954; *The Summer Snowman*, Harper, 1955; *Harry, the Dirty Dog*, Harper, 1956, new edition, 1976; *Really Spring*, Harper, 1956; *Dear Garbage Man*, Harper, 1957; *Jeffie's Party*, Harper, 1957; *No Roses for Harry*, Harper, 1958, new edition, 1976; *The Plant Sitter*, Harper, 1959, new edition, 1976; *Harry and the Lady Next Door*, Harper, 1960; *The Meanest Squirrel I Ever Met*, Scribner, 1962; *The Sugar Mouse Cake*, Scribner, 1964; *Harry By the Sea*, Harper, 1965, new edition, 1976.

Then he planted the cuttings in the little flower pots he'd bought. The book said they would grow. ■ (From *The Plant Sitter* by Gene Zion. Illustrated by Margaret Bloy Graham.)

SIDELIGHTS: Born in New York City and raised in Ridge-field, New Jersey where "life was rural and included a barn with cows, chickens, and pigeons." His artistic career began in kindergarten when his teacher praised his crayon border around a piece of paper.

As a child Zion loved to read and would sit on the grass in front of the library trying to finish his books before he took them home. He earned money by painting oil pictures upon request on the backs of his classmates' yellow rain slickers.

He returned to New York City during his high school years and later graduated from Pratt Institute. He further studied art at the New School in New York. In 1936 he won a trip to Europe from a national travel poster competition. During that trip he became interested in book design.

After serving in the Army during World War II, Zion joined the art department of Columbia Broadcasting System and later the Condé Nast Publications. By 1949, however, he was free-lancing as a designer and art director.

His wife, Margaret Bloy Graham, and Ursula Nordstrom of Harper & Brothers encouraged Zion to write children's books. According to Zion, "no creative effort has been more gratifying . . . than writing picture books for children."

A sketch of children gathering apples in an orchard done by his wife several years earlier in Canada was the inspiration for Eugene Zion's first children's book, *All Falling Down.* "It might seem oversimple were it not that the pictures have such charm and offer so many details for further talk," commented a *New York Herald Tribune Book Review* critic. "The scenes are in city or country, and the many moods so happily translated into action are worth the long look. . . ."

As collaborators, Zion and his wife are probably best known for their stories about Harry the dog. The first one, *Harry, the Dirty Dog,* received the following comments from a *New York Times* reviewer: "Harry is sure to be loved; especially by those pre-school children to whom dirt is an ever-delight-ful thing. The illustrations by Margaret Bloy Graham are bright, animated, and expressive, and are a bold complement to the direct and charming text." Concerning *Plant Sitter,* the *London Times Literary Supplement* observed: "The happy blend of unanswerable logic and wild improbability that is the special gift of American children's writers is as strong as ever."

FOR MORE INFORMATION SEE: New York Herald Trib-une Book Review, November 11, 1951; *New York Times,* September 16, 1956; *Times Literary Supplement,* May 29, 1959; Muriel Fuller, editor, *More Junior Authors,* H. W. Wilson, 1963; Obituaries—*New York Times,* December 9, 1975; *Publishers Weekly,* December 29, 1975; *A. B. Book-man's Weekly,* March 22, 1976.

(Died December 5, 1975)

Gene Zion, with Margaret Bloy Graham.

He slid down a coal chute and got the dirtiest of all. In fact, he changed from a white dog with black spots, to a black dog with white spots. ■ (From *Harry the Dirty Dog* by Gene Zion. Illustrated by Margaret Bloy Graham.)

CUMULATIVE INDEX TO
ILLUSTRATIONS AND AUTHORS

Illustrations Index

(In the following index, the number of the volume in which an illustrator's work appears is given *before* the colon, and the page on which it appears is given *after* the colon. For example, a drawing by Adams, Adrienne appears in Volume 2 on page 6, another drawing by her appears in Volume 3 on page 80, another drawing in Volume 8 on page 1, and another drawing in Volume 15 on page 107.)

YABC

Index citations including this abbreviation refer to listings appearing in *Yesterday's Authors of Books for Children,* also published by the Gale Research Company, which covers authors who died prior to 1960.

Aas, Ulf, *5:* 174
Abbé, S. van. *See* van Abbé, S., *16:* 142
Abel, Raymond, *6:* 122; *7:* 195; *12:* 3
Accorsi, William, *11:* 198
Acs, Laszlo, *14:* 156
Adams, Adrienne, *2:* 6; *3:* 80; *8:* 1; *15:* 107; *16:* 180
Adams, John Wolcott, *17:* 162
Adkins, Jan, *8:* 3
Agard, Nadema, *18:* 1
Aichinger, Helga, *4:* 5, 45
Akasaka, Miyoshi, *YABC 2:* 261
Akino, Fuku, *6:* 144
Alajalov, *2:* 226
Albright, Donn, *1:* 91
Alcorn, John, *3:* 159; *7:* 165
Alden, Albert, *11:* 103
Alexander, Martha, *3:* 206; *11:* 103; *13:* 109
Alexeieff, Alexander, *14:* 6
Aliki, *See* Brandenberg, Aliki
Allamand, Pascale, *12:* 9
Alland, Alexander, *16:* 255
Alland, Alexandra, *16:* 255
Allen, Gertrude, *9:* 6
Almquist, Don, *11:* 8; *12:* 128; *17:* 46
Aloise, Frank, *5:* 38; *10:* 133
Altschuler, Franz, *11:* 185
Ambrus, Victor G., *1:* 6-7, 194; *3:* 69; *5:* 15; *6:* 44; *7:* 36; *8:* 210; *12:* 227; *14:* 213; *15:* 213
Ames, Lee J., *3:* 12; *9:* 130; *10:* 69; *17:* 214
Amon, Aline, *9:* 9
Amoss, Berthe, *5:* 5
Amundsen, Dick, *7:* 77
Amundsen, Richard E., *5:* 10
Ancona, George, *12:* 11
Anderson, Alasdair, *18:* 122
Anderson, C. W., *11:* 10
Anderson, Carl, *7:* 4
Anderson, Laurie, *12:* 153, 155
Andrews, Benny, *14:* 251

Angelo, Valenti, *14:* 8; *18:* 100
Anglund, Joan Walsh, *2:* 7, 250-251
Anno, Mitsumasa, *5:* 7
Antal, Andrew, *1:* 124
Appleyard, Dev, *2:* 192
Archer, Janet, *16:* 69
Ardizzone, Edward, *1:* 11, 12; *2:* 105; *3:* 258; *4:* 78; *7:* 79; *10:* 100; *15:* 232; *YABC 2:* 25
Arenella, Roy, *14:* 9
Armer, Austin, *13:* 3
Armer, Laura Adams, *13:* 3
Armer, Sidney, *13:* 3
Armitage, Eileen, *4:* 16
Armstrong, George, *10:* 6
Arno, Enrico, *1:* 217; *2:* 22, 210; *4:* 9; *5:* 43; *6:* 52
Arrowood, Clinton, *12:* 193
Artzybasheff, Boris, *13:* 143; *14:* 15
Aruego, Ariane, *6:* 4
    See also Dewey, Ariane
Aruego, Jose, *4:* 140; *6:* 4; *7:* 64
Asch, Frank, *5:* 9
Ashby, Gail, *11:* 135
Ashmead, Hal, *8:* 70
Atene, Ann, *12:* 18
Atkinson, J. Pricstman, *17:* 275
Atwood, Ann, *7:* 9
Austin, Margot, *11:* 16
Austin, Robert, *3:* 44
Averill, Esther, *1:* 17
Axeman, Lois, *2:* 32; *11:* 84; *13:* 165
Ayer, Jacqueline, *13:* 7
Ayer, Margaret, *15:* 12

B.T.B. *See* Blackwell, Basil T., *YABC 1:* 68, 69
Babbitt, Natalie, *6:* 6; *8:* 220
Bacon, Bruce, *4:* 74
Bacon, Paul, *7:* 155; *8:* 121
Bacon, Peggy, *2:* 11, 228
Baker, Charlotte, *2:* 12
Balet, Jan, *11:* 22
Balian, Lorna, *9:* 16

Ballis, George, *14:* 199
Banner, Angela. *See* Maddison, Angela Mary
Bannon, Laura, *6:* 10
Bare, Arnold Edwin, *16:* 31
Bargery, Geoffrey, *14:* 258
Barkley, James, *4:* 13; *6:* 11; *13:* 112
Barling, Tom, *9:* 23
Barnett, Moneta, *16:* 89
Barney, Maginel Wright, *YABC 2:* 306
Barnum, Jay Hyde, *11:* 224
Barrer-Russell, Gertrude, *9:* 65
Barrett, Ron, *14:* 24
Barron, John N., *3:* 261; *5:* 101; *14:* 220
Barrows, Walter, *14:* 268
Barry, Ethelred B., *YABC 1:* 229
Barry, James, *14:* 25
Barry, Katharina, *2:* 159; *4:* 22
Barry, Robert E., *6:* 12
Barth, Ernest Kurt, *2:* 172; *3:* 160; *8:* 26; *10:* 31
Barton, Byron, *8:* 207; *9:* 18
Bartram, Robert, *10:* 42
Bartsch, Jochen, *8:* 105
Bate, Norman, *5:* 16
Bauernschmidt, Marjorie, *15:* 15
Baum, Willi, *4:* 24-25; *7:* 173
Baumhauer, Hans, *11:* 218; *15:* 163, 165, 167
Baynes, Pauline, *2:* 244; *3:* 149; *13:* 133, 135, 137-141
Beame, Rona, *12:* 40
Beard, J. H., *YABC 1:* 158
Bearden, Romare, *9:* 7
Beardsley, Aubrey, *17:* 14
Beaucé, J. A., *18:* 103
Beck, Charles, *11:* 169
Beck, Ruth, *13:* 11
Becker, Harriet, *12:* 211
Beckhoff, Harry, *1:* 78; *5:* 163
Beech, Carol, *9:* 149
Behr, Joyce, *15:* 15
Behrens, Hans, *5:* 97
Belden, Charles J., *12:* 182

Bell, Corydon, *3:* 20
Bemelmans, Ludwig, *15:* 19, 21
Benda, W. T., *15:* 256
Bendick, Jeanne, *2:* 24
Bennett, F. I., *YABC 1:* 134
Bennett, Rainey, *15:* 26
Bennett, Richard, *15:* 45
Bennett, Susan, *5:* 55
Benton, Thomas Hart, *2:* 99
Berelson, Howard, *5:* 20; *16:* 58
Berenstain, Jan, *12:* 47
Berenstain, Stan, *12:* 47
Berg, Joan, *1:* 115; *3:* 156; *6:* 26, 58
Berger, William M.,
    14: 143; *YABC 1:* 204
Bering, Claus, *13:* 14
Berkowitz, Jeanette, *3:* 249
Bernadette. *See* Watts, Bernadette
Berrill, Jacquelyn, *12:* 50
Berry, Erick. *See* Best, Allena.
Berry, William A., *6:* 219
Berry, William D., *14:* 29
Berson, Harold, *2:* 17-18;
    4: 28-29, 220; *9:* 10; *12:* 19;
    17: 45; *18:* 193
Bertschmann, Harry, *16:* 1
Best, Allena, *2:* 26
Bethers, Ray, *6:* 22
Bettina. *See* Ehrlich, Bettina
Betts, Ethel Franklin,
    17: 161, 164-165; *YABC 2:* 47
Bewick, Thomas,
    16: 40-41, 43-45, 47;
    YABC 1: 107
Bianco, Pamela, *15:* 31
Bible, Charles, *13:* 15
Biggers, John, *2:* 123
Bileck, Marvin, *3:* 102
Bimen, Levent, *5:* 179
Birch, Reginald,
    15: 150; *YABC 1:* 84;
    YABC 2: 34, 39
Bird, Esther Brock, *1:* 36
Birmingham, Lloyd, *12:* 51
Biro, Val, *1:* 26
Bjorklund, Lorence, *3:* 188, 252;
    7: 100; *9:* 113;
    10: 66; *YABC 1:* 242
Blackwell, Basil T., *YABC 1:* 68, 69
Blades, Ann, *16:* 52
Blaisdell, Elinore, *1:* 121; *3:* 134
Blake, Quentin, *3:* 170; *9:* 21;
    10: 48; *13:* 38
Blass, Jacqueline, *8:* 215
Blegvad, Erik, *2:* 59; *3:* 98; *5:* 117;
    7: 131; *11:* 149; *14:* 34, 35;
    18: 237; *YABC 1:* 201
Bloch, Lucienne, *10:* 12
Blumenschein, E. L.,
    YABC 1: 113, 115
Boardman, Gwenn, *12:* 60
Bock, Vera, *1:* 187
Bock, William Sauts, *8:* 7; *14:* 37;
    16: 120
Bodecker, N. M., *8:* 13; *14:* 2;
    17: 55-57

Bolian, Polly, *3:* 270; *4:* 30; *13:* 77
Bolognese, Don, *2:* 147, 231;
    4: 176; *7:* 146; *17:* 43
Bond, Arnold, *18:* 116
Booth, Franklin, *YABC 2:* 76
Bordier, Georgette, *16:* 54
Bornstein, Ruth, *14:* 44
Borten, Helen, *3:* 54; *5:* 24
Bottner, Barbara, *14:* 46
Bourke-White, Margaret,
    15: 286-287
Bozzo, Frank, *4:* 154
Bradford, Ron, *7:* 157
Bradley, William, *5:* 164
Brady, Irene, *4:* 31
Bramley, Peter, *4:* 3
Brandenberg, Aliki, *2:* 36-37
Brandon, Brumsic, Jr., *9:* 25
Bransom, Paul, *17:* 121
Brick, John, *10:* 15
Bridwell, Norman, *4:* 37
Briggs, Raymond, *10:* 168
Brinckloe, Julie, *13:* 18
Brock, C. E.,
    15: 97; *YABC 1:* 194, 196, 203
Brock, Emma, *7:* 21
Brock, Henry Matthew, *15:* 81;
    16: 141
Bromhall, Winifred, *5:* 11
Brooke, L. Leslie,
    16: 181-183, 186; *17:* 15-17;
    18: 194
Brooker, Christopher, *15:* 251
Brotman, Adolph E., *5:* 21
Brown, David, *7:* 47
Brown, Denise, *11:* 213
Brown, Judith Gwyn, *1:* 45; *7:* 5;
    8: 167; *9:* 182, 190
Brown, Marc Tolon, *10:* 17, 197;
    14: 263
Brown, Marcia, *7:* 30; *YABC 1:* 27
Brown, Margery W., *5:* 32-33; *10:* 3
Browne, Dik, *8:* 212
Browne, Gordon, *16:* 97
Browne, Hablot K., *15:* 80
Browning, Coleen, *4:* 132
Brule, Al, *3:* 135
Bryson, Bernarda, *3:* 88, 146
Buba, Joy, *12:* 83
Buchanan, Lilian, *13:* 16
Buck, Margaret Waring, *3:* 30
Buehr, Walter, *3:* 31
Bull, Charles Livingston, *18:* 207
Bullen, Anne, *3:* 166, 167
Burchard, Peter, *3:* 197; *5:* 35;
    6: 158, 218
Burger, Carl, *3:* 33
Burkert, Nancy Ekholm,
    18: 186; *YABC 1:* 46
Burn, Doris, *6:* 172
Burningham, John, *9:* 68; *16:* 60-61
Burns, Howard M., *12:* 173
Burns, Raymond, *9:* 29
Burr, Dane, *12:* 2
Burra, Edward, *YABC 2:* 68
Burridge, Marge Opitz, *14:* 42

Burris, Burmah, *4:* 81
Burton, Virginia Lee,
    2: 43; *YABC 1:* 24
Busoni, Rafaello, *1:* 186; *3:* 224;
    6: 126; *14:* 5; *16:* 62-63
Butterfield, Ned, *1:* 153
Buzzell, Russ W., *12:* 177
Byfield, Barbara Ninde, *8:* 18
Byrd, Robert, *13:* 218

Caddy, Alice, *6:* 41
Cady, Harrison, *17:* 21, 23
Caldecott, Randolph, *16:* 98, 103;
    17: 32-33, 36, 38-39;
    YABC 2: 172
Calder, Alexander, *18:* 168
Campbell, Ann, *11:* 43
Campbell, Walter M., *YABC 2:* 158
Caraway, James, *3:* 200-201
Carle, Eric, *4:* 42; *11:* 121; *12:* 29
Carrick, Donald, *5:* 194
Carroll, Ruth, *7:* 41; *10:* 68
Carter, Helene,
    15: 38; *YABC 2:* 220-221
Carty, Leo, *4:* 196; *7:* 163
Cary, *4:* 133; *9:* 32
Cary, Page, *12:* 41
Case, Sandra E., *16:* 2
Cassel, Lili, *3:* 247
Cassels, Jean, *8:* 50
Cassel-Wronker, Lili.
    See also Wronker, Lili Cassel
Castle, Jane, *4:* 80
Cather, Carolyn, *3:* 83; *15:* 203
Cellini, Joseph, *2:* 73; *3:* 35; *16:* 116
Chalmers, Mary, *3:* 145; *13:* 148
Chambers, C. E., *17:* 230
Chambers, Dave, *12:* 151
Chambers, Mary, *4:* 188
Chapman, C. H., *13:* 83, 85, 87
Chapman, Frederick T., *6:* 27
Chappell, Warren, *3:* 172
Charlip, Remy, *4:* 48
Charlot, Jean, *1:* 137, 138; *8:* 23;
    14: 31
Charmatz, Bill, *7:* 45
Chartier, Normand, *9:* 36
Chase, Lynwood M., *14:* 4
Chastain, Madye Lee, *4:* 50
Chen, Tony, *6:* 45
Cheney, T. A., *11:* 47
Chess, Victoria, *12:* 6
Chew, Ruth, *7:* 46
Cho, Shinta, *8:* 126
Chorao, Kay, *7:* 200-201; *8:* 25;
    11: 234
Christensen, Gardell Dano, *1:* 57
Christy, Howard Chandler,
    17: 163-165, 168-169
Church, Frederick, *YABC 1:* 155
Chute, Marchette, *1:* 59
Chwast, Jacqueline, *1:* 63; *2:* 275;
    6: 46-47; *11:* 125; *12:* 202;
    14: 235

Chwast, Seymour, *3:* 128-129;
　18: 43
Cirlin, Edgard, *2:* 168
Clayton, Robert, *9:* 181
Cleaver, Elizabeth, *8:* 204
Clevin, Jörgen, *7:* 50
Coalson, Glo, *9:* 72, 85
Cober, Alan, *17:* 158
Cochran, Bobbye, *11:* 52
CoConis, Ted, *4:* 41
Coerr, Eleanor, *1:* 64
Coggins, Jack, *2:* 69
Cohen, Alix, *7:* 53
Cohen, Vivien, *11:* 112
Colbert, Anthony, *15:* 41
Colby, C. B., *3:* 47
Cole, Olivia H. H., *1:* 134; *3:* 223;
　9: 111
Collier, David, *13:* 127
Connolly, Jerome P., *4:* 128
Cooke, Donald E., *2:* 77
Coombs, Patricia, *2:* 82; *3:* 52
Cooney, Barbara, *6:* 16-17, 50;
　12: 42; *13:* 92; *15:* 145;
　16: 74, 111;
　18: 189; *YABC 2:* 10
Cooper, Marjorie, *7:* 112
Copelman, Evelyn, *8:* 61; *18:* 25
Corcos, Lucille, *2:* 223; *10:* 27
Corey, Robert, *9:* 34
Corlass, Heather, *10:* 7
Cornell, Jeff, *11:* 58
Corrigan, Barbara, *8:* 37
Corwin, Judith Hoffman, *10:* 28
Cosgrove, Margaret, *3:* 100
Cox, Charles, *8:* 20
Crane, Alan H., *1:* 217
Crane, H. M., *13:* 111
Crane, Walter,
　18: 46-49, 53-54, 56-57, 59-61
Credle, Ellis *1:* 69
Crowell, Pers, *3:* 125
Cruikshank, George, *15:* 76, 83
Crump, Fred H., *11:* 62
Cruz, Ray, *6:* 55
Cuffari, Richard, *4:* 75; *5:* 98; *6:* 56;
　7: 13, 84, 153; *8:* 148, 155;
　9: 89; *11:* 19; *12:* 55, 96, 114;
　15: 51, 202; *18:* 5
Cunningham, David, *11:* 13
Cunningham, Imogene, *16:* 122, 127
Curry, John Steuart, *2:* 5

D'Amato, Alex, *9:* 48
D'Amato, Janet, *9:* 48
Darley, F.O.C.,
　16: 145; *YABC 2:* 175
Darling, Lois, *3:* 59
Darling, Louis, *1:* 40-41; *2:* 63; *3:* 59
Darrow, Whitney, Jr., *13:* 25
Dauber, Liz, *1:* 22; *3:* 266
Daugherty, James, *3:* 66; *8:* 178;
　13: 27-28, 161;
　18: 101; *YABC 1:* 256;
　YABC 2: 174

d'Aulaire, Edgar, *5:* 51
d'Aulaire, Ingri, *5:* 51
Davis, Bette J., *15:* 53
Davis, Marguerite, *YABC 1:* 126,
　230
de Angeli, Marguerite,
　1: 77; *YABC 1:* 166
De Bruyn, M(onica) G., *13:* 30-31
De Cuir, John F., *1:* 28-29
De Grazia, *14:* 59
de Groat, Diane, *9:* 39; *18:* 7
de Groot, Lee, *6:* 21
de Larrea, Victoria, *6:* 119, 204
Delessert, Etienne,
　7: 140; *YABC 2:* 209
Delulio, John, *15:* 54
Denetsosie, Hoke, *13:* 126
Dennis, Morgan, *18:* 68-69
Dennis, Wesley, *2:* 87; *3:* 111;
　11: 132; *18:* 71-74
Denslow, W. W., *16:* 84-87;
　18: 19-20, 24
de Paola, Tomie, *8:* 95; *9:* 93; *11:* 69
Detmold, Edmund J., *YABC 2:* 203
de Veyrac, Robert, *YABC 2:* 19
DeVille, Edward A., *4:* 235
Devito, Bert, *12:* 164
Devlin, Harry, *11:* 74
Dewey, Ariane, *7:* 64
　See also Aruego, Ariane
Dick, John Henry, *8:* 181
Dickey, Robert L., *15:* 279
DiFiore, Lawrence, *10:* 51; *12:* 190
Dillard, Annie, *10:* 32
Dillon, Corinne B., *1:* 139
Dillon, Diane, *4:* 104, 167; *6:* 23;
　13: 29; *15:* 99
Dillon, Leo, *4:* 104, 167; *6:* 23;
　13: 29; *15:* 99
Dines, Glen, *7:* 66-67
Dinsdale, Mary, *10:* 65; *11:* 171
Dobrin, Arnold, *4:* 68
Dodd, Ed, *4:* 69
Dodgson, Charles L., *YABC 2:* 98
Dodson, Bert, *9:* 138; *14:* 195
Dohanos, Stevan, *16:* 10
Dolson, Hildegarde, *5:* 57
Domanska, Janina,
　6: 66-67; *YABC 1:* 166
Donahue, Vic, *2:* 93; *3:* 190; *9:* 44
Donald, Elizabeth, *4:* 18
Donna, Natalie, *9:* 52
Doré, Gustave, *18:* 169, 172, 175
Doremus, Robert, *6:* 62; *13:* 90
Dorfman, Ronald, *11:* 128
Dougherty, Charles, *16:* 204; *18:* 74
Douglas, Goray, *13:* 151
Dowd, Vic, *3:* 244; *10:* 97
Dowden, Anne Ophelia, *7:* 70-71;
　13: 120
Drawson, Blair, *17:* 53
Drew, Patricia, *15:* 100
Drummond, V. H., *6:* 70
du Bois, William Pene, *4:* 70;
　10: 122
Duchesne, Janet, *6:* 162

Duke, Chris, *8:* 195
Dulac, Edmund, *YABC 1:* 37;
　YABC 2: 147
Dulac, Jean, *13:* 64
Dunn, Phoebe, *5:* 175
Dunn, Tris, *5:* 175
Dunnington, Tom, *3:* 36; *18:* 281
Dutz, *6:* 59
Duvoisin, Roger, *2:* 95; *6:* 76-77;
　7: 197
Dypold, Pat, *15:* 37

Eagle, Michael, *11:* 86
Earle, Olive L., *7:* 75
Eaton, Tom, *4:* 62; *6:* 64
Ebel, Alex, *11:* 89
Ebert, Len, *9:* 191
Edrien, *11:* 53
Edwards, Gunvor, *2:* 71
Eggenhofer, Nicholas, *2:* 81
Egielski, Richard, *11:* 90; *16:* 208
Ehrlich, Bettina, *1:* 83
Eichenberg, Fritz, *1:* 79;
　9: 54; *YABC 1:* 104-105;
　YABC 2: 213
Einsel, Naiad, *10:* 35
Einsel, Walter, *10:* 37
Einzig, Susan, *3:* 77
Eitzen, Allan, *9:* 56; *12:* 212;
　14: 226
Elgin, Kathleen, *9:* 188
Elliott, Sarah M., *14:* 58
Emberley, Ed, *8:* 53
Englebert, Victor, *8:* 54
Erhard, Walter, *1:* 152
Erickson, Phoebe, *11:* 83
Escourido, Joseph, *4:* 81
Estrada, Ric, *5:* 52, 146; *13:* 174
Ets, Marie Hall, *2:* 102
Eulalie, *YABC 2:* 315
Evans, Katherine, *5:* 64
Ewing, Juliana Horatia, *16:* 92

Falls, C. B., *1:* 19
Faulkner, Jack, *6:* 169
Fava, Rita, *2:* 29
Fax, Elton C., *1:* 101; *4:* 2; *12:* 77
Feelings, Tom, *5:* 22; *8:* 56;
　12: 153; *16:* 105
Feiffer, Jules, *3:* 91; *8:* 58
Fellows, Muriel H., *10:* 42
Fenton, Carroll Lane, *5:* 66
Fenton, Mildred Adams, *5:* 66
Fetz, Ingrid, *11:* 67; *12:* 52;
　16: 205; *17:* 59
Fiammenghi, Gioia, *9:* 66; *11:* 44;
　12: 206; *13:* 57, 59
Field, Rachel, *15:* 113
Fink, Sam, *18:* 119
Fiorentino, Al, *3:* 240
Fisher, Leonard Everett, *3:* 6;
　4: 72, 86; *6:* 197; *9:* 59;
　16: 151, 153; *YABC 2:* 169
Fitschen, Marilyn, *2:* 20-21

Fitzgerald, F. A., *15:* 116
Fitzhugh, Louise, *1:* 94; *9:* 163
Fitzhugh, Susie, *11:* 117
Fitzsimmons, Arthur, *14:* 128
Flack, Marjorie, *YABC 2:* 122
Flagg, James Montgomery, *17:* 227
Flax, Zeona, *2:* 245
Fleishman, Seymour, *14:* 232
Fleming, Guy, *18:* 41
Floethe, Richard, *3:* 131; *4:* 90
Floherty, John J., Jr., *5:* 68
Flora, James, *1:* 96
Floyd, Gareth, *1:* 74; *17:* 245
Flynn, Barbara, *7:* 31; *9:* 70
Fogarty, Thomas, *15:* 89
Folger, Joseph, *9:* 100
Forberg, Ati, *12:* 71, 205; *14:* 1
Ford, H. J., *16:* 185-186
Foreman, Michael, *2:* 110-111
Fortnum, Peggy,
    6: 29; *YABC 1:* 148
Foster, Genevieve, *2:* 112
Foster, Gerald, *7:* 78
Foster, Laura Louise, *6:* 79
Fox, Charles Phillip, *12:* 84
Fox, Jim, *6:* 187
Fracé, Charles, *15:* 118
Frame, Paul, *2:* 45, 145; *9:* 153;
    10: 124
Frank, Lola Edick, *2:* 199
Frank, Mary, *4:* 54
Frascino, Edward, *9:* 133
Frasconi, Antonio, *6:* 80
Fraser, Betty, *2:* 212; *6:* 185; *8:* 103
Freeman, Don, *2:* 15; *13:* 249;
    17: 62-63, 65, 67-68; *18:* 243
French, Fiona, *6:* 82-83
Frith, Michael K., *15:* 138; *18:* 120
Frost, A. B.,
    17: 6-7; *YABC 1:* 156-157, 160;
    YABC 2: 107
Fry, Guy, *2:* 224
Fry, Rosalie,
    3: 72; *YABC 2:* 180-181
Fuchs, Erich, *6:* 84
Funk, Tom, *7:* 17, 99

Gag, Flavia, *17:* 49, 52
Gag, Wanda, *YABC 1:* 135, 137-
    138, 141, 143
Gagnon, Cécile, *11:* 77
Gal, Laszlo, *14:* 127
Galdone, Paul, *1:* 156, 181, 206;
    2: 40, 241; *3:* 42, 144; *4:* 141;
    10: 109, 158; *11:* 21;
    12: 118, 210; *14:* 12; *16:* 36-37;
    17: 70-74; *18:* 111, 230
Galster, Robert, *1:* 66
Gammell, Stephen, *7:* 48; *13:* 149
Gannett, Ruth Chrisman, *3:* 74;
    18: 254
Garnett, Eve, *3:* 75
Garraty, Gail, *4:* 142
Geary, Clifford N., *1:* 122; *9:* 104

Geer, Charles, *1:* 91; *3:* 179; *4:* 201;
    6: 168; *7:* 96; *9:* 58; *10:* 72;
    12: 127
Geisel, Theodor Seuss,
    1: 104-105, 106
Geldart, Bill, *15:* 121
Genia, *4:* 84
Gentry, Cyrille R., *12:* 66
George, Jean, *2:* 113
Geritz, Franz, *17:* 135
Gervase, *12:* 27
Gilbert, John, *YABC 2:* 287
Gill, Margery, *4:* 57; *7:* 7
Gilman, Esther, *15:* 124
Giovanopoulos, Paul, *7:* 104
Githens, Elizabeth M., *5:* 47
Gladstone, Gary, *12:* 89; *13:* 190
Gladstone, Lise, *15:* 273
Glanzman, Louis S., *2:* 177; *3:* 182
Glaser, Milton, *3:* 5; *5:* 156; *11:* 107
Glass, Marvin, *9:* 174
Glattauer, Ned, *5:* 84; *13:* 224;
    14: 26
Glauber, Uta, *17:* 76
Gleeson, J. M., *YABC 2:* 207
Gliewe, Unada, *3:* 78-79
Glovach, Linda, *7:* 105
Gobbato, Imero, *3:* 180-181; *6:* 213;
    7: 58; *9:* 150; *18:* 39
Godfrey, Michael, *17:* 279
Goffstein, M. B., *8:* 71
Golbin, Andrée, *15:* 125
Goldfeder, Cheryl, *11:* 191
Goldsborough, June, *5:* 154-155;
    8: 92; *14:* 266
Goldstein, Leslie, *5:* 8; *6:* 60;
    10: 106
Goldstein, Nathan, *1:* 175; *2:* 79;
    11: 41, 232; *16:* 55
Goodall, John S., *4:* 92-93;
    10: 132; *YABC 1:* 198
Goode, Diane, *15:* 126
Goodwin, Harold, *13:* 74
Goodwin, Philip R., *18:* 206
Gordon, Gwen, *12:* 151
Gordon, Margaret, *4:* 147; *5:* 48-49;
    9: 79
Gorecka-Egan, Erica, *18:* 35
Gorey, Edward, *1:* 60-61; *13:* 169;
    18: 192
Gorsline, Douglas, *1:* 98; *6:* 13;
    11: 113; *13:* 104;
    15: 14; *YABC 1:* 15
Gosner, Kenneth, *5:* 135
Gotlieb, Jules, *6:* 127
Graham, A. B., *11:* 61
Graham, L., *7:* 108
Graham, Margaret Bloy, *11:* 120;
    18: 305, 307
Grahame-Johnstone, Anne, *13:* 61
Grahame-Johnstone, Janet, *13:* 61
Gramatky, Hardie, *1:* 107
Grant, Gordon,
    17: 230, 234; *YABC 1:* 164
Grant, (Alice) Leigh, *10:* 52; *15:* 131
Gray, Reginald, *6:* 69

Green, Eileen, *6:* 97
Greenaway, Kate,
    17: 275; *YABC 1:* 88-89;
    YABC 2: 131, 133, 136, 138-
    139, 141
Greenwald, Sheila, *1:* 34; *3:* 99;
    8: 72
Greiffenhagen, Maurice, *16:* 137
Greifferhager, Maurice,
    YABC 2: 288
Greiner, Robert, *6:* 86
Gretz, Susanna, *7:* 114
Gretzer, John, *1:* 54; *3:* 26; *4:* 162;
    7: 125; *16:* 247; *18:* 117
Grieder, Walter, *9:* 84
Grifalconi, Ann, *2:* 126; *3:* 248;
    11: 18; *13:* 182
Gringhuis, Dirk, *6:* 98; *9:* 196
Gripe, Harald, *2:* 127
Grisha, *3:* 71
Grose, Helen Mason,
    YABC 1: 260; *YABC 2:* 150
Grossman, Robert, *11:* 124
Groth, John, *15:* 79
Gschwind, William, *11:* 72
Guggenheim, Hans, *2:* 10; *3:* 37;
    8: 136

Haas, Irene, *17:* 77
Hader, Berta H., *16:* 126
Hader, Elmer S., *16:* 126
Haldane, Roger, *13:* 76; *14:* 202
Hale, Kathleen, *17:* 79
Hall, Douglas, *15:* 184
Hall, H. Tom, *1:* 227
Halpern, Joan, *10:* 25
Hamberger, John, *6:* 8; *8:* 32; *14:* 79
Hamil, Tom, *14:* 80
Hamilton, Helen S., *2:* 238
Hammond, Elizabeth, *5:* 36, 203
Hampshire, Michael, *5:* 187;
    7: 110-111
Hampson, Denman, *10:* 155;
    15: 130
Handville, Robert, *1:* 89
Hane, Roger, *17:* 239
Hanley, Catherine, *8:* 161
Hanson, Joan, *8:* 76; *11:* 139
Hardy, David A., *9:* 96
Hardy, Paul, *YABC 2:* 245
Harlan, Jerry, *3:* 96
Harnischfeger, *18:* 121
Harper, Arthur, *YABC 2:* 121
Harrington, Richard, *5:* 81
Harrison, Harry, *4:* 103
Hart, William, *13:* 72
Hartelius, Margaret, *10:* 24
Hartshorn, Ruth, *5:* 115; *11:* 129
Harvey, Gerry, *7:* 180
Hassell, Hilton, *YABC 1:* 187
Hasselriis, Else, *18:* 87; *YABC 1:* 96
Hauman, Doris, *2:* 184
Hauman, George, *2:* 184
Hausherr, Rosmarie, *15:* 29

Hawkinson, John, *4:* 109; *7:* 83
Haydock, Robert, *4:* 95
Haywood, Carolyn, *1:* 112
Healy, Daty, *12:* 143
Hechtkopf, H., *11:* 110
Henneberger, Robert, *1:* 42; *2:* 237
Henry, Thomas, *5:* 102
Henstra, Friso, *8:* 80
Herbster, Mary Lee, *9:* 33
Hergé. *See* Remi, Georges
Hermanson, Dennis, *10:* 55
Herrington, Roger, *3:* 161
Heyduck-Huth, Hilde, *8:* 82
Heyman, Ken, *8:* 33
Higginbottom, J. Winslow, *8:* 170
Hildebrandt, Greg, *8:* 191
Hildebrandt, Tim, *8:* 191
Himler, Ronald, *6:* 114; *7:* 162;
　　8: 17, 84, 125; *14:* 76
Hirsh, Marilyn, *7:* 126
Hitz, Demi, *11:* 135; *15:* 245
Ho, Kwoncjan, *15:* 132
Hoban, Lillian, *1:* 114
Hoberman, Norman, *5:* 82
Hodges, C. Walter, *2:* 139; *11:* 15;
　　12: 25; *YABC 2:* 62-63
Hodges, David, *9:* 98
Hofbauer, Imre, *2:* 162
Hoff, Syd, *9:* 107; *10:* 128
Hoffman, Rosekrans, *15:* 133
Hoffmann, Felix, *9:* 109
Hogan, Inez, *2:* 141
Hogarth, Paul, *YABC 1:* 16
Hogenbyl, Jan, *1:* 35
Hogner, Nils, *4:* 122
Hogrogian, Nonny, *3:* 221;
　　4: 106-107; *5:* 166; *7:* 129;
　　15: 2; *16:* 176; *YABC 2:* 84, 94
Holberg, Richard, *2:* 51
Holiday, Henry, *YABC 2:* 107
Holland, Janice, *18:* 118
Holland, Marion, *6:* 116
Holling, Holling C., *15:* 136-137
Hollinger, Deanne, *12:* 116
Holmes, B., *3:* 82
Holmes, Bea, *7:* 74
Holz, Loretta, *17:* 81
Homar, Lorenzo, *6:* 2
Homer, Winslow, *YABC 2:* 87
Honigman, Marian, *3:* 2
Hood, Susan, *12:* 43
Hook, Jeff, *14:* 137
Hoover, Russell, *12:* 95; *17:* 2
Horder, Margaret, *2:* 108
Horvat, Laurel, *12:* 201
Hough, Charlotte, *9:* 112; *13:* 98;
　　17: 83
Houlihan, Ray, *11:* 214
Houston, James, *13:* 107
Howard, Alan, *16:* 80
Howard, J. N., *15:* 234
Howe, Stephen, *1:* 232
Howell, Pat, *15:* 139
Hudnut, Robin, *14:* 62
Huffaker, Sandy, *10:* 56
Huffman, Joan, *13:* 33
Huffman, Tom, *13:* 180; *17:* 212

Hughes, Shirley, *1:* 20, 21; *7:* 3;
　　12: 217; *16:* 163
Hülsmann, Eva, *16:* 166
Hummel, Lisl, *YABC 2:* 333-334
Humphrey, Henry, *16:* 167
Hunt, James, *2:* 143
Hurd, Clement, *2:* 148, 149
Hurd, Peter, *YABC 2:* 56
Hustler, Tom, *6:* 105
Hutchins, Pat, *15:* 142
Hutchinson, William M., *6:* 3, 138
Hutton, Clarke, *YABC 2:* 335
Hyman, Trina Schart, *1:* 204;
　　2: 194; *5:* 153; *6:* 106;
　　7: 138, 145; *8:* 22; *10:* 196;
　　13: 96; *14:* 114; *15:* 204; *16:* 234

Ide, Jacqueline, *YABC 1:* 39
Ilsley, Velma, *3:* 1; *7:* 55; *12:* 109
Inga, *1:* 142
Ipcar, Dahlov, *1:* 124-125
Irvin, Fred, *13:* 166; *15:* 143-144
Ives, Ruth, *15:* 257

Jacobs, Barbara, *9:* 136
Jacobs, Lou, Jr., *9:* 136; *15:* 128
Jacques, Robin, *1:* 70; *2:* 1; *8:* 46;
　　9: 20; *15:* 187; *YABC 1:* 42
Jagr, Miloslav, *13:* 197
Jakubowski, Charles, *14:* 192
Jambor, Louis, *YABC 1:* 11
James, Gilbert, *YABC 1:* 43
James, Harold, *2:* 151; *3:* 62; *8:* 79
Janosch, *See* Eckert, Horst
Jansson, Tove, *3:* 90
Jaques, Faith, *7:* 11, 132-133
Jauss, Anne Marie, *1:* 139; *3:* 34;
　　10: 57, 119; *11:* 205
Jeffers, Susan, *17:* 86-87
Jefferson, Louise E., *4:* 160
Jeruchim, Simon, *6:* 173; *15:* 250
John, Diana, *12:* 209
John, Helen, *1:* 215
Johnson, Bruce, *9:* 47
Johnson, Crockett, *See* Leisk,
　　David
Johnson, Harper, *1:* 27; *2:* 33;
　　18: 302
Johnson, James David, *12:* 195
Johnson, James Ralph, *1:* 23, 127
Johnson, Milton, *1:* 67; *2:* 71
Johnson, Pamela, *16:* 174
Johnstone, Anne, *8:* 120
Johnstone, Janet Grahame, *8:* 120
Jones, Carol, *5:* 131
Jones, Elizabeth Orton,
　　18: 124, 126, 128-129
Jones, Harold, *14:* 88
Jones, Wilfred, *YABC 1:* 163
Jucker, Sita, *5:* 93
Jupo, Frank, *7:* 148-149

Kakimoto, Kozo, *11:* 148

Kamen, Gloria, *1.* 41; *9.* 119;
　　10: 178
Kane, Henry B., *14:* 90; *18:* 219-220
Kane, Robert, *18:* 131
Karlin, Eugene, *10:* 63
Kaufman, Angelika, *15:* 156
Kaufman, John, *13:* 158
Kaufmann, John, *1:* 174; *4:* 159;
　　8: 43, 192; *10:* 102; *18:* 133-134
Kaye, Graham, *1:* 9
Keane, Bil, *4:* 135
Keats, Ezra Jack, *3:* 18, 105, 257;
　　14: 101, 102
Keegan, Marcia, *9:* 122
Keeping, Charles, *9:* 124, 185;
　　15: 28, 134; *18:* 115
Keith, Eros, *4:* 98; *5:* 138
Kelen, Emery, *13:* 115
Kellogg, Steven, *8:* 96; *11:* 207;
　　14: 130; *YABC 1:* 65, 73
Kelly, Walt,
　　18: 136-141, 144-146, 148-149
Kemble, E. W., *YABC 2:* 54, 59
Kennedy, Paul Edward, *6:* 190;
　　8: 132
Kennedy, Richard, *3:* 93;
　　12: 179; *YABC 1:* 57
Kent, Rockwell, *5:* 166; *6:* 129
Kepes, Juliet, *13:* 119
Kessler, Leonard, *1:* 108; *7:* 139;
　　14: 107, 227
Kettelkamp, Larry, *2:* 164
Key, Alexander, *8:* 99
Kiakshuk, *8:* 59
Kidder, Harvey, *9:* 105
Kindred, Wendy, *7:* 151
King, Robin, *10:* 164-165
Kingman, Dong, *16:* 287
Kingsley, Charles, *YABC 2:* 182
Kipling, John Lockwood,
　　YABC 2: 198
Kipling, Rudyard, *YABC 2:* 196
Kirk, Ruth, *5:* 96
Kirmse, Marguerite, *15:* 283;
　　18: 153
Klapholz, Mel, *13:* 35
Knight, Christopher, *13:* 125
Knight, Hilary, *1:* 233; *3:* 21;
　　15: 92, 158-159; *16:* 258-260;
　　18: 235; *YABC 1:* 168-169, 172
Kocsis, J. C., *4:* 130
Koering, Ursula, *3:* 28; *4:* 14
Koerner, W. H. D., *14:* 216
Komoda, Kiyo, *9:* 128; *13:* 214
Konashevicha, V., *YABC 1:* 26
Konigsburg, E. L., *4:* 138
Korach, Mimi, *1:* 128-129; *2:* 52;
　　4: 39; *5:* 159; *9:* 129; *10:* 21
Koren, Edward, *5:* 100
Kossin, Sandy, *10:* 71
Kovacević, Zivojin, *13:* 247
Krahn, Fernando, *2:* 257
Kramer, Frank, *6:* 121
Kraus, Robert, *13:* 217
Kredel, Fritz, *6:* 35;
　　17: 93-96; *YABC 2:* 166, 300

Krementz, Jill, *17:* 98
Krush, Beth, *1:* 51, 85; *2:* 233;
    4: 115; *9:* 61; *10:* 191; *11:* 196;
    18: 164-165
Krush, Joe, *2:* 233; *4:* 115; *9:* 61;
    10: 191; *11:* 196; *18:* 164-165
Kubinyi, Laszlo, *4:* 116; *6:* 113;
    16: 118; *17:* 100
Kuhn, Bob, *17:* 91
Künstler, Mort, *10:* 73
Kurelek, William, *8:* 107
Kuriloff, Ron, *13:* 19
Kuskin, Karla, *2:* 170

La Croix, *YABC 2:* 4
Laimgruber, Monika, *11:* 153
Laite, Gordon, *1:* 130-131; *8:* 209
Lamb, Jim, *10:* 117
Lambo, Don, *6:* 156
Landa, Peter, *11:* 95; *13:* 177
Landshoff, Ursula, *13:* 124
Lane, John, *15:* 176-177
Lane, John R., *8:* 145
Lang, Jerry, *18:* 295
Langler, Nola, *8:* 110
Lantz, Paul, *1:* 82, 102
Larsen, Suzanne, *1:* 13
La Rue, Michael D., *13:* 215
Lasker, Joe, *7:* 186-187; *14:* 55
Latham, Barbara, *16:* 188-189
Lathrop, Dorothy,
    14: 117, 118-119; *15:* 109;
    16: 78-79, 81; *YABC 2:* 301
Lattimore, Eleanor Frances, *7:* 156
Lauden, Claire, *16:* 173
Lauden, George, Jr., *16:* 173
Laune, Paul, *2:* 235
Lawson, Carol, *6:* 38
Lawson, George, *17:* 280
Lawson, Robert, *5:* 26; *6:* 94;
    13: 39; *16:* 11; *YABC 2:* 222,
    224-225, 227-235, 237-241
Lazarevich, Mila, *17:* 118
Lazzaro, Victor, *11:* 126
Leacroft, Richard, *6:* 140
Lear, Edward, *18:* 183-185
Lebenson, Richard, *6:* 209; *7:* 76
Le Cain, Errol, *6:* 141; *9:* 3
Lee, Doris, *13:* 246
Lee, Manning de V., *2:* 200;
    17: 12; *YABC 2:* 304
Lee, Robert J., *3:* 97
Leech, John, *15:* 59
Lees, Harry, *6:* 112
Legrand, Edy, *18:* 89, 93
Lehrman, Rosalie, *2:* 180
Leichman, Seymour, *5:* 107
Leisk, David, *1:* 140-141; *11:* 54
Leloir, Maurice, *18:* 77, 80, 83, 99
Lemke, Horst, *14:* 98
Lemon, David Gwynne, *9:* 1
Lenski, Lois, *1:* 144
Lent, Blair, *1:* 116-117; *2:* 174;
    3: 206-207; *7:* 168-169

Lerner, Sharon, *11:* 157
Levin, Ted, *12:* 148
Lewin, Ted, *4:* 77; *8:* 168
Lewis, Allen, *15:* 112
Liese, Charles, *4:* 222
Lilly, Charles, *8:* 73
Lindberg, Howard, *10:* 123; *16:* 190
Linden, Seymour, *18:* 200-201
Linell. *See* Smith, Linell
Lionni, Leo, *8:* 115
Lipinsky, Lino, *2:* 156
Lippman, Peter, *8:* 31
Lisker, Sonia O., *16:* 274
Lissim, Simon, *17:* 138
Little, Harold, *16:* 72
Lloyd, Errol, *11:* 39
Lo, Koon-chiu, *7:* 134
Lobel, Anita, *6:* 87; *9:* 141; *18:* 248
Lobel, Arnold, *1:* 188-189; *5:* 12;
    6: 147; *7:* 167, 209; *18:* 190-191
Loefgren, Ulf, *3:* 108
Lofting, Hugh, *15:* 182-183
Lonette, Reisie, *11:* 211; *12:* 168;
    13: 56
Longtemps, Ken, *17:* 123
Looser, Heinz, *YABC 2:* 208
Lopshire, Robert, *6:* 149
Lorraine, Walter H., *3:* 110; *4:* 123;
    16: 192
Loss, Joan, *11:* 163
Louderback, Walt, *YABC 1:* 164
Low, Joseph, *14:* 124, 125; *18:* 68
Lowenheim, Alfred, *13:* 65-66
Lowitz, Anson, *17:* 124; *18:* 215
Lowrey, Jo, *8:* 133
Lubell, Winifred, *1:* 207; *3:* 15;
    6: 151
Lubin, Leonard B., *YABC 2:* 96
Luhrs, Henry, *7:* 123; *11:* 120
Lupo, Dom, *4:* 204
Lynch, Charles, *16:* 33
Lyon, Elinor, *6:* 154
Lyon, Fred, *14:* 16
Lyons, Oren, *8:* 193

Maas, Dorothy, *6:* 175
MacDonald, Norman, *13:* 99
Macguire, Robert Reid, *18:* 67
MacIntyre, Elisabeth, *17:* 127-128
Mack, Stan, *17:* 129
Mackay, Donald, *17:* 60
Mackinstry, Elizabeth, *15:* 110
Maclise, Daniel, *YABC 2:* 257
Madden, Don, *3:* 112-113;
    4: 33, 108, 155;
    7: 193; *YABC 2:* 211
Maddison, Angela Mary, *10:* 83
Maestro, Giulio, *8:* 124; *12:* 17;
    13: 108
Maik, Henri, *9:* 102
Maitland, Antony, *1:* 100, 176;
    8: 41; *17:* 246
Malvern, Corrine, *2:* 13
Mangurian, David, *14:* 133

Manning, Samuel F., *5:* 75
Maraja, *15:* 86;
    YABC 1: 28; *YABC 2:* 115
Marchiori, Carlos, *14:* 60
Marino, Dorothy, *6:* 37; *14:* 135
Markham, R. L., *17:* 240
Mars, W. T., *1:* 161; *3:* 115;
    4: 208, 225; *5:* 92, 105, 186;
    8: 214; *9:* 12; *13:* 121
Marsh, Christine, *3:* 164
Marsh, Reginald, *17:* 5
Marshall, Anthony D., *18:* 216
Marshall, James, *6:* 160
Martin, Fletcher, *18:* 213
Martin, Rene, *7:* 144
Martin, Stefan, *8:* 68
Martinez, John, *6:* 113
Mason, George F., *14:* 139
Massie, Diane Redfield, *16:* 194
Matsubara, Naoko, *12:* 121
Matsuda, Shizu, *13:* 167
Matthews, F. Leslie, *4:* 216
Matthieu, Joseph, *14:* 33
Matulay, Laszlo, *5:* 18
Matus, Greta, *12:* 142
Mawicke, Tran, *9:* 137; *15:* 191
Maxwell, John Alan, *1:* 148
Mayan, Earl, *7:* 193
Mayer, Mercer, *11:* 192; *16:* 195-196
Mayhew, Richard, *3:* 106
Mays, Victor, *5:* 127; *8:* 45, 153;
    14: 245
McCann, Gerald, *3:* 50; *4:* 94; *7:* 54
McClary, Nelson, *1:* 111
McClintock, Theodore, *14:* 141
McCloskey, Robert, *1:* 184-185;
    2: 186-187; *17:* 209
McClung, Robert, *2:* 189
McCrady, Lady, *16:* 198
McCrea, James, *3:* 122
McCrea, Ruth, *3:* 122
McCully, Emily, *2:* 89;
    4: 120-121, 146, 197; *5:* 2, 129;
    7: 191; *11:* 122; *15:* 210
McCurdy, Michael, *13:* 153
McDermott, Beverly Brodsky,
    11: 180
McDermott, Gerald, *16:* 201
McDonald, Jill, *13:* 155
McDonald, Ralph J., *5:* 123, 195
McDonough, Don, *10:* 163
McFall, Christie, *12:* 144
McGee, Barbara, *6:* 165
McKay, Donald, *2:* 118
McKee, David, *10:* 48
McKie, Roy, *7:* 44
McLachlan, Edward, *5:* 89
McNaught, Harry, *12:* 80
McPhail, David, *14:* 105
McVay, Tracy, *11:* 68
Melo, John, *16:* 285
Meng, Heinz, *13:* 158
Merrill, Frank T., *16:* 147;
    YABC 1: 226, 229, 273
Merryweather, Jack, *10:* 179
Meyer, Renate, *6:* 170

Meyers, Bob, *11:* 136
Micale, Albert, *2:* 65
Middleton-Sandford, Betty, *2:* 125
Mikolaycak, Charles, *9:* 144;
   12: 101; *13:* 212
Miles, Jennifer, *17:* 278
Milhous, Katherine, *15:* 193; *17:* 51
Millar, H. R., *YABC 1:* 194-195,
   203
Miller, Don, *15:* 195; *16:* 71
Miller, Grambs, *18:* 38
Miller, Jane, *15:* 196
Miller, Marcia, *13:* 233
Miller, Marilyn, *1:* 87
Miller, Shane, *5:* 140
Mizumura, Kazue, *10:* 143; *18:* 223
Mochi, Ugo, *8:* 122
Mohr, Nicholasa, *8:* 139
Montresor, Beni, *2:* 91; *3:* 138
Moon, Eliza, *14:* 40
Mordvinoff, Nicolas, *15:* 179
Morrill, Leslie, *18:* 218
Morrow, Gray, *2:* 64; *5:* 200;
   10: 103, 114; *14:* 175
Morton, Marian, *3:* 185
Moses, Grandma, *18:* 228
Moss, Donald, *11:* 184
Mozley, Charles, *9:* 87; *YABC 2:* 89
Mugnaini, Joseph,, *11:* 35
Mullins, Edward S., *10:* 101
Munari, Bruno, *15:* 200
Munowitz, Ken, *14:* 148
Munson, Russell, *13:* 9
Murphy, Bill, *5:* 138
Mutchler, Dwight, *1:* 25
Myers, Bernice, *9:* 147
Myers, Lou, *11:* 2

Nakatani, Chiyoko, *12:* 124
Nason, Thomas W., *14:* 68
Navarra, Celeste Scala, *8:* 142
Naylor, Penelope, *10:* 104
Neebe, William, *7:* 93
Needler, Jerry, *12:* 93
Negri, Rocco, *3:* 213; *5:* 67;
   6: 91, 108; *12:* 159
Neill, John R., *18:* 8, 10-11, 21, 30
Ness, Evaline, *1:* 164-165; *2:* 39;
   3: 8; *10:* 147; *12:* 53
Neville, Vera, *2:* 182
Newberry, Clare Turlay, *1:* 170
Newfeld, Frank, *14:* 121
Nicholson, William, *15:* 33-34;
   16: 48
Nickless, Will, *16:* 139
Nicolas, *17:* 130, 132-133;
   YABC 2: 215
Niebrugge, Jane, *6:* 118
Nielsen, Jon, *6:* 100
Nielsen, Kay, *15:* 7;
   16: 211-213, 215, 217;
   YABC 1: 32-33
Ninon, *1:* 5
Nixon, K., *14:* 152
Noonan, Julia, *4:* 163; *7:* 207

Nordenskjold, Birgitta, *2:* 208
Norman, Michael, *12:* 117
Nussbaumer, Paul, *16:* 219

Oakley, Graham, *8:* 112
Oakley, Thornton, *YABC 2:* 189
Obligado, Lilian, *2:* 28, 66-67;
   6: 30; *14:* 179; *15:* 103
Obrant, Susan, *11:* 186
Oechsli, Kelly, *5:* 144-145; *7:* 115;
   8: 83, 183; *13:* 117
Ohlsson, Ib, *4:* 152; *7:* 57; *10:* 20;
   11: 90
Olschewski, Alfred, *7:* 172
Olsen, Ib Spang, *6:* 178-179
Olugebefola, Ademola, *15:* 205
O'Neil, Dan IV, *7:* 176
Ono, Chiyo, *7:* 97
Orbaan, Albert, *2:* 31; *5:* 65, 171;
   9: 8; *14:* 241
Ormsby, Virginia H., *11:* 187
Orozco, José Clemente, *9:* 177
Osmond, Edward, *10:* 111
O'Sullivan, Tom, *3:* 176; *4:* 55
Oudry, J. B., *18:* 167
Oughton, Taylor, *5:* 23
Overlie, George, *11:* 156
Owens, Carl, *2:* 35
Owens, Gail, *10:* 170; *12:* 157
Oxenbury, Helen, *3:* 150-151

Padgett, Jim, *12:* 165
Page, Homer, *14:* 145
Pak, *12:* 76
Palazzo, Tony, *3:* 152-153
Palladini, David, *4:* 113
Palmer, Heidi, *15:* 207
Palmer, Juliette, *6:* 89; *15:* 208
Palmer, Lemuel, *17:* 25, 29
Panesis, Nicholas, *3:* 127
Papas, William, *11:* 223
Papish, Robin Lloyd, *10:* 80
Paraquin, Charles H., *18:* 166
Parker, Lewis, *2:* 179
Parker, Nancy Winslow, *10:* 113
Parker, Robert, *4:* 161; *5:* 74; *9:* 136
Parker, Robert Andrew, *11:* 81
Parnall, Peter, *5:* 137; *16:* 221
Parrish, Maxfield,
   14: 160, 161, 164, 165; *16:* 109;
   18: 12-13; *YABC 1:* 149, 152,
   267; *YABC 2:* 146, 149
Parry, Marion, *13:* 176
Pascal, David, *14:* 174
Pasquier, J. A., *16:* 91
Paterson, Diane, *13:* 116
Paterson, Helen, *16:* 93
Paton, Jane, *15:* 271
Payne, Joan Balfour, *1:* 118
Payson, Dale, *7:* 34; *9:* 151
Peake, Mervyn, *YABC 2:* 307
Peat, Fern B., *16:* 115
Peck, Anne Merrimann, *18:* 241
Pederson, Sharleen, *12:* 92

Pedersen, Vilhelm, *YABC 1:* 40
Peet, Bill, *2:* 203
Peltier, Leslie C., *13:* 178
Pendle, Alexy, *7:* 159; *13:* 34
Peppe, Rodney, *4:* 164-165
Perl, Susan, *2:* 98; *4:* 231;
   5: 44-45, 118; *6:* 199; *8:* 137;
   12: 88; *YABC 1:* 176
Pesek, Ludek, *15:* 237
Petersham, Maud, *17:* 108, 147-153
Petersham, Miska, *17:* 108, 147-153
Peterson, R. F., *7:* 101
Peterson, Russell, *7:* 130
Petie, Haris, *2:* 3; *10:* 41, 118;
   11: 227; *12:* 70
Peyton, K. M., *15:* 212
Pfeifer, Herman, *15:* 262
Phillips, Douglas, *1:* 19
Phillips, F. D., *6:* 202
"Phiz." *See* Browne, Hablot K.,
   15: 65
Piatti, Celestino, *16:* 223
Picarella, Joseph, *13:* 147
Pickard, Charles, *12:* 38; *18:* 203
Pienkowski, Jan, *6:* 183
Pimlott, John, *10:* 205
Pincus, Harriet, *4:* 186; *8:* 179
Pinkney, Jerry, *8:* 218; *10:* 40;
   15: 276
Pinkwater, Manus, *8:* 156
Pinto, Ralph, *10:* 131
Pitz, Henry C.,
   4: 168; *YABC 2:* 95, 176
Pogany, Willy, *15:* 46, 49
Politi, Leo, *1:* 178; *4:* 53
Polseno, Jo, *1:* 53; *3:* 117; *5:* 114;
   17: 154
Ponter, James, *5:* 204
Poortvliet, Rien, *6:* 212
Portal, Colette, *6:* 186; *11:* 203
Porter, George, *7:* 181
Potter, Beatrix, *YABC 1:* 208-210,
   212, 213
Potter, Miriam Clark, *3:* 162
Powers, Richard M., *1:* 230; *3:* 218;
   7: 194
Price, Christine, *2:* 247;
   3: 163, 253; *8:* 166
Price, Garrett, *1:* 76; *2:* 42
Price, Hattie Longstreet, *17:* 13
Price, Norman, *YABC 1:* 129
Prince, Leonora E., *7:* 170
Prittie, Edwin J., *YABC 1:* 120
Pudlo, *8:* 59
Purdy, Susan, *8:* 162
Puskas, James, *5:* 141
Pyk, Jan, *7:* 26
Pyle, Howard,
   16: 225-228, 230-232, 235

Quackenbush, Robert, *4:* 190;
   6: 166; *7:* 175, 178; *9:* 86;
   11: 65, 221
Quirk, Thomas, *12:* 81

Rackham, Arthur,
  15: 32, 78, 214-227;
  17: 105, 115;
  18: 233; *YABC 1:* 25, 45, 55,
  147; *YABC 2:* 103, 142, 173,
  210
Rafilson, Sidney, *11:* 172
Raible, Alton, *1:* 202-203
Ramsey, James, *16:* 41
Rand, Paul, *6:* 188
Rappaport, Eva, *6:* 190
Raskin, Ellen, *2:* 208-209; *4:* 142;
  13: 183
Rau, Margaret, *9:* 157
Raverat, Gwen, *YABC 1:* 152
Ravielli, Anthony, *1:* 198; *3:* 168;
  11: 143
Ray, Deborah, *8:* 164
Ray, Ralph, *2:* 239; *5:* 73
Razzi, James, *10:* 127
Relf, Douglas, *3:* 63
Relyea, C. M., *16:* 29
Remi, Georges, *13:* 184
Renlie, Frank, *11:* 200
Reschofsky, Jean, *7:* 118
Rethi, Lili, *2:* 153
Reusswig, William, *3:* 267
Rey, H. A., *1:* 182; *YABC 2:* 17
Reynolds, Doris, *5:* 71
Ribbons, Ian, *3:* 10
Rice, Elizabeth, *2:* 53, 214
Richards, Henry, *YABC 1:* 228, 231
Richardson, Ernest, *2:* 144
Richardson, Frederick, *18:* 27, 31
Rieniets, Judy King, *14:* 28
Riger, Bob, *2:* 166
Ringi, Kjell, *12:* 171
Rios, Tere. *See* Versace, Marie
Ripper, Charles L., *3:* 175
Rivkin, Jay, *15:* 230
Roach, Marilynne, *9:* 158
Roberts, Cliff, *4:* 126
Roberts, Doreen, *4:* 230
Robinson, Charles, *3:* 53; *5:* 14;
  6: 193; *7:* 150; *7:* 183; *8:* 38;
  9: 81; *13:* 188; *14:* 248-249
Robinson, Charles [1870-1937],
  17: 157, 171-173, 175-176;
  YABC 2: 308-310, 331
Robinson, Jerry, *3:* 262
Robinson, Joan G., *7:* 184
Robinson, T. H., *17:* 179, 181-183
Robinson, W. Heath,
  17: 185, 187, 189, 191, 193,
  195, 197, 199, 202;
  YABC 1: 44; *YABC 2:* 183
Rocker, Fermin, *7:* 34; *13:* 21
Rockwell, Anne, *5:* 147
Rockwell, Gail, *7:* 186
Rockwell, Norman, *YABC 2:* 60
Rodriguez, Joel, *16:* 65
Roever, J. M., *4:* 119
Rogers, Carol, *2:* 262; *6:* 164
Rogers, Frances, *10:* 130

Rogers, William A.,
  15: 151, 153-154
Rojankovsky, Feodor, *6:* 134, 136;
  10: 183
Rose, Carl, *5:* 62
Rosenblum, Richard, *11:* 202;
  18: 18
Rosier, Lydia, *16:* 236
Ross, Clare, *3:* 123
Ross, John, *3:* 123
Ross, Tony, *17:* 204
Roth, Arnold, *4:* 238
Rouille, M., *11:* 96
Rounds, Glen, *8:* 173; *9:* 171;
  12: 56; *YABC 1:* 1-3
Rubel, Nicole, *18:* 255
Rud, Borghild, *6:* 15
Rudolph, Norman Guthrie, *17:* 13
Ruffins, Reynold, *10:* 134-135
Russell, E. B., *18:* 177, 182
Ruth, Rod, *9:* 161
Ryden, Hope, *8:* 176

Sacker, Amy, *16:* 100
Sagsoorian, Paul, *12:* 183
Sale, Morton, *YABC 2:* 31
Sambourne, Linley, *YABC 2:* 181
Sampson, Katherine, *9:* 197
Samson, Anne S., *2:* 216
Sandberg, Lasse, *15:* 239, 241
Sandin, Joan, *4:* 36; *6:* 194; *7:* 177;
  12: 145, 185
Sapieha, Christine, *1:* 180
Sarg, Tony, *YABC 2:* 236
Sargent, Robert, *2:* 217
Saris, *1:* 33
Sarony, *YABC 2:* 170
Sasek, Miroslav, *16:* 239-242
Sassman, David, *9:* 79
Savage, Steele, *10:* 203
Savitt, Sam, *8:* 66, 182; *15:* 278
Scabrini, Janet, *13:* 191
Scarry, Richard, *2:* 220-221; *18:* 20
Schaeffer, Mead, *18:* 81, 94
Scheel, Lita, *11:* 230
Schick, Joel, *16:* 160; *17:* 167
Schindelman, Joseph, *1:* 74; *4:* 101;
  12: 49
Schindler, Edith, *7:* 22
Schlesinger, Bret, *7:* 77
Schmid, Eleanore, *12:* 188
Schmidt, Elizabeth, *15:* 242
Schoenherr, John, *1:* 146-147, 173;
  3: 39, 139; *17:* 75
Schomburg, Alex, *13:* 23
Schongut, Emanuel, *4:* 102; *15:* 186
Schoonover, Frank,
  17: 107; *YABC 2:* 282, 316
Schramm, Ulrik, *2:* 16; *14:* 112
Schreiber, Elizabeth Anne, *13:* 193
Schreiber, Ralph W., *13:* 193
Schreiter, Rick, *14:* 97
Schroeder, E. Peter, *12:* 112
Schroeder, Ted, *11:* 160; *15:* 189

Schulz, Charles M., *10:* 137-142
Schwartz, Charles, *8:* 184
Schwartzberg, Joan, *3:* 208
Schweitzer, Iris, *2:* 137; *6:* 207
Scott, Anita Walker, *7:* 38
Scribner, Joanne, *14:* 236
Sebree, Charles, *18:* 65
Sedacca, Joseph M., *11:* 25
Sejima, Yoshimasa, *8:* 187
Selig, Sylvie, *13:* 199
Seltzer, Isadore, *6:* 18
Seltzer, Meyer, *17:* 214
Sempé, *YABC 2:* 109
Sendak, Maurice, *1:* 135, 190;
  3: 204; *7:* 142; *15:* 199;
  17: 210; *YABC 1:* 167
Sengler, Johanna, *18:* 256
Seredy, Kate, *1:* 192; *14:* 20-21;
  17: 210
Sergeant, John, *6:* 74
Servello, Joe, *10:* 144
Seton, Ernest Thompson,
  18: 260-269, 271
Seuss, Dr. *See* Geisel, Theodor
Severin, John Powers, *7:* 62
Seward, Prudence, *16:* 243
Sewell, Helen, *3:* 186; *15:* 308
Sewell, Marcia, *15:* 8
Shanks, Anne Zane, *10:* 149
Sharp, William, *6:* 131
Shaw, Charles G., *13:* 200
Shecter, Ben, *16:* 244
Shekerjian, Haig, *16:* 245
Shekerjian, Regina, *16:* 245
Shenton, Edward, *YABC 1:* 218-
  219, 221
Shepard, Ernest H., *3:* 193; *4:* 74;
  16: 101;
  17: 109; *YABC 1:* 148, 153,
  174, 176, 180-181
Shepard, Mary, *4:* 210
Sherwan, Earl, *3:* 196
Shields, Charles, *10:* 150
Shields, Leonard, *13:* 83, 85, 87
Shimin, Symeon, *1:* 93; *2:* 128-129;
  3: 202; *7:* 85; *11:* 177; *12:* 139;
  13: 202-203
Shinn, Everett, *16:* 148; *18:* 229
Shore, Robert, *YABC 2:* 200
Shortall, Leonard, *4:* 144; *8:* 196;
  10: 166
Shulevitz, Uri, *3:* 198-199; *17:* 85
Sibley, Don, *1:* 39; *12:* 196
Sidjakov, Nicolas, *18:* 274
Siebel, Fritz, *3:* 120; *17:* 145
Siegl, Helen, *12:* 166
Sills, Joyce, *5:* 199
Silverstein, Alvin, *8:* 189
Silverstein, Virginia, *8:* 189
Simon, Eric M., *7:* 82
Simon, Howard, *2:* 175; *5:* 132
Simont, Marc, *2:* 119; *4:* 213;
  9: 168; *13:* 238, 240; *14:* 262;
  16: 179; *18:* 221
Singer, Edith G., *2:* 30
Slackman, Charles B., *12:* 201

Sloan, Joseph, *16:* 68
Slobodkin, Louis, *1:* 200; *3:* 232;
    5: 168; *13:* 251; *15:* 13, 88
Slobodkina, Esphyr, *1:* 201
Smalley, Janet, *1:* 154
Smee, David, *14:* 78
Smith, Alvin, *1:* 31, 229; *13:* 187
Smith, E. Boyd, *YABC 1:* 4-5,
    240, 248-249
Smith, Edward J., *4:* 224
Smith, Eunice Young, *5:* 170
Smith, Jessie Willcox, *15:* 91;
    16: 95;
    18: 231; *YABC 1:* 6;
    YABC 2: 180, 185, 191, 311,
    325
Smith, Linell Nash, *2:* 195
Smith, Maggie Kaufman, *13:* 205
Smith, Ralph Crosby, *2:* 267
Smith, Robert D., *5:* 63
Smith, Susan Carlton, *12:* 208
Smith, Terry, *12:* 106
Smith, Virginia, *3:* 157
Smith, William A., *1:* 36; *10:* 154
Smyth, M. Jane, *12:* 15
Snyder, Jerome, *13:* 207
Sofia, *1:* 62; *5:* 90
Solbert, Ronni, *1:* 159; *2:* 232;
    5: 121; *6:* 34; *17:* 249
Solonevich, George, *15:* 246; *17:* 47
Sommer, Robert, *12:* 211
Sorel, Edward, *4:* 61
Sotomayor, Antonio, *11:* 215
Spaenkuch, August, *16:* 28
Spanfeller, James, *1:* 72, 149; *2:* 183
Sparks, Mary Walker, *15:* 247
Spier, Jo, *10:* 30
Spier, Peter, *3:* 155; *4:* 200; *7:* 61;
    11: 78
Spilka, Arnold, *5:* 120; *6:* 204;
    8: 131
Spivak, I. Howard, *8:* 10
Spollen, Christopher J., *12:* 214
Sprattler, Rob, *12:* 176
Spring, Bob, *5:* 60
Spring, Ira, *5:* 60
Staffan, Alvin E., *11:* 56; *12:* 187
Stahl, Ben, *5:* 181; *12:* 91
Stamaty, Mark Alan, *12:* 215
Stanley, Diana, *3:* 45
Steig, William, *18:* 275-276
Stein, Harve, *1:* 109
Stephens, Charles H., *YABC 2:* 279
Steptoe, John, *8:* 197
Stern, Simon, *15:* 249-250; *17:* 58
Stevens, Mary, *11:* 193; *13:* 129
Stewart, Charles, *2:* 205
Stirnweis, Shannon, *10:* 164
Stobbs, William, *1:* 48-49; *3:* 68;
    6: 20; *17:* 117, 217
Stone, David, *9:* 173
Stone, David K., *4:* 38; *6:* 124;
    9: 180
Stone, Helen V., *6:* 209
Stratton-Porter, Gene,
    15: 254, 259, 263-264, 268-269

Strong, Joseph D., Jr.,
    YABC 2: 330
Ströyer, Poul, *13:* 221
Stubis, Talivaldis, *5:* 182, 183;
    10: 45; *11:* 9; *18:* 304
Stubley, Trevor, *14:* 43
Stuecklen, Karl W., *8:* 34, 65
Stull, Betty, *11:* 46
Suba, Susanne, *4:* 202-203; *14:* 261
Sugarman, Tracy, *3:* 76; *8:* 199
Sumichrast, Jözef, *14:* 253
Summers, Leo, *1:* 177; *2:* 273;
    13: 22
Svolinsky, Karel, *17:* 104
Sweet, Darryl, *1:* 163; *4:* 136
Sweetland, Robert, *12:* 194
Szasz, Susanne, *13:* 55, 226; *14:* 48
Szekeres, Cyndy, *2:* 218; *5:* 185;
    8: 85; *11:* 166; *14:* 19;
    16: 57, 159

Tait, Douglas, *12:* 220
Takakjian, Portia, *15:* 274
Takashima, Shizuye, *13:* 228
Talarczyk, June, *4:* 173
Tallon, Robert, *2:* 228
Tamburine, Jean, *12:* 222
Tandy, H. R., *13:* 69
Tarkington, Booth, *17:* 224-225
Teale, Edwin Way, *7:* 196
Teason, James, *1:* 14
Tee-Van, Helen Damrosch,
    10: 176; *11:* 182
Tempest, Margaret, *3:* 237, 238
Templeton, Owen, *11:* 77
Tenggren, Gustaf,
    18: 277-279; *YABC 2:* 145
Tenniel, John, *YABC 2:* 99
Thelwell, Norman, *14:* 201
Thistlethwaite, Miles, *12:* 224
Thollander, Earl, *11:* 47; *18:* 112
Thomas, Martin, *14:* 255
Thomson, Arline K., *3:* 264
Thorvall, Kerstin, *13:* 235
Thurber, James,
    13: 239, 242-245, 248-249
Tichenor, Tom, *14:* 207
Timmins, Harry, *2:* 171
Tinkelman, Murray, *12:* 225
Tolford, Joshua, *1:* 221
Tolkien, J. R. R., *2:* 243
Tolmie, Ken, *15:* 292
Tomes, Jacqueline, *2:* 117; *12:* 139
Tomes, Margot, *1:* 224; *2:* 120-121;
    16: 207; *18:* 250
Toner, Raymond John, *10:* 179
Toothill, Harry, *6:* 54; *7:* 49
Toothill, Ilse, *6:* 54
Toschik, Larry, *6:* 102
Totten, Bob, *13:* 93
Tremain, Ruthven, *17:* 238
Trez, Alain, *17:* 236
Trier, Walter, *14:* 96
Tripp, Wallace, *2:* 48; *7:* 28; *8:* 94;
    10: 54, 76; *11:* 92

Trnka, Jiri, *YABC 1:* 30-31
Troyer, Johannes, *3:* 16; *7:* 18
Tsinajinie, Andy, *2:* 62
Tsugami, Kyuzo, *18:* 198-199
Tuckwell, Jennifer, *17:* 205
Tudor, Bethany, *7:* 103
Tudor, Tasha,
    18: 227; *YABC 2:* 46, 314
Tunis, Edwin, *1:* 218-219
Turkle, Brinton, *1:* 211, 213;
    2: 249; *3:* 226; *11:* 3;
    16: 209; *YABC 1:* 79
Turska, Krystyna, *12:* 103
Tusan, Stan, *6:* 58
Tzimoulis, Paul, *12:* 104

Uchida, Yoshiko, *1:* 220
Ulm, Robert, *17:* 238
Unada. *See* Gliewe, Unada
Ungerer, Tomi, *5:* 188; *9:* 40; *18:* 188
Unwin, Nora S., *3:* 65, 234-235;
    4: 237; *YABC 1:* 59;
    YABC 2: 301
Utpatel, Frank, *18:* 114
Utz, Lois, *5:* 190

Van Abbé, S., *16:* 142;
    18: 282; *YABC 2:* 157, 161
Van Everen, Jay,
    13: 160; *YABC 1:* 121
Van Loon, Hendrik Willem,
    18: 285, 289, 291
Van Stockum, Hilda, *5:* 193
Van Wely, Babs, *16:* 50
Vasiliu, Mircea, *2:* 166, 253; *9:* 166;
    13: 58
Vavra, Robert, *8:* 206
Vawter, Will, *17:* 163
Veeder, Larry, *18:* 4
Ver Beck, Frank, *18:* 16-17
Verney, John, *14:* 225
Verrier, Suzanne, *5:* 20
Versace, Marie, *2:* 255
Vestal, H. B., *9:* 134; *11:* 101
Viereck, Ellen, *3:* 242; *14:* 229
Vigna, Judith, *15:* 293
Vilato, Gaspar E., *5:* 41
Vo-Dinh, Mai, *16:* 272
Vogel, Ilse-Margret, *14:* 230
von Schmidt, Eric, *8:* 62
Vosburgh, Leonard, *1:* 161; *7:* 32;
    15: 295-296
Vroman, Tom, *10:* 29

Wagner, John, *8:* 200
Wagner, Ken, *2:* 59
Wainwright, Jerry, *14:* 85
Waldman, Bruce, *15:* 297
Walker, Charles, *1:* 46; *4:* 59;
    5: 177; *11:* 115

Walker, Dugald Stewart, *15:* 47
Walker, Gil, *8:* 49
Walker, Jim, *10:* 94
Walker, Mort, *8:* 213
Walker, Stephen, *12:* 229
Wallner, Alexandra, *15:* 120
Wallner, John C., *9:* 77; *10:* 188; *11:* 28; *14:* 209
Wallower, Lucille, *11:* 226
Walters, Audrey, *18:* 294
Walton, Tony, *11:* 164
Waltrip, Lela, *9:* 195
Waltrip, Mildred, *3:* 209
Waltrip, Rufus, *9:* 195
Wan, *12:* 76
Ward, Keith, *2:* 107
Ward, Lynd, *1:* 99, 132, 133, 150; *2:* 108, 158, 196, 259; *18:* 86
Warner, Peter, *14:* 87
Warren, Betsy, *2:* 101
Warren, Marion Cray, *14:* 215
Waterman, Stan, *11:* 76
Watkins-Pitchford, D. J., *6:* 215, 217
Watson, Aldren, *2:* 267; *5:* 94; *13:* 71; *YABC 2:* 202
Watson, Karen, *11:* 26
Watson, Wendy, *5:* 197; *13:* 101
Watts, Bernadette, *4:* 227
Webber, Helen, *3:* 141
Webber, Irma E., *14:* 238
Weber, William J., *14:* 239
Webster, Jean, *17:* 241
Wegner, Fritz, *14:* 250
Weihs, Erika, *4:* 21; *15:* 299
Weil, Lisl, *7:* 203; *10:* 58
Weiner, Sandra, *14:* 240
Weisgard, Leonard, *1:* 65; *2:* 191, 197, 204, 264-265; *5:* 108; *YABC 2:* 13
Weiss, Emil, *1:* 168; *7:* 60
Weiss, Harvey, *1:* 145, 223
Wells, Frances, *1:* 183
Wells, Rosemary, *6:* 49; *18:* 297

Werenskiold, Erik, *15:* 6
Werth, Kurt, *7:* 122; *14:* 157
Wetherbee, Margaret, *5:* 3
Wheatley, Arabelle, *11:* 231; *16:* 276
Wheelright, Rowland, *15:* 81; *YABC 2:* 286
Whistler, Rex, *16:* 75
White, David Omar, *5:* 56; *18:* 6
Whithorne, H. S., *7:* 49
Whitney, George Gillett, *3:* 24
Wiese, Kurt, *3:* 255; *4:* 206; *14:* 17; *17:* 18-19
Wiesner, William, *4:* 100; *5:* 200, 201; *14:* 262
Wiggins, George, *6:* 133
Wikland, Ilon, *5:* 113; *8:* 150
Wilde, George, *7:* 139
Wildsmith, Brian, *16:* 281-282; *18:* 170-171
Wilkinson, Gerald, *3:* 40
Williams, Garth, *1:* 197; *2:* 49, 270; *4:* 205; *15:* 198, 302-304, 307; *16:* 34; *18:* 283, 298-301; *YABC 2:* 15-16, 19
Williams, Maureen, *12:* 238
Williams, Patrick, *14:* 218
Wilson, Charles Banks, *17:* 92
Wilson, Dagmar, *10:* 47
Wilson, Edward A., *6:* 24; *16:* 149; *20*
Wilson, Jack, *17:* 139
Wilson, Peggy, *15:* 4
Wilwerding, Walter J., *9:* 202
Winchester, Linda, *13:* 231
Windham, Kathryn Tucker, *14:* 260
Winter, Milo, *15:* 97; *YABC 2:* 144
Wise, Louis, *13:* 68
Wiseman, B., *4:* 233
Wishnefsky, Phillip, *3:* 14
Wiskur, Darrell, *5:* 72; *10:* 50; *18:* 246
Woehr, Lois, *12:* 5

Wohlberg, Meg, *12:* 100; *14:* 197
Wolf, J., *16:* 91
Wondriska, William, *6:* 220
Wonsetler, John C., *5:* 168
Wood, Myron, *6:* 220
Wood, Owen, *18:* 187
Wood, Ruth, *8:* 11
Woodson, Jack, *10:* 201
Worboys, Evelyn, *1:* 166-167
Worth, Wendy, *4:* 133
Wrenn, Charles L., *YABC 1:* 20, 21
Wright, George, *YABC 1:* 268
Wronker, Lili Cassel, *10:* 204
Wyeth, Andrew, *13:* 40; *YABC 1:* 133-134
Wyeth, N. C., *13:* 41; *17:* 252-259, 264-268; *18:* 181; *YABC 1:* 133, 223; *YABC 2:* 53, 75, 171, 187, 317

Yang, Jay, *1:* 8; *12:* 239
Yap, Weda, *6:* 176
Yashima, Taro, *14:* 84
Yohn, F. C., *YABC 1:* 269
Young, Ed, *7:* 205; *10:* 206; *YABC 2:* 242
Young, Noela, *8:* 221

Zacks, Lewis, *10:* 161
Zalben, Jane Breskin, *7:* 211
Zallinger, Jean, *4:* 192; *8:* 8, 129; *14:* 273
Zallinger, Rudolph F., *3:* 245
Zelinsky, Paul O., *14:* 269
Zemach, Margot, *3:* 270; *8:* 201
Zemsky, Jessica, *10:* 62
Zinkeisen, Anna, *13:* 106
Zweifel, Francis, *14:* 274

Author Index

(In the following index, the number of the volume in which an author's sketch appears is given *before* the colon, and the page on which it appears is given *after* the colon. For example, the sketch of Aardema, Verna, appears in Volume 4 on page 1).

YABC

Index citations including this abbreviation refer to listings appearing in *Yesterday's Authors of Books for Children,* also published by the Gale Research Company, which covers authors who died prior to 1960.

Aardema, Verna, *4:* 1
Aaron, Chester, *9:* 1
Abbott, Alice. *See* Borland, Kathryn Kilby, *16:* 54
Abbott, Alice. *See* Speicher, Helen Ross (Smith), *8:* 194
Abbott, Manager Henry. *See* Stratemeyer, Edward L., *1:* 208
Abdul, Raoul, *12:* 1
Abel, Raymond, *12:* 2
Abell, Kathleen, *9:* 1
Abercrombie, Barbara (Mattes), *16:* 1
Abernethy, Robert G., *5:* 1
Abisch, Roslyn Kroop, *9:* 3
Abisch, Roz. *See* Abisch, Roslyn Kroop, *9:* 3
Abodaher, David J. (Naiph), *17:* 1
Abrahall, C. H. *See* Hoskyns-Abrahall, Clare, *13:* 105
Abrahall, Clare Hoskyns. *See* Hoskyns-Abrahall, Clare, *13:* 105
Abrahams, Robert D(avid), *4:* 3
Abrams, Joy, *16:* 2
Ackerman, Eugene, *10:* 1
Adair, Margaret Weeks, *10:* 1
Adams, Adrienne, *8:* 1
Adams, Andy, *YABC 1:* 1
Adams, Harriet S(tratemeyer), *1:* 1
Adams, Harrison. *See* Stratemeyer, Edward L., *1:* 208
Adams, Hazard, *6:* 1
Adams, Richard, *7:* 1
Adams, Ruth Joyce, *14:* 1
Adamson, Graham. *See* Groom, Arthur William, *10:* 53
Adamson, Joy, *11:* 1
Addona, Angelo F., *14:* 1
Addy, Ted. *See* Winterbotham, R(ussell) R(obert), *10:* 198
Adelberg, Doris. *See* Orgel, Doris, *7:* 173
Adelson, Leone, *11:* 2

Adkins, Jan, *8:* 2
Adler, David A., *14:* 2
Adler, Irene. *See* Storr, Catherine (Cole), *9:* 181
Adler, Irving, *1:* 2
Adler, Ruth, *1:* 4
Adoff, Arnold, *5:* 1
Adorjan, Carol, *10:* 1
Adshead, Gladys L., *3:* 1
Agapida, Fray Antonio. *See* Irving, Washington, *YABC 2:* 164
Agard, Nadema, *18:* 1
Agle, Nan Hayden, *3:* 2
Agnew, Edith J(osephine), *11:* 3
Ahern, Margaret McCrohan, *10:* 2
Aichinger, Helga, *4:* 4
Aiken, Clarissa (Lorenz), *12:* 4
Aiken, Conrad, *3:* 3
Aiken, Joan, *2:* 1
Ainsworth, Norma, *9:* 4
Ainsworth, Ruth, *7:* 1
Aistrop, Jack, *14:* 3
Aitken, Dorothy, *10:* 2
Akers, Floyd. *See* Baum, L(yman) Frank, *18:* 7
Alberts, Frances Jacobs, *14:* 4
Albrecht, Lillie (Vanderveer), *12:* 5
Alcott, Louisa May, *YABC 1:* 7
Alden, Isabella (Macdonald), *YABC 2:* 1
Alderman, Clifford Lindsey, *3:* 6
Aldis, Dorothy (Keeley), *2:* 2
Aldon, Adair. *See* Meigs, Cornelia, *6:* 167
Aldrich, Thomas Bailey, *17:* 2
Aldridge, Josephine Haskell, *14:* 5
Alegria, Ricardo E., *6:* 1
Alexander, Anna Cooke, *1:* 4
Alexander, Frances, *4:* 6
Alexander, Linda, *2:* 3
Alexander, Lloyd, *3:* 7
Alexander, Martha, *11:* 4
Alexander, Sue, *12:* 5
Alexeieff, Alexandre A., *14:* 5
Alger, Horatio, Jr., *16:* 3

Alger, Leclaire (Gowans), *15:* 1
Aliki. *See* Brandenberg, Aliki, *2:* 36
Alkema, Chester Jay, *12:* 7
Allamand, Pascale, *12:* 8
Allan, Mabel Esther, *5:* 2
Allee, Marjorie Hill, *17:* 11
Allen, Adam [Joint pseudonym]. *See* Epstein, Beryl and Samuel, *1:* 85
Allen, Allyn. *See* Eberle, Irmengarde, *2:* 97
Allen, Betsy. *See* Cavanna, Betty, *1:* 54
Allen, Gertrude E(lizabeth), *9:* 5
Allen, Leroy, *11:* 7
Allen, Samuel (Washington), *9:* 6
Allerton, Mary. *See* Govan, Christine Noble, *9:* 80
Allison, Bob, *14:* 7
Allred, Gordon T., *10:* 3
Almedingen, Martha Edith von. *See* Almedingen, E. M., *3:* 9
Allsop, Kenneth, *17:* 13
Almedingen, E. M., *3:* 9
Almquist, Don, *11:* 8
Alsop, Mary O'Hara, *2:* 4
Alter, Robert Edmond, *9:* 8
Altsheler, Joseph A(lexander), *YABC 1:* 20
Alvarez, Joseph A., *18:* 2
Ambrus, Victor G(ozo), *1:* 6
Amerman, Lockhart, *3:* 11
Ames, Evelyn, *13:* 1
Ames, Gerald, *11:* 9
Ames, Lee J., *3:* 11
Amon, Aline, *9:* 8
Amoss, Berthe, *5:* 4
Anckarsvard, Karin, *6:* 2
Ancona, George, *12:* 10
Andersen, Hans Christian, *YABC 1:* 23
Andersen, Ted, *See* Boyd, Waldo T., *18:* 35
Anderson, C(larence) W(illiam), *11:* 9

Anderson, Ella. *See* MacLeod, Ellen Jane (Anderson), *14:* 129
Anderson, Eloise Adell, *9:* 9
Anderson, George. *See* Groom, Arthur William, *10:* 53
Anderson, J(ohn) R(ichard) L(ane), *15:* 3
Anderson, Joy, *1:* 8
Anderson, (John) Lonzo, *2:* 6
Anderson, Lucia (Lewis), *10:* 4
Anderson, Mary, *7:* 4
Andrews, J(ames) S(ydney), *4:* 7
Andrews, Julie, *7:* 6
Angell, Madeline, *18:* 3
Angelo, Valenti, *14:* 7
Angier, Bradford, *12:* 12
Anglund, Joan Walsh, *2:* 7
Angrist, Stanley W(olff), *4:* 9
Annett, Cora. *See* Scott, Cora Annett, *11:* 207
Annixter, Jane. *See* Sturtzel, Jane Levington, *1:* 212
Annixter, Paul. *See* Sturtzel, Howard A., *1:* 210
Anno, Mitsumasa, *5:* 6
Anrooy, Frans van. *See* Van Anrooy, Francine, *2:* 252
Anthony, C. L. *See* Smith, Dodie, *4:* 194
Anticaglia, Elizabeth, *12:* 13
Anton, Michael (James), *12:* 13
Appiah, Peggy, *15:* 3
Appleton, Victor [Collective pseudonym], *1:* 9
Appleton, Victor II [Collective pseudonym], *1:* 9
Apsler, Alfred, *10:* 4
Aquillo, Don. *See* Prince, J(ack) H(arvey), *17:* 155
Arbuthnot, May Hill, *2:* 9
Archer, Jules, *4:* 9
Archer, Marion Fuller, *11:* 12
Archibald, Joseph S. *3:* 12
Arden, Barbie. *See* Stoutenburg, Adrien, *3:* 217
Ardizzone, Edward, *1:* 10
Arenella, Roy, *14:* 9
Armer, Alberta (Roller), *9:* 11
Armer, Laura Adams, *13:* 2
Armour, Richard, *14:* 10
Armstrong, George D., *10:* 5
Armstrong, Gerry (Breen), *10:* 6
Armstrong, Richard, *11:* 14
Armstrong, William H., *4:* 11
Arnett, Carolyn. *See* Cole, Lois Dwight, *10:* 26
Arnold, Elliott, *5:* 7
Arnold, Oren, *4:* 13
Arnoldy, Julie. *See* Bischoff, Julia Bristol, *12:* 52
Arnov, Boris, Jr., *12:* 14
Arnstein, Helene S(olomon), *12:* 15
Arntson, Herbert E(dward), *12:* 16
Arora, Shirley (Lease), *2:* 10
Arquette, Lois S(teinmetz), *1:* 13
Arthur, Ruth M., *7:* 6

Artis, Vicki Kimmel, *12:* 17
Artzybasheff, Boris (Miklailovich), *14:* 14
Aruego, Ariane. *See* Dewey, Ariane, *7:* 63
Aruego, Jose, *6:* 3
Arundel, Honor, *4:* 15
Asbjörnsen, Peter Christen, *15:* 5
Asch, Frank, *5:* 9
Ashabranner, Brent (Kenneth), *1:* 14
Ashe, Geoffrey (Thomas), *17:* 14
Ashey, Bella. *See* Breinburg, Petronella, *11:* 36
Ashford, Daisy. *See* Ashford, Margaret Mary, *10:* 6
Ashford, Margaret Mary, *10:* 6
Ashley, Elizabeth. *See* Salmon, Annie Elizabeth, *13:* 188
Asimov, Isaac, *1:* 15
Asinof, Eliot, *6:* 5
Aston, James. *See* White, T(erence) H(anbury), *12:* 229
Atene, Ann. *See* Atene, (Rita) Anna, *12:* 18
Atene, (Rita) Anna, *12:* 18
Atkinson, M. E. *See* Frankau, Mary Evelyn, *4:* 90
Atkinson, Margaret Fleming, *14:* 15
Atticus. *See* Fleming, Ian (Lancaster), *9:* 67
Atwater, Florence (Hasseltine Carroll), *16:* 11
Atwater, Montgomery Meigs, *15:* 10
Atwood, Ann, *7:* 8
Austin, Elizabeth S., *5:* 10
Austin, Margot, *11:* 15
Austin, Oliver L. Jr., *7:* 10
Averill, Esther, *1:* 16
Avery, Al. *See* Montgomery, Rutherford, *3:* 134
Avery, Gillian, *7:* 10
Avery, Kay, *5:* 11
Avery, Lynn. *See* Cole, Lois Dwight, *10:* 26
Avi. *See* Wortis, Avi, *14:* 269
Ayars, James S(terling), *4:* 17
Ayer, Jacqueline, *13:* 7
Ayer, Margaret, *15:* 11
Aylesworth, Thomas G(ibbons), *4:* 18

Baastad, Babbis Friis. *See* Friis-Baastad, Babbis, *7:* 95
Babbis, Eleanor. *See* Friis-Baastad, Babbis, *7:* 95
Babbitt, Natalie, *6:* 6
Bach, Richard David, *13:* 7
Bachman, Fred, *12:* 19
Bacmeister, Rhoda W(arner), *11:* 18
Bacon, Elizabeth, *3:* 14
Bacon, Margaret Hope, *6:* 7
Bacon, Martha Sherman, *18:* 4
Bacon, Peggy, *2:* 11

Baden-Powell, Robert (Stephenson Smyth), *16:* 12
Baerg, Harry J(ohn), *12:* 20
Bagnold, Enid, *1:* 17
Bailey, Alice Cooper, *12:* 22
Bailey, Bernadine Freeman, *14:* 16
Bailey, Carolyn Sherwin, *14:* 18
Bailey, Jane H(orton), *12:* 22
Bailey, Maralyn Collins (Harrison), *12:* 24
Bailey, Matilda. *See* Radford, Ruby L., *6:* 186
Bailey, Maurice Charles, *12:* 25
Bailey, Ralph Edgar, *11:* 18
Baity, Elizabeth Chesley, *1:* 18
Bakeless, John (Edwin), *9:* 12
Bakeless, Katherine Little, *9:* 13
Baker, Augusta, *3:* 16
Baker, Betty (Lou), *5:* 12
Baker, Charlotte, *2:* 12
Baker, Elizabeth, *7:* 12
Baker, Jeffrey J(ohn) W(heeler), *5:* 13
Baker, Laura Nelson, *3:* 17
Baker, Margaret, *4:* 19
Baker, Margaret J(oyce), *12:* 25
Baker, Mary Gladys Steel, *12:* 27
Baker, (Robert) Michael, *4:* 20
Baker, Nina (Brown), *15:* 12
Baker, Rachel, *2:* 13
Baker, Samm Sinclair, *12:* 27
Balaam. *See* Lamb, G(eoffrey) F(rederick), *10:* 74
Balch, Glenn, *3:* 18
Balducci, Carolyn Feleppa, *5:* 13
Baldwin, Anne Norris, *5:* 14
Baldwin, Clara, *11:* 20
Baldwin, Gordo. *See* Baldwin, Gordon C., *12:* 30
Baldwin, Gordon C., *12:* 30
Baldwin, James (Arthur), *9:* 15
Balet, Jan (Bernard), *11:* 21
Balian, Lorna, *9:* 16
Ball, Zachary. *See* Masters, Kelly R., *3:* 118
Ballard, Lowell Clyne, *12:* 30
Ballard, (Charles) Martin, *1:* 19
Balogh, Penelope, *1:* 20
Balow, Tom, *12:* 31
Bamfylde, Walter. *See* Bevan, Tom, *YABC 2:* 8
Bamman, Henry A., *12:* 32
Bancroft, Griffing, *6:* 8
Bancroft, Laura. *See* Baum, L(yman) Frank, *18:* 7
Baner, Skulda V(anadis), *10:* 8
Banner, Angela. *See* Maddison, Angela Mary, *10:* 82
Bannon, Laura, *6:* 9
Barbary, James. *See* Baumann, Amy (Brown), *10:* 9
Barbary, James. *See* Beeching, Jack, *14:* 26
Barbour, Ralph Henry, *16:* 27
Barclay, Isabel. *See* Dobell, I. M. B., *11:* 77

Barc, Arnold Edwin, *16.* 31
Barish, Matthew, *12:* 32
Barker, Albert W., *8:* 3
Barker, Melvern, *11:* 23
Barker, S. Omar, *10:* 8
Barker, Will, *8:* 4
Barkley, James Edward, *6:* 12
Barnaby, Ralph S(tanton), *9:* 17
Barnum, Richard [Collective
    pseudonym], *1:* 20
Barr, George, *2:* 14
Barr, Jene, *16:* 32
Barrett, Ron, *14:* 23
Barrie, J(ames) M(atthew),
    YABC 1: 48
Barry, James P(otvin), *14:* 24
Barry, Katharina (Watjen), *4:* 22
Barry, Robert, *6:* 12
Barth, Edna, *7:* 13
Barthelme, Donald, *7:* 14
Bartlett, Philip A. [Collective
    pseudonym], *1:* 21
Bartlett, Robert Merill, *12:* 33
Barton, Byron, *9:* 17
Barton, May Hollis [Collective
    pseudonym], *1:* 21
Bartos-Hoeppner, Barbara, *5:* 15
Bashevis, Isaac. *See* Singer, Isaac
    Bashevis, *3:* 203
Bate, Lucy, *18:* 6
Bate, Norman, *5:* 15
Bates, Barbara S(nedeker), *12:* 34
Batten, Mary, *5:* 17
Batterberry, Ariane Ruskin, *13:* 10
Battles, Edith, *7:* 15
Baudouy, Michel-Aime, *7:* 18
Bauer, Helen, *2:* 14
Bauernschmidt, Marjorie, *15:* 14
Baum, L(yman) Frank, *18:* 7
Baum, Willi, *4:* 23
Baumann, Amy (Brown), *10:* 9
Baumann, Hans, *2:* 16
Bawden, Nina. *See* Kark, Nina
    Mary, *4:* 132
Baylor, Byrd, *16:* 33
BB. *See* Watkins-Pitchford, D. J.,
    6: 214
Beach, Charles Amory [Collective
    pseudonym], *1:* 21
Beach, Edward L(atimer), *12:* 35
Beachcroft, Nina, *18:* 31
Bealer, Alex W(inkler III), *8:* 6
Beals, Carleton, *12:* 36
Beame, Rona, *12:* 39
Beaney, Jan. *See* Udall, Jan
    Beaney, *10:* 182
Beard, Charles Austin, *18:* 32
Beatty, Hetty Burlingame, *5:* 18
Beatty, Jerome, Jr., *5:* 19
Beatty, John (Louis), *6:* 13
Beatty, Patricia (Robbins), *1:* 21
Bechtel, Louise Seaman, *4:* 26
Beck, Barbara L., *12:* 41
Becker, Beril, *11:* 23
Becker, John (Leonard), *12:* 41
Beckman, Gunnel, *6:* 14

Bedford, A. N. *See* Watson, Jane
    Werner, *3:* 244
Bedford, Annie North. *See*
    Watson, Jane Werner, *3:* 244
Beebe, B(urdetta) F(aye), *1:* 23
Beech, Webb. *See* Butterworth,
    W. E., *5:* 40
Beeching, Jack, *14:* 26
Beeler, Nelson F(rederick), *13:* 11
Beers, Dorothy Sands, *9:* 18
Beers, Lorna, *14:* 26
Beers, V(ictor) Gilbert, *9:* 18
Behn, Harry, *2:* 17
Behnke, Frances L., *8:* 7
Behr, Joyce, *15:* 15
Behrman, Carol H(elen), *14:* 27
Beiser, Germaine, *11:* 24
Belknap, B. H. *See* Ellis, Edward
    S(ylvester), *YABC 1:* 116
Bell, Corydon, *3:* 19
Bell, Emily Mary. *See* Cason,
    Mabel Earp, *10:* 19
Bell, Gertrude (Wood), *12:* 42
Bell, Gina. *See* Iannone, Jeanne,
    7: 139
Bell, Janet. *See* Clymer, Eleanor,
    9: 37
Bell, Margaret E(lizabeth), *2:* 19
Bell, Norman (Edward), *11:* 25
Bell, Raymond Martin, *13:* 13
Bell, Thelma Harrington, *3:* 20
Bellairs, John, *2:* 20
Belloc, (Joseph) Hilaire (Pierre),
    YABC 1: 62
Bell-Zano, Gina. *See* Iannone,
    Jeanne, *7:* 139
Belpré, Pura, *16:* 35
Belting, Natalie Maree, *6:* 16
Belvedere, Lee. *See* Grayland,
    Valerie, *7:* 111
Bemelmans, Ludwig, *15:* 15
Benary, Margot. *See* Benary-
    Isbert, Margot, *2:* 21
Benary-Isbert, Margot, *2:* 21
Benasutti, Marion, *6:* 18
Benchley, Nathaniel, *3:* 21
Benchley, Peter, *3:* 22
Bendick, Jeanne, *2:* 23
Bendick, Robert L(ouis), *11:* 25
Benedict, Dorothy Potter, *11:* 26
Benedict, Lois Trimble, *12:* 44
Benedict, Rex, *8:* 8
Benét, Laura, *3:* 23
Benét, Stephen Vincent,
    YABC 1: 75
Benezra, Barbara, *10:* 10
Benj. F. Johnson, of Boone. *See*
    Riley, James Whitcomb,
    17: 159
Bennett, John, *YABC 1:* 84
Bennett, Rainey, *15:* 27
Benson, Sally, *1:* 24
Bentley, Phyllis (Eleanor), *6:* 19
Berelson, Howard, *5:* 20
Berenstain, Janice, *12:* 44
Berenstain, Stan(ley), *12:* 45

Berg, Jean Horton, *6:* 21
Berger, Melvin H., *5:* 21
Berger, Terry, *8:* 10
Berkowitz, Freda Pastor, *12:* 48
Berliner, Franz, *13:* 13
Berna, Paul, *15:* 27
Bernadette. *See* Watts,
    Bernadette, *4:* 226
Bernard, Jacqueline (de Sieyes),
    8: 11
Bernstein, Joanne E(ckstein),
    15: 29
Bernstein, Theodore M(enline),
    12: 49
Berrien, Edith Heal. *See* Heal,
    Edith, *7:* 123
Berrill, Jacquelyn (Batsel), *12:* 50
Berrington, John. *See* Brownjohn,
    Alan, *6:* 38
Berry, B. J. *See* Berry, Barbara,
    J., *7:* 19
Berry, Barbara J., *7:* 19
Berry, Erick. *See* Best, Allena
    Champlin, *2:* 25
Berry, William D(avid), *14:* 28
Berson, Harold, *4:* 27
Berwick, Jean. *See* Meyer, Jean
    Shepherd, *11:* 181
Best, (Evangel) Allena Champlin,
    2: 25
Best, (Oswald) Herbert, *2:* 27
Beth, Mary. *See* Miller, Mary
    Beth, *9:* 145
Bethancourt, T. Ernesto, *11:* 27
Bethell, Jean (Frankenberry), *8:* 11
Bethers, Ray, *6:* 22
Bethune, J. G. *See* Ellis, Edward
    S(ylvester), *YABC 1:* 116
Bettina. *See* Ehrlich, Bettina, *1:* 82
Betz, Eva Kelly, *10:* 10
Bevan, Tom, *YABC 2:* 8
Bewick, Thomas, *16:* 38
Beyer, Audrey White, *9:* 19
Bialk, Elisa, *1:* 25
Bianco, Margery (Williams), *15:* 29
Biblc, Charles, *13:* 14
Biegel, Paul, *16:* 49
Bierhorst, John, *6:* 23
Billout, Guy René, *10:* 11
Birmingham, Lloyd, *12:* 51
Biro, Val, *1:* 26
Bischoff, Julia Bristol, *12:* 52
Bishop, Claire (Huchet), *14:* 30
Bishop, Curtis, *6:* 24
Bisset, Donald, *7:* 20
Bixby, William, *6:* 24
Black, Algernon David, *12:* 53
Black, Irma S(imonton), *2:* 28
Blackburn, John(ny) Brewton,
    15: 35
Blackett, Veronica Heath, *12:* 54
Blades, Ann, *16:* 51
Bladow, Suzanne Wilson, *14:* 32
Blaine, John. *See* Goodwin,
    Harold Leland, *13:* 73

Blaine, John. *See* Harkins, Philip, 6: 102
Blaine, Marge. *See* Blaine, Margery Kay, 11: 28
Blaine, Margery Kay, 11: 28
Blair, Ruth Van Ness, 12: 54
Blair, Walter, 12: 56
Blake, Quentin, 9: 20
Blake, Walker E. *See* Butterworth, W. E., 5: 40
Bland, Edith Nesbit. *See* Nesbit, E(dith), YABC 1: 193
Bland, Fabian [Joint pseudonym]. *See* Nesbit, E(dith), YABC 1: 193
Blassingame, Wyatt (Rainey), 1: 27
Bleeker, Sonia, 2: 30
Blegvad, Erik, 14: 33
Blegvad, Lenore, 14: 34
Blishen, Edward, 8: 12
Bliss, Ronald G(ene), 12: 57
Bliven, Bruce Jr., 2: 31
Bloch, Lucienne, 10: 11
Bloch, Marie Halun, 6: 25
Bloch, Robert, 12: 57
Block, Irvin, 12: 59
Blough, Glenn O(rlando), 1: 28
Blue, Rose, 5: 22
Blume, Judy (Sussman), 2: 31
Blyton, Carey, 9: 22
Boardman, Fon Wyman, Jr., 6: 26
Boardman, Gwenn R., 12: 59
Bobbe, Dorothie, 1: 30
Bock, Hal. *See* Bock, Harold I., 10: 13
Bock, Harold I., 10: 13
Bock, William Sauts Netamux'we, 14: 36
Bodecker, N. M., 8: 12
Boden, Hilda. *See* Bodenham, Hilda Esther, 13: 16
Bodenham, Hilda Esther, 13: 16
Bodie, Idella F(allaw), 12: 60
Bodker, Cecil, 14: 39
Boeckman, Charles, 12: 61
Boesch, Mark J(oseph), 12: 62
Boesen, Victor, 16: 53
Boggs, Ralph Steele, 7: 21
Boles, Paul Darcy, 9: 23
Bolian, Polly, 4: 29
Bolliger, Max, 7: 22
Bolton, Carole, 6: 27
Bolton, Evelyn. *See* Bunting, Anne Evelyn, 18: 38
Bond, Gladys Baker, 14: 41
Bond, J. Harvey. *See* Winterbotham, R(ussell) R(obert), 10: 198
Bond, Michael, 6: 28
Bond, Ruskin, 14: 43
Bonehill, Captain Ralph. *See* Stratemeyer, Edward L., 1: 208
Bonham, Barbara, 7: 22
Bonham, Frank, 1: 30
Bontemps, Arna, 2: 32

Boone, Pat, 7: 23
Bordier, Georgette, 16: 53
Borland, Hal, 5: 22
Borland, Harold Glen. *See* Borland, Hal, 5: 22
Borland, Kathryn Kilby, 16: 54
Bornstein, Ruth, 14: 44
Borski, Lucia Merecka, 18: 34
Borten, Helen Jacobson, 5: 24
Borton, Elizabeth. *See* Trevino, Elizabeth B. de, 1: 216
Bortstein, Larry, 16: 56
Bosco, Jack. *See* Holliday, Joseph, 11: 137
Boshell, Gordon, 15: 36
Boshinski, Blanche, 10: 13
Bothwell, Jean, 2: 34
Bottner, Barbara, 14: 45
Bourne, Leslie. *See* Marshall, Evelyn, 11: 172
Bourne, Miriam Anne, 16: 57
Bova, Ben, 6: 29
Bowen, Betty Morgan. *See* West, Betty, 11: 233
Bowen, Catherine Drinker, 7: 24
Bowie, Jim. *See* Stratemeyer, Edward L., 1: 208
Bowman, John S(tewart), 16: 57
Boyd, Waldo T., 18: 35
Boyle, Ann (Peters), 10: 13
Boz. *See* Dickens, Charles, 15: 55
Bradbury, Bianca, 3: 25
Bradbury, Ray (Douglas), 11: 29
Brady, Irene, 4: 30
Bragdon, Elspeth, 6: 30
Brandenberg, Aliki Liacouras, 2: 36
Brandenberg, Franz, 8: 14
Brandon, Brumsic, Jr., 9: 25
Brandon, Curt. *See* Bishop, Curtis, 6: 24
Branfield, John (Charles), 11: 36
Branley, Franklyn M(ansfield), 4: 32
Bratton, Helen, 4: 34
Braymer, Marjorie, 6: 31
Brecht, Edith, 6: 32
Breck, Vivian. *See* Breckenfeld, Vivian Gurney, 1: 33
Breckenfeld, Vivian Gurney, 1: 33
Breda, Tjalmar. *See* DeJong, David C(ornel), 10: 29
Breinburg, Petronella, 11: 36
Brennan, Joseph L., 6: 33
Brenner, Barbara (Johnes), 4: 34
Brent, Stuart, 14: 47
Brewster, Benjamin. *See* Folsom, Franklin, 5: 67
Brewton, John E(dmund), 5: 25
Brick, John, 10: 14
Bridges, William (Andrew) 5: 27
Bridwell, Norman, 4: 36
Brier, Howard M(axwell), 8: 15
Brimberg, Stanlee, 9: 25
Brinckloe, Julie (Lorraine), 13: 17
Brindel, June (Rachuy), 7: 25
Brink, Carol Ryrie 1: 34

Brinsmead, H(esba) F(ay), 18: 36
Britt, Dell, 1: 35
Brock, Betty, 7: 27
Brock, Emma L(illian), 8: 15
Brockett, Eleanor Hall, 10: 15
Broderick, Dorothy M., 5: 28
Brokamp, Marilyn, 10: 15
Bronson, Lynn. *See* Lampman, Evelyn Sibley, 4: 140
Brooke, L(eonard) Leslie, 17: 15
Brooks, Anita, 5: 28
Brooks, Gwendolyn, 6: 33
Brooks, Lester, 7: 28
Brooks, Polly Schoyer, 12: 63
Brooks, Walter R(ollin), 17: 17
Brosnan, James Patrick, 14: 47
Brosnan, Jim. *See* Brosnan, James Patrick, 14: 47
Broun, Emily. *See* Sterne, Emma Gelders, 6: 205
Brower, Millicent, 8: 16
Browin, Frances Williams, 5: 30
Brown, Alexis. *See* Baumann, Amy (Brown), 10: 9
Brown, Bill. *See* Brown, William L., 5: 34
Brown, Billye Walker. *See* Cutchen, Billye Walker, 15: 51
Brown, Bob. *See* Brown, Robert Joseph, 14: 48
Brown, Dee (Alexander), 5: 30
Brown, Eleanor Frances, 3: 26
Brown, George Earl, 11: 40
Brown, Irene Bennett, 3: 27
Brown, Ivor, 5: 31
Brown, Marc Tolon, 10: 17
Brown, Marcia, 7: 29
Brown, Margaret Wise, YABC 2: 9
Brown, Margery, 5: 31
Brown, Marion Marsh, 6: 35
Brown, Myra Berry, 6: 36
Brown, Pamela, 5: 33
Brown, Robert Joseph, 14: 48
Brown, Rosalie (Gertrude) Moore, 9: 26
Brown, William L(ouis), 5: 34
Browne, Matthew. *See* Rands, William Brighty, 17: 156
Browning, Robert, YABC 1: 85
Brownjohn, Alan, 6: 38
Bruce, Mary, 1: 36
Bryant, Bernice (Morgan), 11: 40
Bryson, Bernarda, 9: 26
Buchan, John, YABC 2: 21
Buchwald, Art(hur), 10: 18
Buchwald, Emilie, 7: 31
Buck, Lewis, 18: 37
Buck, Margaret Waring, 3: 29
Buck, Pearl S(ydenstricker), 1: 36
Buckeridge, Anthony, 6: 38
Buckley, Helen E(lizabeth), 2: 38
Buckmaster, Henrietta, 6: 39
Budd, Lillian, 7: 33
Buehr, Walter, 3: 30
Bulla, Clyde Robert, 2: 39

Bunting, A. E.. *See* Bunting, Anne
  Evelyn, *18:* 38
Bunting, Anne Evelyn, *18:* 38
Bunting, Eve. *See* Bunting, Anne
  Evelyn, *18:* 38
Burch, Robert J(oseph), *1:* 38
Burchard, Peter D(uncan), *5:* 34
Burchardt, Nellie, *7:* 33
Burford, Eleanor. *See* Hibbert,
  Eleanor, *2:* 134
Burger, Carl, *9:* 27
Burgess, Em. *See* Burgess, Mary
  Wyche, *18:* 39
Burgess, Mary Wyche, *18:* 39
Burgess, Robert F(orrest), *4:* 38
Burgess, Thornton W(aldo), *17:* 19
Burgwyn, Mebane H., *7:* 34
Burland, C. A. *See* Burland, Cottie
  A., *5:* 36
Burland, Cottie A., *5:* 36
Burlingame, (William) Roger, *2:* 40
Burman, Ben Lucien, *6:* 40
Burn, Doris, *1:* 39
Burnett, Frances (Eliza) Hodgson,
  YABC 2: 32
Burnford, S. D. *See* Burnford,
  Sheila, *3:* 32
Burnford, Sheila, *3:* 32
Burningham, John (Mackintosh),
  16: 58
Burns, Paul C., *5:* 37
Burns, Ray. *See* Burns, Raymond
  (Howard), *9:* 28
Burns, Raymond, *9:* 28
Burns, William A., *5:* 38
Burroughs, Polly, *2:* 41
Burt, Olive Woolley, *4:* 39
Burton, Hester, *7:* 35
Burton, Virginia Lee, *2:* 42
Burton, William H(enry), *11:* 42
Busoni, Rafaello, *16:* 61
Butler, Beverly, *7:* 37
Butters, Dorothy Gilman, *5:* 39
Butterworth, Oliver, *1:* 40
Butterworth, W(illiam)
  E(dmund III), *5:* 40
Byars, Betsy, *4:* 40
Byfield, Barbara Ninde, *8:* 19

Cable, Mary, *9:* 29
Cadwallader, Sharon, *7:* 38
Cain, Arthur H., *3:* 33
Cain, Christopher. *See* Fleming,
  Thomas J(ames), *8:* 19
Cairns, Trevor, *14:* 50
Caldecott, Randolph (J.), *17:* 31
Caldwell, John C(ope), *7:* 38
Calhoun, Mary (Huiskamp), *2:* 44
Calkins, Franklin. *See*
  Stratemeyer, Edward L.,
  1: 208
Call, Hughie Florence, *1:* 41
Cameron, Edna M., *3:* 34

Cameron, Eleanor (Butler), *1.* 42
Cameron, Elizabeth. *See* Nowell,
  Elizabeth Cameron, *12:* 160
Cameron, Polly, *2:* 45
Camp, Walter (Chauncey),
  YABC 1: 92
Campbell, Ann R., *11:* 43
Campbell, Bruce. *See* Epstein,
  Samuel, *1:* 87
Campbell, Jane. *See* Edwards,
  Jane Campbell, *10:* 34
Campbell, R. W. *See* Campbell,
  Rosemae Wells, *1:* 44
Campbell, Rosemae Wells, *1:* 44
Canfield, Dorothy. *See* Fisher,
  Dorothy Canfield, *YABC 1:* 122
Canusi, Jose. *See* Barker, S.
  Omar, *10:* 8
Capps, Benjamin (Franklin), *9:* 30
Caras, Roger A(ndrew), *12:* 65
Carbonnier, Jeanne, *3:* 34
Carey, Bonnie, *18:* 40
Carey, Ernestine Gilbreth, *2:* 45
Carini, Edward, *9:* 30
Carle, Eric, *4:* 41
Carleton, Captain L. C. *See* Ellis,
  Edward S(ylvester),
  YABC 1: 116
Carlisle, Clark, Jr. *See* Holding,
  James, *3:* 85
Carlsen, Ruth C(hristoffer), *2:* 47
Carlson, Bernice Wells, *8:* 19
Carlson, Dale Bick, *1:* 44
Carlson, Natalie Savage, *2:* 48
Carlson, Vada F., *16:* 64
Carol, Bill J. *See* Knott, William
  Cecil, Jr., *3:* 94
Carpelan, Bo (Gustaf Bertelsson),
  8: 20
Carpenter, Allan, *3:* 35
Carpenter, Frances, *3:* 36
Carpenter, Patricia (Healy Evans),
  11: 43
Carr, Glyn. *See* Styles, Frank
  Showell, *10:* 167
Carr, Harriett Helen, *3:* 37
Carr, Mary Jane, *2:* 50
Carrick, Carol, *7:* 39
Carrick, Donald, *7:* 40
Carroll, Curt. *See* Bishop, Curtis,
  6: 24
Carroll, Latrobe, *7:* 40
Carroll, Laura. *See* Parr, Lucy,
  10: 115
Carroll, Lewis. *See* Dodgson,
  Charles Lutwidge,
  YABC 2: 297
Carse, Robert, *5:* 41
Carson, Captain James. *See*
  Stratemeyer, Edward L.,
  1: 208
Carson, John F., *1:* 46
Carter, Bruce. *See* Hough, Richard
  (Alexander), *17:* 83
Carter, Dorothy Sharp, *8:* 21
Carter, Helene, *15:* 37

Carter, (William) Hodding, *2:* 51
Carter, Katharine J(ones), *2:* 52
Carter, Phyllis Ann. *See* Eberle,
  Irmengarde, *2:* 97
Carter, William E., *1:* 47
Cartner, William Carruthers, *11:* 44
Cartwright, Sally, *9:* 30
Cary. *See* Cary, Louis F(avreau),
  9: 31
Cary, Louis F(avreau), *9:* 31
Caryl, Jean. *See* Kaplan, Jean
  Caryl Korn, *10:* 62
Case, Marshal T(aylor), *9:* 33
Case, Michael. *See* Howard,
  Robert West, *5:* 85
Casewit, Curtis, *4:* 43
Casey, Brigid, *9:* 33
Casey, Winifred Rosen. *See*
  Rosen, Winifred, *8:* 169
Cason, Mabel Earp, *10:* 19
Cass, Joan E(velyn), *1:* 47
Cassel, Lili. *See* Wronker, Lili
  Cassell, *10:* 204
Cassel-Wronker, Lili. *See*
  Wronker, Lili Cassell, *10:* 204
Castellanos, Jane Mollie
  (Robinson), *9:* 34
Castillo, Edmund L., *1:* 50
Castle, Lee. [Joint pseudonym].
  See Ogan, George F. and
  Margaret E. (Nettles), *13:* 171
Caswell, Helen (Rayburn), *12:* 67
Catherall, Arthur, *3:* 38
Catlin, Wynelle, *13:* 19
Catton, (Charles) Bruce, *2:* 54
Catz, Max. *See* Glaser, Milton,
  11: 106
Caudill, Rebecca, *1:* 50
Causley, Charles, *3:* 39
Cavallo, Diana, *7:* 43
Cavanah, Frances, *1:* 52
Cavanna, Betty, *1:* 54
Cawley, Winifred, *13:* 20
Cebulash, Mel, *10:* 19
Ceder, Georgiana Dorcas, *10:* 21
Cerf, Bennett, *7:* 43
Cerf, Christopher (Bennett), *2:* 55
Cetin, Frank (Stanley), *2:* 55
Chadwick, Lester [Collective
  pseudonym], *1:* 55
Chaffee, Allen, *3:* 41
Chaffin, Lillie D(orton), *4:* 44
Chalmers, Mary, *6:* 41
Chambers, Aidan, *1:* 55
Chambers, Margaret Ada
  Eastwood, *2:* 56
Chambers, Peggy. *See* Chambers,
  Margaret, *2:* 56
Chandler, Edna Walker, *11:* 45
Chandler, Ruth Forbes, *2:* 56
Channel, A. R. *See* Catherall,
  Arthur, *3:* 38
Chapman, Allen [Collective
  pseudonym], *1:* 55
Chapman, (Constance) Elizabeth
  (Mann), *10:* 21

Chapman, Walker. See Silverberg, Robert, 13: 206
Chappell, Warren, 6: 42
Charles, Louis. See Stratemeyer, Edward L., 1: 208
Charlip, Remy, 4: 46
Charlot, Jean, 8: 22
Charmatz, Bill, 7: 45
Charosh, Mannis, 5: 42
Chase, Alice. See McHargue, Georgess, 4: 152
Chase, Mary (Coyle), 17: 39
Chase, Mary Ellen, 10: 22
Chastain, Madye Lee, 4: 48
Chauncy, Nan, 6: 43
Chaundler, Christine, 1: 56
Chen, Tony, 6: 44
Chenault, Nell. See Smith, Linell Nash, 2: 227
Cheney, Cora, 3: 41
Cheney, Ted. See Cheney, Theodore Albert, 11: 46
Cheney, Theodore Albert, 11: 46
Chernoff, Goldie Taub, 10: 23
Cherryholmes, Anne, See Price, Olive, 8: 157
Chetin, Helen, 6: 46
Chew, Ruth, 7: 45
Chidsey, Donald Barr, 3: 42
Childress, Alice, 7: 46
Childs, (Halla) Fay (Cochrane), 1: 56
Chimaera, See Farjeon, Eleanor, 2: 103
Chipperfield, Joseph E(ugene), 2: 57
Chittenden, Elizabeth F., 9: 35
Chittum, Ida, 7: 47
Chorao, (Ann Mc)Kay (Sproat), 8: 24
Chrisman, Arthur Bowie, YABC 1: 94
Christensen, Gardell Dano, 1: 57
Christgau, Alice Erickson, 13: 21
Christian, Mary Blount, 9: 35
Christopher, Matt(hew F.), 2: 58
Chu, Daniel, 11: 47
Chukovsky, Kornei (Ivanovich), 5: 43
Church, Richard, 3: 43
Churchill, E. Richard, 11: 48
Chute, B(eatrice) J(oy), 2: 59
Chute, Marchette (Gaylord), 1: 58
Chwast, Jacqueline, 6: 46
Chwast, Seymour, 18: 42
Ciardi, John (Anthony), 1: 59
Clapp, Patricia, 4: 50
Clare, Helen, See Hunter Blair, Pauline, 3: 87
Clark, Ann Nolan, 4: 51
Clark, Frank J(ames), 18: 43
Clark, Margaret Goff, 8: 26
Clark, Mavis Thorpe, 8: 27
Clark, Merle. See Gessner, Lynne, 16: 119
Clark, Patricia (Finrow), 11: 48

Clark, Ronald William, 2: 60
Clark, Van D(eusen), 2: 61
Clark, Virginia. See Gray, Patricia, 7: 110
Clark, Walter Van Tilburg, 8: 28
Clarke, Arthur C(harles), 13: 22
Clarke, Clorinda, 7: 48
Clarke, John. See Laklan, Carli, 5: 100
Clarke, Mary Stetson, 5: 46
Clarke, Michael. See Newlon, Clarke, 6: 174
Clarke, Pauline. See Hunter Blair, Pauline, 3: 87
Clarkson, Ewan, 9: 36
Cleary, Beverly (Bunn), 2: 62
Cleaver, Carole, 6: 48
Cleishbotham, Jebediah. See Scott, Sir Walter, YABC 2: 280
Cleland, Mabel. See Widdemer, Mabel Cleland, 5: 200
Clemens, Samuel Langhorne, YABC 2: 51
Clemons, Elizabeth. See Nowell, Elizabeth Cameron, 12: 160
Clerk, N. W. See Lewis, C. S., 13: 129
Cleven, Cathrine. See Cleven, Kathryn Seward, 2: 64
Cleven, Kathryn Seward, 2: 64
Clevin, Jörgen, 7: 49
Clewes, Dorothy (Mary), 1: 61
Clifford, Eth. See Rosenberg, Ethel, 3: 176
Clifford, Harold B., 10: 24
Clifford, Margaret Cort, 1: 63
Clifford, Martin. See Hamilton, Charles Harold St. John, 13: 77
Clifford, Peggy. See Clifford, Margaret Cort, 1: 63
Clifton, Harry. See Hamilton, Charles Harold St. John, 13: 77
Clifton, Martin. See Hamilton, Charles Harold St. John, 13: 77
Clinton, Jon. See Prince, J(ack) H(arvey), 17: 155
Clive, Clifford. See Hamilton, Charles Harold St. John, 13: 77
Clymer, Eleanor, 9: 37
Coates, Belle, 2: 64
Coates, Ruth Allison, 11: 49
Coats, Alice M(argaret), 11: 50
Coatsworth, Elizabeth, 2: 65
Cobb, Vicki, 8: 31
Cobbett, Richard. See Pluckrose, Henry (Arthur), 13: 183
Cober, Alan E., 7: 51
Cobham, Sir Alan. See Hamilton, Charles Harold St. John, 13: 77
Cocagnac, A(ugustin) M(aurice-Jean), 7: 52
Cochran, Bobbye A., 11: 51
Cockett, Mary, 3: 45
Coe, Douglas [Joint pseudonym]. See Epstein, Beryl and Samuel, 1: 87

Coerr, Eleanor, 1: 64
Coffin, Geoffrey. See Mason, F. van Wyck, 3: 117
Coffman, Ramon Peyton, 4: 53
Coggins, Jack (Banham), 2: 68
Cohen, Barbara, 10: 24
Cohen, Daniel, 8: 31
Cohen, Joan Lebold, 4: 53
Cohen, Peter Zachary, 4: 54
Cohen, Robert Carl, 8: 33
Coit, Margaret L(ouise), 2: 70
Colbert, Anthony, 15: 39
Colby, C. B., 3: 46
Cole, Annette. See Steiner, Barbara A(nnette), 13: 213
Cole, Davis, See Elting, Mary, 2: 100
Cole, Jack. See Stewart, John (William), 14: 189
Cole, Jackson. See Schisgall, Oscar, 12: 187
Cole, Lois Dwight, 10: 26
Cole, William (Rossa), 9: 40
Collier, Christopher, 16: 66
Collier, James Lincoln, 8: 33
Collins, David, 7: 52
Colman, Hila, 1: 65
Colonius, Lillian, 3: 48
Colt, Martin. See Epstein, Samuel, 1: 87
Colum, Padraic, 15: 42
Columella. See Moore, Clement Clarke, 18: 224
Colver, Anne, 7: 54
Colwell, Eileen (Hilda), 2: 71
Comfort, Jane Levington. See Sturtzel, Jane Levington, 1: 212
Comfort, Mildred Houghton, 3: 48
Comins, Ethel M(ae), 11: 53
Cone, Molly (Lamken), 1: 66
Conford, Ellen, 6: 48
Conklin, Gladys (Plemon), 2: 73
Connolly, Jerome P(atrick), 8: 34
Conquest, Owen. See Hamilton, Charles Harold St. John, 13: 77
Conway, Gordon. See Hamilton, Charles Harold St. John, 13: 77
Cook, Bernadine, 11: 55
Cook, Fred J(ames), 2: 74
Cook, Joseph J(ay), 8: 35
Cook, Lyn. See Waddell, Evelyn Margaret, 10: 186
Cooke, David Coxe, 2: 75
Cooke, Donald Ewin, 2: 76
Cookson, Catherine (McMullen), 9: 42
Coolidge, Olivia E(nsor), 1: 67
Coombs, Charles, 3: 49
Coombs, Chick. See Coombs, Charles, 3: 49
Coombs, Patricia, 3: 51
Cooney, Barbara, 6: 49
Cooper, James R. See Stratemeyer, Edward L., 1: 208

Cooper, John R. [Collective pseudonym], *1:* 68
Cooper, Kay, *11:* 55
Cooper, Lee (Pelham), *5:* 47
Cooper, Susan, *4:* 57
Copeland, Helen, *4:* 57
Coppard, A(lfred) E(dgar), *YABC 1:* 97
Corbett, Scott, *2:* 78
Corbin, William. *See* McGraw, William Corbin, *3:* 124
Corby, Dan. *See* Catherall, Arthur, *3:* 38
Corcoran, Barbara, *3:* 53
Corcos, Lucille, *10:* 27
Cordell, Alexander. *See* Graber, Alexander, *7:* 106
Cormack, M(argaret) Grant, *11:* 56
Cormier, Robert Edmund, *10:* 28
Cornell, J. *See* Cornell, Jeffrey, *11:* 57
Cornell, Jeffrey, *11:* 57
Correy, Lee. *See* Stine, G. Harry, *10:* 161
Corrigan, Barbara, *8:* 36
Cort, M. C. *See* Clifford, Margaret Cort, *1:* 63
Corwin, Judith Hoffman, *10:* 28
Coskey, Evelyn, *7:* 55
Courlander, Harold, *6:* 51
Cousins, Margaret, *2:* 79
Cowie, Leonard W(allace), *4:* 60
Cowley, Joy, *4:* 60
Cox, Jack. *See* Cox, John Roberts, *9:* 42
Cox, John Roberts, *9:* 42
Coy, Harold, *3:* 53
Craig, John Eland. *See* Chipperfield, Joseph, *2:* 57
Craig, M. Jean, *17:* 45
Craig, Margaret Maze, *9:* 43
Craig, Mary Francis, *6:* 52
Crane, Caroline, *11:* 59
Crane, Stephen (Townley), *YABC 2:* 94
Crane, Walter, *18:* 44
Crane, William D(wight), *1:* 68
Crary, Margaret (Coleman), *9:* 43
Crawford, Deborah, *6:* 53
Crawford, John E., *3:* 56
Crawford, Phyllis, *3:* 57
Crayder, Dorothy, *7:* 55
Crayder, Teresa. *See* Colman, Hila, *1:* 65
Crayon, Geoffrey. *See* Irving, Washington, *YABC 2:* 164
Crecy, Jeanne. *See* Williams, Jeanne, *5:* 202
Credle, Ellis, *1:* 68
Cresswell, Helen, *1:* 70
Cretan, Gladys (Yessayan), *2:* 82
Crew, Helen (Cecilia) Coale, *YABC 2:* 95
Crichton, (J.) Michael, *9:* 44
Cromie, William J(oseph), *4:* 62

Crompton, Richmal. *See* Lamburn, Richmal Crompton, *5:* 101
Cronbach, Abraham, *11:* 60
Crone, Ruth, *4:* 63
Crosby, Alexander L., *2:* 83
Crosher, G(eoffry) R(obins), *14:* 51
Cross, Wilbur Lucius, III, *2:* 83
Crossley-Holland, Kevin, *5:* 48
Crouch, Marcus, *4:* 63
Crout, George C(lement), *11:* 60
Crowe, Bettina Lum, *6:* 53
Crowell, Pers, *2:* 84
Crowfield, Christopher. *See* Stowe, Harriet (Elizabeth) Beecher, *YABC 1:* 250
Crownfield, Gertrude, *YABC 1:* 103
Crowther, James Gerald, *14:* 52
Crump, Fred H., Jr., *11:* 62
Cruz, Ray, *6:* 54
Cuffari, Richard, *6:* 55
Cullen, Countee, *18:* 64
Culp, Louanna McNary, *2:* 85
Cummings, Betty Sue, *15:* 51
Cummings, Parke, *2:* 85
Cummins, Maria Susanna, *YABC 1:* 103
Cunliffe, John Arthur, *11:* 62
Cunningham, Captain Frank. *See* Glick, Carl (Cannon), *14:* 72
Cunningham, Dale S(peers), *11:* 63
Cunningham, E. V. *See* Fast, Howard, *7:* 80
Cunningham, Julia W(oolfolk), *1:* 72
Curie, Eve, *1:* 73
Curry, Jane L(ouise), *1:* 73
Curry, Peggy Simson, *8:* 37
Curtis, Peter. *See* Lofts, Norah Robinson, *8:* 119
Cushman, Jerome, *2:* 86
Cutchen, Billye Walker, *15:* 51
Cutler, (May) Ebbitt, *9:* 46
Cutler, Samuel. *See* Folsom, Franklin, *5:* 67
Cutt, W(illiam) Towrie, *16:* 67
Cuyler, Stephen. *See* Bates, Barbara S(nedeker), *12:* 34

Dahl, Borghild, *7:* 56
Dahl, Roald, *1:* 74
Dahlstedt, Marden, *8:* 38
Dale, Jack. *See* Holliday, Joseph, *11:* 137
Dalgliesh, Alice, *17:* 47
Daly, Jim. *See* Stratemeyer, Edward L., *1:* 208
Daly, Maureen, *2:* 87
D'Amato, Janet, *9:* 47
Damrosch, Helen Therese. *See* Tee-Van, Helen Damrosch, *10:* 176
D'Andrea, Kate. *See* Steiner, Barbara A(nnette), *13:* 213
Dangerfield, Balfour. *See* McCloskey, Robert, *2:* 185

Daniel, Anne. *See* Steiner, Barbara A(nnette), *13:* 213
Daniel, Hawthorne, *8:* 39
Daniels, Guy, *11:* 64
Darby, J. N. *See* Govan, Christine Noble, *9:* 80
Darby, Patricia (Paulsen), *14:* 53
Darby, Ray K., *7:* 59
Daringer, Helen Fern, *1:* 75
Darke, Marjorie, *16:* 68
Darling, Lois M., *3:* 57
Darling, Louis, Jr., *3:* 59
Darling, Kathy. *See* Darling, Mary Kathleen, *9:* 48
Darling, Mary Kathleen, *9:* 48
Darrow, Whitney. *See* Darrow, Whitney, Jr., *13:* 24
Darrow, Whitney, Jr., *13:* 24
Daugherty, Charles Michael, *16:* 70
Daugherty, James (Henry), *13:* 26
d'Aulaire, Edgar Parin, *5:* 49
d'Aulaire, Ingri (Maartenson Parin) *5:* 50
Daveluy, Paule Cloutier, *11:* 65
Davenport, Spencer. *See* Stratemeyer, Edward L., *1:* 208
David, Jonathan. *See* Ames, Lee J., *3:* 11
Davidson, Basil, *13:* 30
Davidson, Jessica, *5:* 52
Davidson, Margaret, *5:* 53
Davidson, Marion. *See* Garis, Howard R(oger), *13:* 67
Davidson, Mary R., *9:* 49
Davis, Bette J., *15:* 53
Davis, Burke, *4:* 64
Davis, Christopher, *6:* 57
Davis, Daniel S(heldon), *12:* 68
Davis, Julia, *6:* 58
Davis, Mary L(ee), *9:* 49
Davis, Mary Octavia, *6:* 59
Davis, Paxton, *16:* 71
Davis, Robert, *YABC 1:* 104
Davis, Russell G., *3:* 60
Davis, Verne T., *6:* 60
Dawson, Elmer A. [Collective pseudonym], *1:* 76
Dawson, Mary, *11:* 66
Day, Thomas, *YABC 1:* 106
Dazey, Agnes J(ohnston), *2:* 88
Dazey, Frank M., *2:* 88
Deacon, Richard. *See* McCormick, (George) Donald (King), *14:* 141
Dean, Anabel, *12:* 69
de Angeli, Marguerite, *1:* 76
DeArmand, Frances Ullmann, *10:* 29
deBanke, Cecile, *11:* 67
De Bruyn, Monica, *13:* 30
de Camp, Catherine C(rook), *12:* 70
DeCamp, L(yon) Sprague, *9:* 49
Decker, Duane, *5:* 53
DeGering, Etta, *7:* 60
de Grummond, Lena Young, *6:* 61

Deiss, Joseph J., *12:* 72
DeJong, David C(ornel), *10:* 29
de Jong, Dola, *7:* 61
De Jong, Meindert, *2:* 89
de Kay, Ormonde, Jr., *7:* 62
de Kiriline, Louise. *See* Lawrence,
    Louise de Kirilene, *13:* 126
deKruif, Paul (Henry) *5:* 54
De Lage, Ida, *11:* 67
de la Mare, Walter, *16:* 73
Delaney, Harry, *3:* 61
Delaune, Lynne, *7:* 63
DeLaurentis, Louise Budde, *12:* 73
Delderfield, Eric R(aymond), *14:* 53
De Leeuw, Adele Louise, *1:* 77
Delmar, Roy. *See* Wexler, Jerome
    (LeRoy), *14:* 243
Delton, Judy, *14:* 54
Delulio, John, *15:* 54
Delving, Michael. *See* Williams,
    Jay, *3:* 256
Demarest, Doug. *See* Barker, Will,
    8: 4
Demas, Vida, *9:* 51
Dennis, Morgan, *18:* 68
Dennis, Wesley, *18:* 70
Denslow, W(illiam) W(allace),
    16: 83
de Paola, Thomas Anthony, *11:* 68
de Paola, Tomie. *See* de Paola,
    Thomas Anthony, *11:* 68
deRegniers, Beatrice Schenk
    (Freedman), *2:* 90
Derleth, August (William) *5:* 54
Derman, Sarah Audrey, *11:* 71
Derry Down Derry. *See* Lear,
    Edward, *18:* 182
Derwent, Lavinia, *14:* 56
De Selincourt, Aubrey, *14:* 56
Desmond, Alice Curtis, *8:* 40
Detine, Padre. *See* Olsen, Ib
    Spang, *6:* 177
Deutsch, Babette, *1:* 79
Devaney, John, *12:* 74
Devereux, Frederick L(eonard),
    Jr., *9:* 51
Devlin, Harry, *11:* 73
Devlin, (Dorothy) Wende, *11:* 74
DeWaard, E. John, *7:* 63
Dewey, Ariane, *7:* 63
Dick, Trella Lamson, *9:* 51
Dickens, Charles, *15:* 55
Dickens, Monica, *4:* 66
Dickinson, Peter, *5:* 55
Dickinson, Susan, *8:* 41
Dickinson, William Croft, *13:* 32
Dickson, Naida, *8:* 41
Dietz, David H(enry), *10:* 30
Dietz, Lew, *11:* 75
Dillard, Annie, *10:* 31
Dillon, Diane, *15:* 98
Dillon, Eilis, *2:* 92
Dillon, Leo, *15:* 99
Dines, Glen, *7:* 65
Dinsdale, Tim, *11:* 76
DiValentin, Maria, *7:* 68

Dixon, Franklin W. [Collective
    pseudonym], *1:* 80.
    See also Svenson, Andrew E.,
    2: 238; Stratemeyer, Edward,
    1: 208
Dixon, Peter L., *6:* 62
Doane, Pelagie, *7:* 68
Dobell, I(sabel) M(arian) B(arclay),
    11: 77
Dobler, Lavinia G., *6:* 63
Dobrin, Arnold, *4:* 67
"Dr. A." *See* Silverstein, Alvin,
    8: 188
Dodd, Ed(ward) Benton, *4:* 68
Dodge, Bertha S(anford), *8:* 42
Dodgson, Charles Lutwidge,
    YABC 2: 97
Dodson, Kenneth M(acKenzie),
    11: 77
Doherty, C. H., *6:* 65
Dolson, Hildegarde, *5:* 56
Domanska, Janina, *6:* 65
Donalds, Gordon. *See* Shirreffs,
    Gordon D., *11:* 207
Donna, Natalie, *9:* 52
Doob, Leonard W(illiam), *8:* 44
Dor, Ana. *See* Ceder, Georgiana
    Dorcas, *10:* 21
Dorian, Edith M(cEwen) *5:* 58
Dorian, Harry. *See* Hamilton,
    Charles Harold St. John, *13:* 77
Dorian, Marguerite, *7:* 68
Dorman, Michael, *7:* 68
Doss, Margot Patterson, *6:* 68
Dougherty, Charles, *18:* 74
Douglas, James McM. *See*
    Butterworth, W. E., *5:* 40
Douglas, Marjory Stoneman, *10:* 33
Douty, Esther M(orris), *8:* 44
Dow, Emily R., *10:* 33
Dowdell, Dorothy (Florence)
    Karns, *12:* 75
Dowden, Anne Ophelia, *7:* 69
Dowdey, Landon Gerald, *11:* 80
Downey, Fairfax, *3:* 61
Downie, Mary Alice, *13:* 32
Draco, F. *See* Davis, Julia, *6:* 58
Dragonwagon, Crescent, *11:* 81
Drake, Frank. *See* Hamilton,
    Charles Harold St. John, *13:* 77
Drawson, Blair, *17:* 52
Drew, Patricia (Mary), *15:* 100
Drewery, Mary, *6:* 69
Drummond, V(iolet) H., *6:* 71
Drummond, Walter. *See*
    Silverberg, Robert, *13:* 206
Drury, Roger W(olcott), *15:* 101
du Blanc, Daphne. *See* Groom,
    Arthur William, *10:* 53
du Bois, William Pene, *4:* 69
DuBose, LaRocque (Russ), *2:* 93
Ducornet, Erica, *7:* 72
Dudley, Nancy. *See* Cole, Lois
    Dwight, *10:* 26
Dudley, Ruth H(ubbell), *11:* 82
Dugan, Michael (Gray), *15:* 101

du Jardin, Rosamond (Neal), *2:* 94
Dumas, Alexandre (the elder),
    18: 74
Duncan, Gregory. *See*
    McClintock, Marshall, *3:* 119
Duncan, Julia K. [Collective
    pseudonym], *1:* 81
Duncan, Lois. *See* Arquette, Lois
    S., *1:* 13
Duncan, Norman, *YABC 1:* 108
Dunlop, Agnes M. R., *3:* 62
Dunn, Judy. *See* Spangenberg,
    Judith Dunn, *5:* 175
Dunn, Mary Lois, *6:* 72
Dunnahoo, Terry, *7:* 73
Dunne, Mary Collins, *11:* 83
Dupuy, T(revor) N(evitt), *4:* 71
Durrell, Gerald (Malcolm), *8:* 46
Du Soe, Robert C., *YABC 2:* 121
Dutz. *See* Davis, Mary Octavia,
    6: 59
Duvall, Evelyn Millis, *9:* 52
Duvoisin, Roger (Antoine), *2:* 95
Dwiggins, Don, *4:* 72
Dwight, Allan. *See* Cole, Lois
    Dwight, *10:* 26

Eagar, Frances, *11:* 85
Eager, Edward (McMaken), *17:* 54
Eagle, Mike, *11:* 86
Earle, Olive L., *7:* 75
Earnshaw, Brian, *17:* 57
Eastman, Charles A(lexander),
    YABC 1: 110
Eastwick, Ivy O., *3:* 64
Eaton, George L. *See* Verral,
    Charles Spain, *11:* 255
Ebel, Alex, *11:* 88
Eberle, Irmengarde, *2:* 97
Eckert, Horst, *8:* 47
Edell, Celeste, *12:* 77
Edmonds, I(vy) G(ordon), *8:* 48
Edmonds, Walter D(umaux), *1:* 81
Edmund, Sean. *See* Pringle,
    Laurence, *4:* 171
Edsall, Marian S(tickney), *8:* 50
Edwards, Bertram. *See* Edwards,
    Herbert Charles, *12:* 77
Edwards, Bronwen Elizabeth. *See*
    Rose, Wendy, *12:* 180
Edwards, Dorothy, *4:* 73
Edwards, Harvey, *5:* 59
Edwards, Herbert Charles, *12:* 77
Edwards, Jane Campbell, *10:* 34
Edwards, Julie. *See* Andrews,
    Julie, *7:* 6
Edwards, Julie. *See* Stratemeyer,
    Edward L., *1:* 208
Edwards, Monica le Doux
    Newton, *12:* 78
Edwards, Sally, *7:* 75
Eggenberger, David, *6:* 72
Egielski, Richard, *11:* 89
Egypt, Ophelia Settle, *16:* 88

Ehrlich, Bettina (Bauer), *1:* 82
Eichberg, James Bandman. *See*
　　Garfield, James B., *6:* 85
Eichenberg, Fritz, *9:* 53
Eichner, James A., *4:* 73
Eifert, Virginia S(nider), *2:* 99
Einsel, Naiad, *10:* 34
Einsel, Walter, *10:* 37
Eiseman, Alberta, *15:* 102
Eisenberg, Azriel, *12:* 79
Eitzen, Allan, *9:* 57
Eitzen, Ruth (Carper), *9:* 57
Elam, Richard M(ace, Jr.), *9:* 57
Elfman, Blossom, *8:* 51
Elia. *See* Lamb, Charles, *17:* 101
Eliot, Anne. *See* Cole, Lois
　　Dwight, *10:* 26
Elkin, Benjamin, *3:* 65
Elkins, Dov Peretz, *5:* 61
Elliott, Sarah M(cCarn), *14:* 57
Ellis, Edward S(ylvester),
　　YABC 1: 116
Ellis, Ella Thorp, *7:* 76
Ellis, Harry Bearse, *9:* 58
Ellis, Mel, *7:* 77
Ellison, Virginia Howell, *4:* 74
Ellsberg, Edward, *7:* 78
Elspeth. *See* Bragdon, Elspeth,
　　6: 30
Elting, Mary, *2:* 100
Elwart, Joan Potter, *2:* 101
Emberley, Barbara A(nne), *8:* 51
Emberley, Ed(ward Randolph),
　　8: 52
Embry, Margaret (Jacob), *5:* 61
Emerson, Alice B. [Collective
　　pseudonym], *1:* 84
Emery, Anne (McGuigan), *1:* 84
Emrich, Duncan (Black
　　Macdonald), *11:* 90
Emslie, M. L. *See* Simpson,
　　Myrtle L(illias), *14:* 181
Engdahl, Sylvia Louise, *4:* 75
Engle, Eloise Katherine, *9:* 60
Englebert, Victor, *8:* 54
Enright, Elizabeth, *9:* 61
Epstein, Beryl (Williams), *1:* 85
Epstein, Samuel, *1:* 87
Erdman, Loula Grace, *1:* 88
Ericson, Walter. *See* Fast,
　　Howard, *7:* 80
Erlich, Lillian (Feldman), *10:* 38
Ervin, Janet Halliday, *4:* 77
Estep, Irene (Compton), *5:* 62
Estes, Eleanor, *7:* 79
Estoril, Jean. *See* Allan, Mabel
　　Esther, *5:* 2
Ets, Marie Hall, *2:* 102
Eunson, Dale, *5:* 63
Evans, Katherine (Floyd), *5:* 64
Evans, Mari, *10:* 39
Evans, Patricia Healy. *See*
　　Carpenter, Patricia, *11:* 43
Evarts, Hal G. (Jr.), *6:* 72
Evernden, Margery, *5:* 65
Ewen, David, *4:* 78

Ewing, Juliana (Horatia Gatty),
　　16: 90
Eyerly, Jeannette Hyde, *4:* 80

Fabe, Maxene, *15:* 103
Faber, Doris, *3:* 67
Faber, Harold, *5:* 65
Fadiman, Clifton (Paul), *11:* 91
Fair, Sylvia, *13:* 33
Fairfax-Lucy, Brian, *6:* 73
Fairman, Joan A(lexandra), *10:* 41
Faithfull, Gail, *8:* 55
Falconer, James. *See* Kirkup,
　　James, *12:* 120
Falkner, Leonard, *12:* 80
Fall, Thomas. *See* Snow, Donald
　　Clifford, *16:* 246
Fanning, Leonard M(ulliken), *5:* 65
Faralla, Dana, *9:* 62
Faralla, Dorothy W. *See* Faralla,
　　Dana, *9:* 62
Farb, Peter, *12:* 81
Farjeon, (Eve) Annabel, *11:* 93
Farjeon, Eleanor, *2:* 103
Farley, Carol, *4:* 81
Farley, Walter, *2:* 106
Farnham, Burt. *See* Clifford,
　　Harold B., *10:* 24
Farquhar, Margaret C(utting),
　　13: 35
Farr, Finis (King), *10:* 41
Farrell, Ben. *See* Cebulash, Mel,
　　10: 19
Fassler, Joan (Grace), *11:* 94
Fast, Howard, *7:* 80
Father Xavier. *See* Hurwood,
　　Bernhardt J., *12:* 107
Fatio, Louise, *6:* 75
Faulhaber, Martha, *7:* 82
Feagles, Anita MacRae, *9:* 63
Feague, Mildred H., *14:* 59
Fecher, Constance, *7:* 83
Feelings, Muriel (Grey), *16:* 104
Feelings, Thomas, *8:* 55
Feelings, Tom. *See* Feelings,
　　Thomas, *8:* 55
Feiffer, Jules, *8:* 57
Feil, Hila, *12:* 81
Feilen, John. *See* May, Julian,
　　11: 175
Fellows, Muriel H., *10:* 41
Felsen, Henry Gregor, *1:* 89
Felton, Harold William, *1:* 90
Felton, Ronald Oliver, *3:* 67
Fenner, Carol, *7:* 84
Fenner, Phyllis R(eid), *1:* 91
Fenten, D. X., *4:* 82
Fenton, Carroll Lane, *5:* 66
Fenton, Edward, *7:* 86
Feravolo, Rocco Vincent, *10:* 42
Ferber, Edna, *7:* 87
Ferguson, Bob. *See* Ferguson,
　　Robert Bruce, *13:* 35
Ferguson, Robert Bruce, *13:* 35

Fergusson, Erna, *5:* 67
Fermi, Laura, *6:* 78
Fern, Eugene A., *10:* 43
Ferris, James Cody [Collective
　　pseudonym], *1:* 92
Fiammenghi, Gioia, *9:* 64
Fiarotta, Noel, *15:* 104
Fiarotta, Phyllis, *15:* 105
Fichter, George S., *7:* 92
Fidler, Kathleen, *3:* 68
Fiedler, Jean, *4:* 83
Field, Edward, *8:* 58
Field, Eugene, *16:* 105
Field, Rachel (Lyman), *15:* 106
Fife, Dale (Odile), *18:* 110
Fighter Pilot, A. *See* Johnston,
　　H(ugh) A(nthony) S(tephen),
　　14: 87
Figueroa, Pablo, *9:* 66
Fijan, Carol, *12:* 82
Fillmore, Parker H(oysted),
　　YABC 1: 121
Finkel, George (Irvine), *8:* 59
Finlayson, Ann, *8:* 61
Firmin, Peter, *15:* 113
Fischbach, Julius, *10:* 43
Fisher, Aileen (Lucia), *1:* 92
Fisher, Dorothy Canfield,
　　YABC 1: 122
Fisher, John (Oswald Hamilton),
　　15: 115
Fisher, Laura Harrison, *5:* 67
Fisher, Leonard Everett, *4:* 84
Fitch, Clarke. *See* Sinclair, Upton
　　(Beall), *9:* 168
Fitch, John, IV. *See* Cormier,
　　Robert Edmund, *10:* 28
Fitzgerald, Captain Hugh. *See*
　　Baum L(yman) Frank, *18:* 7
Fitzgerald, F(rancis) A(nthony),
　　15: 115
Fitzhardinge, Joan Margaret, *2:* 107
Fitzhugh, Louise, *1:* 94
Flack, Marjorie, *YABC 2:* 123
Flash Flood. *See* Robinson, Jan
　　M., *6:* 194
Fleischman, (Albert) Sid(ney), *8:* 61
Fleming, Alice Mulcahey, *9:* 67
Fleming, Ian (Lancaster), *9:* 67
Fleming, Thomas J(ames), *8:* 64
Fletcher, Charlie May, *3:* 70
Fletcher, Helen Jill, *13:* 36
Flexner, James Thomas, *9:* 70
Flitner, David P., *7:* 92
Floethe, Louise Lee, *4:* 87
Floethe, Richard, *4:* 89
Flood, Flash. *See* Robinson, Jan
　　M., *6:* 194
Flora, James (Royer), *1:* 95
Flynn, Barbara, *9:* 71
Flynn, Jackson. *See* Shirreffs,
　　Gordon D., *11:* 207
Folsom, Franklin (Brewster), *5:* 67
Forbes, Esther, *2:* 108
Forbes, Graham B. [Collective
　　pseudonym], *1:* 97

Forbes, Kathryn. *See* McLean, Kathryn (Anderson), *9:* 140
Ford, Albert Lee. *See* Stratemeyer, Edward L., *1:* 208
Ford, Elbur. *See* Hibbert, Eleanor, *2:* 134
Ford, Marcia. *See* Radford, Ruby L., *6:* 186
Foreman, Michael, *2:* 110
Forrest, Sybil. *See* Markun, Patricia M(aloney), *15:* 189
Forester, C(ecil) S(cott), *13:* 38
Forman, Brenda, *4:* 90
Forman, James Douglas, *8:* 64
Forsee, (Frances) Aylesa, *1:* 97
Foster, Doris Van Liew, *10:* 44
Foster, E(lizabeth) C(onnell), *9:* 71
Foster, Elizabeth, *10:* 45
Foster, Elizabeth Vincent, *12:* 82
Foster, F. Blanche, *11:* 95
Foster, Genevieve (Stump), *2:* 111
Foster, John T(homas), *8:* 65
Foster, Laura Louise, *6:* 78
Fowke, Edith (Margaret), *14:* 59
Fox, Charles Philip, *12:* 83
Fox, Eleanor. *See* St. John, Wylly Folk, *10:* 132
Fox, Freeman. *See* Hamilton, Charles Harold St. John, *13:* 77
Fox, Lorraine, *11:* 96
Fox, Michael Wilson, *15:* 117
Fox, Paula, *17:* 59
Frances, Miss. *See* Horwich, Frances R., *11:* 142
Franchere, Ruth, *18:* 111
Francis, Dorothy Brenner, *10:* 46
Francis, Pamela (Mary), *11:* 97
Frank, Josette, *10:* 47
Frankau, Mary Evelyn, *4:* 90
Frankel, Bernice, *9:* 72
Franklin, Harold, *13:* 53
Franklin, Steve. *See* Stevens, Franklin, *6:* 206
Franzén, Nils-Olof, *10:* 47
Frasconi, Antonio, *6:* 79
Frazier, Neta Lohnes, *7:* 94
Freedman, Russell (Bruce), *16:* 115
Freeman, Don, *17:* 60
French, Allen, *YABC 1:* 133
French, Dorothy Kayser, *5:* 69
French, Fiona, *6:* 81
French, Paul. *See* Asimov, Isaac, *1:* 15
Frewer, Glyn, *11:* 98
Frick, C. H. *See* Irwin, Constance Frick, *6:* 119
Frick, Constance. *See* Irwin, Constance Frick, *6:* 119
Friedlander, Joanne K(ohn), *9:* 73
Friedman, Estelle, *7:* 95
Friendlich, Dick. *See* Friendlich, Richard, *11:* 99
Friendlich, Richard J., *11:* 99
Friermood, Elisabeth Hamilton, *5:* 69

Friis, Babbis. *See* Friis-Baastad, Babbis, *7:* 95
Friis-Baastad, Babbis, *7:* 95
Friskey, Margaret Richards, *5:* 72
Fritz, Jean (Guttery), *1:* 98
Froman, Elizabeth Hull, *10:* 49
Froman, Robert (Winslow), *8:* 67
Frost, Lesley, *14:* 61
Frost, Robert (Lee), *14:* 63
Fry, Rosalie, *3:* 71
Fuchs, Erich, *6:* 84
Fujita, Tamao, *7:* 98
Fujiwara, Michiko, *15:* 120
Fuller, Catherine L(euthold), *9:* 73
Fuller, Iola. *See* McCoy, Iola Fuller, *3:* 120
Fuller, Lois Hamilton, *11:* 99
Funk, Thompson. *See* Funk, Tom, *7:* 98
Funk, Tom, *7:* 98
Funke, Lewis, *11:* 100

Gág, Wanda (Hazel), *YABC 1:* 135
Gage, Wilson. *See* Steele, Mary Q., *3:* 211
Galdone, Paul, *17:* 69
Gallant, Roy (Arthur), *4:* 91
Gallico, Paul, *13:* 53
Galt, Thomas Franklin, Jr., *5:* 72
Galt, Tom. *See* Galt, Thomas Franklin, Jr., *5:* 72
Gamerman, Martha, *15:* 121
Gannett, Ruth Stiles, *3:* 73
Gannon, Robert (Haines), *8:* 68
Gard, Joyce. *See* Reeves, Joyce, *17:* 158
Gard, Robert Edward, *18:* 113
Garden, Nancy, *12:* 85
Gardner, Jeanne LeMonnier, *5:* 73
Gardner, Martin, *16:* 117
Gardner, Richard A., *13:* 64
Garfield, James B., *6:* 85
Garfield, Leon, *1:* 99
Garis, Howard R(oger), *13:* 67
Garner, Alan, *18:* 114
Garnett, Eve C. R., *3:* 75
Garrison, Frederick. *See* Sinclair, Upton (Beall), *9:* 168
Garst, Doris Shannon, *1:* 100
Garst, Shannon. *See* Garst, Doris Shannon, *1:* 100
Garthwaite, Marion H., *7:* 100
Gates, Doris, *1:* 102
Gatty, Juliana Horatia. *See* Ewing, Juliana (Horatia Gatty), *16:* 90
Gault, William Campbell, *8:* 69
Gay, Kathlyn, *9:* 74
Geis, Darlene, *7:* 101
Geisel, Theodor Seuss, *1:* 104
Geldart, William, *15:* 121
Gelinas, Paul J., *10:* 49
Gelman, Steve, *3:* 75
Gemming, Elizabeth, *11:* 104
Gentleman, David, *7:* 102

George, Jean Craighead, *2:* 112
George, John L(othar), *2:* 114
George, S(idney) C(harles), *11:* 104
Georgiou, Constantine, *7:* 102
Gessner, Lynne, *16:* 119
Gibbs, Alonzo (Lawrence), *5:* 74
Gibson, Josephine. *See* Joslin, Sesyle, *2:* 158
Gidal, Sonia, *2:* 115
Gidal, Tim N(ahum), *2:* 116
Giegling, John A(llan), *17:* 75
Gilbert, (Agnes) Joan (Sewell), *10:* 50
Gilbert, Nan. *See* Gilbertson, Mildred, *2:* 116
Gilbert, Sara (Dulaney), *11:* 105
Gilbertson, Mildred Geiger, *2:* 116
Gilbreath, Alice (Thompson), *12:* 87
Gilbreth, Frank B., Jr., *2:* 117
Gilfond, Henry, *2:* 118
Gill, Derek L(ewis) T(heodore), *9:* 75
Gillett, Mary, *7:* 103
Gillette, Henry Sampson, *14:* 71
Gilman, Dorothy. *See* Dorothy Gilman Butters, *5:* 39
Gilman, Esther, *15:* 123
Gilson, Barbara. *See* Gilson, Charles James Louis, *YABC 2:* 124
Gilson, Charles James Louis, *YABC 2:* 124
Ginsburg, Mirra, *6:* 86
Giovanopoulos, Paul, *7:* 104
Gipson, Frederick B., *2:* 118
Gittings, Jo Manton, *3:* 76
Gittings, Robert, *6:* 88
Gladstone, Gary, *12:* 88
Glaser, Milton, *11:* 106
Glaspell, Susan, *YABC 2:* 125
Glauber, Uta (Heil), *17:* 75
Glazer, Tom, *9:* 76
Glick, Carl (Cannon), *14:* 72
Gliewe, Unada, *3:* 77
Glovach, Linda, *7:* 105
Glubok, Shirley, *6:* 89
Glynne-Jones, William, *11:* 107
Godden, Rumer, *3:* 79
Gode, Alexander. *See* Gode von Aesch, Alexander (Gottfried Friedrich), *14:* 74
Gode von Aesch, Alexander (Gottfried Friedrich), *14:* 74
Goettel, Elinor, *12:* 89
Goffstein, M(arilyn) B(rooke), *8:* 70
Golann, Cecil Paige, *11:* 109
Golbin, Andrée, *15:* 124
Gold, Sharlya, *9:* 77
Goldfeder, Cheryl. *See* Pahz, Cheryl Suzanne, *11:* 189
Goldfeder, Jim. *See* Pahz, James Alon, *11:* 190
Goldfrank, Helen Colodny, *6:* 89
Goldin, Augusta, *13:* 72
Goldston, Robert (Conroy), *6:* 90
Goodall, John S(trickland), *4:* 92

Author Index

Goode, Diane, *15:* 125
Goodman, Elaine, *9:* 78
Goodman, Walter, *9:* 78
Goodwin, Hal. *See* Goodwin,
    Harold Leland, *13:* 73
Goodwin, Harold Leland, *13:* 73
Gordon, Colonel H. R. *See* Ellis,
    Edward S(ylvester),
    YABC 1: 116
Gordon, Esther S(aranga), *10:* 50
Gordon, Frederick [Collective
    pseudonym], *1:* 106
Gordon, Hal. *See* Goodwin,
    Harold Leland, *13:* 73
Gordon, John, *6:* 90
Gordon, Lew. *See* Baldwin,
    Gordon C., *12:* 30
Gordon, Margaret (Anna), *9:* 79
Gordon, Selma. *See* Lanes, Selma
    G., *3:* 96
Gordon, Sol, *11:* 111
Gordon, Stewart. *See* Shirreffs,
    Gordon D., *11:* 207
Gorelick, Molly C., *9:* 80
Gorham, Michael. *See* Folsom,
    Franklin, *5:* 67
Gorsline, Douglas (Warner), *11:* 112
Gottlieb, Gerald, *7:* 106
Goudge, Elizabeth, *2:* 119
Goulart, Ron, *6:* 92
Gould, Jean R(osalind), *11:* 114
Gould, Lilian, *6:* 92
Gould, Marilyn, *15:* 127
Govan, Christine Noble, *9:* 80
Graber, Alexander, *7:* 106
Graff, Polly Anne. *See* Colver,
    Anne, *7:* 54
Graff, (S.) Stewart, *9:* 82
Graham, Ada, *11:* 115
Graham, Eleanor, *18:* 116
Graham, Frank, Jr., *11:* 116
Graham, John, *11:* 117
Graham, Lorenz B(ell), *2:* 122
Graham, Margaret Bloy, *11:* 119
Graham, Robin Lee, *7:* 107
Grahame, Kenneth, *YABC 1:* 144
Gramatky, Hardie, *1:* 107
Grange, Peter. *See* Nicole,
    Christopher Robin, *5:* 141
Granstaff, Bill, *10:* 51
Grant, Bruce, *5:* 75
Grant, Eva, *7:* 108
Grant, (Alice) Leigh, *10:* 52
Grant, Matthew C. *See* May,
    Julian, *11:* 175
Grant, Neil, *14:* 75
Graves, Charles Parlin, *4:* 94
Gray, Elizabeth Janet, *6:* 93
Gray, Genevieve S., *4:* 95
Gray, Jenny. *See* Gray, Genevieve
    S., *4:* 95
Gray, Nicholas Stuart, *4:* 96
Gray, Patricia, *7:* 110
Gray, Patsey. *See* Gray, Patricia,
    7: 110

Grayland, V. Merle. *See* Grayland,
    Valerie, *7:* 111
Grayland, Valerie, *7:* 111
Great Comte, The. *See*
    Hawkesworth, Eric, *13:* 94
Greaves, Margaret, *7:* 113
Green, Adam. *See* Weisgard,
    Leonard, *2:* 263
Green, D. *See* Casewit, Curtis,
    4: 43
Green, Jane, *9:* 82
Green, Mary Moore, *11:* 120
Green, Morton, *8:* 71
Green, Norma B(erger), *11:* 120
Green, Roger (Gilbert) Lancelyn,
    2: 123
Green, Sheila Ellen, *8:* 72
Greenaway, Kate, *YABC 2:* 129
Greenberg, Harvey R., *5:* 77
Greene, Bette, *8:* 73
Greene, Carla, *1:* 108
Greene, Constance C(larke),
    11: 121
Greene, Wade, *11:* 122
Greening, Hamilton. *See*
    Hamilton, Charles Harold St.
    John, *13:* 77
Greenleaf, Barbara Kaye, *6:* 95
Greenwald, Sheila. *See* Green,
    Sheila Ellen, *8:* 72
Gregori, Leon, *15:* 129
Grendon, Stephen. *See* Derleth,
    August (William), *5:* 54
Gretz, Susanna, *7:* 114
Gretzer, John, *18:* 117
Grey, Jerry, *11:* 123
Grice, Frederick, *6:* 96
Grieder, Walter, *9:* 83
Griese, Arnold A(lfred), *9:* 84
Grifalconi, Ann, *2:* 125
Griffith, Jeannette. *See* Eyerly,
    Jeanette, *4:* 80
Griffiths, Helen, *5:* 77
Grimm, William C(arey), *14:* 75
Grimsley, Gordon. *See* Groom,
    Arthur William, *10:* 53
Gringhuis, Dirk. *See* Gringhuis,
    Richard H. *6:* 97
Gringhuis, Richard H., *6:* 97
Grinnell, George Bird, *16:* 121
Gripe, Maria (Kristina), *2:* 126
Grohskopf, Bernice, *7:* 114
Grol, Lini Richards, *9:* 85
Groom, Arthur William, *10:* 53
Gross, Sarah Chokla, *9:* 86
Grossman, Robert, *11:* 124
Gruenberg, Sidonie M(atsner),
    2: 127
Gugliotta, Bobette, *7:* 116
Guillaume, Jeanette G. (Flierl),
    8: 74
Guillot, Rene, *7:* 117
Gunston, Bill. *See* Gunston,
    William Tudor, *9:* 88
Gunston, William Tudor, *9:* 88
Gunther, John, *2:* 129

Gurko, Leo, *9:* 88
Gurko, Miriam, *9:* 89
Gustafson, Sarah R. *See* Riedman,
    Sarah R., *1:* 183
Guy, Rosa (Cuthbert), *14:* 77

Haas, Irene, *17:* 76
Habenstreit, Barbara, *5:* 78
Haber, Louis, *12:* 90
Hader, Berta (Hoerner), *16:* 122
Hader, Elmer (Stanley), *16:* 124
Hadley, Franklin. *See*
    Winterbotham, R(ussell)
    R(obert), *10:* 198
Hafner, Marylin, *7:* 119
Haggard, H(enry) Rider, *16:* 129
Haggerty, James J(oseph) *5:* 78
Hagon, Priscilla. *See* Allan, Mabel
    Esther, *5:* 2
Hahn, Emily, *3:* 81
Hahn, Hannelore, *8:* 74
Hahn, James (Sage), *9:* 90
Hahn, (Mona) Lynn, *9:* 91
Haig-Brown, Roderick
    (Langmere), *12:* 90
Haines, Gail Kay, *11:* 124
Haining, Peter, *14:* 77
Haldane, Roger John, *13:* 75
Hale, Edward Everett, *16:* 143
Hale, Helen. *See* Mulcahy, Lucille
    Burnett, *12:* 155
Hale, Kathleen, *17:* 78
Hale, Linda, *6:* 99
Hall, Adele, *7:* 120
Hall, Anna Gertrude, *8:* 75
Hall, Elvajean, *6:* 100
Hall, Jesse. *See* Boesen, Victor,
    16: 53
Hall, Lynn, *2:* 130
Hall, Malcolm, *7:* 121
Hall, Rosalys Haskell, *7:* 121
Hallard, Peter. *See* Catherall,
    Arthur, *3:* 38
Hallas, Richard. *See* Knight, Eric
    (Mowbray), *18:* 151
Hallin, Emily Watson, *6:* 101
Hall-Quest, Olga W(ilbourne),
    11: 125
Hallstead, William F(inn) III,
    11: 126
Hallward, Michael, *12:* 91
Halsell, Grace, *13:* 76
Hamberger, John, *14:* 79
Hamil, Thomas Arthur, *14:* 80
Hamil, Tom. *See* Hamil, Thomas
    Arthur, *14:* 80
Hamilton, Charles Harold St.
    John, *13:* 77
Hamilton, Clive. *See* Lewis, C. S.,
    13: 129
Hamilton, Dorothy, *12:* 92
Hamilton, Robert W. *See*
    Stratemeyer, Edward L.,
    1: 208

Hamilton, Virginia, *4:* 97
Hammer, Richard, *6:* 102
Hammerman, Gay M(orenus), *9:* 92
Hammontree, Marie (Gertrude), *13:* 89
Hampson, (Richard) Denman, *15:* 129
Hamre, Leif, *5:* 79
Hancock, Sibyl, *9:* 92
Hanff, Helene, *11:* 128
Hanlon, Emily, *15:* 131
Hanna, Paul R(obert), *9:* 93
Hano, Arnold, *12:* 93
Hanser, Richard (Frederick), *13:* 90
Hanson, Joan, *8:* 75
Harald, Eric. *See* Boesen, Victor, *16:* 53
Hardwick, Richard Holmes Jr., *12:* 94
Hardy, Alice Dale [Collective pseudonym], *1:* 109
Hardy, David A(ndrews), *9:* 95
Hardy, Stuart. *See* Schisgall, Oscar, *12:* 187
Hark, Mildred. *See* McQueen, Mildred Hark, *12:* 145
Harkaway, Hal. *See* Stratemeyer, Edward L., *1:* 208
Harkins, Philip, *6:* 102
Harlan, Glen. *See* Cebulash, Mel, *10:* 19
Harmelink, Barbara (Mary), *9:* 97
Harnan, Terry, *12:* 94
Harnett, Cynthia (Mary), *5:* 79
Harper, Wilhelmina, *4:* 99
Harrington, Lyn, *5:* 80
Harris, Christie, *6:* 103
Harris, Colver. *See* Colver, Anne, *7:* 54
Harris, Dorothy Joan, *13:* 91
Harris, Janet, *4:* 100
Harris, Joel Chandler, *YABC 1:* 154
Harris, Leon A., Jr., *4:* 101
Harris, Rosemary (Jeanne), *4:* 101
Harrison, Deloris, *9:* 97
Harrison, Harry, *4:* 102
Hartshorn, Ruth M., *11:* 129
Harwin, Brian. *See* Henderson, LeGrand, *9:* 104
Harwood, Pearl Augusta (Bragdon), *9:* 98
Haskell, Arnold, *6:* 104
Haskins, James, *9:* 100
Haskins, Jim. *See* Haskins, James, *9:* 100
Haugaard, Erik Christian, *4:* 104
Hauser, Margaret L(ouise), *10:* 54
Hausman, Gerald, *13:* 93
Hausman, Gerry. *See* Hausman, Gerald, *13:* 93
Hautzig, Esther, *4:* 105
Havenhand, John. *See* Cox, John Roberts, *9:*
Havighurst, Walter (Edwin), *1:* 109
Haviland, Virginia, *6:* 105
Hawes, Judy, *4:* 107

Hawk, Virginia Driving. *See* Sneve, Virginia Driving Hawk, *8:* 193
Hawkesworth, Eric, *13:* 94
Hawkins, Quail, *6:* 107
Hawkinson, John, *4:* 108
Hawley, Mable C. [Collective pseudonym], *1:* 110
Hawthorne, Captain R. M. *See* Ellis, Edward S(ylvester), *YABC 1:* 116
Hawthorne, Nathaniel, *YABC 2:* 143
Hay, John, *13:* 95
Hay, Timothy. *See* Brown, Margaret Wise, *YABC 2:* 9
Haycraft, Howard, *6:* 108
Haycraft, Molly Costain, *6:* 110
Hayes, Carlton J. H., *11:* 129
Hayes, John F., *11:* 129
Hayes, Will, *7:* 122
Hayes, William D(imitt), *8:* 76
Hays, Wilma Pitchford, *1:* 110
Haywood, Carolyn, *1:* 111
Head, Gay. *See* Hauser, Margaret L(ouise), *10:* 54
Headley, Elizabeth. *See* Cavanna, Betty, *1:* 54
Headstrom, Richard, *8:* 77
Heady, Eleanor B(utler), *8:* 78
Heal, Edith, *7:* 123
Heath, Veronica. *See* Blackett, Veronica Heath, *12:* 54
Heaven, Constance. *See* Fecher, Constance, *7:* 83
Hecht, Henri Joseph, *9:* 101
Hechtkopf, Henryk, *17:* 79
Hegarty, Reginald Beaton, *10:* 54
Heiderstadt, Dorothy, *6:* 111
Heinlein, Robert A(nson), *9:* 102
Heins, Paul, *13:* 96
Helfman, Elizabeth S., *3:* 83
Helfman, Harry, *3:* 84
Hellman, Hal. *See* Hellman, Harold, *4:* 109
Hellman, Harold, *4:* 109
Helps, Racey, *2:* 131
Hemming, Roy, *11:* 130
Henderley, Brooks [Collective pseudonym], *1:* 113
Henderson, LeGrand, *9:* 104
Henderson, Zenna (Chlarson) *5:* 81
Hendrickson, Walter Brookfield, Jr., *9:* 104
Henry, Joanne Landers, *6:* 112
Henry, Marguerite, *11:* 131
Henry, O. *See* Porter, William Sydney, *YABC 2:* 259
Henry, Oliver. *See* Porter, William Sydney, *YABC 2:* 259
Henstra, Friso, *8:* 80
Herald, Kathleen. *See* Peyton, Kathleen (Wendy), *15:* 211
Herbert, Cecil. *See* Hamilton, Charles Harold St. John, *13:* 77
Herbert, Don, *2:* 131

Herbert, Frank (Patrick), *9:* 105
Hergé. *See* Remi, Georges, *13:* 183
Hermanson, Dennis (Everett), *10:* 55
Herrmanns, Ralph, *11:* 133
Herron, Edward A(lbert), *4:* 110
Hess, Lilo, *4:* 111
Hewett, Anita, *13:* 97
Heyduck-Huth, Hilde, *8:* 81
Heyerdahl, Thor, *2:* 132
Heyliger, William, *YABC 1:* 163
Hibbert, Christopher, *4:* 112
Hibbert, Eleanor Burford, *2:* 134
Hickman, Janet, *12:* 97
Hicks, Eleanor B. *See* Coerr, Eleanor, *1:* 64
Hicks, Harvey. *See* Stratemeyer, Edward L., *1:* 208
Hieatt, Constance B(artlett), *4:* 113
Hiebert, Ray Eldon, *13:* 98
Higdon, Hal, *4:* 115
Hightower, Florence, *4:* 115
Hildick, E. W. *See* Hildick, Wallace, *2:* 135
Hildick, (Edmund) Wallace, *2:* 135
Hill, Grace Brooks [Collective pseudonym], *1:* 113
Hill, Grace Livingston, *YABC 2:* 162
Hill, Kathleen Louise, *4:* 116
Hill, Kay. *See* Hill, Kathleen Louise, *4:* 116
Hill, Lorna, *12:* 97
Hill, Monica. *See* Watson, Jane Werner, *3:* 244
Hill, Robert W(hite), *12:* 98
Hill, Ruth A. *See* Viguers, Ruth Hill, *6:* 214
Hill, Ruth Livingston. *See* Munce, Ruth Hill, *12:* 156
Hillerman, Tony, *6:* 113
Hillert, Margaret, *8:* 82
Hilton, Irene (P.), *7:* 124
Hilton, Ralph, *8:* 83
Hilton, Suzanne, *4:* 117
Himler, Ann, *8:* 84
Himler, Ronald, *6:* 114
Hirsch, S. Carl, *2:* 137
Hirsh, Marilyn, *7:* 126
Hiser, Iona Seibert, *4:* 118
Hitte, Kathryn, *16:* 158
Hitz, Demi, *11:* 134
Ho, Minfong, *15:* 131
Hoban, Russell C(onwell), *1:* 113
Hobart, Lois, *7:* 127
Hoberman, Mary Ann, *5:* 82
Hochschild, Arlie Russell, *11:* 135
Hodge, P(aul) W(illiam), *12:* 99
Hodges, C(yril) Walter, *2:* 138
Hodges, Carl G., *10:* 56
Hodges, Elizabeth Jamison, *1:* 114
Hodges, Margaret Moore, *1:* 116
Hoexter, Corinne K., *6:* 115
Hoff, Carol, *11:* 136
Hoff, Syd(ney), *9:* 106
Hoffman, Phyllis M., *4:* 120

Hoffman, Rosekrans, *15:* 133
Hoffmann, Felix, *9:* 108
Hogan, Inez, *2:* 140
Hogan, Bernice Harris, *12:* 99
Hogarth, Jr. *See* Kent, Rockwell,
  6: 128
Hogg, Garry, *2:* 142
Hogner, Dorothy Childs, *4:* 121
Hogrogian, Nonny, *7:* 128
Hoke, Helen (L.), *15:* 133
Hoke, John, *7:* 129
Holbeach, Henry. *See* Rands,
  William Brighty, *17:* 156
Holberg, Ruth Langland, *1:* 117
Holbrook, Peter. *See* Glick, Carl
  (Cannon), *14:* 72
Holbrook, Stewart Hall, *2:* 143
Holding, James, *3:* 85
Holisher, Desider, *6:* 115
Holl, Adelaide (Hinkle), *8:* 84
Holland, Isabelle, *8:* 86
Holland, Janice, *18:* 117
Holland, Marion, *6:* 116
Hollander, John, *13:* 99
Holliday, Joe. *See* Holliday,
  Joseph, *11:* 137
Holliday, Joseph, *11:* 137
Holling, Holling C(lancy), *15:* 135
Holm, (Else) Anne (Lise), *1:* 118
Holman, Felice, *7:* 131
Holmes, Rick. *See* Hardwick,
  Richard Holmes Jr., *12:* 94
Holmquist, Eve, *11:* 138
Holt, Margaret, *4:* 122
Holt, Michael (Paul), *13:* 100
Holt, Stephen. *See* Thompson,
  Harlan H., *10:* 177
Holt, Victoria. *See* Hibbert,
  Eleanor, *2:* 134
Holton, Leonard. *See* Wibberley,
  Leonard, *2:* 271
Holz, Loretta (Marie), *17:* 81
Homze, Alma C., *17:* 82
Honig, Donald, *18:* 119
Honness, Elizabeth H., *2:* 145
Hood, Joseph F., *4:* 123
Hooks, William H(arris), *16:* 159
Hoopes, Roy, *11:* 140
Hoover, Helen (Drusilla
  Blackburn), *12:* 100
Hope, Laura Lee [Collective
  pseudonym], *1:* 119
Hope Simpson, Jacynth, *12:* 102
Hopf, Alice L(ightner) *5:* 82
Hopkins, Joseph G(erard)
  E(dward), *11:* 141
Hopkins, Lee Bennett, *3:* 85
Hopkins, Lyman. *See* Folsom,
  Franklin, *5:* 67
Hopkins, Marjorie, *9:* 110
Horgan, Paul, *13:* 102
Hornblow, Arthur, (Jr.), *15:* 138
Hornblow, Leonora (Schinasi),
  18: 120
Horner, Dave, *12:* 104
Horvath, Betty, *4:* 125

Horwich, Frances R(appaport),
  11: 142
Hosford, Jessie, *5:* 83
Hoskyns-Abrahall, Clare, *13:* 105
Hough, (Helen) Charlotte, *9:* 110
Hough, Richard (Alexander), *17:* 83
Houghton, Eric, *7:* 132
Houlehen, Robert J., *18:* 121
Household, Geoffrey (Edward
  West), *14:* 81
Houston, James A(rchibald),
  13: 106
Howard, Prosper. *See* Hamilton,
  Charles Harold St. John, *13:* 77
Howard, Robert West, *5:* 85
Howarth, David, *6:* 117
Howell, Pat, *15:* 139
Howell, S. *See* Styles, Frank
  Showell, *10:* 167
Howell, Virginia Tier. *See* Ellison,
  Virginia Howell, *4:* 74
Howes, Barbara, *5:* 87
Hoyle, Geoffrey, *18:* 121
Hoyt, Olga (Gruhzit), *16:* 161
Hubbell, Patricia, *8:* 86
Hudson, Jeffrey. *See* Crichton, (J.)
  Michael, *9:* 44
Huffaker, Sandy, *10:* 56
Hughes, Langston, *4:* 125
Hughes, Monica, *15:* 140
Hughes, Richard (Arthur Warren),
  8: 87
Hughes, Shirley, *16:* 162
Hull, Eric Traviss. *See* Harnan,
  Terry, *12:* 94
Hull, H. Braxton. *See* Jacobs,
  Helen Hull, *12:* 112
Hülsmann, Eva, *16:* 165
Hults, Dorothy Niebrugge, *6:* 117
Hume, Lotta Carswell, *7:* 133
Humphrey, Henry (III), *16:* 167
Hungerford, Pixie. *See* Brinsmead,
  H(esba) F(ay), *18:* 36
Hunt, Francis. *See* Stratemeyer,
  Edward L., *1:* 208
Hunt, Irene, *2:* 146
Hunt, Mabel Leigh, *1:* 120
Hunter, Dawe. *See* Downie, Mary
  Alice, *13:* 32
Hunter, Hilda, *7:* 135
Hunter, Kristin (Eggleston), *12:* 105
Hunter, Mollie. *See* McIllwraith,
  Maureen, *2:* 193
Hunter Blair, Pauline, *3:* 87
Huntington, Harriet E(lizabeth),
  1: 121
Huntsberry, William E(mery), *5:* 87
Hurd, Clement, *2:* 147
Hurd, Edith Thacher, *2:* 150
Hurwood, Bernhardt J., *12:* 107
Hutchins, Carleen Maley, *9:* 112
Hutchins, Pat, *15:* 141
Hutchins, Ross E(lliott), *4:* 127
Hutchmacher, J. Joseph, *5:* 88
Hyde, Dayton O(gden), *9:* 113

Hyde, Hawk. *See* Hyde, Dayton
  O(gden), *9:* 113
Hyde, Margaret Oldroyd, *1:* 122
Hyde, Wayne F., *7:* 135
Hylander, Clarence J., *7:* 137
Hyman, Robin P(hilip), *12:* 108
Hyman, Trina Schart, *7:* 137
Hymes, Lucia M., *7:* 139
Hyndman, Jane Andrews, *1:* 122
Hyndman, Robert Utley, *18:* 123

Iannone, Jeanne, *7:* 139
Ibbotson, Eva, *13:* 108
Ibbotson, M. C(hristine), *5:* 89
Ilsley, Velma (Elizabeth), *12:* 109
Ingham, Colonel Frederic. *See*
  Hale, Edward Everett, *16:* 143
Ingraham, Leonard W(illiam),
  4: 129
Inyart, Gene, *6:* 119
Ionesco, Eugene, *7:* 140
Ipcar, Dahlov (Zorach), *1:* 125
Irvin, Fred, *15:* 143
Irving, Robert. *See* Adler, Irving,
  1: 2
Irving, Washington, *YABC 2:* 164
Irwin, Constance Frick, *6:* 119
Irwin, Keith Gordon, *11:* 143
Ish-Kishor, Judith, *11:* 144
Ish-Kishor, Sulamith, *17:* 84
Israel, Elaine, *12:* 110
Iwamatsu, Jun Atsushi, *14:* 83

Jackson, C. Paul, *6:* 120
Jackson, Caary. *See* Jackson, C.
  Paul, *6:* 120
Jackson, Jesse, *2:* 150
Jackson, O. B. *See* Jackson, C.
  Paul, *6:* 120
Jackson, Robert B(lake), *8:* 89
Jackson, Sally. *See* Kellogg, Jean,
  10: 66
Jackson, Shirley, *2:* 152
Jacobs, Flora Gill, *5:* 90
Jacobs, Helen Hull, *12:* 112
Jacobs, Lou(is), Jr., *2:* 155
Jacobson, Daniel, *12:* 113
Jacopetti, Alexandra, *14:* 85
Jagendorf, Moritz (Adolf), *2:* 155
James, Andrew. *See* Kirkup,
  James, *12:* 120
James, Dynely. *See* Mayne,
  William, *6:* 162
James, Harry Clebourne, *11:* 144
James, Josephine. *See* Sterne,
  Emma Gelders, *6:* 205
James, T. F. *See* Fleming, Thomas
  J(ames), *8:* 64
Jane, Mary Childs, *6:* 122
Janosch. *See* Eckert, Horst, *8:* 47
Jansen, Jared. *See* Cebulash, Mel,
  10: 19

Janson, H(orst) W(oldemar), *9:* 114
Jansson, Tove, *3:* 88
Jarman, Rosemary Hawley, *7:* 141
Jarrell, Randall, *7:* 141
Jauss, Anne Marie, *10:* 57
Jayne, Lieutenant R. H. *See* Ellis,
   Edward S(ylvester),
   YABC 1: 116
Jeake, Samuel Jr. *See* Aiken,
   Conrad, *3:* 3
Jefferies, (John) Richard, *16:* 168
Jeffers, Susan, *17:* 86
Jefferson, Sarah. *See* Farjeon,
   Annabel, *11:* 93
Jeffries, Roderic, *4:* 129
Jenkins, Marie M., *7:* 143
Jenkins, William A(twell), *9:* 115
Jennings, Gary (Gayne), *9:* 115
Jennings, Robert. *See* Hamilton,
   Charles Harold St. John, *13:* 77
Jennings, S. M. *See* Meyer,
   Jerome Sydney, *3:* 129
Jennison, C. S. *See* Starbird,
   Kaye, *6:* 204
Jennison, Keith Warren, *14:* 86
Jensen, Virginia Allen, *8:* 90
Jewett, Eleanore Myers, *5:* 90
Jewett, Sarah Orne, *15:* 144
Johns, Avery. *See* Cousins,
   Margaret, *2:* 79
Johnson, A. E. [Joint pseudonym]
   See Johnson, Annabell and
   Edgar, *2:* 156, 157
Johnson, Annabell Jones, *2:* 156
Johnson, Charles R., *11:* 146
Johnson, Chuck. *See* Johnson,
   Charles R., *11:* 146
Johnson, Crockett. *See* Leisk,
   David Johnson, *1:* 141
Johnson, Dorothy M., *6:* 123
Johnson, Edgar Raymond, *2:* 157
Johnson, Elizabeth, *7:* 144
Johnson, Eric W(arner), *8:* 91
Johnson, Gaylord, *7:* 146
Johnson, James Ralph, *1:* 126
Johnson, LaVerne B(ravo), *13:* 108
Johnson, Lois S(mith), *6:* 123
Johnson, of Boone, Benj. F. *See*
   Riley, James Whitcomb,
   17: 159
Johnson, (Walter) Ryerson, *10:* 58
Johnson, Shirley K(ing), *10:* 59
Johnson, William Weber, *7:* 147
Johnston, Agnes Christine. *See*
   Dazey, Agnes J., *2:* 88
Johnston, H(ugh) A(nthony)
   S(tephen), *14:* 87
Johnston, Johanna, *12:* 115
Johnston, Portia. *See* Takakjian,
   Portia, *15:* 273
Johnston, Tony, *8:* 94
Jones, Adrienne, *7:* 147
Jones, Diana Wynne, *9:* 116
Jones, Elizabeth Orton, *18:* 123
Jones, Evan, *3:* 90

Jones, Gillingham. *See* Hamilton,
   Charles Harold St. John, *13:* 77
Jones, Harold, *14:* 87
Jones, Hortense P., *9:* 118
Jones, Mary Alice, *6:* 125
Jones, Weyman, *4:* 130
Jonk, Clarence, *10:* 59
Jordan, Hope (Dahle), *15:* 150
Jordan, June, *4:* 131
Jordan, Mildred, *5:* 91
Jorgenson, Ivar. *See* Silverberg,
   Robert, *13:* 206
Joslin, Sesyle, *2:* 158
Joyce, J(ames) Avery, *11:* 147
Jucker, Sita, *5:* 92
Judd, Frances K. [Collective
   pseudonym], *1:* 127
Jumpp, Hugo. *See* MacPeek,
   Walter G., *4:* 148
Jupo, Frank J., *7:* 148
Juster, Norton, *3:* 91
Justus, May, *1:* 127

Kabdebo, Tamas. *See* Kabdebo,
   Thomas, *10:* 60
Kabdebo, Thomas, *10:* 60
Kakimoto, Kozo, *11:* 147
Kalashnikoff, Nicholas, *16:* 173
Kaler, James Otis, *15:* 151
Kalnay, Francis, *7:* 149
Kamen, Gloria, *9:* 118
Kane, Henry Bugbee, *14:* 91
Kane, Robert W., *18:* 131
Kaplan, Irma, *10:* 61
Kaplan, Jean Caryl Korn, *10:* 62
Karen, Ruth, *9:* 120
Kark, Nina Mary, *4:* 132
Karlin, Eugene, *10:* 62
Karp, Naomi J., *16:* 174
Kashiwagi, Isami, *10:* 64
Kästner, Erich, *14:* 91
Katchen, Carole, *9:* 122
Kathryn. *See* Searle, Kathryn
   Adrienne, *10:* 143
Katz, Bobbi, *12:* 116
Katz, Fred, *6:* 126
Katz, William Loren, *13:* 109
Kaufman, Mervyn D., *4:* 133
Kaufmann, Angelika, *15:* 155
Kaufmann, John, *18:* 132
Kaula, Edna Mason, *13:* 110
Kay, Helen. *See* Goldfrank, Helen
   Colodny, *6:* 89
Kay, Mara, *13:* 111
Kaye, Geraldine, *10:* 64
Keane, Bil, *4:* 134
Keating, Bern. *See* Keating, Leo
   Bernard, *10:* 65
Keating, Leo Bernard, *10:* 65
Keats, Ezra Jack, *14:* 99
Keegan, Marcia, *9:* 121
Keen, Martin L., *4:* 135
Keene, Carolyn. *See* Adams,
   Harriet S., *1:* 1

Keeping, Charles (William James),
   9: 123
Keir, Christine. *See* Pullein-
   Thompson, Christine, *3:* 164
Keith, Carlton. *See* Robertson,
   Keith, *1:* 184
Keith, Harold (Verne), *2:* 159
Kelen, Emery, *13:* 114
Keller, B(everly) L(ou), *13:* 115
Keller, Charles, *8:* 94
Keller, Gail Faithfull. *See*
   Faithfull, Gail, *8:* 55
Kellin, Sally Moffet, *9:* 125
Kellogg, Gene. *See* Kellogg, Jean,
   10: 66
Kellogg, Jean, *10:* 66
Kellogg, Steven, *8:* 95
Kellow, Kathleen. *See* Hibbert,
   Eleanor, *2:* 134
Kelly, Eric P(hilbrook),
   YABC 1: 165
Kelly, Ralph. *See* Geis, Darlene,
   7: 101
Kelly, Regina Z., *5:* 94
Kelly, Walt(er Crawford), *18:* 135
Kelsey, Alice Geer, *1:* 129
Kempner, Mary Jean, *10:* 67
Kempton, Jean Welch, *10:* 67
Kendall, Carol (Seeger), *11:* 148
Kendall, Lace. *See* Stoutenburg,
   Adrien, *3:* 217
Kennedy, John Fitzgerald, *11:* 150
Kennedy, Joseph, *14:* 104
Kennedy, X. J. *See* Kennedy,
   Joseph, *14:* 104
Kennell, Ruth E., *6:* 127
Kenny, Herbert A(ndrew), *13:* 117
Kent, Margaret, *2:* 161
Kent, Rockwell, *6:* 128
Kenworthy, Leonard S., *6:* 131
Kenyon, Ley, *6:* 131
Kepes, Juliet A(ppleby), *13:* 118
Kerigan, Florence, *12:* 117
Kerr, Jessica, *13:* 119
Kerry, Frances. *See* Kerigan,
   Florence, *12:* 117
Kerry, Lois. *See* Arquette, Lois
   S., *1:* 13
Kessler, Leonard P., *14:* 106
Kesteven, G. R. *See* Crosher,
   G(eoffry) R(obins), *14:* 51
Kettelkamp, Larry, *2:* 163
Key, Alexander (Hill), *8:* 98
Khanshendel, Chiron. *See* Rose,
   Wendy, *12:* 180
Kherdian, David, *16:* 175
Kiddell, John, *3:* 93
Killilea, Marie (Lyons), *2:* 165
Kilreon, Beth. *See* Walker,
   Barbara K., *4:* 219
Kimbrough, Emily, *2:* 166
Kimmel, Eric A., *13:* 120
Kindred, Wendy, *7:* 150
Kines, Pat Decker, *12:* 118
King, Arthur. *See* Cain, Arthur H.,
   3: 33

King, Billie Jean, *12:* 119
King, Cynthia, *7:* 152
King, Martin. *See* Marks,
    Stan(ley), *14:* 136
King, Martin Luther, Jr., *14:* 108
King, Reefe. *See* Barker, Albert
    W., *8:* 3
King, Stephen, *9:* 126
Kingman, (Mary) Lee, *1:* 133
Kingsland, Leslie William, *13:* 121
Kingsley, Charles, *YABC 2:* 179
Kinney, C. Cle, *6:* 132
Kinney, Harrison, *13:* 122
Kinney, Jean Stout, *12:* 120
Kinsey, Elizabeth. *See* Clymer,
    Eleanor, *9:* 37
Kipling, (Joseph) Rudyard,
    YABC 2: 193
Kirk, Ruth (Kratz), *5:* 95
Kirkup, James, *12:* 120
Kirtland, G. B. *See* Joslin, Sesyle,
    2: 158
Kishida, Eriko, *12:* 123
Kisinger, Grace Gelvin, *10:* 68
Kissin, Eva H., *10:* 68
Kjelgaard, James Arthur, *17:* 88
Kjelgaard, Jim. *See* Kjelgaard,
    James Arthur, *17:* 88
Klass, Morton, *11:* 152
Kleberger, Ilse, *5:* 96
Klein, H. Arthur, *8:* 99
Klein, Leonore, *6:* 132
Klein, Mina C(ooper), *8:* 100
Klein, Norma, *7:* 152
Klimowicz, Barbara, *10:* 69
Knickerbocker, Diedrich. *See*
    Irving, Washington,
    YABC 2: 164
Knight, Damon, *9:* 126
Knight, David C(arpenter), *14:* 111
Knight, Eric (Mowbray), *18:* 151
Knight, Francis Edgar, *14:* 112
Knight, Frank. *See* Knight,
    Francis Edgar, *14:* 112
Knight, Hilary, *15:* 157
Knight, Mallory T. *See* Hurwood,
    Bernhardt J., *12:* 107
Knott, Bill. *See* Knott, William
    Cecil, Jr., *3:* 94
Knott, William Cecil, Jr., *3:* 94
Knowles, John, *8:* 101
Knox, Calvin. *See* Silverberg,
    Robert, *13:* 206
Knudson, R. R. *See* Knudson,
    Rozanne, *7:* 154
Knudson, Rozanne, *7:* 154
Koch, Dorothy Clarke, *6:* 133
Kohn, Bernice (Herstein), *4:* 136
Kohner, Frederick, *10:* 70
Komisar, Lucy, *9:* 127
Komoda, Kiyo, *9:* 127
Komroff, Manuel, *2:* 168
Konigsburg, E(laine) L(obl), *4:* 137
Koning, Hans. *See* Koningsberger,
    Hans, *5:* 97
Koningsberger, Hans, *5:* 97

Konkle, Janet Everest, *12:* 124
Korach, Mimi, *9:* 128
Koren, Edward, *5:* 98
Korinetz, Yuri (Iosifovich), *9:* 129
Korty, Carol, *15:* 159
Kossin, Sandy (Sanford), *10:* 71
Koutoukas, H. M.. *See* Rivoli,
    Mario, *10:* 129
Kouts, Anne, *8:* 103
Krantz, Hazel (Newman), *12:* 126
Krasilovsky, Phyllis, *1:* 134
Kraus, Robert, *4:* 139
Krauss, Ruth, *1:* 135
Krautter, Elisa. *See* Bialk, Elisa,
    1: 25
Kredel, Fritz, *17:* 92
Krementz, Jill, *17:* 96
Kristof, Jane, *8:* 104
Kroeber, Theodora (Kracaw),
    1: 136
Kroll, Francis Lynde, *10:* 72
Krumgold, Joseph, *1:* 136
Krush, Beth, *18:* 162
Krush, Joe, *18:* 163
Krüss, James, *8:* 104
Kubinyi, Laszlo, *17:* 99
Kumin, Maxine (Winokur), *12:* 127
Künstler, Morton, *10:* 73
Kuratomi, Chizuko, *12:* 128
Kurelek, William, *8:* 106
Kurland, Gerald, *13:* 123
Kuskin, Karla (Seidman), *2:* 169
Kuttner, Paul, *18:* 165
Kvale, Velma R(uth), *8:* 108
Kyle, Elisabeth. *See* Dunlop,
    Agnes M. R., *3:* 62

Lacy, Leslie Alexander, *6:* 135
Lader, Lawrence, *6:* 135
Lady of Quality, A. *See* Bagnold,
    Enid, *1:* 17
La Farge, Phyllis, *14:* 113
La Fontaine, Jean de, *18:* 166
Lagerlöf, Selma (Ottiliana Lovisa),
    15: 160
Laimgruber, Monika, *11:* 153
Laklan, Carli, *5:* 100
la Mare, Walter de. *See* de la
    Mare, Walter, *16:* 73
Lamb, Charles, *17:* 101
Lamb, G(eoffrey) F(rederick),
    10: 74
Lamb, Lynton, *10:* 75
Lamb, Mary Ann, *17:* 112
Lamb, Robert (Boyden), *13:* 123
Lamburn, Richmal Crompton,
    5: 101
Lamplugh, Lois, *17:* 116
Lampman, Evelyn Sibley, *4:* 140
Lamprey, Louise, *YABC 2:* 221
Lancaster, Bruce, *9:* 130
Land, Barbara (Neblett), *16:* 177

Land, Jane [Joint pseudonym] *See*
    Borland, Kathryn Kilby,
    16: 54. *See* Speicher, Helen
    Ross (Smith), *8:* 194
Land, Myrick (Ebben), *15:* 174
Land, Ross [Joint pseudonym].
    See Borland, Kathryn Kilby,
    16: 54. *See* Speicher, Helen
    Ross (Smith), *8:* 194
Landau, Elaine, *10:* 75
Landeck, Beatrice, *15:* 175
Landin, Les(lie), *2:* 171
Landshoff, Ursula, *13:* 124
Lane, Carolyn, *10:* 76
Lane, John, *15:* 175
Lanes, Selma G., *3:* 96
Lang, Andrew, *16:* 178
Lange, John. *See* Crichton, (J.)
    Michael, *9:*
Lange, Suzanne, *5:* 103
Langner, Nola, *8:* 110
Langstaff, John, *6:* 135
Langstaff, Launcelot. *See* Irving,
    Washington, *YABC 2:* 164
Langton, Jane, *3:* 97
Lanier, Sidney, *18:* 176
Larrick, Nancy G., *4:* 141
Larsen, Egon, *14:* 115
Larson, Eve. *See* St. John, Wylly
    Folk, *10:* 132
Larson, William H., *10:* 77
Lasher, Faith B., *12:* 129
Lasker, Joe, *9:* 131
Lasky, Kathryn, *13:* 124
Lassalle, C. E. *See* Ellis, Edward
    S(ylvester), *YABC 1:* 116
Latham, Barbara, *16:* 187
Latham, Frank B., *6:* 137
Latham, Jean Lee, *2:* 171
Latham, Mavis. *See* Clark, Mavis
    Thorpe, *8:* 27
Latham, Philip. *See* Richardson,
    Robert S(hirley), *8:* 164
Lathrop, Dorothy P(ulis), *14:* 116
Lattimore, Eleanor Frances, *7:* 155
Lauber, Patricia (Grace), *1:* 138
Laugesen, Mary E(akin), *5:* 104
Laughbaum, Steve, *12:* 131
Laughlin, Florence, *3:* 98
Laurence, Ester Hauser, *7:* 156
Lauritzen, Jonreed, *13:* 125
Lavine, Sigmund A., *3:* 100
Lawrence, Louise de Kiriline,
    13: 126
Lawrence, Mildred, *3:* 101
Lawson, Don(ald Elmer), *9:* 132
Lawson, Robert, *YABC 2:* 222
Laycock, George (Edwin) *5:* 105
Lazarevich, Mila, *17:* 118
Leacroft, Helen, *6:* 139
Leacroft, Richard, *6:* 139
Lear, Edward, *18:* 182
LeCain, Errol, *6:* 141
Lee, Carol. *See* Fletcher, Helen
    Jill, *13:* 36
Lee, Dennis (Beynon), *14:* 120

Lee, (Nelle) Harper, *11:* 154
Lee, Mary Price, *8:* 111
Lee, Mildred, *6:* 142
Lee, Robert J., *10:* 77
Lee, Tanith, *8:* 112
Lefler, Irene (Whitney), *12:* 131
Le Gallienne, Eva, *9:* 133
LeGrand. *See* Henderson,
    LeGrand, *9:* 104
Le Guin, Ursula K(roeber), *4:* 142
Legum, Colin, *10:* 78
Lehr, Delores, *10:* 79
Leichman, Seymour, *5:* 106
Leighton, Margaret, *1:* 140
Leipold, L. Edmond, *16:* 189
Leisk, David Johnson, *1:* 141
Leitch, Patricia, *11:* 155
L'Engle, Madeleine, *1:* 141
Lengyel, Emil, *3:* 102
Lens, Sidney, *13:* 127
Lenski, Lois, *1:* 142
Lent, Blair, *2:* 172
Lent, Henry Bolles, *17:* 119
Leodhas, Sorche Nic. *See* Alger,
    Leclaire (Gowans), *15:* 1
Leong Gor Yun. *See* Ellison,
    Virginia Howell, *4:* 74
Lerner, Marguerite Rush, *11:* 156
Lerner, Sharon (Ruth), *11:* 157
LeSieg, Theo. *See* Geisel, Theodor
    Seuss, *1:* 104
Leslie, Robert Franklin, *7:* 158
Lester, Julius B., *12:* 132
Le Sueur, Meridel, *6:* 143
Levin, Marcia Obrasky, *13:* 128
Levine, I(srael) E., *12:* 134
Levine, Joan Goldman, *11:* 157
Levine, Rhoda, *14:* 122
Levitin, Sonia, *4:* 144
Lewis, C(live) S(taples), *13:* 129
Lewis, Claudia (Louise), *5:* 107
Lewis, Elizabeth Foreman,
    YABC 2: 243
Lewis, Francine. *See* Wells,
    Helen, *2:* 266
Lewis, Lucia Z. *See* Anderson,
    Lucia (Lewis), *10:* 4
Lewis, Richard, *3:* 104
Lewiton, Mina, *2:* 174
Lexau, Joan M., *1:* 144
Ley, Willy, *2:* 175
Libby, Bill. *See* Libby, William
    M., *5:* 109
Libby, William M., *5:* 109
Liberty, Gene, *3:* 106
Liebers, Arthur, *12:* 134
Lietz, Gerald S., *11:* 159
Lifton, Betty Jean, *6:* 143
Lightner, A. M. *See* Hopf, Alice
    L. *5:* 82
Limburg, Peter R(ichard), *13:* 147
Lincoln, C(harles) Eric, *5:* 111
Linde, Gunnel, *5:* 112
Lindgren, Astrid, *2:* 177
Lindop, Edmund, *5:* 113
Lindquist, Jennie Dorothea, *13:* 148

Lingard, Joan, *8:* 113
Lionni, Leo, *8:* 114
Lipkind, William, *15:* 178
Lipman, Matthew, *14:* 122
Lippincott, Joseph Wharton,
    17: 120
Lipsyte, Robert, *5:* 114
Lisle, Seward D. *See* Ellis,
    Edward S(ylvester),
    YABC 1: 116
Liss, Howard, *4:* 145
List, Ilka Katherine, *6:* 145
Liston, Robert A., *5:* 114
Litchfield, Ada B(assett), *5:* 115
Little, (Flora), Jean, *2:* 178
Littledale, Freya (Lota), *2:* 179
Lively, Penelope, *7:* 159
Liversidge, (Henry) Douglas, *8:* 116
Livingston, Myra Cohn, *5:* 116
Livingston, Richard R(oland),
    8: 118
Llewellyn Lloyd, Richard Dafydd
    Vyvyan, *11:* 160
Llewellyn, Richard. *See* Llewellyn
    Lloyd, Richard Dafydd
    Vyvyan, *11:* 160
Llewellyn, T. Harcourt. *See*
    Hamilton, Charles Harold St.
    John, *13:* 77
Lloyd, (Mary) Norris, *10:* 79
Lobel, Anita, *6:* 146
Lobel, Arnold, *6:* 147
Lobsenz, Amelia, *12:* 135
Lobsenz, Norman M., *6:* 148
Lochlons, Colin. *See* Jackson, C.
    Paul, *6:* 120
Locke, Clinton W. [Collective
    pseudonym], *1:* 145
Locke, Lucie, *10:* 81
Löfgren, Ulf, *3:* 106
Loeper, John J(oseph), *10:* 81
Lofting, Hugh, *15:* 180
Lofts, Norah (Robinson), *8:* 119
Lomas, Steve. *See* Brennan,
    Joseph L., *6:* 33
London, Jack, *18:* 195
London, Jane. *See* Geis, Darlene,
    7: 101
London, John Griffith. *See*
    London, Jack, *18:* 195
Lonergan, (Pauline) Joy (Maclean),
    10: 82
Long, Helen Beecher [Collective
    pseudonym], *1:* 146
Longman, Harold S., *5:* 117
Longtemps, Kenneth, *17:* 123
Longway, A. Hugh. *See* Lang,
    Andrew, *16:* 178
Loomis, Robert D., *5:* 119
Lopshire, Robert, *6:* 149
Lord, Beman, *5:* 119
Lord, (Doreen Mildred) Douglas,
    12: 136
Lord, Nancy. *See* Titus, Eve,
    2: 240
Lord, Walter, *3:* 109

Lorraine, Walter (Henry), *16:* 191
Loss, Joan, *11:* 162
Lot, Parson. *See* Kingsley,
    Charles, *YABC 2:* 179
Lourie, Helen. *See* Storr,
    Catherine (Cole), *9:* 181
Love, Katherine, *3:* 109
Lovelace, Delos Wheeler, *7:* 160
Lovelace, Maud Hart, *2:* 181
Low, Alice, *11:* 163
Low, Elizabeth Hammond, *5:* 120
Low, Joseph, *14:* 123
Lowe, Jay, Jr.. *See* Loper, John
    J(oseph), *10:* 81
Lowenstein, Dyno, *6:* 150
Lowitz, Anson C., *18:* 214
Lowitz, Sadyebeth (Heath), *17:* 125
Lowry, Peter, *7:* 160
Lubell, Cecil, *6:* 150
Lubell, Winifred, *6:* 151
Luckhardt, Mildred Corell, *5:* 122
Ludlum, Mabel Cleland. *See*
    Widdemer, Mabel Cleland,
    5: 200
Lueders, Edward (George), *14:* 125
Luhrmann, Winifred B(ruce),
    11: 165
Luis, Earlene W., *11:* 165
Lum, Peter. *See* Crowe, Bettina
    Lum, *6:* 53
Lund, Doris (Herold), *12:* 137
Lunn, Janet, *4:* 146
Lutzker, Edythe, *5:* 124
Luzzati, Emanuele, *7:* 161
Lydon, Michael, *11:* 165
Lyle, Katie Letcher, *8:* 121
Lynch, Lorenzo, *7:* 161
Lynch, Patricia, *6:* 153
Lynch, Patricia (Nora), *9:* 134
Lynn, Mary. *See* Brokamp,
    Marilyn, *10:* 15
Lynn, Patricia. *See* Watts, Mabel
    Pizzey, *11:* 227
Lyon, Elinor, *6:* 154
Lyon, Lyman R. *See* De Camp,
    L(yon) Sprague, *9:* 49
Lyons, Dorothy, *3:* 110
Lystad, Mary (Hanemann), *11:* 166

Maas, Selve, *14:* 127
MacBeth, George, *4:* 146
MacClintock, Dorcas, *8:* 122
MacDonald, Anson. *See* Heinlein,
    Robert A(nson), *9:* 102
MacDonald, Betty (Campbell
    Bard), *YABC 1:* 167
Macdonald, Blackie. *See* Emrich,
    Duncan, *11:* 90
Mac Donald, Golden. *See* Brown,
    Margaret Wise, *YABC 2:* 9
Macdonald, Marcia. *See* Hill,
    Grace Livingston, *YABC 2:* 162
Macdonald, Zillah K(atherine),
    11: 167

MacFarlane, Iris, *11:* 170
MacGregor-Hastie, Roy, *3:* 111
MacIntyre, Elisabeth, *17:* 125
Mack, Stan(ley), *17:* 128
MacKellar, William, *4:* 148
Mackenzie, Dr. Willard. *See*
   Stratemeyer, Edward L.,
   1: 208
MacLeod, Beatrice (Beach), *10:* 82
MacLeod, Ellen Jane (Anderson),
   14: 129
MacMillan, Annabelle. *See* Quick,
   Annabelle, *2:* 207
MacPeek, Walter G., *4:* 148
MacPherson, Margaret, *9:* 135
Macrae, Hawk. *See* Barker, Albert
   W., *8:* 3
MacRae, Travis. *See* Feagles,
   Anita (MacRae), *9:* 63
Macumber, Mari. *See* Sandoz,
   Mari, *5:* 159
Madden, Don, *3:* 112
Maddison, Angela Mary, *10:* 82
Maddock, Reginald, *15:* 184
Madian, Jon, *9:* 136
Madison, Arnold, *6:* 155
Madison, Winifred, *5:* 125
Maestro, Giulio, *8:* 123
Maher, Ramona, *13:* 149
Mahon, Julia C(unha), *11:* 171
Mahony, Elizabeth Winthrop,
   8: 125
Mahy, Margaret, *14:* 129
Maidoff, Ilka List. *See* List, Ilka
   Katherine, *6:* 145
Maik, Henri. *See* Hecht, Henri
   Joseph, *9:* 101
Malcolmson, Anne. *See* Storch,
   Anne B. von, *1:* 221
Malcolmson, David, *6:* 157
Malmberg, Carl, *9:* 136
Malo, John, *4:* 149
Manchel, Frank, *10:* 83
Mangione, Jerre, *6:* 157
Mangurian, David, *14:* 131
Maniscalco, Joseph, *10:* 85
Manley, Seon, *15:* 185
Mann, Peggy, *6:* 157
Mannheim, Grete (Salomon), *10:* 85
Manning, Rosemary, *10:* 87
Manning-Sanders, Ruth, *15:* 186
Manton, Jo. *See* Gittings, Jo
   Manton, *3:* 76
Manushkin, Fran, *7:* 161
Mapes, Mary A. *See* Ellison,
   Virginia Howell, *4:* 74
Mara, Jeanette. *See* Cebulash,
   Mel, *10:* 19
Marasmus, Seymour. *See* Rivoli,
   Mario, *10:* 129
Marcellino. *See* Agnew, Edith J.,
   11: 3
Marchant, Bessie, *YABC 2:* 245
Marchant, Catherine. *See*
   Cookson, Catherine
   (McMullen), *9:* 42

Marcher, Marion Walden, *10:* 87
Marcus, Rebecca B(rian), *9:* 138
Margolis, Richard J(ules), *4:* 150
Marino, Dorothy Bronson, *14:* 134
Mark, Pauline (Dahlin), *14:* 136
Mark, Polly. *See* Mark, Pauline
   (Dahlin), *14:* 136
Markins, W. S. *See* Jenkins, Marie
   M., *7:* 143
Marks, J(ames) M(acdonald),
   13: 150
Marks, Mickey Klar, *12:* 139
Marks, Peter. *See* Smith, Robert
   Kimmel, *12:* 205
Marks, Stan(ley), *14:* 136
Markun, Patricia M(aloney),
   15: 189
Marlowe, Amy Bell [Collective
   pseudonym], *1:* 146
Marokvia, Mireille (Journet), *5:* 126
Mars, W. T. *See* Mars, Witold
   Tadeusz, J., *3:* 114
Mars, Witold Tadeusz, J., *3:* 114
Marsh, J. E. *See* Marshall, Evelyn,
   11: 172
Marsh, Jean. *See* Marshall,
   Evelyn, *11:* 172
Marshall, Anthony D(ryden),
   18: 215
Marshall, (Sarah) Catherine, *2:* 182
Marshall, Douglas. *See*
   McClintock, Marshall, *3:* 119
Marshall, Evelyn, *11:* 172
Marshall, James, *6:* 161
Martin, Eugene [Collective
   pseudonym], *1:* 146
Martin, Fredric. *See* Christopher,
   Matt, *2:* 58
Martin, J(ohn) P(ercival), *15:* 190
Martin, Jeremy. *See* Levin, Marcia
   Obransky, *13:* 128
Martin, Marcia. *See* Levin, Marcia
   Obransky, *13:* 128
Martin, Nancy. *See* Salmon, Annie
   Elizabeth, *13:* 188
Martin, Patricia Miles, *1:* 146
Martin, Peter. *See* Chaundler,
   Christine, *1:* 56
Martin, Vicky. *See* Storey,
   Victoria Carolyn, *16:* 248
Martineau, Harriet, *YABC 2:* 247
Martini, Teri, *3:* 116
Marzani, Carl (Aldo), *12:* 140
Mason, F. van Wyck, *3:* 117
Mason, Frank W. *See* Mason, F.
   van Wyck, *3:* 117
Mason, George Frederick, *14:* 138
Mason, Miriam E(vangeline), *2:* 183
Mason, Tally. *See* Derleth, August
   (William), *5:* 54
Mason, Van Wyck. *See* Mason, F.
   van Wyck, *3:* 117
Massie, Diane Redfield, *16:* 193
Masters, Kelly R., *3:* 118
Masters, William. *See* Cousins,
   Margaret, *2:* 79

Mathis, Sharon Bell, *7:* 162
Matson, Emerson N(els), *12:* 141
Matsui, Tadashi, *8:* 126
Matsuno, Masako, *6:* 161
Matus, Greta, *12:* 142
Maves, Mary Carolyn, *10:* 88
Maves, Paul B(enjamin), *10:* 88
Mawicke, Tran, *15:* 190
Maxon, Anne. *See* Best, Allena
   Champlin, *2:* 25
Maxwell, Arthur S., *11:* 173
Maxwell, Edith, *7:* 164
May, Charles Paul, *4:* 151
May, Julian, *11:* 175
Mayberry, Florence V(irginia
   Wilson), *10:* 89
Mayer, Ann M(argaret), *14:* 140
Mayer, Mercer, *16:* 195
Mayne, William, *6:* 162
Mays, (Lewis) Victor, (Jr.), *5:* 126
McCaffrey, Anne, *8:* 127
McCain, Murray, *7:* 165
McCall, Edith S., *6:* 163
McCall, Virginia Nielsen, *13:* 151
McCallum, Phyllis, *10:* 90
McCarthy, Agnes, *4:* 152
McCarty, Rega Kramer, *10:* 91
McCaslin, Nellie, *12:* 143
McClintock, Marshall, *3:* 119
McClintock, Mike. *See*
   McClintock, Marshall, *3:* 119
McClintock, Theodore, *14:* 140
McClinton, Leon, *11:* 178
McCloskey, Robert, *2:* 185
McClung, Robert M., *2:* 188
McCord, David (Thompson
   Watson), *18:* 217
McCormick, (George) Donald
   (King), *14:* 141
McCoy, Iola Fuller, *3:* 120
McCoy, J(oseph) J(erome), *8:* 127
McCrady, Lady, *16:* 197
McCrea, James, *3:* 121
McCrea, Ruth, *3:* 121
McCullough, Frances Monson,
   8: 129
McCully, Emily Arnold, *5:* 128
McCurdy, Michael, *13:* 153
McDermott, Beverly Brodsky,
   11: 179
McDermott, Gerald, *16:* 199
McDole, Carol. *See* Farley, Carol,
   4: 81
McDonald, Gerald D., *3:* 123
McDonald, Jill (Masefield), *13:* 154
McDonald, Lucile Saunders, *10:* 92
McDonnell, Lois Eddy, *10:* 94
McFall, Christie, *12:* 144
McFarland, Kenton D(ean), *11:* 180
McGaw, Jessie Brewer, *10:* 95
McGee, Barbara, *6:* 165
McGiffin, (Lewis) Lee (Shaffer),
   1: 148
McGinley, Phyllis, *2:* 190
McGovern, Ann, *8:* 130
McGowen, Thomas E., *2:* 192

McGowen, Tom. *See* McGowen, Thomas, *2:* 192
McGrady, Mike, *6:* 166
McGraw, Eloise Jarvis, *1:* 149
McGraw, William Corbin, *3:* 124
McGregor, Craig, *8:* 131
McGuire, Edna, *13:* 155
McHargue, Georgess, *4:* 152
McIlwraith, Maureen, *2:* 193
McKay, Robert W., *15:* 192
McKown, Robin, *6:* 166
McLean, Kathryn (Anderson), *9:* 140
McMeekin, Clark. *See* McMeekin, Isable McLennan, *3:* 126
McMeekin, Isabel McLennan, *3:* 126
McMullen, Catherine. *See* Cookson, Catherine (McMullen), *9:* 42
McNair, Kate, *3:* 127
McNeer, May, *1:* 150
McNeill, Janet, *1:* 151
McNulty, Faith, *12:* 144
McPherson, James M., *16:* 202
McQueen, Mildred Hark, *12:* 145
Mead, Russell (M., Jr.), *10:* 96
Meade, Ellen (Roddick), *5:* 130
Meader, Stephen W(arren), *1:* 153
Meadowcroft, Enid LaMonte. *See* Wright, Enid Meadowcroft, *3:* 267
Means, Florence Crannell, *1:* 154
Medary, Marjorie, *14:* 143
Medearis, Mary, *5:* 130
Mee, Charles L., Jr., *8:* 132
Meeker, Oden, *14:* 144
Meeks, Esther MacBain, *1:* 155
Mehdevi, Alexander, *7:* 166
Mehdevi, Anne (Marie) Sinclair, *8:* 132
Meigs, Cornelia Lynde, *6:* 167
Melcher, Marguerite Fellows, *10:* 96
Melin, Grace Hathaway, *10:* 96
Mellersh, H(arold) E(dward) L(eslie), *10:* 97
Meltzer, Milton, *1:* 156
Melzack, Ronald, *5:* 130
Memling, Carl, *6:* 169
Mendel, Jo. [House pseudonym]. *See* Bond, Gladys Baker, *14:* 41
Meng, Heinz (Karl), *13:* 157
Mercer, Charles (Edward), *16:* 203
Meredith, David William. *See* Miers, Earl Schenck, *1:* 160
Merriam, Eve, *3:* 128
Merrill, Jean (Fairbanks), *1:* 158
Metcalf, Suzanne. *See* Baum, L(yman) Frank, *18:* 7
Meyer, Carolyn, *9:* 140
Meyer, Edith Patterson, *5:* 131
Meyer, F(ranklyn) E(dward), *9:* 142
Meyer, Jean Shepherd, *11:* 181
Meyer, Jerome Sydney, *3:* 129

Meyer, June. *See* Jordan, June, *4:* 131
Meyer, Louis A(lbert), *12:* 147
Meyer, Renate, *6:* 170
Meynier, Yvonne (Pollet), *14:* 146
Micklish, Rita, *12:* 147
Miers, Earl Schenck, *1:* 160
Miklowitz, Gloria D., *4:* 154
Mikolaycak, Charles, *9:* 143
Miles, Betty, *8:* 132
Miles, Miska. *See* Martin, Patricia Miles, *1:* 146
Milhous, Katherine, *15:* 192
Militant. *See* Sandburg, Carl (August), *8:* 177
Millar, Barbara F., *12:* 149
Miller, Albert G(riffith), *12:* 150
Miller, Don, *15:* 194
Miller, Eddie. *See* Miller, Edward, *8:* 134
Miller, Edward, *8:* 134
Miller, Helen M(arkley), *5:* 133
Miller, Jane (Judith), *15:* 196
Miller, John. *See* Samachson, Joseph, *3:* 182
Miller, Mary Beth, *9:* 145
Milne, A(lan) A(lexander), *YABC 1:* 174
Milne, Lorus J., *5:* 133
Milne, Margery, *5:* 134
Milotte, Alfred G(eorge), *11:* 181
Minarik, Else Holmelund, *15:* 197
Miner, Lewis S., *11:* 183
Minier, Nelson. *See* Stoutenburg, Adrien, *3:* 217
Mintonye, Grace, *4:* 156
Mirsky, Jeannette, *8:* 135
Mirsky, Reba Paeff, *1:* 161
Miskovits, Christine, *10:* 98
Miss Francis. *See* Horwich, Francis R., *11:* 142
Miss Read. *See* Saint, Dora Jessie, *10:* 132
Mitchell, (Sibyl) Elyne (Keith), *10:* 98
Mizumura, Kazue, *18:* 222
Moffett, Martha (Leatherwood), *8:* 136
Mohn, Viola Kohl, *8:* 138
Mohr, Nicholasa, *8:* 138
Molarsky, Osmond, *16:* 204
Molloy, Paul, *5:* 135
Monjo, F(erdinand) N., *16:* 206
Monroe, Lyle. *See* Heinlein, Robert A(nson), *9:* 102
Montgomery, Elizabeth Rider, *3:* 132
Montgomery, L(ucy) M(aud), *YABC 1:* 182
Montgomery, Rutherford George, *3:* 134
Montresor, Beni, *3:* 136
Moody, Ralph Owen, *1:* 162
Moon, Sheila (Elizabeth), *5:* 136
Moore, Anne Carroll, *13:* 158
Moore, Clement Clarke, *18:* 224

Moore, Fenworth. *See* Stratemeyer, Edward L., *1:* 208
Moore, Janet Gaylord, *18:* 236
Moore, John Travers, *12:* 151
Moore, Margaret Rumberger, *12:* 154
Moore, Regina. *See* Dunne, Mary Collins, *11:* 83
Moore, Rosalie. *See* Brown, Rosalie (Gertrude) Moore, *9:* 26
Mordvinoff, Nicolas, *17:* 129
More, Caroline. *See* Cone, Molly Lamken, *1:* 66
More, Caroline. *See* Strachan, Margaret Pitcairn, *14:* 193
Morey, Charles. *See* Fletcher, Helen Jill, *13:* 36
Morey, Walt, *3:* 139
Morgan, Lenore, *8:* 139
Morgan, Shirley, *10:* 99
Morrah, Dave. *See* Morrah, David Wardlaw, Jr., *10:* 100
Morrah, David Wardlaw, Jr., *10:* 100
Morris, Desmond (John), *14:* 146
Morris, Robert A., *7:* 166
Morrison, Gert W. *See* Stratemeyer, Edward L., *1:* 208
Morrison, Lillian, *3:* 140
Morrison, Lucile Phillips, *17:* 134
Morrison, William. *See* Samachson, Joseph, *3:* 182
Morriss, James E(dward), *8:* 139
Morrow, Betty. *See* Bacon, Elizabeth, *3:* 14
Morton, Miriam, *9:* 145
Moscow, Alvin, *3:* 142
Mosel, Arlene, *7:* 167
Moss, Don(ald), *11:* 183
Mountfield, David. *See* Grant, Neil, *14:* 75
Mowat, Farley, *3:* 142
Mulcahy, Lucille Burnett, *12:* 155
Muller, Billex. *See* Ellis, Edward S(ylvester), *YABC 1:* 116
Mullins, Edward S(wift), *10:* 101
Mulvihill, William Patrick, *8:* 140
Munari, Bruno, *15:* 199
Munce, Ruth Hill, *12:* 156
Munowitz, Ken, *14:* 149
Munson(-Benson), Tunie, *15:* 201
Munzer, Martha E., *4:* 157
Murphy, Barbara Beasley, *5:* 137
Murphy, E(mmett) Jefferson, *4:* 159
Murphy, Pat. *See* Murphy, E(mmett) Jefferson, *4:* 159
Murphy, Robert (William), *10:* 102
Murray, Marian, *5:* 138
Murray, Michele, *7:* 170
Musgrave, Florence, *3:* 144
Mussey, Virginia T. H. *See* Ellison, Virginia Howell, *4:* 74
Mutz. *See* Kunstler, Morton, *10:* 73

Myers, Bernice, 9: 146
Myers, Hortense (Powner), 10: 102

Nash, Linell. See Smith, Linell
    Nash, 2: 227
Nash, (Frediric) Ogden, 2: 194
Nast, Elsa Ruth. See Watson, Jane
    Werner, 3: 244
Nathan, Dorothy (Goldeen), 15: 202
Nathan, Robert, 6: 171
Navarra, John Gabriel, 8: 141
Naylor, Penelope, 10: 104
Naylor, Phyllis Reynolds, 12: 156
Nazaroff, Alexander I., 4: 160
Neal, Harry Edward, 5: 139
Nee, Kay Bonner, 10: 104
Needleman, Jacob, 6: 172
Negri, Rocco, 12: 157
Neigoff, Anne, 13: 165
Neigoff, Mike, 13: 166
Neilson, Frances Fullerton
    (Jones), 14: 149
Neimark, Anne E., 4: 160
Nelson, Esther L., 13: 167
Nesbit, E(dith), YABC 1: 193
Nesbit, Troy. See Folsom,
    Franklin, 5: 67
Nespojohn, Katherine V., 7: 170
Ness, Evaline (Michelow), 1: 165
Neufeld, John, 6: 173
Neumeyer, Peter F(lorian), 13: 168
Neurath, Marie (Reidemeister),
    1: 166
Neville, Emily Cheney, 1: 169
Neville, Mary. See Woodrich,
    Mary Neville, 2: 274
Newberry, Clare Turlay, 1: 170
Newell, Edythe W., 11: 185
Newlon, Clarke, 6: 174
Newman, Robert (Howard), 4: 161
Newman, Shirlee Petkin, 10: 105
Newton, Suzanne, 5: 140
Nic Leodhas, Sorche. See Alger,
    Leclaire (Gowans), 15: 1
Nichols, Cecilia Fawn, 12: 159
Nichols, (Joanna) Ruth, 15: 204
Nickelsburg, Janet, 11: 185
Nickerson, Betty. See Nickerson,
    Elizabeth, 14: 150
Nickerson, Elizabeth, 14: 150
Nicol, Ann. See Turnbull, Ann
    (Christine), 18: 281
Nicolas. See Mordvinoff, Nicolas,
    17: 129
Nicolay, Helen, YABC 1: 204
Nicole, Christopher Robin, 5: 141
Nielsen, Kay (Rasmus), 16: 210
Nielsen, Virginia. See McCall,
    Virginia Nielsen, 13: 151
Nixon, Joan Lowery, 8: 143
Nixon, K. See Nixon, Kathleen
    Irene (Blundell), 14: 152
Nixon, Kathleen Irene (Blundell),
    14: 152

Noble, Iris, 5: 142
Nodset, Joan M. See Lexau, Joan
    M., 1: 144
Nolan, Jeannette Covert, 2: 196
Noonan, Julia, 4: 163
Nordstrom, Ursula, 3: 144
North, Andrew. See Norton, Alice
    Mary, 1: 173
North, Captain George. See
    Stevenson, Robert Louis,
    YABC 2: 307
North, Joan, 16: 218
North, Robert. See Withers, Carl
    A., 14: 261
North, Sterling, 1: 171
Norton, Alice Mary, 1: 173
Norton, Andre. See Norton, Alice
    Mary, 1: 173
Norton, Browning. See Norton,
    Frank R(owland) B(rowning),
    10: 107
Norton, Frank R(owland)
    B(rowning), 10: 107
Norton, Mary, 18: 236
Nowell, Elizabeth Cameron,
    12: 160
Nussbaumer, Paul (Edmond),
    16: 218
Nye, Robert, 6: 174

Oakes, Vanya, 6: 175
Oakley, Don(ald G.), 8: 144
Oakley, Helen, 10: 107
Obrant, Susan, 11: 186
O'Carroll, Ryan. See Markun,
    Patricia M(aloney), 15: 189
O'Connell, Peg. See Ahern,
    Margaret McCrohan, 10: 2
O'Connor, Patrick. See Wibberley,
    Leonard, 2: 271
O'Dell, Scott, 12: 161
Odenwald, Robert P(aul), 11: 187
Oechsli, Kelly, 5: 143
Offit, Sidney, 10: 108
Ofosu-Appiah, L(awrence)
    H(enry), 13: 170
Ogan, George F., 13: 171
Ogan, M. G. [Joint pseudonym].
    See Ogan, George F. and
    Margaret E. (Nettles), 13: 171
Ogan, Margaret E. (Nettles),
    13: 171
Ogburn, Charlton, Jr., 3: 145
O'Hara, Mary. See Alsop, Mary
    O'Hara, 2: 4
Ohlsson, Ib, 7: 171
Olds, Elizabeth, 3: 146
Olds, Helen Diehl, 9: 148
Oldstyle, Jonathan. See Irving,
    Washington, YABC 2: 164
O'Leary, Brian, 6: 176
Olmstead, Lorena Ann, 13: 172
Olney, Ross R., 13: 173
Olschewski, Alfred, 7: 172

Olsen, Ib Spang, 6: 177
Olugebefola, Ademole, 15: 204
O'Neill, Mary L(e Duc), 2: 197
Opie, Iona, 3: 148
Opie, Peter, 3: 149
Oppenheim, Joanne, 5: 146
Orgel, Doris, 7: 173
Orleans, Ilo, 10: 110
Ormondroyd, Edward, 14: 153
Ormsby, Virginia H(aire), 11: 187
Osborne, Chester G., 11: 188
Osborne, David. See Silverberg,
    Robert, 13: 206
Osborne, Leone Neal, 2: 198
Osmond, Edward, 10: 110
Otis, James. See Kaler, James
    Otis, 15: 151
Ousley, Odille, 10: 111
Owen, Caroline Dale. See
    Snedecker, Caroline Dale
    (Parke), YABC 2: 296
Owen, Clifford. See Hamilton,
    Charles Harold St. John, 13: 77
Oxenbury, Helen, 3: 151

Page, Eileen. See Heal, Edith,
    7: 123
Page, Eleanor. See Coerr, Eleanor,
    1: 64
Pahz, (Anne) Cheryl Suzanne,
    11: 189
Pahz, James Alon, 11: 190
Paice, Margaret, 10: 111
Paine, Roberta M., 13: 174
Paisley, Tom. See Bethancourt, T.
    Ernesto, 11: 27
Palazzo, Anthony D., 3: 152
Palazzo, Tony. See Palazzo,
    Anthony D., 3: 152
Palder, Edward L., 5: 146
Palmer, C(yril) Everard, 14: 153
Palmer, (Ruth) Candida, 11: 191
Palmer, Heidi, 15: 206
Palmer, Juliette, 15: 208
Panetta, George, 15: 210
Pansy. See Alden, Isabella
    (Macdonald), YABC 2: 1
Panter, Carol, 9: 150
Papashvily, George, 17: 135
Papashvily, Helen (Waite), 17: 141
Pape, D(onna) L(ugg), 2: 198
Paradis, Adrian A(lexis), 1: 175
Paradis, Marjorie (Bartholomew),
    17: 143
Parish, Peggy, 17: 144
Parker, Elinor, 3: 155
Parker, Nancy Winslow, 10: 113
Parker, Richard, 14: 156
Parker, Robert. See Boyd, Waldo
    T., 18: 35
Parkinson, Ethelyn M(inerva),
    11: 192
Parks, Edd Winfield, 10: 114
Parks, Gordon (Alexander
    Buchanan), 8: 145

Author Index

Parlin, John. *See* Graves, Charles
    Parlin, *4:* 94
Parnall, Peter, *16:* 220
Parr, Lucy, *10:* 115
Parrish, Mary. *See* Cousins,
    Margaret, *2:* 79
Parrish, (Frederick) Maxfield,
    14: 158
Parry, Marian, *13:* 175
Pascal, David, *14:* 174
Paschal, Nancy. *See* Trotter,
    Grace V(iolet), *10:* 180
Paterson, Katherine (Womeldorf),
    13: 176
Paton, Alan (Stewart), *11:* 194
Paton Walsh, Gillian, *4:* 164
Patterson, Lillie G., *14:* 174
Paul, Aileen, *12:* 164
Pauli, Hertha, *3:* 155
Paulson, Jack. *See* Jackson, C.
    Paul, *6:* 120
Pavel, Frances, *10:* 116
Payson, Dale, *9:* 150
Payzant, Charles, *18:* 239
Paz, A. *See* Pahz, James Alon,
    11: 190
Paz, Zan. *See* Pahz, Cheryl
    Suzanne, *11:* 189
Pearce, (Ann) Philippa, *1:* 176
Peare, Catherine Owens, *9:* 152
Pease, Howard, *2:* 199
Peck, Anne Merriman, *18:* 240
Peck, Richard, *18:* 242
Peeples, Edwin A., *6:* 181
Peet, Bill. *See* Peet, William B.,
    2: 201
Peet, William Bartlett, *2:* 201
Pelaez, Jill, *12:* 165
Pelta, Kathy, *18:* 245
Peltier, Leslie C(opus), *13:* 177
Pembury, Bill. *See* Groom, Arthur
    William, *10:* 53
Pender, Lydia, *3:* 157
Pendery, Rosemary, *7:* 174
Penn, Ruth Bonn. *See* Rosenberg,
    Ethel, *3:* 176
Pennage, E. M. *See* Finkel,
    George (Irvine), *8:* 59
Penrose, Margaret. *See*
    Stratemeyer, Edward L.,
    1: 208
Peppe, Rodney, *4:* 164
Percy, Charles Henry. *See* Smith,
    Dodie, *4:* 194
Perera, Thomas Biddle, *13:* 179
Perl, Lila, *6:* 182
Perlmutter, O(scar) William, *8:* 149
Perrine, Mary, *2:* 203
Peters, Caroline. *See* Betz, Eva
    Kelly, *10:* 10
Peters, S. H. *See* Porter, William
    Sydney, *YABC 2:* 259
Petersham, Maud (Fuller), *17:* 146
Petersham, Miska, *17:* 149
Peterson, Hans, *8:* 149
Peterson, Harold L(eslie), *8:* 151

Peterson, Helen Stone, *8:* 152
Petie, Haris, *10:* 118
Petrovskaya, Kyra. *See* Wayne,
    Kyra Petrovskaya, *8:* 213
Petry, Ann (Lane), *5:* 148
Pevsner, Stella, *8:* 154
Peyton, K. M. *See* Peyton,
    Kathleen (Wendy), *15:* 211
Peyton, Kathleen (Wendy), *15:* 211
Pfeffer, Susan Beth, *4:* 166
Phelan, Mary Kay, *3:* 158
Phillips, Irv. *See* Phillips, Irving
    W., *11:* 196
Phillips, Irving W., *11:* 196
Phillips, Jack. *See* Sandburg, Carl
    (August), *8:* 177
Phillips, Loretta (Hosey), *10:* 119
Phillips, Louis, *8:* 155
Phillips, Mary Geisler, *10:* 119
Phillips, Prentice, *10:* 119
Phipson, Joan. *See* Fitzhardinge,
    Joan M., *2:* 107
Phleger, Marjorie Temple, *1:* 176
Piatti, Celestino, *16:* 222
Picard, Barbara Leonie, *2:* 205
Pienkowski, Jan, *6:* 182
Pierce, Katherine. *See* St. John,
    Wylly Folk, *10:* 132
Pierce, Ruth (Ireland), *5:* 148
Pierik, Robert, *13:* 180
Pilarski, Laura, *13:* 181
Pilgrim, Anne. *See* Allan, Mabel
    Esther, *5:* 2
Pilkington, Francis Meredyth,
    4: 166
Pilkington, Roger (Windle), *10:* 120
Pine, Tillie S(chloss), *13:* 182
Pinkwater, Manus, *8:* 156
Piper, Roger. *See* Fisher, John
    (Oswald Hamilton), *15:* 115
Piro, Richard, *7:* 176
Pitrone, Jean Maddern, *4:* 167
Pitz, Henry C., *4:* 167
Place, Marian T., *3:* 160
Plaidy, Jean. *See* Hibbert,
    Eleanor, *2:* 134
Plimpton, George (Ames), *10:* 121
Plowman, Stephanie, *6:* 184
Pluckrose, Henry (Arthur), *13:* 183
Plummer, Margaret, *2:* 206
Podendorf, Illa E., *18:* 247
Pohlmann, Lillian (Grenfell),
    11: 196
Pointon, Robert. *See* Rooke,
    Daphne (Marie), *12:* 178
Pola. *See* Watson, Pauline, *14:* 235
Polatnick, Florence T., *5:* 149
Polder, Markus. *See* Krüss, James,
    8: 104
Politi, Leo, *1:* 177
Polking, Kirk, *5:* 149
Polland, Madeleine A., *6:* 185
Polseno, Jo, *17:* 153
Pond, Alonzo W(illiam), *5:* 150
Poole, Gray Johnson, *1:* 179
Poole, Josephine, *5:* 152

Poole, Lynn, *1:* 179
Portal, Colette, *6:* 186
Porter, William Sydney,
    YABC 2: 259
Posell, Elsa Z., *3:* 160
Posten, Margaret L(ois), *10:* 123
Potter, (Helen) Beatrix,
    YABC 1: 205
Potter, Marian, *9:* 153
Potter, Miriam Clark, *3:* 161
Powell, Richard Stillman. *See*
    Barbour, Ralph Henry, *16:* 27
Powers, Anne. *See* Schwartz,
    Anne Powers, *10:* 142
Powers, Margaret. *See* Heal,
    Edith, *7:* 123
Price, Christine, *3:* 162
Price, Jennifer. *See* Hoover, Helen
    (Drusilla Blackburn), *12:* 100
Price, Lucie Locke. *See* Locke,
    Lucie, *10:* 81
Price, Olive, *8:* 157
Prieto, Mariana B(eeching), *8:* 160
Prince, J(ack) H(arvey), *17:* 155
Pringle, Laurence, *4:* 171
Proctor, Everitt. *See* Montgomery,
    Rutherford, *3:* 134
Provensen, Alice, *9:* 154
Provensen, Martin, *9:* 155
Pryor, Helen Brenton, *4:* 172
Pugh, Ellen T., *7:* 176
Pullein-Thompson, Christine, *3:* 164
Pullein-Thompson, Diana, *3:* 165
Pullein-Thompson, Josephine,
    3: 166
Purdy, Susan Gold, *8:* 161
Purscell, Phyllis, *7:* 177
Putnam, Arthur Lee. *See* Alger,
    Horatio, Jr., *16:* 3
Pyle, Howard, *16:* 224
Pyne, Mable Mandeville, *9:* 155

Quackenbush, Robert M., *7:* 177
Quammen, David, *7:* 179
Quarles, Benjamin, *12:* 166
Queen, Ellery, Jr. *See* Holding,
    James, *3:* 85
Quick, Annabelle, *2:* 207
Quin-Harkin, Janet, *18:* 247

Rabe, Berniece, *7:* 179
Rabe, Olive H(anson), *13:* 183
Rackham, Arthur, *15:* 213
Radford, Ruby L(orraine), *6:* 186
Radlauer, Edward, *15:* 227
Radlauer, Ruth (Shaw), *15:* 229
Raebeck, Lois, *5:* 153
Raftery, Gerald (Bransfield),
    11: 197
Raiff, Stan, *11:* 197
Ralston, Jan. *See* Dunlop, Agnes
    M. R., *3:* 62

Ramal, Walter. *See* de la Mare, Walter, *16:* 73
Ranadive, Gail, *10:* 123
Rand, Paul, *6:* 188
Randall, Florence Engel, *5:* 154
Randall, Janet. *See* Young, Janet & Robert, *3:* 268-269
Randall, Robert. *See* Silverberg, Robert, *13:* 206
Randall, Ruth Painter, *3:* 167
Randolph, Lieutenant J. H. *See* Ellis, Edward S(ylvester), *YABC 1:* 116
Rands, William Brighty, *17:* 156
Ranney, Agnes V., *6:* 189
Rapaport, Stella F(read), *10:* 126
Rappaport, Eva, *6:* 189
Raskin, Edith (Lefkowitz), *9:* 156
Raskin, Ellen, *2:* 209
Raskin, Joseph, *12:* 166
Rathjen, Carl H(enry), *11:* 198
Rau, Margaret, *9:* 157
Raucher, Herman, *8:* 162
Ravielli, Anthony, *3:* 169
Rawlings, Marjorie Kinnan, *YABC 1:* 218
Ray, Deborah, *8:* 163
Ray, Irene. *See* Sutton, Margaret Beebe, *1:* 213
Ray, JoAnne, *9:* 157
Ray, Mary (Eva Pedder), *2:* 210
Raymond, Robert. *See* Alter, Robert Edmond, *9:* 8
Razzell, Arthur (George), *11:* 199
Razzi, James, *10:* 126
Read, Elfreida, *2:* 211
Redding, Robert Hull, *2:* 212
Redway, Ralph. *See* Hamilton, Charles Harold St. John, *13:* 77
Redway, Ridley. *See* Hamilton, Charles Harold St. John, *13:* 77
Reed, Betty Jane, *4:* 172
Reed, Gwendolyn, *7:* 180
Reed, William Maxwell, *15:* 230
Reeder, Colonel Red. *See* Reeder, Russell P., Jr., *4:* 174
Reeder, Russell P., Jr., *4:* 174
Rees, Ennis, *3:* 169
Reeves, James, *15:* 231
Reeves, Joyce, *17:* 158
Reeves, Ruth Ellen. *See* Ranney, Agnes V., *6:* 189
Reggiani, Renée, *18:* 248
Reid, Eugenie Chazal, *12:* 167
Reinfeld, Fred, *3:* 170
Reiss, Johanna de Leeuw, *18:* 250
Remi, Georges, *13:* 183
Rendina, Laura Cooper, *10:* 127
Renick, Marion (Lewis), *1:* 180
Renlie, Frank H., *11:* 200
Renvoize, Jean, *5:* 157
Retla, Robert. *See* Alter, Robert Edmond, *9:* 8
Reuter, Carol (Joan), *2:* 213
Rey, H(ans) A(ugusto), *1:* 181

Reyher, Becky. *See* Reyher, Rebecca Hourwich, *18:* 253
Reyher, Rebecca Hourwich, *18:* 253
Rhys, Megan. *See* Williams, Jeanne, *5:* 202
Ricciuti, Edward R(aphael), *10:* 110
Rice, Elizabeth, *2:* 213
Rice, Inez, *13:* 186
Rich, Elaine Sommers, *6:* 190
Rich, Josephine , *10:* 129
Richard, Adrienne, *5:* 157
Richards, Frank. *See* Hamilton, Charles Howard St. John, *13:* 77
Richards, Hilda. *See* Hamilton, Charles Howard St. John, *13:* 77
Richards, Laura E(lizabeth Howe), *YABC 1:* 224
Richardson, Grace Lee. *See* Dickson, Naida, *8:* 41
Richardson, Robert S(hirley), *8:* 164
Richoux, Pat, *7:* 180
Richter, Conrad, *3:* 171
Richter, Hans Peter, *6:* 191
Ridge, Antonia, *7:* 181
Ridley, Nat, Jr. *See* Stratemeyer, Edward L., *1:* 208
Riedman, Sarah R(egal), *1:* 183
Rikhoff, Jean, *9:* 158
Riley, James Whitcomb, *17:* 159
Ringi, Kjell. *See* Ringi, Kjell Arne Sörensen, *12:* 168
Ringi, Kjell Arne Sörensen, *12:* 168
Rinkoff, Barbara (Jean), *4:* 174
Rios, Tere. *See* Versace, Marie Teresa, *2:* 254
Ripley, Elizabeth Blake, *5:* 158
Ripper, Charles L., *3:* 174
Ritchie, Barbara (Gibbons), *14:* 176
Riverside, John. *See* Heinlein, Robert A(nson), *9:* 102
Rivoli, Mario, *10:* 129
Roach, Marilynne K(athleen), *9:* 158
Roach, Portia. *See* Takakjian, Portia, *15:* 273
Robbins, Raleigh. *See* Hamilton, Charles Harold St. John, *13:* 77
Robbins, Ruth, *14:* 177
Roberts, David. *See* Cox, John Roberts, *9:* 42
Roberts, Jim. *See* Bates, Barbara S(nedeker), *12:* 34
Roberts, Terence. *See* Sanderson, Ivan T., *6:* 195
Robertson, Barbara (Anne), *12:* 172
Robertson, Don, *8:* 165
Robertson, Dorothy Lewis, *12:* 173
Robertson, Jennifer (Sinclair), *12:* 174
Robertson, Keith, *1:* 184
Robins, Seelin. *See* Ellis, Edward S(ylvester), *YABC 1:* 116

Robinson, Adjai, *8:* 165
Robinson, Barbara (Webb), *8:* 166
Robinson, Charles, *6:* 192
Robinson, Charles [1870-1937], *17:* 171
Robinson, Jan M., *6:* 194
Robinson, Jean O., *7:* 182
Robinson, Joan (Mary) G(ale Thomas), *7:* 183
Robinson, Maudie (Millian Oller), *11:* 200
Robinson, T(homas) H(eath), *17:* 178
Robinson, W(illiam) Heath, *17:* 184
Robison, Bonnie, *12:* 175
Robottom, John, *7:* 185
Roche, A. K. [Joint pseudonym with Boche Kaplan]. *See* Abisch, Roslyn Kroop, *9:* 3
Rockwell, Thomas, *7:* 185
Rockwood, Roy [Collective pseudonym], *1:* 185
Rodgers, Mary, *8:* 167
Rodman, Emerson. *See* Ellis, Edward S(ylvester), *YABC 1:* 116
Rodman, Maia. *See* Wojciechowska, Maia, *1:* 228
Rodman, Selden, *9:* 159
Roe, Harry Mason. *See* Stratemeyer, Edward L., *1:* 208
Rogers, (Thomas) Alan (Stinchcombe), *2:* 215
Rogers, Frances, *10:* 130
Rogers, Matilda, *5:* 158
Rogers, Pamela, *9:* 160
Rogers, Robert. *See* Hamilton, Charles Harold St. John, *13:* 77
Rokeby-Thomas, Anna E(lma), *15:* 233
Roland, Albert, *11:* 201
Rolerson, Darrell A(llen), *8:* 168
Roll, Winifred, *6:* 194
Rollins, Charlemae Hill, *3:* 175
Rongen, Björn, *10:* 131
Rood, Ronald (N.), *12:* 177
Rooke, Daphne (Marie), *12:* 178
Rose, Anne, *8:* 168
Rose, Florella. *See* Carlson, Vada F., *16:* 64
Rose, Wendy, *12:* 180
Rosen, Sidney, *1:* 185
Rosen, Winifred, *8:* 169
Rosenbaum, Maurice, *6:* 195
Rosenberg, Ethel, *3:* 176
Rosenberg, Nancy Sherman, *4:* 177
Rosenberg, Sharon, *8:* 171
Rosenblum, Richard, *11:* 202
Rosenburg, John M., *6:* 195
Ross, Tony, *17:* 203
Rothkopf, Carol Z., *4:* 177
Rothman, Joel, *7:* 186
Rounds, Glen (Harold), *8:* 171
Rourke, Constance (Mayfield), *YABC 1:* 232

Rowland, Florence Wightman,
    8: 173
Roy, Liam. See Scarry, Patricia,
    2: 218
Rubel, Nicole, 18: 255
Ruchlis, Hy, 3: 177
Rudomin, Esther. See Hautzig,
    Esther, 4: 105
Ruedi, Norma Paul. See
    Ainsworth, Norma, 9: 4
Ruhen, Olaf, 17: 204
Rumsey, Marian (Barritt), 16: 236
Rushmore, Helen, 3: 178
Rushmore, Robert (William), 8: 174
Ruskin, Ariane, 7: 187
Russell, Charlotte. See Rathjen,
    Carl H(enry), 11: 198
Russell, Franklin, 11: 203
Russell, Helen Ross, 8: 175
Russell, Patrick. See Sammis,
    John, 4: 178
Russell, Solveig Paulson, 3: 179
Ruth, Rod, 9: 160
Ruthin, Margaret, 4: 178
Rutz, Viola Larkin, 12: 181
Ryan, Peter (Charles), 15: 235
Rydell, Wendell. See Rydell,
    Wendy, 4: 178
Rydell, Wendy, 4: 178
Ryden, Hope, 8: 176

Sabin, Edwin Legrand,
    YABC 2: 277
Sabuso. See Phillips, Irving W.,
    11: 196
Sachs, Marilyn, 3: 180
Sackett, S(amuel) J(ohn), 12: 181
Sackson, Sid, 16: 237
Sadie, Stanley (John), 14: 177
Sage, Juniper [Joint pseudonym].
    See Brown, Margaret Wise,
    YABC 2: 9
Sage, Juniper. See Hurd, Edith,
    2: 150
Sagsoorian, Paul, 12: 183
Saint, Dora Jessie, 10: 132
St. Briavels, James. See Wood,
    James Playsted, 1: 229
St. George, Judith, 13: 187
St. John, Wylly Folk, 10: 132
St. Meyer, Ned. See Stratemeyer,
    Edward L., 1: 208
Saito, Michiko. See Fujiwara,
    Michiko, 15: 120
Salmon, Annie Elizabeth, 13: 188
Salter, Cedric. See Knight, Francis
    Edgar, 14: 112
Samachson, Dorothy, 3: 182
Samachson, Joseph, 3: 182
Sammis, John, 4: 178
Samson, Anne S(tringer), 2: 216
Samson, Joan, 13: 189
Samuels, Charles, 12: 183
Samuels, Gertrude, 17: 206
Sanchez-Silva, Jose Maria, 16: 237

Sandberg, (Karin) Inger, 15: 238
Sandberg, Lasse (E. M.), 15: 239
Sandburg, Carl (August), 8: 177
Sandburg, Charles A. See
    Sandburg, Carl (August),
    8: 177
Sandburg, Helga, 3: 184
Sanderlin, George, 4: 180
Sanderlin, Owenita (Harrah),
    11: 204
Sanderson, Ivan T., 6: 195
Sandin, Joan, 12: 185
Sandoz, Mari (Susette), 5: 159
Sanger, Marjory Bartlett, 8: 181
Sarac, Roger. See Caras, Roger
    A(ndrew), 12: 65
Sarg, Anthony Fredrick. See Sarg,
    Tony, YABC 1: 233
Sarg, Tony, YABC 1: 233
Sargent, Robert, 2: 216
Sargent, Shirley, 11: 205
Sarnoff, Jane, 10: 133
Sasek, Miroslav, 16: 239
Sattler, Helen Roney, 4: 181
Saunders, Caleb. See Heinlein,
    Robert A(nson), 9: 102
Saunders, Keith, 12: 186
Savage, Blake. See Goodwin,
    Harold Leland, 13: 73
Savery, Constance (Winifred),
    1: 186
Savitt, Sam, 8: 181
Savitz, Harriet May, 5: 161
Sawyer, Ruth, 17: 207
Sayers, Frances Clarke, 3: 185
Sazer, Nina, 13: 191
Scabrini, Janet, 13: 191
Scagnetti, Jack, 7: 188
Scanlon, Marion Stephany, 11: 206
Scarf, Maggi. See Scarf, Maggie,
    5: 162
Scarf, Maggie, 5: 162
Scarry, Patricia (Murphy), 2: 218
Scarry, Patsy. See Scarry,
    Patricia, 2: 218
Scarry, Richard (McClure), 2: 218
Schaefer, Jack, 3: 186
Schechter, Betty (Goodstein),
    5: 163
Scheer, Julian (Weisel), 8: 183
Scheffer, Victor B., 6: 197
Schell, Orville H., 10: 136
Scherf, Margaret, 10: 136
Schick, Eleanor, 9: 161
Schiff, Ken, 7: 189
Schisgall, Oscar, 12: 187
Schlein, Miriam, 2: 222
Schloat, G. Warren, Jr., 4: 181
Schmid, Eleonore, 12: 188
Schmidt, Elizabeth, 15: 242
Schneider, Herman, 7: 189
Schneider, Nina, 2: 222
Schnirel, James R(einhold), 14: 178
Schoen, Barbara, 13: 192
Scholastica, Sister Mary. See
    Jenkins, Marie M., 7: 143

Scholefield, Edmund O. See
    Butterworth, W. E., 5: 40
Schoor, Gene, 3: 188
Schreiber, Elizabeth Anne
    (Ferguson), 13: 192
Schreiber, Ralph W(alter), 13: 194
Schulman, L(ester) M(artin),
    13: 194
Schultz, James Willard,
    YABC 1: 238
Schulz, Charles M(onroe), 10: 137
Schurfranz, Vivian, 13: 194
Schutzer, A. I., 13: 195
Schwartz, Alvin, 4: 183
Schwartz, Anne Powers, 10: 142
Schwartz, Charles W(alsh), 8: 184
Schwartz, Elizabeth Reeder, 8: 184
Scoppettone, Sandra, 9: 162
Scott, Cora Annett (Pipitone),
    11: 207
Scott, Dan [House pseudonym].
    See Barker, S. Omar, 10: 8
Scott, Dan. See Stratemeyer,
    Edward L., 1: 208
Scott, John, 14: 178
Scott, John M(artin), 12: 188
Scott, Sir Walter, YABC 2: 280
Scribner, Charles Jr., 13: 195
Seamands, Ruth (Childers), 9: 163
Searight, Mary W(illiams), 17: 211
Searle, Kathryn Adrienne, 10: 143
Sears, Stephen W., 4: 184
Sebastian, Lee. See Silverberg,
    Robert, 13: 206
Sechrist, Elizabeth Hough, 2: 224
Sedges, John. See Buck, Pearl S.,
    1: 36
Seed, Jenny, 8: 186
Seeger, Pete(r), 13: 196
Segal, Lore, 4: 186
Seidelman, James Edward, 6: 197
Seidman, Laurence (Ivan), 15: 244
Seigal, Kalman, 12: 190
Seixas, Judith S., 17: 212
Sejima, Yoshimasa, 8: 186
Selden, George. See Thompson,
    George Selden, 4: 204
Selig, Sylvie, 13: 199
Selsam, Millicent E(llis), 1: 188
Seltzer, Meyer, 17: 213
Sendak, Maurice (Bernard), 1: 190
Sengler, Johanna, 18: 255
Serage, Nancy, 10: 143
Seredy, Kate, 1: 193
Seroff, Victor I(lyitch), 12: 190
Serraillier, Ian (Lucien), 1: 193
Servello, Joe, 10: 143
Serwer, Blanche L., 10: 144
Seton, Anya, 3: 188
Seton, Ernest Thompson, 18: 257
Seuling, Barbara, 10: 145
Seuss, Dr. See Geisel, Theodor
    Seuss, 1: 104
Severn, Bill. See Severn, William
    Irving, 1: 195

Severn, David. *See* Unwin, David S(torr), *14:* 217

Severn, William Irving, *1:* 195

Seward, Prudence, *16:* 242

Sexton, Anne (Harvey), *10:* 146

Seymour, Alta Halverson, *10:* 147

Shafer, Robert E(ugene), *9:* 164

Shahn, Bernarda Bryson. *See* Bryson, Bernarda, *9:* 26

Shanks, Ann Zane (Kushner), *10:* 148

Shapp, Martha, *3:* 189

Sharfman, Amalie, *14:* 179

Sharma, Partap, *15:* 244

Sharmat, Marjorie Weinman, *4:* 187

Sharp, Margery, *1:* 196

Sharpe, Mitchell R(aymond), *12:* 191

Shaw, Arnold, *4:* 189

Shaw, Charles (Green), *13:* 200

Shaw, Ray, *7:* 190

Shaw, Richard, *12:* 192

Shay, Arthur, *4:* 189

Shecter, Ben, *16:* 243

Sheehan, Ethna, *9:* 165

Shekerjian, Regina Tor, *16:* 244

Sheldon, Ann [Collective pseudonym], *1:* 198

Sheldon, Aure, *12:* 194

Shelton, William Roy, *5:* 164

Shemin, Margaretha, *4:* 190

Shepard, Ernest Howard, *3:* 191

Shephard, Esther, *5:* 165

Shepherd, Elizabeth, *4:* 191

Sherburne, Zoa, *3:* 194

Sherman, Diane (Finn), *12:* 194

Sherman, Elizabeth. *See* Friskey, Margaret Richards, *5:* 72

Sherman, Nancy. *See* Rosenberg, Nancy Sherman, *4:* 177

Sherrod, Jane. *See* Singer, Jane Sherrod, *4:* 192

Sherry, (Dulcie) Sylvia, *8:* 187

Sherwan, Earl, *3:* 195

Shields, Charles, *10:* 149

Shimin, Symeon, *13:* 201

Shippen, Katherine B(inney), *1:* 198

Shipton, Eric, *10:* 151

Shirreffs, Gordon D(onald), *11:* 207

Shotwell, Louisa R., *3:* 196

Showalter, Jean B(reckinridge), *12:* 195

Shub, Elizabeth, *5:* 166

Shulevitz, Uri, *3:* 197

Shulman, Alix Kates, *7:* 191

Shulman, Irving, *13:* 204

Shura, Mary Francis. *See* Craig, Mary Francis, *6:* 52

Shuttlesworth, Dorothy, *3:* 200

Shyer, Marlene Fanta, *13:* 205

Sibley, Don, *12:* 195

Siculan, Daniel, *12:* 197

Sidjakov, Nicolas, *18:* 272

Silcock, Sara Lesley, *12:* 199

Silver, Ruth. *See* Chew, Ruth, *7:* 45

Silverberg, Robert, *13:* 206

Silverman, Mel(vin Frank), *9:* 166

Silverstein, Alvin, *8:* 188

Silverstein, Virginia B(arbara Opshelor), *8:* 190

Simon, Charlie May. *See* Fletcher, Charlie May, *3:* 70

Simon, Joe. *See* Simon, Joseph H., *7:* 192

Simon, Joseph H., *7:* 192

Simon, Martin P(aul William), *12:* 200

Simon, Mina Lewiton. *See* Lewiton, Mina, *2:* 174

Simon, Norma, *3:* 201

Simon, Seymour, *4:* 191

Simon, Shirley (Schwartz), *11:* 210

Simonetta, Linda, *14:* 179

Simonetta, Sam, *14:* 180

Simont, Marc, *9:* 167

Simpson, Colin, *14:* 181

Simpson, Myrtle L(illias), *14:* 181

Sinclair, Upton (Beall), *9:* 168

Singer, Isaac. *See* Singer, Isaac Bashevis, *3:* 203

Singer, Isaac Bashevis, *3:* 203

Singer, Jane Sherrod, *4:* 192

Singer, Susan (Mahler), *9:* 170

Sisson, Rosemary Anne, *11:* 211

Sivulich, Sandra (Jeanne) Stroner, *9:* 171

Skelly, James R(ichard), *17:* 215

Skinner, Constance Lindsay, *YABC 1:* 247

Skinner, Cornelia Otis, *2:* 225

Skorpen, Liesel Moak, *3:* 206

Skurzynski, Gloria (Joan), *8:* 190

Slackman, Charles B., *12:* 200

Slade, Richard, *9:* 171

Sleator, William, *3:* 207

Sleigh, Barbara, *3:* 208

Slicer, Margaret O., *4:* 193

Slobodkin, Florence (Gersh), *5:* 167

Slobodkin, Louis, *1:* 199

Slobodkina, Esphyr, *1:* 201

Slote, Alfred, *8:* 192

Small, Ernest. *See* Lent, Blair, *2:* 172

Smaridge, Norah, *6:* 198

Smiley, Virginia Kester, *2:* 227

Smith, Beatrice S(chillinger), *12:* 201

Smith, Betty, *6:* 199

Smith, Bradford, *5:* 168

Smith, Datus C(lifford) Jr., *13:* 208

Smith, Dodie, *4:* 194

Smith, Dorothy Stafford, *6:* 201

Smith, E(lmer) Boyd, *YABC 1:* 248

Smith, Eunice Young, *5:* 169

Smith, Frances C., *3:* 209

Smith, Gary R(ichard), *14:* 182

Smith, George Harmon, *5:* 171

Smith, Howard Everett Jr., *12:* 201

Smith, Hugh L(etcher), *5:* 172

Smith, Imogene Henderson, *12:* 203

Smith, Jean. *See* Smith, Frances C., *3:* 209

Smith, Jean Pajot, *10:* 151

Smith, Johnston. *See* Crane, Stephen (Townley), *YABC 2:* 84

Smith, Lafayette. *See* Higdon, Hal, *4:* 115

Smith, Linell Nash, *2:* 227

Smith, Marion Hagens, *12:* 204

Smith, Marion Jaques, *13:* 209

Smith, Mary Ellen, *10:* 152

Smith, Mike. *See* Smith, Mary Ellen, *10:* 152

Smith, Nancy Covert, *12:* 204

Smith, Norman F., *5:* 172

Smith, Robert Kimmel, *12:* 205

Smith, Ruth Leslie, *2:* 228

Smith, Sarah Stafford. *See* Smith, Dorothy Stafford, *6:* 201

Smith, Susan Carlton, *12:* 207

Smith, Vian (Crocker), *11:* 213

Smith, William A., *10:* 153

Smith, William Jay, *2:* 229

Smith, Z. Z. *See* Westheimer, David, *14:* 242

Snedeker, Caroline Dale (Parke), *YABC 2:* 296

Sneve, Virginia Driving Hawk, *8:* 193

Sniff, Mr. *See* Abisch, Roslyn Kroop, *9:* 3

Snodgrass, Thomas Jefferson. *See* Clemens, Samuel Langhorne, *YABC 2:* 51

Snow, Donald Clifford, *16:* 246

Snow, Dorothea J(ohnston), *9:* 172

Snyder, Anne, *4:* 195

Snyder, Zilpha Keatley, *1:* 202

Snyderman, Reuven K., *5:* 173

Sobol, Donald J., *1:* 203

Soderlind, Arthur E(dwin), *14:* 183

Softly, Barbara (Frewin), *12:* 209

Sohl, Frederic J(ohn), *10:* 154

Solbert, Romaine G., *2:* 232

Solbert, Ronni. *See* Solbert, Romaine G., *2:* 232

Solonevich, George, *15:* 245

Solot, Mary Lynn, *12:* 210

Sommer, Elyse, *7:* 192

Sommer, Robert, *12:* 211

Sommerfelt, Aimee, *5:* 173

Sonneborn, Ruth, *4:* 196

Sorche, Nic Leodhas. *See* Alger, Leclaire (Gowans), *15:* 1

Sorensen, Virginia, *2:* 233

Sorrentino, Joseph N., *6:* 203

Sortor, June Elizabeth, *12:* 212

Sortor, Toni. *See* Sortor, June Elizabeth, *12:* 212

Soskin, V. H. *See* Ellison, Virginia Howell, *4:* 74

Sotomayor, Antonio, *11:* 214

Soudley, Henry. *See* Wood, James Playsted, *1:* 229

Soule, Gardner (Bosworth), *14:* 183

Soule, Jean Conder, *10:* 154

Southall, Ivan, *3:* 210

Spangenberg, Judith Dunn, 5: 175
Spar, Jerome, 10: 156
Sparks, Mary W., 15: 247
Spaulding, Leonard. See
    Bradbury, Ray, 11: 29
Speare, Elizabeth George, 5: 176
Spearing, Judith (Mary Harlow),
    9: 173
Specking, Inez, 11: 217
Speicher, Helen Ross (Smith),
    8: 194
Spellman, John W(illard), 14: 186
Spencer, Ann, 10: 156
Spencer, Cornelia. See Yaukey,
    Grace S. 5: 203
Spencer, Elizabeth, 14: 186
Spencer, William, 9: 175
Sperry, Armstrong W., 1: 204
Sperry, Raymond, Jr. [Collective
    pseudonym], 1: 205
Spiegelman, Judith M., 5: 179
Spier, Peter (Edward), 4: 198
Spilhaus, Athelstan, 13: 209
Spilka, Arnold, 6: 203
Spink, Reginald (William), 11: 217
Spinossimus. See White, William,
    16: 276
Spollen, Christopher, 12: 213
Sprigge, Elizabeth, 10: 157
Spykman, E(lizabeth) C., 10: 157
Squire, Miriam. See Sprigge,
    Elizabeth, 10: 157
Squires, Phil. See Barker, S.
    Omar, 10: 8
S-Ringi, Kjell. See Ringi, Kjell,
    12: 168
Stadtler, Bea, 17: 215
Stahl, Ben(jamin), 5: 179
Stamaty, Mark Alan, 12: 214
Stambler, Irwin, 5: 181
Stanhope, Eric. See Hamilton,
    Charles Harold St. John, 13: 77
Stankevich, Boris, 2: 234
Stanley, Robert. See Hamilton,
    Charles Harold St. John, 13: 77
Stanstead, John. See Groom,
    Arthur William, 10: 53
Stapp, Arthur D(onald), 4: 201
Starbird, Kaye, 6: 204
Stark, James. See Goldston,
    Robert, 6: 90
Starkey, Marion L., 13: 211
Starret, William. See McClintock,
    Marshall, 3: 119
Staunton, Schuyler. See Baum,
    L(yman) Frank, 18: 7
Stearns, Monroe (Mather), 5: 182
Steele, Chester K. See
    Stratemeyer, Edward L.,
    1: 208
Steele, Mary Q., 3: 211
Steele, (Henry) Max(well), 10: 159
Steele, William O(wen), 1: 205
Steig, William, 18: 275
Stein, M(eyer) L(ewis), 6: 205
Stein, Mini, 2: 234

Steinbeck, John (Ernst), 9: 176
Steinberg, Alfred, 9: 178
Steinberg, Fred J., 4: 201
Steiner, Barbara A(nnette), 13: 213
Steiner, Stan(ley), 14: 187
Stephens, Mary Jo, 8: 196
Steptoe, John (Lewis), 8: 198
Sterling, Dorothy, 1: 206
Sterling, Helen. See Hoke, Helen
    (L.), 15: 133
Sterling, Philip, 8: 198
Stern, Madeleine B(ettina), 14: 188
Stern, Philip Van Doren, 13: 215
Stern, Simon, 15: 248
Sterne, Emma Gelders, 6: 205
Steurt, Marjorie Rankin, 10: 159
Stevens, Carla M(cBride), 13: 217
Stevens, Franklin, 6: 206
Stevens, Peter. See Geis, Darlene,
    7: 101
Stevenson, Anna (M.), 12: 216
Stevenson, Augusta, 2: 235
Stevenson, Janet, 8: 199
Stevenson, Robert Louis,
    YABC 2: 307
Stewart, A(gnes) C(harlotte),
    15: 250
Stewart, Charles. See Zurhorst,
    Charles (Stewart, Jr.), 12: 240
Stewart, Elizabeth Laing, 6: 206
Stewart, John (William), 14: 189
Stewart, George Rippey, 3: 213
Stewart, Mary (Florence Elinor),
    12: 217
Stewart, Robert Neil, 7: 192
Stiles, Martha Bennett, 6: 207
Stillerman, Robbie, 12: 219
Stine, G(eorge) Harry, 10: 161
Stinetorf, Louise, 10: 162
Stirling, Arthur. See Sinclair,
    Upton (Beall), 9: 168
Stirling, Nora B., 3: 214
Stirnweis, Shannon, 10: 163
Stobbs, William, 17: 216
Stoddard, Edward G., 10: 164
Stoddard, Hope, 6: 207
Stoddard, Sandol. See Warburg,
    Sandol Stoddard, 14: 234
Stoiko, Michael, 14: 190
Stokes, Jack (Tilden), 13: 218
Stolz, Mary (Slattery), 10: 165
Stone, Alan [Collective
    pseudonym], 1: 208.
    See also Svenson, Andrew E.,
    2: 238
Stone, D(avid) K(arl), 9: 179
Stone, Eugenia, 7: 193
Stone, Gene. See Stone, Eugenia,
    7: 193
Stone, Helen V., 6: 208
Stone, Irving, 3: 215
Stone, Raymond [Collective
    pseudonym], 1: 208
Stone, Richard A. See
    Stratemeyer, Edward L.,
    1: 208

Stonehouse, Bernard, 13: 219
Storch, Anne B. von. See von
    Storch, Anne B., 1: 221
Storey, (Elizabeth) Margaret
    (Carlton), 9: 180
Storey, Victoria Carolyn, 16: 248
Storme, Peter. See Stern, Philip
    Van Doren, 13: 215
Storr, Catherine (Cole), 9: 181
Stoutenburg, Adrien, 3: 217
Stover, Allan C(arl), 14: 191
Stover, Marjorie Filley, 9: 182
Stowe, Harriet (Elizabeth)
    Beecher, YABC 1: 250
Strachan, Margaret Pitcairn,
    14: 193
Stratemeyer, Edward L., 1: 208
Stratton-Porter, Gene, 15: 251
Strayer, E. Ward. See
    Stratemeyer, Edward L.,
    1: 208
Street, Julia Montgomery, 11: 218
Strong, Charles. See Epstein,
    Samuel, 1: 87
Ströyer, Poul, 13: 221
Stuart, Forbes, 13: 222
Stuart, (Hilton) Jesse, 2: 236
Stuart, Sheila. See Baker, Mary
    Gladys Steel, 12: 27
Stubis, Talivaldis, 5: 183
Sture-Vasa, Mary. See Alsop,
    Mary, 2: 4
Sturton, Hugh. See Johnston,
    H(ugh) A(nthony) S(tephen),
    14: 87
Sturtzel, Howard A(llison), 1: 210
Sturtzel, Jane Levington, 1: 212
Styles, Frank Showell, 10: 167
Suba, Susanne, 4: 202
Subond, Valerie. See Grayland,
    Valerie, 7: 111
Suhl, Yuri, 8: 200
Sullivan, George E(dward), 4: 202
Sullivan, Mary W(ilson), 13: 224
Sullivan, Thomas Joseph, Jr.,
    16: 248
Sullivan, Tom. See Sullivan,
    Thomas Joseph, Jr., 16: 248
Surge, Frank, 13: 225
Susac, Andrew, 5: 184
Sutcliff, Rosemary, 6: 209
Sutherland, Margaret, 15: 271
Sutton, Margaret (Beebe), 1: 213
Svenson, Andrew E., 2: 238
Swarthout, Kathryn, 7: 194
Swenson, May, 15: 271
Swift, David. See Kaufmann,
    John, 18: 132
Swiger, Elinor Porter, 8: 202
Swinburne, Laurence, 9: 183
Swinnerton, (Neville) Ronald, 2: 239
Synge, (Phyllis) Ursula, 9: 184
Sypher, Lucy Johnston, 7: 195
Szasz, Suzanne Shorr, 13: 226
Szekeres, Cyndy, 5: 184

Tabrah, Ruth Milander, *14:* 194
Tait, Douglas, *12:* 220
Takakjian, Portia, *15:* 273
Takashima, Shizuye, *13:* 227
Talbot, Charlene Joy, *10:* 169
Talbot, Toby, *14:* 195
Talker, T. *See* Rands, William
    Brighty, *17:* 156
Tallcott, Emogene, *10:* 170
Talmadge, Marian, *14:* 196
Tamarin, Alfred, *13:* 229
Tamburine, Jean, *12:* 221
Tannenbaum, Beulah, *3:* 219
Tanner, Louise S(tickney), *9:* 185
Tapio, Pat Decker. *See* Kines, Pat
    Decker, *12:* 118
Tarkington, (Newton) Booth,
    17: 218
Tarry, Ellen, *16:* 250
Tarshis, Jerome, *9:* 186
Tashjian, Virginia A., *3:* 220
Tasker, James, *9:* 187
Tate, Ellalice. *See* Hibbert,
    Eleanor, *2:* 134
Tate, Joan, *9:* 188
Tatham, Campbell. *See* Elting,
    Mary, *2:* 100
Taylor, Barbara J., *10:* 171
Taylor, Carl, *14:* 196
Taylor, David, *10:* 172
Taylor, Elizabeth, *13:* 230
Taylor, Florance Walton, *9:* 190
Taylor, Florence M(arion
    Tompkins), *9:* 191
Taylor, Mildred D., *15:* 275
Taylor, Robert Lewis, *10:* 172
Taylor, Sydney (Brenner), *1:* 214
Taylor, Theodore, *5:* 185
Teal, Val, *10:* 174
Teale, Edwin Way, *7:* 196
Tee-Van, Helen Damrosch, *10:* 176
Temko, Florence, *13:* 231
Templar, Maurice. *See* Groom,
    Arthur William, *10:* 53
Tenggren, Gustaf, *18:* 277
Tennant, Kylie, *6:* 210
ter Haar, Jaap, *6:* 211
Terhune, Albert Payson, *15:* 277
Terris, Susan, *3:* 221
Terry, Luther L(eonidas), *11:* 220
Terry, Walter, *14:* 198
Terzian, James P., *14:* 199
Thacher, Mary McGrath, *9:* 192
Tharp, Louise Hall, *3:* 223
Thayer, Jane. *See* Woolley,
    Catherine, *3:* 265
Thayer, Peter. *See* Wyler, Rose,
    18: 303
Thelwell, Norman, *14:* 200
Thieda, Shirley Ann, *13:* 233
Thiele, Colin (Milton), *14:* 201
Thistlethwaite, Miles, *12:* 223
Thomas, J. F. *See* Fleming,
    Thomas J(ames), *8:* 64
Thomas, Joan Gale. *See* Robinson,
    Joan G., *7:* 183

Thomas, Lowell (Jackson), Jr.,
    15: 290
Thompson, Christine Pullein. *See*
    Pullein-Thompson, Christine,
    3: 164
Thompson, David H(ugh), *17:* 236
Thompson, Diana Pullein. *See*
    Pullein-Thompson, Diana,
    3: 165
Thompson, George Selden, *4:* 204
Thompson, Harlan H., *10:* 177
Thompson, Josephine Pullein. *See*
    Pullein-Thompson, Josephine,
    3: 166
Thompson, Kay, *16:* 257
Thompson, Vivian L., *3:* 224
Thorndyke, Helen Louise
    [Collective pseudonym], *1:* 216
Thorne, Ian. *See* May, Julian,
    11: 175
Thornton, W. B. *See* Burgess,
    Thornton Waldo, *17:* 19
Thorvall, Kerstin, *13:* 233
Thum, Marcella, *3:* 226
Thundercloud, Katherine. *See*
    Witt, Shirley Hill, *17:* 247
Thurber, James (Grover), *13:* 235
Thwaite, Ann (Barbara Harrop),
    14: 206
Tichenor, Tom, *14:* 206
Timmins, William F., *10:* 177
Tinkelman, Murray, *12:* 224
Titus, Eve, *2:* 240
Tobias, Tobi, *5:* 187
Todd, Anne Ophelia. *See* Dowden,
    Anne Ophelia, *7:* 69
Todd, Barbara K., *10:* 178
Todd, H(erbert) E(atton), *11:* 221
Tolkien, J(ohn) R(onald) R(euel),
    2: 242
Tolles, Martha, *8:* 203
Tolmie, Ken(neth Donald), *15:* 291
Tomfool. *See* Farjeon, Eleanor,
    2: 103
Tomlinson, Jill, *3:* 227
Tompert, Ann, *14:* 208
Toner, Raymond John, *10:* 179
Toonder, Martin. *See* Groom,
    Arthur William, *10:* 53
Toothaker, Roy Eugene, *18:* 280
Tooze, Ruth, *4:* 205
Topping, Audrey R(onning), *14:* 209
Tor, Regina. *See* Shekerjian,
    Regina Tor, *16:* 244
Totham, Mary. *See* Breinburg,
    Petronella, *11:* 36
Townsend, John Rowe, *4:* 206
Toye, William E(ldred), *8:* 203
Traherne, Michael. *See* Watkins-
    Pitchford, D. J., *6:* 214
Trapp, Maria (Augusta) von,
    16: 260
Travers, P(amela) L(yndon), *4:* 208
Trease, (Robert) Geoffrey, *2:* 244
Tredez, Alain, *17:* 236
Treece, Henry, *2:* 246

Tregaskis, Richard, *3:* 228
Trell, Max, *14:* 211
Tremain, Ruthven, *17:* 237
Trent, Timothy. *See* Malmberg,
    Carl, *9:* 136
Tresselt, Alvin, *7:* 197
Trevino, Elizabeth B(orton) de,
    1: 216
Trevor, (Lucy) Meriol, *10:* 180
Trez, Alain. *See* Tredez, Alain,
    17: 236
Tripp, Eleanor B., *4:* 210
Tripp, Paul, *8:* 204
Trost, Lucille Wood, *12:* 226
Trotter, Grace V(iolet), *10:* 180
Tucker, Caroline. *See* Nolan,
    Jeannette, *2:* 196
Tully, John (Kimberley), *14:* 212
Tunis, Edwin (Burdett), *1:* 217
Turkle, Brinton, *2:* 248
Turlington, Bayly, *5:* 187
Turnbull, Agnes Sligh, *14:* 213
Turnbull, Ann (Christine), *18:* 281
Turner, Alice K., *10:* 181
Turner, Ann W(arren), *14:* 214
Turner, Elizabeth, *YABC 2:* 332
Turner, Josie. *See* Crawford,
    Phyllis, *3:* 57
Turner, Philip, *11:* 222
Turngren, Ellen, *3:* 230
Twain, Mark. *See* Clemens,
    Samuel Langhorne,
    YABC 2: 51
Tweedsmuir, Baron. *See* Buchan,
    John, *YABC 2:* 21
Tyler, Anne, *7:* 198

Ubell, Earl, *4:* 210
Uchida, Yoshiko, *1:* 219
Udall, Jan Beaney, *10:* 182
Udry, Janice May, *4:* 212
Ullman, James Ramsey, *7:* 199
Ulm, Robert, *17:* 238
Ulyatt, Kenneth, *14:* 216
Unada. *See* Gliewe, Unada, *3:* 77
Uncle Gus. *See* Rey, H. A., *1:* 181
Uncle Ray. *See* Coffman, Ramon
    Peyton, *4:* 53
Underhill, Alice Mertie, *10:* 182
Ungerer, Jean Thomas, *5:* 187
Ungerer, Tomi. *See* Ungerer, Jean
    Thomas, *5:* 187
Unkelbach, Kurt, *4:* 213
Unnerstad, Edith, *3:* 230
Unrau, Ruth, *9:* 192
Unstead R(obert) J(ohn), *12:* 226
Unsworth, Walt, *4:* 215
Untermeyer, Louis, *2:* 250
Unwin, David S(torr), *14:* 217
Unwin, Nora S., *3:* 233
Usher, Margo Scegge. *See*
    McHargue, Georgess, *4:* 152
Uttley, Alice Jane, *3:* 235
Uttley, Alison. *See* Uttley, Alice
    Jane, *3:* 235

Utz, Lois, *5:* 189

Vaeth, J(oseph) Gordon, *17:* 239
Valens, Evans G., Jr., *1:* 220
Van Abbé, Salaman, *18:* 282
Van Anrooy, Francine, *2:* 252
Van Anrooy, Frans. *See* Van
    Anrooy, Francine, *2:* 252
Vance, Eleanor Graham, *11:* 223
Vandenburg, Mary Lou, *17:* 240
Vander Boom, Mae M., *14:* 219
Van der Veer, Judy, *4:* 216
Van Duyn, Janet, *18:* 283
Van Dyne, Edith. *See* Baum,
    L(yman) Frank, *18:* 7
Van Leeuwen, Jean, *6:* 212
Van Loon, Hendrik Willem, *18:* 284
Van Orden, M(erton) D(ick), *4:* 218
Van Rensselaer, Alexander (Taylor
    Mason), *14:* 219
Van Riper, Guernsey, Jr., *3:* 239
Van Stockum, Hilda, *5:* 191
Van Tuyl, Barbara, *11:* 224
Van Vogt, A(lfred) E(lton), *14:* 220
Van Wyck Mason. *See* Mason, F.
    van Wyck, *3:* 117
Van-Wyck Mason, F. *See* Mason,
    F. van Wyck, *3:* 117
Varley, Dimitry V., *10:* 183
Vasiliu, Mircea, *2:* 254
Vaughan, Harold Cecil, *14:* 221
Vaughan, Sam(uel) S., *14:* 222
Vaughn, Ruth, *14:* 223
Vavra, Robert James, *8:* 206
Vecsey, George, *9:* 192
Veglahn, Nancy (Crary), *5:* 194
Venable, Alan (Hudson), *8:* 206
Verney, John, *14:* 224
Vernon, (Elda) Louise A(nderson),
    14: 225
Vernor, D. *See* Casewit, Curtis,
    4: 43
Verral, Charles Spain, *11:* 225
Versace, Marie Teresa Rios, *2:* 254
Vesey, Paul. *See* Allen, Samuel
    (Washington), *9:* 6
Vestly, Anne-Cath(arina), *14:* 228
Vicker, Angus. *See* Felsen, Henry
    Gregor, *1:* 89
Victor, Edward, *3:* 240
Viereck, Ellen K., *14:* 229
Viereck, Phillip, *3:* 241
Viertel, Janet, *10:* 183
Vigna, Judith, *15:* 292
Viguers, Ruth Hill, *6:* 214
Villiers, Alan (John), *10:* 184
Vincent, Mary Keith. *See* St.
    John, Wylly Folk, *10:* 132
Vining, Elizabeth Gray. *See* Gray,
    Elizabeth Janet, *6:* 93
Viorst, Judith, *7:* 200
Visser, W(illiam) F(rederick)
    H(endrik), *10:* 186
Vo-Dinh, Mai, *16:* 271

Vogel, Ilse-Margret, *14:* 231
Vogel, John H(ollister), Jr., *18:* 292
Vogt, Esther Loewen, *14:* 231
Voight, Virginia Frances, *8:* 208
von Almedingen, Martha Edith.
    See Almedingen, E. M., *3:* 9
von Storch, Anne B., *1:* 221
Vosburgh, Leonard (W.), *15:* 294
Voyle, Mary. *See* Manning,
    Rosemary, *10:* 87

Waddell, Evelyn Margaret, *10:* 186
Wagner, Sharon B., *4:* 218
Wagoner, David (Russell), *14:* 232
Wahl, Jan, *2:* 256
Walden, Amelia Elizabeth, *3:* 242
Waldman, Bruce, *15:* 297
Waldron, Ann Wood, *16:* 273
Walker, Barbara K., *4:* 219
Walker, David Harry, *8:* 210
Walker, Diana, *9:* 193
Walker, Holly Beth. *See* Bond,
    Gladys Baker, *14:* 41
Walker, (Addison) Mort, *8:* 211
Walker, Stephen J., *12:* 228
Wallace, Barbara Brooks, *4:* 221
Wallace, John A., *3:* 243
Wallace, Nigel. *See* Hamilton,
    Charles Harold St. John, *13:* 77
Wallner, John C., *10:* 189
Wallower, Lucille, *11:* 226
Walsh, Jill Paton. *See* Paton
    Walsh, Gillian, *4:* 164
Walter, Villiam Christian. *See*
    Andersen, Hans Christian,
    YABC 1: 23
Walters, Audrey, *18:* 293
Walton, Richard J., *4:* 223
Waltrip, Lela (Kingston), *9:* 194
Waltrip, Rufus (Charles), *9:* 195
Walworth, Nancy Zinsser, *14:* 233
Warbler, J. M. *See* Cocagnac,
    A. M., *7:* 52
Warburg, Sandol Stoddard, *14:* 234
Ward, Lynd (Kendall), *2:* 257
Ward, Martha (Eads), *5:* 195
Wardell, Dean. *See* Prince, J(ack)
    H(arvey), *17:* 155
Ware, Leon (Vernon), *4:* 224
Warner, Frank A. [Collective
    pseudonym], *1:* 222
Warner, Gertrude Chandler, *9:* 195
Warren, Billy. *See* Warren,
    William Stephen, *9:* 196
Warren, Joyce W(illiams), *18:* 294
Warren, Mary Phraner, *10:* 190
Warren, William Stephen, *9:* 196
Warshofsky, Isaac. *See* Singer,
    Isaac Bashevis, *3:* 203
Washburne, Heluiz Chandler,
    10: 192
Waters, John F(rederick), *4:* 225
Watkins-Pitchford, D. J., *6:* 214
Watson, Clyde, *5:* 196

Watson, James, *10:* 192
Watson, Jane Werner, *3:* 244
Watson, Pauline, *14:* 235
Watson, Sally, *3:* 245
Watson, Wendy (McLeod), *5:* 198
Watt, Thomas, *4:* 226
Watts, Bernadette, *4:* 226
Watts, Mabel Pizzey, *11:* 227
Waugh, Dorothy, *11:* 228
Wayne, Kyra Petrovskaya, *8:* 213
Wayne, Richard. *See* Decker,
    Duane, *5:* 53
Weales, Gerald (Clifford), *11:* 229
Weaver, Ward. *See* Mason, F. van
    Wyck, *3:* 117
Webb, Christopher. *See*
    Wibberley, Leonard, *2:* 271
Webber, Irma E(leanor Schmidt),
    14: 237
Weber, Alfons, *8:* 215
Weber, Lenora Mattingly, *2:* 260
Weber, William John, *14:* 239
Webster, Alice (Jane Chandler),
    17: 241
Webster, David, *11:* 230
Webster, Frank V. [Collective
    pseudonym], *1:* 222
Webster, James, *17:* 242
Webster, Jean. *See* Webster, Alice
    (Jane Chandler), *17:* 241
Weddle, Ethel H(arshbarger),
    11: 231
Weihs, Erika, *15:* 297
Weik, Mary Hays, *3:* 247
Weil, Ann Yezner, *9:* 197
Weil, Lisl, *7:* 202
Weilerstein, Sadie Rose, *3:* 248
Weiner, Sandra, *14:* 240
Weingarten, Violet, *3:* 250
Weingartner, Charles, *5:* 199
Weir, LaVada, *2:* 261
Weisgard, Leonard (Joseph), *2:* 263
Weiss, Adelle, *18:* 296
Weiss, Harvey, *1:* 222
Weiss, Malcolm E., *3:* 251
Weiss, Miriam. *See* Schlein,
    Miriam, *2:* 222
Weiss, Renee Karol, *5:* 199
Welch, Jean-Louise. *See*
    Kempton, Jean Welch, *10:* 67
Welch, Pauline. *See* Bodenham,
    Hilda Esther, *13:* 16
Welch, Ronald. *See* Felton,
    Ronald Oliver, *3:* 67
Wellman, Manly Wade, *6:* 217
Wellman, Paul I., *3:* 251
Wells, Helen, *2:* 266
Wells, J. Wellington. *See* DeCamp,
    L(yon) Sprague, *9:* 49
Wells, Rosemary, *18:* 296
Wels, Byron G(erald), *9:* 197
Welty, S. F. *See* Welty, Susan F.,
    9: 198
Welty, Susan F., *9:* 198
Werner, Jane. *See* Watson, Jane
    Werner, *3:* 244

Werner, K. *See* Casewit, Curtis, 4: 43

Wersba, Barbara, 1: 224

Werstein, Irving, 14: 240

West, Barbara. *See* Price, Olive, 8: 157

West, Betty, 11: 233

West, James. *See* Withers, Carl A., 14: 261

West, Jerry. *See* Stratemeyer, Edward L., 1: 208

West, Jerry. *See* Svenson, Andrew E., 2: 238

West, Ward. *See* Borland, Hal, 5: 22

Westervelt, Virginia (Veeder), 10: 193

Westheimer, David, 14: 242

Westwood, Jennifer, 10: 194

Wexler, Jerome (LeRoy), 14: 243

Wheatley, Arabelle, 16: 275

Wheeler, Captain. *See* Ellis, Edward S(ylvester), YABC 1: 116

Wheeler, Janet D. [Collective pseudonym], 1: 225

Whelan, Elizabeth M(urphy), 14: 244

Whitcomb, Jon, 10: 195

White, Anne Terry, 2: 267

White, Dale. *See* Place, Marian T., 3: 160

White, Dori, 10: 195

White, E(lwyn) B(rooks), 2: 268

White, Eliza Orne, YABC 2: 333

White, Florence M(eiman), 14: 244

White, Laurence B., Jr., 10: 196

White, Ramy Allison [Collective pseudonym], 1: 225

White, Robb, 1: 225

White, T(erence) H(anbury), 12: 229

White, William, Jr., 16: 276

Whitehead, Don(ald) F., 4: 227

Whitehouse, Arch. *See* Whitehouse, Arthur George, 14: 246

Whitehouse, Arthur George, 14: 246

Whitinger, R. D. *See* Place, Marian T., 3: 160

Whitney, Alex(andra), 14: 249

Whitney, Phyllis A(yame), 1: 226

Wibberley, Leonard, 2: 271

Widdemer, Mabel Cleland, 5: 200

Widenberg, Siv, 10: 197

Wier, Ester, 3: 252

Wiese, Kurt, 3: 254

Wiesner, Portia. *See* Takakjian, Portia, 15: 273

Wiesner, William, 5: 200

Wiggin, Kate Douglas (Smith), YABC 1: 258

Wilbur, Richard (Purdy), 9: 200

Wilde, Gunther. *See* Hurwood, Bernhardt, J., 12: 107

Wilder, Laura Ingalls, 15: 300

Wildsmith, Brian, 16: 277

Wilkins, Frances, 14: 249

Wilkinson, Brenda, 14: 250

Wilkinson, Burke, 4: 229

Will. *See* Lipkind, William, 15: 178

Willard, Barbara (Mary), 17: 243

Willard, Mildred Wilds, 14: 252

Willey, Robert. *See* Ley, Willy, 2: 175

Williams, Barbara, 11: 233

Williams, Beryl. *See* Epstein, Beryl, 1: 85

Williams, Charles. *See* Collier, James Lincoln, 8: 33

Williams, Clyde C., 8: 216

Williams, Eric (Ernest), 14: 253

Williams, Frances B. *See* Browin, Frances Williams, 5: 30

Williams, Garth (Montgomery), 18: 298

Williams, Guy R., 11: 235

Williams, Hawley. *See* Heyliger, William, YABC 1: 163

Williams, J. R. *See* Williams, Jeanne, 5: 202

Williams, Jay, 3: 256

Williams, Jeanne, 5: 202

Williams, Maureen, 12: 238

Williams, Michael. *See* St. John, Wylly Folk, 10: 132

Williams, Patrick J. *See* Butterworth, W. E., 5: 40

Williams, Selma R(uth), 14: 256

Williams, Slim. *See* Williams, Clyde C., 8: 216

Williams, Ursula Moray, 3: 257

Williamson, Joanne Small, 3: 259

Wilma, Dana. *See* Faralla, Dana, 9: 62

Wilson, Beth P(ierre), 8: 218

Wilson, Carter, 6: 218

Wilson, Dorothy Clarke, 16: 283

Wilson, Ellen (Janet Cameron), 9: 200

Wilson, (Leslie) Granville, 14: 257

Wilson, Hazel, 3: 260

Wilson, Walt(er N.), 14: 258

Wilton, Elizabeth, 14: 259

Wilwerding, Walter Joseph, 9: 201

Winders, Gertrude Hecker, 3: 261

Windham, Kathryn T(ucker), 14: 259

Winfield, Arthur M. *See* Stratemeyer, Edward L., 1: 208

Winfield, Edna. *See* Stratemeyer, Edward L., 1: 208

Winter, R. R.. *See* Winterbotham, R(ussell) R(obert), 10: 198

Winterbotham, R(ussell) R(obert), 10: 198

Winthrop, Elizabeth. *See* Mahony, Elizabeth Winthrop, 8: 125

Wirtenberg, Patricia Z., 10: 199

Wise, William, 4: 230

Wise, Winifred E., 2: 273

Wiseman, B(ernard), 4: 232

Withers, Carl A., 14: 261

Witt, Shirley Hill, 17: 247

Wizard, Mr. *See* Herbert, Don, 2: 131

Wohlrabe, Raymond A., 4: 234

Wojciechowska, Maia, 1: 228

Wolcott, Patty, 14: 264

Wolfe, Burton H., 5: 202

Wolfe, Louis, 8: 219

Wolff, Robert Jay, 10: 199

Wolkstein, Diane, 7: 204

Wondriska, William, 6: 219

Wood, Edgar A(llardyce), 14: 264

Wood, James Playsted, 1: 229

Wood, Kerry. *See* Wood, Edgar A(llardyce), 14: 264

Wood, Nancy, 6: 220

Woodard, Carol, 14: 266

Woodburn, John Henry, 11: 236

Woodrich, Mary Neville, 2: 274

Woods, Margaret, 2: 275

Woods, Nat. *See* Stratemeyer, Edward L., 1: 208

Woodson, Jack. *See* Woodson, John Waddie, Jr., 10: 200

Woodson, John Waddie, Jr., 10: 200

Woodward, Cleveland, 10: 201

Woody, Regina Jones, 3: 263

Woolley, Catherine, 3: 265

Woolsey, Janette, 3: 266

Worcester, Donald Emmet, 18: 301

Worline, Bonnie Bess, 14: 267

Worth, Valerie, 8: 220

Wortis, Avi, 14: 269

Wriggins, Sally Hovey, 17: 248

Wright, Enid Meadowcroft, 3: 267

Wright, Esmond, 10: 202

Wright, Frances Fitzpatrick, 10: 202

Wright, Judith, 14: 270

Wright, R(obert) H., 6: 220

Wrightson, Patricia, 8: 220

Wronker, Lili Cassel, 10: 204

Wyeth, N(ewell) C(onvers), 17: 249

Wyler, Rose, 18: 303

Wyndham, Lee. *See* Hyndman, Jane Andrews, 1: 122

Wyndham, Robert. *See* Hyndman, Robert Utley, 18: 123

Wynter, Edward (John), 14: 271

Wynyard, Talbot. *See* Hamilton, Charles Harold St. John, 13: 77

Wyss, Thelma Hatch, 10: 205

Yamaguchi, Marianne, 7: 205

Yang, Jay, 12: 239

Yashima, Taro. *See* Iwamatsu, Jun Atsushi, 14: 83

Yates, Elizabeth, 4: 235

Yaukey, Grace S(ydenstricker), 5: 203

Yep, Laurence M., *7:* 206
Yolen, Jane H., *4:* 237
York, Andrew. *See* Nicole,
    Christopher Robin, *5:* 141
Yonge, Charlotte Mary, *17:* 272
York, Carol Beach, *6:* 221
Young, Bob. *See* Young, Robert
    W., *3:* 269
Young, Clarence [Collective
    pseudonym], *1:* 231
Young, Ed, *10:* 205
Young, Edward. *See* Reinfeld,
    Fred, *3:* 170

Young, Jan. *See* Young, Janet
    Randall, *3:* 268
Young, Janet Randall, *3:* 268
Young, Margaret B(uckner), *2:* 275
Young, Miriam, *7:* 208
Young, Robert W., *3:* 269
Young, Scott A(lexander), *5:* 204

Zalben, Jane Breskin, *7:* 211
Zallinger, Jean (Day), *14:* 272
Zappler, Lisbeth, *10:* 206

Zemach, Harve, *3:* 270
Ziemienski, Dennis, *10:* 206
Zillah. *See* Macdonald, Zillah K.,
    11: 167
Zim, Herbert S(pencer), *1:* 231
Zimmerman, Naoma, *10:* 207
Zindel, Paul, *16:* 283
Ziner, (Florence) Feenie, *5:* 204
Zion, (Eu)Gene, *18:* 305
Zolotow, Charlotte S., *1:* 233
Zurhorst, Charles (Stewart, Jr.),
    12: 240
Zweifel, Frances, *14:* 273

Author Index